MEDIEVAL RELIGIOUS HOUSES
SCOTLAND

MEDIEVAL
RELIGIOUS HOUSES
SCOTLAND

*With an Appendix on the
Houses in the Isle of Man*

By
IAN B. COWAN
and
DAVID E. EASSON

With a Foreword by
DAVID KNOWLES

and Maps by
R. NEVILLE HADCOCK

Second Edition

LONGMAN
LONDON AND NEW YORK

LONGMAN GROUP LIMITED
London

*Associated companies, branches and representatives throughout
the world*

Published in the United States of America
by Longman Inc., New York

© Longman Group Limited 1957, 1976

First published 1957
Second edition 1976

Library of Congress Cataloging in Publication Data

Cowan, Ian Borthwick.
Medieval religious houses, Scotland.

Edition for 1957 entered under D. E. Easson.
Includes index.
1. Monasteries—Scotland. I. Easson, David Edward, 1897—
Medieval religious houses, Scotland. II. Title

BX2597.E2   1976   271'.009411   75-42083
ISBN 0-582-12069-1

Set in 10 point and 8 point Baskerville

Printed in Great Britain by Whitstable Litho Ltd.

CONTENTS

MAPS

Following the index

The first map is based on *An Historical Atlas of Scotland*, by permission of the trustees. The other maps are based on the Ordnance Survey Map of Monastic Britain (North Sheet), by permission of the Director General.

FOREWORD

WITHIN the area of north-western Europe there were, in the tenth century, roughly speaking three regions in the matter of religion: that covered by the organized Church, connected with Rome by bonds of varying strength; that of Celtic Christianity embracing Ireland, Scotland and (though less definitely) Wales; and that of the pagan north, in which the first seeds of Christianity were being planted by the Irish and the Anglo-Saxon missionaries. Monasticism was common to the whole of western Christendom, but whereas in the organized Church it was the life of individual communities, entirely separate from the clergy and hierarchy, in the Celtic lands it contained within itself the priesthood and even the episcopate, and was indeed the only powerful religious and cultural force in the land. In form, too, the monastic body differed greatly in the two regions. In the organized Church it was now almost entirely dominated by the Rule of St. Benedict and a common set of liturgical and disciplinary customs, while the more austere and individualistic monachism of the Celtic lands had never aimed at or attained more than a loose kind of union or uniformity.

In the late tenth century these differences were greatly accentuated. The missionary achievements and the golden age of Celtic monasticism lay in the distant past, and in Ireland, Wales and Scotland alike what had been a class of great social and intellectual importance had now become a scattering of small groups and individuals living a solitary, or at least an isolated, existence. In continental Europe, on the other hand, the great expansion of Western civilization had begun, helped rather than hindered in the long run by the migrations of the Northmen and the Normans. Scandinavia and its island dependencies, hitherto almost virgin soil, received Christianity from England and Germany along with all its contemporary developments, as every new institution gradually made its way to the frontier. The Celtic lands had various fortunes. Wales, within easy reach of England, became, by a mixture of conquest and peaceful penetration, at least superficially similar in church matters to England. Ireland, a prey to disorder for many centuries before the Norman Conquest, remained throughout the Middle Ages as a shifting sand beneath a surface of the familiar western pattern artificially imposed upon it. Scotland's religious history was determined by the racial affinities of its

Celtic west and Nordic east, by its relationship, at first friendly, but later hostile, with England, and by the gradual emergence of a national spirit and character.

Scotland, unlike England, had in the eleventh century no past traditions of the monastic life as one of the elements of its national greatness, and no associations in the past history of great and wealthy abbeys, and of notable monk-bishops and reformers. Her many Celtic saints were revered as holy individuals and as figures of legend rather than of history. The Culdees had neither the strength nor the organization to resist or to influence the newcomers; they were gradually absorbed into the new system, or disappeared before it. Scotland, therefore, which in the mid-eleventh century had for the first time attained something like political unity, was more potentially receptive of external influences than at any time since her first conversion to Christianity. With Celtic Christianity losing its shape and force she was in many respects a *tabula rasa*, like the Scandinavian lands, but with the possession of Christian faith and practice she was more open to religious influences.

It was at this very moment in the history of Europe that the vast multiplication and proliferation of the monastic life began. Starting with the reforms and developments of the traditional Benedictine or 'black' monks, of which the most spectacular example was the growth of the 'order' of Cluny, it continued with the emergence of powerful new monastic and canonical bodies, of which the greatest by far were the Cistercian (or 'white') monks and the Premonstratensian (or 'white') canons, and after producing in the four chief orders of friars the most characteristic creation of the later Middle Ages, dwindled to its last manifestation, a shadow of its old self, in the collegiate church of the fifteenth century. These waves, issuing from France and Italy, swept outwards across Europe and normally reached Scotland late, but as with tides, so with human movements, an obstacle or a free passage can change rhythms and seasons, and personal or political accidents could on occasion bring to Scotland a religious family that had not yet arrived in England, or perhaps never was to arrive.

It is generally acknowledged that the infiltration of what Scottish historians are agreed in calling Roman monastic life was directly due to the influence of Queen Margaret, daughter of Edward the Atheling, who became the second wife of King Malcolm III in 1069. The moment was propitious, for in England also a great stirring and development was on the point of taking place. Margaret had chosen as her somewhat remote spiritual director the new Italian archbishop of Canterbury, and when she had thoughts of introducing monks to Scotland it was to him she turned. Lanfranc met her request by sending three of his Canterbury monks, and they formed the nucleus of the house that was afforced fifty years later by another colony from Christ Church and became to the Scottish monarchy something of what Westminster and St. Denis were in England and France. Dunfermline became wealthy and its abbot was a person of distinction, but it remained the only sizeable independent house of the Benedictines.

Dunfermline owed its splendour to Margaret's son, King David I, and in his long reign the monastic map of Scotland was firmly blocked in. David, half English in blood through his mother, and earl of Huntingdon and Northampton by his marriage with Maude, daughter of the earl Waltheof who had been beheaded by the Conqueror, had many personal and feudal connections with England, where he had spent much of his youth. At that time the border between England and Scotland was still fluid: Cumberland, Northumberland and Durham were not yet finally part of either country, and communications between them and Teviotdale and Lothian were open and free. David, at home in England and Scotland alike, turned naturally, as did his Norman vassals, both to England and the Continent for help in his task of religious plantation. Thus the Augustinian houses of Holyrood, Scone (under Alexander I) and perhaps St. Andrews were founded from Merton (Surrey) and Nostell (Yorks), while the Premonstratensian abbey at Dryburgh was a daughter of Alnwick (Northumberland). Still more striking was the filiation of the Cistercians. Melrose, the first Scottish house, had as its founding abbot the king's stepson, St. Waldef. Waldef was a monk of Rievaulx, and the whole family of eleven Cistercian abbeys in Scotland, the most compact and in some ways the most remarkable group of monasteries in the country, was derived at one remove or more from Rievaulx, either through Melrose or through another daughter, yet another of the king's foundations, Dundrennan in Kirkcudbrightshire. King David, however, was catholic in his choice and went further than England to find what he needed. Thus for Cambuskenneth and Jedburgh he summoned canons from Arrouaise and Beauvais, while for Selkirk (later Kelso) he introduced into Scotland an order all but unknown in England, the monks of the reform of Tiron in Brittany, and it is probable that he visited Tiron itself to secure his purpose. Kelso in its early maturity was probably the most populous abbey in Scotland, while Arbroath, another Tironian house founded in Angus by William the Lion, was the wealthiest. Whether judged by their number, their size, their wide distribution or the variety of their rule, the foundations of David I must rank as the most remarkable of any Scottish monarch, or indeed of any monarch of the age.

The monastic family continued to grow in Scotland for half-a-century or so after expansion had ceased in England. While some orders, such as those of Grandmont and Fontevrault, never came so far north, and others, such as the Carthusians and Gilbertines, either came late or failed to make a lasting stay, the chief families of men were well represented. Nunneries were always few, and relatively small and poor, and Scotland lacked almost entirely the galaxy of small priories and cells that covered the face of medieval England. By far the greater number of these were 'alien priories', the lesser Cluniac dependencies and the small establishments set up by Norman and French abbeys on their English estates, often simply as a *pied-à-terre* or centre of economic administration. By the time of King David, the high tide of this expansion had passed, and the number of small monastic establishments in Scotland in his day barely exceeded half-a-dozen. This was no loss; indeed, it eliminated one great source of religious weakness and one great temptation for the confiscator.

The friars, who needed neither abbey nor benefaction nor even a summons to attract them, reached Scotland within a few years of arriving in London, and the country soon had its quota. All four orders were represented, but the Augustinian friars had only a single house and the splinter orders barely reached the north. On the other hand, an order of canons, the Trinitarians, sometimes known as 'red friars', was relatively strong, and there were three houses of a family unknown to England, that of the Valliscaulians, a minor monastic group not unlike the Cistercians. The friars reached the north through England, and during the whole of the thirteenth century the bonds of religious and intellectual unity were stronger than the forces of separation throughout Europe.

With the fourteenth century, a time of change throughout Europe, the break came also in Scotland. Henceforth the Border was not only a real barrier, but also an area of destruction in which the Scottish abbeys fared worse than the English, for in England there were no rich houses north of Durham and Carlisle, which were never overrun, whereas in Scotland a group of the fairest and wealthiest abbeys lay to hand unprotected in the basin of the Tweed. These and other houses near the Firth of Forth had to suffer again and again a fate that no English abbey endured between the Conquest and the Dissolution—fire and ruin at the hands of a merciless enemy.

The pattern of the religious life in Scotland deviates most markedly from that of any other part of the British Isles in the fifteenth and early six-

teenth centuries. Whereas in England, Wales and Ireland, though in
different ways, the rhythm of life becomes universally slower, and scarcely
any new feature appears until the abrupt end, in Scotland development
and deterioration continue side by side. While England was absorbed in
the French war and internal disputes, Scotland maintained its continental
associations; in consequence, the new reform of the Franciscans, that of the
Observants, found entry half-a-century before it came to England, and
provided a body of friars, small in number but influential in an age of
waning fervour. Similarly, the solitary Scottish Charterhouse of Perth,
though probably owing its conception to the English memories of Jane
Beaufort, drew its first community from the Continent. A further development was that of the secular colleges. Whereas in England the great
extension of numbers took place before 1450, in Scotland foundations
were made with the greatest frequency throughout the period 1440–1540.
In one of the earliest, St. Mary's at St. Andrews, a lingering group of
Culdees was transformed; of the remainder, a certain number were parish
churches of which the revenue had been augmented and parcelled into
prebends, but more than a third were 'chantry' colleges or incorporations
of chaplains. A type almost peculiar to Scotland was that of the large
burgh church, with a number of endowed altars, which became (or was on
the way to becoming) collegiate, and was the centre of all kinds of civic
activity.

Alongside of these developments the decline of observance in the
monasteries was hastened by their occupation by lay 'abbots'. The system
of commendam, common on the Continent but unknown in England,
was introduced into Scotland in the last decades of the fifteenth century.
The abbey and title of abbot was given to a commendator, often a bishop
or court official or high-born cleric, who enjoyed the revenues and allowed
the monks their 'portions'; in later years he was often a layman who
installed himself, as at Melrose, in a house adjacent to the abbey. Simultaneously, the feuing of monastic lands and the allotment of individual
incomes to the religious were destroying both the property and the spirit
of the communities. In addition, the houses near the Border and the Forth
experienced the brutality of the disgraceful expedition of the Earl of
Hertford in 1544. Nevertheless, the end came far more slowly in Scotland
than in England, and it was both more violent and more gentle in different
houses. As neither James V nor the Earl of Arran took the forthright
advice of Henry VIII to imitate his own successful action, the religious
houses were never confiscated *en bloc* at the Reformation. While the urban
houses, especially those of the friars, were sacked by the lawless element

among the reformers, the abbeys held or controlled by the great lairds continued to exist, but with diminishing communities who had lost every vestige of traditional monastic routine, until their annexation to the Crown in 1587, and even then in many cases did not legally come to an end till they almost insensibly became lay property at the turn of the century, when one by one they were irrevocably secularized by crown charters and acts of parliament.

Owing to the late introduction of regular monasticism to Scotland, when the 'Benedictine centuries' were about to end, the country owed little of its artistic or literary capital, and none of its religious tradition, to the black monks. There was no centres of manuscript illumination and literary composition comparable to St. Albans, Canterbury and Durham. Similarly, the age of saints was passing, and after the death of St. Waldef at Melrose it is difficult to name a monk or friar of outstanding sanctity or reputation. There were relatively few monk-bishops, and the monks came too late to provide a creative statesman of the type of Lanfranc or Suger.

The monastic map of Scotland is for the most part sparsely covered, and much of its area is entirely barren of houses. If a line is drawn from Inverness to Perth, and thence to Glasgow, the only sizeable house north and west of this is the revived abbey of Iona. Most of this area is indeed mountain or moorland, but it may seem at first surprising that the Cistercians and Premonstratensians, who penetrated to the Alps and the Pyrenees, never sought out the fertile glens and islands of the west. Possibly the Celtic temperament and system of clans were not susceptible of a life ordered upon the needs and habits of Latin lands; possibly those in search of 'noble wild prospects' could find them to hand without crossing the Highland line.

Though a few abbeys were well endowed and populous, no Scottish house was great or inordinately wealthy by continental or even by English standards, nor were their buildings of any great complexity or architectural distinction, save in the region between Forth and Tay, and, above all, in the wide basin of the Tweed. There, more than anywhere else, at Jedburgh, Dryburgh and Melrose, a regional version of Gothic architecture was produced which resembled that of Yorkshire, but had an idiom of its own. Melrose is a particular jewel in the treasury of the Middle Ages, just as, by Solway Firth, Dundrennan and Sweetheart, for all their conformity to strict Cistercian planning, have a colour and texture of their own.

DAVID KNOWLES

PREFACE

FURTHER research, particularly in the Vatican Archives, into the history of the medieval Church in Scotland, has been undertaken since the late Rev. Dr. David E. Easson published his edition of this work in 1957. Consequently this new edition, which appears under the same title, is more than a reprint with corrections, but has been expanded and revised at all points to incorporate additions, corrections and further information about commendation. Figures of the monastic population, which the original editor demurred from attempting to estimate, have also been supplied where relevant evidence is available. Among other important new material may be mentioned the separate list of early religious foundations (not only of those surviving into the medieval period), an entirely new section on the Schottenklöster (Appendix II, contributed by the Rev. Mark Dilworth, O.S.B.), the inclusion of forty hitherto unrecorded hospital foundations and the attempt to provide, with as much exactitude as possible, information as to the names and numbers of prebends founded in collegiate churches and cathedrals. As a result of all these additions and changes the second edition is in many respects a new book. Nevertheless, the present edition still owes an overwhelming debt to the scholarship of David Easson. Few of his original judgments have proved to be wrong, and most of the information which appeared in the first edition has been incorporated in this new version. His account of the development of monasticism in Scotland has likewise withstood the test of time, and with the exception of minor corrections and the addition of prefatory material on early monastic foundations, appears in much the same form as he wrote it. So too with his account of the contributions made by earlier scholars towards the compilation of a Scottish *Monasticon*, although this would inevitably have been incomplete without some evaluation of his own outstanding work in this particular field.

The layout of the volume has, however, been changed. In the first edition the notes were at the foot of the page below the names of a small series of houses. Here as in the companion volumes, *Medieval Religious Houses: Ireland* and the revised edition of *Medieval Religious Houses: England and Wales*, each list of the houses of a particular order is followed by the relevant notes printed continuously. But in a number of respects it still differs, necessarily, from the English and Irish volumes. The lists are primarily inclusive of houses accepted as authentic, while in each section a subsidiary list of doubtful and unauthentic foundations is appended. This procedure has been deemed advisable because, in certain cases, such as the Trinitarians and Dominicans, the number of unauthentic houses mentioned is considerable and these, if included, would have formed a disproportionate as well as a confusing element in the lists. Again, because reliable works on Scottish religious foundations are lamentably few, the lists and notes are based to a large extent on material drawn from original sources. These sources, it is hoped, are sufficiently indicated on pp. 32–45 where the list of references and abbreviations serves in some measure as a bibliography. The lists include a properly computed statement of the incomes of the religious houses and other foundations in 1561, that is at the Reformation, so far as these incomes can be ascertained from existing records. These revenues purport to be set forth in various works which allude to the Scottish monasteries (e.g. Keith, *History of Church and State in Scotland*, Book III, Appendix); but as a rule, the figures given cover only the money income and no attempt has hitherto been made to assess and include their victual total and thus to arrive at an estimate of their total resources. A debt of gratitude is owed to Professor Gordon Donaldson not only for making this computation but for supplying a valuable note (see Appendix III) explaining its sources and basis. A further difficulty in relation to the Scottish lists arises from the fact that 'dissolution' and 'suppression' are terms which cannot be applied to the Scottish houses in the sense in which they are applicable to the English monasteries. Those houses which became extinct before the Reformation are noted as 'dissolved' or, in some cases where the term is appropriate, 'suppressed'. But in the case of communities which continued till the Reformation the column recording their extinction is headed 'secularized', and the date there given is generally that of the formal erection of the abbey or priory into a temporal lordship. Such an erection was usually made in terms of a crown charter and an act of parliament and the date listed is that on which the erection is first recorded. But it should be noted that all Scottish monastic houses effectively came to an end with the abolition of the mass on 24 August 1560. Thereafter, although communities of the religious might continue, until the death of its members, to constitute the convent in a legal and technical sense, their significance as religious institutions was at an end. Collegiate churches were equally brought to an end by the abolition of the mass, but in the case of hospitals, whereas some were terminated, others continued to maintain their primary function of providing for the poor, infirm or aged.

The period covered by this work is from the introduction of Christianity to 1560. No apology is needed for including among Scottish foundations those at Berwick-on-Tweed. The religious houses and hospitals at Berwick were founded within the period when it was indisputably a Scottish burgh and situated in the diocese of St. Andrews. Again the Cistercian nunnery and the Dominican priory were founded by Scottish kings; the Trinitarian house was the foundation of a Scottish countess; the house at Segden is specifically described as Scottish; and, in 1333, Edward III gave orders for the removal of the Scottish friars from the four friaries. After 1482, when Berwick finally passed from Scottish possession, its surviving monasteries had little more than half a century of continued existence. The case for the inclusion of the houses at Berwick in this volume seems obvious.

As the houses of the Isle of Man do not appear in the English volume, it has been thought desirable to include them in the present work (Appendix I). The listing and annotation of the Manx foundations will, it is hoped, suffice without special commentary to illustrate the main features of their history.

It should be mentioned that customary Scottish terminology has been retained. Thus 'Augustinian' is preferred to 'Austin' as a designation of regular canons and friars. On the other hand, although the Trinitarian are sometimes described by writers (but not in medieval records) as 'red friars', this term is avoided as inaccurate—the Trinitarians were not, strictly speaking, friars. 'Collegiate church' is employed, in accordance with the usage of Scottish records and writers, as signifying a college of secular priests; the term 'provostry', often used in the same sense, is only admitted where sources which are cited make use of it. Scottish writers, legal and ecclesiastical, do not speak of 'peculiars'. 'Lazar house' is not found; the usual term is 'leper house'. 'Teinds' are the Scottish equivalent of 'tithes' and, except in references to English records, 'sasine' appears instead of 'seisin'.

Attention may be drawn to the maps which illustrate the distribution of (*a*) early religious foundations (*b*) the houses of monks, regular canons, etc., and nuns, (*c*) the houses of friars, and (*d*) the cathedrals, collegiate churches and hospitals in the late fifteenth and sixteenth centuries. With the exception of the first which is based on maps in *An Historical Atlas of Scotland* (1975) these maps, revised and redrawn for this edition, are the contribution of Mr. R. Neville Hadcock, of whose skill and ingenuity in devising their details warm appreciation should be expressed.

In the compilation of the first edition Dr. Easson recorded his gratitude to such scholars as Dr. A. O. Anderson, the Rev. W. J. Anderson, Professor G. W. S. Barrow, Professor Gordon Donaldson, Professor A. A. M. Duncan, Dr. Annie I. Dunlop, Dr. I. F. Grant, Mr. T. R. Harley, Dr. C. T. McInnes, Dr. C. A. Malcolm, Mr. B. R. S. Megaw, Colonel L. Nowosilski, the Rev. W. E. K. Rankin, Mr. R. C. Reid, Professor W. Stanford Reid and Mr. D. J. Withrington. He also recognized his indebtedness to the Roman Catholic bishops of Scotland for their permission to make use of the Brockie MSS for the purposes of his work. With the passage of time, some of these scholars are unhappily no longer with us, but the present editor's debt of gratitude to all those who contributed to the making of the first edition, is no less than that expressed by Dr Easson eighteen years ago. Several of the above have also contributed, with others too numerous to mention individually, to the making of this new edition. Members of the Scottish Medievalists Conference have in particular responded to pleas for assistance and particular mention may be made of the generous contributions received from Dr. John Bannerman, Mr. F. M. Cowe, the Rev. Mark Dilworth and Dr. D. E. R. Watt. Above all, I am grateful to Dr. J. Durkan who generously supplied me with information, derived from a lifelong study of manuscript sources, which not only facilitated the inclusion of a considerable number of new entries in the hospital section but also solved many of the problems in relation to hospitals, academic colleges and collegiate churches. Recognition should also be made of the assistance received from former Ross Fund scholars, Mr. Thomas Graham, the Rev. F. Kennedy, Dr. N. McDougall, Mr. P. Murray and Mr. T. Smyth, but for whose labours in the Vatican archives additions to these lists would have been considerably fewer. In this respect also, I am grateful to Monsignor C. Burns and Mr. F. McGurk for access to their manuscript calendars of the Papal Letters of Clement VII and Benedict XIII respectively, both of which are to be published shortly by the Scottish History Society. These will constitute memorial volumes to the late Dr. Annie Dunlop whose manuscript calendar of Scottish Supplications to Rome, 1433–79, has likewise been an invaluable source of information. I would equally like to acknowledge the encouragement and help which I received from the late Dom. David Knowles. He above all was the inspirer and guiding light behind this series, playing a major part in editing the English volume and instilling an equal sense of dedication in the editors of the companion volumes for Ireland and Scotland. If the task of compiling a *Monasticon* for all these countries is still not at an end, and it is hoped that this volume like its predecessor will produce a goodly quota of further emendations, these volumes as they stand constitute a permanent memorial to his endeavours to advance the study of monasticism in the British Isles.

IAN B. COWAN

Glasgow
January 1975

RES MONASTICAE

SCOTTISH religious foundations were catalogued more than once during the Middle Ages. The earliest lists are given in the writings of English chroniclers, one in the *Mappa Mundi* of Gervase of Canterbury, a work which has been dated *c.* 1207 or –1216, and another appended to the Chronicle of Henry of Silgrave, *c.* 1272. These lists have considerable similarities, but the latter is the more accurate. The first list of Scottish *provenance* appears in the addition to the *Scotichronicon* which purports to be the composition of Robert Scot. On his own statement, Scot completed this supplement in May 1510; but internal evidence suggests that the list which it incorporates belongs to the latter part of the preceding century.[1] That this list was the prototype of many later compilations of a similar nature can hardly be doubted; for they often reproduce its arrangement— the grouping of entries under abbeys, priories, houses of friars and of lesser orders, secular colleges (which are called 'praefecturae' or 'praepositurae') and nunneries, though not invariably in that sequence; while its idiosyncrasies, for example its reference to St. Columba as the founder of the houses in Iona, its mention of the mysterious Trinitarian foundation of 'Crennach', and its inclusion of the apocryphal nunneries of Gullane and Elbottle, become stock features of post-Reformation lists. A less complete list of slightly later date (1523–41?) occurs in 'Law's MS.' in Edinburgh University Library (MS. Dc. 7. 63).

Catalogues of two main types emerge in the seventeenth century: (1) MS. lists, under such a heading as 'Nomina monasteriorum', which contain entries of foundations grouped after the fashion of the *Scotichronicon* list[2] (from which they very probably derive), but often with the addition of a section giving the names of 'chori oppidani' ('town choirs', i.e. burgh churches with a quasi-collegiate organization). The usual though not invariable entry, in the case of the abbeys, priories, nunneries and colleges, has the name of the house, its location, its order and its founder, with an occasional note of the date of foundation. In the sections dealing with the houses of friars and of the smaller orders, no details beyond the names of these are given. There was undoubtedly something

---

[1] Cf. the reference to the contemporary building of the collegiate churches of Roslin and Dunglass.

[2] It is convenient to refer to it thus, though it is later in date than the *Scotichronicon*, because it is included in Goodall's edition of that work.

like a *textus receptus* of these lists, which, as with the analogous lists of
kings, were copied again and again. Examples are found in MS. collections
in the National Library of Scotland (e.g. MSS. 22.1.14, 33.2.12) and in an
Edinburgh University Library MS. (Db. 6.19).[1] A list of like character
appears in Thomas Dempster's *Apparatus ad historiam Scoticam* (1622). This
writer may have had before him the *Scotichronicon* (or a similar) list, though
he introduces some dubious items of his own.[2] (2) Lists which give a more
discursive account of the religious houses and are independent of the
Scotichronicon list. Such a compilation is included in Habukkuk Bisset's
Rolment of Courtis (1626?) and, taking a different form, in the *De Scotorum
Fortitudine, Doctrina et Pietate* (1631) of David Camerarius (Chalmers).
These lists, although the former has a few points of interest, are confused
and rambling performances, with an admixture of legendary matter. Of
the lists emanating from this period it cannot be said that they show any
advance on the catalogue appended to the *Scotichronicon*.

A curious feature of one of the foregoing lists (in National Library of
Scotland MS. 22.1.14) is that the scribe appears to have blundered by
including under the Friars Preachers items which properly belong to, and
elsewhere are placed in, the section on 'chori oppidani'. This confusion
reappears in the list of religious houses, attributed to Thomas Middleton,
which is appended to the 1677 edition of archbishop Spottiswoode's
History of the Church of Scotland, and, whether through dependence on
Middleton or otherwise, has misled other writers. Hence the number of
Dominican foundations has sometimes been falsified and exaggerated.

The eighteenth century saw the preparation of catalogues of religious
houses on a more ambitious scale. Thus, Fr. Richard Augustine Hay's
Scotia Sacra (1700), which exists in MS. in the National Library of
Scotland, is an *omnium gatherum*, dealing at length with Scottish foundations
and including also much material of a biographical and hagiographical
character. Hay is a voluminous but by no means critical writer. In the
same library is his Diplomatum Veterum Collectio, a collection of transcripts which also comprises an elaborated catalogue of Scottish Trinitarian
houses. The latter, unfortunately, is of no historical value. Hay's interest in
records, as manifested by his collections, is not matched by the use he
made of them; he was a hagiographer rather than a historian. More

---

[1] One of the best specimens among lists of this type belonged to the late William
Saunders, Edinburgh, who lent it to the present writer for transcription. It is cited *infra*
as 'MS. Saunders'.

[2] Dempster is an unreliable writer whose blunders and inventions cannot be justified by
the suggestion (cf. Backmund, *Monast. Praemon.*, ii, 112 n) that he made use of sources no
longer available.

significant is the work of John Spottiswoode (a layman, to be distinguished
from his kinsman the archbishop) which, under the title *An Account of all
the Religious Houses that were in Scotland at the time of the Reformation,* was
published in 1734 as an appendix to Hope's *Minor Practicks* and in 1755
as part of Keith's *Historical Catalogue of Scottish Bishops.* This treatise covers
the houses, under their orders, of monks, friars, and nuns with an account
of the secular colleges and, for the first time, of the hospitals. Though it has
manifest inaccuracies and misinterpretations and borrows too much that
is legendary from previous writers (e.g. Hay), Spottiswoode's production
is more comprehensive and more systematically constructed than any
preceding catalogue; moreover, it makes considerable reference to records.[1]
That this work long maintained its ground was due to its unquestionable
(though not outstanding) merits. William Maitland, who included a list
of religious houses in his *History and Antiquities of Scotland* (1757), closely
followed Spottiswoode (to the extent of faithfully reproducing his errors),
though he added details of the revenues in money and victual of the
various houses. The same period saw the composition by Fr. Marianus
Brockie of his monumental Monasticon Scoticum, the MS. of which is
preserved in the Scottish Catholic Archives at Columba House, Edinburgh. Brockie's collection of transcripts and *notitiae* is in the tradition of
Hay. Comparatively little use of this material was made by subsequent
writers[2] as its historical value was not rated highly. This was fortunate as it
has subsequently been proved that Brockie was guilty of blatant forgery
and much of his work is of his own invention.[3] Other writers were no less
imaginative and it is evident that a number of fresh errors came into
circulation in the later seventeenth and earlier eighteenth centuries. How
these errors originated is often difficult to ascertain, but as there was a good
deal of dependence of one writer on another, mistaken statements were apt
to be repeated and expanded.

In the later part of the eighteenth century, George Henry Hutton
(d. 1827), an English artillery officer who rose to be a lieutenant-general,
became, while stationed in Scotland, deeply interested in its monastic
antiquities, pursuing his inquiries by an extensive correspondence and
collecting copies of records and drawings. In the *Dictionary of National
Biography,* Hutton is stated to have gathered these materials 'with a view

[1] It is unnecessary to investigate here the question of how far these were due to his own
researches. Spottiswoode wrote mainly on legal subjects and his *Religious Houses,* as appears
supra, was originally a contribution to a legal treatise.
[2] It was used by Gordon, with not too happy results, for his *Monasticon* (1875). A few
Coupar Angus items from this source appear in *Rental Bk. of the Cist. Abbey of Cupar-Angus*
(Grampian Club, 1880), ii, 284 ff.
[3] Rev. Henry Docherty, 'The Brockie Forgeries', *Innes Review,* xvi (1965), 79–127.

to compiling a "Monasticon Scotiae" '. If this was the case, he did not
carry out his intention. But his collections, covering much of the country,
are deposited in the National Library of Scotland. By its nature, this
miscellany of letters, notes and transcripts varies in value. Hutton's
correspondents too often reveal the limitations of contemporary knowledge of monastic institutions and history.

Reference is not uncommonly made by writers on the Scottish monasteries to George Chalmers's *Caledonia* (originally published in three
volumes, 1807, 1811, 1824; later in eight volumes, 1887–1902). This is not
a Monasticon nor yet a catalogue of religious houses—it is described as 'a
historical and topographical account of North Britain from the most
ancient to the present time'; but it has much to say on Scottish religious
foundations. Of Chalmers Cosmo Innes declares: 'He laboured under the
disadvantage of defective scholarship of which he was quite unconscious.
. . . In charter study . . . he worked with faulty copies.'[1] Nevertheless it is
unwise to reject this work completely as it embodies information from
documents and rentals which are no longer extant.

With the earlier nineteenth century came a recrudescence of interest in
the discovery and publication of records which seemed propitious for the
more exact study of monasticism in Scotland. The Bannatyne and Maitland Clubs, precursors of many other historical and antiquarian societies,
were founded respectively in 1823 and 1828 and among the volumes
issued under their auspices monastic chartularies took a prominent place;
thus a valuable and growing contribution was made to the sources readily
available for an account of the Scottish religious houses. This was recognized by, among others, W. B. D. D. Turnbull, an enthusiast rather than a
scholar, whose anonymous *Fragmenta Scoto-Monastica* (1842) has as its
subtitle 'Memoir of what has been already done, and what materials exist
towards the formation of a Scotish [*sic*] Monasticon'. That these newly
accessible materials were not utilized at the time to the best advantage,
though they have since become indispensable to the student of Scottish
monastic history, was due in large measure to the fact that they were
regarded from an antiquarian rather than a historical standpoint. They
were an addition to the lore of what was quaint and curious. It was the
age of Scott—himself a prominent member of the Bannatyne Club—who
was not exempt from the foibles of his own Monkbarns.

Among those who were well aware of the significance for the historian of
the new publications was Cosmo Innes, professor of constitutional law and

---

[1] *Scotch Legal Antiquities*, 17; cf. Somerville, *My Own Life and Times* (Edinburgh, 1861),
312–13.

history at the University of Edinburgh (1846–74), who edited many of the Bannatyne volumes and whose works *Scotland in the Middle Ages* (1860), *Sketches of Early Scotch History* (1861) and *Scotch Legal Antiquities* (1872) were, at the time, epoch-making for the study of Scottish medieval history. In 1851 and 1854–5 appeared as one of the publications of the Bannatyne Club *Origines Parochiales Scotiae*, for the editing of which Innes was largely responsible. How marked an advance this work displayed is seen by comparing its historical standard with that of other works which, to a certain extent, cover the same ground, such as the *Statistical Account of Scotland* (in twenty-one volumes, 1791–9) and the *New Statistical Account of Scotland* (in fifteen volumes, 1845). These were made up of contributions (answers to something like a questionnaire) on all the parishes in Scotland, supplied by parish ministers and concerned primarily with contemporary social and ecclesiastical conditions; but local antiquities are also designedly mentioned and, with a few exceptions, dealt with ineptly—ruins, to take a common instance, are much too readily identified as 'monasteries'.[1] *Origines Parochiales* is on a different level. Here we find carefully prepared and adequately documented accounts of the religious foundations which occur in the parishes included in this work. It is noticeable that, in their anxiety to omit no details, the editors sometimes admit unsatisfactory statements from the *Statistical Accounts* and conjectural interpretations of place-names. But, on the whole, *Origines Parochiales* is a sound and useful compilation. Unfortunately it is incomplete; the editors did not carry it beyond the dioceses of Glasgow, Argyll, the Isles, Ross and Caithness.

So far the nineteenth century had passed without a specific attempt to construct a Monasticon, although the materials for such a work were accumulating. Besides the publications of the historical clubs and James Raine's *History and Antiquities of North Durham* (1852), with its important appendix of Coldingham charters, the Acts of Parliament and certain of the public records of Scotland, as well as English records like *Rotuli Scotiae*, had been published; while Augustinus Theiner's *Vetera Monumenta Hibernorum et Scotorum historiam illustrantia* (1864) for the first time provided from the Vatican archives an extensive collection of records bearing on Scottish ecclesiastical history. It is a sad anticlimax to mention, in this promising period, the *Scoti-Monasticon* (otherwise *The Ancient Church in*

---

[1] For a good example, *v.* Fintray, p. 70 *infra*. In this connection may be mentioned the description by Robert Louis Stevenson of the farm at Swanston, in the neighbourhood of Edinburgh: 'It was first a grange of Whitekirk abbey, tilled and inhabited by rosy friars' (*Picturesque Notes*, Edinburgh, Tusitala edn., p. 193). It is enough to say of this ludicrous statement that no such abbey existed. This type of identification is not extinct. Cf. the fanciful statement regarding the church of Durrisdeer in Dumfriesshire that 'the oldest part was a monastery' (*Scotsman*, 2 August 1954).

Scotland, 1874) of Mackenzie Walcott, precentor of Chichester; for, so far as this egregious writer was concerned, these accumulations of valuable source material might never have been made. Depending on secondary sources often of poor quality, Walcott used these uncritically and to their errors added, through his gross carelessness and ignorance both of Scotland and of Scottish history, a number of choice blunders of his own.[1] It is unfortunate that this slipshod work, *faute de mieux*, has been so frequently quoted. Another *Monasticon,* the compilation of J. F. S. Gordon, an Episcopalian clergyman, appeared in 1875. This is in no sense a product of research; it is incomplete and it borrows its statements (and errors) from earlier writers, notably Brockie. Lists of religious houses appeared in various subsequent publications, but they were of no authority and as often as not were derived from Walcott or Gordon.

If a survey of the work which had been done on Scottish monastic antiquities and history by the close of the nineteenth century is on the whole depressing and a record largely of shortcomings and failures, the explanation of the ill-success of many of the efforts which have been narrated is not far to seek. We do not expect to find in the majority of these catalogues and treatises an anticipation of the historical outlook and methods of the twentieth century; yet it is fair to say that the general reason for the defects of these accounts, over a considerable period, was a lack of reference to primary sources. That these were often inaccessible to writers who embarked on the making of a Monasticon (or catalogue of foundations) goes without saying. But the want of them did not sufficiently act as a deterrent; and it made for the uncritical repetition of the statements of other compilers, encouraged too ready a resort to tradition and legend, and opened a wide door to conjecture and improvised opinions. The 'Scot Abroad', intent on glorifying the past of his country (like Camerarius) or his Church (like Dempster or Brockie) was beset with a tendency to overdraw the picture. The Scot in his own country, unfamiliar with but attracted to its monastic past, romanticized it, read into it ideas which were fanciful, ill-informed, unhistorical.

By the twentieth century the sources available for the making of a Monasticon had greatly multiplied, since collections of monastic charters began to be published in the early nineteenth century. Surviving chartularies and collections of monastic charters had now in the main been edited. But while considerable material existed for the history of the religious foundations of the south-eastern, central and eastern Lowlands,

---

[1] One instance will suffice. Writing on the Carmelite friary at Aberdeen, Walcott declares: 'In 1560, the church was sacked by the Covenanters' (*Scoti-Monasticon,* 336).

the monastic (as well as the episcopal) records of Galloway were missing; not a single chartulary of the notable group of religious houses in that region is known to be extant. There was likewise a dearth of sources for the history of the monasteries situated in the western and northern Highlands and the Hebrides; while the foundations in Orkney and Shetland raised problems of peculiar difficulty. On the other hand, much that is important for Scottish monastic history had come to light in the Vatican records. Equally useful was work done on the history of individual orders in Scotland. Dr. W. Moir Bryce's volumes, *The Scottish Greyfriars*, supplied a well-documented study of the Franciscans, and Fr. Norbert Backmund, in *Monasticon Praemonstratense*, II (1952), dealt in detail with the Scottish houses of white canons. This admirably industrious writer was at times somewhat uncritical in his use of sources and his acquaintance with Scottish ecclesiastical history and topography has limitations; but his work makes a valuable contribution to our knowledge of the development of Premonstratensian organization in Scotland. The late Professor R. K. Hannay did much to shed light on the later history of the medieval church in Scotland and the publication of the *Letters of James IV* (1953) and the *Letters of James V* (1954), which he was responsible for collecting, made available material which is highly significant for the last half century (or thereby) of the monasteries' career.

Nevertheless, until the late David Easson published his *Medieval Religious Houses Scotland* in 1957, a reliable account of Scottish religious foundations continued to be a *desideratum*. The author's self-avowed purpose was to list and annotate the houses of which the existence could be verified; and in the notes an attempt was made to indicate the significant features of their history, so far as these were ascertainable. To set forth all the erroneous statements that had figured in lists and other accounts of the Scottish foundations would have been an impossible and, in any case, an invidious and somewhat unprofitable task. But an effort was made to include the typical and recurring errors (which, as regards certain orders, were numerous) so that at least no pretext would be provided for their reappearance. The result was a notable contribution to Scottish ecclesiastical history. Dr. Easson's notes both clarified medieval sources and exposed the fabrications of previous antiquaries. But if many problems were resolved the author of Scotland's first properly documented Monasticon was well aware of difficulties which remained unsolved. Much work in this field remained to be done before even the revised lists could be regarded as other than provisional and in this respect Dr. Easson laid great store on sources 'furth of Scotland'.

That wish has been partially fulfilled. For over a decade, the Ross Fund
of Glasgow University has financed a systematic examination of all pre-
Reformation records in the Vatican archives. Manuscript calendars of
Scottish petitions to the Pope gifted to the university by Dr. Annie I.
Dunlop, who spent a lifetime working in these archives, has been supplemented by a vast microfilm collection of Scottish material derived from
papal records. This collection above all has made possible this revised
edition of Dr. Easson's pioneer volume. But many problems still remain
unresolved, and this new edition can only lay claim to have advanced our
knowledge of Scottish monasticism some little way along the road to the
more definitive edition which further endeavour and research can alone
bring.

THE DEVELOPMENT OF MONASTICISM
IN SCOTLAND

(i)

IT is impossible to say with certainty when monasticism was first introduced into Scotland. The traditional account of St. Ninian's settlement at Whithorn, as given by Bede and later elaborated by Ailred, has sometimes been taken as pointing to the establishment in Galloway of an outpost of Martinian monasticism, since those writers associate Candida Casa and its founder with the founder of Marmoutier and bishop of Tours. But the connection of St. Ninian with St. Martin cannot be substantiated and the type of organizational structure established by Ninian at Whithorn in the early fifth century was apparently not monastic. A more definite landmark in the monastic history of Scotland is the founding of a monastery at Iona in 565, following the arrival in Scotland of St. Columba and his companions from Ireland in 563. In the years which followed the arrival of Columba many such monasteries were to be founded. Among them were those of Artchain and Mag Luinge, both situated on the isle of Tiree, and other island monasteries in Eigg, Eileach an Naoimh in the Garvelloch islands, Hinba (Jura) and Lismore. These were all founded during the lifetime of Columba (d. 597), as was Cella Diuni on Loch Awe. According to twelfth-century Gaelic tradition, Aberdour and Turriff in Aberdeenshire were personally founded by Columba, but this may be doubted and their foundation should possibly be attributed with that of Applecross, Abernethy and Kingarth in Bute to the century after the saint's death. Other monasteries, including one on the island of Rum, may have been founded during this period, but it is clear that the principal achievement of the Columban church was not the conversion of Pictland and the Northern Isles, but its southwards expansion which culminated in the resuscitation of Christianity in Northumbria.

In the course of this expansion between 635 and 663, two early episcopal centres at Old Melrose and Abercorn appear to have been transformed into monasteries based on Lindisfarne, and at Whithorn a similar development seems to have taken place in this period. Archaeological evidence would appear to suggest that Govan likewise became monastic at this time. The southward expansion of this monastic church, which was also accompanied by the foundation of a monastery at Coldingham, inevitably brought it into collision with a fast expanding missionary church with which it was at variance on a number of issues. The ultimate decision in favour of Roman usage was made at Whitby in 663 and as a verdict binding upon the whole of Northumbria its effect was to reverberate to the Forth and eventually beyond that line.

South of the Forth–Clyde line, Whithorn, and for a brief period Abercorn, became established episcopal centres, while other churches in this area, such as Applegarth, Govan, Hoddam and Kirkcudbright, appear to have approximated in organization to English minsters rather than to monasteries of a conventual nature. Such monasteries may have continued to exist at Old Melrose and Coldingham, and a new monastic foundation was traditionally established at Tyninghame by Baldred (d. 756). But Coldingham and Tyninghame were both destroyed by the Norse in *c.* 870 and 941 respectively, and Old Melrose was deserted before 1074.

North of the Forth–Clyde line, the pattern presents a very similar appearance. The effects of the decision made at Whitby, which found acceptance in Pictland in the early eighth century, coupled with Norse raids, appears to have terminated the existence of most Columban foundations. In the meantime other churches were being established. An episcopal centre appeared at Abernethy by the early eighth century. Other bishops may have been appointed at the same time and Ross, with its centre at Rosemarkie and its dedication to St. Peter, has at least a legendary claim to be regarded as one of them. However, the episcopal centre at Abernethy proved to be short lived, and following the union of the Picts and the Scots (843–850), Dunkeld which may have been the site of an older Columban monastery, became the chief ecclesiastical centre of the united kingdom. Tradition associates with this site a group of Culdee clergy who may have acted as the bishop's *familia*. The nature of those Culdees is not entirely certain. But, whatever their origins in Ireland, where they initially constituted an elite of monks who strictly observed their rule, it is clear that in Scotland, as indeed in Ireland where few Culdee communities maintained their initial fervour, they became akin to groups of secular clerks living in a community or *muintir*. Such a community is also found at Brechin where 'the great city' was offered to the Lord by Kenneth II (971–5). Likewise at Kilrimont (St. Andrews) which by the beginning of the tenth century had wrested the primacy from Dunkeld, a similar situation is evident. An early monastic site appears to have existed, and two identifiable communities, one associated with the earlier monastic community and the other with the Culdees, eventually emerged. The members of the former became secularized, but the Culdees appear to have functioned in association with the bishops of St. Andrews until an attempt was made to replace them by canons regular in the twelfth century.

Not all ministrations were provided from diocesan centres, however, and the area north of the Forth–Clyde line demonstrates close similarities in this respect to the pattern established in the south. Here too communities of secular priests, frequently but not invariably called Culdees, are found serving from their houses considerable areas which were deemed to be their *parochia*. The existence of some such communities is well attested, but caution must be exercised in relation to others (see p. 52 below). Lesser communities which are clearly identifiable as religious centres founded between the eighth and eleventh centuries can be classified as Culdee and non-Culdee. Of the latter, Clova in Aberdeenshire, Deer with its *canonici* in the twelfth century and Methven, with a similar group of clerks, are most readily identifiable with the minsters of the south.

Among the Culdee churches, two significant groupings can be assessed, firstly the communities of Culdees which have the hallmark of communities of secular priests and are significantly at the episcopal centres at St. Andrews, Brechin and Dunkeld or older episcopal centres such as Abernethy and Muthil. Secondly those who by their location appear to be of a more eremitical nature, such as those at Inchaffray, where the community is not specifically called Culdees but brethren, and at Loch Leven, where the donation of churches to this institution in the eleventh century nevertheless points to service by members of the community who must have been clerks. In the nature of the evidence the remaining Culdee communities cannot be assigned with any certainty to one category or another. Monifieth is an enigma; and although Monymusk is one of the best documented of these houses the nature of the original foundation must remain in question, but it was evidently not following a strict monastic rule.

Indeed, with the exception of Iona, the only apparent approach to an old Columban type monastery is found at Turriff where in 1131—1132 an abbot and a lector (*fer-léginn*) who was head of a monastic school, appear on record. The evidence is indeterminate and only at Iona is there any clear indication of a monastic community with a Culdee community situated alongside it. This is very much in the Irish tradition in which the Culdee elite were often to be found in the midst of a larger community who respected them, but did not share their devotions and austerities. However, even here by this latter stage the larger community may have ceased to be regular monks.

In addition to the Culdees, who lived in a community, there were also hermits who perpetuated an earlier ascetic tradition. Of this type, it would seem, were the 'very many men, shut up in cells apart, in various places in the district of the Scots' of Turgot's account, who, according to the same writer, 'led the life of angels upon earth' and were held in respect and visited by Queen Margaret (Anderson, *Early Sources*, ii, 76). Such also, may have been, the solitary of the island of Inchcolm, who, it is narrated in the *Scotichronicon*, succoured King Alexander I and his companions; and, to cite medieval charters, it is probable that John the hermit, who, in the later twelfth century, was granted an island in the loch of 'Lunnin' by William the Lion, and Gillemichel, 'the late hermit', whose hermitage was bestowed, in the early thirteenth century, upon Coupar Angus abbey, were followers of a pre-medieval tradition.

Nevertheless, by the mid-eleventh century monastic communities survived at best in a few isolated centres of which Iona alone presents sufficient evidence of a community to justify a firm conclusion about its status. Indeed it would seem that Iona was not only the first Irish monastery to be founded in Scotland, but was one of the few to survive the organizational changes of the eighth century and retain its links with Ireland. Elsewhere, with the possible exception of Turriff, the so-called monasteries approximate more closely to minsters in their organization than to communities following a monastic rule.

(ii)

It was with the coming to Scotland of the Saxon princess, Margaret, Edward Aetheling's daughter, who, in 1068/9, married Malcolm III [Canmore], that the way was opened for the introduction of monasticism of the medieval type in the northern kingdom. Not infrequently Margaret has been described as the instigator of a 'new order' within the ecclesiastical sphere in Scotland. This, however, is an exaggeration. Ere her time, Roman influences had, almost inevitably, been infiltrating into Scotland; and her 'innovations', significant as they may have been for the future, were modest contributions towards the alignment of Scottish ecclesiastical institutions with those of Western Christendom. The saintly queen 'initiated no reforms in the administration or organization of the church'[1] and set herself rather to rectify certain of its prevailing customs and usages. So far from showing antagonism to the Celtic clergy, Margaret and her husband maintained towards them the benevolent policy of their predecessors. Thus Margaret and Malcolm are found bestowing a bene-

[1] *A Source Book of Scottish History*, i (1952), 42.

faction upon the Culdees of Loch Leven; and it is said by Ordericus
Vitalis that the queen rebuilt the monastery of Iona and 'gave monks
fitting revenues for the work of the Lord'.[1] But it is of much significance
that, before 1089, Lanfranc, at Queen Margaret's request, sent Goldwin
and two other 'brethren' to Scotland. Little enough is known of this
settlement of Benedictine monks, presumably at Dunfermline, the first of
its kind in Scottish territory. But it is clear that, in bringing them into her
realm, Margaret was not reviving Benedictinism, as it was revived in
England. By this step, the queen inaugurated the policy of encouraging
the establishment of the monastic orders in Scotland, a policy which was to
be greatly developed by her sons and successors. The Crown, in the next two
centuries, was to play a leading part in fostering the spread of monasticism.

Three younger sons of Margaret in turn held the throne of Scotland. In
the reign of Edgar (1097–1106/7) took place the foundation at Coldingham which developed into a second Benedictine monastery, a priory
linked with Durham.[2] With Alexander I (1106/7–1124), Augustinian
canons were brought to Scone—it is said, from Nostell. In 1113, Earl
David, Margaret's sixth son, introduced at Selkirk Benedictines of Tiron
and thus signalized the outstanding favour he was later to show, as king of
Scotland, towards the religious orders. His reign, as David I (1124–53),
is justly described as 'one of the most momentous in all Scots history'.[3] The
elements of far-reaching changes were present in Scotland when he came
to the throne; David of set policy expedited these developments. The
characteristic features of his reign were the settlement of Normans, with
royal encouragement, in the country and their acquisition of lands; the
steady extension of feudal administration in the kingdom; and, as the
counterpart of these secular movements, the marked expansion of the
organization and institutions of the medieval church.

More especially, this reign is notable for the planting of religious houses
on a scale unmatched in any other period of Scottish history. The new
abbeys were, in many cases, of David's own foundation and endowment—
to an extent which evoked the jibe attributed to James I that David was a
'sair sanct for the croun'—and their first inhabitants came from England
or, in some cases, from France. A few years after his accession, David
appears to have secured for Dunfermline the status of a Benedictine

[1] *Patr. Lat.*, 188, col. 620. If the chronicler's statement is reliable, it is difficult to suppose
that these could have been other than Celtic monks.
[2] A letter of Anselm, archbishop of Canterbury to Alexander I, in 1107, mentions 'our
brothers whom we have sent into Scotland according to the desire of your brother [King
Edgar]' (*ESC*, no. xxv). If the reference is to monks sent from Canterbury, it remains
incapable of explanation.
[3] I. F. Grant, *Social and Economic Development of Scotland* (1930), 13.

abbey, having brought the first abbot and a fresh influx of monks from Canterbury. From Rievaulx came the Cistercians who colonized the first Scottish house of that order, the abbey which the king had founded at Melrose (1136), parent-house of at least five abbeys, among which Newbattle (1140) and Kinloss (1150 or 1151) were likewise of David's foundation. Another community from Rievaulx went to the abbey of Dundrennan (1142) which David had instituted and which became the mother-house of two later abbeys in Galloway. To the king also were due the Augustinian foundations of Holyrood (1128), a daughter-house of Merton; of Jedburgh (c. 1138), whose canons were derived from Beauvais; and of Cambuskenneth (c. 1140), an offshoot of Arrouaise. In addition to these royal foundations, the Augustinian priory of St. Andrews (1144) was established by the bishop of that see; and a house of Premonstratensians at Dryburgh (1150) had as its founder Hugh de Moreville, constable of Scotland, the canons being brought from Alnwick; King David, again, founded the Benedictine priories of Urquhart (c. 1136) and the Isle of May (–1153), the priory of Lesmahagow (1144) of the order of Tiron and the earliest Scottish Cistercian nunnery, at Berwick-on-Tweed (–1153). He also introduced the military orders, the Knights Templars and the Hospitallers. David's foundations were widely distributed, from the Borders to the Moray Firth, from Lothian to Galloway.

(iii)

Succeeding rulers followed King David's example. Thus, Malcolm IV (1153–65) had founded by 1164 the abbey of white monks at Coupar Angus, the Cistercian nunnery of Manuel and the Augustinian hospital of Soutra. Only second to the Crown in their promotion of religious foundations were the Scoto-Norman magnates and it was Walter FitzAlan, Steward of Scotland, who for the first time brought Cluniac monks (from Wenlock) to Scotland and settled them at Paisley (c. 1169); while a de Moreville endowed a house of the order of Tiron at Kilwinning (1162 × 89). Of the two or more Cistercian nunneries founded during Malcolm's reign, Haddington (–1159), the largest of the Scottish houses of women, owed its inception to the king's mother, the countess Ada, who, like her son, is said to have been influenced by St. Waltheof in showing favour to this order. Two Tironensian houses arose in the reign of Malcolm's brother and successor, William the Lion (1165–1214): the great abbey of Arbroath, dedicated to St. Thomas of Canterbury, which the king himself founded in 1178; and the abbey of Lindores (1191), founded by David, earl of Huntingdon, his younger brother.

It may be noted that in the period covered by these reigns religious foundations took place in outlying parts of the kingdom through the initiative of local potentates who, in a scarcely homogeneous Scotland, were the virtual rulers of these regions. Successive lords of Galloway— Fergus, Roland, Alan—established the Premonstratensians at Soulseat (–1161) (and perhaps Whithorn, *c.* 1175) as well as at Tongland (1218), and the Cistercians at Glenluce (1191/2), while the Benedictine nunnery of Lincluden (–1174) is said to have been founded by Uchtred, son of Fergus of Galloway. Again, the Benedictine abbey (–1203) and the Augustinian nunnery (–1208) of Iona, and the Cistercian house of Saddell (–1207) in Kintyre had as their founder Reginald, son of Somerled, lord of the Isles. These groups of foundations were mainly situated in dioceses— Galloway (Candida Casa) and Sodor—which, until the fifteenth century, were in a position extraneous to the diocesan structure of the church in Scotland, since the former was under the jurisdiction of York and the latter under the jurisdiction of Nidaros in Norway.

The reign of Alexander II (1214–49) has some features important for Scottish monastic history. Three further Cistercian foundations, at Culross (–1217), Deer (1219) and Balmerino (*c.* 1227), took place, the last of these effected by the king and his mother, Queen Ermengarde. A projected establishment of Gilbertines at Dalmilling in Ayrshire, the only attempt to extend this order beyond England forms an interesting episode in the years between 1219 and 1238; the project, however, was abandoned. But, in the third decade of this century, an order which is not represented in England came to occupy three Scottish houses. This was the order of Val des Choux (Vallis Caulium), which was instituted at the place of that name in the diocese of Langres in Burgundy by Viard, a former *conversus* of the Carthusian monastery of Louvigny, towards the end of the twelfth century. Its rule, confirmed by Pope Innocent III, in 1205, has affinities with the rules of the Cistercians and the Carthusians. In 1230 the order was introduced into Scotland; for this, it is said, William de Malvoisin, bishop of St. Andrews, was responsible; and the king founded for its monks the priory of Pluscarden (1230 or 1231). The Valliscaulian houses were placed in isolated regions in the north and west of Scotland. A significant feature of the same decade is the arrival of the friars. In 1230 the Black-friars appear at Edinburgh; and their coming to Scotland is said to have been due, once more, to Bishop de Malvoisin. Of the nine Dominican houses which came into being in this reign all save one were royal foundations. The Greyfriars were established at Berwick in 1231 and friaries at Roxburgh and Haddington followed. It is uncertain whether the Trinitarians settled in Scotland as early as the reign of William the Lion, though he is stated to have provided for a house at Aberdeen. But towards the middle of the thirteenth century they had been placed at Berwick and Dunbar.

It remains to add that the reign of Alexander III (1249–1285/6) saw the foundation of the first Scottish house of Carmelites at Tullilum near Perth (1262). Franciscan foundations increased and for a short time the Friars of the Sack were housed at Berwick. We may note also the latest of the Cistercian plantations—the abbey of Sweetheart, which Devorgilla de Balliol founded in 1273.

(iv)

As the end of the thirteenth century marks an epoch in the history of the religious orders in Scotland it is appropriate to comment at this point on the first and most important stage of the development of monasticism in Scotland which we have rapidly surveyed. Before 1300 all the greater orders, if we except the Carthusians, were present in the kingdom. Of these the most conspicuous were the orders of Cîteaux and Tiron and the Augustinian canons. The Cistercians had six houses established between 1136 and 1164; thereafter, until 1273, foundations of this order occur at longer intervals, a slowing- down which was probably the belated effect of the act of the General Chapter of 1152, forbidding new plantations. As early as 1157 Scottish abbots were given the concession of attending at Cîteaux only once in four years, But Scottish Cistercian affairs are the subject of statutes of the General Chapter from time to time until 1282, when there is a significant and protracted break in the record of the relations of the Scottish abbeys with the mother-house of the order. From the Chronicle of Melrose we learn of the crisis that overtook the Scottish Cistercians in 1216–18, when the monks were involved in a struggle with the legate, Gualo, in defence of their privileges. But the white monks stood high in the favour of the royal house and the feudal lords and such was their vogue that, *c.* 1240, it appeared possible that the Cluniacs of Paisley, at that time the one Scottish community of that order, might be superseded by Cistercians.[1]

Of the original Benedictine monasteries only two were major foundations—Dunfermline abbey and Coldingham priory; but to these the Benedictines of the order of Tiron, who were relatively stronger in Scotland than in England, added four abbeys, including the important foundations of Kelso and Arbroath. Among the houses of Augustinian canons were

[1] See p. 65 below.

the prominent abbeys of Scone, Holyrood, Jedburgh and Cambuskenneth, but their chief foundation was the priory of St. Andrews, whose canons formed the chapter of the cathedral. The Premonstratensians also contributed a monastic chapter at Whithorn. Again, the three orders of friars, Dominican, Franciscan and Carmelite, had become well established; and the older orders of nuns, Benedictine, Cistercian, Augustinian, were now represented in Scotland. By the end of Alexander III's reign, the tale of monastic establishments in Scotland was relatively complete. A number of mendicant houses were yet to be founded and the Carthusians do not appear till the fifteenth century. But all the greater monastic foundations had been made.

The geographical distribution of the monasteries was uneven. Although they spread into the Hebrides and perhaps as far as the Orkneys, the great majority were situated in central and southern Scotland. Of the larger houses a number were located in Lothian and the proximity of the Border, advantageously, if only for their economic development, in time of peace, but precariously, as the later centuries of their history would show, in days of war and invasion.

In this period, which witnessed the settlement and extension of the religious orders, we detect the signs of tensions which were to become accentuated by the worsening relations of Scotland and her neighbour. Thus priories which were sited within Scottish territory but affiliated to English houses came to occupy the invidious position vividly displayed in the later contentious history of Coldingham. Already in the reign of Alexander III an attempt was made—and, in the end, successfully—to sever the priory of May from its mother-house at Reading and to associate it with the priory of St. Andrews. Again, as the orders present in Scotland had in many cases been brought originally from England, they were not infrequently within the sphere of jurisdiction of English authorities. In the thirteenth century the first movement was made (by the Greyfriars) to secure independence of English control. The Scottish friars, whose earlier foundations were included in the custody of Newcastle (though for a short time they had the name if not the reality of a province) enlisted the aid of King Alexander III to obtain for themselves, through the good offices of the Pope, a Provincial Minister; and, although this request was rejected by the Franciscan Chapter at Narbonne in 1260, there is, according to Moir Bryce, 'a strong presumption that they enjoyed a *de facto* autonomy'.[1] A Scottish vicariate was ultimately formed in 1329.

---

[1] *Grey Friars*, i, 11.

(v)

From the eleventh to the thirteenth centuries, few conspicuous names appear in the annals of the Scottish monasteries.[1] In 1148, St. Waltheof, who had been a canon of Nostell and prior of Kirkham, and later a monk at Wardon and Rievaulx, crossed the Border to become abbot of Melrose; he ruled that abbey till his death in 1159. Clement, who as the able bishop of Dunblane (1233–56/58) was responsible for the revival of that decrepit see, belonged to the Dominican order, though the legend that he was appointed by St. Dominic to bring the first colony of Blackfriars into Scotland must be regarded as doubtful. Two more notable figures have a brief and somewhat uncertain association with the orders in Scotland Adam 'the Scot', author of *On the Tripartite Tabernacle*, homilies on *The Order, Habit and Profession of Premonstratensian Canons* and other contemplative works, and also known as Adam of Dryburgh, was in all likelihood a canon of the Premonstratensian abbey of that name rather than of the priory of that order at Whithorn, where he has sometimes been located; he eventually joined the Carthusians at Witham, *c.* 1189.

(vi)

In the troubled years of the late thirteenth century emerged the political situation which lasted more or less till the end of the medieval period; the relations of Scotland and England were uneasy, strained and often overtly hostile, while the Scots resorted to alliance and made common cause with France. This situation was primarily the outcome of the disputed succession which followed the death of 'the Maid of Norway', the heiress to Alexander III's throne, and the opportunity it afforded Edward I of asserting overlordship of Scotland. How the War of Independence which developed out of the resistance movements of Wallace and Bruce affected the Scottish religious houses is too complicated a question to enter on in detail here. It must suffice to note that warfare and occupation of the country did not leave the monasteries unscathed. This is seen more especially in the case of the abbey of Scone, from which, in 1296, Edward I removed the Stone of Destiny on which the Scottish kings were crowned, while in 1298, for some unexplained reason, but probably because of its connection with the Scottish dynasty, the abbey was sacked and destroyed.

[1] John Duns Scotus can no longer be accounted among this number as the story of his birth at Littledean in Maxton parish and his purported reception of the Franciscan habit in the house of the Friars Minor at Dumfries have been exposed as bogus—'the high water mark of Marianus Brockie's catalogue of bogus charters, fictitious histories, imaginative history, outright mendacity and crass effrontery' (Henry Docherty, 'The Brockie forgeries' in *Innes Review*, xvi (1965), 79–127).

Neither Bruce's victory in 1314 nor the treaty of Northampton which officially ended hostilities in 1328, brought immunity from the effects of invasion to the religious houses in the south of Scotland. Kelso, Melrose, Dryburgh, Holyrood had suffered, and would suffer again. Meanwhile, the attitude of Robert I towards the monasteries, once he had become effective ruler of Scotland, maintained the tradition of royal benevolence. Three small foundations, an Augustinian priory at Strathfillan (1317/18), a Carmelite house at Banff (1321–4) and a Franciscan house at Lanark (1328–9) were of his creating. But the considerable number of his charters to the religious houses, confirming their properties and granting them new endowments, suggests that the king who, in 1319, proclaimed his policy of protecting 'holy church and holy religion' was concerned to succour the monasteries and revive them.

But a period of marked decline was now to overtake them; and the fourteenth century is, in the main, a bleak and undistinguished stage in their history. One of the last documents of King Robert's reign is a letter exhorting his son and successors to augment rather than diminish the grants he has made to Melrose abbey and to protect it against 'invaders and enviers'. The fulfilment of this counsel was beyond the power of the weak kings who followed him; and the religious houses, in a period vexed with unstable government, insecurity and intermittent war, shared in the demoralization of the kingdom. Isolation likewise befell them, for their contacts with motherhouses beyond the Border and the general chapters of their orders in France were broken as a result of hostilities with England, the Hundred Years' War and, eventually, the schism in the Church. Favour also fell away from them; their prestige declined and the former profusion of endowments ceased. It is tempting to suppose that the Black Death, which devastated the English religious houses, must have added to the adversities of the Scottish monasteries. That pestilence came to Scotland in 1349–50 and there were later visitations of plague in the same century. How far the monasteries were affected remains uncertain; on this subject, save for a reference in the *Scotichronicon* to the death from plague of twenty-four canons of St. Andrews, records are surprisingly silent. Nor is there any clear indication of monasteries becoming defunct from this cause. The effect of war rather than of pestilence accounts for the extinction of the Cistercian nunnery at Berwick.

One point of interest emerges in the fourteenth century. To what extent episcopal visitation of non-exempt houses was maintained in Scotland we have no means of knowing, for apart from such a record as appears in 1345 acknowledging that the bishops of Moray had visited the priory of

Pluscarden since its foundation and that the monks of that house had no exemption of privilege to the contrary—from which no inference on the regularity of visitation can be drawn—evidence is almost entirely lacking. The only visitation records, two in number, come to us from the later part of this century. From them we learn that William de Landallis, bishop of St. Andrews, visited the abbey of Scone in January 1365/6 and October 1369, and his ordinances on discipline and obedience are set forth in detail. There is no indication that the state of this abbey was such as to demand the special attention of the bishop. De Landallis, we may gather from these isolated records, was acting simply as a conscientious diocesan.

A few houses of friars were endowed in this period. But before the end of the fourteenth century, foundations non-monastic and of a type new to Scotland had begun, very sporadically, to appear. These were colleges of secular clergy, an innovation inasmuch as Scotland, unlike England, had, apart from cathedral chapters, no early incorporations of secular canons after the pattern of Ripon or Southwell to be revived in the later Middle Ages. The first of these collegiate bodies came into existence when, towards 1250, the Culdee community at St. Andrews, with its property became dissociated from the cathedral and was set up as a secular college which figures thereafter as the collegiate church of St. Mary on the Rock and for some time as a chapel royal. Not till the first half of the next century was well advanced were further colleges inaugurated. In 1342 a college for a dean, archpriest and eight prebendaries was founded in the parish church of Dunbar, in its constitution unlike later Scottish collegiate churches and somewhat reminiscent of an Italian *pieve*. Again, at Abernethy what had once been a Culdee house and was latterly a priory of Augustinian canons became a secular college before 1345.

Towards the end of this century, a succession of collegiate foundations begins with Maybole (1383/4), Lincluden (a suppressed house of Benedictine nuns) (1389) and Bothwell (1397/8) and continues to the eve of the Reformation; the last of the Scottish colleges was founded at Biggar (1545/6). In general, these foundations come within two categories: a *collegium* might be instituted in a parish church of which the revenues were augmented to maintain a number of prebendaries or canons or chaplains (for the clergy of such churches are variously designated), with provision for the parochial cure of souls; or a group of chantry priests was incorporated to serve a church or chapel which had no parochial commitments. At the head of a secular college was a provost or, occasionally, a dean; but the most ambitious of these foundations, the Chapel Royal of Stirling, ultimately had a bishop and dean (i.e. a dean of episcopal status) and dignitaries after the pattern of a cathedral. Two of the academic foundations—St. Salvator's College, St. Andrews, and King's College, Aberdeen—were primarily collegiate churches. The founders of the secular colleges were in many cases barons or 'lairds'; a few colleges were royal foundations. It is noteworthy that in the sixteenth century there was a marked tendency on the part of the more important Scottish burghs to secure for their parish churches, in which the numerous choir and chantry priests constituted a quasi-collegiate organization, formal collegiate status, with a provost or president. This development is seen at Peebles, Aberdeen, Haddington and Stirling. In progress elsewhere, it was halted by the Reformation.

(vii)

We may regard the reigns of the first five Jameses, extending from 1406 to 1542, as covering approximately the last phase of the active history of the Scottish religious houses. It is convenient to note, first of all, the progress of monastic foundations in this their final period. In 1429 James I was responsible for introducing the Carthusians, belatedly, into Scotland; the Charterhouse at Perth, established in that year, was the most considerable foundation since the thirteenth century. During the reign of the second James, the Franciscans of the Observantine reform had their first Scottish settlement at Edinburgh (*c.* 1462–3). Of the eight houses of that order which arose in the next half-century several were royal foundations, while some, on the other hand, may have been due to the characteristic initiative of the burgesses in the burghs where they were placed. It is significant that Observant friars were settled in St. Andrews (1458) by Bishop James Kennedy, who, eight years previously, by establishing his college of St. Salvator, had manifested his desire to vitalize the first Scottish university. The presence of the university likewise induced the development of the Dominican house in that city; in 1516, the provincial chapter envisaged its enlargement for friars 'engaged continually in the study of sacred letters'. Of the four mendicant orders, the Augustinian friars (or hermits) are of least account in the monastic annals of Scotland. They are, indeed, represented only be a transient unidentified foundation and a house at Berwick which appears in the earlier fourteenth century, when from it, as from the other Berwick friaries, Edward III ordered the Scottish friars to be removed and English friars substituted. Much later, this austere order commended itself to James IV, who, in 1506, made an ineffective attempt to displace the nuns of the Cistercian priory of Manuel and to introduce in their stead Augustinian friars; and *c.* 1511, the same king designed unsuccessfully the conversion of the hospital of St. Laurence at Haddington into a house of this order. Three nunneries appear among these later foundations: small houses of Franciscan nuns at Aberdour (1486) and Dundee (1501/2) and the more imposing establishment of Dominican nuns at Sciennes, Edinburgh (1517). Latest among the Scottish foundations were a Dominican priory at Dundee (*c.* 1521), destined to be destroyed after a brief existence, and a Carmelite house at Greenside, Edinburgh (1520–5).

While foundations continued to be made until the third decade of the sixteenth century, the later Middle Ages saw a number of houses, mostly small and sometimes non-conventual, in straits which led to their extinction. In these, religious observance had ceased or was barely maintained; and they were commonly merged in larger foundations. Before 1423 the obscure Cistercian nunnery of St. Evoca in Galloway, a foundation unknown until the evidence of Vatican records was forthcoming, had dwindled and expired; and, about 1434, the Augustinian nunnery of St. Leonard at Perth was extinguished—its revenues were annexed to the Charterhouse. The Benedictine priory of Urquhart, in 1453/4, was united to the priory of Pluscarden, in which Benedictines had replaced the order of Val des Choux; while the once important house of that order at Coldingham, where the community is said, in 1461, to have been reduced to two monks, barely survived the unexampled vicissitudes of its later career; the long and tortuous struggle to dissever this priory from Durham and its varied exploitation by ecclesiastics and laymen make its history more tangled than that of any other Scottish monastery. In the fifteenth century, a house of Friars Preachers at Haddington is mentioned twice in records—and disappears. Again, in the beginning of the sixteenth century, the Cistercian abbey of Saddell, isolated in Kintyre, had fallen on evil days and was beyond revival. In 1519 the Dominicans at Cupar were incorporated in the friary at St. Andrews. Lastly, the Trinitarian house of Peebles, before the middle of the sixteenth century, had absorbed the small defunct settlements of that order at Berwick, Dunbar and Houston.

The state of certain of the religious houses in the earlier fifteenth century, when Scotland had lately renounced the antipope Benedict XIII and adhered to Pope Martin V, is disclosed in a well-known document, the letter which in 1425 James I directed to the abbots and priors of the Benedictine monks and the Augustinian canons. Thus early in his active reign, for only in the previous year had he returned from captivity, the first energetic ruler whom Scotland had seen for well nigh a century addressed himself to the condition of the monasteries. Deploring the decadence of monasticism in his realm, he urges upon these heads of religious houses the reformation of their orders, especially by the holding of general chapters,[1]

lest through your negligence and idleness the munificence of kings, who formerly for their preservation and the salvation of their subjects notably endowed your monasteries in olden days and enriched them, may repent of having erected walls of marble.

The king enjoins the strengthening of discipline to 'take away all these occasions of decay' and promises the monasteries, thus reinvigorated, his protection.[2] It may have been that King James was influenced by Henry V's concern for the failure of these orders in England to hold general chapters; but the cases of Coldingham and Inchaffray suggest that his remonstrance was not without some justification; and his almost contemporary foundation of the Perth Charterhouse amounted to a direct encouragement of strict religious observance. The veiled threat which we may read between the lines of his letter to the Benedictines and the Augustinians is not, however, to be ignored. James I may or may not have carped at the liberality of his ancestor, King David;[3] but the suggestion conveyed in the letter would seem to be that failure on the part of the orders to amend might be met by the withholding of their endowments. James did not go beyond this threat; but its implication—that as the Crown had endowed the monasteries, so it might also recall these endowments—was significant for their future history. Later rulers were to treat monastic wealth as virtually at the disposal of the Crown; and the annexation of the monasteries to the Crown, as yet a long way ahead, was enacted in 1587 on the ground that the revenues granted to the abbeys 'of auld' had been Crown property.

From Cistercian records we learn something of the state of this the most prominent order in Scotland, at the same period. Before the end of the

[1] The evidence concerning the holding of chapters in Scotland is almost nil. One of the few indications is in a record of 17 September 1326, whereby the abbot of Dunfermline who is designated 'conservator of the general chapter of monks of the order of St. Benedict in the realm of Scotland', summons the abbot of Arbroath, in terms of the Lateran statute requiring a triennial general chapter in each kingdom or province, to attend a forthcoming chapter at Dunfermline abbey on 21 October (*Arbroath Liber*, ii, no. 356).

[2] See *Source Book of Scottish History*, ii, 97–9.

[3] John Major's version is that James, 'when he visited the tomb of David, is reputed to have said: "There abide, king most pious, but likewise to Scotland's state and kings most unprofitable." meaning thereby that on the establishment of some very wealthy communities he had lavished more than was right of the royal revenues' (*Hist. of Greater Britain*, 135–6).

schism, relations between the Scottish abbeys and Cîteaux had been resumed;[1] and in 1408 the abbot of Balmerino is found at the mother-house of the order, where, in consideration of the 'lamentable desolation' of the abbey of Coupar Angus, he obtained release of that monastery from arrears and remission of part of its future dues. Forty years later, the same abbey was allowed by the General Chapter to compound for its dues in respect of its poverty. That the Cistercians were beset with economic problems need not surprise us, for even the recently endowed Carthusians were soon to find the times stringent and to have difficulty in paying their debts. How far the white monks had otherwise declined is by no means easy to say. Ferrerius speaks of the abbot of Pontigny, who came to Scotland in 1417, as an emissary of the General Chapter sent to restore monastic observance which had fallen away, but it appears that this was not the sole object of the abbot's visit. Again, a statute of 1433 mentions disorders prevalent in Scottish as well as English, Welsh and Irish houses which are attributed to the absence of the abbots of these regions from the Chapter because of wars and the dangers of travel, while in 1445 and later, commissaries were appointed to deal with their reform. More specific evidence does not become available till the following century.

(viii)

We may credit James I with a sincere desire to restore the vitality of the Scottish religious houses. But the beginnings of a system which thwarted their revival were soon to appear; and already in King James's reign took place the first phases of a struggle which was fraught for them with un-happy consequences. The practice of granting an abbey or priory to an already beneficed churchman as a commend (*in commendam*) was originally designed as a temporary and exceptional measure; for example, to provide for the administration of a house and its revenues during a vacancy in its government. In 1439 the provision of the abbey of Scone to the bishop of St. Andrews *in commendam* (though that prelate probably did not obtain possession, as an abbot elected by the convent appears to have held his ground) set an unfortunate precedent; and the grant of a pension from Paisley abbey in 1459, to placate a rival claimant to the commend, exemplified a practice which was to become too common. The grant of Paisley *in commendam* to Patrick Graham, bishop of St. Andrews in 1466 sparked off a spate of legislation starting with a statute of the Scottish Parliament which forbade the holding of commends 'of new nor aulde' and

[1] It is said that a prior of Kinloss attended the General Chapter in 1371 (*Kinloss Recs*, xl).

inhibited under penalties, the purchasing of them. Nevertheless, if the recipient, unlike Graham, had royal approval the practice thereafter was widely condoned. In consequence the system of granting commends in perpetuity, which eventually attained disastrous dimensions in Scotland, meant that these were to be little more than a source of emolument to their holders; it led increasingly to the exploitation and demoralization of the monasteries; and its development is closely bound up with the involved and long-drawn struggle between the Papacy and the Crown for the control of appointments to benefices.

The source of this tension between the Pope and the Scottish kings had its roots in the growth and extension of the custom of reserving for papal provision benefices which were otherwise elective. So far as monasteries were concerned, regular churches of which the heads were ordinarily elected, priories and offices of administration in monasteries and priories were reserved to papal disposal by Pope John XXII (1316–34). This procedure was endorsed by his successors, who added little to general rules of provision which were already so sweeping that few new categories were open to even the most inventive papal mind. The extent to which these claims were implemented is patently demonstrated during the pontificate of Benedict XIII (1394–1418) when provision was made to no less than nineteen Scottish religious houses of all orders and widely differing valuations. Nevertheless, papal intervention rarely went beyond the formal provision of the chapter nominee, behind the choice of which royal or other lay influence frequently lurked. In such circumstances a purely papal nominee had little chance and only in infrequent cases of internal conflict did papal provision become in any sense more meaningful. With the end of the Schism the situation remained unchanged and unchallenged, and it is unlikely that the reaffirmation by Pope Eugenius IV (1431–47) and Pope Nicholas V (1447–55) of pre-Schismatic chancery rules relating to provision and reservation caused in themselves any hostility between the Crown and the Papacy. Royal action, initiated by James I and his successors, against papal provision can hardly have been motivated by the fear of losing influence over the choice of churchmen, but were more probably an attempt to curb the outflow of money to pay for the rubber stamping of decisions effectively made in Scotland. Thus during the reign of James I legislative restraints were placed upon the export of money and upon the quest of benefices or pensions by purchase and without royal licence.[1] Thereafter, in addition to the legislation of 1466 forbidding the holding of commends, stress was also laid on the right of 'free election' in

[1] This constituted the punishable offence of 'barratry'.

abbeys and other elective benefices which, it was erroneously claimed, had
not been subject to papal provision. In 1471 it was enacted (rendering the
Scots statute into English) 'that no such abbey nor other benefices which
were never at the court of Rome before be purchased by no secular nor
religious person but that the said places have free election of the same use
and custom has been in the said places'. No further annexations were to
be permitted and those made since the accession of James III (1460–88)
were to be revoked; while any contravention of this statute was to be
accounted treason. If much of this legislation arose out of the personal
animosity between the king and Patrick Graham, who in the course of the
struggle secured the elevation of his see to an archbishopric, repeated
legislation on the same lines suggests that James III was determined to
prevent any recurrence of a situation which had temporarily allowed an
effective demonstration of papal authority.

The concern for the maintenance of 'free election', manifested in the
acts of parliament of this period, is specious and misleading. The course
of events shows quite clearly that the term was not intended to mean the
unimpeded exercise by the monks of the right to elect their head, subject,
in some cases, to the ratification of the bishop of the diocese and, in others,
to the confirmation of the mother-house. In practice, it signified royal
nomination without papal interference.[1] Bishop Lesley, in one version of
his *History*, leaves us in no doubt of this. For he cites the case of Dunfermline, where the monks elected an abbot only to have him superseded
by James III's nominee, the former abbot of Paisley; and he adds that to
Paisley, thus vacated, the king proceeded to nominate a secular priest, the
rector of Minto. It is to these practices which, he notes, 'the Pope allows
. . . at the king's request', that he traces the mischief that soon befell the
monasteries.

> From this proceeded the first and foul slander that after infected monasteries
> and monks through all Scotland; when secular persons were begun to have
> place in cloisters, and through the king's force, in a manner, and his authority,
> began to rule and have dominion in religious places. . . . Then in religious
> places crept idleness, deliciousness, and all bodily pleasure, fertility in worldly
> affairs; then God's service began to be neglected and cool; then hospitality . . .
> began to be contemned, and what cloisters respected most was worldly

[1] The royal notion of 'free election' is illustrated in a communication (6 April 1530)
which the duke of Albany is to make to the Pope on behalf of James V. 'Albany is to
request that henceforth by apostolic grant monks may be allowed . . . to elect a suitable
abbot or prior from the fraternity at the royal recommendation, or, if election cannot be
held, to nominate an abbot or prior, the persons thus elected . . . to be admitted, confirmed
and blessed by the ordinary, so that there may be no need for the Roman see to look into
the matter or send a representative' (*James V Letters*, 175).

wealth. . . . The monks now elect not abbots who are most godly and devout, but kings choose abbots who are lustiest and most with them in favour.[1]

Lesley's strictures are more applicable to the proceedings of James IV than to those of James III. Meanwhile, in the reign of the latter king, legislation against the 'impetration' and purchase of benefices at Rome was renewed in 1482 and 1484. Eventually, in 1485, a petition to the Pope sought a delay of six months in provision to 'prelacies or dignities elective' so that the king's supplication on behalf of recommended candidates might reach Rome; and in 1487 an indult was granted to James III whereby Pope Innocent VIII consented to postpone for eight months appointments to cathedrals and monasteries whose income exceeded two hundred florins, and to await royal nominations. The indult was a concession given to King James, late in his reign, at the same time as other tokens of papal favour. Its interpretation, which had marked and serious consequences for the monasteries, lay with his successors.

(ix)

We may pause to notice certain developments internal to the religious orders. The formation of units of monastic administration on a national basis originated, as we have seen, with the Franciscans, who secured the erection of a Scottish vicariate in 1329. Though this vicariate was suppressed by the General Chapter in 1359, the decree may have been a dead letter, for a vicar-general is mentioned in 1375; and the ensuing schism, during which Scotland and England adopted different allegiances, contributed to perpetuate the separation of the Scottish Greyfriars from the English province. A Conventual province was apparently in existence before the end of the fifteenth century, while the General Chapter of the Observants sanctioned the erection of a Scottish province in 1467. In 1481, the petition of James III led to the creation of a province of Scotland by the Dominican General Chapter; and towards the end of this century, the acts of the Premonstratensian General Chapter refer to a *circaria* of Scotland as existing in its own right. The one Scottish Charterhouse, originally associated with the province of Further Picardy, was united, *c.* 1456, to the English province of the Carthusians; but in 1460, at the request of the Scottish king, it was transferred to the province of Geneva. In the early sixteenth century the General Chapters of the Cistercians and the Premonstratensians show an increasing concern for the visitation of Scottish houses of these orders and the same period provides the only

---

[1] *Historie of Scotland* (Scottish Text Society, 1895), ii, 90–1, cf. *ibid.* (Bannatyne Club, 1830), 39–40.

indications of contact between the Valliscaulian priories, now only two in number, with the motherhouse of Val des Choux. In 1506 the prior of Beauly received directions on the visitation of the priory of Ardchattan, and, again, on the relations of his house with the bishop of Ross, with an admonition from the head of the order to attend the General Chapter, which his predecessor, despite the concession of appearing there only once in six years, had failed to do and, moreover, to send to Bruges or Valenciennes (whence it would be taken to Dijon) the fish 'called salmon', which his predecessor had promised. It is unlikely that either behest was heeded. The contact was not maintained and a few years later Beauly became a Cistercian dependency.[1]

(x)

In the chronicle known as the *Diurnal of Occurrents*, there is a character-sketch of James IV which dwells on his foundation of 'mony religious places' and his personal piety; it adds significantly that 'without counsel of spiritual estate', he gave such benefices as became vacant in his time to his 'familiars'. With this king and still more with his successor appears the ambivalent royal policy which on the one hand added to the number of monasteries and showed an ostensible concern for monastic reform, and on the other exploited and crippled the religious houses. James's foundation of friaries has been mentioned elsewhere. We find the Cistercian General Chapter empowering, in 1491, the abbots of Coupar Angus, Melrose and Culross to visit the Scottish houses of that order because it had been brought to the notice of the Chapter by letters of the Scottish king how much these houses stand in need of visitation and reform; and in 1506 he writes to the Pope at length on the situation of the monastery of Melrose. Again, the king communicates more than once with the Prior-General of the Dominicans (1506) on the affairs of that order in Scotland; and, in 1506/7, he appeals to the Pope on behalf of the Observants. On the other hand the assertion of royal control over nominations to the monasteries did not relax. The indult of 1487 was not explicitly renewed by Pope Innocent VIII's successors. But not only did the Scots act on the assumption that it was a perpetual privilege; it was held to apply not merely to benefices of a certain value but to all which were elective. Moreover the desire to counteract the device of 'resignation in favour', by which the holder of a benefice transferred his title to a successor but retained a life rent, thus precluding a vacancy and an occasion for the

---

[1] On the state of Ardchattan priory, which seems to have remained—at least nominally a Valliscaulian house, see *James V Letters*, 345–6.

exercise of patronage, may well have prompted the act of parliament of 1496 which forbade resort to Rome without licence of the king or his chancellor. At the same time, the former indignation at the system of commends conveniently subsided; they were (in Hannay's phrase) 'now no longer offensive when directed according to royal wish' and in encouraging them the Crown was the arch-offender. Thus James Stewart, duke of Ross, the king's brother, who in 1497 had been made administrator of the diocese of St. Andrews at the age of eighteen, was given, in the same year, the commend of the abbey of Holyrood; three years later, that of the abbey of Dunfermline; and in 1503 the commend of the abbey of Arbroath. The king exerted himself to have Tongland abbey bestowed on the bishop of Galloway, Glenluce abbey on a secular clerk who was his Lord High Treasurer, the abbey of Cambuskenneth on his Secretary, the celebrated Patrick Panter, who was not even in priest's orders; and contrived the annexation of the priories of Restennet and Inchmahome to his new Chapel Royal at Stirling. From the later years of James IV, the hold of the commendatory system upon the Scottish monasteries became firmly established. Some abbeys, like Inchaffray, from 1495, were in the hands of commendators continuously for the rest of their career.

(xi)

In 1513 James IV fell at Flodden. His policy towards the monasteries was continued and extended by his successor. When he came to rule in person, James V, as his *Letters* display, evinced a considerable interest in the affairs —and reform—of the religious houses. We find him, in 1524, protesting to the Pope against the granting of a pension from the church of Dunkeld to a Dominican as a proceeding unworthy of the Blackfriars. In 1530/1 he requests the abbot of Cîteaux and the *diffinitores* of the General Chapter, in view of the shortcomings of the order in Scotland, to provide an abbot to visit and reform it, promising his cooperation, and the abbot of Chaalis was duly sent. Professing his anxiety to do his best for the state of the religious in Scotland, he appeals to the Pope, in 1531/2, for the conservation of the rules and privileges of the Observants. In 1532 he vouches his support to the abbot of Soulseat, commissioned by the Premonstratensian General Chapter to visit the monasteries of that order; and five years later gives the like undertaking in regard to the representative whom the Prior General of the Carmelites shall send, at his somewhat peremptory invitation, to report on the Scottish Whitefriars. Again, when Henry VIII sought to prevail upon the Scottish king to follow his example in dealing with the monasteries and the English emissary dwelt, in terms of his instructions, upon the misdemeanours of the monks, James is said to have proclaimed his ability to reform them. But there are reasons, as will presently appear, for discounting James's zeal for monastic reform. Meanwhile, insistence on the royal right of nomination was maintained. During James's minority, Pope Leo X, after some contention with the Governor, had confirmed the indult of 1487; and, in 1526, on the ground that there had been violations of the rule that when bishoprics or abbeys were vacant, the nomination belonged to the king and provision to the Pope, an act of parliament declared that any who entered upon possession of such benefices without the king's 'command, letters or charges, or desire of the convents thereof' should 'incur the crime of treason'. But a new factor soon entered into the situation. The English Reformation had begun and the Scottish king could advance the price of his allegiance to the Pope; and, on 7 March 1534/5, James secured from Pope Paul III a bull explicitly recognizing the royal right of nomination and extending the period to twelve months, giving the king likewise the right to use the temporalities of vacant prelacies (including Cluniac, Cistercian and Premonstratensian abbeys) in the first year of a vacancy at his discretion.

The results for the monasteries of the increasing exploitation of vacancies were deplorable. Already during the king's minority, when the Governor Albany exercised control of ecclesiastical affairs, we find such situations as that which appears at Glenluce, where in 1516 there were three candidates with conflicting claims on the abbey: the papal nominee, the Cardinal of St. Eusebius; the royal nominee, David, bishop of Lismore; the monks' nominee, Alexander Cunningham, who had been elected by his brethren with the confirmation of the father-abbot and whose claim to the benefice brought upon him imprisonment.[1] Again, in 1523/4 the election of a monk of Coupar Angus as abbot by the convent, 'made without advice of the Crown and contrary to its privileges', was quashed and the monks ordered to choose according to the Governor's nomination, the abbot of Melrose who had confirmed the election being forced to annul it. Worse was to follow. Between 1534 and 1541 five of the greater monasteries, Kelso, Melrose, St. Andrews, Holyrood and Coldingham, were granted to three of the king's illegitimate children.

The deteriorating economic situation of the monasteries from the fifteenth century onwards is demonstrated by the increase in leases of their lands as well as by the difficulties and compromises which appear in their dealings with General Chapters regarding the payment of their dues.

---

[1] The General Chapter, in 1518, protested against the supersession of the monks' choice (Canivez, *Statuta*, vi, 543–4).

James V was now to add to their embarrassments by imposing upon them crippling financial demands. In vain Henry VIII had besought the king of Scots to adopt his ecclesiastical policy; James would not consent to extinguish the religious houses, but he would exact a price for their survival. Thus was inaugurated what has been aptly called 'the Scottish alternative to the dissolution of the monasteries'.[1] The king was able to extract from Pope Clement VII, in 1531, a bull sanctioning the taxation of the Church. The pretext was the obtaining of funds for the establishment of a College of Justice, but the primary aim was the replenishing of the royal treasury; and the subsidy for the College of Justice became a precedent for further demands, e.g. for the defence of the realm. The effect on the monasteries of this repeated drain on their resources was not only that they frequently fell into arrears, and abbots, on occasion, were distrained for debt; they were driven to raise money by the expedient of 'feuing' their lands. Feu-holding, a usage peculiar to Scotland, has been described as 'a heritable tenure,[2] granted in return for a fixed and single rent and for certain casualties'.[3] It had hitherto been applied to Crown lands. Now its extension to the lands of the monasteries brought about a 'rapid dissolution' of monastic property.

... The real ownership of the Church's property passed from its hands. ... Once the Church's power was broken, it was comparatively easy for the feuars to assume complete ownership. On the other hand, it was correspondingly difficult for the crown or parliament to get possession of the land, once it had passed into the hands of the feuars. Consequently church lands disbursed by the clergy to meet the demands of taxation never again left the hands of those to whom they were granted.[4]

The feuing of monastic lands led straight to their alienation.

The financial demands of the Crown were by no means the only factor which contributed to the secularization of monastic property. As the sixteenth century progressed, lay control of the monasteries' lands and possessions proceeded apace. From 1529 onwards the farming of religious houses—Coupar Angus, Kilwinning, St. Mary's Isle, Dundrennan, Inchaffray, Holyrood, Kelso, Melrose, Holywood—was in vogue. A

---

[1] W. Stanford Reid, *Cath. Hist. Rev.*, xxxv (1948), 152.

[2] As contrasted with a terminable lease or (*Scottice*) tack.

[3] I. F. Grant, *Social and Economic Development of Scotland*, 256

[4] W. Stanford Reid, 'Clerical taxation; the Scottish alternative to the dissolution of the monasteries, 1530–1560', *Cath. Hist. Rev.*, xxxv (1948), 152. This is a valuable discussion of the subject. Cf. also R. K. Hannay, 'Church lands at the Reformation', *SHR*, xvi (1918–19); Grant, *op. cit.*, 269 ff.

commendator, even if he was a court official who, by holding a quasi-monastic office, drew a revenue from a monastery, was, in the earlier stages of the system, usually a secular priest who took the habit of the order to which his house belonged; but, in the course of the sixteenth century, laymen are mentioned as holding commends. In various ways, indeed, the 'land-hungry nobility' (in the phrase of the editor of *The Letters of James V*) and lairds established a hold upon the monasteries which they were able, in many cases, to maintain until, during and after the Reformation. Thus a Colville, called rector of Dysart, but recommended as the king's 'familiar' for his father's services to James IV, and out of regard for his brother as a royal official, secured a family hold on the abbey of Culross; an Erskine, who, according to James V was 'a young noble with proved personal qualities and strong family connections', staked a claim for himself and his successors in the case of Dryburgh abbey, by obtaining the commend in 1541, despite an attempt at the provision to that house of the blind theologian, Robert Wauchope; a Stewart, aged fourteen, but described as 'a noble and studious youth', became titular abbot of Inchcolm in 1544, and paved the way for the Stewarts, Lords St. Colm, who were to come after him. Again, at Glenluce, in the fourth decade of the century, the acquisitive rivalry of the earl of Cassillis and Gordon of Lochinvar led to the invasion of that abbey by both parties in turn, the molestation of the convent and the spoliation of its possessions. Before the Reformation lay encroachment upon the Scottish monasteries had gone far. The fact can merely be illustrated here. Only by a study of the records of the period can its extent and ramifications be realized.

(xii)

What of the internal life of the monasteries in this period of exploitation and inevitable decadence ? The correspondence of the ambiguous monarch, James V, commonly adduces as a reason for nomination to monastic office the suitability of the candidate for restoring the *morale* of a monastery or for repairing its dilapidations. No doubt we may discount many of these protestations—the prevalence of royal nominees tended to debase rather than to enhance the quality of those who held office as abbots. Yet in some cases the royal recommendations were justified; and in certain fortunate monasteries, where the abbots were notable and conscientious rulers of their houses, we see definite attempts at reform. The conspicuous examples are Kinloss and Cambuskenneth. Thomas Chrystall, who held Kinloss from *c.* 1504 to 1535, not only exerted himself to recover the alienated patrimony of the monastery but sought to raise the standard of monastic life and education and added to the number of the monks. In 1528 the regress of the abbot's office was granted to Robert Reid, already a pluralist, who, on becoming bishop of Orkney in 1541, continued to hold Kinloss as well as the priory of Beauly *in commendam*. Reid, who was prominent in state affairs and in this and other respects a typical churchman of his time, was exceptional in that he displayed a practical interest in the wellbeing of his commended monasteries. To Kinloss he brought the Italian scholar, Ferrerius, who spent a number of years in the instruction of the monks of that abbey as well as of the novices from Beauly and among whose writings is an account of the course of study pursued in the monastery. In 1516 Alexander Myln, who had been official of Dunkeld, was nominated by the duke of Albany, the Governor, for the abbey of Cambuskenneth, and, on taking up office, exhibited an assiduous interest in the reform of observance and education in his monastery; to this end, he proposed, in 1522, the sending of his novices to the abbey of St. Victor at Paris. It was to this outstanding abbot that Robert Richardson (Richardinus), himself a canon of the same order and abbey, dedicated his *Commentary on the Rule of St. Augustine*.[1] That the plans of Robert Reid and Alexander Myln for reviving education in their monasteries were by no means misplaced is shown by the tardy attempt of the Church in Scotland to promote reform in this direction by legislation. Thus, a provincial council in 1549 enacted, in order that 'the study of the holy scriptures and the virtues pleasing to God Himself may, as in time past so now again, flourish in the monasteries', that there should be a theologian maintained in each house, who should daily expound holy writ and preach; and, further, that in proportion to their revenues, monasteries should send one or two monks to the universities, there to spend at least four years in the study of theology and holy scripture.[2] The records of the university of St. Andrews supply some instances of monks matriculating after this date, including, curiously enough, in 1545, the abbot of Glenluce, who had been the Governor's secretary and must have been from forty to fifty years of age. This remedy for monastic decline came too late to be effective. The fact, however, is significant that, in this period when the monasteries appear at a low ebb, men were still entering the religious life and there is no abrupt drop in the numbers of monastic personnel.

We have seen that James V professed his zeal for the reformation of certain orders and the opportunity was accordingly taken by their General

---

[1] Myln, like Reid, played a conspicuous part in state affairs and became the first president of the College of Justice.

[2] Subjoined to this statute is a list showing the number of monks to be sent from each house, with a secular priest representing each of two nunneries.

Chapters to provide for the visitation of Scottish houses. It is somewhat intriguing to find the king claiming the countenance of his lieutenants for the abbot of Soulseat, who in 1532 was about to undertake the visitati on of the Premonstratensians

> howbeit he dredis that the . . . abbottis, prioris and religious personis wald nocht obey, bot be the contrary resist and withstand to the same, without our supple, help, mainteinance and assistance.

The abbot of Chaalis, who came to visit the Cistercian houses in 1531, appears to have raised more problems than he solved. There is extant a lengthy list of ordinances on the religious life sent by him from Coupar Angus to the abbey of Deer 'to which we ourselves have not been able to go'. It is doubtful if these were much more than counsels of perfection; yet he saw enough of Scottish Cistercianism to discover local irregularities, with which he dealt without *finesse*. According to King James's letters to the General Chapter (1 March 1531/2), the visitor 'failed to ask himself whether he was dealing a blow at country and custom by his expedients hastily imposed to alter the immemorial manner of monastic life', 'gave strange and unusual orders to the monks which they could not put into practice without mature consideration', and, having put the religious under ecclesiastical censures, departed from Scotland. What were the local customs of which the French abbot disapproved? It appears from the ensuing controversy that they were relaxations of the principle of cor-porate possession, instances of the 'damnable vice of ownership' which the visitor, for once hitting the mark, had denounced in his communication to the monks of Deer. In 1534 the abbots of Coupar Angus and Glenluce, as visitors of the Scottish houses, dealt with the abbot of Melrose who is said to have been chiefly responsible for impeding the reform of the order in regard to this prevailing deviation; and it transpires that the monks of Melrose, as well as those of its daughter-houses, Newbattle and Balmerino, had been in the habit of holding private gardens, of treating their portions as individual possessions and of receiving sums of money for the purchase of clothing and other necessities. The monks of the three monasteries urged against the discontinuance of these relaxations that Scotland was less fertile and less abundant in the requisites of monastic life than France and other countries and that their predecessors from time immemorial had lived in this way. James V seems to have intervened in the controversy on the side of the Scottish monks; for, pointing out that the obstacles to reform were the geographical position of the country and the customs which the Scottish Cistercians had always observed, he asked Cîteaux (28 March

1534 or 1535) to permit 'what the old superiors of the order observed without sacrificing its weal'. We find the monks of Deer obtaining in 1537 a specific relaxation from the constitutions of the abbot of Chaalis 'on account of the inconvenient situation of the place and the maliciousness of the times'. Yet in the same year the abbot and convent of that monastery made a compact that they should henceforth lead a regular and reformed life and, after providing for the brethren and officers of the abbey, have its fruits and rents in common. Nor is this the only sign that the Cistercians, at the eleventh hour, were persuaded to take steps towards counteracting the 'vice' to which the abbot of Chaalis had drawn attention. Thus in 1553 the community at Coupar Angus resolved 'to lead a regular life and to order our manners according to the reformers of the Cistercian order', and that the abbot and convent should possess and use in common the fruits, income and provision of the monastery. How far the communities carried out these reforms is impossible to tell; but the fact that after the Reformation surviving monks continued to receive their portions points to the perpetuation of the idea that these were personal perquisites.[1]

(xiii)

To the monasteries in the area between Tay and Tweed, where many of the great houses were situated, came in the sixteenth century the devastating experience of repeated invasion. In 1523 damage was done by English armies to the Border abbeys of Kelso, Jedburgh and Dryburgh, and the last was to suffer again in 1542. But from 1544, when Hertford began his operations in Scotland, to 1549, the havoc wrought by the invaders was systematic and widespread.[2] The abbeys, nunneries, friaries and hospitals of the Borders, Lothian and the Merse underwent terrible destruction and the invaders carried their forays to the Firth of Tay, burning the abbey of Balmerino, the nunnery of Elcho and the friaries of Dundee. From these devastations the religious houses had no chance of recovering. To the decade of the later English invasions belongs also the first display of popular hostility towards the monasteries—the attack by a mob upon the friars' houses of Dundee and the expulsion of the monks from Lindores abbey in 1543;[3] and in 1546 an act of the Lords of Council, ratified by parliament, on the preamble that 'it is dred and ferit' that

---

[1] Monks' portions were treated as private property when, after the Reformation, they were secularized. Thus in 1588 portions of deceased monks of Coupar Angus were granted to the children of the king's master-saddler (*Coupar Angus Chrs.*, ii, no. cclxxxvi).

[2] A contemporary list of the buildings destroyed by Hertford's forces in September 1545 is given in *Source Bk. of Scottish History*, ii, 127–8.

[3] The expulsion of the monks in this case was temporary.

evilly disposed persons will invade, destroy and cast down abbeys and other religious structures, institutes the severest penalties for those who are guilty of such destruction.

On the eve of the Reformation (1556), Cardinal Sermonetta presented to Pope Paul IV a gloomy picture of the state of the Scottish monasteries, dwelling on the alienation of their property to the nobles and deploring the condition of their buildings which, he declared, were 'reduced to ruins by hostile inroads or through the avarice and neglect of those placed in charge . . . crumbling to decay'.[1] It must suffice to remark that while secularization of the religious houses and their possessions had passed beyond ecclesiastical control, there was, after the death of James V in 1542, no strong ruler to resist the vested interests which laymen steadily established in monastic property; the Crown played no part in the disposal of the monasteries until a much later stage. When the Reformation came, the commendators remained. Now, however, their pretensions to monastic status mattered little and their virtual possession of monastic property counted for much. The annexation of the monasteries to the Crown in 1587, a quarter of a century after they had ceased to function, came as a belated measure, an afterthought, and its effect was restricted by the fact that by this date not a little of the monasteries' possessions had been alienated beyond recall. There followed the gradual disposal by the Crown of what remained, once the convents had ceased to exist, through the erection of abbeys into temporal lordships. The monks remaining in an abbey, it is to be noted, were not dislodged but were allowed to die out; thereafter the suppression of the monastery took place and it became irrevocably secularized. Contrary to a common notion, there was no concerted destruction of monastic fabrics.

(xiv)

One modification of the foregoing statement falls to be made. Although, as in England, the friars continued, in the sixteenth century, to receive small bequests (for example, they are often mentioned in wills), and although, within that century, houses of friars were still being founded, there are unmistakable evidences of their unpopularity; and from the time of the mob attack on the friaries in Dundee (1543), many of their houses were damaged or destroyed. The houses of friars, indeed, rather than the greater monasteries, were the objects of violence at the Reformation. It is not easy to account for this, though the fact that friaries were situated in towns and were of little interest to the gentry who had established a hold

[1] *Papal Negotiations with Queen Mary*, 529.

upon the abbeys may partly explain it. Some, as at Aberdeen, Elgin, Inverness and Glasgow, are mentioned in 1561/2 as 'undemolished'; it was, in fact, left to twentieth-century vandalism to erase the church of the Aberdeen Greyfriars. In general, the friars' properties passed to the possession of the burghs where they were located.

Religious foundations for women in Scotland were only fifteen in number and of these four expired before the Reformation. Most of the Scottish nunneries were small—the largest seem to have been those of Haddington and North Berwick—and none ranked higher than a priory. Their history is in many respects obscure. Nine are described as of the Cistercian order; two were Augustinian; one (Lincluden) is called Benedictine. There were also three late foundations of the mendicant orders: two small houses of Franciscan nuns and one larger house of Dominican sisters. These designations, however, raise some problems. The so-called Cistercian houses, which formed the majority of the Scottish nunneries, were in a somewhat anomalous position in regard to the order; and it is impossible to say how they stood towards each other. We find the nuns of North Berwick denied recognition as Cistercian because they did not wear the habit of the order;[1] and no mention of the Scottish Cistercian nunneries occurs in the records of the General Chapter till 1530, when the seven remaining houses are listed for assessment by the commissary of the Chapter in Scotland.[2] It is noteworthy that an earlier attempt (*c.* 1516) to include the Scottish nunneries among the houses to be visited by a Cistercian commissary concerned with the levying of contributions to the order was challenged by the archbishop of St. Andrews, who claimed an immemorial right to visit them; and the appointment by the General Chapter of the abbot of Glenluce in 1530 for a similar purpose was met at the instigation of the archbishop, by resolutions of the Lords of Council (31 January 1530/1; 23 July 1531) inhibiting him from visiting nunneries because the archbishop and his predecessors had always had that right.

Though evidence is forthcoming that Scottish nuns exercised the right of electing their prioresses in the sixteenth century—the communities at Haddington (1517) and Coldstream (1537/8) furnish instances—there was a marked tendency at this period for a nunnery to become 'the perquisite of some noble house', with the consequence that 'as it passed from member to member, the revenues were alienated to their kinsfolk'.[3] Thus North Berwick nunnery became virtually the family benefice of the

---

[1] See p. 148 below.
[2] Their names, presumably, were supplied by the commissary.
[3] G. Donaldson, 'The Cistercian nunnery of St. Mary, Haddington', *East Lothian Trans.*, v (1952), 14.

Humes of Polwarth, and Haddington of the Hepburns (though these were later displaced by the Maitlands). It may be added that the situation of most of the nunneries in the south-east of Scotland made them particularly vulnerable to destruction and spoliation in times of war.

So far in this account little mention has been made of the medieval hospitals of Scotland. These were of the types familiar in England and elsewhere—for the sick, lepers, the poor, travellers and pilgrims. Sometimes these types overlapped; occasionally, the original type of a hospital in course of time was changed. Some hospitals were in the hands of religious orders; thus, St. Germains was a house of Bethlehemites, a congregation rarely exemplified in Britain; Soutra and Segden were Augustinian; St. Anthony's, Leith, belonged to the order of St. Anthony of Vienne, and was specially intended for sufferers from erysipelas. Of the hospitals originally maintained by religious orders only St. Anthony's survived till the Reformation. A number of hospitals were attached to colleges of secular canons and formed, with their bedesmen, as at Trinity College, Edinburgh, an integral part of such foundations. Among the secular hospitals are some rarely mentioned and probably shortlived.

originally maintained by religious only St. Anthony's survived till the Reformation. A number of hospitals were attached to colleges of secular canons and formed, with their bedesmen, as at Trinity College, Edinburgh, an integral part of such foundations. Among the secular hospitals are some rarely mentioned and probably shortlived.

The state of the hospitals in the fifteenth century was such that by an act of parliament of 12 March 1424/5—early in the reign of James I—it was enacted that those which had been founded by the Crown for the poor and the sick were to be visited by the chancellor, 'as has been done in the king's progenitors' times'—the usage has English parallels; while those founded by bishops and other spiritual and temporal lords were to have visitation of the diocesan bishop, in order (in both cases) to reform them in accordance with their original foundations. The specific defects prevailing in the hospitals are not disclosed; nor does any remedial action seem to have been taken. But a further act of 9 October 1466 for the reformation of the hospitals provided that their holders should be warned to produce the foundation charters for the perusal of the bishop and chancellor, so that these institutions might be 'reducit [brought back] to thare first fundacione'. Where such a document could not be exhibited, the income of the hospital was to be allocated to 'poor and miserable' persons according to the extent of the endowments. Again on 20 November 1469 the king's almoner-general is empowered by another act to put into operation the statute of 1466. The one known instance of the almoner's activity in this regard is his framing of a new constitution for St. Laurence's hospital at Haddington, the solitary example of a constitution devised for a Scottish medieval hospital. But the reform, in this case, was only on paper and took no effect. It is, indeed, more than doubtful whether any reformation of the hospitals resulted from the acts of parliament. The hospitals tended to become mere benefices and sinecures. Yet some there were which maintained their services to the ailing and the poor and persisted not only to the Reformation but long after it.[1]

(xv)

It is fair to state, in conclusion, that any account of the medieval religious houses in Scotland must be partial and incomplete because a reconstruction of their development is based on imperfect knowledge. Not only are there great gaps in the available records. Existing documents may enable us in some degree to recognize the external aspects of monasticism in the five centuries of its existence in Scotland. But the information conveyed to us regarding the domestic life of the Scottish monasteries is sparse, fragmentary and seldom intimate. Only in the sixteenth century do we find such items as the record which shows that the monks of Newbattle had gone on strike, since the abbot had refused to grant them larger portions;[2] and the recital of the involved dispute in the priory of Monymusk, where the canons were at odds with the prior and the formal Latin is relieved with an account of the sentence passed on one of the brethren couched in the robust Scots of the period.[3] Much that we would wish to know—and not least of the devotional life of the monasteries—eludes us. But if so many points remain 'greatly dark', their obscurity serves to temper our judgments; on the other hand, such knowledge as we can attain of a great religious and social institution deserves to be frankly set forth, not without anticipation of shortcomings and blunders, but also in the hope that it may be amended and augmented.

[1] This was particularly so in the north-eastern counties (Aberdeen and Banff).
[2] *St. Andrews Formulare*, i, no. 261.
[3] *Aberdeen–Banff Illustrations*, iii, 490–1.

ABBREVIATIONS

1. Symbols
   * In charge of the Ministry of Works or the National Trust.
   ¶ Scheduled as an Ancient Monument.
   ‡ Church, or part(s) of church, in ecclesiastical use.
   § Remains of importance, in private hands and not necessarily open to the public.
   −(before date)   before that year.
   +(after date)   after that year.
   ×(before date)   not later than.
   ×(between two dates)   not earlier than . . . and not later than.
   †(in tables)   died in.

2. Abbreviations

ab./abs.	abbot/abbots
abp./abps.	archbishop/s
bp./bps.	bishop/s
c. (after date)	century/ies
c. (before date)	*circa:* about
ch.	church
D (under date in tables)	Dissolved (usually by union to another house) before the Reformation
d. (in the notes)	died, died of
ded.	dedicated to
dep.	dependent/dependency
dioc.	diocese
e.	earl of
fd.	founded or established
fd'n.	foundation
hosp.	hospital
hosps.	hospitallers
k.	king
kt/kts.	knight/s
mk./mks.	monk/s
mon./mons.	monastery/ies
pr./prs.	prior/s
prot.	protestant
q.	queen
r.	*recte*
sec.	secularized
supp.	suppressed before the Reformation
t.	*tempe*
term.	terminated
val.	value (per annum)

Abbrev. Feu Chrs	Abbreviates of Feu Charters of Kirklands, SRO.
Abdn. Reg.	*Registrum Episcopatus Aberdonensis* (Spalding and Maitland Clubs, 1845).
Abdn., St. Nich. Cart.	*Cartularium Ecclesiae Sancti Nicholai Aberdonensis* (New Spalding Club, 1888–92).
Aberdeen–Banff Coll.	*Collections for a History of the Shires of Aberdeen and Banff* (Spalding Club, 1843).
Aberdeen–Banff Illus.	*Illustrations of the Topography and Antiquities of the Shires of Aberdeen and Banff* (Spalding Club, 1847–69).
Aberdeen Council Register	*Extracts from the Council Register of the Burgh of Aberdeen* (Spalding Club, 1844–8).

32

Aberdeen Description	*Aberdoniae utriusque descriptio: A description of both towns of Aberdeen* (Spalding Club, 1842).
Aberdeen Ecclesiastical Records	*Selections from the Kirk Session, Presbytery, and Synod of Aberdeen* (Spalding Club, 1846).
Aberdeen Ecclesiol. Trans.	*Transactions of the Aberdeen Ecclesiological Society* (1886–1905).
Aberdeen Fasti	*Fasti Aberdonenses: Selections from the Records of the University and King's College of Aberdeen* (Spalding Club, 1854).
Aberdeen Friars	*Aberdeen Friars: Red, Black, White, Grey*, ed. P. J. Anderson (Aberdeen, 1909).
Acta Sanctorum	*Acta Sanctorum*, ed. the Bollandists (Antwerp/ Brussels, 1643–).
Acts of Council [*ADC*]	*The Acts of the Lords of Council in Civil Causes*, ed. T. Thomson and others (Edinburgh, 1839 and 1918–).
Acts of Council (Public Affairs) [*ADCP*]	*Acts of the Lords of Council in Public Affairs 1501– 1554: Selections from Acta Dominorum Concilii*, ed. R. K. Hannay (Edinburgh, 1932).
Acts of Lords Auditors [*ADA*]	*The Acts of the Lords Auditors of Causes and Complaints*, ed. T. Thomson (Edinburgh, 1839).
Acts Parl. Scot. [*APS*]	*The Acts of the Parliaments of Scotland*, ed. T. Thomson and C. Innes (Edinburgh, 1814–75).
Adomnán, *Columba*	*Adomnán's Life of Columba*, ed. A. O. and M. O. Anderson (Edinburgh, 1961).
AI	*Annals of Inisfallen*, ed. Seán Mac Airt (Dublin, 1951).
Analecta F.P.	*Analecta sacri ordinis Fratrum Praedictorum.*
Ancient Burgh Laws	*Ancient Laws and Customs of the Burghs of Scotland* (SBRS, 1868–1910).
Anderson, *Early Sources* [*ES*]	*Early Sources of Scottish History 500 to 1286*, ed. A. O. Anderson (Edinburgh, 1922).
Anderson, *Kings and Kingship*	M. Anderson, *Kings and Kingship in Early Scotland* (Edinburgh, 1974).
Anderson, *Oliphants*	J. Anderson, *The Oliphants in Scotland* (Edinburgh, 1879).
Anderson, *Orkneyinga Saga*	*Orkneyinga Saga*, ed. J. Anderson (Edinburgh, 1873).
Anderson, *Scottish Annals* [*SA*]	*Scottish Annals from English Chroniclers 500 to 1286*, ed. A. O. Anderson (London, 1908).
Annales Minorum	*Annales Minorum seu trium ordinum a S. Francisco institutorum*, ed. L. Wadding (2nd edition, 1753).
Antiquity	*Antiquity* (1927–).
APS	See *Acts Parl. Scot.*
Arb. Lib.	*Liber S. Thome de Aberbrothoc* (Bannatyne Club, 1848–56).
Arch. Francisc Hist.	*Archivum Franciscanum Historicum.*
Arran Bk.	*The Book of Arran* (Arran Society of Glasgow, 1910–14).
A. Tig.	See *Tig. Annals.*
AU	See *Ulster Annals.*
Ayr Burgh Accts	*Ayr Burgh Accounts 1534–1624*, ed. G. S. Pryde (SHS, 1937).
Ayr Friars	*Charters of the Friars Preachers of Ayr* (AHCAG, 1881).
Ayr-Galloway Coll. [*AHCAG*]	*Archeological and Historical Collections relating to Ayrshire and Galloway (1878–99; volumes for 1878– 84 bear the title . . . relating to the Counties of Ayr and Wigton).*
Ayrshire Coll.	*Collections of the Ayrshire Archeological and Natural History Society* (1947–).

Backmund, *Monasticon Praemonstratense*
Backmund, *Monasticon Praemonstratense* (Straubing, 1952).

Balm. Lib.
Liber Sancte Marie de Balmorinach (Abbotsford Club, 1841).

Bamff Chrs
Bamff Charters 1232–1703, ed. J. H. Ramsay (Oxford, 1915).

Bannatyne Misc.
The Bannatyne Miscellany (Bannatyne Club, 1827–55).

Barrow, *Kingdom of the Scots*
G. W. S. Barrow, *The Kingdom of the Scots* (London, 1973).

Beauly Chrs
The Charters of the Priory of Beauly (Grampian Club, 1877).

Bede, *History*
Bede's Ecclesiastical History of the English People, ed. B. Colgrave and R. A. B. Mynors (Oxford, 1969).

Bede, *Life of St. Cuthbert*
See Colgrave, *Two Lives of St. Cuthbert*.

Berwickshire Hist. [HBNC]
History of Berwickshire Naturalists' Club (1831–).

Boece, *Historiae*
Hector Boethius, *Scotorum Historiae*, 2nd ed. (Paris, 1574).

Bisset, *Rolment of Courtis*
Habbakuk Bisset's Rolment of Courtis, ed. P. Hamilton-Grierson (STS, 1920–6).

Book of Assumption
Books of the Assumption of the Benefices in SRO.

Brady, *Episcopal Succession*
W. M. Brady, *The Episcopal Succession in England, Scotland and Ireland, 1400–1875* (Rome, 1876–7).

Brech. Reg.
Registrum Episcopatus Brechinensis (Bannatyne Club, 1856).

British Museum Maps
Maps held in the British Museum, London.

Brockie
MS. collections of Fr. Marianus Brockie, in Scottish Catholic Archives, Edinburgh.

Bryce, *Grey Friars*
W. Moir Bryce, *The Scottish Grey Friars* (Edinburgh, 1909).

BUK
Booke of the Universall Kirk of Scotland (Bannatyne Club, 1839–45).

Cal. Close Rolls
Calendar of the Close Rolls preserved in the Public Record Office (London, 1892–).

Cal. Docs. Scot. [CDS]
Calendar of Documents relating to Scotland, ed. J. Bain (Edinburgh, 1881–8).

Cal. Inquis.
Calendarium Inquisitionum post mortem sive escaetarum, ed. J. Caley (London, 1806–28).

Cal. Inquis. Miscell.
Calendar of Inquisitions miscellaneous (Chancery) preserved in the Public Record Office (London, 1916–).

Cal. Papal Letters [CPL]
Calendar of Entries in the Papal Registers relating to Great Britain and Ireland: Papal Letters, ed. W. H. Bliss and others (London, 1893–).

Cal. Papal Petitions [CPP]
Calendar of Entries in the Papal Registers relating to Great Britain and Ireland: Petitions to the Pope, ed. W. H. Bliss, (London, 1896).

Cal. Pat. Rolls
Calendar of the Patent Rolls preserved in the Public Record Office (London, 1891–).

Cal. Scot. Supp., i [*CSSR*, i]
Calendar of Scottish Supplications to Rome 1418–22, ed. E. R. Lindsay and A. I. Cameron (SHS, 1934).

Cal. Scot. Supp., ii [*CSSR*, ii]
Calendar of Scottish Supplications to Rome 1423–28, ed. A. I. Dunlop (SHS, 1956).

Cal. Scot. Supp., iii [*CSSR*, iii]
Calendar of Scottish Supplications to Rome 1428–32, ed. I. B. Cowan and A. I. Dunlop (SHS, 1970).

Cal. State Papers
Calendar of State Papers, Domestic, 1547–1625, ed. R. Lemon and M. E. A. Green (London, 1856–72).

Cal. State Papers Scot.
Calendar of the State Papers relating to Scotland 1547–1603, ed. J. Bain and others (Edinburgh, 1898–).

Cal. State Papers (*Thorpe*)	*Calendar of State Papers relating to Scotland 1509–1603*, ed. M. J. Thorpe (London, 1858).
Camb. Reg.	*Registrum Monasterii S. Marie de Cambuskenneth* (Grampian Club, 1872).
Camerarius, *De Scotorum*	Camerarius, *De Scotorum Fortitudine, Doctrina et Pietate* (Paris, 1631).
Cameron, *Apostolic Camera*	*The Apostolic Camera and Scottish Benefices 1418–88*, ed. A. I. Cameron (Oxford, 1934).
Campbell, *Balmerino*	J. Campbell, *Balmerino and its Abbey* (Edinburgh, 1899).
Canivez, *Statuta*	*Statuta Capitulorum Generalium Ordinis Cisterciensis*, 1116– ed. J. M. Canivez (1933).
Cant, *Coll. of St. Salvator*	R. G. Cant., *The College of St. Salvator* (Edinburgh, 1950).
Cant., *University of St. Andrews*	R. G. Cant., *The University of St. Andrews* (Edinburgh, 1970).
Carnwath Court Bk	*The Court Book of the Barony of Carnwath 1523–43*, ed. W. C. Dickinson (SHS, 1937).
Cath. Hist. Rev.	*Catholic Historical Review.*
Cawdor Bk	*The Book of the Thanes of Cawdor* (Spalding Club, 1859).
Chalmers, *Caledonia*	G. Chalmers, *Caledonia* (Paisley, 1887–92).
Chron. Bower	*Joannis de Fordun Scotichronicon cum Supplementis et Continuatione Walteri Boweri*, ed. Goodall (Edinburgh, 1759).
Chron. Extracta	*Extracta e Variis Cronicis Scocie* (Abbotsford Club, 1842).
Chron. Fordun	*Johannis de Fordun, Chronica Gentis Scotorum*, ed. W. F. Skene (Edinburgh, 1872).
Chron. Frasers	*Chronicles of the Frasers: The Wardlaw MS.* (SHS, 1905).
Chron. Holyrood	*A Scottish Chronicle known as the Chronicle of Holyrood*, ed. M. O. Anderson (SHS, 1938).
Chron. Lanercost	*Chronicon de Lanercost* (Maitland Club, 1839).
Chron. Man	*The Chronicle of Man and the Sudreys*, ed. P. A. Munch and Rev. Dr. Goss (Manx Society, Douglas, 1874).
Chron. Melrose	*Chronica de Mailros* (Bannatyne Club, 1835).
Chron. Picts-Scots	*Chronicles of the Picts: Chronicles of the Scots*, ed. W. F. Skene (Edinburgh, 1867).
Chron. Pluscarden	*Liber Pluscardensis*, ed. F. J. H. Skene (Edinburgh, 1877–80).
Chron. Stephen	*Chronicles of the reigns of Stephen, Henry II and Richard I* (Rolls Series, 1885–90).
Chron. Wyntoun	*Androw of Wyntoun, The Orygynale Cronykil of Scotland*, ed. D. Laing (Edinburgh, 1872–9).
CKS	*Chronicle of the Kings of Scotland* in *Chron. Picts–Scots.*
Cluny	*Recueil des chartes de l'abbaye de Cluny*, ed. Bruel (Collections des documents inédits, Paris 1876–1903).
Cold. Corr.	*The Correspondence, Inventories, Account Rolls and Law Proceedings of the Priory of Coldingham*, ed. J. Raine (Surtees Society, London, 1841).
Cold. Cart.	*Chartulary of the Cistercian Priory of Coldstream* (Grampian Club, 1879).
Coldingham, Liber Vitae	*Liber Vitae Ecclesiae Dunelmensis* (Surtees Soc., 1923).
Colgrave, *Two Lives at St. Cuthbert*	*Two Lives of St. Cuthbert*, ed. B. Colgrave (Cambridge, 1956).
Coll. de Rebus Alban.	*Collectanea de Rebus Albancis* (Iona Club, 1847).

Coupar Angus Chrs	*Charters of the Abbey of Coupar Angus*, ed. D. E. Easson (SHS, 1947).
Coupar Angus Rental	*Rental Book of the Cistercian Abbey of Cupar Angus* (Grampian Club, 1879–80).
Cowan, *Parishes*	I. B. Cowan, *The Parishes of Medieval Scotland* (SRS, 1967).
Crail Register	*Register of the Collegiate Church of Crail* (Grampian Club, 1877).
Cramond, *Church and Churchyard of Cullen*	W. Cramond, *The Church and Churchyard of Cullen* (Aberdeen, 1883).
Cramond, *Church and Churchyard of Rathven*	W. Cramond, *The Church and Churchyard of Rathven* (Banff, 1885).
Cross. Chrs	*Charters of the Abbey of Crosraguel* (AHCAG, 1886).
CS	*Chronicon Scotorum*, ed. W. M. Hennessy (Rolls Series, 1866).
Dalyell, *Fragments of Scottish History*	J. G. Dalyell, *Fragments of Scottish History* (Edinburgh, 1798).
Deeds	Register of Deeds (Books of Council and Session), in SRO.
Dempster, *Apparatus*	T. Dempster, *Apparatus ad historiam Scoticam* (Bologna, 1622).
Dickinson, Austin Canons	J. C. Dickinson, *The Origins of the Austin Canons and their Introduction into England* (London, 1950).
Diplom. Norv.	*Diplomatarium Norvegicum* (Kristiania, 1849–1919).
Diurnal of Occurrents	*A Diurnal of Remarkable Occurrents that have passed within the country of Scotland, since the death of King James the Fourth till the year 1575* (Bannatyne and Maitland Clubs, 1833).
Dobson, *Durham Priory*	R. B. Dobson, *Durham Priory 1400–1450* (Cambridge, 1973).
Donaldson, 'Scottish bishops' sees'	Donaldson 'Scottish bishops sees before the reign of David I' in *PSAS*, lxxxvii (1952–3), 106ff.
Dowden, *Bishops*	J. Dowden, *The Bishops of Scotland* (Glasgow, 1912).
Dowden, *Medieval Church*	J. Dowden, *The Medieval Church in Scotland* (Glasgow, 1910).
Dryb. Lib.	*Liber S. Marie de Dryburgh* (Bannatyne Club, 1847).
Duckett, *Visitation*	G. F. Duckett, *Visitation of English Cluniac Foundations* (London, 1890).
Dugdale, *Monasticon Anglicanum*	*Monasticon Anglicanum . . .* , ed. R. Dodsworth and W. Dugdale, 3 vols (1655–73).
Dundas Chrs	Dundas Charters in NLS.
Dumfries. Trans. [*TDGAS*]	*Transactions of the Dumfriesshire and Galloway Natural History and Antiquarian Society* (1862–).
Dundas Papers	*Royal Letters and other Historical Documents selected from the Family Papers of Dundas of Dundas*, ed. W. Macleod (Edinburgh, 1897).
Dundee Chrs	*Charters, Writs and Public Documents of the Royal Burgh of Dundee*, ed. W. Hay (Dundee, 1880).
Dunf. Reg.	*Registrum de Dunfermelyn* (Bannatyne Club, 1842).
Dunfermline Court Bk	*Regality of Dunfermline Court Book 1531–1538*, ed. J. M. Webster and A. A. M. Duncan (Dunfermline, 1953).
Dunfermline Burgh Recs	*The Burgh Records of Dunfermline*, ed. E. Beveridge (Edinburgh, 1917).
Dunkeld Rentale	*Rentale Dunkeldense* (SHS, 1915).
Dunlop, *James Kennedy*	A. I. Dunlop, *The Life and Times of James Kennedy, Bishop of St. Andrews* (Edinburgh, 1950).
Durham Wills and Inventories	*Durham Wills and Inventories* (Surtees Soc., 1835–1929).

Eadmer, *Historia Novorum*	Eadmer, *Historia Novorum in Anglia* (Rolls Series, 1884).
East Lothian Deeds	*Deeds relating to East Lothian*, ed. J. G. Wallace-James (Haddington, 1899).
East Lothian Trans.	*Transactions of the East Lothian Antiquarian and Field Naturalists' Society* (1924–).
Edinburgh Black Friars	W. M. Bryce, *The Black Friars of Edinburgh* (Edinburgh, 1911).
Edinburgh Commissariot Records.	*Commissariot Record of Edinburgh: Register of Testaments* (SRS, 1897–9).
Edinburgh Recs	*Extracts from the Records of the Burgh of Edinburgh* (SBRS, 1869–92).
Edinburgh, Hammermen	*The Hammermen of Edinburgh and their Altar in St. Giles' Church*, ed. J. Smith (Edinburgh, 1905).
Edinburgh Sciennes Lib.	*Liber Conventus S. Katherine Senensis prope Edinburgum* (Abbotsford Club, 1841).
Edinburgh Trinity Chrs	*Charters and Documents relating to the Collegiate Church and Hospital of the Holy Trinity and the Trinity Hospital, Edinburgh* (SBRS, 1871).
EU	Manuscript in Edinburgh University Library.
Elgin Recs	*The Records of Elgin* (New Spalding Club, 1903–8).
Ep. Regum Scotorum	*Epistolae Jacobi Quarti, Jacobi Quinti et Mariae Regum Scotorum*, ed. T. Ruddiman (Edinburgh, 1722–4).
ES	See Anderson, *Early Sources*.
ESC	See Lawrie, *Charters*.
Essays on Scottish Reformation	*Essays on the Scottish Reformation*, ed. D. McRoberts (Glasgow, 1962).
Exch. Rolls [*ER*]	*The Exchequer Rolls of Scotland*, ed. J. Stuart and others (Edinburgh, 1878–1908).
Family of Rose	*A Genealogical Deduction of the Family of Rose of Kilravock* (Spalding Club, 1848).
Fasti Dunelmensis	*Fasti Dunelmensis* (Surtees Soc., 1926).
Ferguson, *Ecclesia Antiqua*	J. Ferguson, *Ecclesia Antiqua, or a history of an ancient church, St. Michael's, Linlithgow* (Edinburgh and London, 1905).
Ferrerius, *Historia*	*Ferrerii Historia Abbatum de Kynlos* (Bannatyne Club, 1839).
Fittis, *Eccles. Annals of Perth*	R. S. Fittis, *Ecclesiastical Annals of Perth* (Edinburgh and Perth, 1885).
Foedera	*Foedera, Conventiones, Litterae et Cuiuscunque Generis Acta Publica*, ed. T. Rymer (London, 1816–69).
Forbes, *St. Ninian and St. Kentigern*	R. F. Forbes, *Lives of St. Ninian and St. Kentigern* (Edinburgh, 1874).
Four Masters [*FM*]	*Annals of Ireland by the Four Masters*, ed. J. O'Donovan (Dublin, 1848–51).
Fraser, *Buccleuch*	W. Fraser, *The Scotts of Buccleuch* (Edinburgh, 1878).
Fraser, *Colquhoun Cartulary*	W. Fraser, *Cartulary of Colquhoun of Colquhoun and Luss* (Edinburgh, 1873).
Fraser, *Cromartie*	W. Fraser, *The Earls of Cromartie* (Edinburgh, 1876).
Fraser, *Douglas*	W. Fraser, *The Douglas Book* (Edinburgh, 1885).
Fraser, *Grant*	W. Fraser, *The Chiefs of Grant* (Edinburgh, 1883).
Fraser, *Haddington*	W. Fraser, *Memorials of the Earls of Haddington* (Edinburgh, 1889).
Fraser, *Lennox*	W. Fraser, *The Lennox* (Edinburgh, 1874).
Fraser, *Menteith*	W. Fraser, *The Red Book of Menteith* (Edinburgh, 1880).

Fraser Papers — *Papers from the Collection of Sir William Fraser* (SHS, 1924).

Fraser, *Pollock-Maxwell* — W. Fraser, *The Cartulary of Pollock-Maxwell* (Edinburgh, 1875).

Fraser, *Southesk* — W. Fraser, *History of Carnegies, Earls of Southesk* (Edinburgh, 1867).

Fraser, *Stirling. of Keir* — W. Fraser, *The Stirlings of Keir* (Edinburgh, 1858).

Fraser, *Wemyss* — W. Fraser, *Memorials of the Family of Wemyss of Wemyss* (Edinburgh, 1888).

Furness Coucher Bk — *The Coucher Book of Furness Abbey* (Chetham Society, 1915–19).

Gillies, *In Famed Breadalbane* — W. A. Gillies, *In Famed Breadalbane* (Perth, 1938).

Glasgow Archeol. Trans. — *Transactions of the Glasgow Archeological Society* (1857–).

Glasgow Chrs. — *Charters and other Documents relating to the City of Glasgow* (SBRS, 1894–1906).

Glas. Friars — *Munimenta Fratrum Predicatorum de Glasgu* (Maitland Club, 1846).

Glasgow Protocols — *Abstracts of Protocols of Town Clerks of Glasgow*, ed. R. Renwick (Glasgow, 1894–1900).

Glas. Reg. — *Registrum Episcopatus Glasguensis* (Bannatyne and Maitland Clubs, 1843).

Glasgow St. Mary Lib. — *Liber Collegii Nostre Domine: Registrum Ecclesie B.V. Marie et S. Anne infra Muros Civitatis Glasguensis 1549* (Maitland Club, 1846).

Glas. Mun. — *Munimenta Alme Universitatis Glasguensis* (Maitland Club, 1854).

Glencairn Chrs — Glencairn Charters in SRO.

Goudie, *Shetland Antiquities* — G. Goudie, *The Celtic and Scandinavian Antiquities of Shetland* (Edinburgh, 1904).

Gwynn and Hadcock, *Medieval Religious Houses Ireland* — A. Gwynn and R. N. Hadcock, *Medieval Religious Houses Ireland* (London, 1970).

Haddan & Stubbs, *Councils* — A. W. Haddan and W. Stubbs, *Councils and Ecclesiastical Documents relating to Great Britain and Ireland* (Oxford, 1869–78).

Hamilton of Wishaw, *Lanarkshire* — W. Hamilton, *Description of the Sheriffdoms of Lanark and Renfrew*, ed. Dillon and Fullarton (Maitland Club, 1831).

Hamilton Papers — *The Hamilton Papers*, ed. J. Bain (Edinburgh, 1890–92).

Hawick Trans. — *Transactions of the Hawick Archeological Society* (1863–).

Hay, *Diplomatum* — Father R. A. Hay, Diplomatum Veterum Collectio. MS. 34.1.10 in NLS.

Hay of Park — Hay of Park MSS in SRO.

Hay, *Sainteclaires* — *Genealogie of the Sainteclaires of Rosslyn*, ed. R. A. Hay (Edinburgh, 1835).

Hay, Scotia Sacra — Father R. A. Hay, Scotia Sacra, MS. 34.1.18 in NLS.

Herkless and Hannay, *Archbishops* — J. Herkless and R. K. Hannay, *The Archbishops of St. Andrews* (Edinburgh, 1907–15).

Herkless and Hannay, *Coll. of St. Leonard* — J. Herkless and R. K. Hannay, *The College of St. Leonard* (Edinburgh, 1905).

Hermans, *Annales* — C. R. Hermans, *Annales Canonicorum regularium S. Augustini ordinis S. Crucis*, i–iii (Bois-le-Duc, 1858), *Highland Papers*, ed. J. R. N. Macphail (SHS. 1914–34).

Highland Papers

Hist. Chapel Royal — *History of the Chapel Royal of Scotland* (Grampian Club, 1882).

Hist. Mon. Comm. (Orkney) — Reports of the Royal Commission on Ancient and Historical Monuments and Constructions of Scotland, e.g. *Orkney* (Edinburgh, 1909–).

Hist. MSS. Comm. [HMC] — Reports of the Royal Commission on Historical Manuscripts (London, 1870–).

Historia Dunelmensis scriptores tres — Historia Dunelmensis scriptores tres (Surtees Soc., 1839).

Hist. Papers and Letters from Northern Registers — Historical Papers and Letters from the Northern Registers, ed. J. Raine (Chronicles and Memorials of Great Britain, London, 1873).

Hodgson, *History of Northumberland* — J. Hodgson and J. H. Hinde, *A History of Northumberland* (Newcastle, 1820–58).

Holy. Lib. — Liber Cartarum Sancte Crucis (Bannatyne Club, 1840).

Hurry, *Reading Abbey* — J. P. Hurry, *Reading Abbey* (London, 1906).

Hutton's Coll. — Hutton's Collections in NLS.

Huyshe, *Devorgilla, Lady of Galloway* — W. Huyohe, *Devorgilla, Lady of Galloway* (Edinburgh, 1913).

Inchaff Chrs — Charters, Bulls and other Documents relating to the Abbey of Inchaffray (SHS, 1908).

Inchaff Liber — Liber Insule Missarum (Bannatyne Club, 1847).

Inchcolm Chrs — Charters of the Abbey of Inchcolm, ed. D. E. Easson and A. Macdonald (SHS, 1938).

Innes Rev. [IR] — The Innes Review (1950–).

Inquis. Retorn. Abbrev. [Retours] — Inquisitionum ad Capellam Domini Regis Retornatarum, quae in publicis archivis Scotiae adhuc servantur, Abbreviatio, ed. T. Thomson (1811–16).

Irons, *Leith and Its Antiquities* — J. C. Irons, *Leith and Its Antiquities* (2 vols, Edinburgh, 1897).

Jackson, *Gaelic Notes* — K. Jackson, *Gaelic Notes in the Book of Deer* (Cambridge, 1972).

Jaffé–Loewenfeld, *Regesta* — P. Jaffé, *Regesta Pontificum Romanorum*, ed. S. Loewenfeld (Leipzig, 1881–8).

James IV Letters — The Letters of James the Fourth 1505–13, ed. R. K. Hannay and R. L. Mackie (SHS, 1953).

James V Letters — The Letters of James V, ed. R. K. Hannay and D. Hay (Edinburgh, 1954).

Janauschek, *Orog. Cist.* — Leopoldus Janauschek, *Originum Cisterciensium* (Wien, 1877).

Journ. Brit. Arch. Assoc. — Journal of the British Archaeological Association.

Journ. Eccles. Hist. — Journal of Ecclesiastical History (London/Cambridge, 1950–).

Kalendars of Scottish Saints — A. P. Forbes, *Kalendars of Scottish Saints* (Edinburgh, 1872).

Keith, *Bishops* — R. Keith, *An Historical Catalogue of the Scottish Bishops*, ed. M. Russel (Edinburgh, 1824).

Kel. Lib. — Liber S. Marie de Calchou (Bannatyne Club, 1846).

Kinlos Recs. — Records of the Monastery of Kinloss, ed. J. Stuart (Edinburgh, 1872).

Knowles, *The Monastic Order in England* — D. Knowles, *The Monastid Order in England* (Cambridge, 1949).

Knowles and Hadcock, *Medieval Religious Houses: England and Wales* — D. Knowles and R. N. Hadcock, *Medieval Religious Houses England and Wales* (London, 1971).

Knox, *Works* — The Works of John Knox, ed. D. Laing (Edinburgh, 1846–64).

Lag Chrs — The Lag Charters, 1400–1720 (SRS, 1958).

Laing Chrs — Calendar of the Laing Charters, 854–1837, ed. J. Anderson (Edinburgh, 1899).

Lanark Recs — Extracts from the Records of the Royal Burgh of Lanark, ed. R. Renwick (Glasgow, 1893).

Langley, *Registrum*
 Register of Thomas Langley, bishop of Durham (Surtees Society).

Lawrie, *Annals*
 Annals of the Reigns of Malcolm and William, Kings of Scotland, ed. A. C. Lawrie (Glasgow, 1910).

Lawrie, *Charters* [*ESC*]
 Early Scottish Charters prior to 1153, ed. A. C. Lawrie (Glasgow, 1905).

Lees, *Abbey of Paisley*
 J. C. Lees, *The Abbey of Paisley* (Paisley, 1878).

Le Paige, *Bibliotheca Praem. Ord.*
 J. Le Paige, *Bibliotheca Praemonstratensis Ordinis* (Paris, 1633).

Lesley, *De Origine*
 J. Lesley, *De Origine, Moribus et Rebus Gestis Scotorum Libri Decem* (Rome, 1578).

Lesley, *History*
 J. Lesley, *The History of Scotland from the Death of King James I in the Year 1436 to the Year 1561* (Bannatyne Club, 1830).

Liber quotidianus
 Liber quotidianus contrarotulatoris garderobae (Society of Antiquaries, 1797).

Lind. Cart.
 Chartulary of the Abbey of Lindores (SHS,, 1903).

Little, *Franciscan Papers*
 A. G. Little, *Franciscan Papers, Lists and Documents* (Manchester, 1943).

Lives of the Lindsays
 Lord Lindsay, *Lives of the Lindsays* (London, 1858).

Low, *Memorials of the Parish Church of Montrose*
 J. C. Low, *Memorials of the Church of St. John the Evangelist, the Parish Church of Montrose* (Montrose, 1891).

LP *Henry VIII*
 Letters and Papers, foreign and domestic of the reign of Henry VIII, ed. J. S. Brewer and others (London, 1864–1932).

Macdonald, *The Clan Donald*
 A. Macdonald, *History and Genealogy of the Clan Donald* (Inverness, 1896–1904).

McDowall, *Chronicles of Lincluden*
 W. McDowall, *Chronicles of Lincluden* (Edinburgh, 1886).

Macfarlane, *Genealogical Coll.*
 Genealogical Collections concerning Families in Scotland made by Walter Macfarlane (SHS, 1900).

Macfarlane, *Geographical Coll.*
 Geographical Collections relating to Scotland made by Walter Macfarlane (SHS, 1906–08).

McGibbon and Ross, *Eccles. Archit.*
 D. McGibbon and T. Ross, *The Ecclesiastical Architecture of Scotland* (Edinburgh, 1896–7).

Mackie, *University of Glasgow*
 J. D. Mackie, *The University of Glasgow* (Glasgow, 1954).

MacKinlay, *Dedications*
 J. M. MacKinlay, *Ancient Church Dedications in Scotland. Scriptural*, 1910; *Non-scriptural*, 1914.

MacKinlay, *Place Names*
 J. M. MacKinlay, *The Influence of the pre-Reformation Church on Scottish Place Names* (Edinburgh and London, 1904).

Macphail, *Pluscardyn*
 S. R. Macphail, *History of the Religious House of Pluscardyn* (Edinburgh, 1881).

McPherson, *The Kirk's Care of the Poor*
 J. N. McPherson, *The Kirk's Care of the Poor* (Aberdeen, n.d.).

McNaught, *Kilmaurs Parish and Burgh*
 D. McNaught, *Kilmaurs Parish and Burgh* (Paisley, 1912).

Maitland, *History of Edinburgh*
 W. Maitland, *The History of Edinburgh from its foundation to the present time* (1742).(Edinburgh 1753).

Maitland, *History*
 W. Maitland, *The History and Antiquities of Scotland* (London, 1757).

Major, *History*
 J. Major, *A History of Greater Britain* (SHS, 1892).

Manx Society
 Publications of the Manx Society.

Martine, *Reliquiae*
 G. Martine, *Reliquiae Divi Andreae* (St. Andrews, 1797).

Mary of Lorraine Corresp.
 The Scottish Correspondence of Mary of Lorraine (SHS, 1927).

Mathew of Westminster, *Flores Historiarum*
Flores Historiarum per Mattheum Westmonasterien em collecti (Frankfort, 1601).

Maxwell, *Old Dundee*
A. Maxwell, *Old Dundee, ecclesiastical, burghal and social, prior to the Reformation* (Dundee, 1891).

May Recs
Records of the Priory of the Isle of May, ed. J. Stuart (Edinburgh, 1868).

Melr. Lib.
Liber Sancte Marie de Melros (Bannatyne Club, 1837).

Mem. de Parl.
Memoranda de Parliamento (Rolls Series, 1893).

Memorie of the Somervilles
James Lord Somerville's Memorie of the Somervilles, ed. Sir W. Scott (Edinburgh, 1815).

Midlothian Chrs
Charters of the Hospital of Soltre, of Trinity College, Edinburgh, and other Collegiate Churches in Midlothian (Bannatyne Club, 1861).

Migne, *Patr. Lat.*
B. Migne, *Patrologia Cursus completa*, Series Latina (Paris, 1844–64).

Mon. ord. F.P. Hist.
Monumenta ordinis Fratrum Praedictorum Historica (1898).

Monro, *Western Isles*
Monro's Western Isles of Scotland and Genealogies of the Clans 1549, ed. R. W. Munro (Edinburgh, 1961).

Moray Reg.
Registrum Episcopatus Moraviensis (Bannatyne Club, 1837).

Morris, *Provostry of Methven*
T. Morris, *The Provosts of Methven* (Edinburgh, 1875).

Morton, *Monastic Annals*
J. Morton, *The Monastic Annals of Teviotdale* (Edinburgh, 1832).

Mort. Reg.
Registrum Honoris de Morton (Bannatyne Club, 1853).

Munro Writs
Calendar of Writs of Munro of Foulis 1299–1823, ed. C. T. McInnes (SRS, 1940)

Myln, *Vitae*
A. Myln, *Vitae Dunkeldensis Ecclesiae Episcoporum* (Bannatyne Club, 1831).

Nat. MSS. Scot.
Facsimiles of the National Manuscripts of Scotland (London, 1867–71).

N.B·Chrs
Carte Monialium de Northberwic (Bannatyne Club, 1847).

Newb. Reg.
Registrum S. Marie de Newbotle (Bannatyne Club 1849).

New Stat. Acct. [*NSA*]
The New Statistical Account of Scotland (Edinburgh, 1834–45).

NLS. MS.
Manuscript in National Library of Scotland.

Notes and Queries (S. N. & Q.)
Scottish Notes and Queries (1887–1935).

Obit. Prem.
Obituaire de l'abbaye de Prémontré ed. R. V. Waefelghem (Brussels, 1913).

Origines Parochiales [*OPS*]
Origines Parochiales Scotiae (Bannatyne Club, 1851–5).

Pais. Reg.
Registrum Monasterii de Passelet (Maitland Club, 1832: New Club, 1877).

Palgrave, *Docs Hist. Scot.*
Documents and Records illustrating the History of Scotland, ed. F. Palgrave (London, 1837).

Panmure Reg.
Registrum de Panmure, ed. J. Stuart (Edinburgh, 1874).

Papal Negotiations with Queen Mary
Papal Negotiations with Mary Queen of Scots during her reign in Scotland, 1561–1567 (SHS, 1901).

Peebles Chrs
Charters and Documents relating to the Burgh of Peebles (SBRS, 1872).

Peebles Recs.
Extracts from the Records of the Burgh of Peebles (SBRS, 1910).

Pennant, *Tour of Scotland*
T. Pennant, *A Tour in Scotland, 1769 and 1772*, fifth edition, 3 vols (London, 1790).

Perth Blackfriars	*The Blackfriars of Perth*, ed. R. Milne (Edinburgh, 1893).
Perth Hammermen Book	*Book of the Perth Hammermen, 1518 to 1568*, ed. C. A. Hunt (Perth, 1889).
Pitcairn, *Trials*	*Criminal Trials in Scotland from 1488 to 1624*, ed. R. Pitcairn (Bannatyne Club, 1833).
Pitscottie, *Historie*	R. Lindesay of Pitscottie, *The Historie and Cronicles of Scotland* (STS, 1899–1911).
Powis Papers	*Powis Papers, 1507–1894*, ed. J. G. Burnett (Third Spalding Club, 1951).
Prestwick Recs.	*Records of the Burgh of Prestwick in the Sheriffdom of Ayr* (Maitland Club, 1834).
PRO	Public Record Office.
Proc. Soc. Antiq. Scot. [*PSAS*]	*Proceedings of the Society of Antiquaries of Scotland* (1851–).
Prot. Bk Brounhill	Protocol Book of Andrew Brounhill (MS. SRO).
Prot. Bk Feyrn	Protocol Book of John Feyrn (MS. SRO).
Prot. Bk Foular	*Protocol Book of John Foular, 1501–28*, ed. W. Macleod and M. Wood (SRS, 1930–53).
Prot. Bk Foulis	*Protocol Book of James Foulis 1546–53* (SRS, 1927).
Prot. Bk Gaw	*Protocol Book of Sir Alexander Gaw, 1540–58* (SRS, 1910).
Prot. Bk Grote	*Protocol Book of Mr. Gilbert Grote 1552–73* (SRS, 1914).
Prot. Bk Ireland	Protocol Book of Thomas Ireland (MS., Dundee City Archives).
Prot. Bk Johnsoun	*Protocol Books of Dominus Thomas Johnsoun 1528–78* (SRS, 1920).
Prot. Bk Ros	*Protocol Book of Gavin Ros, 1512–32* (SRS, 1908).
Prot. Bk Simon	*Liber Protocollorum M. Cuthberti Simonis Notarii Publici et Scribae Capituli Glasguensis 1499–1513* (Grampian Club, 1875).
Prot. Bk Steven	Protocol Book of Thomas Steven (MS. in Haddington Burgh Records, SRO).
Prot. Bk Strathauchin	Protocol Book of Vincent Strathauchin (MS., SRO).
Prot. Bk Thounis	*Protocol Book of Nicol Thounis 1559–64* (SRS, 1927).
Prot. Bk Young	*Protocol Book of James Young 1485–1515*, ed. G. Donaldson (SRS, 1952).
PSAS	See *Proc. Soc. Antiq. Scot.*
Purves, *Revenues of the Scottish Crown (1681)*	W. Purves, *Revenues of the Scottish Crown (1681)* (Edinburgh, 1897).
Raine, *North Durham*	J. Raine, *The History and Antiquities of North Durham* (London, 1852).
Rait, *Universities of Aberdeen*	R. S. Rait, *The Universities of Aberdeen* (Aberdeen, 1895).
Recs. Scot. Church Hist. Soc. [*RSCHS*]	*Records of the Scottish Church History Society* (1923–).
Reeves, *Culdees*	W. Reeves, *The Culdees of the British Islands* (Dublin, 1864).
Reg. Aven.	Registra Avinionensia in Vat. Arch.
Regesta Regum Scottorum	*Regesta Regum Scottorum*, ed. G. W. S. Barrow and others (Edinburgh, 1960–).
Reg. Gregoire IX	*Les Registres de Gregoire IX* (Écoles de Athenes et de Rome, 1896–1910).
Reginald of Durham, *Libellus*	Reginald of Durham, *Libellus de amirandis Beati Cuthberti virtibus quae novellis patratae sunt temporibus* (Surtees Society, 1835).
Reg. Lat.	Registra Lateranensia in Vat. Arch.
Reg. of Walter Gray, archbishop of York	*Register of Walter Grey, archbishop of York* (Surtees Society, 1870–2).

Reg. Mag. Sig. [*RMS*]	*Registrum Magni Sigilii Regum Scotorum*, ed. J. M. Thomson and others (Edinburgh, 1882–1914).
Reg. Pres.	Register of Presentations to Benefices (MS., SRO).
Reg. Privy Council [*RPC*]	*The Register of the Privy Council of Scotland*, ed. J. H. Burton and others (Edinburgh, 1877–).
Reg. Sec. Sig. [*RSS*]	*Registrum Secreti Sigilli Regum Scotorum*, ed. M. Livingstone and others (Edinburgh, 1908–).
Reg. Supp.	Registra Supplicationum in Vat. Arch. (MS. Calendar of Entries held by department of Scottish History, University of Glasgow).
Reg. Vat.	Registra Vaticana in Vat. Arch.
Reliquiae Celticae	*Reliquiae Celticae, Texts, papers and studies in Gaelic literature and philology*, ed. A. Macbain and J. Kennedy (Inverness, 1892).
Renwick, *Gleanings from the Burgh Records*	R. Renwick, *Gleanings from the Records of the Royal Burgh of Peebles* (Peebles, 1912).
Renwick, *Peebles Aisle and Monastery*	R. Renwick, *Aisle and Monastery* (Glasgow, 1897).
Renwick, *Peebles during the Reign of Queen Mary*	R. Renwick, *Peebles during the Reign of Queen Mary* (Peebles, 1903).
Rep. on State of Certain Parishes	*Reports on the State of Certain Parishes in Scotland . . . mdcxxvii* (Maitland Club, 1835).
Retours	See *Inquis. Retorn. Abbrev.*
Ross Estate Muniments	MS., Ross Estate Muniments in SRO.
Rot. Scot.	*Rotuli Scotiae in Turri Londinensi et in Domo Capitulari Westmonasteriensi Asservati*, ed. D. Macpherson and others (1814–19).
SA	See Anderson, *Scottish Annals.*
St. A. Lib.	*Liber Cartarum Prioratus Sancti Andree in Scotia* (Bannatyne Club, 1841).
St. Andrews Acta	*Acta facultatis Artium Universitatis Sancti Andree 1413–1588*, ed. A. I. Dunlop (SHS, 1964).
St. Andrews Chrs.	Charters of the city of St. Andrews (notes supplied by Rev. W. E. K. Rankin, D.D.).
St. Andrews Copiale	*Copiale Prioratus Sanctiandree*, ed. J. H. Baxter (Oxford, 1930).
St. Andrews Formulare	*St. Andrews Formulare 1514–46*, ed. G. Donaldson and C. Macrae (Stair Society, 1942–4).
St. Andrews Rentale	*Rentale Sancti Andree* (SHS, 1913).
St. Andrews Univ. Recs	*Early Records of the University of St. Andrews* (SHS, 1926).
St. Bees Reg.	*Register of the Priory of St. Bees* (Surtees Society, 1915).
St. Giles Reg.	*Registrum Cartarum Ecclesiae Sancti Egidii de Edinburgh* (Bannatyne Club, 1859).
Saunders MS	MS. in possession of the late William Saunders, Edinburgh.
Scalacronica	*Scalacronica, by Sir Thomas Gray of Heton Knight* (Maitland Club, 1836).
Scone Lib.	*Liber Ecclesie de Scon* (Bannatyne and Maitland Clubs, 1843).
Scot. Antiq.	*Scottish Antiquary* (1886–1903: volumes for 1886–90 bear the title *Northern Notes and Queries.*
Scot. Arch. Forum	*Scottish Archaeological Forum.*
Scot. Hist. Rev. [*SHR*]	*The Scottish Historical Review* (1903–28, 1947–).
Scotichronicon	See *Chron. Bower.*
Scots Peerage	*The Scots Peerage*, ed. Sir J. Balfour Paul (Edinburgh, 1904–14).
Scott, *Berwick-upon-Tweed*	J. Scott, *Berwick-upon-Tweed; the history of the town and guild . . .* (London, 1888).

Scott Letters	*The Letters of Sir Walter Scott*, ed. Grierson (London, 1932–7).
Shetland Court Bk	*The Court Book of Shetland* (SRS, 1954).
SHS Misc.	*The Miscellany of the Scottish History Society* (SHS, 1893–).
Sibbald, *Fife*	R. Sibbald, *The History, Ancient and Modern, of the Sheriffdoms of Fife and Kinross* [ed. L. Adamson] (Cupar–Fife, 1803).
Skene, *Celtic Scotland*	W. F. Skene, *Celtic Scotland* (Edinburgh, 1867).
Smith, *Strathendrick*	J. G. Smith, *Strathendrick and its inhabitants* (Glasgow, 1896).
Speed, *Historie of Great Britaine*	John Speed, *The Historie of Great Britaine under the conquests of the Romans, Saxons, Danes and Normans* (London, 1611).
Spalding Misc.	*Miscellany of the Spalding Club* (Spalding Club, 1841–52).
Spottiswoode, *History*	J. Spottiswoode, *History of the Church of Scotland* (London, 1677). This edition has an appendix containing lists of religious houses. This appendix is also found as a separate publication—An Appendix to the History of the Church of Scotland (London, 1677). It is anonymous but attributed to T. Middleton.
Spottiswoode	J. Spottiswoode, *An account of all the Religious Houses that were in Scotland at the time of the Reformation;* included in R. Keith, *An Historical Catalogue of the Scottish Bishops* (Edinburgh, 1824).
Spottiswoode Misc.	*The Spottiswoode Miscellany* (Spottiswoode Society, 1844–5).
SRO	Scottish Record Office.
SRO Chrs	Scottish Record Office Charters.
State Papers Henry VIII	*State Papers during the Reign of Henry the Eighth* (Record Commission, 1830–52).
Stephen, *Hist. of Inverkeithing*	W. Stephen, *History of Inverkeithing and Rosyth* (Aberdeen, 1921).
Stevenson, *Documents*	*Documents Illustrative of the History of Scotland 1286–1306*, ed. J. Stevenson (Edinburgh, 1870).
Stirling Chrs	*Charters and other Documents relating to the Royal Burgh of Stirling*, ed. R. Renwick (Glasgow, 1884).
Stirling Recs	*Extracts from the Records of the Royal Burgh of Stirling*, ed. R. Renwick (Glasgow, 1887–9).
Stirling Trans.	*Transactions of the Stirling Natural History and Archaeology Society* (1878–).
Symeon of Durham, *Hist. Dunelm. Eccl.*	Symeon of Durham, *Historia Dunelmensis Ecclesiae* (Rolls Series, 1882).
Symeon of Durham, *Hi t. Regum.*	Symeon of Durham, *Historia Regum* in *Symeonis Monachi Opera Omnia*, ed. T. Arnold (Rolls Series, 1882–5).
Symeon of Durham, *Opera Omnia*	*Symeonis Monachi Opera Omnia*, ed. T. Arnold (Roll Series, 1882–5).
Symington Grieve, *The Book of Colonsay and Oronsay*	Symington Grieve, *The Book of Colonsay and Oronsay*, 2 vols (Edinburgh, 1923).
Templaria	*Templaria; Papers relative to the history of the Scottish Knights Templars and to the Knights of St. John* (1828).
Theiner, *Vet. Mon.*	*Vetera Monumenta Hibernorum et Scotorum Historiam Illustrantia*, ed. A. Theiner (Rome, 1864).
The Lennox	*The Lennox* (Edinburgh, 1874).
Thirds of Benefices	*Accounts of the Collectors of Thirds of Benefices 1561–1572* (SHS, 1949).

Thomas, *Early Christian Archaeology* — C. Thomas, *Early Christian Archaeology of North Britain* (Oxford, 1971).

Thomson, *Lauder and Lauderdale* — A. Thomson, *Lauder and Lauderdale* (Galashiels, 1904.)

Tig. Annals [*A. Tig.*] — *Annals of Tigernach*, ed. Whitley Stokes in *Revue Celtique*, xvi–xviii, 1895–7.

Torphichen Chrs — *Abstracts of charters and other papers recorded in the chartulary of Torphichen from 1581 to 1596* (Edinburgh, 1830).

Trans. Royal Hist. Soc. [*Trans. RHS*] — *Transactions of the Royal Historical Society* (London, 1800–).

Trans. Scot. Ecclesiol. Soc. [*TSES*] — *Transactions of the Scottish Ecclesiological Society* (1903–).

Treasurer Accts [*TA*] — *Accounts of the Lord High Treasurer of Scotland*, ed. T. Dickson and Sir J. Balfour Paul (Edinburgh, 1877–1916).

Tyninghame Letter Bk — Tyninghame Letter Book; abstracts in SRO.

Ulster Annals [*AU*] — *Annals of Ulster*, ed. W. M. Hennessy and B. Mac-Carthy (Dublin, 1887–1901).

Univ. Evidence — *Evidence, oral and documentary, taken and received by the Commissioners . . . for visiting the Universities of Scotland* (London, 1837).

Vat. Arch. — Vatican Archives.

Vat. Trans. — Vatican Transcripts in SRO.

Wallace-James, Notebooks — MS. Notebooks of Dr. J. G. Wallace-James, SRO.

Watson, *Celtic Place-names* — W. J. Watson, *The History of the Celtic Place-Names of Scotland* (Edinburgh, 1926).

Watt, *Fasti* — *Fasti Ecclesiae Scoticanae Medii Aevi ad annum 1638*, ed. D. E. R. Watt (SRS, 1969).

Wigtown Charter Chest — *Charter Chest of the Earldom of Wigtown* (SRS, 1910).

Wigtownshire Chrs — *Wigtownshire Charters*, ed. R. C. Reid (*SHS*, 1960).

Wilson, *Folklore and Genealogies of Uppermost Nithsdale* — W. Wilson, *Folklore and Genealogies of Uppermost Nithsdale* (Dumfries, 1904).

Yester Writs — *Calendar of Writs preserved at Yester House 1166–1503*, ed. C. C. H. Harvey and J. Macleod (SRS, 1930).

EARLY RELIGIOUS FOUNDATIONS

GENERAL NOTES

EARLY Scottish foundations prior to the twelfth century are listed in the following section. For the development of monastic life in Scotland from the arrival of St. Ninian at Whithorn in the early fifth century, see p. 1 ff. above. Other religious institutions, and their relationship to those of a monastic character, are discussed by Ian B. Cowan, 'The post-Columban Church', *Recs Scot. Church Hist. Soc.*, xviii, p. 245ff.

ABERCORN, Co. West Lothian. Probably fd. 635 × 663, Trumwine made this monastery the centre of his episcopal activities 681–5 but was forced to leave after the battle of Nechtansmere (Bede, *History*, 42, 220, 428). Still in existence in early eighth c. (*ibid.*, 42). According to a twelfth-c. account, which incorporates earlier source material, the mon. survived in 854 as a fd'n. pertaining to the bp. of Lindisfarne (*SA*, 60n).

ABERDOUR, Co. Aberdeen. According to twelfth-c. Gaelic tradition, founded by Colum Cille (d. 597) and his disciple Drostan, son of Coscrach, at the same time as the mon. of Deer (Jackson, *Gaelic Notes*, 30, 33). Its provenance at this early date must remain doubtful. Although the twelfth-c. wording gives no indication that it had ceased to function at that date, no positive evidence is forthcoming. See DEER.

ABERNETHY, Co. Perth. Traditionally fd. *c.* 600 by Nechtank. of the Picts (Anderson, *Kings and Kingship*, 92–3). A shortlived episcopal centre may have been established here in the early eighth c.. but the evidence is late and uncorroborated (*Chron. Bower* iv, xii). Round tower dated to second half of eleventh c. (C. A. Ralegh Radford, *Antiquity*, xvi, 3–4). A community of Céli Dé apparently shared the house with ordinary clerics, *c.* 1100. *Sacerdotes* of both communities mentioned (Mael-nethe, son of Beollan, Maei-Brigte, Tuathal, Augustinus) and Berheadh, *rector scholarum* (Lawrie, *Charters*, 11–12). The Céli Dé are mentioned 1189 × 1239 (*Arb. Lib.*, 25–6, 147–8; *Lind. Cart.*, 55, 60). Gill-Anndrais (Andreas), pr., occurs 1235–9 (*ibid.*, 55, 60). By the mid-thirteenth c. this community with its pr. had been transformed into a house of regular canons, who in turn gave place to a collegiate ch. in the mid-fourteenth c. See under Augustinian canons and Secular colleges.

AILECH, Co. Argyll; see GARVELLOCH ISLANDS.

APPLECROSS, Co. Ross and Cromarty. Mael-rubai abbot of Bangor, went to Scotland in 671 (*AU; FM*). He founded the mon. in 673 (*AU*) and died there in 722 (*AU*). A successor, Failbe, was drowned in 737 (*A. Tig.*). Mac-oigi of Applecross, ab. of Bangor, d. 802 (*AU*).

ARTCHAIN, Isle of Tiree, Co. Argyll. Findchan, *presbyter*, was founder and ab. He was a contemporary of Colum Cille (d. 597) (Adomnán, *Columba*, I, c. 36).

BLEDACH, Isle of Tiree, Co. Argyll. F. in Heth (Tiree) by Brendan, founder abbot of Clonfert (d. 577) (*ES*, i, 18 and *n*).

BRECHIN, Co. Angus. Kenneth II (971–5) 'Offered the great *civitas* of Brechin to the Lord' (*CKS*. 10), either a record of its fd'n., or perhaps more likely, of a grant to an existing community of their freedom from secular exaction. A round tower of eleventh-c. date. Leot, ab., 1131 × 1150, was almost certainly a layman and his successors, who are mentioned till *c.* 1219, certainly were so (Jackson, *Gaelic Notes*, 31, 61; Lawrie, *Charters*, 181; *Brech. Reg.* i, iv–v). Community of Céli Dé is on record in the second half of the twelfth c. and first half of the thirteenth c. (*Arb. Lib.*, i, 49, 52, 122–3, 125–8, 130, 132–4). Gille-Brigte or Mael-Brigte (Bricius), pr., Gille-Fali and Mathalan, witnesses 1178 × 1189 (*ibid.*, 50). Mael-Brigte, pr., 1204–14 (*ibid.*, 49, 52, 122–3, 125–8, 130, 132–3). During this period the prior and the community were acting as the bp's *familia* (*ibid.*, 130, 133). The formalization of this body into a chapter of secular canons was evidently completed by 18 Feb. 1249/50 when a bull of Pope Innocent IV refers to the fact that 'the brethren who have been wont to be in the church of Brechen were called Keledei and now by change of name are styled canons' (*Lind. Cart.*, no. xcix). See under Cathedrals.

CELLA DIUNI, Loch Awe, Co. Argyll. Diun was presumably the founder and his probable successor was his brother Cailtan. Cailtan, a disciple of Colum Cille, d. –597. The monastery was still functioning in the time of Adomnán (d. 704). (Adomnán, *Columba*, I, c. 31).

CLOVA, Co. Aberdeen. Occurs in a bull of Pope Adrian IV in 1157 in which the '*monasterium Cloveth*' is confirmed to bp. of Aberdeen (*Abdn. Reg.*, i, 6, 85).

COLDINGHAM, Co. Berwick. A double mon. of both monks and nuns fd. by Ebba, daughter of K. Ethelfred of Northumbria, before 661 × 664 (Bede, *Life of St. Cuthbert*, x). The buildings were burnt *c.* 683 and most of the convent subsequently departed (Bede, *History*, 392, 420, 426). It continued, according to a twelfth-c. account, which contains earlier material, as a fd'n. pertaining to the bps. of Lindisfarne in 854 (*SA*, 60n). By this period it had become exclusively a female house, which was burnt and sacked by the Danes *c.* 870 (*SA*, 61).

DEER, Co. Aberdeen. According to twelfth-c. Gaelic tradition, fd. by Colum Cille (d. 597) and his disciple Drostan, son of Cosrach (Jackson, *Gaelic Notes*, 30, 33, 94–6). This fd'n. legend is of doubtful provenance (*ibid.*, 2–7, 97–102). Deer's claim to be regarded as an early mon. rests rather on the identification of Vineus, ab. of Ner, d. 623 (*AU*) and Nechtan of Ner, d. 679 (*AU*) as heads of this house (*ibid.*, 6–7). This may be held to be non-proven and the Drostan who died at Ardbraccan in 719, may have an equal claim as its founder (*ibid.*, 7). Grants of land were being received by a religious community from *c.* 1000 to 1150, but whatever its origins there is no evidence that this was specifically a monastic community at this date (*ibid.*, 42–3). A reference to the *clerici* of Deer in the mid-twelfth c. would rather point to the existence of a community of secular priests, some of the property pertaining to which eventually passed to the Cistercian mon. fd., at Deer in 1218 (Lawrie, *Charters*, no. ccxxiii; *ES*, ii, 181n).

DUNBLANE, Co. Perth. Mac-bethad, *rex scholarum* and a reference to *scolastici*, occurs 1214 × 1223 (*Lind. Cart.*, 49). See under Cathedrals.

DUNKELD, Co. Perth. Built by Kenneth, son of Alpin, K. of Scots before 849. In that year Kenneth caused the relics of Colum Cille to be brought there from Iona, thereby. transferring the administrative centre of the ch. to Dunkeld (*CKS*, 8; *AU*, 849 A.D.) Plundered by the Danes, 849 × 858 (*CKS*, 8). Tuathal, son of Artgus, abbot and *primepscop* (chief bp.) of Fortrui, d. 865 (*AU*). Flaithbertach, son of Muirchertach, ab. d. 873 (*AU*). Duncan, ab., was killed in 965 in a battle between Dub and Culen, who succeeded one another in the kingship of the Scots (*AU*; *CKS*, 10). Burned in 1027 (*AU*). Crinán, ab, killed in battle 1045 (*AU*). His wife was Bethoc, daughter of Malcolm II (1005–34), and their son was Duncan I (1034–40) (*AU*; *CKS*, 152). Before this date the office of bp. had evidently become disassociated from the abbotship, the successive holders of which appear to have been laymen. Ethelred, son of Malcolm III, ab., 1093 × 1107 (*Lawrie*, 11). Donald Bán (1093–7) was buried at Dunkeld, after which his remains were transferred to Iona (*CKS*, 175). Late traditions that a community of the early church continued to function in the twelfth c., at least, seem to be confirmed by a reference to *macleins et scolloci*, 1214 × 1229 (*Lind. Cart.*, 35–6) but whether it was a community of Céli Dé, as was claimed, is not proven. See under Cathedrals.

ECCLESGREIG, Co. Kincardine. The church of Ecclesgyrg *'cum terra abbacie'* was granted to the priory of St. Andrews by Richard, bp. of St. Andrews (1165–78), and the land of the 'abbacie de Eglesgirig' with certain other rights throughout its entire *'parochia'* was confirmed to the canons by William the Lion 1189 × 1195 (*St. A. Lib.*, 138, 229–30). Not conclusive in itself, a reference to a pr. of the priory of Ecclesgirg (*ibid.*, 27) provides the necessary further evidence of an ecclesiastical community previously settled at this site.

EIGG, Co. Inverness. Donnan founder, martyred with community in 617 (*A. Tig.; AU*). Eogan, ab., d. 725 (*AU*). See also A. Macdonald, 'Two major early monasteries of Scottish Dalriata: Lismore and Eigg', *Scot. Arch. Forum*, v (1973), 57–64.

GARVELLOCH ISLANDS, Co. Argyll. The monastery of Ailech traditionally fd. by Brendan, founder ab. of Clonfert (d.577) was probably situated on the island of Eileach an Naoimh in the Garvelloch group on which comparatively well preserved remains of monastic buildings of an early ch. are located (*ES*, i, 17; Watson, *Celtic Place-names*, 81; OPS ii[1], 277).

GOVAN, Co. Lanark. Traditionally a monastery fd. by Constantine in the late sixth c. (*Chron. Bower*, i, 130). Documentary evidence for this fd. is wanting, but archaeological evidence would appear to suggest that a mon. was in existence on this site during the seventh c. Sculptured stones, notably those of the hog-back variety, can be attributed to the second half of the tenth c., and attest to the continued existence of a religious community who may have acted in association with the early bps. of Cumbria (R. C. Ralegh Radford, 'The Early Christian Monuments at Govan and Inchinnan', *Glasgow Archaeol. Trans.*, xv (4), 173–88).

HETH, Co. Argyll, see TIREE.

HINBA, Co. Argyll. Probably the island of Jura (Watson, *Celtic Place-names*, 82–3). Fd. by Colum Cille some years before his death in 597. Before that his uncle Ernan, whom he had sent there as abbot, had also died (Adomnán, *Columba*, I, cs. 21, 45). Virgno became a mk. on Hinba after Colum Cille's death and lived as an anchorite for the last twelve years of his life (*ibid.*, III, c. 23).

HODDAM, Co. Dumfries. Traditionally associated with Kentigern (d. 612) who reputedly built a ch. at Hoddam and placed his see there for a time (Forbes, *St. Ninian and St. Kentigern*, 93, 217). Archaeological evidence from this site which includes sculptured stones and part of a tenth-c. staff or crozier shrine points to the existence of an important ecclesiastical centre at this site (R. A. Ralegh Radford, 'Hoddam' *Dumfries. Trans.*, 3rd ser., xxl, 174 ff).

INCHAFFRAY, Co. Perth. Gilbert, e. of Strathearn, in founding the Augustinian house *c*. 1200, provided that Mael-Isu, presbyter and hermit would administer the new fd'n. and that those who were associated with him would be instructed in the service of God according to the rule of St. Augustine (*Inchaff. Chrs.*, no. ix) Community referred to as *fratres* of St. John of Strathearn and therefore presumably not Céli Dé, but ordinary clerics comparable to those at Deer (*ibid.*, nos vii, ix).

INCHINNAN, Co. Renfrew. Sculptured stones of the tenth or early eleventh c., closely resembling those at Govan, in association with medieval acknowledgment to the church's traditional founder Conval whose relics continued to be venerated, point to the existence of a flourishing ecclesiastical centre at this site (R. A. Ralegh Radford, 'The Early Christian monuments at Govan and Inchinnan', *Glasgow Archaeol. Trans.*, xv (4), 173—88).

IONA. Colum Cille, born 518, left Ireland for Scotland in 563, (*AU; CS*) and two years later founded the monastery (Bede *History*, III, c. 4). Iona became the religious centre of the kingdom of Dalriada and head of the widespread *paruchia* of Columban mon. in Scotland, in Ireland and eventually also in England. Colum Cille himself became the paramount saint of the Scots. His first biographer, Cummine, was ab. from 657 to 669 and his second biographer, Adomnán, was ab. from 679–704. The mon. was plundered by the

Norse in 795 (*AI*) and 802 (*AU*). Sixty-eight of the community killed in 806 (*AU*). Martyrdom of Blathmac, ab., in 825 (*AU*). In 849 a division of the relics of Colum Cille, some going to Dunkeld and others to Kells in Ireland (*AU*; *CKS*, 8). Although the religious capital of the Scots was now Dunkeld, Iona continued to be the spiritual centre and almost all the kings of Scots are said to have been buried there until and including Donald Bán, whose reign ended in 1097. Indrechtach, ab. martyred by *Saxoni* on his way to Rome in 854 (*AI*). Fland, ab., d. 891 (*AU*). Oengus, son of Muirchertach, scholar, anchorite, and tanist-ab., d. 937 (*AU*). Fingan, bp., d. 966 (*CS*). Olaf, son of Sictric, K. of the foreigners of Dublin, died on pilgrimage to Iona in 980 (*A. Tig.*). The abbot and fifteen of the community killed by Danes on Christmas Eve, 986 (*AU*). A dispute in the community may have caused the death of the ab. in 1070 (*AU*). An untrustworthy twelfth-c. account credits Q. Margaret (1069×1093) with the rebuilding of the mon. and the endowment of mks. (*SA*, 116). Dondchad, ab., d. 1099 (*AU*). The dignatories of the community in 1164, when the ab. of Derry, Flaithbertach Ua Brolchain was unsuccessfully invited to take charge as ab., were Augustin, *sacart*, Dub-shide, *fer-léginn*; Mac Gille-duib, *disertach*, and Mac Forchellaig, head of the Céli Dé (*AU*). This last implies that the Céli Dé formed a separate community within the mon., not unusual in Irish houses of the period. In 1174 Mael-Pádruig, bp. of Connor, died at Iona and the obits of other pilgrims are recorded in 1188 and 1200 (*AU*). In 1203 Iona became a Benedictine mon., although not without opposition from Northern Ireland, especially from the abbot and community of Derry which had succeeded Kells as head of the Columban mons. in Ireland about the middle of the previous century. In 1204 the Irish clergy, with two bps. and the abps. of Armagh and Derry, raided Iona and razed this mon. (*AU*). See under Benedictine Monks.

JEDBURGH, Co. Roxburgh. Ecgred, bp. of Lindisfarne (830×846), who, *c*. 830, granted the two vills called Jedworth to the ch. of Lindisfarne (Symeon of Durham, *Hist. Dunelm Eccl.*, i, 52–3; *Hist. Regum*, ii, 101) is said to have built a ch. in Jedburgh (Annals of Lindisfarne, cited *SA*, 60*n*). This ch. occurs *c*. 1080 (Symeon of Durham, *Hist. Regum*, ii, 198). It was probably sited at Old Jedburgh, about five miles from the site of the Augustinian priory, fd. by David I, *c*. 1138, and to which that king confirmed the *monasterium Jeddewrde* (Lawrie, *Charters*, nos. clxxxix, cxc; *Nat. MSS. Scot.*, i, no. xxxviii; *OPS*, i, 367–9).

JURA, Co. Argyll, see HINBA.

KILRIMONT, St. Andrews, Co. Fife. Cill-rigmonaid or earlier Cenn-rigmonaid, traditionally fd. by Ungus, son of Urguist (Watson, *Celtic Place-names*, 396–8 Anderson, *Kings and Kingship*, 97–99). Tuathalan, ab., d. 747 (*AU*). Constantine, K. of Scots (900–*c*. 943), abdicated to become ab. of the Céli Dé (CKS., 9, 151) by which time, evidently Kilrimont had succeeded Dunkeld as the administrative centre of the early ch. The death of a pilgrim, presumably from Ireland is recorded in 963 (*CS; ES*, i, 472). Succession of bps. associated with Kilrimont, apparently beginning in the tenth c., bearing such titles as 'bishop of the Scots' or 'bishop of Scotland' (see G. Donaldson, 'Scottish bishops' sees before David I' in *PSAS*, lxxxvii, 110) are exactly equivalent to similar titles borne by bps. resident in the mon. of Armagh, the administrative centre of the church in Ireland. The office of abbot, the only other known holder of what does not appear on record until 1180×1186, eventually fell into lay hands (*St. A. Lib.*, 353). Thereafter in a manner similar to Abernethy, two groups of clergy are identifiable neither of which appears to have functioned as an integrated monastic community, and the office of fer-léginn, which is recorded *c*. 1211, was assumed by the archdeacons of St. Andrews who first appear on record 1147×1152 (*ibid.*, 317; and see W. J. Watson, 'Inscription on a cross from Kilchoman, Islay' in *PSAS*, lxvi, 442). Both groups of clergy served the bp's cathedral (i.e. the modern St. Rule's ch.). Nevertheless, no regular service was provided at the high altar in 1124 (*Chron. Picts-Scots*, 190) though its revenues were divided into seven portions, five of which supported 'personages' held by married clergy (*personae*) who did not lead a communal life and whose only duties lay in providing hospitality to pilgrims and strangers (*ibid.*, 189). The community of Céli Dé, who numbered thirteen *c*. 1144 (*ibid.*, 183) held their prebends hereditarily and though they had no rights connected with the ch. of St. Andrew at this date, and celebrated their offices at a side altar of that ch., their position may be compared with the Céli Dé at Armagh who were responsible for the choral and other services in that Ch. (Gwynn and Hadcock, *Medieval Religious Houses, Ireland*, 29; see also Barrow, *Kingdom of the Scots*, 212–32; Watt, *Fasti*, 299–302; see also under Cathedrals.) After the fd'n. of the Augustinian priory in 1144, a bull of Pope Eugenius III ordained that as the Céli Dé died out, their places should be taken by regular canons, 30 Aug. 1147 (*St. A. Lib.*, 49); and, about the same date, David I issued a mandate to the prior and canons providing that they should receive the Céli Dé of Kilrimont, with their possessions and revenues, as canons, if such they were willing to become. If they were unwilling, those then living might hold their possessions for their lifetime and, after their death, as many canons as there were Céli Dé were to be instituted in the ch. of St. Andrews, the possessions of the Céli Dé being converted to the canons' use (*ibid.*, 186). The Céli Dé community, however, maintained its existence and entered into agreements with the priory regarding lands and revenues –1161 (*ibid.*, 203) and 1198–9 (*ibid.*, 318). By 1250 this community, with its prior, had been formalized as a college of secular canons. See under Secular Colleges.

KINGARTH, Co. Bute. Daniel, bp. of Kingarth, d. 660 (*AU*). Iolan, bp., d. 689 (*AU*). Temnen, *religiosus clericus*, d. 732 (*A. Tig.*; *AU*). Ronan, ab., d. 737 (*AU*). Mael-manaig, ab., d. 776 (*AU*). Noah, ab., d. 790 (*AU*).

KIRKCUDBRIGHT, Co. Kirkcudbright. *Scollofthes* or scholars of a religious community which apparently served a religious foundation situated on this site were still in possession of the church in 1164 (Reginald of Durham, *Libellus*, 179).

LISMORE, Co. Argyll. Lugaid or Moluag, founder, d. 592 (*AU*). Neman, ab., d. *c.* 611 (*A. Tig.*). Eochaid, ab., d. 635 (*ibid.*). See also A. Macdonald, 'Two major early monasteries of Scottish Dalriata: Lismore and Eigg', *Scot. Arch. Forum*, v (1973), 47–57).

LOCH LEVEN, Co. Kinross. Traditionally fd. by Brude, son of Dergard, last K. of the Picts, but it is more likely that Brude, son of Ferat, is intended, ×842 (Anderson, *Kings and Kingship*, 100). Grants of land by early Scottish kings and bps. of St. Andrews to the community of Céli Dé at Loch Leven are recorded from the middle of the eleventh c. to *c.* 1107 (Lawrie, *Charters*, 5–7, 9, 11, 19) originally recorded in an 'old volume written in the ancient idiom of the Scots', that is Gaelic (*St. A. Lib.*, 113). One grant may date to the middle of the tenth c. (Lawrie, *Charters*, 4), in which case Ronan was ab. at the time. It has been suggested that the transcription of Adomnán's *Life of Columba* commissioned by Alexander I (1107–24) was made at Loch Leven (Adomnán, *Columba*, 10). Dubthach, *sacerdos* and ab., Eogan (*Eugenius*), *monachus*, Cathan, *senex*, appear *c.* 1128 (Lawrie, *Charters*, 67). Granted to the canons regular of St. Andrews by David I, *c.* 1150, with leave to expel those Céli Dé who refused to become canons (*St. A. Lib.*, 188–9, Raine, *North Durham*, App. no. xxvi, Lawrie, *Charters*, 187).

MAG LUINGE, Isle of Tiree, Co. Argyll. Probably situated at Soroby on the south-east of the island, Baithine its abbot before 597 succeeded to the abbacy of Iona on Colum Cille's death (*Adomnán, Columba*, I cs. 30, 41; II, c. 15). The mon. was burned in 673 (*AU*) Connal of Mag Lunge, killed in 775, may have been the monastic head of the restored mon. (*AU*).

MELROSE, Co. Roxburgh, see OLD MELROSE.

METHVEN, Co. Perth. Clerks of Methfyn who appear in a quitclaim 1214×1223 testifies to the existence of a community of secular priests on this site at some period before this date. The agreement then made was sealed by the bp. of St. Andrews as the clerks, who evidently regarded themselves as a corporation, had no seal of their own. (*Lind. Cart.* no. xlviii).

MONIFIETH, Co. Angus. Céli Dé are recorded in the twelfth c. (*Arb. Lib.*, i, 82). A charter of Matilda, countess of Angus, grants to Arbroath abbey in 1242–3 the land 'on the south side of the church of Monifieth which the Céli Dé held in the lifetime of my father' (i.e. Malcolm, E. of Angus (*c.* 1214–42)) (*ibid.*, i, no. 115). Their property had evidently become secularized *c.* 1220 as at that date Earl Malcolm made a grant of all the land of the *abthein* of Monifieth (*ibid.*, i, 330–1) to Nicolas, who witnesses Countess Matilda's charters, 1242–3, as 'abbot' (i.e. lay-abbot) of Monifieth (*ibid.*, i, nos. 49, 114).

MONYMUSK, Co. Aberdeen. Grants of land and revenue to Céli Dé throughout the twelfth c. (*St. A. Lib.*, 369–75, and see W. D. Simpson, 'Augustinian Priory and parish church of Monymusk', *PSAS*, lix (1925), 40–44). Probably replaced by Augustinian canons in 1245 (see Augustinian Canons). Reference to *scollatis* or *scolcc*'s land in the vicinity (Simpson, 'Augustinian Priory', 43).

MORTLACH, Co. Banff. Traditionally the original site of the bishopric of Aberdeen. The clergy associated with the *monasterium de murthillach* which was confirmed, with five chs. which had evidently pertained to it, to the bp. of Aberdeen by Pope Adrian IV in 1157, may have originally served as the early bps. familia. (*Chron. Bower*, iv, p. xliv, *Abdn. Reg.*, i, 6, 85).

MUTHILL, Co. Perth. References to a community of Céli Dé are recorded, 1178 × 1236. Mael-Poil, pr., Sitach and Mael-Coluim witnessed a charter 1178 × 1195 (*N.B. Chrs.*, 7). Mael-domnaig, *rex scolarum*, and a reference to *scolastici* occurs, 1213 × 1223 (*Lind. Cart.*, 50) Muiredach (Mauricius), pr., appears 1235 (*ibid.*, 55). A prior of Muthill witnesses a charter of William, bp. of Dunblane (1284–96), but the fd'n. must have laicized by this date (*Moray Reg.*, 469). See Dunblane, under Cathedrals.

OLD MELROSE, Co. Roxburgh. Possibly founded from Iona during the episcopate of Aidan between 635 and 651, the year to which can be attributed the entry of Cuthbert to the monastery under its abbot Eata and its prior Boisil (Colgrave, *Two Lives of St. Cuthbert*, 166–7, 172–3; Bede, *History*, 430–3). Eata remained as ab. until 663/4 (*ibid.*, 430–1). Drythelm, an ascetic, became a mk. in a separate dwelling at Melrose at the end of the seventh c. (*ibid.*, 488–9). Burned down by Kenneth MacAlpin in 839 (*Chron. Picts-Scots*, 8). According to a twelfth-c. account which incorporates earlier source material the mon. survived in 854 as a fd'n. pertaining to the bps. of Lindisfarne, one of whom Edilwald is credited as ab. of Melrose in 746 in a treatise on the Benedictine order (*SA*, 60n; *Kalendars of Scottish Saints*, 330). The mon. was deserted in 1074 when an attempt by Aldwin of Jarrow to restore it for Benedictine mks. failed (*SA*, 97–8). The mon. was succeeded by a ch. dedicated to St. Cuthbert and dependent on the priory of Durham till 1124 × 1136 when David I exchanged it for the ch. of Berwick and annexed it to the Cistercian mon. fd. at Melrose in 1136 (see under Cistercian Abbeys).

ST. ANDREWS, Co. Fife, see KILRIMONT.

TIREE, Co. Argyll, see ARTCHAIN and MAG LUINGE. Another mon. founded in Heth (Tiree) by Comgall, founder-abbot of Bangor, *c.* 564–565 was apparently shortlived as Pictish raids caused Comgall to return to Ireland with 'many holy men' (*ES*, i, 52–4).

TURRIFF, Co. Aberdeen. Domangart, fer-léginn occurs 1131 × 1132. Cormac, ab. of Turbruaid appears *c.* 1150. These entries constitute clear evidence for the existence of an early monastery at this site, and a community was apparently still in existence at this date (Jackson, *Gaelic Notes*, 31–2, 79, 84, 89).

TYNINGHAME, Co. East Lothian. Traditionally fd. by Baldred (d. 756) who according to a twelfth-c. source had lived as an anchorite at this site (*Chron. Melrose*, 29; *ES*, i, 242 n; *SA*, 56). The same chronicler describes it as mon. pertaining to the bishopric of Lindisfarne in 854 (*ibid.*, 60 and n). Its destruction by the Norse is recorded in 941 (*Chron. Melrose*, 29; Symeon of Durham, *Hist. Regum*, ii, 94).

WHITHORN, Co. Wigtown. An existing Christian community may have existed at this site even before the arrival, as its bp. in the late fourth c., of Ninian who built 'a church of stone' (E. A. Thompson, 'The origin of Christianity in Scotland', *SHR* xxxvii (1958), 17–22; Bede, *History*, 222–3). This early ch. does not appear to have been monastic but had apparently become such by the eighth c., the change perhaps stemming from the activities of Irish Christian monks in the late sixth c. (Thomas, *Early Christian Archaeology*, 97, 100). A succession of bps. commences about 725–20 (Pechthelm, d. 735; Frithwald, 735–63; Pechtwin 763–76; Ethelbert 777–89; Badulf, 790— (*SA*, 53, 55, 58–9)). Thereafter the bishopric appears to have lapsed, but status of ch. from which bp. Gilla-

Aldan took his title in 1128 is obscure and a community of sorts may have been in existence at that date (Watt, *Fasti*, 133–4). See under Cathedrals.

UNIDENTIFIED FOUNDATIONS

General Notes. These monasteries may have been situated in Ireland but as they are equally unidentifiable there, their inclusion as probable Scottish foundations may be justified.

Cailli au Finde. According to Adomnán, Finten, son of Aid, founded this unidentified monastery (Adomnán *Columba*, II, 31).

Elen, Isle of. According to Adomnán, one of Columba's followers, Lugne mocu-Min became ab. of a monastery on this unidentified island (Adomnán *Columba*, II, 18).

UNCERTAIN FOUNDATIONS

General Notes. This list could be expanded on the strength of sources such as the Life of Brendan of Clonfert which would add a monastery at Bledoch on the isle of Tiree (Anderson, *Early Sources*, i, 18), and the Life of Comgall of Bangor who also apparently founded a shortlived monastery on the same island (*ibid.*, i, 52–4). Late sources such as Walter Bowers continuation of John of Fordun's *Scotichronicon* would add Inchcolm, on which a hermit is said to have dwelt before the foundation of the Augustinian monastery in 1123 (*Chron. Bower*, v, xxxvii) and the Aberdeen Breviary could provide several otherwise unauthenticated foundations. However, unless reasonably contemporary sources exist or archaeological evidence corroborates suspect sources, it has been deemed advisable to omit such alleged foundations from these lists.

Applegarth, Co. Dumfries. Archaeological evidence and the possible identification of certain lands in Dryfesdale, which were to be held (*c.* 1215) 'in wood and plain, monastery and mill' as pertaining to Applegarth has led to the suggestion that this was the site of an ecclesiastical foundation which probably continued until early twelfth c. (see *Dumfries. Trans.* 3rd ser., xxxv, 14–19; *CDS*, i, no. 635).

Arbilot, Co. Angus. Maurice, ab. of Arbirlot, witnesses charters at the beginning of the thirteenth c. (1201 × 1214) (*Arb. Lib.*, i, 29, 32, 47). His office may have been titular and no record of foundation or community.

Dornoch, Co. Sutherland. Monks, whom David I ordered Reinwald, E. of Orkney to respect, appear 1127 × 1153 (*Dunf. Reg.*, no. 23). No evidence as to whether members of an early community on this site, which is traditionally associated with the Céli Dé, *c.* 1272, or attempt at twelfth-c. fd'n (*ES*, ii, 700).

Falkirk, Co. Stirling. John, son of Harvey, ab. of Varia Capella, relinquished to abbey of Holyrood in 1257 rights and titles to land which his father had previously possessed. (*Holy. Lib.*, no. 91). Harvey's office may have been titular, but an ecclesiastical institution, previously known as Eaglis Breac, had evidently been in existence at some earlier date.

Glasgow, Co. Lanark. Traditionally associated with Kentigern who is reputed to have established his church in the mid-sixth c. at 'Deschu'. This is identified with Glasgow by a twelfth-c. chronicler, but this cannot be substantiated, and a cathedral dedicated to Kentigern does not appear on record until the early twelfth c. (Forbes, *St. Ninian and St. Kentigern*, 55, 182). See GLASGOW, under Cathedrals.

Glendochart, Co. Perth. The 'abbot of Glendochir (or Glendocheroch)', who is mentioned as a local magnate, along with the E. of Atholl, in the reign of William the Lion (1165–1214) (*APS*, i, 50, 239) was a layman. There is no record of such a fd'n. or community.

Kilspindie, Co. Perth. Malcolm, ab. of Kilspindie, witnesses a charter, 1211–25 (*Scone Lib.*, no. 84). His office may have been titular, but no evidence of monastery or community.

Kinkell, Co. Aberdeen. The church is called a *plebania* in an account of its erection as a prebend of Aberdeen cathedral in 1420 (*Abdn. Reg.* ii, 253). It had closely associated with it, six chapels or *membrums* in Drumblade, Dyce, Kemnay, Kinnellar, Kintore and Skene (*Reg. Supp.*, 608, fo. 247). This connection, which was obviously of long standing, may have arisen if Kinkell's origin was that of an ecclesiastical foundation with an extensive *parochia*.

Mow, Co. Roxburgh. The church, *cum parochiis*, was confirmed to Kelso by Herbert, bp. of Glasgow, 1147 × 1164, and this may indicate that at one period the ch. had served as an institution serving a fairly wide area (*Kel. Lib.*, no. 416).

Old Roxburgh, Co. Roxburgh. The church was granted by Malcolm IV, 1153 × 1156 to the see of Glasgow in *capelliis et parochis* (*Glas. Reg.*, no. 12). This and the close association between the mother ch. and the other chs. of Roxburgh might indicate that this ch. initially acted as a foundation with an extensive *parochia* (*OPS.*, i, 450ff.).

Restennet, Co. Angus. Claims that this may have been the site of the church of stone dedicated to St. Peter built *c.* 710 at the instance of Nechtan, K. of the Picts who had sought advice from Ab. Ceolfrith of Jarrow are unsubstantiated (*SA*, 47–49). Nevertheless, architectural detail in one of the towers of the later medieval priory ch. points to the existence of a ch. of early Saxon design on this site (Gordon Donaldson, 'Scotland's earliest church buildings', *RSCHS*, xviii, 1–9).

Rosemarkie, Co. Ross and Cromarty. The association of Curitan as founder of Rosemarkie is not in doubt but whether he is to be associated with the bp. and ab. of Ros-mic- bairend who was present at a council in Ireland in 697 is uncertain. This association of Curitan with Rosemarkie and further attempts to identify him with the legendary Boniface who 'foundit' Rosmarkyne' cannot be substantiated (*ES*, i, 205, 211; Skene, *Celtic Scotland*, ii, 229–32).

Rum, Co. Inverness. The ŏnly cleric on record is Beccán, d. 677 (*AU*), but it is nowhere stated that he was an anchorite or hermit and the likelihood is that he was an abbot of a monastic community on the island.

Stobo, Co. Peebles. Possibly the site of a sixth-c. diocesan centre in the Tweed valley (Thomas, *Early Christian Archaeology*, 17–18), the ch. with its wide *parochia* and large number of dependent chapels at Lyne, Broughton, Drummelzier and Dawick, possesses the physical characteristics of a pre-twelfth c. religious fd'n. (*Glas. Reg.* nos. 48, 84; *OPS*, i, 196–208).

The list of religious houses given by Gervase of Canterbury (–1216) (*SA*, 327–8) and Henry of Silgrave (*c.* 1272) (*ES*, ii, 699–700) show Céli Dé not only under the bishopric of Dunkeld (above) but also under the bishoprics of Dunblane, Ross, Caithness and Argyll. In none of the latter instances, however, is there definite evidence of the existence of Céli Dé. (See Skene, *Celtic Scotland*, ii, 377–408.)

Supposed Foundations

General Notes. The terms *apdaine* (*abland, abthania, abthen*) and *scoloc* should not be used as evidence of a community when they appear alone or together. The abdaine or 'abbey lands' were often in the vicinity of the monastery to which it belonged, but it could also be at some distance away, and the more important the monastery the more likely it was to have had lands granted to it elsewhere than its immediate vicinity. Hence the *abdaine* of Iona in Galloway.

The same applies for the *scoloc*. When a grant of land was made to a monastery, the people already occupying that land became in effect monastic tenants. The first born son of each tenant was given to the church to receive an ecclesiastical education and inherited his share of the family land, farming it on more liberal terms than other tenants. He was called a *scoloc* or scholar and came under the jurisdiction of the *fer-léginn* while receiving his education. Later, probably, the term was applied to all monastic tenants and this would explain its decline in meaning to 'farm servant' in present day Gaelic. Like the abbey lands which he occupied, the *scoloc* need not necessarily have lived in the vicinity of the monastery whose tenant he was.

For the significance of 'Eccles', denoting an early ecclesiastical site, see G. W. S. Barrow, *The Kingdom of the Scots*, 60–4; the significance of 'Annat' as a similar pointer is discussed in Aidan MacDonald, 'Annat in Scotland: A Provisional Review' in *Scottish Studies*, 17, pp. 135–46.

Airlie, Co. Angus. The '*abbathein de Erolyn*' was leased by William, bp. of St. Andrews to the abbot and convent of Coupar Angus in 1212 (*Coupar Angus Chrs.*, i, 47). No evidence of a foundation.

Arbuthnott, Co. Angus. Tenants called parsons had held the kirk town, from which 'divers scolocs' had been removed at the end of the twelfth c. (*Spalding Misc.*, v, 62–6). No indication of fd'n. or community on this site.

Dull, Co. Perth. The *abthania de Dul* appears in a charter confirming the ch. of Dull to the priory of St. Andrews, 1214 × 1249 (*St. A. Lib.*, 296–7), but no evidence of fd'n. or community.

Ellon, Co. Aberdeen. Lands held by the scolocs of Ellon were leased by Gameline, bp. of St. Andrews in 1265 (*Aberdeen-Banff Coll.*, 311–12). No indication of fd'n. or community on this site.

Fetteresso, Co. Kincardine. Dufscolok of Fetheressau appears in an early thirteenth-c. charter, but no evidence for an institution or community (*Arb. Lib.*, i, no. 89).

Kettins, Co. Angus. The '*abthenagium de Ketenes*' appears in a grant of Hugh de Ever, lord of Kettins to Coupar Angus abbey, 1292–96 (*Coupar Angus Chrs.*, i, 136). No indication of a fd'n.

Kinghorn, Co. Fife. Skene (*Chron. Fordun*, ii, 417) claims to have seen record evidence for this *abthania*, but the original source has not been located.

Kirkmichael in Strathardle, Co. Perth. The *abbethayne de Kylmichel* appears in a charter of 1297 in which the abbey lands were quit-claimed by Dunfermline abbey to John of Inchmartin (*Dunf. Reg.*, no. 297). No evidence for fd'n. or community.

Madderty, Co. Perth. The land of Maddyrn which of old was called *abbacia* was granted to the priory of Inchaffray by Gilbert, E. of Strathearn, 1200 × 1203 (*Inchaff. Lib.*, no. 13). Further confirmations followed, but no indication of a religious institution (*ibid.*, nos. 24, 74).

Melginch, Co. Perth. The church of Megginch with the land called in Gaelic *abthen* was confirmed to Holyrood abbey by William the Lion, 1189 × 1199 (*Holy. Lib.*, no. 48). Other confirmations followed, but no indication of a religious institution (*ibid.*, 53–4, 177).

Montrose, Co. Angus. A charter of William the Lion grants to Hugh of Roxburgh, 1178 × 1184, the *terram abbacie de Munros*, (*Arb. Lib.*, i, 67). No indication of a community.

Rossie, Co. Angus. Part of the *abbacia de Rossim* was granted to Matthew, archdeacon of St. Andrews by David I, c. 1150 × 1153, and this was later confirmed by Malcolm IV, 1153 × 1159 (*St. A. Lib.*, 200). No evidence of a community.

Rothesay, Co. Bute. Described as the *abbacie* of Rothesay in 1407 (SRO, Macgregor Coll., Lamont Papers, Shuttle 1, Bundle 1 (1)).

THE BENEDICTINE (BLACK) MONKS

GENERAL NOTES

INCLUDED in the list of the Benedictine houses is the priory of May, frequently regarded as Cluniac, as well as the more doubtful foundation of Rindalgros (Rhynd). These are taken as following the development of the abbey of Reading (of which they were dependencies), which, originating as in some sort a Cluniac foundation, appears from the thirteenth century onwards as a Benedictine house (see Hurry, *Reading Abbey*, 65; Knowles and Hadcock, *Medieval Religious Houses: England and Wales*, 74).

THE BENEDICTINE HOUSES

Name	County	Rank	Minimum income (1561)	Fd.	Date D. or Sec.	Dependent on or (note)
¶‡COLDINGHAM	Berwick	Priory	£2600(?)	−1139	1606	Durham
*‡DUNFERMLINE	Fife	Priory		c. 1070		
		Abbey	£9630	1128	1593	
¶‡IONA	Argyll	Abbey	?	−1203	1587/8(?)	
MAY	Fife	Priory	See Pitten-weem	−1153	See notes	Reading
‡ §PLUSCARDEN	Moray	Priory	£3570	See notes	1587	Dunfermline
RINDALGROS (RHYND)	Perth	?		1147–53(?)	−1231	Reading see notes
URQUHART	Moray	Priory		c. 1136	1453/4 (united to Pluscarden)	Dunfermline

COLDINGHAM. Statements (Spottiswoode, 465; Raine, *North Durham*, 374) that K. Edgar rebuilt the monastery burned by the Danes (see under Early Religious Foundations) cannot be substantiated. About 1098, Edgar granted the shire of Coldingham, with 'all the lands which they have in Lothian', to the monks of Durham (*ibid.*, App., no. ix). A ch., not yet monastic, was built and Edgar was present at its dedication, *c.* 1100 (*ibid.*, App., no. iv). But Edgar can hardly be regarded as the founder of the monastery. This was the view of one fifteenth-c. prior who stated: 'Edgar, king of Scots, gave this place . . . to the monastery of Durham; but as time passed the prior and brethren at Durham preferred to erect a church and place their own monks there' (Dobson, *Durham Priory*, 317). 'Coldingham priory' it has been said 'cannot be assigned to a single founder, though it grew from Edgar's gift' (Barrow, *Kingdom of the Scots*, 169). It undoubtedly originated from the necessity of sending monks from Durham to take charge of the Scottish estates and the 'monk of Coldingham' who appears, −1136 (Raine, *North Durham*, App. no. clxxxiv) is more probably one of these rather than a member of a religious community at Coldingham. Only the ch. of Coldingham is mentioned in 1127 (*Liber Vitae* (Surtees Soc., 1923), fos. 44, 47), but in 1139 and again in 1140–1, charters of David I and Earl Henry, his son, refer to the mks serving the ch. of St. Mary and St. Cuthbert of Coldingham (Raine, *North Durham*, App., nos. xx, ciii). The first prior of Coldingham appears on record, *c.* 1147 (*Dunf. Reg.,* no. 4), but the priory was obviously founded before this date (cf. Lawrie, *Charters*, 251). In Jan. (?) 1215/16 the priory was plundered by K. John's forces (*Chron. Melrose*, 122; *Chron. Lanercost*, 18). It was proposed, *c.* 1235, that there should always be thirty resident monks (besides the prior) at Coldingham as opposed to seventy at Durham (R. B. Dobson, 'The last English monks on Scottish soil', *SHR*, xlvi (1967), 2n), but the number of resident brethren had dropped well below this figure by the early fourteenth c. There were only seven resident monks in 1304 (*Cold. Corr.*, 5) and it was alleged by the Scots that by April 1379 (Raine, *North Durham*, App. no. dxci) the number had fallen from twenty-four to three or four. During the Anglo-Scottish wars of the early fourteenth c. the monks were compelled for a time to abandon Coldingham (Dobson, 'Last English monks on Scottish soil', 3). In spite of Robert I's confirmation of Durham's possession of the priory, 14 November 1326 (*RMS*, i, App. I, no. 19), Edward III's Scottish campaigns again threatened to break the connection between Coldingham and Durham.

A period of stability from 1340 onwards was shattered by Robert II's decision in July 1378 to expel the Durham monks from the priory and replace them by other Benedictines from Dunfermline abbey (*Chron. Bower*, ii, 161–3; Hay, *Diplomatum*, i, 380; *CPL*, iv, 236; Raine, *North Durham*, App. no. dxci). 'The struggle between the monks of Durham and Dunfermline for possession of Coldingham provides the main interest of the priory's history between 1378 and June 1442, when James II admitted the English candidate, John Oll, to the cell' (Dobson, 'Last English monks on Scottish soil, 3n). Dunfermline monks enjoyed possession of the priory for most, though not all, of the period between 1378 and 1424 (see A. L. Brown, 'The Priory of Coldingham in the late fourteenth century', *Innes Review*, xxiii (1972), 91–101). There are complaints of the intrusion of a monk of Dunfermline into the priory (*Cold. Corr.*, no. xlviii ff.); and in 1379 (Swinton Chrs., no. 3), 1380/1 (*Dunf. Reg.*, no. 392) and later the abbot figures as superior of Coldingham, which is described as a dependency or cell of Dunfermline, in 1390 (*CPP*, i, 575) and in 1419 (*CSSR*, i, 123). In spite of assurances that Robert II was willing conditionally to restore the priory to Durham (*CDS*, iv, no. 291), a confirmation by charter of the possessions of the priory by Robert III, 26 Jan. 1391/2 (*RMS*, i, no. 839) and temporary repossession of the priory in 1419 (Dobson, *Durham Priory*, 319), it was not until the release of James I in March 1424 that English mks. returned to Coldingham on a more secure basis. In that year a precept was given by the Scottish king to the (English) prior for the repair of this house which had been partially destroyed in 1419 by serious fire for which the Scots blamed the then English pr. (*RMS*, ii, no. 2; *APS*, ii, 25; *Chron. Bower*, ii, 163–5). Despite litigation at the Curia by monks of Dunfermline, the position of the priory remained stable for some years and in 1436 Henry VI of England took the priory into his special protection (*Rot. Scot.*, ii, 298). After the death of the prior in 1441, Dunfermline made a further bid to secure the priory but was again thwarted after the admission of an English prior by James, II, 11 June 1442 (Dunlop, *James Kennedy*, 48–54). During this period the number of mks varied; the pr. had only one fellow mk in January 1438 but three in June 1446 (Dobson, *Durham Priory*, 300n).

By this date a contest had arisen for the office of bailie of Coldingham between members of the family of Home, the victor, Sir Alexander Home, who had supported Durham priory in its struggle against Dunfermline, being rewarded by the conferment of the bailiary of Coldingham upon him for life 14 May 1442 and upon himself, or his son, for sixty years on 4 Jan. 1443 (Dobson, *Durham Priory*, 321–7). The position of the English prior and of Sir Alexander, son of the former bailie, was jointly threatened on 6 Aug. 1461 when a Patrick Home, a kinsman of the bailies, obtained a papal mandate to deprive the prior, who it was claimed had allowed the complement of monks to fall from eighteen to two, and was himself to be appointed *in commendam* for life (*CPL*, xi, 425–6). Durham mks. continued to reside at Coldingham for some time after this bull, and as late as 31 March 1462, two more monks were despatched from Durham to increase the community, but by mid-May 1462 the English mks. had been expelled (Dobson, 'Last English Monks on Scottish soil', 8). Thereafter, the mks. of Durham were permanently excluded from the priory and, although continuing their litigation for several years, eventually abandoned their attempts to regain the priory in Oct. 1478 'to such season as it may pleas God and Seynt Cuthbert that we may have better spede than we can have yit' (*ibid.*, 8–24). In the meantime, the struggle between Patrick Home and Sir Alexander Home had resulted in

the deprivation and expulsion of Patrick before 10 Dec. 1464 and the provision of Sir
Alexander's son John, as commendator (*CPL*, xii, 232–4; Reg. Supp., 577, fo. 196;
Durham, Muniments and Manuscripts of the Dean and Chapter, Misc. Chrs., no. 1491).
The Homes thereafter successfully resisted the counterclaims of Durham and Patrick
Home and also attempts at suppression by James III who obtained papal consent to annex
the non-conventional priory to the collegiate ch. of St. Mary (the Chapel Royal), St.
Andrews (*CPL*, xiii, 14, 16; Cameron, *Apostolic Camera*, 172).

More success attended James III's attempt on 3 April 1473 to convert the priory into a
collegiate ch., to be called the Chapel Royal of Coldingham (see under Secular Colleges)
of which Patrick Home was to be dean with an allocation from the revenues (in what proportion is not clear) to the Chapel Royal of St. Mary, St. Andrews, of which John Home
was already dean (Reg. Supp., 639, fo. 147v; *CPL*, xiii, 19; Theiner, *Vet. Mon.*, 472–3;
Fraser, *Lennox*, ii, 93). Nevertheless, nothing was done to erect prebends, other than the
deanery, which was acquired following the resignation of Patrick Home (1474 × 1478) by
John Home who subsequently styles himself dean rather than prior (Watt, *Fasti*, 346–8).
On 16 Dec. 1484, however, he misused royal letters of recommendation to Pope Innocent
VIII to obtain a revocation of the proceedings subsequent to the mandate of 3 April 1473,
the partially erected collegiate ch. being suppressed and the priory restored (*CPL*, xiv,
46–47). Parliament on 26 May 1485 decided that the Pope should be asked to overturn his
act of revocation and adhere to the scheme of 3 April 1473 (*APS*, ii, 171). But although the
Pope eventually agreed to this on 28 April 1487, and parliament declared it was treason to
try and upset the erection of the collegiate ch. at Coldingham, the restoration of the
political fortunes of the Homes on the death of James III on 11 June 1488 saw the end of
this scheme to restore and complete the collegiate ch. and John Home appears soon after
as prior (not dean) of Coldingham (*CPL*, xiv, 47–48; *APS*, ii, 179, 215; *ADA*, 143; see also
Norman Macdougall, 'The struggle for the Priory of Coldingham', *Innes Rev.*, xxiii (1972),
102–14). Successive members of the Home family obtained the priorship, but about Dec.
1509, in a letter to Pope Julius II, James IV revived a more ancient claim when stating
that while, 130 years before, the Scottish council [*sic*] decided that the priory should be
united to Dunfermline, it had latterly ceased to be under that abbey's control, and went
on to request that the priory, when vacant, should be annexed to Dunfermline, which is
held *in commendam* by his son, abp. of St. Andrews, or given to the abp. for his lifetime
(*James IV Letters*, no. 287). The request was successful and the annates were promised,
23 Feb. 1510 (Vat. Arch. Libri Annatarum, 52, fo. 68v). Following the death of the
commendator at Flodden, Henry VIII petitioned the Pope, 12 Oct. 1513, for the reunion
of the priory to Durham (*LP Henry VIII*, i, 2355; Theiner, *Vet. Mon.*, no. dcccxcix). The
Scottish crown's nomination of David Home (*James V. Letters*, 3) was, however, accepted
and he held it until his death in 1517 (M. Dilworth, 'Coldingham Priory and the Reformation' in *Innes Rev.*, xxiii (1972), 120–1).

A long struggle between the Homes and the Douglases for possession of the priory broke
out in 1519 following the murder of Home's successor, Robert Blackadder, and lasted
until 1528 (*ibid.*, 122–5). Thereafter a series of commendators drawn from a variety of
families, including Home and Stewart (*ibid.*, 125–31), held the priory until the final
triumph of Alexander Home who obtained the commendatorship, 10 Aug. 1592 (*HMC
Home*, no. 316) and had this priory, along with the abbey of Jedburgh, erected into a temporal
lordship in his favour, in parliament, 1606 (*APS*, iv, 360–1), and by charter, 1610 (*RMS*,
vii, no. 290). The dispute for possession of the lordship of Coldingham between the Homes
and the Stewarts continued long after this date and resulted in the latter re-obtaining the
priory between 1620 and 1643 when repossession was effected by the Homes. (Dilworth,
'Coldingham Priory and the Reformation' 132–3).

In the sixteenth c., the priory suffered severely during invasions and was garrisoned
both by Scottish and English forces. Coldingham was burned in Oct. 1532, though the
priory is not specifically mentioned (*LP Henry VIII*, v. no. 1460; *Diurnal*, 16). In Nov.
1542, Coldingham 'with the abbey', appears in a list of places burned by Hertford's army
(*LP Henry VIII*, xvii, nos. 1086, 1197); while, on 17 June 1544, the priory buildings, except
the ch., suffered a similar fate (*ibid.*, xix[1], no. 762). They were being 'held' for the [English]
king's use', Nov.–Feb. 1544/5 (*ibid.*, xix[2], no. 625, xx[1], no. 129); and the Scots in the same
period, were besieging the garrisoned 'abbey and steeple' (*RSS*, iii, nos. 990, 1013). The
priory underwent further destruction in Hertford's invasion, Aug. 1545 (*LP Henry VIII*,
xx[2], no. 494); and in Oct. 1547, it was proposed to be razed (*Cal. State Papers Scot.*, i, no.

57). On 4 Feb. 1551/2, it is stated that 'the priorie hes bene wastit be the weiris [wars] thir yeiris bigane, mekle of the place and kirk brint [burned] and distroyit' (*ADCP*, 614). The Coldingham mks. were evicted during the upheavals of 1532, 1542 and 1544/5, but remained a corporate body which, in addition to the prior, and in spite of two mks. having gone to Dunfermline, numbered eleven in 1543, after which date no new mk. entered the community which consisted of at least six mks. at the Reformation (Dilworth, *op cit.*, 133–5). In 1648 most of the remaining buildings were destroyed by Cromwell.

DUNFERMLINE. The charter purporting to record the fd'n. of the abbey by Malcolm III, 1070–93 (*Dunf. Reg.*, 417) is spurious (Lawrie, *Charters*, 237). According to Turgot, Q. Margaret, after her marriage to Malcolm, 1068–9, built a church here in honour of the Holy Trinity (*Vitae S. Margaretae Scotorum Reginae* in *Symeonis Dunelmensis Opera et Collectanea*, i (Surtees Soc., 1868), 238–9), in which a priory was established; a letter of Lanfranc, abp. of Canterbury, announces the sending of Goldwine and other two brethren, at the queen's request (*Scalachronica*, 222, Lawrie, *Charters*, no. ix). These monks formed the nucleus 'of what in time became a full Benedictine convent under a prior' (Barrow, *Kingdom of the Scots*, 195). A letter of David I, 1126 × 1128, states that 'the first foundation of the monastery of Dunfermline took from the church of Canterbury, with the advice and assistance of the monks of that church' (*Regesta Regum Scottorum*, i, no. 8; cf. *SHR*, xxxi, 18–19), and this confirms that Christ Church of Holy Trinity of Dunfermline was founded by Queen Margaret as a daughter house of Christ Church or Holy Trinity of Canterbury. It was to this ch. that St. Anselm, 1100 × 1107, sent monks from Canterbury at King Edgar's request, afterwards asking King Alexander I to protect the monks of Canterbury who were in Scotland (Lawrie, *Charters*, no. xxv), and from this ch., Peter, 'monk and prior' of the ch. of Dunfermline was sent as an envoy to Canterbury to negotiate the appointment of Eadmer to the see of St. Andrews (Eadmer, *Historia Novorum*, 279). In 1128 Geoffrey, pr. of Canterbury, was sent, at the request of David I to be the first abbot of Dunfermline (*Regesta Regum Scottorum*, i, no. 8; John of Worcester in Anderson, *Scottish Annals*, 166). This has sometimes been taken (e.g. *Chron. Holyrood*, 121*n*), that K. David, in that year, refounded the monastery as a Benedictine abbey. The source of the idea of refoundation is evidently the assertion in the *Scotichronicon* (lib. v, cap. xlviii; *Chron. Bower*, i, 301) that David I brought thirteen mks. as a convent from Canterbury. But K. David's charter, *c.* 1128, grants anew to the ch. of Dunfermline lands bestowed by his parents [Malcolm III and Margaret] (*Dunf. Reg.*, no. 1); and the *Scotichronicon* (lib. v, cap. xliv (*Chron. Bower*, i, 297)) speaks of that ch. as 'first founded by [King David's] father and mother, augmented in buildings and possessions by his brother [Alexander I], while he himself enriched it, as now built, with more abundant gifts and honours'. These references, with the dedication to the Holy Trinity establish the continuity of Margaret's original foundation (see Barrow, *Kingdom of the Scots*, 193–8).

The abbey ch. was dedicated in 1150 (*Chron. Holyrood*, 121). On 24 April 1245 Pope Innocent IV granted the abbot the use of the mitre (Theiner, *Vet. Mon.*, no. cxiii). The abbey, except for the ch. was largely destroyed by Edward I's forces in 1303 (Mathew of Westminster, *Flores Historiarium*, 446). For most of the early sixteenth c. the abbey was held *in commendam* by abps. of St. Andrews (*Dunf. Reg.*, xvi), but this link was severed with the death of James Beaton in 1539. Thereafter George Dury, who had been provided to the abbey, 23 May 1526 (Reg. Lat. 1482, fos. 53v–57), finally obtained the commendatorship to which he had had some claim since 1532 (Vat. Arch. Resignationes A, 46, fo. 310; *Dunf. Reg.*, 386–9). The number of mks. remained fairly constant in this period, 26 being recorded in 1520, 28 in 1555 and 25 in 1559 (Dilworth, 'Monks and ministers after 1560', *RSCHS* xviii, 216). Part of the buildings were demolished by the reforming lords, 26 March 1560 (Pitscottie, *Historie*, ii, 168).

At the Reformation, George Dury went to France, 29 Jan. 1560/1 (*Diurnal of Occurrents*, 64) but continued to be considered usufructuar or principal commendator, while in Scotland, Robert Pitcairne exercised authority as commendator-designate (*RSS*, v, no. 2064; *RMS*, iv, no. 1659). Having succeeded to the office on Dury's death, Pitcairne held the commendatorship until 1583, which then passed in turn to Patrick, master of Gray and George, earl of Huntly (*APS*, iii, 412, 473). Thereafter, the lordship of Dunfermline, with its lands, etc., north of the Forth was granted to Q. Anne, consort of James VI, 24 Nov. 1589 (*ibid.*, iv, 24). From *c.* 1587, other portions of the abbey lands were separately erected: the lordship of Musselburghshire for Sir John Maitland, afterwards Lord Thirlestane (1587) (*ibid.*, iii, 628–9); the barony of Burntisland for Sir Robert Melville (ratified 1592) (*ibid.*, iii, 601); which was expressly excepted when the abbey was annexed to the Crown in 1593 (*ibid.*, iv, 23). Alexander Seton, its hereditary baillie on the south side of the Forth (*ibid.*, iv, 249–52) was cr. E. of Dunfermline, 4 March 1605 (*RMS*, vi, no. 1565).

Dependencies: Urquhart; Pluscarden (15–16 c.); Coldingham (14–15 c.).

IONA. Formerly a Columban monastery. See under Early Religious Foundations. This house was founded by Reginald, son of Somerled, lord of the Isles (1164–1207) for black monks (Book of Clanranald in *Reliquiae Celticae*, ii, 157; *Highland Papers*, i, 82). The fd'n. took place previous to 9 Dec. 1203, when Pope Innocent III directed a letter to the abbot and convent taking the mon. under his protection and confirming its possessions (*Diplom. Norv.*, vii, 4–5, no. 4; *SHR*, viii, (1911), 259). Spottiswoode (414) includes Iona (Icolmkill) under Cluniac houses; and it is described as 'of the Cluniac order' in a charter, 8 Aug. 1532 (*Cawdor Bk.*, 156). But the papal letter of 1203 and other papal records, as well as the *Scotichronicon* (lib. ii, cap. x; *Chron. Bower*, i, 45) speak of it as Benedictine. An attempt to demonstrate that it belonged to the order of Tiron is unconvincing (W. F. Skene, 'Notes on the history of the ruins of Iona', *PSAS*, x, 1875, 206–7). On 22 April 1247 the Pope, on account of the distance of the abbey from Norway, gave the abbot the use of the mitre and ring and other episcopal privileges (*Diplom. Norv.*, vii, 16) and, on the same date, declared that the ab. and convent of Iona, in the diocese of Sodor, Norway were not to be summoned to the general chapter of the Benedictines in Scotland (*CPL*, i, 231). By 1289 the abbey was also exempt from the jurisdiction of the bp. of Sodor (*ibid.*, i, 504). The abbey remained within the dioc. of Sodor but, from time to time, papal commissions were granted to bps. to act as ordinary for the abbey on behalf of the Pope. Thus, the bp. of Dunkeld acting as its ordinary in 1320 confirmed the election of Finlay as ab. (*Chron. Extracta*, 147), and in 1431 the ab. made manual obedience to the bp. of the see (*ibid.*, 233). In petitions granted 3, 5 and 17 Dec. 1421, the abbey is described as improverished and its buildings destroyed (*Highland Papers*, iv, 168–75; *CSSR*, i, 271–2, 275–6). A letter to the Pope 'for the erection of the Abbacy of Colmkyll in the bishopis sete of the Ilis, quhil his principall kirk in the Ile of Man be recoverit fra Inglismen' is recorded 1 April 1498, the suppliant being the earl of Argyll (*RSS*, i, no. 384); and, on 15 June 1499 the Pope granted the abbey *in commendam* to the bp. of Sodor (Reg. Lat., 1049, fo. 141; *Highland Papers*, iv, 185). However, there is no evidence to prove that the abbey ever became the cathedral, or that the Benedictine mks. ever formed the chapter, of the dioc. of the Isles (see under Cathedrals). But successive bps. did hold the abbey *in commendam*. Thus, on 24 May 1530 Ferquhard, bp. of Sodor, had a precept of admission to the temporality of the bishopric and to the abbacy of Colmkill annexed to it (*RSS*, ii, no. 685). Besides the bishop-commendator, the pr. and six mks. attest a charter, 8 Aug. 1532 (*Cawdor Bk.*, 158). In 1551 the mon. had been occupied by master Patrick McLean and his brother Hector McLean of Duart (later to obtain possession of the abbey) (*ADCP*, 610, 614). A declaration (Hay, Scotia Sacra, 487) that in 1560 the mon. was destroyed and the mks. driven away cannot be verified, but if destruction took place, it could only have been partial. On 6 June 1581 James VI constituted Alexander Campbell for his lifetime, abbot and commendator of Icolmkill, granting him both the spirituality and temporality, which his father, John Campbell, bp. of the Isles had resigned in his favour (*RMS*, v, no. 208). On 19 March 1587/8, the island, with the houses and other property formerly belonging to the monastery, was bestowed on Hector McLean, son of Lachlan McLean of Duart, to be held of the commendator and the community (*ibid.*, v, no. 1491). The abbey was eventually annexed, before Alexander Campbell's death, to the bishopric of the Isles, in 1615 (*Cawdor Bk.*, 223; *APS*, iv, 554).

MAY. The history of this house abounds in problems and the account of the priory given by Stuart in *Records of the Priory of the Isle of May* is in many respects unsatisfactory. The following notes owe much to A. A. M. Duncan, 'Documents relating to the priory of the Isle of May *c.* 1140–1313', *PSAS*, xc, (1956–7), 52–80. It has generally been,assumed, in accordance with statements made in records of 1292–3, that the priory was founded by David I, who is said to have granted it to Reading abbey for nine monks of that house (*May Recs.*, lxxxvi–lxxxviii). But the date of the foundation and that of the grant to Reading are alike difficult to ascertain. A prior of May is mentioned in one of K. David's charters dated ?1144–?1147, by A. O. Anderson (*Early Sources* ii, 194); 1142–53, by Professor Duncan. The grant of the priory to Reading is assigned by Lawrie to a date probably after 1135, when Henry I, K. David's brother-in-law, was buried at Reading (Lawrie, *Charters*, 387). The Isle of May, described as the gift of David I, was confirmed to Reading by Pope Alexander III (1159–81) (BM. Egerton MS., 67v–68r, 70v). In a charter of William the Lion, 1166 × 71, it is stated that the king confirms the priory's possessions 'so that a convent of thirteen mks. of the Cluniac order may be maintained there' (*May Recs.*, no. 12). It is described as Benedictine, 17 Jan. 1257/8 (*CPL*, i, 340) and as Cluniac, on the following 25 Feb. (*Ibid.*, i, 344). Cf. Reading, occasionally mentioned as Cluniac after it became specifically Benedictine (Hurry, *Reading Abbey*, 65).

From *c*. 1270, the priory's history presents a series of complications and discrepancies. According to the *Scotichronicon* (lib. x, cap. xxvi (*Chron. Bower*, ii, 110–11)), K. Alexander III, in 1269, after a monk of Reading had been admitted as prior, was alarmed at the danger of English espionage and bought back the island, its purchase price (700 marks) being paid by William Wishart, bp. of St. Andrews, who conferred it upon St. Andrews priory. But this account conflicts with record evidence. A grant by Reading to the countess of Warwick of 10 marks yearly from the priory of May, 25 Dec. 1284 (Hurry, *op. cit.*, 180) implies that at this date the priory was still in Reading's possession. According to the petition of the ab. of Reading to the Scottish king [John Balliol] and parliament in 1292–3, the priory of May was alienated by ab. Robert de Burghgate, who sold it to William [Fraser], bp. of St. Andrews for £1,000. This transaction, it is stated, the bp., as a guardian of the realm of Scotland (which was without a king) sworn to maintain the royal patrimony, had no right to carry through; while, in consequence of it, de Burghgate, who had acted without the assent of the majority of his convent, was deposed. The bp. is said to have paid only 214 marks of the purchase price and the procurators of Reading sought the arrears of the fruits for the four years previous to Palm Sunday (22 March 1292/3) (*May Recs.*, lxxxvi–lxxxvii). (It may be noted that they were asked if they were prepared to return to the bp. of St. Andrews the sum of 1100 marks which he had paid to Reading (*ibid.*, lxxxvi).) The sale of the priory to the bp. must have taken place between 2 April 1286, when Fraser was appointed a guardian, and –Oct. 1288 (according to Professor Duncan's emendation of the date in *CDS*), when Edward I summoned Ralph de Broughton, *custos* of the mon. of Reading, to answer for connivance at the alienation of the priory of May from that abbey (*CDS*, iv. no. 1765) (Professor Duncan shows that de Broughton was appointed *custos* 16 March 1286/7, on the suspension of de Burghgate (BM. Harleian MS., 1708 (Chartulary of Reading) fo. 232v)). It is further stated that the abbot of Reading enfeoffed William Fresel [Fraser], bp. of St. Andrews (†1297) in the priory of Pittenweem (which may be equivalent to May) and that Fraser in turn enfeoffed in it the ch. (i.e. the priory) of St. Andrews (*Mem. de Parl.*, no. 317). From a writ of 24 March 1305/6, it appears that the Isle of May and its manor of Pittenweem were restored to Reading after the rebellion of John Balliol (1296) and that May was held as a cell of that abbey until the monks were ejected by Wallace (1297 or 1298) (*Cal. Close Rolls*, 1302–7, 249). But although, according to the same writ, Edward I ordered Reading to have seisin of May and Pittenweem 'as before the commencement of the last war', we find that king writing to Aymer de Valence, 2 Sept. 1306, regarding a complaint of the ab. of Reading that the bp. and pr. of St. Andrews had invaded the Isle of May and manor of Pittenweem, seized and taken away the monks' goods and beaten, wounded and ill-treated their men there (PRO. Ancient Corresp., xlvii/89).

It is not possible to say precisely when St. Andrews priory entered into possession of May or when the priory of May was finally transferred to Pittenweem. A petition, dated 1306–7 in *CDS*, is directed to Edward I by Thomas de Houburn, canon of St. Andrews and liegeman of the English king. who is described as having been ousted by the Scots from his priory of Pittenweem (*CDS*. ii, no. 1964), but its significance is not clear; it may have been that St. Andrews had taken possession of May and/or Pittenweem with the consent of Edward I, who had then intruded an English prior. There is a mention of a prior of May, 3 Aug. 1313 (*Scone Liber*, no. 148). Eventually, on 1 July 1318, a specific indication is given that the connection with Reading was at an end; for on that date, William de Lamberton, bp. of St. Andrews, in virtue of the transference to the mon. of St. Andrews of 'all right of the monastery of Reading in England which it had in the priory of May and Pittenweem', granted to St. Andrews priory the annual pension of 16 marks formerly paid by May to Reading (*May Recs.*, xci–xcii). See further Pittenweem under the Augustinian Canons. On 30 Jan. 1549/50, the prior of Pittenweem granted a lease of the Isle of May, which is said to be now lying waste (*ibid.*, xcvii).

PLUSCARDEN. For the earlier history of this fd'n. see under Valliscaulian Monks. The house became a Benedictine priory, dependent on Dunfermline Abbey, after its union with Urquhart (*q.v.*) in 1454. In 1457 the buildings are said to be collapsed (*CPL*, xi, 330), the prior who was then appointed being described in 1460 as '*prior prioratum de Pluschardyn et Urcharde*' (*Dunf. Reg.*, 353). On 13 Oct. 1508 a charter is subscribed by the pr. and eight mks. (Macphail, *Pluscardyn*, 236–7); the pr. and twelve mks. occur, 16 Dec. 1524 (*ibid.*, 237–9) and 24 June 1548 (*ibid.*, 240–1). At the Reformation there were at least nine mks. besides the pr. in the community (*ibid.*, 125). The last pre-Reformation pr., Alexander Dunbar, who had been provided 20 May 1529 (Reg. Lat. 1525, fos. 333–5) continued to hold office until he d. 1560/1, following which, George, fifth, Lord Seton was appointed 'commissar and iconymus', 17 April 1561 (*RSS*, v, no. 891). The priory was gifted to William Cranston, provost of Seton collegiate ch., 18 March 1561/2 (*ibid.*, v, no. 1008), but was thereafter bestowed, 17 Sept. 1565 (*ibid.*, v, nos. 2315, 2317), on Lord Seton's third son, Alexander Seton for whom, after temporary deprivement for nonconformity (*RMS*, iv, no. 2640; *APS*, iii, 276) it was erected into a free barony, in parliament, 1587 (*ibid.*, iii, 485).

RINDALGROS or RINDELGROS (RHYND). David I granted Rindalgros (i.e. the lands) to Reading Abbey, 1143–7, with the proviso that if the augmentation of his gift should enable a monastery to be maintained, that abbey should send a convent there (*May Recs.*, no. 1; *CDS*, ii, no. 1985 (1)). Shortly after (1147–53) the same king ordered his men of the sheriffdom of Perth to pay their teinds of grain and cheese etc., to the mks. of 'Rindelgros' (*May Recs.*, no. 7; *CDS*, ii, no. 1985(7)); and a charter of Malcolm IV, 1153 × 59, bestows upon the mks. of 'Rindelcros' all the teind belonging to the ch. of that vill (*May Recs.*, no. 8; *CDS*, ii, no. 1985(8); *Regesta Regum Scottorum*, i, no. 137). The opinion that 'no monastery was built at Rindalgros' (Lawrie, *Early Charters*, 390) may be correct in respect of actual construction work, but a shortlived community of mks. who either transferred to the Isle of May before 1151 or merged at a later date with the community there, un-doubtedly existed at this site in the mid-twelfth c. (see A. A. M. Duncan, 'Documents relating to the Priory of the Isle of May, *c.* 1140–1313', *PSAS*, xc (1956–7), 52–90). In 1231 the monks of May appear as holding the parish ch. of Rhynd (*May Recs.*, no. 39); and the writ of 1367 which exemplifies a number of May charters describes Rindalgros as 'a place of the . . . cell of May (*ibid.*, no. 7). There is no further mention of a monastery.

URQUHART. David I, who made a grant to the monks here, 1130 × 1150 (*Dunf. Reg.*, no. 34), is usually regarded as the founder of this priory. It appears as a dependency of Dun-fermline abbey in K. David's charter of endowment, 1150–3 (*ibid.*, no. 33; *Moray Reg.*, no. 254). Spottiswoode (404) dates this charter 1124 which is much too early. During the late fourteenth and early fifteenth c., the priorship of this house was in constant dispute (*Moray Reg.*, 350–2; *CSSR*, i, 65, 147; iii, 122, 124, 127 133; *CPL*, viii, 467). On 12 March 1453/4, Pope Nicholas V, on the petition of the prior of Urquhart, containing that there were not more than six mks. in the Valliscaulian priory at Pluscarden and not more than two at Urquhart, consented to the separation of Pluscarden from Val des Choux, made it a dependency of Dunfermline and united it to Urquhart (Macphail, *Pluscardyn*, 223ff.; *CPL*, x, 253–4). As the buildings at Pluscarden were more extensive than those of Urquhart, the united community settled at Pluscarden of which formal possession was taken shortly after 8 Nov. 1454 (*Dunf. Reg.*, no. 442).

UNCERTAIN FOUNDATIONS

Dornoch. The presence of a writ of K. David I (*c.* 1139–51) in the Dunfermline abbey register (*Dunf. Reg.*, no. 23) on behalf of mks. at Dornoch has led to the suggestion that mks. from Dunfermline had established a cell here. However, the wording of the writ does not necessarily imply the existence of a religious house at Dornoch (Barrow, *Kingdom of the Scots*, 187). On the other hand the mks. may have been members of earlier community at this site. See under Early Ecclesiastical Foundations.

Eynhallow. For a discussion of the history of this Orcadian fd'n, the provenance of which rests on a statement in 1175 that the newly elected ab. of Melrose had formerly been an ab. in Orkney (*Chron. Melrose*, 87) and on the remains of what might have been a group of monastic buildings on this island, see *Hist. Mon. Comm.* (*Orkney and Shetland*), ii, 232–4. This gives reasons for abandoning the view that this was a Cistercian house and notes a suggestion that it was probably a Benedictine fd'n. from *c.* 1100 (*ibid*, ii, 233). A 'Description of Orkney' (Macfarlane, *Geographical Coll.*, iii, 306), said to be dated 1529, includes Eynhallow, but makes no mention of a monastery. This omission, and its non-appearance in ecclesiastical records, indicates that the mon. was extinct well before the sixteenth century; but nothing is known with certainty of its career.

Supposed Foundation

Aberdeen. On 3 April 1231 Pope Gregory IX granted to the Benedictine ab. and convent 'de Aberdona' leave to convert the ch. of 'Culdedono' to their own uses for maintaining hospitality (Theiner, *Vet. Mon.*, no. lxviii). 'Aberdono' is a mistranscription. The abbey in question is Abingdon (cf. *CPL*, i, 129, 132). Two 'monks of Aberdeen' appear as witnesses of an episcopal charter, 1239–42 (*Abdn. Reg.* ii, 272), but although their presence does not warrant any inference as to a monastic foundation, it is conceivable that tentative steps had been taken towards the foundation of a regular chapter. See ABERDEEN, under Cathedrals.

Kilconquhar. Spottiswoode, *Hist. of the Ch. of Scotland* (1677 edn.), App. 20, gives under Benedictines: 'the Monastery of Kilconquhar in Galloway, founded by Ethred (or rather Fergus), Lord of Galloway'. There is no such place in Galloway and there was no such monastery. See under Houses of Nuns, *Kilconquhar*, in Fife, which is given erroneously as a nunnery.

THE CLUNIAC MONKS

GENERAL NOTES

CLUNY, near Mâcon in Burgundy, was founded as a strict Benedictine abbey in 909. Its abbots were asked to reform other houses, and gradually an 'order' was built up, the members of which followed the customs of Cluny and were in theory members of the Cluny community. They thus formed an autonomous group within the unorganized Benedictine houses of western Europe. A detailed study of the Scottish Cluniac foundations is a *desideratum*. Unlike many houses of this order, which generally ranked as priories even when populous and wealthy, the two Scottish houses which may be properly regarded as of this order were abbeys, one attaining the status less than fifty years after its foundation and the other having it from the onset. It should be noted that the priory of the Isle of May, a dependency of the abbey of Reading and occasionally described as Cluniac, is listed among the Benedictine houses for reasons which are given in that section.

THE CLUNIAC HOUSES

Name	County	Rank	Minimum income (1561)	Fd	Date D	Dependent on (or mother-house)
* CROSSRAGUEL	Ayr	Oratory		-1214-16		
		Abbey	£1860	-1270	1617	Paisley
‡ §PAISLEY	Renfrew	Priory		c. 1169		Wenlock
		Abbey	£6100	1219	1587	
RENFREW	Renfrew	Priory		c. 1163	1169×73	Wenlock

CROSSRAGUEL. The date of fd'n. of this house cannot be fixed with precision and the circumstances which led up to it are to some extent involved and obscure. These facts, however, can hardly be said to justify the reckless statements made by certain writers. Thus it is asserted by Spottiswoode (413–14) that the abbey 'was founded by Duncan, son of Gilbert, earl of Carrick, in the year 1244, as we are informed by the chartulary of Paisley'. Again the editor of that chartulary declares: 'It appears that Duncan, earl of Carric . . . founded and endowed the house of Crossraguel for monks of Paisley, and so richly that the new abbey aspired immediately to independence, while the mother house endeavoured to keep it as a cell or oratorium to be enjoyed by brethren of their convent and under their immediate control' (*Pais. Reg.*, xviii). Lawrie is no less unsatisfactory: '[Duncan]' granted to Paisley abbey Crossraguel . . . but because the abbot and monks of Paisley did not build a monastery, Duncan himself founded the abbey of Crossraguel and brought Cluniac monks there, to whom he gave the lands previously given to Paisley'

(Lawrie, *Annals*, 327). Duncan, son of Gilbert, was made E. of Carrick, 1214–16 (Anderson, *Early Sources*, 331n). Before that date, he had granted to the mks. of Paisley 'Crosragmol' (Crossraguel) and 'Suthblan', a donation confirmed to Paisley abbey by Pope Honorius III, 23 Jan. 1226/7 (*CPL*, i, 107) (1225, the date given for this bull in *Cross. Chrs.* i, no. 1 is erroneous), and with three chs. in Ayrshire given by Duncan and subsequently confirmed to Paisley by K. Alexander II, 25 Aug. 1236 (*Cross. Chrs.*, no. 2). Later, in a bull of Pope Clement IV, 11 July 1265, it is said that after Duncan's endowment had been made, an oratory was built 'in the said possessions' and Paisley had served it by some of its mks. The donor afterwards asserted that his benefaction had been given on condition that Paisley built a monastery on the lands and the consequent dispute between him and the abbey was remitted to the bp. of Glasgow (*ibid.*, i, no. 4), whose judgment is recorded in a charter of 18 July 1244. This was to the effect that a 'religious house of monks of the order of Paisley' should be built at Crossraguel, the new house to be exempt from the jurisdiction of Paisley 'save only in recognition of the order'; the ab. of Paisley would visit it yearly; the property in Carrick would be given up to the house of Crossraguel by Paisley, to which an annual tribute of 10 marks would be paid (*ibid.*, i, no. 3). After a lapse of about twenty years, Paisley complained to the Pope against the bp's ordinance as 'redounding to its enormous hurt', and on 11 June 1265 and 6 Feb. 1265/6, Pope Clement VI appointed mandatories to investigate the case (*ibid.*, i, no. 4), with what result is not known. Whether the abbey was in being by this date cannot be said with certainty. But some stage in its erection may have provided the occasion for the complaint to the Pope.

The first abbot on record attests a charter, *c.* 1286 (*ibid.*, i, no. 7), but two earlier abs. are named in *Scotichronicon* as holding office, *c.* 1270 (*Chron. Bower*, ii, 112). A visitation of the abbey, probably in 1405, shows that there were then ten monks (*Cross. Chrs.*, i, no. 23). Eight mks. are named along with the ab. in 1548 and 1552 (*ibid.*, i, nos. 64, 67); and at the Reformation, there were at least eleven, besides the commendator and sub-prior (*ibid.*, i, nos. 68, 75, 118). Part of the abbey was 'cast down' by Reformers in 1561 (Knox, *Works*, ii, 168). From 1520, the abbacy was held *in commendam* by members of the Kennedy family. William, brother of the second earl of Cassillis after election by the convent, which the ab. of Paisley, as vicar of Cluny refused to confirm (*ibid.*, i, no. 41) was provided 10 Sept. 1520 (Reg. Supp., 1719, fos. 218–9). He retained the office of ab. until he d. 1547, when he was succeeded by his nephew Quintin Kennedy (*Cross. Chrs.*, i, no. 64; Reg. Vat., 1817, fos. 118–119v), after whose death in 1564 (*Cross. Chrs.*, i, no. 79) a series of commendators held office (*ibid.*, i, xlvi–lv) until 1617 when the abbey was annexed to the bishopric of Dunblane (*APS*, iv, 553).

MAY, see under Benedictine Houses.

PAISLEY. A charter of Walter, son of Alan, steward of Scotland 1161 × 1164 but most probably *c.* 1163 (*Chron. Holyrood*, 163–4; Anderson, *Early Sources*, ii, 251n), declares his intention of founding within his land of Paisley a house of Cluniac monks, adding that he has available thirteen mks. from Wenlock, one of whom will be chosen as prior (*Pais. Reg.*, 1–2). It is possible that these mks. were already settled at Renfrew (see below) when this offer was made. If not, they must have arrived there shortly after. The date of the actual foundation at Paisley is uncertain. Under the year 1169 the Chronicle of Melrose has the statement 'Humbold the prior of Wenlock brought the convent to Paisley which is beside Renfrew' (*Chron. Melrose*, 81) and the *Scotichronicon* makes a similar assertion adding that Walter the steward had founded the monastery at Paisley 'a short time before' (lib. viii, cap. xiii; *Chron. Bower*, i, 460). Again, William of Bondington, bp. of Glasgow, in a letter 1246 × 1249 (*Pais. Reg.*, 15–16), states that the mon. had existed at Paisley for eighty years and more before an abbot was appointed, and while the latter part of the statement is untrue, the date, *c.* 1169, matches the other available evidence for the initial fd'n. on this site (*Chron. Holyrood*, 163n). It is generally assumed that the community at Renfrew was transferred to Paisley, but whether the Melrose chronicler's statement is intended to refer to this or whether it purports to indicate the first arrival of the mks. in Scotland (in which case the date is too late), or to the arrival of further mks. from Wenlock, it is impossible to say.

On 15 July 1219 Pope Honorius III gave permission to the pr. and convent to elect an abbot (*Pais. Reg.*, 9–10), and the first ab. is mentioned, 3 May 1220 (*ibid.*, 325). It is evident that the letter of the ab. and convent of Paisley to the abbey of Cluny regarding the appointment of an ab. (*Cluny*, vi, no. 4934) belongs to about this date rather than *c.* 1250 (cf. *Cluny*). The relations of Cluny were at first indeterminate. But in March 1240/1 and later the bp. of Glasgow took steps to regularize their relationship (*ibid.*, vi, no. 4789; *Pais. Reg.*, 15ff.). (The development of Paisley's relations with Cluny are complex and it should be noted that the dating of some of the records of the period, both in *Pais. Reg.* and *Cluny*, is obviously wrong.) The bp's intervention followed the attempt of Walter (II) the steward and others, sometime between 1232 and 1241, to transform Paisley into a Cistercian house (*Cluny*, vi, no. 4935; see J. Durkan, 'Paisley Abbey: attempt to make it Cistercian' in *Innes Review*, vii, 60–2). The fixed number of mks. is said to have been twenty-five (Duckett, *Visitation*, 37). On 10 Aug. 1395, the abbot was granted the mitre (*Pais. Reg.*, 429; Reg. Aven., 281, fo. 176).

In 1307 this house was burned by the English (*Chron. Bower*, ii, 167). It is said to be collapsed and ruinous, 1 Aug. 1444 (Reg. Supp., 398, fo. 194 v). On 18 Sept. 1471 it was placed under the perpetual protection of the Pope (*ibid.*, 671, fo. 231). At least sixteen mks. constituted the convent at the Reformation (NLS, Paisley Cart., fos. 74, 113; SRO RH6/2112; NLS, Hutton Coll., ii, fo. 27). The abbey was provided *in commendam* to John Hamilton, illegitimate son of James, earl of Arran, 17 May 1525 (Reg. Lat., 1454, fos. 1–2v) and thereafter following some dispute over the succession in 1548–9, by his nephew Claud Hamilton who was provided 5 Dec. 1553 (Vat. Arch., Resignationes, A, 123, fo. 107; Reg. Vat., 1762 fos. 161–4). The abbey was burned by Reformers in 1561 (Knox, *Works*, ii, 167). On 29 July 1587 and 22 March 1591/2, it was erected into a temporal lordship for Lord Claud Hamilton (*RMS*, v, nos. 1320, 2070).

RENFREW. A charter of Malcolm IV, 1163 × 1165, confirms to the priory of St. Mary and St. James of the 'inch' beside Renfrew castle, its possessions, including the ch. of Paisley, as granted by Walter, son of Alan, steward of Scotland (*Regesta Regum Scottorum*, i, no. 254; *Pais. Reg.*, 249). This priory, in which had been placed a prior and convent from Wenlock in Shropshire, was probably founded by Alan, *c.* 1163, from part of the lands which had been confirmed to him by K. Malcolm, 1161–2 (*ibid; Regesta Regum Scottorum*, i, no. 184). It is described as the house of Wenlock at Renfrew, *c.* 1169 (*Pais. Reg.*, 2–3); a charter of the founder, which is not earlier than 1165, refers to the 'lands which the monks first inhabited' (*ibid.*, 6), and a bull of Pope Alexander III, 25 March 1173 describes the mks. as having lived beside the mill at Renfrew. By this date, however, the mks. had removed to the Cluniac priory at Paisley to which their former possessions are confirmed by the Pope (*ibid.*, 408–10). This transference had probably taken place *c.* 1169 (see PAISLEY above).

SUPPOSED FOUNDATION

Fail. Called by Spottiswoode (413) 'Feale' and described by him as a cell or priory dependent on Paisley. Its alleged existence is due to the supposition (unfounded) that the Gilbertine house of Dalmilling (*q.v.*) became a dependency of Paisley and also to confusion with the Trinitarian house of Fail.

THE MONKS OF THE ORDER OF TIRON

GENERAL NOTES

THIS order was founded *c.* 1105 by St. Bernard (of Tiron) and monks of St. Cyprien de Poitiers as a Benedictine reform similar to Cîteaux. But, like the Cluniacs, they formed an autonomous congregation within the unorganized Benedictine houses of Western Europe. The first settlement was not far from the abbey of Savigny in the diocese of Avranches, but it was moved to Tiron in the diocese of Chartres, where building was begun on a new abbey in 1109, and from which, in 1113, monks of this order came to settle at Selkirk. The order, which was never large, possessed in Scotland an influence disproportionate to its total size. It gradually reverted to an observance similar to that of its contemporaries.

HOUSES OF THE ORDER OF TIRON

Name	County	Rank	Minimum income (1561)	Date Fd. D. or	Sec.	Dependent on
* ARBROATH	Angus	Abbey	£10,924	1178	1606	
FOGO	Roxburgh	Priory		1253 × 1297	?	Kelso abbey
FYVIE	Aberdeen	Priory		1285	?	Arbroath abbey
* KELSO	Roxburgh	Abbey	£4830(?) (with Lesma- hagow)	*c.* 1113 (at Selkirk) 1128 (at Kelso)	1607	
¶‡KILWINNING	Ayr	Abbey	£2560	1162 × 89	1592	
LESMAHAGOW	Lanark	Priory	*v.* Kelso	1144	1607	Kelso abbey
¶§LINDORES	Fife	Abbey	£4790	1191	1600	
SELKIRK	Selkirk	Abbey		*c.* 1113	(removed to Kelso *c.* 1128)	

ARBROATH. Founded by William the Lion in 1178 during a vacancy in the see of St. Andrews (*Arb. Lib.*, i, no. 2). The king describes himself as having fd. the abbey in a charter of endowment issued simultaneously with the act of fd'n., or soon after (*Regesta Regum Scottorum*, ii, 250–2). Chronicles also attest to this date of fd'n. (*Chron. Bower*, i, 475) and this is also borne out by a charter of the abbot and convent of Kelso quitclaiming in that year the abbot-elect of Arbroath from subjection and obedience, indicating that monks had been provided from Kelso 'for the building of that house' [Arbroath] and having K. William, 'who has founded that church in honour of St. Thomas [i.e. Becket]' as a witness (*Arb. Lib.*, no. 2). The dedication of the ch. took place 8 May 1233 (*Chron. Melrose*, 143). On 11 May 1350 the ch. is said to have been damaged by assaults from English ships (*Arb. Lib.*, ii, no. 23); and on 11 Feb. 1378/9, the ch. and mon. are stated to have suffered much havoc from English attacks (*ibid.*, ii, no. 36). The ch., in 1380, was ignited by lightning and during its repair its mks. were temporarily removed to other places (*Chron. Extracta*, 194; *CSSR*, i, 92 (*anno*. 1419)). On 26 June 1396 the abbot was given the mitre (*Arb. Lib.* ii, no. 46). Membership of the convent remained fairly constant during the first half of the sixteenth c. There were at least twenty-seven mks. in 1512 (cf. Theiner, *Vet. Mon.*, no. dcccxxvi) and although only seventeen mks. besides the abbot and sub-prior subscribed to a charter in 1527 (*Laing Chrs.*, no. 360), the community at this date numbered twenty-six or more. A total of twenty-seven was again reached in 1543; the sub-prior and twenty mks. attest a charter in 1546 (*Glas. Reg.*, ii, no. 508) and at least twenty-two mks., all of whom survived to the Reformation, formed the convent in 1558 (see M. Dilworth, 'Monks and ministers after 1560', *RSCHS*, xviii, 209 for the above figures).

There are conflicting accounts of the fate of the abbey, of which a detailed description of its buildings and possessions is given in a process of 1517 (Theiner, *Vet. Mon.*, no. dccccxxv, 1). It is said to have been saved by Lord Ogilvie from destruction by the Reformers in 1543 (*Diurnal of Occurrents*, 29). On the other hand, a letter of 5 Sept. 1543 speaks of news that Ogilvy had sacked the abbey (*Hamilton Papers*, ii, no. 14). But the present state of the buildings shows that no serious damage was done. Held by a series of commendators from the early sixteenth c., these included three successive members of the family of Beaton who held office from 1517 until 1551 (Vat. Arch., Acta. Misc., 17, fo. 80; *Arb. Lib.*, ii, no. 583; Reg. Vat., 1667, fos. 328v-331). In that year James Hamilton, third son of the earl of Arran, obtained the commendatorship (Deeds, i, 166; Vat. Arch., Acta. Misc., 4, fo. 70), which he held with two breaks occasioned by forfeiture (*RSS*, vi, nos. 415, 1348; *RMS*, iv, no. 2052), until 1600 when he granted the lands of Arbroath to his son, James Hamilton, 2nd marquis of Hamilton (*ibid.*, vii, no 1033). The abbey was erected into a temporal lordship on his behalf, in parliament, 1606 (*APS*, iv, 321-2) and finally expedited by charter, 1608 (*RMS*, vi, no. 2075).

Dependency: Fyvie. A hospital was attached to this abbey. See Hospitals.

FOGO. The chapel of St. Nicholas of Fogo was granted to Kelso by Patrick Corbet, 1253 × 1297, the mks. being held to provide either three mks., or three secular chaplains in the chapel (*Kel. Lib.*, nos. 305, 308). A monastic community was evidently established. A prior of Fogo occurs in 1465 and 1466 (*ibid.*, nos. 530-1). On 27 Aug. 1537 Andrew Leslie, mk. of Lindores, petitioned the Pope for provision to this priory which is 'conventual and is a dependency of the monastery of Calco [Kelso]' and of which the fruits do not exceed £7 (Reg. Supp., 2258, fos. 37-37v).

FYVIE. It has been asserted that this cell or priory of Arbroath was 'founded with a parish church in honour of the Virgin Mary by Fergus, earl of Buchan, in 1179' (Spottiswoode, 410). This statement almost certainly arose from confusion between the parish ch., dedicated to St. Peter (*Arch. Lib.*, i, no. [235]), which was granted to Arbroath by William the Lion, 1189 × 1194 (*ibid.*, i, no. 28), and the priory ch., dedicated to St. Mary and All Saints (*ibid.*, i, no. [235]). The foundation of the priory took place in or somewhat before 1285. On 16 Oct. of that year, Reginald le Chen [Cheyne] granted to Arbroath and the mks. of that mon. 'dwelling in the religious house built in the land of Ardlogy near the church . . . of Fyvie' the land of Ardlogy and Lethendy (*ibid.*,, i, no. [234]); and the confirmation charter of Henry, bp. of Aberdeen, 18 Oct. 1285, specifically mentions Reginald as founder (*ibid.*, i, no. [235]). The same charter grants the vicarage of Fyvie to the priory, the parish to be served by a chaplain. The head of this small house is frequently called *custos* and there are references to its 'chapel' in 1325 and 1450 (*ibid.*, i, no. 354; ii, no. 92). In 1325 the ab. of Arbroath instructed the *custos* to secure the observance of monastic discipline (*ibid.*, i, no. 354); but a papal letter of 28 March 1450/1 describes this house as non-conventual, valued at no more than £12, while the prior was also parochial vicar (*CPL*, x, 587-9).

On 21 Aug. 1459, Pope Pius II, on the petition of the ab. and convent of Arbroath, united the priory to that abbey (*ibid.*, xi, 405-6). The union did not take effect and mks. of Arbroath continued to be appointed as prs. (Reg. Supp., 538, fo. 237v) until a papal reannexation of the priory by Pope Julius II who granted it in perpetuity to Arbroath, 14 Feb. 1507, the then pr., who was also a mk. of Arbroath, having resigned (Reg. Lat., 1187, fos. 174-5). The ab. of Arbroath obliged himself for the annates of the priory, the value of which does not exceed £18, 24 March 1507 (Vat. Arch., Libri Annatarum, 51, fo. 43v), and on 28 Sept. 1508, the ab. appointed a procurator to take possession of it on his behalf (*Arb. Lib.*, ii, no. 462). The priory, the lands of which were being leased in the latter half of the fifteenth c. (*ibid.*, ii, nos. 143, 144 (*anno* 1462), 368 (*anno* 1496/7), was not immediately extinguished. A dispute over the priorship occurs 7 Jan. 1531 (Reg. Supp., 2034, fo. 8), and about 1546 the priory appears among the benefices taxed for the College of Justice; its contribution is assessed at £2.16s. (*Aberdeen-Banff Illust.*, ii, 424*n*). It is uncertain when its existence was finally terminated, and it may have survived to the Reformation.

KELSO. Founded first at Selkirk (*q.v.*) by Earl David (later David I). The *Scotichronicon*, which must be considered unreliable on this point, declares that 'Herbert was made the third abbot of Selkirk and first of Kelso, because the monastery was transferred thither by King David I in the year of the Lord 1126 and two years after the transference of the community, he founded the church of Kelso'; and, at another point the same chronicle states that in 1128 K. David founded the mon. of Kelso (*op. cit.* lib. viii capp. xxxvi, xl (*Chron. Bower*, i, 286, 296). Again the ch. of Kelso is said to have been fd. 3 May 1128 (*Chron. Melrose*, 69). It has been asserted (Lawrie, *Charters*, 275) that Ab. Herbert 'persuaded the king to remove the monks to Kelso', *c.* 1128, but David's charter to Kelso says that the migration was by the advice of John, bp. of Glasgow, because the site at Selkirk was not convenient (*Kel. Lib.*, no. 2; *Regesta Regum Scottorum*, i, no. 131). The so-called foundation charter (*Kel. Lib.*, no. 2) has been considered spurious (Lawrie, *Charters*, 411), but the information which it contains is undoubtedly authentic (cf. *Regesta Regum Scottorum*, i, no. 131). Spottiswoode (405) declares that the abbey was moved to Roxburgh and then to Kelso; but this is due to the misinterpretation of a phrase in the foundation charter: 'Because there was not a suitable site for the abbey at Roxburgh, I have transferred [the aforesaid monastery] to the church of the Blessed Virgin which is situated . . . in the place which is called Calkou'. The move to Kelso in 1128 may have been prompted by a desire to have a royal fd'n. near this king's burgh and possibly explains the house being designated as St. Mary, Roxburgh, in a papal bull of 16 March 1132 (*Cal. Docs. France*, no. 1007) and Herbert, the first ab. appearing, 1128-47, as 'abbot of Roxburgh' (Lawrie, *Charters*, 64, 79, 82, 85, 93, 138, 140). Arnold, his successor, appears as ab. of Kelso (*ibid.*, 147-8). In 1165 the ab. was granted the mitre, the first ab. of a Scottish house to be thus privileged (*Chron. Melrose*, 80; Lawrie, *Annals*, 100).

In Edward I's parliament of 28 March 1305, the ab. sought remedy for the burning of the abbey's charters and muniments in the war (*Mem. de Parl.*, 188, no. 307); and the monastery is said, *c.* 1316, to have suffered so much spoliation and destruction during war that the mks. were reduced to begging at other houses for food and clothing (*Kel. Lib.*, no. 309). Again a petition of 1420 refers to its precarious situation in the Borders, whence it is often severely damaged by hostile incursions (*CSSR*, i, 177). It was alleged in 1461 it had remained unvisited by its ordinary and his officials for over a hundred years owing to the English occupation of Roxburgh castle, situated about one Italian mile from the abbey (Reg. Supp., 542, fo. 159). The following year, it is said, that only seventeen or eighteen mks. are in the mon. which used to sustain thirty or forty (*ibid.*, 550, fo. 256v). The gatehouse tower was destroyed by Dacre in 1523 (*LP Henry VIII.* iii², nos. 3098, 3135). On 26 Oct. 1542, the abbey was again burned by the English (*Hamilton Papers*, i, 292; *LP Henry VIII*, xvii, nos. 996, 998); and again (probably) in 1544 (*ibid.*, xix², no. 33) and in Sept. 1545 (*ibid.*, xx², no 456).

A detailed description of the buildings and possessions of the monastery in 1517 (Theiner, *Vet. Mon.* no. dccccxxvii) states that in peaceful times there were thirty-six to forty mks. besides the abbot and prior. There were at least twenty-one mks. besides the commendator in 1539/40 (*Laing Chrs.*, no. 441), but by 1560 the number of mks. had evidently been reduced to about twelve (*ibid.*, nos. 857, 934; SRO, RH6/1996/2160; SRO, Fraser Charter, no. 176; *Essays on Scottish Reformation*, 235). Following the provision of Andrew Stewart, bp. of Caithness as commendator, on or shortly before, 6 Nov. 1511 (Vat. Arch., Introitus et Exitus, 549, fo. 64v), the abbey was held *in commendam* by Thomas Ker, provided 2 Dec. 1517 (Vat. Arch., Acta Misc., 17, fo. 80) and James Stewart, nominated 31 Oct. 1534 and provided 12 Jan. 1535 (*James V Letters*, 279; Reg. Supp., 2162, fos. 79-79v). After Stewart's death in 1557 (*RSS*, v, no. 227), the abbey remained for some time in the hands of the crown before the provision of William Ker in 1559 (*ibid.*, v, no. 1428), who held it until his death in 1566 when it was conferred on the queen's nephew Francis Stewart, later E. of Bothwell, 6 Feb. 1566/7 (*ibid.*, no. 3212). Further grants in favour of Sir John Maitland of Thirlstane and Bothwell's son Francis followed (*RMS*, v, no. 1597), but with the forfeiture of Bothwell and his family in 1591 (*RPC*, iv, 643-5), the greater part of the abbey lands fell to Sir Robert Ker of Cesford, later E. of Roxburgh, in whose favour the abbey was erected into a temporal lordship in 1607 (*APS*, iv, 399-400). This house is erroneously called Cistercian in a papal letter of 10 Oct. 1331 (*CPL*, ii, 366) and in NLS. MS. 22. 1. 14, 152; and Premonstratensian in the list given *Scoti-chronicon*, ii, 538).

Dependencies: Fogo, Lesmahagow. See *Merchingley* below.

KILWINNING. The identity of the founder, and the date of fd'n. remain obscure. Spottis-woode (407) gives the fd'n as 1140, but there is no justification for this date, nor for the assertion that the founder was Hugh de Moreville who died in 1162. One account which claims to be based on original sources places date of fd'n in 1157, but names the founder as Richard de Morville (*Ayr-Galloway Coll.*, i, 128). Richard also appears as the founder in the account of Timothy Pont, the cartographer, who saw the abbey's cartulary c. 1608, but as the date of fd'n. is given as 1191, and Richard d. 1189, the date, if not the name of the founder, is certainly false (*ibid.*, i, 115-116, 128-9). The presumption is strong, however, that Richard was the founder of the abbey, 1162 × 1189, rather than his father Hugh who, although frequently referred to as the founder of Dryburgh, receives no such notice in respect of Kilwinning. Record evidence is entirely missing and although the ch. of St. Vinin is mentioned in 1184, it is not until 1202 × 1207 that the abbey is recorded as such (Anderson, *Scottish Annals*, 286, 328; *Glas. Reg.*, i, no. 98). In the absence of further evidence it appears that the question of foundation must rest with the Book of Pluscarden which notes 'Kylwynnyn in Connyngham Tironensis. Fundator Morvile' (*Chron. Pluscarden*, i, 403). Little is known of this abbey's history. The abbot was granted the mitre, 20 Feb. 1409 (Reg. Aven., 333, fo. 432v). The convent consisted of at least sixteen mks. in 1532, seventeen in 1544, twelve in 1557, but only eight for certain in 1560 (Dilworth, 'Monks and ministers after 1560', *RSCHS*, xviii, 206). In 1561 the abbey was 'cast down' by Reformers (Knox, *Works*, ii, 168). In 1512, a determined effort was made to force Abbot William Bunche to resign (*Ayr-Galloway Coll.*, i, 180-3) and after his demission of office, the abbey was repeatedly held by commendators (*James V Letters*, 434). The last of these pre-Reformation commendators, Gavin Hamilton, was nominated by the crown 10 April 1550 (*RSS*, iv., no. 644) and provided by the Pope, 24 June 1550 (Reg. Vat., 1729, fos. 109-110v). After his death and forfeiture the abbey was conferred, 4 July 1571, on Alexander Cunningham, son of the earl of Glencairn (*RSS*, vi, no. 1199; cf. *ibid.*, no. 2090), following whose death, the temporalities of the abbey were erected into a free barony in favour of William Melville, 1592 (*RMS*, v, no. 2085; *APS*, iii, 599).

LESMAHAGOW. In 1144 David I and John, bp. of Glasgow, each of them accrediting the other with the initiative, in turn granted the ch. and lands of Lesmahagow to Kelso abbey so that a prior and monks might be instituted in that ch. (*Kel. Lib.*, nos. 8, 180). The priory is said to have been burned in 1335 by troops under John of Eltham, brother of Edward III (*Chron. Wyntoun*, viii, 30; *Chron. Bower*, ii, 323). The history of the priory is obscure. Five mks. are mentioned in a rental of 1556 (*Kel. Lib.*, ii, 479-80), in which the annual revenues of the priory are reckoned at over £1200. A prior occurs 5 Dec. 1477 (*HMC. 12th Rep.* App. Pt., viii, 122), but at some stage thereafter, and certainly before 1550 (*RSS*, iv, no. 881) the commendatorship of this priory had been assumed, possibly by annexation (see *RSS*, v, no. 3212) by the commendators of Kelso (*q.v.*). Despite the bestowal of the priory and its revenues on James Cunningham, third son of Alexander, E. of Glencairn after the death of James Stewart in 1557 (*RSS*, v, no. 871), the commendatorship appears to have remained with the abs. of Kelso. Cunningham is occasionally described as commendator (*RMS*, iv, no. 2803), but his actual status was 'pensioner of Lesmahagow' (*RSS*, vii, no. 2606). The priory was accordingly included in the erection of Kelso abbey for Robert, earl of Roxburgh, in 1607, but transferred to the marquis of Hamilton in 1623 (*RPC*, 2nd series, i, cxlv).

LINDORES. Founded by David, E. of Huntingdon, c. 1190 × 1191 (*Lind. Cart.*, nos. 1-2; *Regesta Regum Scottorum*, ii, no. 363). The *Scotichronicon* (lib. viii, cap. xxv (*Chron. Bower*, i, 475)) assigns fd'n. to 1178, but this must be regarded as too early. The same chronicle declares that the first abbot had ruled over the house for twenty-eight years before his death in 1219, at which time there were twenty-six mks. in the mon. (*ibid.*, lib. ix, cap. xxcii (*Chron. Bower*, ii, 34)). The ab. was granted the mitre, 19 Sept. 1395 (Reg. Aven., 280, fo. 368). On 16 April 1414 it was represented to the Pope that the monastic building had collapsed and the revenues diminished by robbers and thieves commonly called 'wild Scots' (*ibid.*, 344, fos. 634v–5v; cf. *CPP*, i, 601). Membership of the convent remained at much the same level in the sixteenth c., the figures corresponding closely to that claimed for 1219. There were at least twenty-five monks in 1532, one less in 1538 and nineteen or twenty in 1546, 1552 and 1558 when at least five other names should possibly be added to those recorded (Dilworth, 'Monks and ministers after 1560', *RSCHS*, xviii, 211). The buildings were enlarged in the early sixteenth c. (*James V Letters*, 88). In 1543 Reformers sacked the abbey and temporarily expelled the monks (*Hamilton Papers*, ii, 15); again in 1559, the altars were overthrown by Reformers, who burned statues, books and vestments (Lesley, *History*, 273; Knox, *Works*, vi, 26). Unlike most Scottish abbeys, this house continued to be ruled by a member of the order; the last pre-Reformation ab., John Philp was provided, 24 July 1523 (Reg. Lat., 1417, fos. 173v–5v), the previous ab. Henry Orme having resigned in his favour in 1522 (*James V Letters*, 88 Reg. Lat., 1413, fos. 197v–9v). On 24 Feb. 1566 Philp resigned in favour of John Leslie, later bp. of Ross, who received papal provision as commendator (Reg. Vat., 2017, fo. 595) but was forfeited 19 Aug. 1568 (*APS*, iii, 49–55). Thereafter, the commendatorship passed to Patrick Leslie (*RSS*, vi, no. 822), who was created Lord Lindores when the abbey was erected into a temporal lordship by charter 1600 (*RMS*, vi, no. 1032) and in parliament 1606 (*APS*, iv, 355–6).

SELKIRK. Founded by Earl David (later David I). A marginal note in the chronicle of Melrose (*Chron. Melrose*, 64) under the year 1109 which states: 'And Ralph sent from Tiron became first abbot of Selkirk', and the assignation of the coming of mks. to Selkirk to that year in a derivative statement in the *Scotichronicon* (lib. v, cap. xxxvi, *Chron. Bower*, i, 286), are not trustworthy. The statement of Symeon of Durham (*Hist. Regum*, ii, 247) that the mks. of Tiron came to Selkirk in 1113 and remained there for fifteen years (till 1128) may be accepted as authoritative (Barrow, *Kingdom of the Scots*, 175–6, 199–205). On his return from a visit to Tiron in 1116 or 1117, David brought back a further twelve mks. and an abbot to replace Ralph, the first ab. of Selkirk, who had been elected as ab. of Tiron (*ibid.*, 175; Migne, *Patr. Lat.*, clxxii, 1426). Because the site was deemed unsuitable, the mks. removed to Kelso (*q.v.*) in or about 1128, rather than in 1126 as stated in the *Scotichronicon* (lib. v, cap. xxxvi; *Chron. Bower*, i, 286).

SUPPOSED FOUNDATIONS

Dull. It is suggested by certain writers (e.g. Gordon, *Monasticon*, 438; MacEwen, *Hist. of the Ch. in Scotland*, i, 197) that there was here a house of monks of the order of Tiron. This appears entirely erroneous. If we may judge from the mention of an abthane of Dull (*St. A. Lib.*, 296), this may have been at one time the site of a Celtic community. But there was no medieval mon. here. The parish ch. was granted to St. Andrews priory by Malcolm, earl of Athole (*ibid.*, p. 243).

Fintray. Under the 'antiquities' of this parish (*NSA*, xii, 167–8), there is a reference to the 'foundations of some buildings, supposed to have belonged to the Abbacy of Lindores . . . a branch of which is said to have stood where the principal burying ground of this parish now is. . . . The buildings (denominated the Northern Abbey) are supposed to have been erected about the year 1386, from a stone bearing that date . . . in the dike of the burying ground, which had probably been composed of fragments of the demolished abbey, whereof no vestige now remains above the surface of the ground.' This abbey is entirely imaginary. The lands of Fintray were granted to Lindores abbey by its founder, David E. of Huntingdon, 1198–9 (*Lind. Cart.*, no. ii), and the ch. likewise, 1202–03 (*ibid.*, no. iii). But no priory or cell of Lindores is known to have existed and there was certainly none at Fintray.

Iona. Skene's suggestion that the abbey of Iona belonged to this order (*PSAS*, x. 1875, 206–7) is conjectural and unconvincing. See p. 59.

ADDITIONAL NOTE

Merchingley (*Mercheley*). According to a document in the Kelso chartulary, Walter de Bolbec gives to God and St. Mary and brother William de Mercheley and his successors the hermitage called Merchingley, founded in his waste land beside Merchingburn, with the ch. of St. Mary founded there (*Kel. Lib.*, no. 264). By another charter, Walter, son of Walter de Bolbec, grants this hermitage and ch. to William and Roger, mks. of the order of Kelso, these to be succeeded by one or two mks. of the like habit and order and no other (*ibid.*, no. 265). A charter of this Walter de Bolbec in similar terms emphasizes that two and no more mks. shall have 'the aforesaid [grant in] alms of Mercheley' (*ibid.*, no. 266). We find also a confirmation by Hugh de Balliol of a grant of land by his father, Eustace, to Roger, 'monk of Merchingley' (*ibid.*, no. 267). All these charters are dated *c.* 1280 by the editor of *Kel. Lib.* But among the possessions confirmed to Kelso abbey by Pope Innocent IV (1243-54) is 'in the bishopric of Durham the hermitage which is called Merchingley' (*ibid.*, no. 460); and this reference indicates that the original grant must be dated considerably earlier than *c.* 1280; it also shows that Merchingley was situated in England. The assertion that this fd'n. was located on the Hermitage water in Liddesdale (e.g. Banks, *Scottish Border Country*, p. 84) is erroneous. On its probable site in Slaley or Riding parishes in Northumberland, see Hodgson, *Hist. of Northumberland*, vi., 378. In 1296, the ab. of Kelso's lands of 'Merthenley' appear among those sequestered by Edward I (Stevenson, *Documents*, 48) and they were finally forfeited by Kelso in the reign of Edward II (Hodgson, *op. cit.*, p. 378). It is thus very probable that before or early in the fourteenth c., this site had no longer a monastic character. No trace of the hermitage or ch. remains.

THE CISTERCIAN MONKS

GENERAL NOTES

CÎTEAUX, near Dijon in Burgundy, was founded by St. Robert and monks of Molesme in 1098, and in 1113, when St. Stephen Harding was abbot, the order began to spread rapidly. Each abbey was autonomous in internal matters, but bound to the strict Cistercian observance of the Benedictine rule. The order was bound by the decrees and sanctions of general chapter which met yearly at Cîteaux, and was made up of all the abbots of the order. Cistercian abbeys had the right and duty of 'visiting' their daughter-foundations, even if these lay in different countries.

The dedication of all Scottish Cistercian abbeys was to the Blessed Virgin Mary. A colony, sent by an established abbey to colonise a new abbey, was to consist of at least thirteen monks, including an abbot, and usually with ten or more lay-brothers. Twelve abbeys of the Cistercian order were founded in Scotland, but this number was reduced by one with the suppression of Saddell, c. 1507; and it may be noted that in 1516, when a commissary of Cîteaux proposed to visit the Scottish houses, their number is given as eleven (*RSS*, i, no. 2833).

THE CISTERCIAN ABBEYS

	Name	County	Minimum income (1561)	Date Fd. D. or	Sec.	Mother-house or (note)
*	BALMERINO	Fife	£1773	c. 1227	1603	Melrose
§	COUPAR ANGUS	Perth	£5590	-1164	1606	Melrose
*‡	CULROSS	Fife	£1600	-1217	1589	Kinloss
*	DEER	Aberdeen	£2300	1219 (?-1219)	1587	Kinloss
*	DUNDRENNAN	Kirkcudbright	£500(?)	1142	1606	Rievaulx
*	GLENLUCE	Wigtown	£667	1191/2	1602	Dundrennan
¶	KINLOSS	Moray	£3480	1150	1601	Melrose
*	MELROSE	Roxburgh	£5180	1136	1609	Rievaulx
§	NEWBATTLE	Midlothian	£1500	1140	1587	Melrose
§	SADDELL	Argyll		-1207	c. 1507	Melifont
*	SWEETHEART	Kircudbright	£690	1273	1624	Dundrennan

BALMERINO (ST. EDWARD). The founders were Ermengarde, widow of William the Lion and her son Alexander II. A list of Cistercian fd'ns. (*Kinloss Recs.*, 13) assigns fd'n. to 1227; while the Chronicle of Melrose has the statement: 'In the year of the Lord 1229, the abbey was made by K. Alexander and his mother and the convent was sent to it from Melrose, on the day of St. Lucy the Virgin (13 Dec.)' (*Chron. Melrose*, 141). It is evident that from 1225 Queen Ermengarde was acquiring the land on which the monastery was built and which formed its first endowment; and the Cistercian General Chapter, in 1227, remitted the K. of Scotland's petition for the building of an abbey of that order to the abbots of Rievaulx and Coupar Angus, who, if they were satisfied with the king's proposed endowment, were authorized to grant him a convent from the house of Melrose (Canivez, *Statuta*, ii, 63). It is also to be noted that the abbot of St. Edward's is one of the seven Cistercian abbots who attest an indenture at Kinloss, 20 Sept. 1229 (*Kinloss Recs.*, 119), i.e. before the date given by the Melrose Chronicle for the departure of the convent. This is not necessarily inconsistent with fd'n. taking place in or about 1227 and full conventual life (i.e. at least twelve mks.) being established some two years later. On 3 Feb. 1230/1 Alexander II granted a foundation charter, which implies that it was conferred after the death of his mother (*Balm. Lib.*, no. 1). On the other hand, Q. Ermengarde is said to have died 11 Feb. 1233/4 (*Melrose Chron.*, 143), but as this date in itself raises additional difficulties (see Campbell, *Balmerino*, 122), some uncertainty must remain surrounding the date of the fd'n. charter which, it has been suggested (Anderson, *Early Sources*, ii, 489) may be of later provenance. What seems clear is that the king's charter came at an interval after the fd'n.

The ab. of Melrose occurs as 'father-abbot' of this mon., 4 Aug. 1396 (Reg. Aven., 321, fos. 65v–66). Little is known of its history in the fifteenth c. The abbot and fourteen monks appear in 1537 (Campbell, *Balmerino*, 247), but this does not represent the entire convent, which may have numbered about twenty at this period (*ibid.*, 248). In Dec. 1547 the abbey was burned by the English (*Cal. State Papers* (Thorpe), i, 74), but little diminution of numbers seems to have occurred as at least sixteen mks. can be found at this period (SRO, Dalguise Muniments, no. 1323). Reformers did some destruction at the abbey in June 1559 (Lesley, *History*, 273; *De Origine*, 507), but what this amounted to is difficult to say; the statement (Camerarius, *De Scotorum*, 271) that it was burned lacks confirmation. The last pre-Reformation ab., Robert Foster, was provided 30 Jan. 1511/12 (Reg. Supp., 1379, fos. 130v–1; Vat. Arch., Introitus et Exitus, 550, fo. 26v), and although he made several moves to resign (*James V Letters*, 225–6), he held office until his death shortly before 5 Feb. 1561 (Campbell, *Balmerino*, 257). On 10 Sept. 1561, a gift of the abbey was made to John Hay, parson of Monymusk (*RSS*, v, no. 845) and after his death on 3 Dec. 1573, the commendatorship was held in turn by father and son, Henry and John Kinneir (Campbell, *Balmerino*, 262–79). Following on the death of the son and forfeiture of the father, the abbey was erected by charter into a temporal lordship for Sir James Elphinstone, cr. Lord Balmerino, 21 Feb. 1603 (*RMS*, vi, no. 1411). Despite a grant of the commendatorship, later renounced, to Henry Auchmouty (Campbell, *Balmerino*, 279) the grant of 1603 was confirmed, in parliament, 1606 (*APS*, iv, 341–3) and by charter, 1607 (*RMS*, vi, no. 2001).

COUPAR ANGUS. The fd'n. may have been projected by David I (*Coupar Angus Rental*, i, 321), and was again planned by Malcolm IV on the recommendation of Waltheof of Melrose (Jocelin of Furness, *Vita Waldeni*, iv, 50); the royal manor of Coupar in Gowrie being assigned as the site of the abbey in 1159 (*Regesta Regum Scottorum*, i, 20–1). The actual fd'n. was delayed at this juncture, but the first Cistercians (from Melrose) were established at Coupar before Sept. 1162, and may have been settled there in 1161, to which date Malcolm's 'foundation charter' can probably be assigned (*ibid.*, no. 226; cf. NLS. MS., 33. 2. 5. fo. 9v). On 12 July 1164 the full convent arrived from Melrose and an abbot was appointed (*Chron. Melrose*, 78; cf. Janauschek (*Orig. Cist.*, 152) who assigns fd'n to 1 July 1164). The church was dedicated, 15 May 1233 (*Chron. Melrose*, 143). A petition of the ab. in Edward I's parliament of 28 Feb. 1305 sought remedy for the burning of its granges and other damage (*Mem. de Parl.*, no. 355). The grant of the hosp. of Turriff (*q.v.*) to the abbey in 1379 is said to have been made on account of the ruinous condition of the mon. (Reg. Aven., 229, fos. 377v–8). The ab. became mitred 7 June 1464 (*Coupar Angus Chrs.*, ii, no. clxxiv). The number of mks. remained fairly constant during the first half of the sixteenth c.

A document of 1521 to which 'everilkane' of the mks. had subscribed produces a total of twenty-eight mks. and although numbers may have dropped slightly thereafter, there were at least twenty-four in 1539 and twenty in 1545 and again in 1558–9 (Dilworth, 'Monks and ministers after 1560', *RSCHS*, xviii, 207). Building work was under way in the early part of that century, but according to one seventeenth-c. writer (and there appears to be no other evidence) the abbey was burned by Reformers (Camerarius, *De Scotorum*, 271). In or *c.* 1622, it is described as ruinous (Bisset, *Rolment of Courtis*, ii, 194). The last pre-Reformation ab., Donald Campbell, was provided 24 Sept. 1529 (Reg. Lat., 1525, fos. 115v–6) after controversy over the election of an abbot (see *Coupar Angus Chrs.*, ii, 275–6). After his death, 16 Dec. 1562×20 Jan. 1563, the abbey was conferred on Leonard Leslie, 24 Aug. 1565 (*RSS*, v, no. 2284), but his son failed to effect a precept for his infeftment in the spirituality of the abbey, 7 Feb. 1596/7 (*Coupar Angus Chrs.*, ii, 280). The abbey was later gifted to Andrew Lamb, 24 March 1603, who resigned his claim 24 Jan. 1607, and to Patrick Stirling, 20 May 1607, who failed to make good his claim (*ibid.*, ii, 281). It was erected into a temporal lordship for James Elphinstone, with the title of Lord Coupar, in parliament, 1606 (*APS*, iv, 340–1) and by charter 1607 (*RMS*, vi, no. 2002).

CULROSS. Fd. by Malcolm, E. of Fife. The fd'n. was contemplated by 1214 in which year the Cistercian General Chapter remitted a petition of Earl Malcolm to the abbots of Kinloss, Coupar Angus and Newbattle for inquiry into the suitability of the proposed site and the sufficiency of the endowment and for report to the following Chapter (Canivez, *Statuta* i, 427). As in the case of Balmerino and Coupar Angus (above) mks. may have been present at this site before the convent was sent to Culross from Kinloss, 23 Feb. 1217/18, along with Hugh, formerly pr. of Kinloss, as first ab. of the new foundation, which they reached on 18 March (*Chron. Melrose*, 129). A list of Cistercian foundations gives the date of fd'n. as 13 Feb. 1217(/18) (*Kinloss Recs.* 13). The number of mks. apparently declined before the Reformation. In 1540, besides the commendator and abbot, there were sixteen mks. (*Laing Chrs.*, no. 442), and in 1553 the complement of the house is said, in a description of the abbey, to be fifteen mks. and an abbot (Vat. Arch., Arm. Misc., xii, vol. 214, fos. 204–6). But in 1557 only nine mks. subscribe a charter (SRO RH1/2/611), and the total number may not have exceeded ten (cf. *Laing Chrs.*, no. 782). Following the provision of James Stewart to the abbacy, 6 April 1511 (*HMC, Mar and Kellie Supp. Rept.* (1930), 20), the revenues were held by a series of commendators (see D. McRoberts, 'Culross in the Diocese of Dunblane' in *Soc. of Friends of Dunblane Cathedral*, x, 91–98). From the provision of William Colville on 20 Oct. 1531 (Vat. Arch. Acta Misc., 7, fos. 230v–1) these were invariably drawn from the Colville family, who by divorcing the benefice from its fruits, supplied, on occasions, both an abbot and a commendator (McRoberts, 'Culross in the Diocese of Dunblane', 96–8). The abbey was finally erected into a temporal lordship for James Colville of Easter Wemyss, by charters 1589 and 1609 (*RMS*, v, no. 1675; vii, no. 9), the second charter creating him Lord Colville of Culross.

DEER. Fd. by William Comyn, E. of Buchan (*Chron. Melrose*, 144, which gives no date). A petition of Earl William was remitted by the Cistercian General Chapter, in 1214, to Scottish abbots for inquiry into the suitability of the proposed site and the sufficiency of endowment and for report to the following Chapter (Canivez, *Statuta*, i, 427). The convent was established in 1219, although monks may have been present before this date (see Balmerino, Coupar-Angus, above; Anderson, *Scottish Annals*, ii, 439 and *n*). This was a daughter-house of Kinloss (*CSSR*, ii, 60), but Ferrerius's account of its foundation (Ferrerius, *Historia*, 24) is erroneous. The history of the house is obscure until the sixteenth c. (see *Aberdeen-Banff Illust.*, ii, 409–26). The ab. and eleven mks. occur in 1544 (*ibid.*, ii, 431); thirteen mks. subscribe a rental in 1554 (*ibid.*, iv, 27–9); and twelve subscribe a charter in 1556 (*ibid.*, iv, 31–2). After the resignation on 2 May 1543 of Ab. John Innes (Vat. Arch. Resignationes A, 93, fos. 227–7v) the abbacy was acquired by Robert Keith, brother of William fourth E. Marischal, who was provided, 11 May 1544, following the death of Innes (Reg. Vat., 1634, fos. 170–171v). After his death on 12 June 1551 (*Aberdeen-Banff Illust.*, ii, 422), the commendatorship passed to Robert Keith, son of William, fourth E. Marischal, who was provided 19 Oct. 1552 (Vat. Arch., Arm. Misc., xv, 2 *bis*, fo. 143v) and for whom, as Lord Altrie, the abbey was erected into a temporal lordship, by charter 1587 (*RMS*, v, no. 1309).

DUNDRENNAN. Most writers and lists agree that this was a fd'n. of David I, but a few (Spottiswoode, 417; Lawrie, *Charters*, 362) attribute it to Fergus of Galloway. The date of fd'n. is also generally given as 1142. One list assigns it to 23 July of that year (Anderson, *Early Sources*, ii, 204*n*); an exception is the unreliable Smyth's Chronicle, which gives 1141

(*Kinloss Recs.*, 4). It is averred that the mks. were brought from Rievaulx (Spottiswoode, 417). There is no apparent record evidence that Rievaulx was the mother-house of this abbey (Dundrennan does not appear in the printed Rievaulx charters); but the ab. of Rievaulx is mentioned as in Galloway in 1164 (Lawrie, *Annals*, 90) and abs. of Dundrennan were elected to Rievaulx in 1167 and 1239 (*Chron. Melrose*, 81, 149). In 1299 the convent sought compensation from the English king for loss by destruction and burning amounting to £8000 (*CDS*, ii, no. 1123); and again in 1328 they were seeking from Edward III the restoration of revenues in Ireland and their lands in Meath from which they had been ejected (*ibid.*, ii, nos. 967, 969; cf. no. 1157). The history of the abbey is obscure. The commendator, prior and nine mks. attest a charter, 9 May 1545 (*Laing Chrs.*, no. 497), but at least twelve mks. formed the convent at Reformation (SRO R/H6/1331/1736/1786: NLS, Hutton Coll., i, fo. 35). Its buildings are reputed, 14 Oct. 1529, to be in a state of collapse (*James V Letters*, 160). Provisions *in commendam* were being sought in 1512 (Reg. Supp. 1386, fo. 17v; 1388, fo. 197) and, after the appointment of Abbot James Hay to the bishopric of Ross in 1523 (Watt, *Fasti*, 270), John Maxwell and Henry, bp. of Galloway successively held the commendatorship (*James V Letters*, 94-95, 160). Adam Blacadder, the last pre-Reformation commendator was nominated by the crown 3 July 1541 (*ibid.*, 426) and following his death the commendatorship was granted to Edward Maxwell, son of John Maxwell of Terregles, 14 Aug. 1562 (*RSS*, v, no. 1101). After Maxwell's death, it was conferred, 28 February 1598/9 (*RMS*, vi, no. 864) upon John Murray. The abbey was erected into a temporal lordship for Murray, afterwards E. of Annandale, in parliament, 1606 (*APS*, iv, 326) and by charter, 1609 (*RMS*, vii, no. 35).

GLENLUCE. Said to have been fd. by Roland of Galloway, constable of Scotland (*Chron. Bower*, ii, 538 and other lists; Spottiswoode, 421). A charter of regality, 31 May 1441 refers to charters granted to the abbey by Roland and other lords of Galloway (SRO, Hay of Park MSS., no. 2 calendared in *Wigtownshire Charters*, 57-58). The date is generally given as 1190, but a list of Cistercian foundations (Anderson, *Early Sources*, ii, 328) has it as 21 Jan. 1191/2. The assertion (Spottiswoode, 421) that the mks were brought from Melrose has no apparent foundation, and statutes of 1199 which refer to the ab. of Dundrennan advising his 'son-abbot' to absent himself from the General Chapter and to the ab. of Glenluce as, by the advice of his 'father' staying away from it (Canivez, *Statuta*, i, 238), indicate that Glenluce was a daughter-house of Dundrennan. The abbey was molested in 1235, during a rebellion in Galloway (*Chron. Melrose*, 146). Its history thereafter is obscure. In the sixteenth c., the community suffered considerable disturbance and spoliation. Disputes over the abbacy by a series of commendators (see *Wigtownshire Chrs.*, 41-46) was brought to an end by the provision of Walter Mallen, 13 June 1519 (Reg. Vat., 1119, fos. 8-9), during whose term of office the abbey regained some stability. In 1544, however, the ab. was expelled by the E. of Cassillis (*Hamilton Papers*, ii, 734); and, in 1545-6 the abbey was invaded both by his followers and those of Gordon of Lochinvar, who sought possession of it (*RPC*, 1st ser., ii, 3, 4, 7, 8; *ADCP*, 556) This was followed by Mallen's resignation in favour of James Gordon, brother of James Gordon of Lochinvar, 5 Dec. 1547 (Reg. Vat., 1698, fos. 125-9v, 179-81v). He is described as titular of Glenluce, 22 Aug. 1555 (*Wigtownshire Chrs.*, 75). On his death before March 1560, Lochinvar occupied the abbey and expelled the mks. (*HMC*, 5th Rep., App., 615). A protégé of the E. of Cassillis, Thomas Hay, who had been provided 17 April 1560, was instituted as abbot, 29 Sept. 1560; the institution taking place in the parish ch. owing to the occupation of the abbey (*ibid.*, 615). In that year, a charter is signed by the abbot, prior, sub-prior and thirteen mks. (*Ayr-Galloway Coll.*, v. 161), but this is clearly one or two short of the total number of mks. (*Wigtownshire Chrs.*, nos. 53, 55, 60, 62-3, 65, 68). In 1572 the commendator and five mks. were left (*Ayr-Galloway Coll.*, v, 179). After the Reformation the struggle over the abbey's possessions between Lochinvar and the earls of Cassillis, who recovered possession of the monastic buildings on 17 Nov. 1561 (*HMC 5th Rep.* App., App., 615) and successfully claimed a grant of bailiary continued (see *Wigtownshire Chrs.*, 53-55). Hay remained as commendator until his death in 1580 when it was conferred on Gilbert Moncrief (*RMS*, v, no. 78); he resigned it before 22 Feb. 1581/2 when it was granted to Laurence Gordon (*ibid.*, v, no. 335-6). 'The manor or place of Glenluce called of old the monastery of Glenluce' was granted to Lawrence Gordon, by charter, 1602 (*RMS*, vi, no. 1338), the grant being ratified in parliament, 1606 (*APS*, iv, 327-8). In 1619, the abbey was bestowed on the bp. of Galloway (*ibid.*, v, 72).

KINLOSS. Fd. by David I. The unanimous statement of chroniclers and lists is confirmed by a reference to 'the first foundation by the late King David of good memory' (*Kinloss Recs.*, 111). The date of fd'n. is given as 21 May 1150 (*Melrose Chron.*, 54). Smyth's Chronicle and appended list of Cistercian fd'ns. have this as 21 May 1151 (*Kinloss Recs.*, 5, 113) but as other dates in those lists are demonstrably wrong the earlier date is to be preferred. The date 20 June 1151 (as given *Kinloss Recs.*, x) is probably erroneous; while 12 *Kal. Januarii*, the date mentioned by Spottiswoode (418) is apparently an error for 12 *Kal. Junii*. Cistercian fd'n. lists also assign it to 1151 (Anderson, *Early Sources*, ii, 211). The assertion (Spottiswoode, 419) that the mks. came from Melrose is substantiated by a reference, 13 May 1444, to the ab. of Melrose as 'father-abbot of Kynlos' (*Reg. Supp.*, 397, fo. 55). The ab. of this house is designated ab. of Moray, 1178×1188 (*St. A. Lib.*, 289–90). On 24 Sept. 1395, the ab. was granted the mitre (Reg. Aven., 281, fo. 167v). In 1229 there were twenty-three mks. here, in addition to the ab. and the pr. (*Kinloss Recs.*, 119). A charter is attested, in 1537, by the abbot and nineteen mks. (*ibid.*, lxiv), and there were at least eighteen mks. at the Reformation (*ibid.*, 149, 152, 154; Fraser, *Grant*, iii, 115, GH6/2253/2566). The second-last pre-Reformation abbot, in whose favour Ab. Thomas Chrystall had resigned, 4 July 1528 (Reg. Supp., 1955, fos. 92v–93v) was Robert Reid, sub-dean of Moray, who professed as a monk 11 July 1529 (*Kinloss Recs.*, 11; cf. 49–50) but continued to hold the abbey, along with the commend of the priory of Beauly (*q.v.*), when provided to the bishopric of Orkney in 1541 (Watt, *Fasti*, 254). He resigned in favour of his nephew Walter Reid before 6 April 1553, when Walter received the obedience of the mks., and was himself blessed as abbot, ten days later (Smyth's Chronicle in *Kinloss Recs.*, 12). He granted a deed of demission, reserving a life-rent, in favour of Edward Bruce, 5 July 1583 (*ibid.*, lvi). The abbey was erected into a temporal lordship for Edward Bruce, erected Lord Kinloss, by charters, 1601 and 1608 (*RMS*, vi, nos. 1138, 2074).

MELROSE. Fd. by David I, who *c.* 1136 granted the monks of Durham the ch. of St. Mary in Berwick in exchange for the ch. of Melrose in which they possessed anterior rights (see Old Melrose under Early Religious Foundations). The fd'n. may have been contemplated at an earlier date, however, and the removal of the Tironensians from Selkirk to Kelso (*q.v.*) in 1128 may have been designed to facilitate a new fd'n. at Melrose to which many of the former Tironensian possessions eventually passed (see Barrow, *Kingdom of the Scots*, 205–8). The Cistercian foundation took place not at Old Melrose but at a site about two miles up the river Tweed from the early monastery. The date of the fd'n. is generally given as 1136, but according to the Chronicle of Melrose the abbey was cr. 23 March 1136 (*Chron. Melrose*, 70) i.e. presumably 1236/7 (see also Anderson, *Early Sources*, ii, 195*n*). The fd'n. charter (*Melr. Lib.*, no. 1) is not earlier than 1143–4, though it incorporates a grant made at Earlston previous to that date, probably *c.* 1136 (Lawrie, *Early Charters*, 376; cf. *Regesta Regum Scottorum*, i, 157–8). Melrose was colonized from Rievaulx (*Melr. Lib.*, no. 1). The ch. was dedicated, 28 July 1146 (*Melrose Chron.* 73). On 21 Aug. 1391, the ab. was granted the mitre (Reg. Aven., 268, fo. 431). The abbey suffered much damage from hostile action. Thus the monastic buildings seem to have been partially burned, 1300–07 (*CDS*, ii, no. 1982) and the English sacked it in 1322 (*Scotichronicon*, lib. xii, cap. iv, *Chron. Bower*, ii, 278) and burned it in 1385 (*ibid.*, lib. xiv, cap. i; *Chron. Bower*, ii, 401). Again, Melrose was one of the religious houses burned and destroyed during Hertford's invasion, Sept. 1545 (*LP Henry VIII*, xx², no. 456).

Twenty-nine mks., including the ab. and sub-prior, subscribed a charter, 6 April 1536 (*Melrose Recs.*, iii, 365), but at least three other mks. can also be identified at this time (*ibid.*, iii, 365; cf. *Laing Chrs.*, no. 569; NLS, Hutton Coll. i, fo. 40). Numbers seem to have fallen after its destruction in 1545. Thirteen monks occur in 1555 and 1556, and the names of four others can be found in other sources (*Laing Chrs.*, nos. 569, 628, 642–3; *Melrose Recs.*, iii, 150, 152, 159; Hutton Coll. i, fo. 40), but the convent seems to have numbered no more than seventeen at the Reformation. Protracted litigation over the abbacy between monks and secular clerks characterized the years between 1486 and 1507 (*James IV Letters*, 34–9); the dispute being resolved by the transference of William Turnbull ab. of Melrose to Coupar Angus and the provision of Robert Beaton, ab. of Glenluce, which he was allowed to retain, to Melrose, 19 June 1507 (Vat. Arch. Ob. et. Sol., 88, fo. 118 and v). Following Beaton's death before 2 Dec. 1524, another dispute broke out between John Maxwell and Andrew Dury (*James V Letters*, 110–1), the latter being provided 6 Jan. 1525 (Reg. Lat., 1482, fos. 1–5) and retaining it until appointed bp. of Galloway in 1541 (Watt, *Fasti*, 132). The abbey was then bestowed on James Stewart, commendator of Kelso, as a second *commenda* (*James V Letters*, 426), provision being granted, 16 Aug. 1541 (Reg. Vat., 1511, fos. 146–8). After his death in 1557, James Balfour was provided as commendator, 17 April 1559 (Vat. Arch. Acta Misc., 17, fo. 632) and he obtained a ratification of this provision, 25 March 1564 (*RSS*, v, no. 1656). The commendatorship thereafter passed to James Douglas of Lochleven, 1 May 1569 (*RSS* vi, no. 607). Following upon his resignation, with reservation of a life-rent, the abbey, with the exception of its lands of Kylesmuir in Ayrshire, separately erected for Lord Loudoun, in parliament, 1606 (*APS*, iv, 363–4) and by charter 1608 (*RMS*, vi, no. 2020), was erected into a temporal lordship for John Ramsay, viscount Haddington, cr. Lord Melrose, in parliament, 1609 (*APS*, iv, 461–4).

NEWBATTLE. David I is usually regarded as the founder, but a solemn privilege of Innocent II of Feb.–Sept. 1143 (*Newb. Reg.*, no. 263; cf. Jaffé-Lowenfeld, *Regesta*, no. 8369), links David and his son, Earl Henry, as making the initial endowments (Barrow, *Kingdom of the Scots*, 184n). The date of the foundation is given as 1140 (*Melrose Chron.*, 71). A list of Cistercian foundations gives it as 1 Nov. 1140 (Anderson, *Early Sources*, ii, 202n)—this is the date of K. David's grant of Newbattle to the monks (*Newb. Reg.*, no. 2). The assertion (Spottiswoode, 417) that the convent came from Melrose would appear to be incontestable, the ab. of Melrose being designated 'father-abbot' of this house, 6 Feb. 1412 (Reg. Aven., 332, fos. 151v–2). The ch. was dedicated 13 March 1233/4 (*Chron. Melrose*, 143). The abbey was burned by the English in 1385 (*Scotichronicon*, lib. xiv, cap. i (*Chron. Bower*, ii, 401)) and again on 15 May 1544 (*LP Henry VIII*, xix[1], no. 533) and in June 1548 (*Cal. State Papers Scot.*, i, no. 237), when, it is said, six of the mks. were taken as prisoners to England (Canivez, *Statuta*, vii, 37). The ab. and twenty-four mks. occur in 1528 (*Newb. Reg.*, 284) but numbers had decreased to about fifteen at the Reformation (*Laing Chrs.*, nos. 568, 699, 838, 899; SRO, GH6/1501/1791; SRO, Dalhousie Muniments, nos. 317, 324, 326). The last ab., James Haswell, resigned with retention of the fruits, in favour of Mark Ker, who was provided to the abbacy, 5 Dec. 1547 (Reg. Vat., 1698, fos. 171–8). Haswell continued to administer the abbey and still appears as ab. 12 April 1554 (*APS*, ii, 603) while Ker appears as commendator, 9 Jan. 1556 (*RMS*, iv, no. 1225). His son Mark Ker was presented to the abbacy, during his father's lifetime, 7 April 1567, and this grant was confirmed, 24 Aug. 1584, after his father's death (*RMS*, v, no. 724). The abbey was erected into a temporal lordship in his favour, by charter, 1587 (*RMS*, v, no. 1307).

SADDELL. Fd. by Reginald, son of Somerled, lord of the Isles (d. 1207) (*RMS*, ii, no. 3170; *Highland Papers*, iv, 147). He is stated to have founded at 'Sagadul' a house of Greyfriars (Book of Clanranald in *Reliquiae Celticae*, ii, 157). This as it stands, is erroneous; but 'Greyfriars' should probably be given as 'grey monks' i.e. Cistercians (cf. Chron. Man., 116n). A number of lists (e.g. *Chron. Bower*, ii, 538), have the founder's name as 'Sorly Maclardy', i.e. Somerled, Reginald's father (d. 1164) (Anderson, *Early Sources*, ii, 244–5). This tradition rests on undocumented statements beginning with Cistercian historian Henriquez (*Menologium Cistertiense* (Antwerp, 1630), 148 cited A. L. Brown, 'The Cistercian Abbey of Saddell, Kintyre', *Innes Rev.*, xx, 1969, 131n). Henriquez had access to lost Cistercian records and this gives his assertion some credibility, and this is reinforced if the entry in a list of Cistercian foundations under the year 1160 (Anderson, *Early Sources*, ii, 247) recording the foundation of a monastery of 'Sconedale' refers to Saddell. Somerled may have planned a fd'n., but it seems it was his son Reginald who endowed the house and saw it settled with monks. These mks. almost certainly came from Mellifont abbey in Ireland and not from Rushen in Man. This is indicated by a bull of 12 July 1393 (Reg. Aven., 306, fos. 26v–27) in which it is stated that the name of an abbot-elect had been submitted by the mks., according to their usual custom, to the ab. of Mellifont for confirmation. The history of the house is obscure (see Brown, 'The Cistercian Abbey of Saddell' 133–5). In *c.* 1507, James IV, in a letter to the Cardinal of St. Mark, declared that the house of 'Sagaguil', once Cistercian and fd. by the king's ancestors in the diocese of Lismore (Argyll), had within living memory seen no monastic life and had fallen to the use of laymen. There was no hope of reviving monastic life and the fruits were barely £9 sterling. James asked for a commission to the abp. of Glasgow or some other prelate to investigate and with papal approval to unite the place in perpetuity to the bishopric of Lismore (*James IV Letters*, no. 149). The statement that the abbey was fd. by the king's ancestors is certainly inaccurate and the truth of the allegations is questionable (Brown, 'The Cistercian Abbey of Saddell', 135-7). But the request was successful; the Pope united the abbey to the bp's *mensa* after 26 Nov. 1507 (Reg. Lat., Julius II, *lib*. 8 *anno* 5, fo. 177; this volume has been lost) and on 1 Jan. 1507/8, James IV confirmed to the bishop and his successors, all previous grants made to the abbey, and incorporated them in a free barony of Saddell (*RMS*, ii, nos. 3170, 3208). On 22 April 1512 K. James made the request to Pope Julius II that as the cathedral of Lismore had fallen into ruin and lay deserted, having neither bishop nor chapter nor safe access nor sufficient food, and since the suppressed mon. of 'Sagadul' was united to the episcopal *mensa*, the see might be transferred to that site and a cathedral erected and endowed (*James IV Letters*, no. 446). This proposal had no result. Bps. of Lismore after 1508 are occasionally styled commendators of Saddell.

SWEETHEART (NEW ABBEY). Fd. by Devorgilla, widow of John Balliol. The date of fd'n. is usually given as 1275 (*Scotichronicon*, lib. x, cap. xxxvi; *Chron. Bower*, ii, 124)). But a statute of the Cistercian General Chapter, in 1270, commissions the abs. of Furness and Rievaulx to inspect the site 'in which the widow of John de Balliol intends to found an abbey of monks' (Canivez, *Statuta*, iii, 91); and, on 10 April 1273 Devorgilla granted a charter of endowment 'to God and the church of St. Mary of Sweetheart and the monks of the Cistercian order of the convent of Dundrennan, for the abbey to be built in honour of God' (*Laing Chrs.*, no. 46). A further statute of the General Chapter in 1274 committed to the abs. of Holmcultram and Glenluce the inspection of the abbey 'which, it is said, Devorgilla has founded'; and if they were satisfied to incorporate it to the order and introduce the convent there. It was to be a daughter-house of Dundrennan (Canivez, *Statuta*, iii, 138). In 1299 and 1308, the mks. made complaint to the English king of the damage amounting to more than £5000 through the burning of their granges and destruction of their goods in war (*CDS*, ii, nos. 1122, 1123; iii, no. 69); and in 1397, the abbey buildings are said to have been set on fire by lightning and 'totally burned' (Reg. Vat., 322, fo. 440v), though this no doubt is an exaggeration. The ab. was granted the mitre, 4 July 1398 (Reg. Vat., 322, fo. 536). The ab. and fifteen mks. subscribe a charter, 13 April 1557 (*Laing Chrs.* nos. 530, 669), and this must approximate to the size of the convent at the Reformation. The last pre-Reformation ab., Ab. John Brown, resigned, with reservation of a life-rent, shortly before 23 May 1565, on which date the abbacy was granted to Gilbert Brown (*RSS*, v, no. 2072). He remained an ardent Catholic and in 1579 it was reported that 'there yit stands an high altar in the New Abbay' (*BUK*, ii, 429). After his forfeiture, the abbey was granted to William Lesley in 1586 (Huyshe, *Devorgilla, Lady of Galloway*, 21). In 1624 the abbey was erected into a temporal lordship for Sir Robert Spottiswoode (*RMS*, viii, no. 572).

UNCERTAIN FOUNDATIONS

Soulseat. According to St. Bernard of Clairvaux's account of St. Malachy (Maelmaedoic) of Armagh, that bp. 'after a prosperous crossing (from Ireland) came to Scotland. On the third day he reached a place which is called *Viride Stagnum*, which he had caused to be prepared that he might establish an abbey there.' The account goes on: 'And leaving there some of his sons, our brothers, as a convent of monks and an abbot (for he had brought them with him for that purpose), he bade them farewell and set out'(Vita S. Malachiae, in *Acta Sanctorum*, Nov. ii, Pt. I, 165a; *Patr. Lat.*, 182, col. 1113; see Anderson, *Early Sources*, ii, 208; Lawlor, *Life of St. Malachy of Armagh*, 120). At an earlier point in the narrative, St. Bernard, having described the healing by St. Malachy at Bangor of a clerk named Michael, declares of this man: 'And from that moment he clave to God and to Malachy His servant . . . and at present, as we have heard, he presides over a monastery in the parts of Scotland; and this was the latest of all Malachy's foundations' (*AS*, November, ii. Pt. I, 140; *PL*, 182, col. 1083-4; Lawlor, *op. cit.*, p. 34). The points which emerge in these statements are: (1) This foundation, according to St. Bernard's narrative, took place in the year of St. Malachy's death, 1148; (2) it was, by implication, a house of Cistercians; (3) *Viride Stagnum* came to be identified with Soulseat, in Wigtownshire (perhaps because

Soulseat Loch was regarded as the 'Green Lake'). When this happened seems uncertain. A charter (*Wigtownshire Chrs.*, 110) granted 19 June 1539, by the commendator of Soulseat (viridis stagni alias sedis animarum[1]) (cf. the reference to 'Ecclesia Viridis Stagni alias Sanliesiete [*sic*]' (Le Paige, *Bibliotheca Praem. Ord.* (Paris, 1633), 333)). Dr. Anderson (*Early Sources*, ii, 208 n) offers certain suggestions: (1) Maelmaedoic may have brought mks. from Mellifont (founded for Cistercians in 1140) to Soulseat; in that case, the latter ceased shortly after to be a Cistercian house (Soulseat is not mentioned among the five daughter-houses of Mellifont; Lawlor, *St. Malachy*, 76 n.); (2) this bp. may have founded a Cistercian house at Viride Lignum in Newry County but (while it might have been possible for the names Viride Lignum and Viride Stagnum to be confused, the only possible inference is that the two names stand for different places); (3) as Maelmaedoic had established an abbey of regular canons at Saul, 'it would seem possible that the canons of Soulseat had been brought from Saul' (Soulseat was ultimately to be the site of a Praemonstratensian abbey). This would seem less plausible; but he goes on to state: 'It is difficult to imagine that Bernard should have erred in his belief that the abbey founded in 1148 was Cistercian.' Dr. Anderson believed that if the name 'Saulseat' was derived from the Irish 'Saball', it would have implied that the canons had gone there after their house at Saul had been dispersed. But he later suggested that there is probably no connection between the names and no evidence that Soulseat (Saulseat) had anything to do with Saul:

'The one inference that I incline to make is that Cistercians occupied a place at Viride Stagnum, and Premonstratensians another place called Soulseat. It would appear that the identification of Viride Stagnum with Soulseat must remain unverified. That Maelmaedoic founded a Cistercian abbey at such a place in Scotland is by no means improbable. If so, there is no further evidence concerning it and its career must have been brief. Soulseat was founded for Premonstratensian canons somewhat later in the twelfth century. See under Premonstratensian Canons.

[1] The name is commonly latinized in the latter form.

CISTERCIAN DEPENDENCIES

GENERAL NOTE

THIS list includes recorded 'cells' and granges. Granges were owned by abbeys of the order; they were worked by lay-brothers (*conversi*) and abbey servants. Some of these granges, especially when they were at a distance from the abbey, had buildings of monastic character wherein the lay-brothers could reside. Originally priest-monks were not allowed to stay at granges, but as regulations were relaxed, granges with chapels under one or two priest monks, were not unknown.

CISTERCIAN HOUSES

Name	County	Rank	Date Fd. D. or Sec.		Dependent on
BEAULY	Inverness	Priory	see notes	1634	see notes
GADVAN	Fife	Preceptory	−1475	−1578	Balmerino
Mauchline	Ayr	Grange			Melrose

BEAULY. For the previous history of this house see Valliscaulian Monks (below). On the suppression of that order and the institution of the Cistercian rule, there is no indication that this house was to become dependent on Kinloss, and although two abbots of that house were subsequently to become commendators of this priory, it is nowhere claimed that Beauly was a dependency of Kinloss. After a dispute over the vacant priorship, Robert Reid, ab. of the Cistercian house of Kinloss and later (1541) b. of Orkney, was provided to Beauly priory *in commendam*, 1 Nov. 1531 (Reg. Supp., 2060, fo. 230v). He had already been nominated by James V, 1 Aug. 1531 (*James V Letters*, 194–5) in preference to a canon regular who had been attempting to gain possession of the priory since early 1530 (Reg. Supp., 2024, fo. 164; 2047, fo. 102). It is possible that Reid had *de facto* possession in 1530 as Ferrerius avers (*Beauly Chrs.*, 218; *Kinloss Recs.*, 50). There were six mks here in 1568 (*Beauly Chrs.*, 256) and four in 1571 (*ibid.*, 268). Reid's successor at Kinloss (*q.v.*), his nephew Walter, also held the commendatorship, but he resigned the latter in favour of John Fraser of Lovat, 29 Oct. 1572 (*Kinloss Recs.*, 98; *RSS*, vi, no. 1801). It was thereafter held by a series of commendators (*Beauly Chrs.*, 329). The erection of the priory into a temporal lordship in favour of Lord Hay of Sala is noted under 1612 in *APS*, iv, 522), but this is apparently an error (see *Beauly Chrs.*, 329; *RMS*, vii, no. 702). The priory was finally granted to the bp. of Ross by crown charter, 20 Oct. 1634 (*RMS*, ix, no. 227).

GADVAN. A cell of Balmerino abbey, situated in Dunbog parish. It is called, in 1630, a 'preceptory or ministry' (*RMS*, viii. no. 1543). A prior of Gadvan occurs in 1475 (*Glas. Mun.*, ii, 83). In a letter of James V to Pope Clement VII, 19 March 1529/30, it is described as 'a monastic cell in a hamlet and . . . named Gadwyne, long wont to be governed by a Cistercian of Balmerino, with a second monk as his companion' (*James V Letters*,

p. 169; from Tyninghame Letter Bk.). This house reappears before 10 Oct. 1486, when its head is called 'prior of Dunbolg [Dunbog]' (*Arb. Lib.*, ii, no. 300); he is also designated 'master of the place of Gadvan, annexed to the said monastery [Balmerino]', 25 Jan. 1529/30 (*RMS*, iii. no. 898) and 'preceptor', in 1603 (*Ibid.*, vi. no. 1492). Its chapel, manse and meadow are likewise mentioned in 1603 (*Ibid.*). This house and its property were secularized by 5 April, 1578, when James Beaton of Creich held 'the Gadvan and manor place thereof' (Fraser, *Wemyss*, no. 226 (ii. 302)); and a crown charter of Gadvan, with the manse and meadow (but excluding the chapel) and the lands of Johnstoun, 'formerly held of the monastery [of Balmerino] and of the preceptors of the place of Gadvan annexed to the said monastery', was granted to him, 20 Dec. 1603 (*RMS*, vi. no. 1492).

Mauchline. 'Said to have been founded by David I', according to Spottiswoode (p. 426) and described as a 'cell of Melrose' in lists (e.g. *Chron. Bower*, ii. 539; EU. MS.Db. 6. 19; NLS. MSS. 22.1.14, 31.6.1; NLS. MS. 33.2.12 gives it erroneously as a 'cell of Kelso'). According to Janauschek (*Orig. Cist.*, lxxx), it was not an abbey but a priory subject to Melrose. There is, however, no evidence that it was other than a grange. It appears as the *grangia de Machlyn* in 1527 and 1528 (SRO, Morton Papers, GD. 150, Box 54, fos. 4, 13, 16, 20). Existing charters frequently mention the lands of Mauchline; but neither in the records of Melrose nor elsewhere is there any specific indication of a priory or religious house. The only relevant reference is in 1243, when Richard de Bigre, 'then monk of Mauhelin', is mentioned (*Melrose Liber*, i. no. 191; verified from the original charter in Scottish Record Office). It is difficult to make a definite inference from the appearance of this solitary figure. The lands of Mauchline were granted to Melrose abbey by Walter, son of Alan, steward of Scotland, –1177 (*ibid.*, i. no. 66), i.e. during the reign not of David I but of William the Lion. In this locality the only ch. seems to have been the ch. or chapel of St. Michael mentioned 1204–31 (*ibid.*, i. no. 73), which was given parochial status in 1315 (*ibid.*, ii. nos. 407, 408). The surviving medieval buildings at Mauchline, the so-called 'Castle', are not in the strict sense ecclesiastical. They were probably erected *c.* 1450 and have been described as 'a civil residence for ecclesiastics engaged in managing a large estate' (R. C. Reid, 'Mauchline Castle', *Dumfries. Trans.*, 3rd ser., xvi, 1931, 171). The office of the 'mastership' of Mauchline, granted by the Pope to a mk. of Melrose, 1 Sept. 1487 (Cameron, *Apostolic camera*, 221) was probably connected with the administration of the abbey's lands in this area. These lands were erected separately into the lordship of Kylesmuir, 1606 and 1608. See Melrose above; also Mauchline *hospitium* (p. 199 below).

Supposed Foundations

Ancaria. A place so named appears, in 1530, in a list of Scottish Cistercian monasteries which are to be assessed for contributions to the needs of the order (Canivez, *Statuta*, vi. 689–90). It cannot be identified.

Dron. It is stated in the *New Stat. Acct.* (x. 408) that this chapel, in the parish of Long-forgan, belonged to the abbey of Coupar Angus, though this is doubtful. The statement is also couched in terms which lend themselves to the suggestion that it was the site of a monastic community. This was not the case. The chapel was evidently secular and was probably intended to serve an outlying part of the parish.

Forfar. Adam, 'abbot' of Forfar, who is mentioned in the Coupar Angus *Breviarium* (p. 42), is a mythical personage. The word 'abbas' is apparently an error for 'Albus'. Likewise, the 'monks' of Forfar who appear in the same document are mentioned in error for the monks of Coupar. See *Coupar Angus Chrs.*, i. lxviii, 24.

Hichaten. This name figures in the same list as 'Ancaria' above. It appears as 'Hichaten vel Orcades'; but no place in Orkney can be identified with it.

Lochkindeloch. This was the parish in which Sweetheart abbey was situated. It had a parish ch. but no religious house other than the abbey existed in it.

Roxburgh. With reference to the exemption of the ch. of St. James, Roxburgh (which was held by Kelso abbey) from synodals and episcopal aids, according to a declaration of the papal legate in 1201, A. O. Anderson (*Early Sources*, ii. 183 *n.*) declares: 'It seems therefore to have been occupied by Cistercian monks at this time.' This suggestion seems unfounded. There are no grounds for holding that monks were settled here or that these were Cistercians.

Kerrara. In an inventory of 1292 appears a letter of the ab. and convent of Coupar Angus by which they have obliged themselves to build a chapel at their own expense on the island of 'Karnelay in Arkadia' and to find three mks. to celebrate divine service for the soul cf Alexander, late K. of Scots, apparently in virtue of a sum of money which they had received 'beforehand' from that king (*APS*, i. App. to Preface, 10). This island is Kerrara, off the coast of Argyll, where Alexander II died. There is no evidence that a fd'n. took place or that monks were placed in that island.

THE VALLISCAULIAN MONKS

GENERAL NOTES

The order of Vallis Caulium (or Vallis Olerum) is said to have been introduced into Scotland in 1230 (*Chron. Melrose*, 142). The principles of the rule of this order are given in a bull of Pope Innocent III in 1205 (*Mloray Reg.*, no. 256). The Valliscaulian houses stood in a relation of direct dependence on the mother-house of Val des Choux, in the diocese of Langres, in France. The three Scottish priories of the order are sometimes called Cistercian, but Pluscarden was clearly a Valliscaulian house until it became Benedictine in 1454 and the prior of Val des Choux claimed jurisdiction over Beauly and Ardchattan until at least 1506. The former became Cistercian in 1510.

THE VALLISCAULIAN HOUSES

Name	County	Rank	Minimum income (1561)	Date Fd. D. or Sec.	Dependent on
*ARDCHATTAN	Argyll			1230 or 1231	1602
*BEAULY	Inverness		£674	c.1230	see notes
‡ §PLUSCARDEN	Moray		see under Benedictine Houses	1230 or 1231	1454 (united to Urquhart) see under Benedictines

ARDCHATTAN. Fd. in 1230 or 1231 by Duncan McCowll (or McDougall) (*Chron. Extracta*, 93; MS. lists; *OPS*, ii¹, 149). Its prior and convent swore fealty to Edward I in 1296 (*CDS*, ii, no. 823). With the emergence of the cathedral chapter of Argyll in the early fourteenth c., the pr. of Ardchattan held *ex officio*, the chantership of the cathedral, but he resigned his right in exchange for the ch. of St. Bean in Lower Lorne, *c.* 1371. A later pr. of the mon. which is described as that of St. Mary and St. John the Baptist in 'Beanardaloch' [Benderloch], obtained papal approval for the annulment of this exchange, but this does not appear to have been effective (*CPP*, i, 584; *CSSR*, ii, 112). Its history is largely obscure. It is sometimes described as Cistercian (Maitland, *History*, i, 263), but in 1506, in a commission for its visitation by the prior of Beauly, it is said to be immediately subject to Val des Choux (*Beauly Chrs.*, 140), and there is no evidence that it became Cistercian. There were six mks., –1538 (*James V Letters*, 346) and three or four at the Reformation (*OPS*, ii¹, 149). The abbey was held *in commendam* from 27 Feb. 1545 (Reg. Supp., 2534, fos. 298–9v) by John Campbell, later bp. of the Isles who resigned *commend* in favour of his son Alexander shortly before 5 June 1580 (*RMS.*, iv, no. 3021). The house was erected into a tenandry for Alexander Campbell, its commendatory prior, in 1602 (*APS*, vii, 211). Its annexation to the bishopric of the Isles by charter 1615, and in parliament, 1617 (*ibid.*, iv, 554) was ineffective and tenandry of the priory remained with Alexander's heirs (*Coll. de Rebus Alban.*, 124; Ardchattan Chrs., cited *OPS*, ii[1], 152).

BEAULY. The date of fd'n. of this house and the founder are alike difficult to ascertain. According to the Wardlaw MS., a late and not entirely reliable source (compiled by James Fraser, 1666–99+), John Byset founded and endowed it for Valliscaulian monks, 9 July 1223 (*Chron. Frasers*, 61). It is also asserted in that work that 'these monks came out of France . . . *anno* 1222' (*ibid.*, 63). If the order was not introduced into Scotland until 1230, as is maintained by the Chronicle of Melrose (*Melrose Chron.*, 142), these statements must be rejected. Spottiswoode (427) assigns the fd'n. to *James* Byset and professes to quote the terms of the founder's charter. A bull of Pope Gregory IX, taking the mks. and mon. under his protection as well as its possessions (including those bestowed by John Byset), is, in the existing version, imperfect, as the date is left mainly blank (*Beauly Chrs.*, 14). But if it is identical with the bull mentioned by Spottiswoode (428), it can be regarded as granted by Pope Gregory IX, 5 July 1230 (not 1231 as in *Beauly Chrs.*, 15). In the Wardlaw MS. it is stated that the mks. who 'came out of France' in 1222 were six in number along with a prior. These 'landed at Lovat and the country provided for them during the erection of the mon.; John Bisset in his time taking care of that edifice which afterwards was industriously carried on in Insula de Achinbady' (*Chron. Frasers*, 63). *Insula* here is a translation of the Gaelic *innis*, which means not only 'island' but 'green pastureland' or 'river meadow' (Scottish, 'inch'). This site, the 'Inch of Achinbady' became known as Beauly (*beau lieu*), presumably because it was given that name by the monks. In another (and similar) account by the same writer, it is added that, in 1245, by a bull of Pope Innocent IV, the priory was 'erected' for Valliscaulians to whom Alexander III 'mortified and confirmed . . . all the Lands of Strathalvay, the Monastery to be erected in Insuâ [Insula] de Ackinbady in Strathalvy, where stood a Chappel of St. Michael and John Bisset entrusted with the Erection' (Macfarlane, *Genealogical Coll.* ii, 87). This bull, if the description of it can be trusted, was concerned with the confirmation of the monastery's endowments, including Alexander II's grant, rather than with its erection. The fd'n. must have taken place prior to 1232; a charter of Andrew, bp. of Moray, confirming a donation made to the priory (*Beauly Chrs.*, 38), was granted not later than July of that year. An entry in the Lovat writs which records that Alexander II, on 20 Dec., in the seventeenth year of his reign, (1230, not 1231 as in *Beauly Chrs.*, 17), confirmed a donation made to the priory (*ibid.*), points to the existence of the mon. in that year. The fd'n. is attributed in some lists to John Byset (e.g. *Chron. Bower*, ii, 540; NLS. MS. 33. 2. 12) and in others to Alexander II and Byset (e.g. NLS. MS. 22. 1. 14; EU. MS. Db. 6. 19; MS. Saunders). Beyond these alternatives record evidence (which is insufficient and ambiguous) does not permit further speculation. The pr. of Beauly was present at the parliament of Brigham, 17 March 1289/90 (*APS*, i, 85). In a petition, 18 Jan. 1432, Hugh Fraser, sheriff of Inverness, claims that his ancestors founded and endowed the priory and states that 'the buildings of the priory are falling to the ground', an assertion which must be treated with some suspicion (*CSSR*, iii, 72). In a bull of Pope Alexander VI, 25 Feb. 1497/8, the mon. is described both as of the Cistercian order and as a dependency of the mon. of Val des Choux (*Beauly Chrs.*, 106), as 'of the Cistercian order under the rule of Vallis Caulium' in a form of oath sent to the prior on the same date (*ibid.*, 111), and as of the Cistercian order in a writ of the bp. of Moray (which is also addressed to the ab. of Vallis Caulium), 11 Feb. 1500/1 (*ibid.*, 113). Why it should be called Cistercian in these records is impossible to say; but on 7 May 1506 the pr. of Val des Choux commissions the prior of 'our monastery' at Beauly to make a visitation of the mon. of Ardchattan (*ibid.*, 140), and, on 18 Dec. of the same year, the pr. of Val des Choux as 'head or general' of that order, writers to the pr. and convent of Beauly on the question of episcopal visitation and summons him to the next general chapter of the order (*ibid.*, 157–9). But a bull of 10 May 1510, directed to the pr. and convent of Beauly, extinguished the order of Vallis Caulium there and instituted the Cistercian order (*LP Henry VIII*, i[2], 1522). For the further history of this house see under Cistercian Dependencies.

PLUSCARDEN. Fd. by Alexander II in 1230 (Spottiswoode, 427) or 1231 (*Chron. Pluscarden*, 72) K. Alexander is mentioned as founder in the confirmation charter of Andrew, bp. of Moray, 1233 (Macphail, *Pluscardyn* 201); and his charter of 7 April 1236 is concerned with the granting of endowments, privileges and protection to 'the brethren of the order of Vallis Caulium serving . . . God in the house which we have founded in our forest of Elgin, in the place namely which is called the valley of St. Andrew at Pluscarden' (*ibid.*, 205). By a bull of Pope Urban IV, 5 July 1263, the priory with its possessions was placed under papal protection (*ibid.*, 207–8). In the early fifteenth c. disputes over the priorship became frequent (*CSSR*, ii, 194, 201, 211; iii, 107–8, 174; *CPL*, viii, 568, 609; X, 468–9). On 12 March 1453/4 Pope Nicholas V, on the petition of the Benedictine pr. of Urquhart, containing that there were not more than six mks. at Pluscarden and not more than two at Urquhart, consented to the separation of Pluscarden from Val des Choux, made it a dependency of Dunfermline and united it to Urquhart (Macphail, *Pluscarden*, 223 ff.; *CPL*, X, 253–4). The ab. of Dunfermline, on 8 Nov. 1454, appointed a commissary to take possession of the priory in his name to receive the profession as Benedictines of the mks. (*Dunf. Reg.*, no. 442). For its further history see under Benedictine Monks. This house is erroneously described as of the order of Vallambrosa (Bisset, *Rolment of Courtis*, ii, 122) and as Cistercian (Maitland, *History*, 258).

Supposed Foundation

Dalvey. The statement that Pluscarden had a cell at Dalvey, in the parish of Dyke (*Beauly Chrs.*, 135) is based merely on conjecture. There is no evidence of such a cell.

THE CARTHUSIAN MONKS

GENERAL NOTES

THE Carthusians, founded as a group of hermits at La Grande Chartreuse near Grenoble in 1084, gradually grew into a single claustral complex of cells, each of them a small self-sufficient house with garden and running water. The monks met in their chapel only for certain liturgical acts. Other similar monasteries were founded and they became an order with a constitution similar to that of the Cistercians. Charterhouses were built for multiples of twelve choir monks, in units of twelve self-contained small houses opening off the interior of a large cloister quadrangle. Two or three such units might constitute a monastery. Carthusian lay brothers, who were limited in each house to sixteen, lived a life which was stricter in degree than in most monasteries, but choir monks, who were usually ordained to the priesthood, led a life which was different not only in degree, but in kind: they were hermits living in a community.

On the relations of the Scottish Carthusians with the order, see Miss E. M. Thompson, *The Carthusian Order in England* (London, 1930) in which it is shown (247–8) that the one Carthusian house in Scotland was at first attached to the province of Picardy, about 1456 added to the English province, and in 1460 united to the province of Geneva.

THE CARTHUSIAN HOUSES

Name	County	Rank	Minimum income (1561)	Fd.	Date or	Sec.	Dependent on
PERTH	Perth	Priory	£1680	1429		1569	

PERTH. 'Vale of Virtue.' On 19 Aug. 1426, the pr. of Grande Chartreuse, with the consent of the General Chapter and following on the proposition of James I, authorized the erection of a house near Perth for thirteen mks. (i.e. a pr. and twelve mks.) (Fittis, *Eccles. Annals of Perth*, 216–17). K. James, on 31 March 1429, by a charter in favour of the pr. and convent of the mon. of Vallis Virtutis of the Carthusian order near Perth, bestowed on this house extensive privileges (*ibid.*, 217–18); and it was incorporated by the General Chapter in 1430 (Thompson, *Carthusian Order in England*, 247). By 1434 the nunnery of St. Leonard (*q.v.*) and the hospital of St. Mary Magdalene (*q.v.*) had been annexed to it (Fittis, *op. cit.*, 222). In 1478 the community consisted of the pr., fourteen choirmonks, one novice and two lay-brothers (Thompson, *op. cit.*, 248). This may have been achieved by the pr., his vicar and the procurator living in rooms outside the great cloister. By 1529 the community had reverted to its original total; this was maintained in

1544, but had been reduced to a pr.—who was still a genuine choirmonk—and ten mks. in 1558 (M. Dilworth, 'Monks and ministers after 1560' in *RSCH*, xviii, 205). The Charter-house was sacked and destroyed in May 1559 by Reformers (Lesley, *History*, 272; Knox, *Works*, i, 323; Pitscottie, *Historie*, ii, 146). Of the eleven members of the convent, one subsequently d. and four left for Charterhouses abroad, the remaining six being described in 1565 as 'the convent now beand present in the realme'. Of those, the pr. and another mk. went to continental Charterhouses after Feb. 1567 leaving the remaining four in Scotland. One of these was Adam Steward, illegitimate son of James V, who seems to have been a mk. and, after the Reformation, attempted to call himself pr. and was granted a pension from the revenues (see Dilworth, 'Monks and ministers after 1560', 205). The gardens, mon. and place belonging to the Charterhouse was included in the grant of the friars' lands to the burgh of Perth by James VI, 9 Aug. 1569 (*RMS*, iv, no. 1874). Never-theless, the Charterhouse was held by a series of commendators till 1602 (by which date the convent was extinct), when the priory was finally suppressed (*ibid.*, vi, nos. 851, 1276) and the Town Council apparently obtained effective possession of its property. The charter of 1569 was confirmed by James VI in 1600 (*ibid.*, vi, no. 1098).

PROPOSED FOUNDATION

On 5 June 1419 the Pope granted a petition of Archibald, E. of Douglas, who, out of his 'singular devotion' to the order, had supplicated for licence to found a Carthusian house (*CSSR*, i, 68); but the projected fd'n. was not made.

SUPPOSED FOUNDATION

Makerstoun. It is asserted that 'the priory of Charterhouse in the parish of Mackerston [*sic*], which is said to have been the abode of a small society of Carthusians, possessed half of the Midtoun and Mains of Sprouston' (*OPS*; i. 440, citing Morton, *Monastic Annals*, 173, 321). There is a farm in this parish called Charterhouse, but no evidence of a priory is forthcoming. The lands in the neighbouring parish of Sprouston were bestowed upon the Charterhouse of *Perth* by Archibald, E. of Douglas, 2 Feb. 1433/4 (Fraser, *Douglas*, iii. no. 396; *HMC*, *14th Rep.*, App., Pt. III, 24) and are mentioned in 1603 as 'alleged holden' of the [Perth] Charterhouse (*RPC*, 1st ser., vi, 812); the Mains of Sprouston is specifically described, 20 Dec. 1607, as 'belonging to the priory of Charterhouse' (*RMS*, vi, no. 2003), which must mean the Perth priory.

THE AUGUSTINIAN CANONS

GENERAL NOTES

THE distinct order of regular canons under the rule of St. Augustine
(O.S.A.), this rule being based upon that of St. Augustine of Hippo who
died in 430, did not become fully recognized until after the mid-eleventh
century. Leo IX (1049–54) encouraged the formation of reformed communities of regular canons in order to restore religious discipline, and in
1059 these communities were granted official standing. By 1125 over
thirty important monasteries of Augustinian canons had been established
in England and Wales. Only one Scottish priory at Scone had been
established by this date.

THE AUGUSTINIAN HOUSES

Name	County	Rank	Minimum income (1561)	Date Fd. D. or	Sec.	Dependent on or (note)
ABERNETHY	Perth	Priory		1272 or 1273	early 14c.	
BLANTYRE	Lanark	Priory £131		1238×49	1598/9	Jedburgh abbey
*CAMBUSKENNETH	Stirling	Abbey £3148		c.1140	1604	(Arrouaisian)
CANONBIE	Dumfries	Priory included with Jedburgh		−1165×70	1606	Jedburgh
*HOLYROOD	Midlothian	Abbey £5600		1128	1606	
INCHAFFRAY	Perth	Priory		1200		
		Abbey £667		1220 or 1221	1609– 1669 (V. notes)	
*INCHCOLM	Fife	Priory	c.1153			
		Abbey £1240(?)		1235	1609	
*INCHMAHOME	Perth	Priory £1680		1238+	1604	
*JEDBURGH	Roxburgh	Priory		c.1138	1696	
		Abbey £2480 (with Res- tennet and Canonbie)		c.1154		
LOCH LEVEN (Portmoak)	Kinross	Priory £250		1152/3	1580	St. Andrews
MAY see PITTENWEEM						
‡MONYMSUK	Aberdeen	Priory £400		−1245	1617	(St. Andrews)
ORONSAY	Argyll	Priory ?		−1353	1616	
PITTENWEEM	Fife	Priory £1020		−1318	1606	St. Andrews
PORTMOAK see LOCH LEVEN						

Name	County	Rank	Minimum income (1561)	Date Fd. D. or Sec.		Dependent on or (note)
*RESTENNET	Angus	Priory see Jedburgh		−1153 or 1153–60	1606	Jedburgh
*ST. ANDREWS	Fife	Priory £12500		1144	1592	
ST. MARY'S ISLE (Trail)	Kirkcudbright	Priory		−1173	1608	Holyrood
SCONE	Perth	Priory Abbey £5350		c.1120 c.1164	1606	
STRATHFILLAN	Perth	Priory £40(?)		1317/18	1607	
TRAIL see ST. MARY'S ISLE						

ABERNETHY. Formerly a house of Culdees (see Early Religious Foundations). According to the *Scotichronicon* (lib. x, cap. xxxiii; *Chron. Bower*, ii, 120), 'in this year [it is not clear whether the reference is to 1272 or 1273] the priory of Abernethy was made into regular canons, who were formerly Culdees'. That the Culdees became regular canons is more likely to be true than the statement of Spottiswoode (393): 'At length it became a priory of canons brought from Inchaffray in the year 1273.' There is no evidence that canons were sent to Abernethy from that abbey. The priory appears in the taxation roll of Baiamund for 1274–5 and the prior in the roll for 1275–6 (Theiner, *Vet. Mon.*, no. cclxiv; *SHS Misc.*, vi, 33, 71). This house was transformed into a college of secular canons in the earlier fourteenth c. See under Secular Colleges).

BLANTYRE. Fd. by Patrick (II), E. of Dunbar and his wife Euphemia, 1239 × 1248 (*CPL*, xiii, 531–2; cf. *OPS*, i, 59, where it is said to have been fd. by Alexander II (1214–49). Its pr. was present in the parliament at Brigham on 17 March 1289/90 (*APS*, i, 85). This house, in terms of its fd'n., was a dependency of Jedburgh (*CPL*, xiii, 531–2; *Chron. Bower*, ii, 539, *CPP*, i, 553). Its dedication to the Holy Cross (*CPL*, xiii, 532) explains the reference in 1476 to a 'house or place assigned for regular canons of Holyrood . . . in the land of Blantar, Glasgow diocese' (Cameron, *Apostolic Camera*, 184). On 24 May 1476 it is stated that no canons were being maintained by the pr. and in the earlier sixteenth c. (−24 March 1537/8, according to *RSS*, ii, no. 2745), this priory is described as usually held by a canon of Jedburgh . . . non-conventual and . . . dependent cell of Jedburgh' (*St. Andrews Formulare*, ii, no. 354). Its connection with Jedburgh had become tenuous by this date, and although the pr. of the Augustinian house of Pittenweem was presented by the crown, 24 Sept. 1547 (*RSS*, iii, no. 1547), he had resigned before 6 Oct. 1549 (*ibid.*, iv, no. 446), and the priory was thereafter held by secular priests (*ibid.*, iv, nos. 446, 1683, v, no. 3319). Walter Stewart, son of Sir John Stewart of Minto, occurs as commendator in 1580 (*Scots Peerage*, ii, 82) and the priory was erected as a temporal lordship in his favour, 18 Jan. 1598/9 (*RMS*, vi, no. 833). He was raised to the peerage with title of Lord Blantyre, 10 July 1606 (*Scots Peerage*, ii, 83), and received confirmation in parliament 1617 (*APS*, iv, 563).

CAMBUSKENNETH. David I's charter 29 May—24 Aug. 1147, usually taken as the fd'n. charter, endows an already existing community of canons regular, serving the ch. of St. Mary, Stirling (*Camb. Reg.* no. 51; Lawrie, *Charters*, 400–1). The bull of confirmation of Pope Eugenius III, 30 Aug. 1147, addressed to the ab., refers to the order of Arrouaise as having been set up in this ch. (*Camb. Reg.* no. 23). The fd'n. probably dates from *c.*1140 when David I granted to the ch. of Arrouaise half the hides and a quarter of the tallow of all beasts slaughtered at Stirling (see G. W. S. Barrow, 'The Royal House and the Religious Orders', in *The Kingdom of the Scots*, 182–4). Among K. David's endowments was the land of Cambuskenneth; and from 1201 the abbey was designated by that name (*Camb. Reg.*, no. 27). It is mentioned in 1350 as having been damaged by enemies (*diabolici homines*; *ibid.*, no. 61). In 1378 it is stated that the bell tower which had been struck by lightning had collapsed on the choir of the ch, but there is no architectural evidence to suggest that the bell tower was extensively damaged at this time (Reg. Aven., 222, fo.

620v; *CPL*, iv, 240; *Hist. Mon. Comm. (Stirlingshire)*, i, 122.) The ab. was granted the mitre, 22 March 1406 (*Camb. Reg.*, no. 32). An extensive scheme of reconstruction seems to have been carried out in late medieval times and a new ab.'s hall is mentioned in 1520 (*ibid.*, no. 207; *Hist. Mon. Comm. (Stirlingshire)*, i, 122). This no doubt explains the re-dedication of the ch., buildings and burial-ground which took place, 11 July 1521 (*Camb. Reg.* no. 92). The abbey is said to have been 'ruined and cast down' by the reforming lords in 1559 (Spottiswoode, *History of Church of Scotland*, i, 280); but this is not mentioned by contemporary historians such as Lesley and Knox. The community at that date consisted of approximately nineteen canons (*Laing Chrs.*, nos. 505, 687, 904-5; *Camb. Reg.*, xxxv; SRO, Fraser Chrs., no. 194). During the sixteenth c. the abbey was held by a series of commendators including David Painter, bp. of Ross, who was provided 14 Oct. 1548 (Reg. Vat., 1682, fo. 274) and d. 1 Oct. 1558 (*Camb. Reg.*, ciii). After his death the abbey was gifted by the crown to John, Lord Erskine, who was empowered to appoint an ab. or commendator (*RSS* v, no. 1066). By virtue of this grant Adam Erskine was appointed commendator, 30 June 1562, and retained this title until his death, before 31 May 1608 (*RMS*, vi, no 2093). On that date Alexander Erskine, third son of John, second E. of Mar, in whose favour the abbey, along with Dryburgh abbey and Inchmahome priory had been erected as a temporal lordship, 1604 and 1606 (*APS*, iv, 343), was appointed commendator by his father who on 23 Aug. 1617 permanently bestowed on him the lands of Cambuskenneth (*Camb. Reg.* cxiii).

CANONBIE. A dependency of Jedburgh abbey (*Chron. Bower*, ii, 539). 'The religious house of Liddel' was confirmed to Jedburgh, as a grant of Turgis de Rosdale, by William the Lion, 1165 × 1170 (*Regesta Regum Scottorum*, ii, 163-5). In origin it may have been a church which became a priory with cure (*Glas. Reg.*, no. 114; cf. Knowles, *The Monastic Order in England*, 596-7). It was confirmed to Jedburgh by Alexander II, 28 March 1229 (*RMS*, i, App. 1, no. 94). The history of this house, which is described, 1524-47, as 'the place and cell of Canonbie' (*St. Andrews Formulare*, i, no. 291) is obscure. Henry VIII took upon himself to give orders for the suppression of this priory (which was in the 'Debateable land'), 'as others have been suppressed in England', 30 Nov. 1544 (*LP Henry VIII*, xix², no. 681). It was erected, along with Jedburgh abbey, into a temporal lordship for Alexander, lord Home, in parliament, 1606 (*APS*, iv, 360-1) and by charter, 1610 (*RMS*, vii, no. 290). The buildings were demolished before 1620 (Fraser, *Buccleuch*, i, 252, 256; ii, 465-5).

HOLYROOD. According to the chroniclers, 'the church of Holyrood began to be founded' in 1128 (*Chron. Melrose*, 32, *Chron. Holyrood*, 116, 128). The theory that the canons were originally housed in Edinburgh castle, first put forward by Father Hay in the seventeenth c., seems to be unwarranted (*ibid.*, 117n). The founder was David I, whose 'great charter' (*Holy. Lib.*, no. 1) is, however, later than 1128 (Lawrie, *Charters*, 384, 386). Holyrood was a daughter-house of Merton, in Surrey (Dickinson, *Austin Canons*, 118, n.5). The ab. was granted the mitre, 27 July 1379 (*Holy. Lib.*, 204; Reg. Aven., 216, fo. 28v). In 1322 the abbey was sacked by the English (*Chron. Bower*, ii, 278) and burned by them, in 1385 (*ibid.*, ii, 401n). It was rebuilt in the course of the fifteenth c. (*Hist. Mon. Comm.* (Edinburgh), 130-3). On 6 May 1544 it was burned by Hertford's forces (*Hamilton Papers*, ii, no. 233; *LP Henry VIII*, xix¹ nos. 533, 534; 'the late Expedicion in Scotlande' in Dalyell, *Fragments of Scottish Hist.*, 11), and again in 1547 during Somerset's expedition, when the abbey was found deserted of its canons and the lead and bells were removed (Patten, 'The Expedicion into Scotlande', in Dalyell, *Fragments*, 82). The Reformers appear to have destroyed the altars in 1559 (Lesley, *History*, 275; Knox, *Works*, i, 391). The community which had numbered about twenty-five in 1488 (*Prot. Bk. Young*, no. 103) consisted of at least twenty-one canons at the Reformation (*Holyrood Liber*, 158, 162; SRO, RH6/1904/1818; SRO, Soc. of Antiquities Muniments, i, no. 39; *Laing Chrs.*, nos. 645, 693, 834, 1025). In the sixteenth c. the abbacy was frequently held *in commendam* (*James V Letters*, 357) and the provision of Robert Stewart, infant son of James V, to the perpetual *commenda*, 14 April 1539 (Reg. Vat., 1523, fo. 59) hastened the process of secularization of much of the abbey's wealth. In 1568, Stewart exchanged the commendatorship for the temporalities of the bishopric of Orkney with Adam Bothwell, bp. of that see (*RSS*, vi, no. 506). The abbey and certain of its properties were erected into a temporal lordship for the bp's son John Bothwell, in parliament, 1606 (*APS* iv, 330-2), and by charter, 1607 (*RMS*, vi, no.

2004). The nave of the ch. continued, as in the pre-Reformation era, to be used as the parish ch. of the Canongate until 1686, it thereafter serving as the Chapel Royal until the mid-eighteenth c. (Cowan, *Parishes*, 26; *Hist. Mon. Comm.* (Edinburgh), 131, 154).

Dependency: St. Mary's Isle.

INCHAFFRAY. Originally the site of a community of 'brethren' (see under Early Foundations). Fd. as a priory by Gilbert, E. of Strathearn in 1200 (*Inchaff. Chrs.*, no. ix) and said to have been colonized from Scone (*Chron. Bower*, i, 129). But the first pr., Mael-Isu, who is described as 'presbyter and hermit' and entrusted with the selection of the first members of the new community, may also have been joined by other members of the former community (*Inchaff. Chrs.*, no. ix). It became an abbey in 1220 or 1221 (*ibid.*, 250). On 11 June 1237, a bull of Pope Gregory IX contemplated the transference of the see of Dunblane to Inchaffray, the canons of which were to have the election of the bp. (Theiner, *Vet. Mon.*, no. xc), but this did not take place. Ab. George Murray granted a letter of bailiary in favour of Laurence Lord Oliphant, 25 Jan. 1468/9 (*Inchaff. Chrs.*, 159–60), who on the ab.'s resignation, was provided as commendator 16 November 1495 (Reg. Vat., 792, fos. 287–8v). The abbey thereafter remained in the hands of a series of commendators (*Inchaff. Chrs.*, 255–7); the community consisted of approximately fourteen canons at the Reformation (*ibid.*, nos. xcv, xcviii, xcix, c; *Inchaff. Liber*, 130). On 26 July 1565 the commendatorship was conferred upon James Drummond (*Inchaff. Chrs.*, 246–8) in whose favour, as Lord Maddertie, it was erected into a temporal lordship, 31 Jan. 1609 (*ibid.*, xciii). This did not take effect, and the erection was not finally made until 15 Feb 1669 in favour of William Drummond, later Viscount Strathallan (*ibid.*, 308).

INCHCOLM. This island is said to have been the abode of a hermit (*Chron. Bower*, i, 287). Medieval writers as well as lists (both medieval and later) ascribe the foundation to Alexander I (d. 1124), and the *Scotichronicon* gives the date as *c.* 1123, or, in certain versions, 1124 (*Chron. Bower*, i, 286–7; *Chron. Fordun.*, i, 227). But although a charter, *c.* 1180, speaks of the ch. of Aberdour as having been held by the canons of Inchcolm since the time of K. Alexander (*Inchcolm Chrs.*, no. v), the earliest extant charter of this house, 1162–9, represents Gregory, bp. of Dunkeld, as surrendering and quitclaiming to the canons the island and certain lands, of which, by precept of David I, he has had custody until the canons were settled in the island (*ibid.*, no. i). Since Bp. Gregory did not take office till *c.* 1136×1147 (Watt, *Fasti*, 94), the indication is that the foundation was not complete until the end, or even after, the reign of David I (d. 1153). It may be that Alexander I originally intended to found an Augustinian house at Dunkeld, and when this project failed, the revenues were diverted to Inchcolm. An attribution of the fd'n. to Murdoch, E. of Fife, and description of the community as Cistercian (Purves, *Revenue of the Scottish Crown* (1681), 105) is inaccurate. This house, at first a priory, was erected into an abbey, 22 May 1235 (Theiner, *Vet. Mon.*, no. lxxviii). It is said that the abbey was attacked by the English 1335 and 1385 (*Chron. Bower*, ii, 318, 378) and that, 'for fear of the English', the canons spent part of 1421 on the mainland (*ibid.*, ii, 467). In 1547 the island was occupied by the English (*Inchcolm Chrs.*, xxxix–xl) and in 1548 by the French, the mks. retiring to Dunfermline for the duration of the hostilities (*ibid.*, xl; *Essays on Scottish Reformation*, 424n). The community numbered at least fifteen in 1541 (*Inchcolm Chrs.*, no. lix), but this may have been almost halved by the Reformation (*ibid.*, 70, 72–3, 216; *Laing Chrs.*, nos. 535, 775). By 1564 the convent had finally removed from the island; and only two of the canons appear to survive in 1578 (*Inchcolm Chrs.*, xl, 216). The wealth of the abbey had, however, been gradually secularized following the provision of James Stewart as titular abbot, 13 Aug. 1544 (*ibid.*, nos. lxi–lxii; Reg. Vat., 1622, fo. 105), and his assumption of the commendatorship following the death of 'Abbot' Richard Abercromby on 26 March 1549 (*Inchcolm Chrs.*, 242–3). On his creation as Lord Doune in 1581 the commendatorship was confirmed to his second son Henry Stewart (*APS*, iii, 276), in whose favour, as Lord St. Colme, the abbey and its lands were erected into a temporal lordship, in parliament, 1609 (*ibid.*, iv, 464) and by charter, 1611 (*RMS*, vii, no. 442).

INCHMAHOME. Before the erection of the priory, there was apparently a parish ch. on this island; a parson of 'insula Macholem' is mentioned, *c.* 1210 (*Camb. Reg.*, no. 122). Soon after 1238 the priory was fd. by Walter, E. of Menteith (*Inchaff. Liber*, xxxi; Fraser, *Menteith*, ii, no. 74). Although a priory, this house was not dependent on any place or monastery of regulars' (Reg. Supp., 441, fo. 25v). Its revenues were in dispute before the end of the fifteenth c. (Cameron, *Apostolic Camera*, 160–1, 178, 180, 190, 197, 201, 204, 271, 286, 305, 307). On 3 June 1508, it was annexed by Pope Julius II to the Chapel Royal of Stirling (Reg. Lat., 1208, fo. 289); but the effectiveness of this is questionable. A co-adjutor, with right of succession was appointed 15 June 1517 and resigned as prior, 16 Dec. 1529 (Vat. Arch., Libri Annatarum, 59, fo. 162; Reg. Supp., 1996, fos. 102v–103v). On that date the dissolution of the union of the priory to the Chapel Royal was confirmed, but it is clear from a royal letter of 27 Oct. 1529 that the actual dissolution preceded that date (*ibid.; James V Letters* 161). On 22 April 1536 James V is found writing to the Cardinal of Ravenna resisting the union of this house, as a cell, to Jedburgh Abbey (*ibid.*, 317). By this date the priory, to which Robert, master of Erskine, had been provided as commendator, 16 Dec. 1529 (Reg. Supp., 1996, fos. 102v–103v), was under the control of the family of Erskine from which successive commendators were appointed (*James V Letters*, 338; *Dryb. Lib.*, xxiii–xxx). The priory, which may have contained as many as eleven canons at the Reformation (NLS, Hutton Coll., vii, fos. 70, 71, 73; Fraser, *Menteith*, 331, 333, 335, 362, 365), was erected, with the abbeys of Dryburgh and Cambuskenneth, into a temporal lordship for John Erskine, second E. of Mar, 1604 and 1606 (*APS*, iv, 343).

JEDBURGH. Fd. by David I with the help of John, bp. of Glasgow, *c.* 1138 (Lawrie, *Charters*, no. clxxxix). The date, 1148, given in Smyth's Chronicle (*Kinloss Recs.*, 4) is too late. It is stated by John of Hexham that John, bp. of Glasgow, 'was buried in the church of Jedburgh where he had himself established a convent of regular clergy' (Symeon of Durham, *Opera Omnia*, ii, 321). This cannot be taken as an indication that the bp. was the founder; it must mean that he was instrumental in bringing the Augustinian canons to Jedburgh. The suggestion that 'Jedburgh was an ancient monastic church fallen into decay when David I revived it as a house of Austin canons' (M. Morgan, 'Organisation of the Scottish Church in the twelfth century', *Trans. RHS*, 4th ser., xxix, 1947, 144) is improbable; the earlier ch. referred to was situated at Old Jedburgh about five miles from the site of the Augustinian fd'n. (see under Early Religious Foundations). The original fd'n. was a priory; a prior is mentioned in 1139 (Lawrie, *Charters*, no. cxxi). The canons were apparently brought from Beauvais (see Barrow, *The Kingdom of the Scots*, 180). This house became an abbey, *c.* 1154 (Lawrie, *Annals*, no. xxxii). The declaration (Morton, *Monastic Annals, II*) that in the wars of 1297–1300 the abbey was plundered and destroyed, the lead stripped from the roof of the ch. and retained by Sir Richard Hastings, after its restoration had been ordered by the [English] king, and that the canons were reduced to such destitution that Edward I gave them asylum in England until their monastery should be repaired, is a travesty of the facts. Lead was, however, removed from the roof, *c.* 1305 (*CDS*, ii, no. 1727). In 1296 the election of a pro-English abbot was confirmed by Edward I (*ibid.*, ii, nos. 836, 837, 839). The abbot and eleven canons left the abbey on 28 Feb. 1312/13 (the day after the taking of Roxburgh castle by the Scots), obviously because their pro-English activities had endangered their safety; they were housed at Thornton-on-Humber (*ibid.*, iii, nos. 630 (1318–19), 894 (1314–26), and refused re-admission to the abbey *c.* 1325 (*CPL*, ii, 245). The hospital of Rutherford (*q.v.*) was granted to the abbot and convent, 9 Sept. 1395 (Reg. Aven., 281, fos. 294 and v). On 25 May 1476 the dependent priory of Restennet was to be united to the abbey on the death or resignation of its prior (*CPL*, xii, 507), but although the pr. resigned to facilitate union, 13 Jan. 1477 (Reg. Supp., 746, fos. 78 and v), this appears to have been ineffective. The monastic buildings are said to be in a state of disrepair at this time and in 1502, they are described as ruinous (*ADCP*, ix). On 24 Sept. 1523, the abbey was burned by the English (*LP Henry VIII*, iii², no. 3360), and again 9 June 1544 (*ibid.*, xix¹, no. 762; 'the late Expedicion' in Dalyell, *Fragments*, 14) and in Sept. 1545 (*Cal. State Papers Henry VIII*, v, 518; *LP Henry VIII*, xx², no. 456).

The fate of the convent during these upheavals is obscure, there could have been about eight canons in 1545 (*Essays on Scottish Reformation*, 236) and five named canons have been identified in post-Reformation records (SRO, RH6/2286; RSS, lviii, fo. 73). Conventual life must have been minimal during this period, but the abbey ch. was used for the ordination of clergy in 1550 (Fraser, *Stirlings of Keir*, 399–400). The commendatorship of the abbey was acquired by the Homes in the early sixteenth c. and a series of members of that family acted as commendators (Reg. Vat., 1698, fos. 171–7v) until its erection, along with Coldingham priory, into a temporal lordship for Alexander, Lord Home, in parliament, 1606 (*APS*, iv, 360–1) and by charter, 1610 (*RMS*, vii, no. 290). This house is erroneously called Cluniac (NLS, MS. 33.2.12, 2).

Dependencies: Blantyre, Canonbie, Restennet.

LOCH LEVEN, ST. SERF (PORTMOAK). Formerly a house of Culdees (see under Early Religious Foundations). David I granted the island and its ch. to the canons of St. Andrews *c.* 1150, on condition that canonical order was to be founded there and with provision for expelling those Culdees who refused to become regular canons (Raine, *North Durham*, App., 6; *St. A. Lib.*, 188–9, 219). The priory of the island of Loch Leven was further granted to the priory of St. Andrews, by Robert, bp. of St. Andrews, 1152–3 (*ibid.*, 43). In May 1268 the prior and convent of St. Andrews granted the island priory all the small teinds, obventions, mortuary dues and lands and buildings of the ch. of Portmoak, which, after the death or resignation of the vicar, was to be served by a chaplain (St. Andrews Univ. Muniments, SL 110.01 cited Marinell Ash, 'The administration of the diocese of St. Andrews, 1202–1328', Newcastle Ph.D. thesis, 1972, 228). A confirmation of this in Aug. 1268 clarified the relationship between the priory and its mother-house by ordaining that at the death of a pr. of Loch Leven the chapter of St. Andrews was to provide a new pr. from among the chapter or the cell's membership (*St. A. Lib.*, 121–2). The pr. of Loch Leven was from the thirteenth c. designated as third pr. of St. Andrews (Sibbald, *Fife*, 280; *Moray Reg.*, no. 111). In 1395 the priory, which is said to be 'non-elective', is described as dependent on the priory of St. Andrews and served by one of its canons as pr. (Reg. Aven., 296, fos. 329v–330v). The priory is frequently described as of Portmoak in the fifteenth and sixteenth c. Thus Walter Monypenny is designated pr. of Loch Leven otherwise 'Portmook' 22 Sept. 1465 (Cameron, *Apostolic Camera*, 150); there is a reference to the pr. of St. Serf's in Loch Leven or Portmoak, 9 Oct. 1544 (*RMS*, v, no. 1146), but it is called simply the priory of St. Serfs in Loch Leven, 1 Aug. 1562 (*ibid.*, iv, no. 2934). The use of the designation Portmoak may mean that the canons ultimately resided there rather than on the island, but information about the community, if one existed, is not forthcoming. Following on the resignation of the last pre-Reformation pr., John Winram, who contrary to earlier practice had also held the sub-priorship of St. Andrews, the priory of Portmoak was granted by James VI to St. Leonard's College, St. Andrews, 29 July 1580 (*RMS*, v, no. 1; *APS*, iii, 278).

MAY, see PITTENWEEM.

MONYMUSK. Erroneously called 'Monymaill in Fyfe' (Bisset, *Rolment of Courtis*, ii, 123). This was originally a Culdee community (see Early Religious Foundations). There is a reference to the building of a monastery at Monymusk, at about the end of the twelfth c., by Gilchrist, E. of Mar, 'in the church of St. Mary in which the Culdees formerly were' (*St. A. Lib.*, 374). Gilchrist may be regarded as the founder rather than the unnamed bp. of St. Andrews given as the founder in the list appended to *Scotichronicon* (*Chron. Bower*, ii 540) or Malcolm III (Canmore) (1080+) (*Aberdeen-Banff Coll.* i, 169; Lawrie, *Charters*, 235). But as the result of a complaint by William de Malvoisin, bp. of St. Andrews (who was not the diocesan bp. but who held the vill of Monymusk), that 'certain *keledei* who profess to be canons . . . and certain others in the vill of Monymusk . . . do not fear to establish a kind of regular canonry in opposition to him . . . to the prejudice and hurt of his church', Pope Innocent III, on 23 March 1209/10, appointed commissioners who established an agreement between the bp. and the Culdees. In terms of this the Culdees will have a refectory, a dormitory and an oratory, with burial rights in the cemetery of the parish ch. There will be twelve Culdees, with a thirteenth as prior, on whose death or retirement they will choose three of their number from whom the bp. of St. Andrews shall select a prior. Likewise, it shall not be lawful for the Culdees to adopt 'the life or order of monks or canons regular' without the bishop's consent, nor to exceed their appointed number. The Culdees had confirmation of their lands and revenues and undertook to do nothing to the hurt of the parish ch. of Monymusk (*St. A. Lib.*, 370–2). In charters of Duncan, E. of Mar, 1211–14, the brethren are designated 'Culdees or canons' (*ibid.*, 362) and also merely 'canons' (*ibid.*, 367). Before 19 May 1245 when a bull of Innocent IV is addressed to 'the prior and convent of Monymusk of the order of St. Augustine (*ibid.*, 372), the transformation of the Culdees into canons regular had been completed (cf. W. Douglas Simpson, 'The Augustinian Priory and parish church of Monymusk', *PSAS*, lix, 1925, 44).

The dominant role claimed by the bp. in the selection of prs. of this house indicates that the mon. did not stand initially in the same relationship to St. Andrews priory as its cells at Loch Leven and Pittenweem. These cells (*q.v.*) had been explicitly granted to the chapter of St. Andrews and Monymusk had not (cf. Simpson 'Augustinian Priory of Monymusk', 35). This procedure whereby the convent of Monymusk presented their nominee to the bp. of St. Andrews, who in turn presented the candidate to the bp. of Aberdeen, as diocesan, proved at times divisive, and succession disputes characterized the history of the house in the early fifteenth c. (*CSSR*, iii, 2, 41, 44–5, 64–5, 109–10, 127). In a vacancy shortly before 10 Sept. 1450, only two canons had been present in the priory and one had presented the other to the bp. of St. Andrews as pr. (Reg. Supp., 446, fo. 33v).

Otherwise the history of this house until the sixteenth c. is obscure. On 17 March 1548/9 and 9 Dec. 1550, it is described as ruinous (*Aberdeen-Banff Coll.*, 179, 182); on 11 July 1554 it is mentioned as having through the negligence of the pr. and his servants, been burned (*Aberdeen-Banff Illus.*, iv, 776–9); and on 27 March 1558 it is said of Monymusk that 'the place and religion thereof [are] destroyit' (*Mary of Lorraine Corresp.* no. cclxxvi). The pr. and four canons constituted the community in 1549–50 (*Aberdeen-Banff Coll.*, 180, 182), and the last surviving member of the convent appears on record, 13 Aug. 1574 (*RPC*, 1st ser., ii, 389–90). On the death of the last pre-Reformation pr., John Elphinstone who had been provided by the Pope as coadjutor to the then pr., John Fairlie, on 2 May 1543 (Reg. Supp., 2492, fos. 39v–40; Reg. Vat., 1585, fos. 13–18), the priory was gifted by the crown to John Hay, parson of Monymusk, 20 March 1561/2 (*RSS*, v, no. 1009). On the death of Hay, who was also commendator of Balmerino, the priory was granted, 13 Aug. 1574, to Alexander Forbes (*RMS*, iv, no. 2290) who *c.* 1584, considering that 'the place and monastery . . . is now almost ruined and waste', granted to his kinsman, William Forbes of Monymusk, the dilapidated houses and buildings, with provision for their restoration and the institution of a school (*Aberdeen-Banff Coll.*, 184). It is said, however, that the ruins supplied stone for the building of the Forbeses' castle of Monymusk (*ibid.*, 171). The commendatorship continued with the family of Forbes (*RMS*, v, no. 1267; vi, no. 2121) until 1617 when the priory was annexed to the bishopric of Dunblane, in parliament (*APS*, iv, 553–4).

ORONSAY. The history of this priory is obscure. It is said to have been the site of a Celtic priory which was transformed by a lord of the Isles into a priory of canons regular brought from Holyrood (*Chron. Bower*, i, 5); but there is no mention of it in the Holyrood charters. Its fd'n. has been accredited to John, lord of the Isles (1330–87), but no proof of this statement is forthcoming (Symington–Grieve, *The Book of Colonsay and Oronsay* (Edinburgh, 1923), i, 242). The appearance of the pr. of Oronsay as a papal mandatory in 1353 constitutes the first recorded notice of this house (*CPL*, iii, 490). It is called the conventual priory of St. Columba of the order of St. Augustine, on the island of Orwansay, 15 Oct. 1382 (Reg. Aven., 230, fo. 183v). Occasional notices of both priors and canons occur throughout the fifteenth and early sixteenth c. (*CPP*, i, 632; *CPL*, vii, 457–8; Cameron, *Apostolic Camera*, 92; Reg. Supp., 682, fo. 136, 2285, fos. 131–2). The last known holder of the priorship, Donald Macduffie, resigned title, with life reservation of all fruits, before 6 March 1553 (*RSS*, iv, no. 2485). Further pre-Reformation nominations by the crown appear to have been ineffectual (*ibid.*, nos. 2485, 2961; v, no. 527). On 15 Feb. 1616, James VI granted to the bp. of the Isles the island of Oronsay, along with land in Colonsay formerly belonging to the priory and other properties, all of which are incorporated in a tenandry of Oronsay (*RMS*, vii, no. 1386; *HMC 4th Rep.*, App., 479).

PITTENWEEM, see MAY under Benedictine Monks. The lands of Pittenweem were granted to the monks of May by David I, *c.* 1143 (*May Recs.*, no. 4; the date is given thus by Lawrie (*Charters*, no. clv)). While it is commonly assumed that the priory was established through the transference to Pittenweem of the community in the Isle of May during the late thirteenth or early fourteenth c., i.e. in the period within which the priory of May passed from the possession of the Benedictine abbey of Reading into the possession of the Augustinian priory of St. Andrews, it is impossible to trace the precise course of events which led to this migration or to assign it a specific date. The available evidence presents an abundance of problems and discrepancies. Attention has been drawn to the mention of a prior of Pittenweem at the beginning of the thirteenth c.: 'H. prior de pethneweme' appears as a papal judge-delegate in a record of 1212+ (NLS. MS. 15.1.18, 18)—and it has been suggested that he may be identified with Hugh de Mortimer, pr. of May (–1206) (A. A. M. Duncan, 'Documents relating to the priory of the Isle of May', *PSAS*, xc, 1956–7, 67, 69). If this identification is correct, it would seem to indicate that Pittenweem was used as an alternative designation of May before the priory was transferred from the island; this would explain the mention of a prior of Pittenweem, 25 Oct. 1270 (*APS*, i. Preface, 92) and perhaps also certain later references to prs. of this designation (e.g. *c.* 1300 (*Dryb. Lib.*, nos. 291, 292)). In a petition of the pr. and convent of St. Andrews in Edward I's parliament of 1305 or 1306, it is stated that the ab. of Reading had enfeoffed William Fraser, bp. of St. Andrews, in the priory of Pittenweem; and that he enfeoffed in it the ch. (i.e. the priory) of St. Andrews (see under May, where the sale of *May* to the bishop of St. Andrews is shown to have taken place, 1286–8). The petitioners now seek remedy for their ejection by the ab. of Reading from the priory (*Mem. de Parl.*, no. 317). Another petition in the same parliament seeks remedy on behalf of the ab. of Reading for certain wrongs done to him and his men at Pittenweem (*ibid.*, no. 318); and, on 2 Sept. 1306, Edward I reported to Aymer de Valence a complaint of the abbey of Reading that the bishop and prior of St. Andrews had invaded the Isle of May and the manor of Pittenweem, removed property and molested their men (PRO Ancient Corresp., xlvii/89). It is difficult to explain the facts that Thomas de Houburn, canon of St. Andrews and liegeman of Edward I, describes himself in a petition to that king (dated in *CDS*, 1306–7) as ousted from the priory of Pittenweem by the Scots (*CDS*, ii, no. 1964) (*v.* May) and that, on 20 Dec. 1309, Jordan, pr. of Pittenweem, is mentioned as receiving supplies from the English (*ibid.*, iii, no. 121). A pr. of Pittenweem attended the Scots parliament 6 Nov. 1314 (*APS*, i, 14); and by 1 July 1318, 'all right of the monastery of Reading in England which it had in the priory of May and Pittenweem has been transferred entirely to the monastery of St. Andrews'. To the latter house, on that date, William de Lamberton, bp. of St. Andrews, made payable the pension of 16 marks, formerly paid to Reading by the priory of May (*May Recs.*, xci–xcii). Thereafter the priory is sometimes designated as of May, sometimes as of Pittenweem and May, though, by the sixteenth century, its more usual designation is of Pittenweem. It was held *in commendam* by a number of bps. and abps. of St. Andrews, beginning with James Kennedy, who obtained it, *c.* 1447 (Dunlop, *James Kennedy*, 82). To Kennedy's successor, Patrick Graham, who also held the commend and who became first archbishop of that see, the Pope granted that the priory should be united to the archbishopric, 22 Dec. 1472 (Theiner, *Vet. Mon.*, no. dcccliii). But it appears to have been held *in commendam* rather than as specifically attached to the archbishopric by William Schevez (1477/8–1496/7), who, 26 June 1487, paid annates for the priory, 'which was formerly united and is provided anew' (Cameron, *Apostolic Camera*, 220); while Andrew Forman (1514–20/1) had held it before becoming abp. (Herkless and Hannay, *Archbishops*, ii, 12). On 22 April 1487 it is described as non-conventual (*CPL*, xiv, 157); but a charter of the pr. of Pittenweem and May, 26 April 1542, is subscribed by nine canons (*Yester Writs*, no. 590). In 1593, James VI confirmed the grant of the monastic buildings to the magistrates and community of the burgh of Pittenweem (*RMS*, v, no. 2356). The lands of the priory were erected into a temporal lordship for Frederick Stewart, 1606 *APS* iv, 361).

PORTMOAK, see LOCH LEVEN.

RESTENNET (RESTENNETH). Possibly the site of an early fd'n. (see under Early Religious Foundations). Letters of Patrick, bp. of Brechin (1 May 1361) testify to having seen a charter of David I relating to certain endowments of the ch. of Restennet (*HMC, 14th Rep.*, App., Pt. III, 187–8). There is no reason to doubt the veracity of this statement which must refer to an ecclesiastical establishment of earlier date than the priory on this site. It was this ch. of St. Peter of Restennet which Malcolm IV granted to Jedburgh abbey, 1161 × 1162, in order that a prior and convent might be placed in it (*Regesta Regum Scottorum*, 93–4, 231–2), and the pr. and 'brethren' are mentioned as dependent on Jedburgh, 23 Aug. 1242 (*HMC, 14th Rep.*, App. Pt. III, 188). In 1305 the ab. of Jedburgh obtained from Edward I a writ for the supply of oaks for the repair of the ch. and houses 'in great part destroyed and burned in the war' (*CDS*, ii, nos. 1428, 1704). On 25 May 1476 the priory was united by the Pope to the abbatial *mensa* of Jedburgh (*CPL*, xiii, 507). This annexation, if at all effective, was not complete, as a small community with a prior (Vat. Arch., Armarium xxxix, vol. 25, fos. 104v–5) continued to be maintained in the priory during the sixteenth c. On 2 May 1501 the revenues, amounting to £120 annually, of this priory where it is said only two canons have been wont to reside, were granted by Pope Alexander VI to the Chapel Royal at Stirling, with the reservation of provision for six (regular) canons (*Hist. Chapel Royal*, No. 1). Following a letter of James IV requesting its annexation, 1 March 1507/8 (*James IV Letters*, no. 156), Pope Julius II again united the priory (along with the priory of Inchmahone and the provostry of Lincluden) to the Chapel Royal (*Hist. Chapel Royal*, cxlv; *Reg. Lat.*, 1208, fo. 289). But it transpires, in letters of James IV, Nov. 1508, that the annexation of Restennet to the Chapel Royal had not taken effect and the king now proposed that it should be incorporated into the *mensa* of the abp. of St. Andrews or disponed at the abp's discretion. Neither of these courses was followed, and titular prs. still appear on record, although there is no evidence of a community (Vat. Arch., Resignationes, A, 46, fo. 207v). The priory continued to be regarded as a dependency of Jedburgh at the Reformation (*Thirds of Benefices*, 25, 159). Till 1591 the ch. was in use as a parish ch. (Fraser, *Southesk*, i, xn). The priory, which latterly had been held by a series of commendators, was erected into a temporal lordship for Viscount Fenton, afterwards E. of Kellie, in parliament, 1606 (*APS*, iv, 357) and by charter, 1614 (*RMS*, vii, no. 1024). It may be noted that the editor of the *History of the Chapel Royal of Scotland* (e.g. xxxii, xxxiv), misled apparently by Hay, who stated (Scotia Sacra, 644) that 'Rosneth' was a priory of regular canons (cf. *Hist. Chapel Royal*, xciii), confuses Restennet with Rosneath, which was not a monastic foundation (see below). Confusion also arises in an item (*CPL*, xiii, 625–6) regarding a mk. of Dundrennan who petitions for permission to migrate to the mon. of St. Peter, Ruthtyn, described as of the institution of Bonshommes, OSA, 24 Oct. 1478. The editor adds to the designation of the latter mon.: 'In the diocese of St. Andrews' and the index has 'Ruthtyn, see Restennet'. Both the location of 'Ruthtyn' and its identification with Restennet are erroneous. The Bonshommes were not found in Scotland and this place is Ruthin, in the diocese of Bangor.

ST. ANDREWS. Plans for the fd'n. of a cathedral community of Augustinian canons seem to have been under way in 1124 but the new community was not finally established until 1144 when the priory was eventually fd. and endowed by Robert, bp. of St. Andrews (see Barrow, *The Kingdom of the Scots*, 212–21; *St. A. Lib.*, 122) (On the relations of the priory with the Culdees see KILRIMONT under Early Religious Foundations). In 1147 Pope Eugenius III gave the rights of electing the bp. to the pr. and canons (*ibid.*, 48). (St. Andrews was one of the two Scottish cathedrals whose clergy were regulars; the other was Whithorn which had Premonstratensian canons. See under Monastic Cathedrals.) The relationship between the bp. of St. Andrews and his cathedral mon. is uncertain. In theory the bp. might act as ab., but at St. Andrews the evidence is 'scanty and not very clear cut' (see M. Dilworth, 'The Augustinian Chapter of St. Andrews', *Innes Rev.*, xxv, (1974), 22–25). Free election of their prior was granted by the bp. to the convent in the twelfth and thirteenth c. (*St. A. Lib.*, 126, 171). The pr. became mitred, 27 April 1418 (*ibid.*, 412). The priory had thirty canons in 1555, but nine other canons who are found only in post-Reformation documents were probably members of the community before August. 1560. The number of canons, who were canons of St. Andrews only, for Pittenweem (*q.v.*) remained a separate community, certainly numbered no less than thirty-two and no more than thirty-nine (M. Dilworth, 'The Augustinian Chapter of St. Andrews', 26–7). There is no record of damage done to the priory buildings at the Reformation, but they are described as 'decayit' in 1597 (*APS*, iv, 155). The last pre-Reformation pr. was Patrick Hepburn who had succeeded his uncle John Hepburn in 1526, having previously been provided as his coadjutor (*HMC 9th Rept.*, App., 191) and held office until his appointment as bp. of Moray in 1538 Watt, *Fasti*, 217). Thereafter, James Stewart, later E. of Moray, an illegitimate son of James V, was provided as commendator, 14 June 1538 (Reg. Vat., 1511, fo. 156). After his assassination the commendatorship was granted 9 Oct. 1570 (*RSS*, vi, no. 930), to Robert Stewart, brother of Mathew, E. of Lennox, and he held this until his death; following upon which, Ludovic, Duke of Lennox was appointed commendator, 21 Aug. 1586 (*RMS*, v, no. 1036). The priory was erected into a temporal lordship for the duke, in parliament, 1592 and 1606 (*APS*, iii, 589; iv, 353–5) and by charters 1593 and 1611 (*RMS*, v, no. 2273; vii, no. 464).

Dependencies: Loch Leven; Pittenweem; see also MONYMUSK.

ST. MARY'S ISLE or THE ISLE OF TRAIL. A fabulous account of the fd'n. of this priory attributes its erection to Fergus of Galloway (d.1161) (*Bannatyne Misc.*, ii, 19ff). It is recorded that Fergus gave to the abbey of Holyrood the 'island of Trail' (*Holy. Lib.*, 24. 38) and the attribution of this foundation to him (*Chron. Pluscarden*, i, 405) may be correct, William, prior of Galloway, who occurs with the abbot and prior of Holyrood, *c.* 1173, almost certainly belonged to this house (*St. A. Lib.*, 135). The priory appears on record, 1189×*c.* 1193 when property given by Roland, son of Uchtred, lord of Galloway, was confirmed to it (*Regesta Regum Scottorum*, ii, no. 293). A pr. of the Isle is mentioned in a papal letter, 22 Feb., 1219/20 (Theiner, *Vet. Mon.*, no. xxxii) and William, pr. of the Isle, occurs as an emissary of Alan of Galloway to Henry III, –18 April 1220 (*CDS*, i, no. 754). David, pr. of the Isle, witnesses the fd'n. charter of Sweetheart abbey, 10 April 1273 (*Laing Chrs.*, no. 46). On 1 Aug. 1323, Robert I gave the tenth of the royal pleas between the rivers Cree and Nith to the ab. and convent of Holyrood for the support of the pr. and canons of the Isle of St. Mary (SRO, RH.6/274). It is described as non-conventual, 9 May 1446 (Reg. Supp., 411, fo. 153v). Presentation to the priorship was still being exercised by the ab. and convent of Holyrood in favour of canons from the mother-house in 1484 (Reg. Supp., 833, fo. 254v). But a letter of James IV to the cardinal of St. Mark, 1 March 1511/12, describes this priory as a cell of Holyrood and indicates both that it has become virtually independent of that abbey and threatens to become ruinous. James asks that it should be reunited to Holyrood or granted to the ab. of that house *in commendam* (*James IV Letters*, no. 426). In the event, a relation of the then ab. became prior, but after his death before 7 July 1525 (Reg. Supp., 1858, fos. 51v–52), the priory was held by a series of commendators (*ibid.*, 2213, fos. 257 and v; *James V Letters*, 315, 322; *RSS*, iii, no. 472; v, nos. 379, 3078). On 23 Oct. 1587, James VI granted certain lands of St. Mary's Isle to James Lidderdale (to whom the most part of the priory lands had been leased) and incorporated these in a tenandry (*RMS*, v, no. 1397). The priory lands were finally granted to James Lidderdale and his son Thomas (the priory being suppressed) as a free tenandry, by charter, 10 Feb. 1608 (*ibid.*, vii, no. 2029). See *Dumfries. Trans.*, 3rd series, xxxvi, 1–26.

SCONE. Said to have been originally occupied by Culdees, though this cannot be verified (see under Early Religious Foundations). Scone was an ancient seat of the kings of Scotland. The fd'n. of this house as an Augustinian priory by Alexander I cannot be fixed with certainty. It is ascribed to 1114 by some chroniclers (*Chron. Bower*, i, 286; Edin. Univ. Chronicle cited Anderson, *Early Sources*, ii, 159n) and to 1115 by others (*Chron. Melrose*, 65). It has been averred (Lawrie, *Charters*, 280 ff) that the so-called foundation charter *c.* 1120 (*Scone Lib.* no. 1) is spurious, and that the statement made there and in the *Scotichronicon* that the king had canons sent to Scone from Nostell is doubtful, on the ground that in 1115 St. Oswald's (Nostell) was not yet a house of regular canons (Lawrie, *Charters*, 286); and that Adelwald (Athelwulf), pr. of St. Oswald's, who is said to have acceded to the king's request, did not hold that office until 1128 (*ibid.*, 281). None of these pronouncements are valid. The charter of *c.* 1120 may be genuine (*Regesta Regum Scottorum*, i, 36–7); Athelwulf was the king's contemporary (J. Wilson, 'The foundation of the Austin priories of Nostell and Scone', *SHR*, vii, 1910, 156–7) and the priory of St. Oswald, which had originated in a settlement of hermits *c.* 1114, had adopted the full rule of St. Augustine by Jan. 1120, although a new site at Nostell may not have been occupied until 1122 (Knowles and Hadcock, *Medieval Religious Houses England*, 169). There can be little doubt that Scone was colonized from Nostell as a reference, 4 Feb. 1420/1 to the mon. of St. Oswald in England from which our mon. of Scone took its origin (*St. Andrews Copiale*, 103) adequately proves, but the date of fd'n. may be somewhat later than 1114 or 1115. The suggestion of *c.* 1120 (Barrow, *The Kingdom of the Scots*, 171) would appear to be more acceptable. The priory became an abbey, —5 Dec. 1164 (*Scone Lib.*, no. 18; *Chron. Holyrood*, 139, 140n); a charter of Malcolm IV, 24 May 1163–23 May 1164, declares that after the ch. of Scone had been destroyed by fire, the king had constituted an abbot in it 'for the stability and advancement' of that ch. (*Regesta Regum Scottorum*, i, no. 243). In 1218 there appears to have been an attempt to dislodge the Augustinian canons in favour of Premonstratensians from Hornby in Lancashire (see note by G. O. Sayles, in *SHR*, xxxi, 137–8). The abbey was pillaged and destroyed by an English army in 1298 (*Scone Lib.*, no. 124). The ab. became mitred, 12 Sept. 1395 (*ibid.*, no. 192). The abbey was held *in commendam* by James Kennedy, bp. of Dunkeld, 1439–47 (Dunlop, *James Kennedy*, 38, 82–3), and from 5 Nov. 1518 by Alexander Stewart, who continued to hold the abbey on his appointment to the bishopric of Moray, 13 Sept. 1529 (Reg. Vat., 1092, fos. 33–43;

Vat. Arch., Acta Misc., 17, fo. 175). His successor as bp., Patrick Hepburn, retained the commend to which he was provided, 14 June 1538 (*James V Letters*, 342–3; Vat. Arch., Acta Misc., 17, fo. 233v). The abbey was attacked and burned by Reformers (Lesley, *History*, 274; Knox, *Works*, i, 359–61); the mon., houses and ch. are said, in a charter of 26 Aug. 1559 to be 'now burned to the ground' (*Bamff Chrs.*, no. 59). At this time the community consisted of about sixteen canons (*ibid.*, nos. 59, 73; *Scone Lib.*, 207, 212; *RSS*, vii, no. 272; SRO, RH 6 1701/1851/2025). Following the forfeiture of Hepburn the benefice was conferred on William, lord Ruthven, 2 Sept. 1571 (*RSS*, vi, no. 1267) and on his son John Ruthven, 7 May 1580 (*RMS*, iv, no. 3011). It was erected by charter into a temporal lordship for William, lord Ruthven as E. of Gowrie, 20 Oct. 1581 (*RMS*, v, no. 258); was temporarily lost on the forfeiture of the earl in 1584 (*ibid.*, no. 695), but was restored to his son in 1586 (*APS*, iii, 479). His brother John, who succeeded to the earldom, was ratified in his title and the abbacy of Scone in 1588 (*ibid.*, 591) but was forfeited after the Gowrie conspiracy in 1600 (*ibid.*, iii, 192–3, 195–9, 203–12). The abbey was again erected into a temporal lordship for David Murray, Lord Scone, and later Viscount Stormont in parliament, 1606 (*ibid.*, iv, 328) and by charter, 1608 (*RMS*, vi, no. 2138).

STRATHFILLAN. On 26 Feb. 1317/18, Robert I granted the patronage of the ch. of Killin to Inchaffray abbey so that this house might provide a canon to celebrate divine service in the ch. of Strathfillan (*Inchaff. Chrs.*, no. cxxiii). The development of this fd'n. into a priory is seen in a charter, 28 Oct. 1318, whereby William, bp. of Dunkeld, bestowed this ch. on the ab. of Inchaffray and the canons of that monastery, who by appointment of the ab. shall serve in the chapel of St. Fillan in Glendochart (provided that, according to the capabilities of the place, a sufficient number of canons should be settled there) 'so that all the fruits and revenues of the said church [Killin] should be converted by the ordinance of the abbot to the use of the prior and canons dwelling at the said chapel for divine worship' (*ibid.*, no. cxxvi). There is a record of a grant to the fabric of the ch., in 1329 (*ER*, i, 214). The presentation of a prior by the ab. and convent of Inchaffray, patrons 'from ancient custom' was confirmed by the Pope, 16 July 1414 (Reg. Aven., 343, fo. 362), but thereafter there is difficulty in establishing the succession of prs. until 2 Oct. 1498 (*RMS*, ii, no. 2458). It is described as the mon. or chapel royal of Strathfillan, 28 Feb. 1542–3 (*RMS*, iii, no. 2993). This was evidently a small and poor fd'n.; its rental is given, in 1573, as £40 (*Inchaff. Chrs.*, xlvi). For an account of this house, see *Inchaff. Chrs.*, xliv–xlvi. Spottiswoode (393) declares that it was bestowed on Campbell of Glenorchy; but the revenues of the priory were apparently granted to Archibald Campbell of Glencarradale by the crown, 19 March 1607 (Gillies, *In Famed Breadalbane*, 239).

TRAILL, see ST. MARY'S ISLE.

UNCERTAIN FOUNDATION

Loch Tay. Alexander I granted an island in Loch Tay to the canons of Scone 'so that a church of God may be built there for me and for the soul of the late Sibilla (his queen) and that they may serve God there in religious habit' (*Scone Lib.*, no. 2). This charter must have been given between 13 July 1122 (the date of Queen Sibilla's death) and 23 April 1124 (the date of the king's death). *Scotichronicon* (lib. ii, cap. x (*Chron. Bower*, i, 46)) mentions 'Louch-Tay' as a 'cell of canons of Scone'. But while the island appears among the possessions of Scone in a charter of Malcolm IV, 1163–4 (*Sconee Lib.*, no. 5) and bulls of 1164 and 1226/7 (*ibid.*, nos. 18, 103), there is apparently no reference in records (including those of Scone) to a priory until 29 April 1612, when the 'lands, castles, fisheries, etc.', which belonged to the temporality of the priory of the island of Loch Tay 'appear in a crown charter of confirmation granted to David, Lord Scone (*RMS*, vii, no. 645). A similar reference, to the lands, etc., belonging from of old to the temporality of the priory of Loch Tay is found, 18 May 1642 (*Perth Retours*, no. 507). There is, however, no mention of such a priory in the acts of parliament of 1581 and 1606 erecting the abbey of Scone into a temporal lordship (*APS*, iii, 263; iv, 328); and neither the references to its properties (which are late, formal and exaggerated) nor the statement of Spottiswoode (386) that in his time 'the most part of the buildings' were still extant (since those to which he refers were very probably secular: see Lawrie, *Charters*, 295) can be taken as proving unequivocally that the priory was established. Lawrie is not sure that the charter of Alexander I is genuine and while admitting that 'the story that a priory was built has been generally accepted', doubts the correctness of Spottiswoode's statements, e.g. that 'Loch Tay . . . was a cell or priory belonging to Scone, founded by K. Alexander in the year 1122' (*op. cit.*, pp. 294–5). The existence of this priory must be regarded as uncertain. Sir Walter Scott's description, in *The Fair Maid of Perth*, of a burial at this priory is picturesque but unhistorical and his statement, in a note to that novel, that the last inhabitants of it were three nuns is based on a fanciful explanation of the name of a local fair.

SUPPOSED FOUNDATIONS

Aberuthven. The statement of MacGibbon and Ross that 'this church was a cell of Inchaffray' (*Eccles. Archit.*, iii, 486) is utterly inaccurate. This church was granted to the 'brethren' at Inchaffray, *c.* 1198 (*Inchaff Chrs.*, no. iii) and to the Augustinian canons there, *c.* 1200 (*ibid.*, no. xiii). But it was a parish ch. and in no sense a 'cell' of that abbey.

Carinish. 'Scarinche' in Lewis [*sic*] is described as a cell of Inchaffray in the list appended to *Scotichronicon* (*Chron. Bower*, ii, 540) and by Spottiswoode (393), who also attributes its foundation to 'the Macleods of the Lewis'. Dowden, however, shows that Inchaffray held the chapel and lands of 'Karynch' in *Uist* (*Inchaff. Chrs.*, xlvii–xlviii); there is no evidence of a priory. Monro mentions five parish chs. in Uist (*Western Isles*, pp. 76–7) but no monastery, nor does he mention Scarinche in Lewis. This 'cell' is apocryphal.

Colonsay. *Scotichronicon* (lib. ii, cap. x (*Chron. Bower*, i, 45)) declares that there was an abbey of regular canons here and to this is added by Spottiswoode (390) that it was founded by the lord of the Isles and colonized from Holyrood. Hay (Scotia Sacra, 458) elaborates this by stating that while the founder's name had been lost, there existed at the Vatican a letter addressed to the convent; and he gives alleged details of the first two abbots. Finally, *Origines Parochiales* (ii¹, 281), having accepted the foregoing statements, goes on to make the (absurd) assertion that 'it is traditionally believed that the abbey of Colonsay, which in all probability had been decayed after the retirement of the second abbot recorded by Father Hay, was that of which Oronsay was the priory'. These accounts appear to be without foundation. There is no mention of Colonsay in the Holyrood charters. Monro's description (1549) mentions no monastery (*Western Isles*, 60); and it is impossible to believe that there were Augustinian foundations in both of the closely contiguous islands of Oronsay and Colonsay. According to a bull of 1203, the abbey of Iona held the ch. and island of Colonsay (*Highland Papers*, i, 83). Oronsay priory is also said, in the sixteenth c., to have held land in Colonsay (*HMC Rep.*, iv. App., 479).

Crusay. Mentioned by Spottiswoode (390) as in the Western Isles. The alleged fd'n. appears also in seventeenth-c. MS. lists; it appears to be a misreading for Oronsay. It is not to be identified with Crossaig in Kintyre, at which site, the ecclesiastical remains are not indicative of a monastery.

Kinkell. This was simply a parish ch., granted to Inchaffray abbey, *c.* 1200 (*Inchaff. Chrs.*, no. xv). There is nothing to support the idea that it was a cell of that abbey.

Rodel (*Rowadill*). Monro describes it as 'ane monastery with ane steipell . . . foundit and biggit by McCloyd of Harrey' (*Western Isles*, 86). It is included among Augustinian houses by Spottiswoode (390), who also ascribes its foundation to MacLeod of Harris. Hay (Scotia Sacra, 644) calls it a monastery of canons regular. There is, however, no reason to regard this as other than a parish ch. or perhaps a chapel.

Roslin. Mentioned by Gervase of Canterbury as a priory of black canons (Anderson, *Scottish Annals*, 327). This is obviously an error for 'Rostin[oth]', a form of the name Restennet (see above).

Rosneath. 'It is said by some,' declares Spottiswoode (391), 'that this place was a monastery of canons regular.' He rightly adds: 'It appears it was only a parish church.' See RESTENNET above with which it has been confused.

Roxburgh. An Augustinian house is said to have existed here (Anderson, *Early Sources*, ii, 183 n., 697). This is evidently due to confusion with the Franciscan friary (*q.v.*).

THE PREMONSTRATENSIAN CANONS

GENERAL NOTES

THESE canons regular were also known as the White Canons from their religious habit (originally greyish of unbleached wool). Their founder, St. Norbert, established the first house at Prémontré near Laon in 1120. The order expanded rapidly and eventually there were several hundreds of houses throughout Europe, all under Prémontré as the head house. Norbert placed his canons under the rule of St. Augustine but he organized his new order on Cistercian lines. As in the Cistercian order, new Premonstratensian abbeys were to be colonized by at least thirteen religious, including an abbot, from the mother-houses which were nominated to establish them.

The history of the houses of this order in Scotland is difficult to reconstruct as the only surviving chartulary is that of the abbey of Dryburgh. The foundation of that abbey in 1150 is usually reckoned as marking the establishment of the order in Scotland, but a case can be mounted in support of Soulseat's claim to have been the first Scottish Premonstratensian house.

The development of the Scottish *circariae* and the question of primacy of the abbey of Soulseat (below) have been dealt with by Backmund, *Monasticon Praemonstratense*, ii, 94–6. On the latter point, it may be mentioned that a letter of James IV to the General of the Premonstratensians, 1 May 1507, states that the prior of Whithorn has extorted royal letters to the General asking that his house should be ranked first of the order in Scotland and that he should have the full jurisdiction in visitation and reformation which the abbot of Soulseat, despite his much inferior status, then held. The General complied. But King James referred the question to the archbishop of St. Andrews, who found that Dryburgh, and not Soulseat or Whithorn, was at the head of the order. He accordingly besought the archbishop to put the matter right (*Letters of James IV*, no. 107). On the same date, the archbishop writes to the General asking that the old pre-eminence of Dryburgh should be revived.

THE PREMONSTRATENSIAN HOUSES

Name	County	Rank	Minimum income (1561)	Fd.	Date D. or Sec.		(Mother-house)
* DRYBURGH	Berwick	Abbey	£2210	1150	1606		(Alnwick)
‡ §FEARN	Ross	Abbey	£1010	1221–2 or *c.* 1227 (at Old Fearn) *c.* 1238 (at New Fearn)	1609		(Whithorn)
HOLYWOOD or Dercongal	Dumfries	Abbey	£880(?)	–1225	1609		(Soulseat)
SOULSEAT	Wigtown	Abbey	£810(?)	–1161(?)	1630		(Prémontré)
TONGLAND	Kirkcudbright	Abbey		1218	1612		(Cockersand)
* WHITHORN	Wigtown	Priory	£2540	*c.* 1175	1612		(Soulseat)

DRYBURGH. This house was fd. 10 Nov. 1150 by Hugh de Moreville (*Chron. Melrose*, 74; *Dryb. Lib.*, no. 14); the alleged fd'n. charter (*ibid.*, lxix), which attributes the foundation to David I is spurious (Lawrie, *Charters*, 436); the convent which evidently came from Alnwick arrived on 13 Dec. 1152 (*Chron. Melrose*, 74). (The abbot of Alnwick is called father abbot of Dryburgh, 18 Dec. 1477, when confirmation of the election of abbots of this house is said to belong to him by ancient and approved custom: Reg. Supp., 763, fos. 119v–120). On its pre-eminence in the order in Scotland, see above. On 9 March 1390/1, the abbey was granted the lands and possessions of South Berwick (i.e. Berwick-on-Tweed) nunnery (*RMS*, i, no. 832). This grant and that of the hospitals of Lauder and Smailholm (*q.v.*) were confirmed to the abbey by the Pope 30 Dec. 1429 (*CSSR*, iii, 66–8, 243–4). It was burned by the English in 1322 (*Scotichronicon*, lib. xii, cap. iv; *Chron. Bower*, ii, 278) and in 1385 (*ibid.*, lib. xiv, cap. i; 401). It is again reported as devastated by fire, 13 Aug. 1461, when, on account of being burdened by a father abbot, who resided in England, the ab. and convent sought papal protection (Reg. Supp., 542, fo. 255). The abbey was probably damaged again in 1523 since on 13 Dec. of that year, the duke of Albany, writing to the cardinal of Eusebius, speaks of the mon. having suffered loss and destruction through English raids and the need of an abbot who would revive monastic life and repair the buildings (*James V Letters*, 95); and, again, except the ch., in Nov. 1544 (*LP Henry VIII*, xix2, no. 625) and Sept. 1545 (*ibid.*, xx2, no. 456). The convent which consisted of at least seventeen canons in addition to the abbot in 1537/8 appears to have been reduced to about twelve canons by 1558 (*Dryb. Lib.*, 281, 284, 286, 302; *Laing Chrs.*, no. 727; SRO, Brooke of Biel Muniments, nos. 1180–1). After the death of Ab. Andrew Liderdale in 1506–7 the abbey was held by a series of commendators (*Dryb. Lib.*, xix–xxiii). After the provision of Thomas Erskine, 6 April 1541 (Vat. Arch., Acta Miscellanea, 8, fos. 264–265), the commendatorship continued with that family (*Dryb. Lib.*, xxiii–xxxi). It was erected, along with Cambuskenneth abbey and Inchmahome priory, into the temporal lordship of Cardross in favour of John Erskine, E. of Mar, in parliament, 1604 and 1606 (*APS*, iv, 343 ff.) and by charter, 1610 and 1615 (*RMS*, vii, nos. 301, 1222).

FEARN. Said to have been fd. by Ferquhard, E. of Ross who is reputed to have brought two white canons and relics of St. Ninian from Galloway to 'Farne beside Kincardin in Stracharrin', 1221–2 or *c.* 1227 (Cronicle of Earlis of Ross, cited *OPS*, ii2, 414–5; *Beauly Chrs.*, 313). The case for colonization from Whithorn is strengthened by the presentation of at least three thirteenth-c. abbots by the prior of Whithorn, who also confirmed a four-teenth-c. election (*OPS* ii2, 435; *Moray Reg.*, 282; Balnagown Chrs., cited *OPS*, ii2, 435). About 1238, the abbey was transferred to a site in the parish of Tarbat, after which it was called New Fearn (Cronicle of Earlis of Ross, cited *OPS*, ii2, 435). Pope Urban IV (1261–4) is said to have confirmed conventual regulations (*ibid.*). The abbey was rebuilt between 1338 and 1372 (*ibid*). The pr. of Whithorn confirmed the election of an abbot in 1440 'by observed custom' (Reg. Supp., 369, fo. 168), and further rebuilding appears to have continued through this century (Cronicle of Earlis of Ross, cited *OPS*, ii², 436). Nevertheless, in a letter of James V to Pope Paul III, 9 March 1540/1, the house is described as ruinous and neglected (*James V Letters*, 420–1). If true, this might be attributed to a series of commendators who, commencing with Andrew Stewart, bp. of Caithness, held the mon. from 1508 (Vat. Arch., Introitus et Exitus, 543, fo. 91v; Reg. Vat. 1201, fos. 251–3; Reg. Supp. 1882, fos. 207v–208v). The convent appears to have consisted of five or more canons at the Reformation (NLS, Hutton Coll., xi, part 2, fo. 12). On 1 Feb. 1597/8 the manor of Fearn, 'called of yore the monastery of Fearn,' was granted in feu to Patrick Murray of Geanies (*RMS*, vi, no. 650; cf. *APS*, iv, 240 ff.). The abbey was annexed to the bishopric of Ross, in parliament, 1609 (*APS*, iv, 446).

HOLYWOOD or DERCONGAL. The identity of the founder and the date of fd'n. are unknown. One list (NLS. MS. 33.2.12) gives this house as Cistercian and the founder as Devorgilla, daughter of Alan of Galloway, but this is evidently due to confusion with Sweetheart abbey. An ab. of Dercongal is a papal mandatory, 18 Dec. 1225 (*Pais. Reg.*, 320; this is the reference mentioned by Spottiswoode (399). A poor's hospital was founded within the enclosure or limits of the mon. before 1362 (see under Hospitals). Otherwise the history of the house is obscure and few of its abbots can be identified until the end of the fifteenth c. The abbey was held *in commendam* by William Kennedy, ab. of Crossraguel from 13 Dec. 1523 (Theiner, *Vet Mon.* no. dccccxlv) till his death, following which, Thomas Campbell was provided 22 Feb. 1550 (Reg. Vat. 1729, fos. 69v–71v). He retained the commendatorship until his death in 1580 (*RSS*, vii, nos. 2150, 2378). The convent numbered at least eleven at the Reformation (SRO, RH6/1731/1896/2228). In 1609 the abbey was erected, ineffectively into a temporal lordship for Kirkpatrick of Closeburn (*APS*, iv, 464). It was finally erected for John Murray, afterwards E. of Annandale, in parliament 1617 (*ibid.*, iv, 575) and by charter, 1618 (*RMS*, viii, no. 1817).

SOULSEAT. Said, rather improbably, to have been fd. as a Cistercian abbey in 1148 (see under Cistercian Houses). The Obituary of Prémontré and the Necrology of Newhouse (cited Backmund, *Monasticon Praemonstratense*, ii, 109n) as well as lists of religious houses (e.g. *Chron. Bower*, ii, 538; EU MS. Db. 6. 19; NLS MS. 22. 1. 14; the two later lists describe Soulseat as Cistercian) ascribe the fd'n. of this abbey to Fergus of Galloway (d. 12 May 1161). It has been argued (Backmund, *op. cit.*, ii, 109), from the fact that the Premonstratensian General Chapter gave the primacy in the (Scottish) *circaria* to Soulseat that the latter abbey was presumably first of the order and anterior in fd'n. to Dryburgh, i.e. its fd'n. took place, –1150–2. (On the question of its primacy, see p. 100 above). Counter-arguments to the effect that this abbey, like Whithorn, its daughter-house, must have been founded during the episcopate of Bp. Christian, 1154–86 (C. A. Ralegh Radford 'Ecclesiastical reforms in the twelfth century', *Dumfries. Trans.*, 3rd ser., xxvii, 103–4) are unsubstantiated. Indeed, the Obituary of Prémontré specifically distinguishes between Fergus, as founder of Soulseat and Whithorn (*q.v.*), and Bp. Christian who is accredited only with the fd'n. of the latter (*Annalectes de l'Ordre de Prémontré*, v–viii, 83, 107). The argument for the earlier date of fd'n. is strengthened by the fact that this house is mentioned as a daughter-house of Prémontré (Le Paige, *Bibliotheca Praem. Ord.*, 333), though this may mean that it passed from another order over to the White Canons, and it has been suggested that the house founded by Fergus was Augustinian. (Backmund, 'The Praemonstratensian Order in Scotland', *Innes Rev.*, iv, 36–7). On the other hand the first ab. of this house appears to have been Michael who is described in the obituary of Prémontré as '*primi abbatis ordinis nostris in Galweia*' (*Obit. Prem.*, Oct. 24; cf. Backmund, *op. cit.*, ii, 116). In 1386 the mon. was reputedly in a ruinous and collapsed condition on account of war (Reg. Aven., 273, fos. 548–8v). The history of the house is obscure. It was gifted by the crown 18 Sept. 1532 and thereafter provided *in commendam* to James Johnstone, rector of Johnstone, 18 July 1533 (*RSS*, ii, no. 1404; Reg. Vat., 1410, fos. 9–13v; *James V Letters*, 213), and thereafter passed in 1545 to his successor John Johnstone who remained in office until 1598 (*LP Henry VIII*, i, 295; *RSS*, vii, no. 1938; *RMS*, v, 785). The convent appears to have been much reduced in numbers at the Reformation, only two canons being identifiable at that period (*Wigtownshire Chrs.*, 111; SRO, Acts and Decreets, xcii, 387; *RSS*, vii no. 2243). A series of commendators was appointed 1598–1630 when the abbey was annexed to the parsonage of Portpatrick (*Wigtownshire Chrs.*, 98–99; *APS*, v, 132). See *Wigtownshire Chrs.*, 85–113.

TONGLAND. This fd'n. is ascribed in certain lists (e.g. *Chron. Bower*, ii, 538; NLS. MS. 33.2.12) to Fergus of Galloway, but this is unacceptable. The ch. of 'Tungeland' was granted to the abbey of Holyrood by Uchtred, prince of Galloway (1160 × 1164), and this grant was later confirmed by John, bp. of Galloway (1189 × 1206) (*Holy. Lib.*, nos. 27, 29; App. I, no. 1). This was not a monastic ch., and it was reconveyed to the abbey of Tongland on its fd'n. (Cowan, *Parishes*, 198). The founder, according to other lists (EU MS. Db.6.19; NLS MSS. 22. 1. 14, 31. 6. 1) was Alan of Galloway (d. 1234), and this seems probable. A statement in the Catalogus Ninivensis (2). 'In the diocese of Candida Casa, the daughter house of Cockersand, was founded in the year of grace 1218: Tongland' (Backmund, *Monasticon Praemonstratense*, ii, 111), would seem to bear this out. The prior and the sacrist are said to have been killed during the insurrection in Galloway in 1235 (*Chron. Melrose*, 146). James IV, probably in 1509, requested Pope Julius II to bestow this abbey on David, bp. of Candida Casa, so that he might reform its discipline and repair its ruins (*James IV Letters*, no. 289); and it was held *in commendam* by that bp., 1510–25, and thereafter personally retained by David, who resigned the bishopric in 1526 (*James IV Letters*, no. 289; Reg. Lat. 1470, fos. 157v–160v; Watt, *Fasti*, 132). In 1529, various proposals as to the deposition of the abbacy were made (*James V Letters*, 153–4; Reg. Supp. 1980, fo. 203v), but eventually on 27 Oct. of that year, when the abbey is described as ruinous, although a few mks. remain, James V, in turn, wrote to Pope Clement VII and the cardinal of Ancona seeking the annexation of Tongland to the bishopric of Galloway (*James V Letters*, 161–2); and this union was sanctioned by a bull of 14 Jan. 1529/30 (Reg. Vat. 1403, fos. 137–140), while King James besought confirmation of it from Pope Paul III, 3 July 1541. (*Ep. Regum Scotorum*, ii, 115; *James V Letters*, 425) (see *Dumfries. Trans.*, 3rd ser., xxvii, 128–9). At the Reformation about eleven canons remained in this house (*Wigtownshire Chrs.*, nos. 249, 346; SRO RH6/1667/1712/2126). Except for a period 1588–*c.* 1606, when the abbey was held by William Melville as commendator (*APS*, iv, 156, 308), it remained annexed to the bishopric. This annexation was confirmed in parliament, Oct. 1612 (*RMS*, vii, no. 1238).

WHITHORN. The fd'n. is attributed in numerous lists to Fergus prince of Galloway (d. 1161). The obituary of Prémontré records, under 12 May, the count of Galloway, founder of Soulseat and Candida Casa (*HMC. Rep. Ancaster*, 484). On the other hand, a late source (the Annals of Maurice of Prato) states under 1177, 'about this time Christian, bishop of Candida Casa, in Galloway, . . . changed the canons regular of his cathedral ch. into Praemonstratensians' (Annales quoted in Migne, *Patr. Lat.*, 198, col. 27, cf. coll. 33 and 54). If accurate, the nature of the community in existence before 1175 × 1177 is obscure. A community associated with a 'minster' already situated on this site may have been in existence before this date (see under Early Religious Foundations). On the other hand, arguments have been advanced for a shortlived Augustinian community founded by Fergus (Backmund, *Monasticon Praemonstratense*, ii, 113–14; Watt, *Fasti*, 133–4) and although there is no firm evidence to support this contention, such a transition from Augustinian to Praemonstratensian canons was not unknown in England and on the continent (Knowles and Hadcock, *Medieval Religious Houses, England*, 187–8). The priory appears to have been colonized from Soulseat (*James IV Letters*, no. 107). The names of the prior and twenty canons are recorded, *c.* 1235 (*Reg. of Walter Gray, archbishop of York*, 172–3). There are said to be no more than twelve claustrals in 1408 when the prior and canons are to be compelled to pay half their collective fruits and rents for ten years to help repair the ch. of Whithorn, a popular place of pilgrimage where the blessed Ninian is buried (Reg. Aven., 330, fos. 431–1⁵). A century later the convent consisted of the prior and at least twenty-four other canons, although this number may have been reduced to about sixteen at the Reformation (*Wigtownshire Chrs.*, 26, 35, 125, 248–9; NLS Hutton Coll., i, part 2, fos. 10, 42). From 1515 the priory was held by a series of commendators (for list of whom see G. Donaldson, 'The bishops and priors of Whithorn', *Dumfries. Trans.*, 3rd ser., xxvii, 145 ff.). The priory was granted to the bp. of Galloway in 1605 (RSS, lxxiv, fo. 105), and, in parliament, 1612 (*RMS*, vii, no. 1238). This house is erroneously classed as for white mks., by Gervase of Canterbury (Anderson, *Scottish Annals*, 328) and in lists (Anderson, *Early Sources*, ii, 700). See G. Donaldson, 'The bishop and priors of Whithorn' in *Dumfries. Trans.*, 3rd ser. xxvii, 127 ff and *Wigtownshire Chrs.*, 1–36.

SUPPOSED FOUNDATION

Fidra (Elbottle). The island of Elbottle (now known as Fidra) was granted by William de Vaux to the canons of Dryburgh (*Dryb. Lib.*, no. 105) and, *c.* 1220, canons of that abbey were serving the ch. of St. Nicholas there (*ibid.*, nos. 23, 25, 26, 104). Lawrie calls this a 'cell' (*Charters*, 329), but that term exaggerates its status. About 1240, the foundation is specifically described as a 'chantry' (a somewhat unusual term in Scottish charters) in a charter providing for its termination on the island. Instead, one canon is to celebrate at Stodfald (on the mainland) and another in the abbey of Dryburgh (*Dryb. Lib.*, no. 289).

THE GILBERTINE CANONS AND NUNS

General Notes

This order, founded in 1131 by Master Gilbert, the rector of Sempringham in Lincolnshire, was designed to provide a monastic life for women, following the Benedictine rule as observed by the Cistercians, in association with canons with the rule and customs of the Augustinian and Premonstratensian orders. In addition to nuns and canons, each house of the order had communities of lay-sisters and lay-brothers following the Cistercian rule for *conversi*. The Gilbertines formed an entirely English order, the one attempt to extend the order beyond these bounds proving unsuccessful. The best accounts of the one evanescent foundation in Scotland are given by G. W. S. Barrow, 'The Gilbertine House of Dalmilling', *Ayrshire Coll.*, 2nd ser., 4 (1955–7), 50–67, and by J. Edwards, 'The Order of Sempringham and its connexion with the West of Scotland', *Glasgow Archaeol. Trans.*, ii (1908), 72–90.

PRIORY OF THE GILBERTINE CANONS AND NUNS

Name	County	Fd	Date D.
DALMILLING	Ayr	1219–28	1238

DALMILLING (DALMULIN). An undated letter from Walter II, son of Alan, steward of Scotland, to Roger, master of Sempringham, intimates his intention of founding a house of this order, details the endowments he proposes to give it and seeks the master's approval (*Malton Register, BM MS Cotton Claudius D*, xi, 227; Barrow, 'Gilbertine House of Dalmilling', 58–59). The steward's offer was accepted (cf. Rose Graham, *St. Gilbert of Sempringham and the Gilbertines*, 1901, 46). Nevertheless, although Walter announces in a charter, of date, 1219–28 (Barrow, 'Gilbertine House of Dalmilling', 51–2) that he has founded a house of canons and nuns of the order of Sempringham at a place in the land of 'Mernes' called Dalmilling upon Ayr, this document (*Pais. Reg.*, 21–2) is not in itself evidence that the conventual life was established at Dalmilling. An advance party of canons from Sixthills priory in Lincolnshire (cf. Spottiswoode, 433 who says 'Sixle in Yorkshire') including its prior and two canons visited Scotland in person, as may have Robert, master of the order, but nuns were never present (Barrow, *op. cit.*, 56, 58–9, 61–2). Indeed, it seems that no conventual house was ever established at Dalmilling. The Gilbertines had resigned the lands and possessions granted them by Walter and these had been bestowed upon Paisley abbey before 29 Nov. 1238, when the prs. of Malton and St. Andrews', York, on behalf of the order, formally renounced all right to them, as did the master and chapter of Sempringham, delivering their charters to Paisley (*Pais. Reg.*, 25–7); while the two canons at Dalmulin were instructed to hand over the properties to that abbey and return to England (*Malton Reg.* fo. 227; Barrow, *op. cit.*, 61–2). In an undated charter, *c.* 1238 the steward conveys to Paisley the possessions which the Gilbertines have resigned, with the proviso that Paisley should pay to them yearly at Dryburgh a sum of 40 marks (*Pais. Reg.*, 24). Controversy and litigation arose out of this obligation and continued for over a century (see *Edward, 'Order of Sempringham', 82–90. There is no evidence that Dalmilling became a cell or oratory of Paisley (cf. *ibid.*, 90). Spottiswoode (434) declares that 'the buildings, or rather ruins of this monastery subsisted (as I am informed) not long ago'. This statement probably refers to the earlier eighteenth c., but it must be regarded with considerable dubiety. The charter of James VI, erecting the properties formerly belong to Paisley abbey into a temporal lordship, 29 July 1587, has no mention of a religious house at this site but includes merely 'the lands of Dalmelling with the mill (*RMS*, v, no. 1320).

THE TRINITARIANS

General Notes

Also known as Red Friars, and as such often counted among the friars, but this was not a mendicant order, endowments being allowed. The incomes thus derived were equally divided; to maintain the brethren; to support the poor and poor pilgrims or travellers; and for the redemption or ransom of captives in the hands of the infidels. Each house was for a minister, sometimes called a prior, with three clerks or priest-brethren, and three lay-brothers. This number was sometimes increased and the complement was revised in 1267 to a minister and five brethren. These were under the Augustinian rule.

The number of Trinitarian houses in Scotland has frequently been exaggerated, and a considerable array of unauthentic foundations of this order appears in lists and works on Scottish religious houses. In the case of half the number of the genuine foundations, record evidence of their origin is wanting; and in only one instance, Scotlandwell, is the date of foundation precisely ascertainable. A good, if incomplete, account of the Scottish houses of this order is given by Bain, 'Notes on the Trinitarians or Red Friars in Scotland, etc.', *PSAS*, X (1887–8), 26–32. The unpublished account of the Scottish Trinitarians given by Hay, Diplomatum Veterum Collectio (NLS. MS., 34.1.10), pp. 1065 ff., is at many points unreliable. These are cited in the notes mainly with the negative purpose of exemplifying errors.

THE TRINITARIAN HOUSES

Name	County	Minimum income (1561)	Fd.	Date D. or	Sec.
Aberdeen	Aberdeen	£54	−1274		1561
Berwick			1240–8 –	1488	
Dirleton	East Lothian		15 c.(?)		−1588
Dunbar	East Lothian		1240–8	1529	
Fail	Ayr	£580	−1335		1561 (v. notes)
Houston	East Lothian		c. 1270	1531	
* Peebles	Peebles	£327	−1296		1560/1
Scotlandwell	Kinross	£280	1250/1		−1591/2

107

ABERDEEN. The date of fd'n. is uncertain. Hay gives it as 1181 (Scotia Sacra, 70). It is also said that in 1211 William the Lion gave his royal residence at Aberdeen (*regiam suam Aberdonensem*) to two friars of the order sent to Scotland by Pope Innocent III (Boece, *Historiae*, 279v cited Hay, Diplomatum, iii, 571 [see above] and *Aberdeen Friars*, 11). Bisset seems to indicate that this was a foundation of William and his queen Ermengarde (Bisset, *Rolment of Courtis*, ii, 116), in which case the date would be 1186–1214. Spottis-woode (395) and Brockie (pp. 1170–1) assert that it was founded by King William and mention the lands, etc., with which that ruler endowed it. There is, however, no record evidence regarding the founder or date of fd'n. Trinity friars here appear in 1273 and again in Baiamund's taxation roll for 1274/5 (*Aberdeen Friars*, 13; *SHS Misc.*, vi, 42; Theiner, *Vet Mon.*, no. cclxiv). A small community continued at the Reformation, although buildings seem to have been in a state of disrepair (*Thirds of Benefices*, 8, 97, 225; Aberdeen Burgh Court Books, xxii, 149–50). The house is said to have been sacked in 1560 by the Reforming barons of the Mearns (Lesley, *De Origine*, 563). On 24 Sept. 1561, sasine of the place or monastery of the Trinitarians, with the buildings was granted to Gilbert Menzies of Cowlie (*Aberdeen Friars*, 98); and grants of these properties by Crown appear in 1573/4, 1577 and 1589 (*ibid.*, 104, 110, *RSS*, vi, no. 2345. The ch. is mentioned as still standing in the eighteenth c. (*Aberdeen–Banff Coll.*, 204).

BERWICK. The Trinitarians settled in Berwick before 1240–8 when their fd'n. here was given custody of the new house at Dunbar by Cristiana de Brus (*Yester Writs*, no. 14). They may have established themselves in the hospital of St. Edward or Bridge House (*q.v.*) on their arrival, though it is only from 1306 that there is evidence of their possess-ing Bridge House (*Hist. Papers and Letters from Northern Registers*, no. cxi), while certain identification of the house of the Trinitarians with this hospital comes only from 1386 (*CPL*, iv, 253). This house is described in 1447 as non-conventual (*CPL*, x, 287). In 1456 the buildings are described as being greatly ruined, and a papal commission was empowered to confer the ministry upon a monk of Coupar-Angus (*CPL*, xi, 47–8). Litigation over its endowments continued, and on 2 March 1476 the house is described as so much in ruin that no brother of the order could live therein (*CPL*, xiii, 491; Reg. Supp. 511, fo. 166; *ibid.*, 735, fo. 108). Shortly before this date the house with its revenues had been united by the provincial of the order to the Trinitarian house at Peebles (*ibid.*, 735, fos. 108, 200–200v) an action which was subsequently confirmed by James III (*RSS*, ii, no. 203). See BERWICK, ST. EDWARD under Hospitals.

DIRLETON. According to Bisset, the eighth fd'n. of the Trinitarians in Scotland (Bisset, *Rolment of Courtis*, ii, 126); but this is not certain. The chapel of St. Andrew, Dirleton, founded by the predecessors of Patrick, Lord Haliburton [d. 6 Dec. 1505], is mentioned in 1507 as held by the Trinitarians (*RSS*, i, no. 1470). The minister resigned the house in 1540 'for the augmentation of divine worship at Scotlandwell' though he arranged for a secular priest to remain at Dirleton to pray for its founder, but in fact Dirleton was an-nexed to Scotlandwell (Prot. Bk. Feyrn, fos. 38v, 73, 77v, 129v). The friar lands which formed part of the temporality of the prior of Dirleton had been annexed to the Crown, –1 Aug. 1588 (*RMS*, v, no. 1568).

DUNBAR. Hay (Diplomatum, iii, 575) and Spottiswoode (396) give the date of fd'n. as 1218; Brockie (p. 1073) gives it as *c.* 1218. The first of these writers assigns the fd'n. to George, E. of March (a manifest inaccuracy) and the two latter (more plausibly) to Patrick, E. of Dunbar and March. Cristiana de Brus, countess of Dunbar is, however, stated to have 'biggit and foundit' this house (*RSS*, ii, no. 203); and the fd'n. probably took place 1240–8 when the countess gave the cure and custody of the new house of Dun-bar to the minister of the house of Berwick which was to provide a friar 'to do divine service' at Dunbar (*Yester Writs.*, no. 14). It was a small house with one friar maintaining divine service (*RSS*, ii, no. 203). On 8 March 1528/9 the priory was granted to a secular chaplain (*ibid.*, i, no. 4110), but this was revoked 1 July 1529, when a letter under the privy seal confirmed the Trinitarians of Peebles in possession of its revenues as included with those of the priory of Berwick (*ibid.*, ii, no. 203). After the Reformation its revenues were granted by the Crown to the bailies and community of Dunbar, 31 March 1567 (*RSS*, v, no. 3386).

FAIL or FAILFORD. The date of fd'n. is uncertain. This house does not seem to be mentioned before the fourteenth c., although Hay (Diplomatum, iii, 579) and Spottiswoode (p. 396) state that it was founded in 1252 (Brockie, p. 1078, says c. 1252). Hay and Brockie assign the foundation to Andrew Bruce. James V in 1538 claimed it was 'instituted by the king's ancestors' and the Stewarts of Kyle have probably the strongest claims to be regarded as the founders of this house (*Letters of James V*, 341). A charter was granted there 1335 (*Melr. Lib.*, no. 447) and on 7 Jan. 1337/8, the minister and brethren were given the ch. of Tarbolton (SRO, RH6/148). The burning of the mon. is mentioned in a charter of 21 July 1349 (*RMS*, i, App. 1, no. 145). On 3 Nov. 1459, as the result of a petition of James II and his queen, alleging the notorious decadence of the friars, the Pope appointed mandatories charged, if they found the allegations true, to remove the minister and friars to other Trinitarian houses, to suppress the order at this house and to appropriate it to the new royal foundation of Trinity College and Hospital, Edinburgh (*CPL*, xi, 403). No such steps were taken and on 31 March 1476 it was granted *in commendam* to John Mure, O.P. who became first Scottish provincial of the Blackfriars and 'contrived to maintain and repair in part a house normally monastic' (Cameron *Apostolic Camera*, 188; *James IV Letters*, no. 114). Fifteen years of litigation followed the provincial's death and according to a letter of James IV to Pope Julius II, 2 July 1507, the house had so far deteriorated 'the end must come unless there is succour'. The king asks for the appointment of the new provincial as commendator, in the interests of restoring monastic discipline (*ibid.*, no. 114; cf. no. 119). The minister and six friars occur 7 Nov. 1528 (*Prot. Bk. Ros.*, no. 912); seven friars and the minister appear 9 Feb. 1545/6 (SRO, Fraser Inventory, no. 137) and three friars occur in 1558 (SRO RH6/1741). The house continued to exist till 1561 when it was 'cast down' by Reformers (Knox, *Works*, ii, 168). Nevertheless, two poor men still lived in the convent in 1562 while four old beidmen of the convent lived outside (MS. Rental Book, fos. 48, 52 cited Chalmers, *Caledonia*, v, 493). The ministry was granted to Robert Cunningham, natural son of the E. of Glencairn by the crown 20 Aug. 1540, and retained by him as reformed minister at the Reformation (*James V Letters*, 412; *Thirds of Benefices*, 165, 268, 270). Successive reformed ministers held the benefice until the deposition of the minister in 1638 when it was acquired by Sir William Cochrane of Cowdoun to whom it was confirmed 18 March 1646 (*RMS*, ix, no. 1633). See W. J. Dillon, 'The Trinitarians of Failford', *Ayrshire Coll.*, 2nd ser., 4 (1958), 68–132.

HOUSTON. 'The Grace of God.' In East Lothian, though commonly (and erroneously) located at Houston in Renfrewshire. Hay (Diplomatum, iii, 576) and Spottiswoode (396) give 1226 as the date of fd'n. Brockie (p. 1074), who locates it in Renfrewshier, dates the fd'n. c. 1226, and ascribes it to Hugh lord of Houston. This house was, however, fd. by Cristiana, widow of Sir Roger Mubray, c. 1270 (Sir Roger died on 20 Jan. 1268/9; the fd'n. was confirmed by Alexander III, 26 Jan. 1271/2 (Bain, 'Notes on the Trinitarians or Red Friars', *PSAS*, x (1887–8), 27–8). In 1518 the duke of Albany wrote to the Pope about the state of the Trinitarians in Scotland. He mentions that three or four professed members of the order usually resided at this house, which had recently been given *in commendam* to a secular cleric whom he wished to have replaced by one of the order (Vat. Arch. Armarium xxxix, vol. 32, fos. 113–14). James V, on 2 Dec. 1531, granted the ministry of Houston and its lands, which had been held by a commendator to the house of Peebles (*RSS*, ii, no. 1069), following this up with a letter, 4 Jan. 1531/2 to Pope Clement VII, in which he indicates that the house at Houston had for a long time been reduced to one member, the minister, usually non-resident and (during James's time) a secular, while its lands had been continuously leased to laymen. Having persuaded the minister to resign this for another benefice, the king asks for its annexation to Peebles (*James V Letters*, 204–5). In another letter of the same date, James declares that no one can remember more than a minister and a chapel at Houston and that for many years past there had been no monastic life there (*ibid.*, 205). The annexation was completed and confirmed by a Crown charter, 8 Jan. 1541/2 (*RMS*, iii, no. 2569). See HOUSTON, under Hospitals.

PEEBLES. 'Holy Cross.' The master of this house swore fealty to Edward I in 1296 (*CDS*, ii, no. 823) and this seems to be the earliest mention of it. In the *Scotichronicon* appears the story of the finding at Peebles, on 9 May 1261, in the thirteenth year of the reign of K. Alexander, of a cross of what were said to be relics of 'St. Nicholas the bishop' whence Alexander III had a ch. built there in honour of the Holy Cross (*Chron. Bower*, ii, 96–97).

If the regnal year is correct, the year would be 1262. Another account credits the fd'n. to 1260 and gives the appropriate regnal year as the eleventh, while yet another in giving 1260 as the year maintains the regnal year as the thirteenth (*Chron. Extracta*, 104, 253). In neither account is their mention of the Trinitarians. Hay does not refer to the Cross, but declares that K. Alexander founded the monastery here on the occasion of finding the relics of 'a certain St. Nicholas' (Diplomatum, iii, 532-3). Spottiswoode (397) says it was founded by Alexander III in 1257; while Brockie (pp. 1079-80), who refers to both cross and the relics also attributes it to this king. There is, however, no record evidence of the date of foundation nor the identity of the chapel. The patronage of the chapel lay with the bailies, however, who appear to have sometimes presented a secular priest and at other times a Trinitarian friar to the benefice. The incumbent was removable at will, and when held by a Trinitarian was non-conventual (*Peebles Chrs.*, 115-6, 148; *CPL*, xiii, 169-70).

A community of friars appears to have been established with the approval of the bailies *c.* 1448, but fifteen years later the bailies claimed to have expelled them on the grounds that they had neglected their duty, part of the relic had been cut off and the necklaces, jewels and treasures kept in the chapel were diminished. As a result of their petition and that of the king, the Pope authorized on 21 April 1463, mandatories to approve the friars' expulsion and to erect the chapel into a perpetual benefice for a secular clerk (*CPL*, xii, 168-70). This does not appear to have been effected and a friar appears as master of the Cross Kirk, 1 Oct. 1464 (*Peebles Chrs.*, 151). The Trinitarian community evidently continued in being, and following a petition by James III and his queen who intimated their intention to erect a conventual mon. in the chapel of the Holy Cross; the Minister-General of the order authorized this and consented to the annexation of the house of Berwick to the new foundation on 3 Feb. 1473/4 (Renwick, *Peebles, Aisle and Monastery*, App. viii, 71-74). Dunbar and Houston were later annexed to this house (see above). The minister and four friars occur in 1556 (*Yester Writs*, no. 672) and again in 1562 (Peebles Burgh Recs., MS. Register, 1549-65, fo. 226). It is stated in a record of 1 June 1558 that the house was burnt by the English 'during the last war' (*RMS*, iv, no. 3037); but the Privy Council, 7 Dec. 1560, granted a petition of the burgesses and inhabitants that, since the parish ch. had been burned and destroyed by the English twelve years before, the Trinitarians friars' ch., which 'is as yet standand' should be taken over as the parish ch. (*Peebles Chrs.*, 264), and, on 27 Jan. 1560/1, the minister of the Trinitarians surrendered the keys and ordered the brethren to disperse (*ibid.*, 269-70). In 1597 a warrant for a charter confirming the community in their rights was prepared but this process was not completed until 19 Nov. 1621 (Renwick, *Gleanings from the Burgh Records*, 141-2, *Peebles Chrs.*, 91-2). The ch. was in use till 1784. On 3 Feb. 1624 the lands formerly belonging to this house were erected into a barony for John Hay of Yester (*RMS*, viii, no. 570).

SCOTLANDWELL. The original fd'n. was the hospital of St. Mary (*q.v.* under LOCH LEVEN). On 2 Jan. 1250/1, David de Bernham, bp. of St. Andrews granted it to the Trinitarians (SRO, RH6/48). The date 1249 given by Hay (Diplomatum, iii, 579) is incorrect. This grant evoked protest from St. Andrews priory against the introduction of the Trinitarians within the bounds of its parishes without the canons' consent, and, on 2 July 1255 Pope Alexander IV appointed mandatories to deal with the priory's plea for their removal (NLS. MS. 15. 1. 19). Spottiswoode (p. 396) also mentions a bull of Pope Innocent IV, *c.* 1250, on this subject, but it has not been traced. This attempted removal was unsuccessful and a master occurs in 1274 (*SHS Misc.*, vi, 37, 61). The Trinitarian house at Dirleton (*q.v.*) was annexed to this house in 1539/40 'for the augmentation of divine service' and an increase in the number of brethren was mooted (SRO, Prot. Bk. Feyrn, fos. 38, 73, 77v, 129v), but after a disputed succession over the ministry one of the contestants, Archibald Arnot, and his father occupied the priory in June 1543, ejecting the friars and stopping divine service (*ADCP*, 531). Despite litigation, the house remained in their possession thereafter (*ibid.*, 538, 545, 553, 558, 560-1). Secular possession was confirmed to the family 11 Feb. 1591/2 when lands forming part of the temporality were granted by James VI to David, son of Andrew Arnot, minister (i.e. lay commendator) of Scotlandwell (*RMS*, v, no. 2056); and it is mentioned in 1606 as resigned in the king's hands (*APS*, iv, 334).

SUPPOSED FOUNDATIONS

Ancrum. There is said to have been a house of Red Friars at Nether Ancrum (*Macfarlane Geog. Collns.*, iii, 158). Of this no evidence is forthcoming and the statement is apparently unfounded.

Barra. Scotichronicon (lib. ii, cap. x (*Chron. Bower*, i, 46)) has an entry: 'Barray and there a cell of the Holy Trinity.' This statement may be based on the existence (unrecorded) of a church, perhaps of Celtic origin, dedicated to the Trinity. There is no evidence of Trinitarians here.

Barry. Hay refers to a house which he calls 'domus Barensis', founded by William the Lion in 1212 for thirty-five friars (Diplomatum, iii, 573); and Brockie (p. 1074) locates this at Barry, in Angus, where, he declares, Alexander II erected and endowed a monastery *c.* 1224. This alleged house may have been suggested by the mention of Barra (Barray, above). It can be ruled out as fanciful.

Brechin. Spottiswoode (397) includes this among the 'places . . . mentioned in ancient charters and records, as houses belonging to this order'; but the fact that he does not cite these is suspicious. According to Hay, the founder was Edward, bp. of Brechin, in 1256 (Diplomatum, iii, 579). Brockie (p. 1081) makes a similar statement, but gives the date as *c.* 1258. There was, however, no bp. of that name—the contemporary bp. was Albin (Dowden, *Bishops*, p. 175). Maitland, who suggests David I as the founder (*History*, i, 251), seems to be led astray by the mention of abbots of Brechin (*v.* p. 46–7) and confuses the 'college' (*v.* p. 229) with an entirely suppositious abbey. No reliable evidence of a Trinitarian house at Brechin can be found. There was, however, a 'Trinity Church' at Brechin, viz., the cathedral, dedicated to the Holy Trinity; and this may be the source of the assertion that a Trinitarian monastery existed there.

Brough of Birsay. For the alleged connection of this site with the Red Friars, see *Hist. Mon. Comm. Rep.* (*Orkney and Shetland*), ii, 1, 3). (The statement made there that 'the church and cloister . . . are considerably earlier than the date at which the friars arrived in Northern Europe, while the plan in no way suggests a house of friars' seems to assume unwarrantably that the Trinitarians formed one of the orders properly called friars). Record evidence regarding this monastery is, however, entirely wanting; and it has so far proved impossible to discover the order to which it belonged.

Cara. Hay (Scotia Sacra 458) declares that in this island there was a cell of the Holy Trinity. But Monro (*Western Isles* p. 49) calls Cara 'ane little iyle [isle] with a Chapell in it'; and this chapel is no doubt the 'cell' in question. This was not a Trinitarian site.

Crenach. A site so named is given by Spottiswoode (397) and Brockie (p. 1082), who locate it at Cromarty—the latter appears to suggest that it was founded by Patrick Murray, *c.* 1271; and it figures in lists under various guises, e.g. Crennach (*Scotich.*, ii, 540; NLS. MS. 22.1.14); Crenwathe (NLS. MS. 33.2.12); this may point to Carnwath, in Lanarkshire, but no religious house was situated there; Greenock (NLS. MS. 31.6.1, 33.5.11); there is no evidence of a monastery either at Greenock, in Renfrewshire or in the part of Ayrshire where this place-name occurs. This alleged house cannot be identified; it is probably fictitious.

Cromarty. Mentioned by Spottiswoode (397) and by him identified with Crenach (above). Alleged references to the friars of Cromarty in the Lord High Treasurer's Accounts have been investigated with the result that the entries in this source have been found to refer to the 'feriaris' [ferrymen] of Cromarty (*TA*, i, 324, 363). No evidence of Trinitarians here is forthcoming.

Cupar. Hay gives a foundation here made by James, E. of Fife, in 1277 (Diplomatum, iii, 585). There was no such earl; and no such house.

Dornoch. It is stated by Spottiswoode (397) that, in 1271, Sir Patrick Murray founded a house at 'Dornock, in Sutherland' and that it was given the lands of the ministry of Berwick after that town passed into English possession. Brockie (p. 1083) declares that its foundation is attributed both to Patrick Murray and to the *reguli* of Sutherland, and suggests that Trinitarians were brought to Dornoch by William, 'the younger earl of

Sutherland', *c.* 1272. There appears to be no other evidence of such a foundation and it is missing from MS. lists. If Spottiswoode's phrase, 'after the English had possessed themselves of that city' refers to the final capture of Berwick by the English in 1482, it can be shown that the revenues of the Trinitarian house there were made over to the house at Peebles (see above) before 1488. This foundation cannot be regarded as genuine. See Dornoch under Benedictine monks.

Dundee. Maxwell (*Old Dundee*, 64–5) assumes that there was a Trinitarian house here. But it is difficult to say that there was more than a hospital (*q.v.*) and no convent of this order is mentioned in the burgh charters. A Trinitarian foundation is said to have been made by Sir James Scrymgeour in 1283 (according to Brockie, p. 1085) or 1285 (according to Hay (Diplomatum, iii, 587)); but this is undoubtedly erroneous.

Dunet (in Buchan). This alleged site does not appear in any of the older lists. Hay (Diplomatum, iii, 585) gives the name of a house as '[coenobium] Dumeni', founded, he declares, in 1297. Brockie (p. 1086) mentions this as 'Dunetum' or 'Dumenum', locates it in Buchan and refers to its foundation in the above year. This writer (p. 1087) cites Keith's 'History of the Reformation' (i.e. Keith's *History of the Affairs of Church and State in Scotland from the beginning of the Reformation to the year 1568*) as showing that 'when the monks were driven out', the mons. of Deer and Dunet were granted to the earl Marischal in 1567. Too much, however, is read by Brockie into Keith's statement, viz.: 'Item, Deare, Dunet and Pillorth [Philorth] are given frie to the Erle of Marschell [and others]' (Keith, *op. cit.* (Spottiswoode Socy.), iii, 177). These places are in Buchan but they are not specified here as monasteries. Again, Brockie's account (which is badly paraphrased in Gordon, *Monasticon*, iii, 303) suggests a connection, sufficiently far-fetched, between Dunet and the hospitals at Newburgh and Turriff; his reference to a MS. supplement to Dempster's *Historia Ecclesiastica* as mentioning the connection of a certain William Keith with this monastery carries no weight in authenticating its existence; while his allusion to 'Roger, prior of Dunet' as appearing during the reign of David I in the register of St. Andrews [priory] is based on a misreading (the register does not give 'Roger, prior of Dunet' but 'Roger, prior of Dunfermline' (Rogero priore de Dunef[ermelyn]) (*St. A. Lib.*, p. 182)) and is, in any case, historically impossible. This cannot be regarded as a genuine foundation.

Kettins. This name appears in lists in various and sometimes misleading forms: Katnes (*Scotich.*, ii, 540); Katness (NLS. MS., 31.6.1); Kathness (NLS. MS., 35.3.11); Kattens (NLS. MS., 33.2.12); Ketnes (NLS. MS., 22.1.14). This place is Kettins, in Angus, which was not the site of a Trinitarian house, but the parish church was appropriated to the hospital of the bridge of Berwick (St. Edward's) and thereafter to the Trinitarians. See *Coupar Angus Chrs.*, ii, 19 *n.*

Lochfeal. Mentioned by Spottiswoode (397). There was no house of this designation. 'Lochfeal' is simply Loch Fail or Failford Loch, which was in the close vicinity of the monastery of Fail, apart from which no other house existed in this region.

Luffness. Mentioned by Spottiswoode (397), while Hay (Diplomatum, iii, 587) and Brockie (p. 1068) assign the foundation to 1285, the latter attributing it to one of the earls of Dunbar. This is an obvious confusion with the Carmelite house of Luffness.

St. Andrews. Hay states that a Trinitarian monastery was founded here in 1247 (Diplomatum, iii, 579). This statement is entirely fictitious.

Soutra. On the statement (unfounded) as made by Brockie (p. 1084) that this was a Trinitarian fd'n., see Soutra under Hospitals.

Hay's list includes other foundations which are either fanciful or due to confusion with houses of other orders: [coenobium] 'Benefici', 'which is in the chief [town] of the province of Buchan' (Diplomatum, iii, 585); 'monasterium Farnense', said to have been founded in 1293 (*ibid.*, p. 585)—this may be a confusion with the Premonstratensian house of Fearn; Queensferry (*ibid.*, p. 585)—confused with the Carmelite house there; 'monasterium Ruthnae' (*ibid.*, p. 587). All these may be summarily rejected.

THE CRUTCHED FRIARS

General Notes

Entries (mainly in catalogues dated 1552–1635) of a house of the Polish congregation of Crutched Friars at a site given as 'Pful', 'Phall', 'Faill', 'Fayl in Scotia' (Hermans, *Ann. can. reg. S. Aug. ord. S. Crucis*, ii, 189, 194, 197). This place is presumably Fail, in Ayrshire. But the religious house at Fail (see p. 109) was Trinitarian. Again, although friars of this Order, which does not rank as a mendicant order, have been located at Dunkeld and Hamilton (H. F. Chettle, 'The Friars of the Holy Cross in England', *History*, xxxiv (1949), 205), no reliable evidence of these alleged foundations has been found. There is a reference to the appointment of a visitor 'of the convents of the kingdoms and lands of England, Scotland, Ireland and Wales' (Hermans, *op., cit.*, ii, 388), but the inclusion of Scotland may be no more than 'common form'. It is highly improbable that this order was represented in Scotland.

THE MENDICANT FRIARS

GENERAL NOTES

THESE friars relied almost entirely on charity for subsistence and housing, and little from incomes derived from endowments, as with other religious orders. The persons who are referred to as founders are generally those who gave or procured sites for the friaries, or who paid for their buildings. At the Reformation friars were ejected from their buildings, many of which were destroyed, but compensation, usually at the rate of £16 *per annum*, was paid to friars who wished to avail themselves of those bounties which were usually referred to as 'freiris wageis'.

THE DOMINICAN (BLACK) FRIARS

GENERAL NOTES

INSTITUTED at Toulouse in 1215 by St. Dominic, the founder adopted the existing order of St. Augustine, and a bull of Pope Honorius III, 22 Dec. 1216, formally confirmed the foundation of the new order. The name of Black Friars was given to the Dominicans on account of the black cloak which they wore over a white tunic.

Dominican Friars are said to have appeared in Scotland for the first time in 1230 (*Melrose Chron.*, 142; *Scotichronicon*, lib. ix, cap. xlvii; *Chron Bower*, ii, 58). The *Scotichronicon* says that they were induced to come there by Alexander II, who 'appointed, provided for and founded' places for them; while it is claimed (Spottiswoode, 441) that they were brought to Scotland in that king's reign by William Malvoisin, bishop of St. Andrews. The Scottish houses were nominally part of the English Dominican Province until 1481 when, at the petition of James III, the Dominican General Chapter created a province of Scotland. Five lists or indications of Scottish Dominican foundations are found up to 1564, viz. (1) a writ of 7 March 1296/7, ordaining payments to be made from the fermes of burghs to the Friars Preachers (*Rot. Scotl.*, i. 39); this record may be taken as indicating the houses then in existence; (2) a list, dated 1510, of religious

houses printed as an appendix to the *Scotichronicon* (*Chron. Bower*, ii. 540);
(3) a reference, 14 June 1553 (*ADCP*, 622) to the Friars Preachers, in
which their houses are named; (4) a detailed account of the Scottish
houses in a communication from the Provincial of Scotland to the Master
General, 26 Jan 1557 (?1557/8) (*Analecta F.P.* (1895), 484); (5) an account
of the Blackfriars' foundations in Scotland, said to have been derived from
the account of an octogenarian friar in 1564 (*Chron. Extracta*, 249). The
occurrence of the houses mentioned in these lists may be indicated thus:

Aberdeen	1.2.3.4.5
Ayr	1.2.3.4.5
Berwick	1.5
Cupar	2.5
Dundee	3.4.5
Edinburgh	1.2.3.4.5
Elgin	1.2.3.4.5
Glasgow	1.2.4.5
Inverness	1.2.3.4.5
Montrose	1.2.3.4.5
Perth	1.2.3.4.5
St. Andrews	2.3.4.5
St. Monans'	4.5
Stirling	1.2.3.4.5
Wigtown	1.2.3.4.5

The Blackfriars' house at Haddington, which was evidently of short
duration, does not figure in any of these lists.

That the Friars Preachers had twenty-three houses in Scotland, as
indicated in the Appendix to Spottiswoode's *History of the Church of
Scotland* (1677 edn., p. 16; p. 25 in the Appendix as separately published)
is quite incredible. Lists of religious houses are numerous in the seventeenth c. and their compilers borrowed uncritically from one another. It is
noticeable that the National Library of Scotland MS. 22.1.14, in other
respects comparatively accurate, has an extremely confused list of
Dominican houses; and it may be that the Appendix to Spottiswoode
depends on it. In MSS. of this period, the list of Dominican houses is
sometimes followed (through a purely factitious arrangement) by a list of
chori oppidani containing such names as Linlithgow, Jedburgh, Forres,
Selkirk and these have probably, by some copyist's blunder, found their
way into lists of houses of Black Friars. On the other hand, MS. Saunders,

which belongs to this period, gives a correct list (excluding Berwick and Cupar) of the thirteen houses existing at the Reformation.

THE DOMINICAN (BLACK) FRIARS HOUSES

Name	County	Dedication	Minimum income (1561)	Fd.	Date D. or Sec.
ABERDEEN	Aberdeen	St. John B.	£108	1230–49	1560–87
AYR	Ayr	St. Katherine		c. 1242	1567
BERWICK		St. Peter M. of Milan		–1240/1	1539(?)
CUPAR	Fife	St. Katherine		1348	1519
DUNDEE	Angus	?	£7(?)	c. 1521	1567
EDINBURGH	Midlothian	Assumption of B.V.M.	£67	1230	1566/7
ELGIN	Moray	St. James	£251	1233 or 1234	–1570/1
GLASGOW	Lanark	St. John E.	£73	–1246	1566/7
HADDINGTON	East Lothian			1471	1489–90+
INVERNESS	Inverness	St. Bartholomew	£38	–1240	–1566/7
MONTROSE	Angus	Nativity of B.V.M.	£107	–1275	1570/1
PERTH	Perth	St. Andrew	£93	–1240	1569
* ST. ANDREWS	Fife	Assumption and Coronation of B.V.M.	£67 (with Cupar)	see notes	1567
‡ ST. MONAN'S	Fife	St. Monan		1471	c. 1557
STIRLING	Stirling	St. Laurence	£2(?)	–1249	1567
WIGTOWN	Wigtown	Annunciation of B.V.M.		1267 or –1287	1560–70(?)

ABERDEEN. Said to have been fd. by Alexander II, 1230 × 1249 (*Chron. Extracta*, 249; *Aberdeen–Banff Coll.*, 201; *Aberdeen Friars*, 12). The prior was commissioned as a papal judge 2 Oct. 1257 (Theiner, *Vet. Mon.*, no. cciii). Payments to this house from the Scottish Exchequer are recorded at intervals between 14 Jan. 1328/9 and 11 Aug. 1559 (*ER*, i, 60; xix, 85). A general confirmation detailing the possessions of the house was granted by James III, 30 Sept. 1477 (*RMS*, ii, no. 1311). The prior and thirteen friars occur in 1503 (*Aberdeen–Banff Coll.*, 202). This house was destroyed by Reformers 4 Jan. 1560 (Lesley, *De Origine*, 563; *Aberdeen Description*, 66; *Aberdeen Friars*, 97). Its possessions were granted to George, earl Marischal, 17 May 1587 (*ibid.*, 108), who bestowed them, as part of its endowment, on Marischal College (*ibid.*, 112).

AYR. Fd. before Aug. 1242 by Alexander II, who gave an endowment when the church was dedicated (*Ayr Friars*, xxi–xxii, no. 1). The house continued to receive many donations of property in the early sixteenth c. (*ibid.*, 66–75) though gifts by the 1530s and 1540s were becoming progressively less frequent (*ibid.*, 91–6). Eight friars occur in 1557 (*ibid.*, 98–9). The house, lands, etc., were leased by the crown 4 June 1565 and made over to the burgh of Ayr by a charter of Queen Mary, 14 April 1567 (*RSS*, v, no. 2109; *RMS*, iv, no. 1782; cf. *Ayr Friars*, no. 64). The buildings were demolished after the Reformation (*RSS*, v, no. 2109; *Ayr Burgh Accounts*, 53).

BERWICK. Fd. by Alexander II (*Chron. Extracta*, 249), who gave it an endowment (*ER*, i, 208). There is reference to this community in March 1240/1 (*CDS*, i, 277). On 17 June 1285 the Pope gave mandate to the bp. of St. Andrews to sell to the Friars Preachers, as their house was too far from the town, the former house of the Friars of Penitence (*CPL*, i, 482, 494–5; Theiner, *Vet. Mon.*, nos. cclxxxviii, ccix). On the evidence of grants of pittances made by Edward I it would appear that there were four and six friars in this house on separate occasions in Dec. 1299 (*Liber quotidianus*, 26). Payments from the Scottish Exchequer are recorded in the years 1329–33 (*ER*, i, 208, 312–3, 361, 411). On 10 Aug. 1333, Edward III instructed the provincial of the English Dominicans to remove the Scottish friars in this house to English houses south of the Trent and to substitute English friars (*Rot. Scot.*, i, 258). Orders for the continued payment of the grant of the Scottish kings are made by Edward III of England from time to time up to 1343 (*Rot. Scot.*, i, 318, 399, 486, 526–7, 608, 639; *CDS*, iii, no. 1251). In 1336 their number was stated at different times as fifteen and twenty (BM. MS. Cotton Nero cviii, fos. 203–4). An indulgence for the rebuilding of the house, following its accidental destruction by fire, was granted 25 Feb. 1436 (Reg. Supp., 319, fo. 210). In 1450 the prior is mentioned (*Historiae Dunelmensis scriptores tres. . .* App. cccxxi–cccxxiii). On 25 April 1461, the Scots regained possession of Berwick, Brockie (p. 1121) gives a charter (from the collections of Father Richard Augustine Hay) of James III to the sheriff of Berwick, whereby because Berwick has returned to his obedience, and the Friars Preachers still dwelling there have been defrauded of help by the English, he ordains that the friars may have free transit (*liberum transitum*, i.e. liberty of movement) through the Merse and Lothian in order to collect alms and that their former revenues are to be restored to them. The regnal year is given (=3 Aug. 1467–2 Aug. 1468) but no day or month. This document is almost certainly not genuine. In any case, effect could hardly have been given to such provisions, for Berwick was retaken by the English, 22 Aug. 1482. Thereafter, the history of the house is obscure and there is no definite evidence that this friary survived until the general dissolution of the English monasteries. It is conceivable that the chapel of Ravensdale, a house of friars surrendered in 1539, belonged to the Dominicans (PRO, Ministers Accounts Henry VIII, no. 7364, m 11d). Ravensdale has generally been assumed to be the house of Trinitarians (*q.v.*) but this seems to have ceased to exist before 1473/4. Although the fate of the Augustinians in Berwick is not known, their buildings were in a different part of the town from Ravensdale in the fourteenth c. and probably later (*Newb. Reg.*, no. 188) and the only other possibility, in the absence of further evidence, is that the house dissolved in 1539 was that of the Dominicans.

CUPAR. In 1348 Duncan, E. of Fife, petitioned the Pope for faculty to found a Dominican convent in his castle of Cupar (*CPP*, i, 144). On 21 Nov. of the same year the Pope granted the vicar-general in Scotland of the English provincial permission to receive the land and to build a church with an oratory (*CPL*, iii, 304). On 13 Nov. 1517, the Scottish provincial reported that the house was in a state of collapse and petitioned the Pope that the brethren be moved to the house at St. Andrews (Reg. Supp., 1584, fo. 58v) In the following year, the general chapter at Rome approved this proposal to close the house which contained only two friars (*Acta Cap. Gen. OP.*, ix, 173). This decision was subsequently confirmed by a crown charter on 4 Oct. 1519 which records that, at a chapter held in Edinburgh at Michaelmas of that year, the provincial incorporated the Dominicans' place at Cupar with the Dominican house at St. Andrews, transferring the friars there (*RMS*, iii, no. 196). The Friar Preachers' lands were granted to the burgh of Cupar by James VI, 14 June 1572 (*ibid.*, iv, no. 2075).

DUNDEE. It is impossible to accept as authentic the charters of donation to Friars Preachers at Dundee of Robert I, 4 Sept. 1315, and others (in 1345 and 1388 given by Brockie (pp. 1206–8). On 16 Sept. 1517 the Scottish provincial petitioned the Pope for the erection of a house on the grounds that there was no house of the order in Dundee (Reg. Supp. 1582, fo. 110). The foundation had been effected, apparently through the generosity of Andrew Abercromby, burgess of Dundee, who may be regarded as founder, before 19 March 1521 (*ibid.*, 1730, fo, 241; Maxwell, *Old Dundee*, 62). This house had a brief career. It was sacked by a mob in Aug. 1543 (*Diurnal of Occurrents*, 29, *Hamilton Papers*, ii, nos. 11, 14, 30, 116; Maxwell, *Old Dundee*, 395 (from burgh archives), and it was probably destroyed when the English burned Dundee, in Nov. 1548 (Maxwell, *Old Dundee*, 113). This house is described in 1557 as '*recens natum et erectum*' but also very recently destroyed by heretics and then by the English (*Analecta F.P.* (1895), 484). In 1567 a precept was issued granting the bestowal by a crown charter of its property upon the burgh (*Dundee Chrs.*, 41).

EDINBURGH. Fd. by Alexander II who granted to the friars the place in which the king's manor house was situated (*St. Giles Reg.*, no. 79 from NLS. MS., 34.1.10, i, 466). The exact date of fd'n. is uncertain. The date in these sources is given as 7 June in the eleventh regnal year (i.e. 1225). As this is manifestly incorrect, Moir Bryce (*Edinburgh Black Friars*, 16) attributed this charter to the eleventh year of Alexander III (1260), and identified it as a confirmation of the foundation charter claimed by Spottiswoode (441) to date from the seventeenth regnal year of Alexander II (1230). There is, however, only one charter, and this can not be dated earlier than 1242 and may be dated 7 June 1244 (the thirtieth regnal year of Alexander II) on which date that king made grants to the Black Friars of Perth (*Handlist of the Acts of Alexander II*, ed. J. M. Scoular, Edinburgh, 1959, 45). The same king also granted to the friars ten marks annually from the ferm of Edinburgh (*RMS*, ii, 1125). A general charter of confirmation of donations made to the house was granted by James III 14 May 1473 (*ibid.*, ii, no. 1125). The prior and twelve friars occur in 1479 (*Laing Chrs.*, no. 177); Spottiswoode (422) states that the house was destroyed by fire on 25 April 1528, but this is uncorroborated. The friary was partly burned by the English in May 1544 (*Edinburgh Black Friars*, 51–2). It was destroyed by Reformers in June 1559. Of the two different dates given (*Diurnal of Occurrents*, 53, 269), 14 and 28 June; Knox's account of the destruction of the 'frearis places' by the 'rascheal multitude' (*Works*, i, 366) seems to support the former date; Moir Bryce (*Edinburgh Black Friars*, 56–7 does not make it clear why he accepts the latter date. Only four friars can be positively identified after the Reformation (*ibid.*, 65). The lands and possessions of this house were granted to the magistrates and Town Council 13 March 1566/7 (*RSS*, v, no. 3417).

ELGIN. Fd. by Alexander II in 1233 or 1234 (Spottiswoode, 444); *c*. 1233 (Brockie, p. 1196 where it is mentioned that the foundation charter is lost); *c*. 1235 (*Elgin Recs.*, i, 8). Five chalders of victual were granted to the friars by Alexander III on 29 March 1285 (*RMS*, i, no. 245). The revenues of the Maison Dieu of Elgin were granted to this house 17 Nov. 1520 and this was confirmed by the Pope 21 June 1521 (see ELGIN, under Hospitals). Possession of the revenues of the house was in dispute before 21 Dec. 1526 when the guardian of the house petitioned the Pope to the effect that he had been deprived and violent hands had been laid upon him by Patrick Dunbar, sub-chanter of Moray (Reg. Supp., 1914, fos. 207v–208v; 1915, fo. 56; 1918, fos. 205–6). A general confirmation of previous donations was granted by the crown 9 Oct. 1551 (*RMS*, iv, no. 638). A small community remained at the Reformation (*Thirds of Benefices*, 97) when the lands and revenues of the house appear to have permanently fallen to the Dunbar family, one of whom, Alexander, dean of Moray received crown confirmation of his feu on 7 Jan. 1570/1 (*RMS*, iv, no. 1955). Property formerly belonging to the house was also granted under the great seal, 4 March 1573/4 and 9 Jan. 1575/6 (*RMS*, iv, nos. 2189, 2485).

GLASGOW. Said to have been fd. by the bishop and chapter (*Chron. Extracta*, 249). A bull of 10 July 1246 grants an indulgence to all the faithful who contribute to the completion of the ch. which the Friars Preachers of Glasgow had begun to build (*Glasgow Friars Munimenta*, no. 2). On 15 June 1487 the provincial chapter of the order confirmed the foundation of a perpetual chaplaincy in the ch. of this house to which was appended a promise by the founder to erect houses for the use of the friars between the ch. and their dormitory (*Glasgow Chrs.*, i, pt. ii, 72–79). Ten friars occur, 6 Nov. 1557 and eight on 6 Dec. 1558 (G. U. Archives, Miscellaneous Tacks). On 13 Nov. 1560 the prior and sub-prior feued a tenement 'because the place of the order has become broken up and the brothers dispersed during times of trouble and danger' (*RMS*, iv, no. 1790). The Blackfriars' place with its endowments was bestowed upon the municipality by Queen Mary, 16 March 1566/7 (*Glasgow Friars Munimenta*, lxxviii). The conventual ch. existed till *c*. 1670, when it was destroyed by lightning.

HADDINGTON. The house does not appear in the list of eleven Dominican houses granted payment from their respective burghs, 7 March 1296/7 (*Rot. Scot.*, i, 39). References to a house of this order which is reputed to have stood at the West Port of the burgh (Brockie, p. 1236), first occur on 8–9 Aug. 1471 and 7 May 1482 (*Yester Writs*, nos. 167, 202); and a payment of wheat to it is recorded in the Exchequer account of 1489–90 (*ER*, x, 224). Part of a spurious charter to the Blackfriars here, apparently by John Hay of Yester is dated 30 June 1513 (Brockie, p. 1234); also a forged charter to them by Henry Sinclair of Herdmanston, 29 May 1528 (pp. 1234–5). The date of the extinction of this house is as uncertain as the date of its fd'n. Statements (Brockie, p. 1236) that it was devastated by the English and, *c.* 1558, reduced to ashes 'by the rage of fanatics' are entirely unsubstantiated. It is not mentioned among the Dominican houses surviving in 1557 (see p. 115 above). The likelihood is that it had a somewhat brief existence.

INVERNESS. The date of the fd'n. of this house by Alexander II (*Chron. Extracta*, 249) is not known. The confirmation charter attributed by Hutton (NLS. MS. xi, fo. 68) to that king belongs to his successor Alexander III who on 20 May 1275 confirmed a donation to the friars (*RMS*, iii, no. 962). It is said to be almost ruinous in its structure and buildings, 18 March 1436 (Reg. Supp., 321, fo. 95). A charter of 20 June 1559 records the 'geir' (property) placed by the friars in the custody of the magistrates of Inverness (*Family of Rose*, 226–7). The friars subscribing included the prior and four others, making a community of at least five at this date. This is mentioned as one of the houses still undemolished, 13 Feb. 1561/2 (*RPC*, 1st ser., i, 202), but the friary was disbanded, –19 Jan. 1566/7 (*RMS*, iv, no. 2760).

MONTROSE. Said to have been fd. by Sir Alan Durward (d.1275) (*Chron. Extracta*, 249). It appears to have been abandoned after its destruction in the fourteenth c. On 14 Nov. 1516, James V with the consent of John, duke of Albany, the Governor and the estates of parliament, empowered Patrick Paniter, ab. of Cambuskenneth and master of St. Mary's house (hospital) near Montrose, the king's secretary, to institute a new foundation of the latter house in favour of the Friars Preachers (*RMS*, iii, no. 113; *APS*, ii, 389–92). Hence a mandate of the provincial of the Scottish Dominicans, 18 Dec. 1519, calls him the 'true founder' of this house (Brockie, p. 1202; this document gives the date of Paniter's death as 18 Nov. 1519; but cf. *Camb. Liber*, lxxxiv; *James IV Letters*, xxxii). A petition of the duke of Albany, on behalf of James V to Pope Leo X for the bestowal of the hospital and its lands on the Dominicans, whose house is said to have been burned during war more than a century ago, was granted, 18 May 1517 (*James V Letters*, 45). Another letter (or perhaps another version of the foregoing petition) to this Pope, in 1518 supplicating for the grant of the hospital to the Dominicans, speaks of the latter's house as having been burned by the enemy upwards of two hundred years ago and lying neglected (*Ep. Regum. Scotorum*, i, 290–2; *James V Letters*, 60). This petition was granted and a bull of erection issued, 5 June 1518 (Reg. Supp., 1610, fos. 189–190v; Reg. Vat., 1105, fos. 116–21); and the Dominican General Chapter, in the same year, approved the translation of the house to the hospital (*Mon. Ord. F.P. Hist.*, ix, 173). A charter of 10 May 1524 relates that the king had ordained the return of the friars to their former house, as the situation of the hospital in the public street gave rise to disturbance of the friars' services and devotions (*RMS*, iii, no. 1725; *APS*, ii, 395–6). But the friars evidently retained the hospital buildings until the period of the Reformation. A letter of Francis and Mary dated 22 Feb. 1559 approves the action of the lords of secret council in ordering the ejection of the friars and orders the restoration of the hospital (*HMC, Fifth Report*, App., 640). There were eight friars in this house, 28 Nov. 1531; the prior, sub-prior and two friars occur, 18 May 1564 (*Essays on Scottish Reformation*, 239). On 1 Jan. 1570/1, James VI granted the revenues and other properties of the Friars Preachers to the burgh of Montrose (*RMS*, iv, no. 1874).

PERTH. Said without authority to have been founded by Alexander II in 1231; the first known grant to this house is 31 October 1241 (*Perth Blackfriars*, xviii, no. 1). The church was dedicated 13 May 1240 (Anderson, *Early Sources*, ii, 520). Various councils of the Scottish Church were held here. The friary was attacked by a mob, 14 May 1543 (Fittis, *Eccles. Annals of Perth*, 189) and 11 May 1559 destroyed along with the other religious houses at Perth (Lesley, *History*, 272, where the date is given erroneously as 1558); *Chron. Pitscottie*, ii, 146; Fittis, *op. cit.*, 190). Its lands and revenues were granted to the burgh by James VI, 9 Aug. 1569 (*RMS*, iv, no. 1874).

ST. ANDREWS. Said to have been fd. by William Wishart, bp. of St. Andrews (1273–79) in 1274 (Spottiswoode, 446). There is no evidence for this statement; an alleged charter of Alexander III, 10 March 1285/6, taking under his protection the monastery for Friars Preachers recently erected by William, bp. of St. Andrews who may be William Wishart, 1273–79, or William Fraser, 1279–97: Brockie, p. 1213) is spurious. There are other difficulties in accepting a thirteenth-c. date of foundation, and the fact that St. Andrews does not appear among the eleven Dominican houses granted payment from their respective burghs, 7 March 1296/7 (*Rot. Scot.*, i, 39) would appear to be conclusive. The assumption (D. Henry, 'Dominican friars at St. Andrews', *Aberdeen Ecclesiol. Trans.* (1893), 18 ff.; *Hist. Mon. Comm.* (*Fife and Kinross*), 250) that the sixteenth c. saw the restoration of a thirteenth-c. house which had become impoverished, dilapidated and reduced in personnel, is equally unwarranted. Before 22 Nov. 1464 when the first prior of this house occurs (*Arb. Lib.*, ii, 160) a small oratory or hospice had been founded. If endowed by one of the bps. of St. Andrews this would justify Abp. James Beaton, in 1525, speaking of himself and his predecessors as 'first and principal foundatouris of the forisaid place of Freiris Predicatouries within our cietie forisaid' (Herkless and Hannay, *Archbishops*, iii, 168–9; cf. *Chron. Extracta*. 149 which attributes the foundation 'be the bischop thairof', i.e. St. Andrews). Its early status is revealed by a bull of Pope Sixtus IV, 18 March 1476/7 (*CPL*, xiii, 571), which in response to a petition of James III and the vicar-general of the order in Scotland, grants that the places of the Friars Preachers in St. Andrews and St. Monans, hitherto known as oratories or hospices, shall be named conventual houses and the friars shall have liberty to erect churches and monastic buildings; a concession to which the archdeacon of St. Andrews, as executor deputed by the Pope, gave effect on 24 Dec 1477 (St. Andrews Chrs., no. 75). A payment of alms to the St. Andrews Blackfriars is recorded, 30 Sept. 1504 (*TA*, ii, 264). The developments foreshadowed in the bull of 1476/7 probably remained unfulfilled and one or two friars at the most appear to have been resident (*Abdn. Reg.*, ii, 311–2).

The sixteenth c. saw new developments. On 16 Nov. 1514, provision was made for the bestowal by his executor of the residue of the estate of William Elphinstone, bp. of Aberdeen (d. 25 Oct. 1514), upon the provincial and the order for the building of a convent within the university of St. Andrews (*ibid.*, ii, 310); and a provincial chapter at Stirling, 21 Sept. 1516, decided on the utilization of this sum 'for the fabric of the new convent of St. Andrews, so that there, by the Grace of God, there will be a convent of friars living according to rule and engaged continually in the study of sacred letters where formerly one friar and seldom two were dwelling (*ibid.*, ii, 311–2). It is thus evident that the incentive of the development of the convent at St. Andrews was the presence of the university. In 1518 the Dominican General Chapter signified its approval of the arrangement between the dean of Dunkeld and the provincial of Scotland for the fd'n. 'for five or six students in the convent of the university of St. Andrews' (*Mon. ord. F.P. Hist.*, ix, 173). On the basis of this arrangement and a statement (Myln, *Vitae*, 55–56) concerning this dean (George Hepburn): 'When the order of Preachers in Scotland underwent a reformation by . . . John Adamson, professor of sacred letters, provincial of the order, he was of great assistance; he founded their place in St. Andrews, whence he deservedly bears the title of their founder, and endowed it for the sufficient maintenance of five friars'; it has been suggested (*Edinburgh Blackfriars*, 28) that Hepburn established this new foundation. But his part was restricted to that of executor of Elphinstone's will (*Abdn. Reg.*, 310–2) and Adamson should be credited with the refoundation (*Dunkeld Rentale*, 321). In 1519 the priories of Cupar (see above) and (in part) St. Monan's (see below) and, in 1529, the hospital of St. Nicholas (*q.v.*) were united to the St. Andrews friary. This house was burned by Norman Lesley in 1547 (*RSS*, iii, nos. 2345, 2515); and destroyed by Reformers probably on 14 June 1559— the date lies between 11 June, when Knox preached in St. Andrews (Knox, *Works*, i, 349) and 21 June, when a charter describes the prior and convent as 'violently expelled from their destroyed place' (SRO RH6/1788). On 17 April 1567 Queen Mary granted the property to the municipality of St. Andrews (Reg. of Evidents of the City of St. Andrews, Inventory, no. 4, 15)

·ST. MONAN'S. Erroneously called St. Ninian's (*Chron. Extracta*, p. 249). The church of St. Monan was originally fd. by David II as a chapel with an unspecified number of chaplains, 3 April 1370 (*RMS*, i, no. 304). On 15 Nov. 1471, James III refounded it for 'a certain number of Friars Preachers', to whom he transferred its endowments (*ibid.*, ii, no. 1047). *Chron. Extracta* (249) and Spottiswoode (445) allege that in this the king was instigated by John Muir, vicar-general of the order, so that the number of Dominican houses would justify the formation of a separate Scottish province. Whatever basis there may be for this statement, it is certainly true that the General Chapter, at the petition of the king, erected Scotland in 1481 into a separate province, of which Muir was the first provincial (*Mon. ord. F.P. Hist.*, iii, 369). By a bull of Pope Sixtus IV, 18 March 1476/7, procured by the vicar-general and James III, this house was given conventual status (St. Andrews Chrs., no. 75; *CPL*, xiii, 571). At Michaelmas 1519, the provincial chapter incorporated it in the house at St. Andrews, with provision for the maintenance of two friars of advancing age at St. Monan's (*RMS*, ii, no. 196). It is stated in 1557 that this house had never more than two friars, but at that date it had none, as its revenues were insufficient to maintain a single friar (*Analecta F.P.* (1895), p. 484).

STIRLING. Fd. by Alexander II (*Chron. Extracta*, 249; Spottiswoode, 444). Spottiswoode gives 1233 as the date of foundation. A charter of Robert de London (d. *c.* 1227), the king's stepbrother, to the Friars Preachers of Stirling, which is given by Brockie (p. 1179), is spurious as it refers to the year in which the Galloway rebels were overcome, i.e. 1235. The friary is said to have been destroyed by Reformers in June 1559 (*Chron. Pitscottie*, ii, 160); and there is a retrospective reference, 12 Sept. 1559 to the 'violent ejection' (of the prior) from this place and its 'total destruction' (*RMS*, iv, no. 1373). A precept under the privy seal, 10 May 1560, ordained a charter to be made confirming a grant by the pr. and convent of their lands to Alexander Erskine of Cangnoir (*Stirling Chrs.*, 90; no. xliv). On 15 April 1567 the grant by Queen Mary to the municipality of ecclesiastical properties within the burgh included the lands and revenues of the Friars Preachers (*ibid.*, 94 (no. xlv)); but it has been pointed out that Erskine clung to the Blackfriars' lands and it was not till 1652 that the burgh obtained possession of them (*Stirling Trans.*, 1890–1, 50).

WIGTOWN. Fd. by 'the Maiden of Galloway' (*Chron. Extracta*, p. 249), Devorgilla, daughter of Alan of Galloway, who married John de Balliol, *c.* 1233. Spottiswoode (445) assigns the foundation to Devorgilla to 1267, a date which is probable though not otherwise attested. This house may be taken as having been in existence, –28 January 1289/90 the date of Devorgilla's death (*CDS*, ii, no. 405), and it is mentioned 7 March 1296/7, among the houses in receipt of payments from the fermes of burghs (*Rot. Scot.*, i, 39). One of its priors, Ninian Shanks, appears, 10 May 1490 (*RMS*, ii, no. 2056). The prior and four friars granted a feu charter, 21 December 1560 (*Wigtownshire Chrs.*, 132). The revenues of this house (Bryce, *Grey Friars*, i, 140 *n.*) were probably made over to the burgh at the Reformation, like those of other friaries, but of this no record has been found.

SUPPOSED FOUNDATIONS

Coupar Angus. Listed in the Appendix to Spottiswoode's *Hist. of the Ch. of Scotland* (1677), 16 (25). Brockie (p. 1236) declares that the founder and date of fd'n. are unknown, though at another point (p. 1241) he mentions Thomas, commendator-abbot of Coupar and dean of Dunkeld as the probable founder and (p. 1237) gives *c.* 1480 as a possible date. He also supplies transcripts of charters concerning this house from 26 Feb. 1487/8 onwards (p. 1238). Thus he exemplifies a charter of James Ogilvy of Airlie to the Friars Preachers of Coupar, 28 March 1488 (p. 1237). This document speaks of his donation as made at the 'instigation and request' of Thomas, 'Cistercian abbot of Coupar', who also attests the charter; but the contemporary ab. was John Schanwell (1480–1560) (*Coupar Angus Chrs.*, ii, 274). Again, it refers to Ogilvy's wife, in 1488, as Elizabeth Douglas, but this is almost certainly erroneous (see *SP*, i, 114). There are good grounds for regarding this and other charters (pp. 1238–40) said to pertain to this house as spurious, while the account which Brockie quotes (pp. 1240–1) ostensibly 'from the papers of James Ramsay', of the expulsion of the thirty 'monks' of this house by Donald Campbell, ab. of Coupar, at the Reformation, is entirely incredible. Although Brockie distinguishes this alleged house from the house at Cupar, Fife, he appears to have taken over a supposition that there was a Blackfriars' house at Coupar Angus which is based on a confusion with the Cupar fd'n. It may safely be stated that the house at Coupar Angus is fictitious.

Crail. Brockie (p. 1254) has a charter of Elizabeth Hepburn, abbess of the Cistercian nuns of Haddington, granting the Friars Preachers a site for erecting a ch. and monastery in the burgh of Crail, 28 Sept. 1448. This charter is not genuine. The head of the Cistercian nunnery at Haddington was a prioress and this office was held from –1440 to *c.* 1463 by Mariota de Douglas (*East Lothian Trans.*, v, 7–8). Other charters (Brockie, pp. 1255–7) to this alleged house must likewise be rejected as unauthentic. There is no reliable evidence of a Dominican monastery at Crail.

Dumfries. Included among the Dominican houses listed in NLS. MS. 22.1.14, 153 f., and in the Appendix to Spottiswoode's *Hist. of the Ch. of Scotland* (1677 edn.), 16 (25). This entry is erroneous, as is the reference to the lands of the Friars Preachers (*rectius* Friars Minor) in Dumfries, 1 May 1579 (*RMS*, iv, no. 32).

Dysart. Included in the lists cited for Dumfries. Brockie (p. 1229) has a charter of William Sinclair of Dysart granting the Friars Preachers a site for the building of a monastery, of which the ch. is to be dedicated to St. Cuthbert, 27 March 1466 or 1467 or 1468 (the latter part of the date is blotted and uncertain). One of the witnesses is James, bp. of St. Andrews, who, however, d. 1465 (Dowden, *Bishops*, p. 32). This charter, of which the style itself raises suspicions, cannot be accepted as genuine. The statement is also made, on the authority of the *New Statistical Account*, that 'the chapel at Dysart (dedicated to St. Denis) belonged to a priory of Dominicans' (Mackinlay, *Ancient Ch. Dedications (non-scriptural)*, p. 327). 'Yrland freris' were present at Ravenscraig, near Dysart, 9 April 1540 (*SHS, Misc.*, x, 42) but no reliable evidence of a Dominican house here can be found.

Forres. Included in the lists cited for Dumfries. Other evidence is entirely wanting. This foundation can be rejected.

Inverkeithing. Included in the lists cited for Dumfries and given by Maitland (*History*, i, 262). Brockie (p. 1224) has an undated charter of Hugh de Lundey [*sic*], lord of the burgh of Inverkeithing, granting a site for a Blackfriars' monastery here, with the consent of 'the illustrious king of Scots Robert de Bruis my lord'. The latter phrase, in itself highly suspect, would date the charter 1306+. But among the witnesses are Walter, ab. of Inchcolm (1258–1277+) and Roger de Moubray (d. –23 January 1268/9). This charter must be regarded as unauthentic. Stephen (*Hist. of Inverkeithing*, 301) declares that 'of the existence of a religious house of the Black Friars the evidence is by no means conclusive'. There is a reference to Blackfriars here in the index of *Treasurers Accts.*, ii; but the corresponding entry in the text (*ibid.*, ii, 264) refers merely to the 'Freris of Inverkethin', i.e. almost certainly the Greyfriars.

Jedburgh. Included in the lists cited for Dumfries. The name 'Blackfriars' is used locally but innaccurately (see Watson, 'Hist. of Franciscan Friary of Jedburgh', *HBNC*, 1906, 82). There is also an erroneous reference to a Dominican convent at Jedburgh 'whereof the Lairds of Fairnihurst were patrons' (*Macfarlane Geog. Collns.*, iii, 158). No such convent existed here.

Kinghorn. Included in the lists cited for Dumfries. Brockie, who gives (p. 1228) a vague account of this fd'n., has a charter (*loc. cit.*) of James de Kirkcaldy making a donation to the Friars Preachers at Kinghorn, 28 Sept. 1388. This charter, witnessed by an abbot (Bernard) of Coupar Angus not otherwise known, is very probably spurious. The existence of a monastery here is not otherwise attested in records and may be regarded as very dubious.

Kirkcudbright. There is a reference in 1512 to the Friars Preachers of Kirkcudbright (*ER*, xiii, 472). This is evidently an error for Friars Minor.

Linlithgow. Included in the lists cited for Dumfries. Brockie (p. 1219), who says that the name of the founder and the date of fd'n. are unknown, gives a charter (pp. 1219–20) of John [Balliol], king of Scots, who, 'since for the same friars (i.e. the Blackfriars) a new house has been erected in our town of Linlithgow', takes it under his protection, 19 March 1294/5. This charter can hardly be genuine—Alan, bp. of Caithness and chancellor of Scotland, who died in Oct.–Nov 1291, appears among the witnesses. Again, an indenture between William More, lord of Abercorn, and the Friars Preachers of Linlithgow, 20 May 1348 (Brockie, pp. 1221–3) is said to be attested by the vicar-general of Scotland and sixteen priors attending a chapter at St. Andrews; this detail suggests that the document is a fabrication. References, however, are found in 1451 and 1453 to a croft held on lease by the Friars Preachers of this town (*ER*, v. 457, 544); while, on 29 Oct. 1503, a payment is recorded 'to the Blak Freris of Linlithqw' (*TA*, ii, 255). The existence of a Dominican house here, perhaps for a brief period, cannot be ruled out; but it is difficult to resist the conclusion that the references in the above records are errors for the White Friars of Linlithgow.

St. Ninian's. Given in *Chron. Extracta*, p. 249, clearly in error for St. Monan's.

Selkirk. Included in the lists cited for Dumfries. Brockie (p. 1242) gives a charter (from Tweedie) of James Tweedie of Drumelzier, who has granted the Friars Preachers a site for building a 'new monastery' and ch., which on the instructions of David II, is to be dedicated to St. Ninian, 28 Sept. 1358. This charter purports to bear the seal of Alexander Maxwell, archdeacon of Tweedale (Tuuedaliae). There was no such archdeaconry and even if we take this as referring to Teviotdale, no mention of an archdeacon of this name has been found (Henry de Smalham was appointed to the archdeaconry of Teviotdale in 1354 (*CPL*, ii, 516)). The authenticity of this charter is very questionable; and apart from Brockie there seems to be no evidence of a house of Friars Preachers here.

THE FRANCISCAN (GREY) FRIARS

GENERAL NOTES

ALTHOUGH St. Francis and his first companions received papal approval in 1215, an unwillingness to adopt a formal organization meant that the papal establishment in its final form took place considerably later. Various groups followed the Rule with differing degrees of severity and laxity. In the late fourteenth century a reformed observance was recognized, at first within the order, then as a separate body. When this occurred the main body of the friars became known as the Conventuals and the reformed group as Observants.

(a) THE FRIARS MINOR CONVENTUAL

The Friars Minor are said to have entered Scotland for the first time in 1231 (*Chron. Melrose*, 142). A Scottish province existed from *c.* 1231–3 to 1239, again from 1260 to 1279, and from 1329 to 1359, when the Scottish vicariate was suppressed. This decree may have been ignored as a Scottish vicar-general occurs in 1375. The schism led to the final separation of the Scottish Greyfriars from the English province (cf. Thomas de Eccleston's *Tractatus de adventu Fratrum Minorum in Angliam* ed. D. G. Little (Paris, 1909) p. 50, note b, and the same editor's *Studies in English Franciscan History*, 236–8). In the accompanying notes reference is frequently made to W. Moir Bryce, *The Scottish Greyfriars*. This work has some unsatisfactory features; but its writer made a close investigation of the public records of Scotland and it includes a useful collection of Scottish Franciscan documents.

HOUSES OF THE FRANCISCAN (GREY) FRIARS

(a) THE FRIARS MINOR CONVENTUAL

Name	County	Minimum income (1561)	Fd.	Date D. or Sec.
BERWICK			1231	1538/9

Name	County	Minimum income (1561)	Fd.	Date D. or Sec.
DUMFRIES	Dumfries	£34	1234 –1266	1569
DUNDEE	Angus	£52	–1289	c1560
HADDINGTON	East Lothian		–1242	1566/7
§ INVERKEITHING	Fife		1268(?) or –1384	1559
§ KIRKCUDBRIGHT	Kirkcudbright	£14	1449–56	1569
LANARK	Lanark	£7	1328–9 (?1325–6)	–1566
ROXBURGH	Roxburgh		1232 or 1232–4	1547+

BERWICK. Chronicle sources (*Chron. Melrose*, 142; *Chron. Bower*, ii, 59) would place fd'n. of this house in or about 1231, the year in which the friars entered Scotland (Bryce, *Grey Friars*, i, 6). Brockie (p. 1274), however, gives a charter of Alexander II, who has granted the Friars Minor a 'sufficient place' in the burgh of Berwick for building a convent and has constructed for them a church and other buildings, with an annual endowment of twenty merks from the fermes of Berwick, 28 Sept. 1231. This charter, even if spurious, may embody fact. The church was dedicated by David de Bernham, bp. of St. Andrews, 6 May 1244 (Anderson, *Early Sources*, ii, 525). On the evidence of pittances by Edward I it would appear that there were between five and seven friars in this house in Dec. 1299 (*Liber quotidianus*, 26). In Oct. 1335 the number is stated as thirty, but in Jan. the following year there were only fifteen friars of this order in Berwick (B.M. MSS. Cotton Nero, c, viii, fo. 204). A mandate of Edward III, 10 Aug. 1333, ordered the Scottish friars to be removed and English friars substituted for them (*Rot. Scot.*, i, 258). On 15 Dec. 1337, a payment from the English Exchequer to the friars is authorized (*CDS*, iii, no. 1251). No further record evidence for this house appears in record sources for two centuries, but it is mentioned in the fifteenth-c. poem, 'The Freiris of Berwick' (*Poems of Dunbar*, ed. W. Mackay Mackenzie, 183). This house was suppressed between 10 March 1538/9 (*LP Papers Henry VIII*, xiv[1], no. 494) and Michaelmas 1539 (*PRO*, Ministers' Accounts, Henry VIII, no. 7364, m. 11d).

DUMFRIES (ST. MARY). An alleged charter of fd'n. by Alan of Galloway, 20 April 1234 (Brockie, p. 1268) is undoubtedly spurious as its phraseology and lack of witnesses attest. The idea that Alan may have been the founder is likewise unconfirmed. Other suggested dates or fd'n. such as *c.* 1262 (Bryce, *Grey Friars*, i, 199) and –1305 (Anderson, *Early Sources*, ii, 479n) have equal lack of justification. The house was fd. before 1266 (*ER*, i, 27; cf. Little, *Franciscan Papers*, 221), which might account for the uncorroborated suggestion (Spottiswoode, 448) that the friary was fd. by Devorgilla de Balliol. The friars' ch. was the scene of the slaying of John Comyn by Robert Bruce, 10 Feb. 1305/6. On 9 Sept. 1427, the Pope granted an indulgence in favour of the repair of the conventual buildings (*CSSR*, ii, 168). Twelve brothers are said to be living in the house at that time; in 1548 this number had been reduced to seven (*Cal. State Papers Elizabeth*, 1601–3, 333, 339, 372). The warden and five friars occur between 1555 and 1557 (Bryce, *Grey Friars*, i, 258–61). The burgh had a grant of the revenues and lands of the Greyfriars (with other ecclesiastical properties), 23 April 1569 (*RMS*, iv, no. 1848). By 1570, the Town Council had entered into possession of the friary (Bryce, *Grey Friars*, i, 214).

DUNDEE. Erected before 1296 (Stevenson, *Documents*, ii, no. 484). The house is said to have been fd. by Devorgilla (*Scotichronicon*: lib. viii, cap. xxv; *Chron. Bower*, i, 474; Spottiswoode, 449) (see Bryce, *Grey Friars*, i, 218 and *n* on the alleged fd'n. charter); and if this was the case, the fd'n. must have taken place not later than 1289, the year of her death. But this is unsubstantiated as the alleged charter (Brockie, p. 1435) of John [Balliol], K. of Scots, confirming and amplifying his mother's foundation, 30 March 1294/5, is spurious. It was in the friars' church that the Scottish clergy, 24 Feb. 1309/10, attested their support of Robert Bruce's claims to the Crown (*APS*, i, 100). But it should be noted there are difficulties about accepting this date (*SHR*, xxiii, 284). In 1335 the friary is stated to have been partly burned, as well as much of the town, by 'ships of Newcastle' (*Chron. Lanercost*, 282). Again, according to Froissart, it was totally destroyed by fire during Richard II's invasion in 1385 (Bryce, *Grey Friars*, 223), but there is no other evidence that the English penetrated north of the Forth. Besides the vicar-general of the order, who resided in this house, there were fourteen friars, including the warden, 12 March 1481/2 (Bryce, *Grey Friars*, ii, 129–32), 'but the number of friars resident in 1560 . . . is wholly problematical' (*ibid.*, i, 225). In 1543 the friary was sacked by Reformers (*Hamilton Papers*, i, no. 11; ii, no. 187; Maxwell, *Old Dundee*, 395); and in all probability it was burned, with the other ecclesiastical buildings of Dundee, by the English in Nov. 1548 (Maxwell, *Old Dundee*, 113). The magistrates were in possession of the land and buildings in 1560 (Bryce, *Grey Friars*, i, 227). On 11 Sept. 1564, Queen Mary gave permission for the use of the place and yard formerly belonging to the friars as a public burying ground (*Dundee Chrs.*, 40). It is described (Bryce, *Grey Friars*, i, 229) as 'by far the most wealthy Franciscan community in Scotland', its revenues for 1560 being assessed as £135 (*ibid.*, i, 236).

HADDINGTON. A reference to the burial of Patrick of Athole at the place of the friars Minor at Haddington in 1242 (*Chron. Lanercost*, 50) justifies the statement (Bryce, *Grey Friars*, i, 168) that 'as early as 1242 we find [the friars] in possession of a regular friary' there. A charter of Patrick, E. of Dunbar, which has no witnesses, granting the friars a site for the church and convent, 30 Sept. 1252 (Tweedie MS., cited Brockie, p. 1446) is spurious; and the date of fd'n. (as well as the identity of the founder) remains uncertain. The Greyfriars' church is said (e.g. Major, *History*, 297), to have been called 'the Lamp of Lothian', though this has been contested (James H. Jamieson, ' "The Lamp of Lothian": Parish or Friary Church?' in *East Lothian Trans.*, iii (1938), 112–19). The friary was burned by the English in 1355 (Major, *History*, 297; *Scotichronicon*, lib. xiv, cap. xiii (*Chron. Bower*, ii, 354)). There were eight friars with the warden, in 1478; six with the warden, in 1539 and 1543; three, with the warden, 1557–9 (Bryce, *Grey Friars*, i, 193–4) This house was again burned by the English in May 1544 (*LP Henry VIII*, xix[1], no. 533). Its alienation to the magistrates, 10 Oct. 1555 (Burgh Recs.), and its homologation 9 Oct. 1559 (Bryce, *Grey Friars*, i, 127), was intended to be provisional ('during the present calamity that has fallen upon the religious and churchmen'); and in 1561 stringent orders were issued against the demolition of the friary ch. (*ibid.*, i, 173). But on 24 March 1566/7 the burgh had from Queen Mary a charter of the ecclesiastical properties, including those of the Friars Minor (*RMS*, iv, no. 1776); and in 1572 the Town Council decided on the demolition of the friars' ch. (Bryce, *Grey Friars*, i, 173).

INVERKEITHING. The alleged charter of Philip de Moubray, lord of Barnbougle, narrating his erection of a ch. and convent for the Friars Minor at Inverkeithing with an endowment from the lands of Barnbougle, 28 Oct. 1268 (Brockie, p. 1455) is spurious. The fd'n. does not appear in a list of Franciscan houses, Feb. 1296/7 (*Rot. Scot.*, i, 38). A bull of Pope Clement VI, 29 Nov. 1346 (Bryce, *Grey Friars*, ii, 149) erecting Lanark friary also authorizes the erection of another on a site granted by David II 'far from the attacks of enemies', and this proviso may have been applied to the fd'n. of Inverkeithing friary (Reg. Aven., 88, fos. 191–1v; Bryce, *Grey Friars*, i, 248). A specific reference is found, 10 March 1384/5, when the bailies of Inverkeithing, in accordance with a grant of Robert II, remitted to the Friars Minor a sum due 'from a certain tenement in Inverkeithing which the said friars inhabit' (*ER*, iii, 127 ff., where the date is erroneously given as 1364). Of the community, the warden is alone identifiable in the sixteenth c. (Bryce, *Grey Friars*, i, 258–61; ii, 161). The friary and its garden were conveyed to John Swinton, 4 July 1559 (*ibid.*, i, 249), ii, 165). The hospitium of the friary remains. (See also Stephen, *Hist. of Inverkeithing*, 301–3.)

KIRKCUDBRIGHT. An alleged charter, which has no witnesses, purporting to record the fd'n. of a house here by Roger de Quincy, e. of Winchester, lord of Galloway and constable of Scotland, 16 Sept. 1239 (Tweedie MS. cited Brockie, pp. 1431–2) is spurious. A reference to an offering made by Edward I on the altar of the priory of Kirkcudbright refers to the [Augustinian] priory of St. Mary's Isle (Bryce, *Grey Friars*, i, 36–37). A petition of 29 Dec. 1470 seeking confirmation of the erection of this house names the founder as James II for the souls, weal of himself and his queen; a fact which would seem to place the foundation to a date after his marriage in 1449 (Reg. Supp., 663, fo. 5). A reference, 12 July 1458, to a payment to 'the Friars Minor of the said burgh newly founded by the present King' (*ER*, vi, 406–7) and notices of the Friars Minor of Kirkcudbright occur 17 Sept. 1456, and 15 July 1457 (*ibid.*, vi, 201, 353). A foundation, *c.* 1455 (Bryce, *Grey Friars*, i, 36) would appear to be likely, but available evidence will only support 1449 × 1456. With the exception of the warden, the number in the community at the Reformation is unknown (*ibid.*, i, 258–61). According to one uncorroborated account, 'active Franciscanism in Kirkcudbright was brought to a peaceful termination in the autumn of 1560' (Bryce, *Grey Friars*, i, 254). On 6 Dec. 1569, James VI gave a charter of the place and ch. of the Greyfriars, 'which for a long time past have been destroyed and now lie waste', to Thomas MacLellan of Bombie (*ibid.*, ii, 170), who in turn conveyed those properties to the Town Council, the friars' ch. to become the parish ch., 24 March 1570/1 (*ibid.*, ii, 171).

LANARK. According to an alleged charter, Robert I granted the Friars Minor a site for a convent with a sum for its endowment between 27 March 1325 and 26 March 1326 (Brockie, p. 1459). The charter is spurious, but the fd'n. was projected by Robert. The fdn. has been dated 11 Nov. 1328—15 May 1329 (Bryce, *Grey Friars*, i, 240). The lands granted for a site are mentioned, 7 Aug. 1329 (*ER*, i, 163). The actual fd'n. of the house appears to have been carried out by David II who obtained a bull of erection from Pope Clement VI, 29 Nov. 1346 (Bryce, *Grey Friars*, ii, 149; Reg, Aven, 88, fos. 191–iv), in terms of which there were to be twelve friars, though it is doubtful whether that number was attained. Only two friars are identifiable in the sixteenth c. (Bryce, *Grey Friars*, i 258–61). Before the Reformation (the date is unrecorded), the place and lands of the friary were leased to James Lockhart of Lee (*ibid.*, i, 243; ii, 158). It is not known when the friary was abandoned, but the removal of its stonework had been going on –1566, when it was checked by the Lords of Council (*ibid.*, i, 243).

ROXBURGH. An alleged charter of Alexander II which narrates that the king has granted the Friars Minor a site at Roxburgh and erected for them a ch. and other buildings, 18 Oct. 1232 (Brockie, pp. 1281–2) is spurious. The date of fd'n. may have been 1232–4 (Bryce, *Grey Friars*, i, 161). The friars' cemetery was dedicated 4 May 1235 (*Kel. Lib.*, no. 418). There were four friars here in 1336–7 (Bryce, *Grey Friars*, i, 164). This house ('the friars near Kelso') was burned by the English, 14 Sept. 1545 (*LP Henry VIII*, xx², nos. 456, 533) and was evidently abandoned; in Nov. 1547, it was partially roofed over for military purposes by English troops (*Cal. State Papers Scot.*, i, no. 98). The warden and one friar are found in receipt of pensions after 1560 (*Thirds of Benefices*, 99).

INCOMPLETE FOUNDATION

Elgin. About 1281 William, E. of Ross, gave certain lands for the upkeep of the Friars Minor, 'who for the time or in the future may be in occupation of their house in Elgin beside the cathedral'. If the friars had not taken up residence or were unwilling to remain there, the income of these lands was to be used for the maintenance of two chaplains in the cathedral (*Moray Reg.*, no. 220). The settlement of the friars at this time must have been temporary, as the latter alternative came into operation. See under Observants.

SUPPOSED FOUNDATIONS

Banff. A Franciscan convent, its ch. dedicated to St. John, is mentioned here (*Aberdeen–Banff Coll.*, 205). This is a confusion with the Carmelite house.

Forfar. According to *CDS* (ii, no. 856), Edward I, on 23 Nov. 1296, ordered his treasurer in Scotland to examine the rolls of King Alexander [III] and King John [Balliol] regarding the claims of the Friars Minor in the towns of Berwick, Roxburgh, Haddington, Dumfries and Forfar. But reference to Stevenson, *Documents* (ii, no. cccclxxxiv) shows (under 23 Nov. 1297) that this is an error. The king's mandate is concerned with the friars of

Dundee, who have 10 l. sterling and 20 l. of wax yearly from the ferme of Forfar. There were no Greyfriars at Forfar.

Inverness. The idea that there were Greyfriars here is due to confusion with the Black friars.

THE FRANCISCAN (GREY) FRIARS

(b) THE OBSERVANTS

IN a letter to Pope Julius II, 1 Feb. 1506/7, James IV declares that forty-two years previously his grandmother, Mary of Gueldres, introduced the Observants to Scotland, while he himself 'completed and furnished for them house after house' (*James IV Letters*, no. 76). Both parts of this statement would appear to be accurate. It has been shown (Bryce, *Grey Friars*, i, 58) that K. James had in mind the bull of Pope Pius II, 9 June 1463, addressed to the vicar-general of the ultramontane province of the Observants, in these terms: 'We have learned that, on the account of the devotion of Mary . . . illustrious queen of Scotland and of that people, at the request of certain merchants, you have lately sent your brethren as preachers to that kingdom, in which no house of the Observance of your order has been built. . . . We therefore grant you power to erect, found and build and likewise to receive in that kingdom three or four houses, if you find any who graciously proffer a foundation or erection of this sort' (*ibid.*, ii, 276). The erection of the Edinburgh friary may have started before the receipt of this bull under the terms of which houses were founded at Edinburgh, Aberdeen, Glasgow and St. Andrews, these four being confirmed in possession of their property by James III, 21 Dec. 1479 (*RMS*, ii, no. 1434). It seems likely that these were the only four houses in existence at this date (cf. Bryce, *Grey Friars*, i, 61–2, 299). On 19 March 1481/2, the bp. of Dunkeld received permission from Pope Sixtus IV to found two or three other houses (*CPL*, xiii, 785; Bryce, *Grey Friars*, ii, 250–1). The fulfilment of this dispensation would appear to have been effected by James IV to whom the foundation of Stirling can be certainly attributed while Ayr, Perth, Jedburgh, and Elgin, all of which first appear on record during his reign, may also have been royal foundations. No particulars of the incomes of the Observant houses are available.

HOUSES OF THE FRANCISCAN (GREY) FRIARS

(b) The Observants

Name	County	Fd.	D.	Date or Sec.
ABERDEEN	Aberdeen	1469		1559
AYR	Ayr	1488 × 1497		1567
EDINBURGH	Midlothian	*c.* 1463		1562
‡ ELGIN	Moray	−1494		*c.* 1559(?)
GLASGOW	Lanark	1473–9		1566/7
JEDBURGH	Roxburgh	−1505		?
PERTH	Perth	−1496		1559–60
ST. ANDREWS	Fife	1463 × 66		1559–67
STIRLING	Stirling	1494		1559–67

ABERDEEN. Brockie (p. 1479) gives an alleged letter of the provost, bailies and community of Aberdeen, 28 June 1450, to the vicar of the Observants in Scotland, intimating that as Richard Vaus of Many has informed them that the vicar is agreeable to sending friars to that burgh if these can obtain an 'honest house' to dwell in; and since Vaus has given a site and the community (i.e. of the burgh) has erected a cloister, church, etc., requesting the vicar to supply friars. According to another spurious entry in Brockie (pp. 1480–1), this foundation was confirmed by Pope Nicholas V, 5 Dec. 1450. From references in the Aberdeen Obituary Calendar, Moir Bryce (*Grey Friars*, i, 307) concludes that the friary was 'a foundation of gradual growth dating from . . . 1461', when the Observants reached Aberdeen. It is not till 1 May and 20 July 1469 we find Richard Vaus giving charters of his land to the friars (and it is not mentioned that this was the site of the friary) (*ibid.*, ii, 212, 216), while this donation was confirmed by James III, 9 May 1469 (*ibid.*, ii, 217) and Thomas, bp. of Aberdeen, who speaks of this land as 'for the structure and fabric of the [friars'] church', which may indicate the grant of an endowment rather than a site, 23 May 1469 (*ibid.*, ii, 217–18). That the burgh was associated with Vaus and others in providing for this friary, though their respective contributions are not made clear, is shown by a crown charter of confirmation of the land included in its site, 21 Dec. 1479 (*ibid.*, ii, 195). The statement of Father John Hay (*ibid.*, ii, 176) that this house was constituted in 1470 by the bp. of Aberdeen, who erected a convent beside the university, cannot be accepted. But if the friars were earlier in Aberdeen, it was evidently about this date that their house was built. A new and enlarged ch. was constructed for the friars, 1518–32, by Bp. Gavin Dunbar (*ibid.*, i, 314–16). Moir Bryce regards 12–16 as the maximum number of friars (*ibid.*, i, 318). On 29 Dec. 1559, the friars resigned their entire possessions to the Town Council (*ibid.*, ii, 233; *Aberdeen Friars*, 97), who, on 11 March 1559/60, resolved to maintain the Greyfriars' ch. and place for the town's use (*ibid.*, 97). James VI granted to the Town Council, 30 December 1567, the place of the Friars Minor to be converted into a hospital (*ibid.*, p. 100). It is said that the ch. stood derelict until 1624, when the citizens began to 'reedifie' it (*Aberdeen Description*, 11); and it remained in use as a parish ch. till its removal in 1903. The remaining buildings passed to George, earl Marischal, 22 Sept. 1593 (Bryce, *Grey Friars*, i, 328) and were bestowed by him on Marischal College (*Aberdeen–Banff Coll.*, 200).

AYR. The fd'n. has been attributed to the inhabitants of the town in 1474 (Father John Hay cited Bryce, *Grey Friars*, ii, 176); a similar statement (Spottiswoode, 452) gives the date as 1472. An alleged charter (Brockie, pp. 1491–2) of the provist, bailies and the rest of the community to the vicar-provincial of Scotland narrating their foundation of a ch. and convent for the Observants is dated 28 Oct. 1472, and a spurious bull of Pope Sixtus IV (*ibid.*, p. 1493) purports to confirm the erection, 18 June 1474. But it appears to have been erected as one of the friaries sanctioned by the bull of this Pope, on the petition of James, bp. of Dunkeld, 19 March 1481/2 (Bryce, *Grey Friars*, i, 352; ii, 250). This erection is credited to James IV (1488–1513) (*Diurnal of Occurrents*, 4), and this assertion when coupled to the king's personal claim in 1506/7 (*James IV Letters*, no. 76) to have founded

Observant houses, may have some substance. The house first appears on record 7 March 1497/8 (*TA*, i, 381). It is asserted (Bryce, *Grey Friars*, i, 356) that the friary was sacked at the Reformation; but there is no record of this (*ibid.*, i, 147); or for the assumption (*ibid.*, i, 366), from the fact that there is no record of pensions paid them, that the friars 'quitted the burgh in a body'. A precept for the grant of the lands and possessions of the Grey-friars (and others) to the burgh was given, 14 April 1567 (Bryce, *Grey Friars*, ii, 255).

EDINBURGH. This was the earliest of the Scottish Observant houses. It is alleged that six friars came from Holland in 1447, but this suggestion, and the idea that they occupied their house in 1455 (or, perhaps more correctly, in 1458), after the property had been incorporated by apostolic letters in the Roman Church (Father John Hay cited Bryce, *Grey Friars*, i, 47, 56 and n; ii, 174) is unsubstantiated. Friars of the order were in Scotland, and probably based on Edinburgh before 9 June 1463, but the acquisition of their first Scottish house was probably after this date (*ibid.*, ii, 276). A payment to the friars is entered in the Exchequer account 27 July 1462–26 July 1463 (*ER*, vii, 211) and another, for the repair of their place, appears in the account of 27 July 1463–12 July 1464 (*ibid.*, vii, 284). The repairs may have been to the ch. of St. John the Baptist 'outside the burgh', to their use of which, consent was given, 18 Nov. 1464 (*St. Giles Reg.*, no. 81). The friars had moved to a site within the burgh, bestowed on them by James Douglas of Cassillis and the citizens before 21 Dec. 1479, when they were confirmed in possession of their place and property by James III (Bryce, *Grey Friars*, ii, 195). The convent at this date consisted of twelve friars, including the prior (*Laing Charters*, no. 177). The friary was destroyed by Reformers, 14 June 1559 (*Diurnal of Occurrents*, 269; Lesley, *History*, 275). On 17 Aug. 1562, the Town Council petitioned the queen to grant the yards of the Greyfriars as a burying ground (*Edinburgh Recs.*, 1557–72, 146).

ELGIN. There was a temporary settlement of Greyfriars here in the thirteenth c.: see under Conventual Friars. It is alleged that the Observantine house was fd. by John Innes of Innes in 1479 (Father John Hay cited Bryce, *Grey Friars*, i, 362; ii, 176). The only corroboration for this assertion is a spurious bull of Pope Sixtus IV, which, in response to Innes's petition, confirms his foundation in 1479 (Brockie, p. 1498; no day or month mentioned). The assumption (Bryce, *Grey Friars*, ii, 250) that this was one of the 'two or three' friaries sanctioned by the foregoing Pope, 19 March 1481/2 (*ibid.*) is much more probable, although the house may not have been erected until the reign of James IV (1488–1513) to whom the fd'n. has been attributed (*Diurnal of Occurrents*, 4). A payment to the friars is recorded 5 June 1494–17 August 1495 (*ER*, x, 523). At an unascertained date (probably *c.* 1559), the buildings passed into the possession of the burgh and, from 1563, were used as a Court of Justice (Bryce, *Grey Friars*, i, 364). The Greyfriars' lands were leased by James VI to Robert Innes of Invermarky, 20 April 1573 (*RMS*, iii, no. 2133).

GLASGOW. Allegedly fd. in 1472, its fd'n. is attributed, mistakenly, to the abp. (Father John Hay cited Bryce, *Grey Friars*, ii, 176). According to a spurious bull of Pope Sixtus IV, 1 Dec. 1476 (Brockie, p. 1476), William [Turnbull], bp. of Glasgow (1448–54), introduced the Observants there (cf. Bryce, *Grey Friars*, ii, 276). But as their place was too small for a complete (*integrum*) convent, John [Laing], bp. of Glasgow (1473/4–1482/3), wished to build them a house, of which Thomas Forsyth, canon of Glasgow cathedral and rector of Glasgow, was also a benefactor. The latter part of this statement incorporates fact. Bishop Laing appears as granting the site and Forsyth likewise as a donor in the charter of confirmation given by James III, 21 December 1479 (Bryce, *Grey Friars*, ii, 195). It is stated (Brockie, p. 1477) that the friars' ch. was dedicated (to the Blessed Virgin Mary), on the 8th Sunday after Trinity [3 Aug.], 1477, but this is uncorroborated. At the Reformation the friars were ejected before 19 June 1560 (*Glasgow Protocols*, no. 1370), and on 13 Nov. 1560 the pr. and sub-pr. conveyed their place and yards to John Graham and his wife, who received crown confirmation of this grant, 27 April 1567 (*ibid.*, no. 924; *RMS*, iv, no. 1790). But properties of the Friars Minor were among those granted to the Town Council, 16 March 1566/7 (*Glasgow Chrs.*, Pt. II, no. lix). These were bestowed on the college (university) by the magistrates, 6 Jan. 1572/3 (*ibid.*, no. lxiii). But although the grant to John Graham was set aside by the lords of council and session, 7 June 1578 (*Glasgow Friars Munimenta*, lxvi), the friary appears to have remained in the private ownership of Sir John Stewart of Minto into whose hands it had passed before 1575 (Bryce, *Grey Friars*, i, 348).

JEDBURGH. Allegedly erected in 1513 by the nobles of the Border (Father John Hay cited Bryce, *Grey Friars*, ii, 178) or in the same year by the inhabitants of Jedburgh (Father Richard Augustine Hay, Scotia Sacra, 554; Spottiswoode, 453). Neither of these statements can be corroborated. Friars of the order were present in Jedburgh, 27 March 1505 (*TA*, iii, 508). The bull of erection attributed to Pope Adrian VI, 31 Jan. 1521/2 (Bryce, *Grey Friars*, ii, 262) is spurious. This house had a brief and chequered career. Although it is not specifically mentioned, the friary was probably involved in the destruction of the town by Suffolk's forces, 24 Sept. 1523 (*LP Henry VIII*, iii2, no. 3360); and it was burned by Eure, 9 June 1544 (*ibid.*, xix1, no. 762) and by Hertford in Sept. 1545 (*ibid.*, xx2, no. 456). The assertion (Bryce, *Grey Friars*, i, 379) that 'at the Reformation the site and buildings passed into the possession of the magistrates' is unsubstantiated. The crown grant of ecclesiastical properties (mainly chaplaincies) to the burgh (*RMS*, iii, no. 1897) does not explicitly mention those of the Greyfriars. See Watson, 'History of the Franciscan Friary of Jedburgh', *Berwickshire Hist.*, xx (1910).

PERTH. A payment is erroneously stated to have been made to Greyfriars of Perth in 1358 (Fittis, *Eccles. Annals of Perth*, 267; The entry to which he refers (*ER*, i, 557) is a payment merely to 'Friars', in this case evidently the Blackfriars). The fd'n. of this friary is said by Father John Hay to have been made by Lord Oliphant in 1440, but this is uncorroborated. An alleged charter (Brockie, p. 1488) of the provost, bailies and community of Perth to the vicar-general of the Observants in Scotland, in view of his sending friars to occupy the monastery built by Sir Laurence of Oliphant of Aberdelgie, making provision for the furnishing and upkeep of their house and ch., 28 April 1460; and also (*ibid.*, p. 1487) a purported bull of Pope Pius II, 26 July 1460, confirming the erection of this friary by Sir Laurence Oliphant (who became Lord Oliphant in 1458) are spurious. The absence of this house from the group of Observant houses which had their property confirmed to them by James III, 21 Dec. 1479 (Bryce, *Grey Friars*, ii, 195) would suggest a subsequent date of foundation. It first occurs on record in receipt of royal bounty, 1 Nov. 1492 (*TA*, i, 323), and appears like several other Observant houses to have been founded after the accession of James IV in 1488 (see *James IV Letters*, no. 76). The Perth friary contained eight friars at its destruction by Reformers in May 1559 (Lesley, *History*, 272; Knox, *Works*, i, 323; *Chron. Pitscottie*, ii, 146) and its site became a burying ground in 1580 (Fittis, *Eccles. Annals of Perth*, 269; Bryce, *Grey Friars*, i, 302).

ST. ANDREWS. An alleged bull of fd'n. of Pope Pius II, 24 Nov. 1458 (Brockie, p. 1471), confirming the erection of a house of Observants by James Kennedy, bp. of St. Andrews, is spurious. But that bp. was the founder, and additional endowments conferred on the friars by his successor, Patrick Graham, may well have been in the form of a larger house within the burgh (*ibid.*, p. 1472). These donations by Kennedy and Graham were confirmed by James III, 21 Dec. 1479 (Bryce, *Grey Friars*, ii, 195). The date of foundation is uncertain. It is unlikely to have been before 9 June 1463 (*ibid.*, ii, 276) and as Kennedy d. 24 May 1465 (Watt, *Fasti*, 295) it must have been in existence before this date. The process of fd'n. may not, however, have been complete at Kennedy's death and this may explain, not only Graham's benefaction, but also the petition of the vicar and friars of the Order of the Friars Minor in Scotland for confirmation to them of 'the place called Bethlem in the city of St. Andrews', 14 March 1466 (Reg. Supp., 592, fo. 11v; see ST. ANDREWS, under Carmelite Friars). It is significant that the fd'n. by Bp. Kennedy of the friary at St. Andrews followed on the founding by him of St. Salvator's College (*q.v.*) (see Dunlop, *James Kennedy*, 297). Reputedly founded for twenty-four friars, only six are readily identifiable in the Reformation period (*Essays on Scottish Reformation*, 239). There are references to the burning of this house by Norman Leslie in July 1547 (*RSS*, iii, nos. 2345, 2363). The friary was resigned to the magistrates, 18 May 1559 (Bryce, *Grey Friars*, ii, 202). On or about 14 June following it was destroyed by Reformers (Lesley, *History*, 273) or according to Knox (*Works*, i, 349–50) by the magistrates; and when, on 21 Sept. of that year, the magistrates were invested in the property, the site was described as wasted and the buildings as ruined (Bryce, *Grey Friars*, ii, 202). Along with other ecclesiastical properties, the former possessions of the friars were granted to the burgh by Queen Mary, 17 April 1567 (Reg. of Evidents of the City of St. Andrews, Inventory, no. 4).

STIRLING. Allegedly fd. by James IV in 1494 (Father John Hay cited Bryce, *Grey Friars*, ii, 177), that king, to whom the foundation is accredited in other lists (*Diurnal of Occurents*, 4; Brockie, p. 4510) undoubtedly was its founder. But the bull of erection of Pope Alexander VI, which followed upon that king's petition, is dated 9 Jan. 1497/8 (Bryce, *Grey Friars*, ii, 257–8; ¦Reg. Lat., 1027, fos. 66–67v); while grants towards the building are recorded, 9 and 12 May 1498 (*TA*, i, 390–1). The friary was destroyed by Reformers in 1559 (Lesley, *History*, 274). On 15 April 1567, the former possessions of the friars, along with other ecclesiastical property, was granted to the magistrates (Bryce, *Grey Friars*, ii, 259).

THE CARMELITE FRIARS

GENERAL NOTES

THE origin of the Carmelites is still imperfectly known, but it seems certain that groups of hermits from Mount Carmel, of European nationality, were brought back by Crusaders in the mid-thirteenth century. They settled in England *c.* 1242. It is uncertain when the Carmelites came to Scotland but the assertion that William of Sandwich brought them in 1244 is certainly without foundation (*Bibliotheca Carmelitana*, 2 vols., Rome, 1927, i, 611) Their first appearance in Scotland may have been at Dunkeld in 1262, but the confusing state of the foundation at Berwick-upon-Tweed which also appears in that year makes it uncertain whether the Carmelites came to Scotland before that date.

They were otherwise known as the 'White Friars', and their priories were dedicated to the Blessed Virgin Mary. Until 1291 × 1294, the Scottish houses appear to have been accounted with those pertaining to the English province of the order, but a division of the province appears to have taken place between these dates. As Berwick was politically subject to England for much of the period after 1296, it always appears in chronological lists of the English province, but as no entry for this house appeared in *Medieval Religious Houses in England and Wales*, it has been included among the houses of the Scottish province to which it periodically must have been adjudged.

Valuable information about both the English and Scottish provinces are found in studies by the Very Rev. Keith Egan, O. Carm. entitled 'Medieval Carmelite Houses, England and Wales', and 'Medieval Carmelite Houses, Scotland' in *Carmelus*, xvi (1969) and xix (1972). Fr. Egan, in the course of his researches, came across several lists of representations at general chapters of the order. Examination of extant English lists made it clear that the order of the houses in these lists followed the traditional order of priority in foundation. This enabled him to establish an approximate date for several English houses that was considerably earlier than any extant reference. Only one comparable Scottish list dating from the early sixteenth century (× 1525) has been found. This, with the omission of Berwick and Edinburgh which was founded after its compilation, records the houses in the following order. 1. Tullilum; 2. Aberdeen; 3

Irvine; 4. Luffness; 5. Inverbervie; 6. Banff; 7. Queensferry; 8. Kingussie; 9. Linlithgow (Egan, *Medieval Carmelite Houses, Scotland*, 112, citing Oxford, Bodleian Library, MS. Bodley 73, fo. 48). Adopting this order of priority Fr. Egan suggests considerably earlier dates for Irvine (× 1293); Inverbervie (× 1321–4); Queensferry (× 1401) and Kingussie (× 1401) than extant references would allow. However, as the references themselves appear to argue against such dating at Inverbervie, Queensferry and Kingussie, it must be concluded that this single list is an unreliable guide.

HOUSES OF THE CARMELITE FRIARS

Name	County	Minimum income (1561)	Fd.	Date D. or	Sec.
ABERDEEN	Aberdeen	£96(?)	c. 1273		1560–83
BANFF	Banff		1321–4		1574
BERWICK			1270		1539
EDINBURGH	Midlothian		1520–5		–1563
GREENSIDE					
INVERBERVIE	Kincardine	£94	–1443		–1570
IRVINE	Ayr		–1293		1572
KINGUSSIE	Inverness		–1501		1560+
LINLITHGOW	West Lothian	£33	c. 1401		–1567/8
¶ LUFFNESS	East Lothian		–1293		1560+
‡ QUEENSFERRY	West Lothian		1440/1		–1564/5
TULLILUM	Perth	£16	1262		1559+

ABERDEEN. In 1273 Reginald le Chen made a grant to the Carmelites here 'till their buildings be ready' (*Aberdeen Friars*, 12). A series of grants to this house dating from 1273 to 1350 were confirmed by David II, 7 May 1361 (*ibid.*, 17). Included is a grant by Robert I of annual rents from the fermes of the burgh 'till their church be completed' (*ibid.*, 14). Spottiswoode (455), however, declares that this house is said to have been fd. by Philip de Arbuthnot of that ilk in 1350; while Brockie (p. 1549) has a spurious charter in the form of a letter by Arbuthnot to the provincial of the Carmelites in Scotland, narrating his foundation of a Carmelite house at Aberdeen 'in the place where the castle of that town formerly stood' and dated 'the third weekday after the Assumption of the Blessed Virgin Mary' [i.e. 18 Aug.] 1354. Arbuthnot was undoubtedly a benefactor of the Carmelites, but his grant to them, on 25 April 1355, of an annual rent of 13s 4d from the land of Arbuthnot 'for the repair of the fabric of their church' (*RMS*, i, no. 259) would seem to indicate a restoration rather than the foundation, which can be confidently assigned to the thirteenth c. (Egan, 'Medieval Carmelite Houses, Scotland' 112). A community consisting of at least four friars continued in existence at the Reformation (*Thirds of Benefices*, 97, 154, 219). The house was destroyed in 1560 by the Reforming barons of the Mearns (Lesley, *De Origine*, 563; *Aberdeen Burgh Records*, i, 315, cf. 326). Its lands were thereafter granted to various individuals before being finally granted to the Town Council by James VI, 26 Oct. 1583 (*RMS*, v, no. 618).

BANFF. Our lady chapel near Banff was bestowed on the Carmelites by Robert I, 21 April 1321 (*RMS*, i, App. 1, 91), and confirmed to them by that king, 1 Aug. 1323, along with land for erection of a ch. and monastery (SRO, Forglen Writs, iv, 1; cf. *Aberdeen-Banff Illustrations*, ii, 114–15). Described as priory 'of Bethlem of ye ordour of Carmelits beside Banff' in 1543 (SRO, Forglen Writs, iv, 62); the prior and two friars witness a feu charter 6 Oct. 1544 (*N. & Q.*, 4th ser., vi, 472–3). On the evening of 20 July 1559 the buildings were set on fire 'under sylens of nicht' and considerable destruction 'of the insycht of the kirk and place' occurred (*ibid.*, vi, 521). On 15 Aug. 1559 the pr. with consent of one of the friars leased 'all and haill our place besyde Banff . . . in quhat stait yat ewer yai be for ye tyme be resounn of this present contrawersie' (*ibid.*). On 10 Sept. 1574, James VI granted the lands, buildings and revenues formerly belonging to this house to King's College, Aberdeen (*RMS*, iv, no. 2304; *RSS*, vi, no. 2680).

BERWICK. Said to have been founded in 1270 by Sir John Gray (Speed, *Historie of Great Britaine*, 795). Sir John Gray, mayor of Berwick in 1253 (Raine, *N. Durham*, App. no. ccxxxviii), is known, however, to have been a major benefactor of the Franciscans here (*Chron. Lanercost*, 186), and it may well be that Speed's source confused the tradition of the two houses. On 25 Sept. 1296 the Carmelites were granted land continguous to their site in Berwick by Edward I (*Rot. Scot.*, i, 34). It would appear that there were four friars in this house in Dec. 1299 (*Liber quotidianus*, 26). The community received 40s. from the same king on 5 Jan. 1300 in recompense for damages inflicted on their houses during his stay in Berwick in Dec. 1299 (*ibid.*, 28–9). On 18 June 1310 Isabella, countess of Buchan, was ordered to be removed from her place of imprisonment in Berwick castle to the Carmelite friary (*Rot. Scot.*, i, 85). The friars housed the wardrobe in their buildings at some time in the winter of 1310–11 for that department paid them 5s. for damages sustained then on 31 July 1311 (BM MS. Cott. Nero C. VIII, fo. 51). On 17 Nov. 1317 Edward II granted the request of these friars that they might be allowed to minister in the royal chapel in Berwick castle as friars of their order formerly did (*Cal. Pat. Rolls. Edw. II, 1317–1321*, 53; *CDS*, ii, no. 582). They had an annual grant of £8 from the fermes of Berwick which was paid in part in the year 1327–8 and in full in each of the five years following (*ER*, i, 63, 311, 312, 361, 411). On 10 Aug. 1333 Edward III gave mandate to the prior provincial of the order in England to remove the Scottish friars here to English houses and to substitute English friars (*Rot. Scot.*, i, 258. In Oct. 1335 the number of friars was stated to be ten and by January 1336 it had risen to fifteen (B.M., MS. Cott. Nero C. VIII, fo. 203). The English king continued the annual grant to the friars at irregular intervals and often in curtailed form at least to 1341 (*Cal. Close Rolls, Edw. III, 1337–1339*, 68–69, 223–4; *CDS*, iii, no. 1251; Scott, *Berwick-upon-Tweed* . . . (1888), 341). The house thereafter disappears from record sources for nearly two centuries. Between 10 March and Michaelmas 1539 'the chapel next to the Nesse' in Berwick was dissolved (*LP Henry VIII*, xiv[1], no. 494; P.R.O. Ministers' Accounts, H., VIII, no. 7364, m.11 d.). That this was the Carmelite friary is shown by an account of 1547 (P.R.O. Ministers' Accounts, Edw. VI, no. 355, m. 54).

EDINBURGH, GREENSIDE. On 5 Dec. 1520, the Town Council granted a site at Greenside to the friars of Queensferry, with the permission of the king and the bp. of St. Andrews (*Edinburgh Recs., 1403–1528*, 203). Not till 11 Oct. 1525 were they given possession of the site and had the keys of the Rood Chapel there handed over to them (*ibid.*, 222; *Prot. Bk. Foular*, iii, no. 641). According to a record of 21 March 1529/30, there was friction with Holyrood abbey, resulting in the 'downcasting' of the house where the friars lived (*ADCP*, 325). The friars had ceased to occupy the ch. and buildings and the croft of Greenside, –23 July 1563 (*Edinburgh Recs., 1557–1571*, 168).

INVERBERVIE (BERVIE). Brockie (p. 1552) transcribes a charter purporting to record the fd'n. of this house by David II in 1358 (no day or month are given) and another charter by Mark Rait of Halgreen to the Carmelites of Bervie, 12 Nov. 1388 (pp. 1554 ff.). Neither of these charters (which have no witnesses) are genuine. On 10 Dec. 1443, this house is said to have been 'recently established' (*Aberdeen Friars*, 30) and endowments made on that date by William, E. of Keith and Alexander Strachan of Dullevarde would suggest that one or other, or possibly both, may have been instrumental in securing the foundation (NLS. MS. 29.4.2. vol. 9, fos. 180–183v). Priors occur in 1480 and 1487 (BM. Add. Ms. 8144, fos. 55–55v; SRO, RH6/534) and the prior and one friar who may have then constituted the community occur 20 Feb. 1556 (NLS. MS. 29.4.2, vol. 9, fos. 185–8; *Thirds of Benefices*, 12, 98, 154). On 15 Oct. 1570 a grant was made of lands and other properties formerly belonging to the friars, and on 23 July 1571 these in turn were conveyed to the hospital in Montrose (*RSS*, vi, no. 1217).

IRVINE. On 15 July 1335 Edward III gave 6s. 8d. to the Carmelites of Irvine in whose houses he had been a guest (BM. MS. Cotton Nero VIII, fo. 202v) and foundation by one of the Fullertons of Fullerton may have taken place before 1293 (*Laing Chrs.*, no. 92; Egan, 'Medieval Carmelite Houses, Scotland', 112). On 24 Aug. 1399, Reginald Fullarton made a grant to the friars here for the repairs of the conventual buildings and ch. (MacFarlane, *Genealogical Coll.*, ii, 336); and on 28 June 1412 the patronage of the house was adjudged to belong to Rankin Fullerton whose forbears were described as 'founderis and patronis till our house of Irrwyn' (*Laing Chrs.*, no. 92). A further grant of an annual rent by George Fullerton was made in 1439 and confirmed in 1456 (*ibid.*, nos. 120, 141). Robert Burn was prior at the Reformation (*Essays on Scottish Reformation*, 238). On 8 June 1572 James VI granted its property to the Royal School of Irvine (*RMS*, iv, no. 2071).

KINGUSSIE. Fd. by George, E. of Huntly (d. 1501) (MacFarlane, *Genealogical Coll.*, ii, 416; *RSS*, ii, xxiv). Payments of alms to the friars are recorded, 7 Nov. 1501 and 10 Sept. 1506 (*TA*, ii, 76; *ibid.*, iii, 281). A prior occurs *c.* 1520 (SRO, Forglen Writs, iv, 31) and the pr. and convent received royal protection, 12 Jan. 1530/1 (*RSS*, ii, no. 797). The 'prior de Kingusye' occurs in a rental of 1565 (*Moray Reg.*, 450).

LINLITHGOW. Spottiswoode (455) attributes the fd'n. of this house to the citizens in 1290; while Brockie (p. 540) gives a letter of the provost, bailies and the rest of the community of the burgh to Henry Hann de Brunham, provincial of England and vicar and visitor of the order in Scotland, narrating their foundation of a Carmelite house, 28 Sept. 1280. This document is spurious. On 18 May 1401 an indenture between Sir James Douglas of Dalkeith and the provincial of the Carmelites testifies that the former has granted to the chapel of the Blessed Virgin Mary of Linlithgow and the brethren of the Carmelite order who will celebrate divine service there land for the construction of conventual buildings and a garden (*Mort. Reg.*, ii, no. 210); cf. *ibid.*, no. 211). Payments of alms to the friars are recorded at frequent intervals from 1488 (*TA*, i, 92, 132, 177; *ibid.*, iii, 78, 254). A lease granted in 1544/5 is signed by the pr. and three friars, and another in 1560 by the pr. and one friar (*Laing Chrs.*, nos. 490, 621, 715). This house is said to have been pulled down by the Reformers in 1559 (Lesley, *History*, 274). There is a reference to lands formerly belonging to the friars 25 Feb. 1567/8 (*Prot. Bk. Johnsoun*, no. 523).

LUFFNESS. Occurs 30 Nov. 1293 (*Newb. Reg.*, no. 174). On 13 Nov. 1310 the friars received 40s. for the repair of their houses (PRO. MS. E101/374/7, p. 21 cited Egan, 'Medieval Carmelite Houses, Scotland', 112). In 1335/6 it is recorded that friars of 'Lufnok' receive 10 marks yearly in virtue of a long-standing endowment (*CDS*, iii, 338). This house is also on record 7 May 1361 (*RMS*, i, app. 2 no. 1230 (Index B (2) *n.*); cf. *Aberdeen Friars*, 17). A provincial chapter was held at Luffness in 1480 (BM. Add. MS. 8144, fos. 55–55v) and John Heryng, pr. of the house, occurs 1 March 1497/8 (*Prot. Bk. Young*, no. 1004). The priory is mentioned from 1504/5 to 1512 as in receipt of alms from the king (*TA*, ii, 268; iv, 186). John Rankine, pr. occurs in 1560 (SRO, Prot. Bk. Lawder, fo. 205v). No further references to it have been found, but lands formerly belonging to it were leased by the crown, 4 Jan. 1609 (*RMS*, vi, no. 3).

QUEENSFERRY. According to Spottiswoode (455), this house was fd. by the laird of Dundas in 1330. Brockie (p. 1554) likewise gives what purports to be a letter of James Dundas, laird of Dundas, to the provincial and vicar-general of the Carmelites in Scotland, intimating his fd'n. of a house at Queensferry, 28 Nov. 1333. Again the editor of *Dundas of Dundas* declares, 'There can be no doubt that the family of Dundas of Dundas, as their charter-chest unfolds, introduced the Carmelite order at the present site about A.D. 1330' (*op. cit.*, xlvii). But a confirmation charter of James II, 5 Nov. 1459, incorporates a charter of James Dundas of Dundas, 1 March 1440/1, granting the Carmelites a piece of ground in Queensferry 'for the church of St. Mary the Virgin and for the construction of certain buildings there in the form of a monastery (*in modum monasterii*)' (Dundas Chrs.); and the latter charter was confirmed by Archibald de Dundas, with an additional endowment, 22 June 1455 (*ibid.*). The mon. thus appears to have been a fifteenth c. foundation (cf. also *HMC. 3rd Rep.*, App., 413). David Balbirny was pr. in 1557 (SRO, RH6/1717), but no evidence of a community, and the pr. alone granted a lease of the monastic buildings on 27 Feb. 1564/5 (*RMS*, iv, no. 1607). After 1583, the priory ch. was let by Sir Walter Dundas to the bailies and town council of Queensferry for use as a place of worship (*i.e.* not as a parish ch.) and as a school, with an obligation to remove from it when required. This arrangement probably lasted until 1635 when the present parish ch. was erected (Dundas Chrs., Mac. xxiv, 29).

TULLILUM. Fd. in 1262 when Richard, bp. of Dunkeld, granted the friars a chapel in the suburban area of Perth. (This was the first settlement of the Carmelites in Scotland, *Chron. Bower*, ii, 97; Major, *History*, 188; Oxford, Bodleian Library MS. Selden supra 41, fo. 154v; BM. MS. Harley 3838, fo. 21, cited in Egan, 'Medieval Carmelite Houses, Scotland', 107.) The nave of the ch., which was also called the White Chapel, was rebuilt and the conventual accommodation improved by George Brown, bp. of Dunkeld *c.* 1514 (*Dunkeld Rentale*, 238–9; Myln, *Vitae*, 46 *Fraser Chrs.*, 219). A small community continued at the Reformation when the house is said to have been destroyed by the Reformers in 1559 (*Thirds of Benefices*, 16, 98, 156; Lesley, *History*, 272; Fittis, *Eccles. Annals of Perth*, 208). It is also alleged that Lord Ruthven saved Tullilum from being cast down but abolished the friars (Pitscottie, *Historie*, ii, 146). Feu charters, in favour of Patrick Murray of Tibbermore, of lands pertaining to the priory were confirmed by the Crown, 23 June 1565 (*RSS*, V, no. 2124).

UNCERTAIN FOUNDATION

St. Andrews. Spottiswoode (456) tentatively rejects Dempster's assertion that there were Carmelites here. On the other hand, Brockie (p. 1556) narrates the foundation of a house at St. Andrews by Bishop William de Laverdale [*sic*] in 1370. There was no such bp., though William de Landallis (1341/2–1385) may be meant. Brockie (pp. 1557–8) also gives two spurious charters of alleged benefactors of this house in 1370 and 1378. Nevertheless, a shortlived fd'n. may have existed here, although the evidence is inconclusive.

On 29 March 1466 the Pope appointed a mandatory on the petitions, 14 and 21 March 1466, of the vicar and friars of the Order of the Friars Minor in Scotland, containing that Henry, bp. of St. Andrews (i.e. Henry Wardlaw, 1403–40) had granted them 'the place called Bethlem in the City of St. Andrews' (Reg. Supp., 592, fos. 11v, 100; cf. *CPL*, xii, 53 where the place is called 'Bertheon in the diocese of St. Andrews'). A house with a ch. it is related, had been built there by conventual brothers and had been possessed and served for more than forty years; and supplicating papal confirmation of this grant, permission was sought to receive this house anew with absolution for inhabiting it without papal licence. The nature of this house is obscure, but the brothers in question may have been Carmelite, as on 2 May 1456 land in Market Street is referred to as '*terram fratrum carmelitarum de Bedlem*' (SRO, St. Andrews Charters, BG 65/22/38). The petition for the rehabilitation of this house for Friars Minor appears to be associated with the foundation in St. Andrews of an Observantine house (*q.v.*).

SUPPOSED FOUNDATIONS

Brechin. According to the account given by Brockie (p. 1559), a house was fd. here in the time of Stephen Dempster, bp. of Brechin, who held the see in 1376, by Malcolm Dempster, baron of Careston and nephew of that bp. This statement cannot be accepted. The bp. of Brechin at that period was Patrick de Locrys (1351–83) (Dowden, *Bishops*, 182–3). Brockie (p. 1559) also gives a charter of Robert de Carnegie making a grant to this alleged house, 30 Nov. 1388. But this charter is spurious; for the contemporary Carnegie was John de Carnegie of that ilk who appears 1375–1430 (Fraser, *Southesk*, i, 5). This house is apocryphal.

Drumtochty. No house of Carmelites existed here. In 1403 the Carmelites of Aberdeen were granted the lands of Glensaucht (*Aberdeen Friars*, p. 24), and these are mentioned when leased by the prior to James Keith of Drumtochter, as 'the lands of Easter Glensaucht *alias* the Friars' Glen' (*ibid.*, p. 99). Alleged references to a Carmelite house here, when not merely imaginary, are references to *lands*.

Dunbar. Said by Spottiswoode (455) to have been founded in 1263 by Patrick, E. of March. Brockie (p. 1538) gives what purports to be a charter of foundation by this earl,

28 Jan. 1263. This charter, which adduces the consent to the foundation of William Wishhart, bp. of St. Andrews (the bp. of St. Andrews in 1263 was Gameline (1255–71)) cannot be regarded as genuine. A much later reference, in 1576 (*RMS*, iv, no. 2543), probably rests on a confusion with the Trinitarian foundation at Dunbar (*q.v.*). Dunbar is not mentioned in the list appended to the *Scotichronicon* (*Chron. Bower*, ii, 540).

Elgin. There is a reference in 1581 (*RMS*, vi, no. 303) to lands and rents 'belonging from of old to the White . . . Friars of Elgin'. The reference properly applies to another order, probably the Greyfriars.

THE AUGUSTINIAN FRIARS

GENERAL NOTES

The Augustinian Friars belong to the religious order which is officially known as *Ordo fratrum eremitarum sancti Augustini* (Order of Hermit Friars of St. Augustine). The order as established by a papal act in 1256 was made up piecemeal of several itinerant groups in Italy, some of which spread beyond the Alps before union took place. When united the order received a constitution similar to that of the Dominicans, but like the Carmelites it preserved at least the spiritual tradition of eremetical life.

The earliest Scottish house at Berwick appears to have been deemed to belong to the English province of the order which was under the direction of a prior provincial, and was divided into five districts, called limits, each under a vicar provincial, of which that based upon York comprehended Berwick. Not until the early sixteenth century was an attempt made to found a Scottish province of this order. This attempt is usually deemed to have failed but this surmise was challenged by the late Rev. Francis Roth, O.S.A., in the *English Austin Friars 1249–1538*, i (1966: *History*), and ii (1961: *Sources*), both published in New York. The evidence adduced is in a letter sent in 1535 by the prior general to the vicar general in Scotland and his local priors asking them to work diligently for the indulgence which Pope Paul III had announced for the completion of St. Peter's (Roth, *Austin Friars*, ii, no. 1097). This letter, Roth argues (*ibid.*, i, 132), would not have been sent if the Scottish vicariate had not existed. This has not been substantiated and the sixteenth-century foundations must still be regarded as incomplete.

HOUSES OF THE AUGUSTINIAN FRIARS

Name	County	Fd.	Date D. or Sec
BERWICK		−1299	See notes

BERWICK. The appointment of John of Gubbio as vicar-general of this order in France, England and Scotland in 1260 may point to the foundation of this house before that date (Semple-Chatelain, *Chart. Univ. Paris*, i, 405). On two occasions in Dec. 1299 the friars of St. Augustine of Berwick received alms from Edward I. From the grant of these pittances it would appear that there were six friars in this house on 18 Dec. of that year and four at

Christmas (*Liber quotidianus*, 26). From the Scottish king they had a special grant of £20 for the fabric of their ch., paid in three unequal instalments between 1328 and 1330/1 (*ER*, i, 173-4, 279, 320). On 10 Aug. 1333 Edward III gave mandate to the prior provincial of the Augustinian hermits in England to remove the Scottish friars here to English houses and to substitute English friars (*Rot. Scot.*, i, 258). In Oct. 1335 the number of friars was stated as fifteen and in January 1336 it was twelve (BM. MS. Cott. Nero, C. viii, fo. 203). The account rolls of Lindisfarne priory for the year 1406-7 set down the sum of 26s.8d. as borrowed from the prior of St. Austin at Berwick (Raine, *North Durham*, 115). The house does not appear to have survived to the general suppression of the friaries in England although it may have been one of the three or four houses of friars near Berwick reported as still standing, 10 March 1539/40 (*LP Henry VIII*, xiv, no. 494).

UNIDENTIFIED FOUNDATION

On 19 June and again on 26 June 1453 Thomas Belle, George Halliday and Thomas Sowerby, hermits of the order of St. Augustine, Glasgow diocese, relate that they accepted a church founded by laymen with fields of land annexed to it and made a manse there and lived the life under the said order. They sought papal rehabilitation and requested permission to retain the ch., build as far as need and to choose a prior or minister among themselves (Reg. Supp., 466, fo. 215v; 467, fo. 69v). The ch. is unidentified and no further trace of this foundation occurs.

INCOMPLETE FOUNDATIONS

Haddington. A MS. inventory of the burgh charters includes a sasine in favour of the 'Augustinian friars' of an annuity of 13s.4d., 24 April 1464. This entry is inaccurate; for the document, which has been inspected, is an instrument of that date referring to the Augustinian canons of St. Andrews. An undated letter of James IV to Pope Julius II requests that the hospital of St. Laurence, Haddington, should be converted into a house of Augustinian friars (*James IV Letters*, no. 471; the date suggested for this letter, July 1512, is too late); and, on 13 Oct. 1511, the Pope suppressed the hospital and erected a house of friars (or hermits) of this order *LP Henry VIII*, i2, 1522). But a letter of James V to Pope Leo X, 1513-14, which states that as none of these took up residence, he has conferred it on his chaplain, Walter Ramsay, seeks confirmation of this appointment and the severance of the incorporation of the hospital in this order (*Epp. Reg. Scot.*, i, 193-4; *James V Letters*, p. 8). Payments are recorded, 1511-12, to a master of the hospital who is designated 'friar' (*ER*, xiii, 396, 496) and who may have been an Augustinian. But other friars, to whom payments are made on behalf of this hospital (e.g. *ibid.*, xiv, 206; xv, 76 and later) can be shown to have been Franciscans (*v.* HADDINGTON, St. Laurence, under Hospitals); and it is clear that it did not come into the permanent possession of the Augustinian friars.

Linlithgow. From Sept. to Dec. 1503 royal donations to the Augustinian friars here are recorded, e.g. two grants of £7 'to thair bigging [building]' (*TA*, ii, 254, 255, 256). No evidence, however, is forthcoming to show that this order settled here. That it did not do so seems to be suggested by the attempt, soon after, to place friars at Manuel in the same vicinity.

Manuel. On the petition of James IV, the Pope, on 16 June 1506, provided for the suppression of the Cistercian nunnery here and the introduction of Augustinian friars Observantines (Reg. Lat., 1172, fos. 181-3). This did not take place. See MANUEL under Cistercian Nuns.

THE FRIARS OF THE SACK

GENERAL NOTES

IN the mid-thirteenth century, principally but not solely in Italy, a large number of friar-like groups arose outside the ranks of the Minors and Preachers. The Friars of the Sack, otherwise called the Friars of the Penance of Jesus Christ, formed the largest of these lesser groups in England. At the Second Council of Lyons (1274) all such orders were abolished; that is, they were not allowed to receive further recruitment. The existing houses remained until they were extinct.

HOUSES OF THE FRIARS OF THE SACK

Name	County	Fd.	Date D. or Sec.
BERWICK		1267	1274 × 1285

BERWICK. A charter of Roger, pr. of Coldingham, 18 May 1267, declares that his monastery has conceded to the Friars of Penitence of Jesus Christ that they may erect buildings and an oratory within Coldingham's appropriated parish of Holy Trinity of South Berwick (i.e. Berwick-upon-Tweed). The friars have pledged themselves to do nothing to the prejudice of Coldingham (Raine, *N. Durham*, App. no. dclii). The house did not survive for long after the suppression of the order in 1274, and on 17 June 1285 the bp. of St. Andrews was instructed, as papal mandatory, to sell to the Friars Preachers of Berwick the place in that town 'late held by but now left by the Friars of Penitence' (*CPL*, i, 482; cf. *ibid.*, i, 494–5).

THE HOUSES OF NUNS

General Notes

THERE is some uncertainty regarding the order of nunneries at their foundation. Early foundations were almost invariably Benedictine, but as in England, nunneries which were initially Benedictine may have become Cistercian at a later date. This may explain the presence of only one authenticated Benedictine nunnery.

HOUSES OF BENEDICTINE NUNS

Name	County	Rank	Fd.	Date Supp.
* LINCLUDEN	Kirkcudbright	Priory	–1174	1389

LINCLUDEN. Spottiswoode (459) as well as manuscript and other lists ascribe this fd'n. to Uchtred, son of Fergus, lord of Galloway (d. 1174). This writer and another in Huttons Collections assign the fd'n. to the reign of Malcolm IV (1153-65). The community is generally described as of black nuns; in one source, a papal letter of 7 May 1389, the nunnery is designated 'of the Cluniac order' (Reg. Aven. 259, fos. 471-2v). In 1296 the prioress swore fealty to Edward I (*CDS*, ii, no. 823). The nunnery was suppressed in 1389 on the petition of Archibald Douglas, lord of Galloway, who held the patronage of the priory which it is said his predecessors had founded. It is claimed that the house was sufficiently endowed for eight or nine nuns with a prioress, but the number of nuns, including the prioress, is reduced to four who are to be transferred to some other nunnery of the Cluniac or Benedictine order (Reg. Aven., 259, fos. 471-2v). See LINCLUDEN, under Secular Colleges.

Supposed Foundations

Holystone. As 'Halyston, near Berwick', this house is included by Spottiswoode (459) under Benedictine nunneries. This is erroneous. The house in question is Holystone, in Coquetdale, in the north of England, which appears to have been founded as Benedictine priory but later became Augustinian. (Knowles and Hadcock, *Medieval Religious Houses, England and Wales*, 280-1). The supposition that there was a house of that name near Berwick may be due to confusion with the Cistercian nunnery which was in the vicinity of Halidon, or to the fact that the 'prioresse of Haliston del counte de Berewyk' appears among those who swore fealty to Edward I in 1296 (*CDS*, ii, no. 823). An annual payment granted to it by David I, from the revenues of Berwick which may equally have led to the belief that this was a Scottish house was apparently still being paid in 1332 (*Rot. Scot.*, i, 764a; *ER*, i, 411).

Kilconquhar. Sometimes described as a nunnery in Galloway. It is in fact in Fife, and the suggestion that it was the site of a nunnery is due to a misinterpretation of the fact that the parish ch. was held by North Berwick nunnery (Cowan, *Parishes*, 99).

THE CISTERCIAN NUNS

GENERAL NOTES

THE houses of the Cistercian nuns, like those of the monks, were usually dedicated to St. Mary, and intended for at least thirteen religious, though this number may not always have been reached. Brethren as well as sisters are recorded at some of the nunneries. As in England some of these nunneries appear to have begun as Benedictine, and later claimed to be Cistercian to obtain the privileges of that order.

By way of confirmation of the number of houses included in the following list, it may be noted that a document which records the proposed visitation of Scottish houses by a commissary of Cîteaux in 1516 mentions that there were at this date seven houses of nuns of the Cistercian order (*RSS*, i, no. 2833); and an inhibition by Archbishop Forman of the visitation of these nunneries, *c.* 1516, gives their names as Haddington, North Berwick, Eccles, Coldstream, St. Bothans, Manuel, Elcho (*St. Andrews Formulare*, i, no. 47). A MS. of slightly later date (1524–41?) in Edinburgh University Library (MS. Dc. 7. 63) gives a list of nine Scottish nunneries. These, with the exception of Iona, are the Cistercian houses; South Berwick, North Berwick, Eccles, Coldstream, Haddington, St. Bothan's, Manuel and Elcho. South Berwick (i.e. Berwick-on-Tweed), is probably mentioned in this list retrospectively, as the nunnery was extinct by this time. St. Evoca's, which was extinct about the beginning of the fifteenth century, does not appear.

HOUSES OF CISTERCIAN NUNS

Name	County	Rank	Minimum income (1561)	Fd.	Date D. or Sec.
BERWICK		Priory		–1153	1390/1
COLDSTREAM	Berwick	Priory	£503	–1166	1621
§ ECCLES	Berwick	Priory	£650	1156	1609
ELCHO	Perth	Priory	£193	–1241	1610
HADDINGTON	East Lothian	Priory	£2710	–1159	1621
MANUEL	West Lothian	Priory	£284	–1164	1599+
¶ NORTH BERWICK	East Lothian	Priory	£1880	*c.* 1150	1587/8
ST. BOTHAN'S	Berwick	Priory	£380	13 c.	1622
ST. EVOCA	Kircudbright	Priory		–1423	

144

BERWICK. Usually called the nunnery of South Berwick, to distinguish it from North Berwick. It figures as '[the house] of the Blessed Mary and St. Leonard of South Berwick', *c.* 1284 (*Dryb. Lib.*, xv *n*), and is evidently identical with the nunnery of St. Leonard outside Berwick, mentioned 12 April 1296 (*Rot. Scot.*, i, 23). Chroniclers (Anderson, *Early Sources*, ii, 221, *Chron. Bower*, i, 301) as well as later writers (e.g. Spottiswoode, 460) and lists (except EU. MS. Db. 6. 19, which attributes it to a countess of March) describe it as a foundation of David I. That the nunnery went back to his reign is borne out by a reference, in 1336, to a grant made to it by that king from the ferme of the burgh (*Rot. Scot.*, i, 267a, 416). The nuns appear on record –1177 (*Melr. Lib.*, no. 142). It may have commenced as a Benedictine house, and a number of lists (*Chron. Bower*, ii, 451; NLS. MSS. 22. 1. 14, 33. 2. 12; Bisset, *Rolment of Courtis*, ii, 128 and others) speak of black nuns here. A list given by Gervase of Canterbury (Anderson, *Scottish Annals*, 327) has white (Cistercian) monks, but in Henry of Silgrave's list (*c.* 1272) (Scalacronica, 241; Hadden and Stubbs, *Councils*, iii, 181) and in EU. MS. Db. 6. 19, it appears as a house of white (Cistercian) nuns; and in papal documents of 28 Sept. 1219 and 2 June 1232 (*Dryb. Lib.* nos., 37, 270) as well as later records of 13 May 1420 (*CSSR*, i, 196), the nuns are designated Cistercian. Masters of brethren associated with this house are found in office, 1204 × 1232 (*Dryb. Lib.*, nos. 35–36; *Melr. Lib.*, no. 144). A charter of Edward III, 28 July 1333, making a grant, in commemoration of his victory at Halidon, to 'the nuns beside Berwick' (whose home was situated near the scene of the battle), refers to the conventual ch. and buildings as destroyed and burned and to the nunnery's possessions as largely wasted (*Rot. Scot.*, i, 257); and although he ordered the sheriff of Berwick to undertake repairs, it appears that the nunnery never recovered from the ravages of war.

On 9 March 1390/1 Robert III, since the nunnery was destitute of divine service and regular observance and the nuns were only two in number, granted its lands and possessions to Dryburgh abbey (*RMS*, i, no. 832). Following a petition by the prioress and convent a papal mandate to confirm the foundation of the convent of South Berwick made by K. David, was issued 16 Sept. 1391 (Reg. Aven., 268, fo. 366v), but this was ineffective. The Pope made provision of this house, which had long been void, to Agnes Bron, nun of St. Bothan's, 22 and 29 Jan. 1420 (*CSSR.*, i, 152, 159); but on 13 May following, the ab. and convent of Dryburgh obtained papal confirmation of their possession of it (*ibid.*, 196). On 31 Aug. 1429, the Pope granted a petition of all the prioresses and nuns of the Cistercian order in St. Andrews diocese stating that, although the nunnery was founded by K. David, the prioress and nuns, on account of wars, were driven of necessity to leave it and that the ab. and convent of Dryburgh had had it united to their house and petitioning accordingly that this annexation should be cancelled, the house restored to its pristine state and Agnes Bron provided to it (*CSSR*, iii, 30–31). Dryburgh countered with petitions for confirmation of the union, 30 Dec. 1429 and 7 Aug. 1432 (*ibid.*, 66–7, 243–4). Dryburgh still held it when, 23 July 1466, the Pope appointed mandatories, on the petition of Alexander Lumsden, clerk of St. Andrews diocese, for the administration of the priory, 'since all that region in which the nuns' monastery is situated, was returned to the obedience and fealty of James, K. of Scots (*CPL*, xii, 256). There is no evidence that the nunnery, which is said in 1420 to be so destroyed that scarcely any traces of the buildings remain (*CSSR*, i, 196), was reinstated. This house has sometimes been confused with Holystone (see *Trans. Scot. Ecclesiol. Soc.*, 1940–1, 36).

COLDSTREAM. Fd. by Earl Gospatrick, –1166. From the phrase in the fd'n. charter (*Cold. Cart.*, no. 8), 'Be it known to you that I have given and granted to God and the sisters of Witehou serving God there', it has been alleged (e.g. by Spottiswoode, 461) that 'the nuns of this place were brought from Withow in England'. But no such nunnery apparently existed there (see Knowles and Hadcock, *Medieval Religious Houses, England*), and 'Whitehou' (?Whitehowe) was probably the place where the nunnery was established (see *Cold. Cart.*, viii, *n*). Brethren as well as sisters were established in this house of which masters are found in office between 1256 and 1296 (*ibid.*, nos. 13, 31, 37; *Melr. Lib.*, no. 333; *Hist. MSS. Comm. Rept.*, xii, App. Pt. 8, 174; Stevenson, *Documents*, ii, 32). The chs. of Lennel and Hirsel and the chapel of Bassendean were appropriated to the priory before the end of the twelfth c. (Cowan, *Parishes*, 15, 82, 130) and confirmed to it by papal bull in the early thirteenth c. This bull is mentioned in a list of documents sold in Edinburgh, in Dec. 1934 (see *Scotsman*, 20 Dec. 1934). The document is described as, 'Papal bull of Honorius III in the 8th year of his pontificate (1235)'. This cannot be correct as Honorius was Pope 1216–27. The date may be 1223–4. On the other hand, if 1235 is the true date, it must be a bull of Pope Gregory IX (1227–41).

The priory is described as a house of black nuns by Gervase of Canterbury (Anderson, *Scottish Annals*, 327) and Henry of Silgrave (*Scalachronica*, 241); Scottish lists unanimously call it Cistercian. This nunnery suffered some spoliation and damage by the English, March 1296 (*CDS*, ii, no. 723; Stevenson, *Documents*, ii, 32–25); and it is said in a letter of William de Greenfield, abp. of York, 12 Aug. 1315 that because of war and the destruction of their property by the Scots, the nuns were dispersed (*Hist. Papers and Letters from Northern Regs.*, 197n). Edward III granted letters of protection to the master of the priory and prioress and sisters of that house, 25 July 1333 (*Rot. Scot.*, i, 255–6). An account of the burning of this house by the English is given, 30 Nov. 1542 (*Hamilton Papers*, i, xciii; *LP Henry VIII*, xvii, no. 1157); and it was again burned, during Hertford's invasion, in 1545 (*ibid.*, xx², no. 633). The sub-prioress and ten nuns take part in the election of a prioress, 13 Feb. 1537/8 (*Cold. Cart.*, 83ff), but this number appears to have been reduced to the prioress and seven nuns at the Reformation (*Essays on Scottish Reformation*, 236). Between 1489 and 1566 prioresses were drawn exclusively from the family of Hoppringle, five of whom in succession ruled the priory (*Cold. Cart.*, 50–4, 83–7; *RSS*, v, no. 2912). After the death of the last prioress 29 Oct. 1583 × 12 May 1588, the priory was held by commendators (*RMS*, v, nos. 771, 1538). In 1621, this nunnery was erected into a temporal lordship for Sir John Hamilton of Trabroun, son of the E. of Melrose (*APS*, iv, 647–9).

ECCLES. Said to have been fd. in 1156, when a convent of nuns came there for the second time (*Chron. Melrose*, 75). Other dates are given: 1145 (mentioned by Hay, Scotia Sacra. 213); 1154 (Spottiswoode, 461 citing Hoveden); 1155 (*ibid.*, citing the Book of Coupar), The fd'n. is attributed to Earl Gospatrick (Spottiswoode, 461; Lawrie, *Annals*, 19n., 109n); an unnamed countess of March (perhaps Derdere, wife of Earl Gospatrick (lists in *Chron. Bower*, ii, 541; EU. MS. Db. 6. 19; NLS. MS. 22. 1. 14); and David I (Hay, Scotia Sacra, 213). The last is not admissible if 1156 is the correct date. The ch. of Eccles with its three chapels was confirmed to the priory by David, bp. of St. Andrews in 1250 (*St. A. Lib.*, xxix, no. 59). Masters of brethren associated with this house are found in office in 1209 (Anderson, *Early Sources*, ii, 373) and 1268 × 1278 (*HMC Comm. Rept.*, xii, Pt. viii, 174). The prioress (unnamed) appears in 1297 (Stevenson, *Documents*, ii, 174). The history of the priory is obscure until the sixteenth c. This nunnery suffered in the English invasions of that period. It was threatened with burning by Dacre in 1523 (*LP Henry VIII*, iii², no. 3098). In October 1543 the corn in the abbey [*sic*] was burned (*ibid.*, xix², no. 33); in Sept. 1544, the ch. of Eccles (not certainly the nunnery ch.) was 'won by assault' and eighty men slain in the nunnery and town (*ibid.*, xix², no. 625; xx¹, no. 395). The nunnery was among the places 'brent, rased and cast downe' by the English in Sept. 1545 (*ibid.*, xx², nos. 456, 633). No nuns appear on record during this period, although Marion Hamilton who was granted the temporalities and spiritualities of the benefice as prioress 19 June 1548 is said in a bull of provision 4 May 1549 (Reg. Supp. 2661, fo. 4v; 2673, fo. 125v) to have been elected by the convent. She was still in possession, 21 Aug. 1566, when at the instigation of Sir James Hume of Coldinknowis the priory was granted *in expectationem* to Isobel Home on whose demission, before 26 March 1575, it was conferred on James Hume, second son of Sir James Hume (*RSS*, v, no. 3041, vii, no. 140). It was erected into a temporal lordship for Sir George Hume, 24 June 1609 (*HMC, 12th Rep.*, App. Pt. viii, 131).

ELCHO. This fd'n. is attributed to David Lindsay I, d. 1241 (e.g. MS lists, *Lives of the Lindsays*, i, 206). Spottiswoode (463) associates Lindsay's mother, Lady Marjory, with the foundation. In an undated charter, Lindsay refers to his obligation to pay annually to Dunfermline abbey half a stone of wax 'as a quitclaim of that parcel of land in which the monastery of Elcho is situated' (*Dunf. Reg.*, no. 191). Again a charter regarding a controversy between Lindores abbey and this nunnery, 25 Jan. 1281/2, indicates that the latter was in existence thirty-four years previously, in 1247 (*Lind. Cart.*, no. cxxv). Pope Benedict XIII confirmed the priory's possession of the ch. of Dun and the places and villages of Elcho, Kinnaird, Binning and Standartis in Lothain, 26 May 1418 (Reg. Vat., 329, fo. 18v). The history of the nunnery is obscure. In Dec. 1547, this house was burned by the English (*Cal. State Papers Scot.*, i, 74). Before this destruction a community of at least twelve had formed the convent (*Essays on Scottish Reformation*, 236), but had diminished to about seven at the Reformation. A charter of 26 Sept. 1559, attested by the prioress and six nuns, refers not only to the devastation by the English but also to a later attack by Reformers, who drove out the nuns and completely destroyed their house (Fraser, *Weemys*, ii, no. 120). On 6 Nov. 1570, the nunnery is described as ruinous and uninhabited (*ibid.*, i, 138; *RMS*, iv, no. 1393). The last prioress, Euphemia Leslie, had died, 21 Sept. 1570, when Andrew Moncrief was appointed commendator (*RSS*, vi, no. 911), to be succeeded after his death, 20 Jan. 1601, by Archibald Moncrief, who was then presented by the crown (*RMS*, vii, no. 1135). A pension from the fruits of Scone abbey, apparently in lieu of the commendatorship, was granted to Moncrief in May 1606 (*RPC*, vii, 514). The erection of the priory into a temporal lordship for Lord Scone, afterwards Viscount Stormont, is mentioned, 1606 (*APS*, iv, 339) and is the subject of a charter 1610 (*RMS*, vii, no. 248).

HADDINGTON. Fd. by Ada, countess of Northumberland and Huntingdon (*Scotichronicon*, lib. viii, cap. xxv; *Chron. Bower*, i, 475; *RMS*, ii, no. 610 and lists). The fd'n. took place –1159 (see *East Lothian Trans.*, v, 1952, 3). Masters of brethren associated with this house are found in office between 1172 and *c.* 1255 (*N. B. Chrs.*, nos. 3–4; *St. A. Lib.*, 147–8, 334, 389; *Kel. Lib.*, no. 438; *Newb. Reg.*, no. 74). Its prioresses swore fealty to Edward I in 1291 and 1296 (*CDS*, ii, nos. 508, 833). The nunnery was burned by the English in Feb. 1335/6 (*Chron. Bower*, ii, 354), and again in May 1554 (*LP Henry VIII*, xix[1], no. 533) and perhaps 1545 (*Chron. of John Smyth*, in *Kinloss Recs.*, 10). This was one of the largest Scottish nunneries. It is said to have twenty-four nuns, 21 April 1461 (*CPL*, xii. 115); and there were eighteen in 1560 (*East Lothian Trans.*, v, 18). A feu made by Elizabeth Hepburn, the last prioress, of the lands of the nunnery to William Maitland of Lethington was confirmed by the crown, 30 Dec. 1564 (*RSS*, v, no. 1881), but a subsequent bestowal of the priory was annulled in favour of Isobel Hepburn, 17 March 1565/6 (*ibid.*, v, no. 2685), who still occurs as prioress 21 Aug. 1578 (*RMS*, v, no. 1026). The nunnery was eventually erected into a temporal lordship for John Maitland, master of Lauderdale, in parliament, 1621 and by charter, 1622 (*APS*, iv, 645–7; *RMS*, viii, no. 306).

MANUEL. Fd. by Malcolm IV, –1164 (*Scotichronicon*, lib. viii, cap. vii; *Chron. Bower*, i, 453); his endowment was confirmed by his successor, William the Lion, 1166 × 1171 (*Regesta Regum Scottorum*, ii, 174–5). William subsequently made further grants to the priory, 1196 × 1198 (*ibid.*, ii, 391–2). A master of brethren associated with this house is found in office, *c.* 1243 (*Camb. Lib.*, nos. 80, 86). Its prioresses swore fealty to Edward I in 1291 and 1296 (*CDS*, ii, no. 508; Stevenson, *Documents*, ii, 69). An indulgence is granted to the prioress, 20 Sept. 1379 (Reg. Aven., 220, fo. 503v), but otherwise the history of the house is totally obscure until the sixteenth c. On 16 June 1506 the Pope granted the petition of James IV who, on the ground that the nuns were scarcely five in number, and led a life alien to the Cistercian rule, sought the suppression of the nunnery, the removal of the nuns to another house and the introduction of Augustine Friars Observantine (Reg. Lat., 1172, fos. 181–3v). This did not take place. In 1552 there were still four nuns along with the prioress (Linlithgow Burgh Recs.). Janet Livingstone, the last prioress, was presented by the crown, 24 June 1543 (*RSS*, iii, no. 332), and occurs 27 Nov. 1570 (*RMS*, iv, no. 16). Margaret Livingstone, daughter of William, Lord Livingstone was presented *in expectationem*, 31 May 1566 (*RSS*, v, no. 2866), but it is uncertain whether she held office, her brother Alexander having become commendator before 29 July 1587 (*RMS*, vi, no. 890; cf. *APS*, iii, 431). There appears to be no extant record of the erection of this nunnery into a temporal lordship. On 13 April 1599 James VI renewed the lease of the lands formerly pertaining to it in favour of Alexander, Lord Livingstone (*RMS*, vi, no. 890), and they probably passed into the latter's possession.

NORTH BERWICK. There seems to be no doubt that the founder was Duncan (I), E. of Fife (1136–54). He is mentioned in a charter of Earl Duncan (II), his successor, as having made a donation of land to the nuns (*N. B. Chrs.*, no. 3). A number of writers (*Chron. Bower*, ii, 38, 541; *Chron. Extracta*, 91, Major, *History*, 179; Bisset, *Rolment of Courtis*, ii, 128; Spottiswoode, 463) attribute the fd'n. to Malcolm, E. of Fife (1203–30); but although Malcolm, before succeeding to the earldom, granted the nunnery a charter confirming its possessions, *c.* 1199 (*SHS. Misc.*, iv, 308–9), he cannot be regarded as founder. A wide disparity appears in the dates given for the fd'n., e.g. *c.* 1136 (Lawrie, *Annals*, 15); the third quarter of the twelfth c. (*Hist. Mon. Comm.* (*East Lothian*), 59; 1216

(Spottiswoode, 463); 1218 (*Chron. Pluscarden*, 68). But it was certainly founded 1147 × 1153 (*Regesta Regum Scottorum*, i, 160), and the assignation of the foundation to *c.* 1150 has much to commend it (*SHS Misc.*, iv, 334).

This house is described as for black nuns by Gervase of Canterbury (Anderson, *Scottish Annals*, 327) and by Henry of Silgrave (*Scalachronica*, 241); while it is designated Benedictine in papal letters of 1375 and 1384 (*CPL*, iv, 212, 249; Reg. Aven., 238, fo. 568). But it is called Cistercian in Scottish lists and in a papal bull of 22 Feb. 1258/9 (*N. B. Chrs.*, no. 18) as well as in fifteenth-c. cameral records (Cameron, *Apostolic Camera*, 288 (*anno* 1471), 176 (*anno* 1473). There is a curious record (undated but probably 1418+) in which the nuns of North Berwick are declared to be not of the Cistercian order because they do not wear the Cistercian habit (*St. Andrews Copiale*, 66). They are, however, called Cistercian in an associated document of 1405 (*ibid.*, 55). It would appear that this house may have been fd. as a Benedictine house, and later claimed to be Cistercian to obtain the privileges of that order (see Knowles and Hadcock, *Medieval Religious Houses, England*, 271). A bull of the antipope Clement VII, 18 Feb. 1383/4 (*N. B. Chrs.*, no. 37) is directed to the 'abbess' and convent; but this, and other similar references to an abbess here in 1402 (Reg. Aven., 306, fos. 511v–2) and 1473 (*CPL*. xiii, 23) are manifestly errors; North Berwick like all Scottish houses of nuns was a priory. The ch. was dedicated by David de Bernham, bp. of St. Andrews, 10 Oct. 1242 (Anderson, *Early Sources*, ii, 523). In Clement VII's bull (above) which is erroneously dated 1529 (*N. B. Chrs.*, xvii), this house is said to have suffered frequent devastation by war and to have had its ch. burned by hostile action (*ibid.*, no. 37), but the occasion of the statement is not quite clear (English invasions took place in April and August 1385), and the reference must be retrospective). There were twenty-one nuns besides the prioress in the nunnery, in 1544 (*ibid.*, 60) and at least sixteen at the Reformation (*Essays on Scottish Reformation*, 236). Margaret Hume, the last pre-Reformation prioress, was provided, 27 April 1544 (Reg. Lat., 1749, fos. 226v–8) and had demitted office before 30 June 1566 when the benefice was conferred upon Mariot Cockburn (*RSS*, v, no. 2917). On 7 Aug. 1568 Margaret Hume succeeded to the benefice vacated by Mariot's resignation (*RMS*, iv, no. 1824). The lands and revenues of the priory, the buildings of which were said to be ruinous in 1587 (*APS*, iii, 437), were in turn resigned by Margaret in favour of Alexander Hume in whose favour in 20 March 1587/8. James VI granted 'the place in which the church and cloister were formerly situated', with the nunnery's properties, erected into a free barony (*RMS*, v, no. 1492). The hospitals of North Berwick and Ardross (*q.v.*) were attached to this house.

St. Bothan's. The identity of the founder and the date of fd'n. are alike uncertain. According to Spottiswoode (460), this nunnery 'is said to have been founded by one of the countesses of March, in the reign of William the Lion' (i.e. 1165–1214). the fd'n. has been variously attributed to Ada, natural daughter of William the Lion, who married Earl Patrick in 1184 and died in 1200 (Anderson, *Early Sources*, ii, 307; *Chron. Bower*, i, 515; ii, 541; Lawrie, *Annals*, 251); to Christiana, who married the same earl, –4 December 1214 (EU. Ms. Db. 6. 19; NLS. MS. 22. 1. 14; Bisset, *Rolment of Courtis*, ii, 129) and also to Euphemia, wife of Patrick, sixth E. of Dunbar, who became, by her husband's succession, countess in 1232 and died *c.* 1267 (*Chron. Bower*, ii, 541). St. Bothan's is not mentioned in the lists of Gervase of Canterbury, –1212 and Henry of Silgrave, *c.* 1272. The prioress swore fealty to Edward I in 1296 (*CDS*, ii, no. 823). Little is known of the history of this house. It was burned by the English, 11 Aug. 1545 (*Diurnal of Occurrents*, 35). The prioress Elizabeth Lamb, and three nuns are mentioned 6 March 1557/8 (*HMC Rep. Milne Home MSS.*, 273), and the same prioress and one nun appear 16 June 1565 (*ibid.*, 12th Rep., App. viii, 165), when the whole of its lands were leased to Alexander, Lord Home. On 8 March 1565/6, following the death of Elizabeth Lamb, the priory was conferred on Elizabeth Hume (*RMS*, v, no. 1716). She had demitted office before 23 July 1617 when the benefice was granted to David Lindsay (*RMS*, vii, no. 1663) for whom it was erected into a temporal lordship in 1622 (*ibid.*, viii, no. 295).

St. Evoca. All that is known of this house comes from three sources: (1) A supplication to the Pope (granted 22 May 1423) by John de Innerkethyng, canon of Holyrood, for the grant of it to him to be held, ruled and governed by him for the space of ten years. The house is described as the priory of nuns of St. Evoca the Virgin, of the Cistercian order and diocese of Galloway, wont to be ruled and governed by holy nuns or matrons, now deprived of administration and rule on account of the meagreness of its fruits. It is almost in ruins and at present is not occupied by the nuns or by others in their name. Thus it may be regarded as abandoned by them (*CSSR*, ii, 25–26); (2) A papal letter of 10 January 1463/4 appointing mandatories, on a petition by Robert de Colston, rector of Kirkchrist, in the same diocese, containing that his predecessor held as united to the parish ch., the ch. or chapel of Kyrknok or Kyrkenok (*rectius* Kyrkuoc or Kyrkeuok), situate within the bounds of the said parish, in which ch. or chapel a nun or religious woman used of old to dwell; and that he had continued this possession and now fears interference with it. No nun or religious woman, it is stated, had for thirty years led a regular life there, its buildings were fallen and it had been so long void that there is no certain knowledge of the true way of its voidance. The mandatories, if satisfied, are to ratify this union (*CPL*, xi, 507); (3) In the eighteenth c., Macfarlane incorporates the following note in his *Geographical Collns.* (ii, 132): 'In the parish of Kirkchrist, which is now annexed to Twinam [Twynholm] parish, there was a Nunrie, having the lands called Nuntoun and Nunmill thereunto belonging, but now it is scarce known where the Nunrie was.' Its supposed site is mentioned in *Hist. Mon. Comm. (Kirkcudbright)*, 273. *Dumfries. Trans.*, xxiii.

SUPPOSED FOUNDATIONS

Elbottle. Described as a cell of South Berwick (Spottiswoode, 460; Bisset, *Rolment of Courtis*, ii, 130; EU. MS. Db 6.19; NLS. MS. 22.1.14). Evidence of a nunnery here is, however, altogether lacking. The barony of Elbottle, in the medieval parish of Gullane (now Dirleton), included the island of Elbottle (now Fidra) in the Firth of Forth. About 1220, William de Vaux gave to the Premonstratensian canons of Dryburgh serving the ch. of St. Nicholas in that island the patronage of the ch. of Gullane 'and whatever right I have had . . . in that church . . . saving what the nuns of South Berwick are due to have in the parish of that church' (*Dryb. Lib.*, no. 23). This is the only—and very tenuous—connection of the nunnery of South Berwick with Elbottle. See Gullane (below). The nunnery at Elbottle is apocryphal.

Gullane. Spottiswoode (461) and Hay (Scotia Sacra, 215) allege this to be a foundation of David I and a cell of South Berwick. These statements, although the latter is repeated by the lists cited under Elbottle (above), are not authenticated. The nuns of South Berwick are mentioned as having a 'portion' in the parish of Gullane (*Cold. Corr.*, cxiv) (see under Elbottle), and, as appears from litigation with the canons of Dryburgh and the rector of Gullane, c. 1221, they had claimed the parish ch., which had been granted to Dryburgh abbey, as well as certain teinds (*Dryb. Lib.*, nos. 27, 35, 36, 37). In the record of these proceedings, there is no indication of a nunnery at Gullane. It is stated that in 1369 the prior of Coldingham had submitted to his decision a dispute between the nuns of St. Bothan's and the nuns of Gullane regarding the lands of Fenton (Carr, *Coldingham*, 283); but the source of this assertion cannot be traced. In any case, the existence of a Cistercian nunnery in each of the contiguous parishes of Gullane and North Berwick is inconceivable.

Inishail. 'On the island of Inishail are the remains of a building said to have been a Cistercian nunnery, the temporalities of which, it is also said, were at the Reformation given to Hay, ab. of Inchaffray who embraced the reformed doctrines' (*OPS*, ii¹, 130). This is based on the *New Statistical Account*, which on points of history is often unreliable. There was a parish ch. of St. Findoca of Inishail, which was appropriated to Inchaffray abbey, in 1257 (*Inchaff. Chrs.*, no. lxxxv). But the nunnery is fanciful; and no abbot named Hay is mentioned in the charters of Inchaffray.

Nunraw. This has been described as 'the site of a settlement of Cistercian nuns' (see *East Lothian Trans.*, v (1952), 12). On 29 Feb. 1547/8, it is called a 'place and fortalice', which the prioress of Haddington undertakes to defend against the English (*ADCP* p. 572). There is no evidence that it was the site of a nunnery.

Trefontains. Spottiswoode (460) and others refer to this as a cell of South Berwick. The former mentions David I as founder, while EU. MS. Db. 6.19 and NLS. MS. 22.1.14 attribute its foundation to the countess of March (unspecified). It is impossible to believe that such a house existed about a mile distant from the nunnery of St. Bothan's. In the thirteenth c. there is a reference to 'Trefontaynes, cell of the same' (*Cold. Corr.*, cxiv), without indication of the house of which it was a dependency. On the other hand, it is designated 'the church or hospital of Trefontainys' in a note which states that it was granted to Dryburgh abbey in 1436–7 (NLS. MS. 34.3.12). The lands of Trefontains were, 11 Jan. 1451/2, bestowed on the collegiate ch. of Dunglass (*HMC. 12th Rep.*, App., Pt. VIII, p. 127). By 1481 it is clear that the teinds of Trefontains were being used for the maintenance of two prebends within the collegiate ch. of Dunglass, one of which, the eastern prebend was responsible for parochial services (SRO, RH6/496).

THE AUGUSTINIAN CANONESSES

HOUSES OF AUGUSTINIAN CANONESSES

Name	County	Rank	Minimum income (1561)	Fd.	Date D. or Sec.
¶ IONA	Argyll	Priory		−1208	1574+
PERTH	Perth	Priory		13 c.	c. 1434
ST. LEONARD					annexed to Perth Charterhouse.

IONA, ST. MARY. Said to have been fd. by Reginald, son of Somerled (d. 1207 or 1208), whose sister Bethoc was the first prioress (Skene, 'Notes on the Hist. of the Ruins of Iona', *PSAS*, x (1875), 210; *Highland Papers*, i, 82). Skene notes the statement of the Book of Clanranald (*Reliquiae Celticae*, ii, 157) that the fd'n. was for Black, i.e. Benedictine nuns. Scottish sources (e.g. *Scotichronicon*, lib. ii, cap. x; *Chron. Bower*, i, 45) and appended list (11, 541); *Chron. Pluscarden*, 406; *Chron. Extracta*, 9; Bisset, *Rolment of Courtis*, ii, 128; EU. Ms. Db. 6.19) as well as Vatican records (e.g. a supplication granted, 26 Jan. 1422 (*Highland Papers*, iv, 175–6) describe them as Augustinian. The suggestion made by Skene that 'the nuns may originally have been black or Benedictine nuns . . . but . . . Augustinian nuns may have been substituted' ('Ruins of Iona', 210) seems superfluous. In 1509 James IV granted a letter of protection to the prioress and convent and ordered all his lieges within the Isles not to annoy them in any way (*RSS*, i, no. 1797). Prioresses continued to be appointed until the Reformation but no evidence of a community (*OPS*, ii2, 295–6). In 1574, the nunnery's lands were granted by the prioress and convent in heritage to Hector McLean of Duart (*ibid.*, 296).

PERTH, ST. LEONARD. Spottiswoode (464) includes this house among the Cistercian nunneries and is followed by Fittis (*Eccles. Annals of Perth*, 277). But in lists of Scottish houses appended to the *Chronicon* of Henry of Silgrave, c. 1272 (BM. Cotton MS. Cleopatra A, xii, 56, given *Scalachronica*, 241; Hadden and Stubbs, *Councils*, ii1 182; cf. Anderson, *Early Sources*, ii, 699), a priory for 'black nuns' appears. In a similar list given by Gervase of Canterbury, −1212 (Anderson, *Scottish Annals*, 327), this priory is entered with the manifestly erroneous note, 'black monks'. It is uncertain whether this is intended to refer to St. Leonards. But that house is specifically mentioned as Augustinian in a papal letter 5 Feb. 1292/3 (*CPL*, i, 548). The prioress swore fealty to Edward I in 1926 (*CDS*, ii, no. 823). About 1434 the nunnery and its hospital (*q.v.*) were annexed to the Charterhouse of Perth (Fittis, *Eccles. Annals of Perth*, 219, 278). The prioress renounced all right to the hospital on 24 April 1438 (*ibid.*, 278–9). The nunnery appears to have been suppressed thereafter.

THE DOMINICAN NUNS

HOUSES OF DOMINICAN NUNS

Name	County	Rank	Minimum income (1561)	Fd.	Date Sec.
EDINBURGH SCIENNES	Midlothian	Priory	£245	1517	1569

EDINBURGH, SCIENNES. Spottiswoode (458) states erroneously that 'this house was founded by the Lady Roslin, countess of Caithness'. Brockie, who declares that documentary evidence of the founder's name and the year of erection is wanting (p. 1259) gives a charter of Lady Egidia Douglas, wife of Henry [Sinclair], earl of Orkney and lord of Roslin, purporting to grant a donation to the Dominican nuns 'near Edinburgh', 18 Oct. 1404. This charter cannot be accepted as genuine; it has no witnesses; and Egidia Douglas did not marry Henry Sinclair till *c.* 1407 (*SP*, vi, 570). Other charters to this house transcribed by Brockie are spurious, e.g. an alleged charter of Robert Logan of Restalrig making a grant to the nuns, 28 Sept. 1438 (Brockie, p. 1261) is said to have been sealed by George, dean of the collegiate ch. of Restalrig; but this collegiate ch. was not erected till 1487 and there was no dean of this name till 1575. A bull of 29 Jan. 1517/18 describes the initiators of the petition to the Pope and founders of the house as the ladies of Seton, Glenbervie and Bass (*Edinburgh Scien. Lib.*, no. 11); but while, as has been pointed out (*ibid.*, xix), their influence was used to obtain papal authority for the endowment of the house, the foundation was mainly due to 'Sir' [dominus] John Crawford, who granted St. John's kirk of the Boroughmuir of Edinburgh (which he had founded), with its churchyard, houses and lands, to the sisters 'of the order of St. Katherine of Siena', 5 Jan. 1516/7 (*Edin. Recs., 1403–1528*, pp. 164–5), while Lady Seton contributed to the expense of the building (*Edinburgh Scien. Lib.*, xxi). Further endowment was provided by John Cant, burgess of Edinburgh and Agnes Kerkettil his wife, according to the charter of fd'n., 17 April 1517 (*ibid.*, no. iii); and Crawford's additional grant of land, of which sasine is given to Josina Henrisoun and the other sisters 'of the order of St. Dominic, called St. Katherine of Senis', 5 Dec. 1517, is witnessed, among others, by the provincial of the Friars Preachers (*Prot. Bk. Foular*, ii, no. 60). The erection was for 'a monastery of nuns, of the order of St. Augustine, under the care of the Friars Preachers, for thirty nuns' (*Edinburgh Scien. Lib.*, no. ii; cf. *Prot. Bk. Foular*, iii, no. 655). The annexation of the hospital of St. Laurence, Haddington, to this house is recorded, 29 Aug. 1532 (*Edinburgh Scien. Lib.*, no. iv) and, on 26 Nov. of that year, a letter of James V seeks from the Pope ratification of this union (*James V Letters*, pp. 232–3; from Tyninghame Letter Bk.); it was confirmed by the legate in Scotland, 5 March 1544/5 (*Edinburgh Scien. Lib.*, no. vi). The prioress, sub-prioress and ten nuns subscribe a charter, 18 Feb. 1555/6 (*HMC 14th Rep.*, App., Pt. III, 43). On 5 July 1567, the prioress and convent grant a lease of their lands of the Sciennes 'in their great need immediately after the destruction of their place . . . and their expulsion from it' (*RMS*, iv, no. 1980). The Town Council, finding that the nunnery had been omitted from the grant to them of the properties of religious houses, took steps to rectify this omission, 1 April 1569 (*Edin. Recs., 1557–71*, 260). A house at Sciennes is erroneously given as Franciscan (Spottiswoode, *Hist. of the Ch. of Scotland* (1677 edn.), App., 17; Hay, Scotia Sacra, p. 218; Brockie, p. 1524); see under Franciscan Nuns.

INCOMPLETE FOUNDATION

Glasgow. A Dominican nunnery, dedicated to St. Catherine of Siena, was proposed to be erected near the chapel of St. Thenew about 1510. Three hundred pounds were bequeathed by Roland Blacadyr, subdean of Glasgow, but no steps were ever taken to carry this bequest into execution (*Glasgow St. Mary Liber*, lxxii).

THE FRANCISCAN NUNS

GENERAL NOTES

OTHERWISE called the Grey Sisters, the Minoresses, the Poor Clares, or the Third Order of St. Francis, founded by St. Francis and St. Clare in San Damiano at Assisi.

HOUSES OF FRANCISCAN NUNS

Name	County	Rank	Minimum income (1561)	Fd.	Date Sec.
ABERDOUR	Fife	Pr.		1486	1560
DUNDEE	Angus	Pr.	£2(?)	1501/2	1560

ABERDOUR. The hospital (*q.v.*) founded by James, E. of Morton, was placed under the charge of four sisters of the Third Order, 16 Oct. 1486 (*Mort. Reg.*, ii, 240–2). In the following year (23 June 1487), a bull of Pope Innocent VIII, while confirming the erection of the nunnery, ordained the extinction of the hospital (Theiner, *Vet. Mon.*, no. dccclxxxiv). The nuns continued to be designated the sisters of St. Martha (Bryce, *Grey Friars*, i, 395, 397–8). Brockie (p. 1517) has a charter of Joanetta de Crichton, countess of Morton, making donations to the nunnery and purporting to bear the seal of the convent and six 'senior sisters', 4 Oct. 1492. (This is not an authentic record: one of the witnesses is James, ab. of Inchcolm, but no such abbot is known in this period.) The personnel of the house, which originally consisted of two regular sisters and two novices, who were later joined by four others (*SHR*, xiii, 312), at the Reformation evidently comprised a mother and three sisters (Bryce, *Grey Friars*, i, 392, 395). These, on 18 Aug. 1560, leased to the then E. of Morton their house and land (*ibid.*, ii, 270). The last of the sisters having a life rent of the 'sisteris land' of Aberdour is mentioned in 1584 (*ibid.*, ii, 271). The sisters are erroneously described as of 'Aberdene' (Spottiswoode, *History of Church of Scotland* (1677 edn.), App. 17).

DUNDEE. Brockie (p. 1520) transcribes a charter of James Graham of Fintry and Claverhouse granting a house in Dundee for a prioress and twelve sisters of the Third Order of St. Francis, 28 Oct. 1494. This charter is spurious; for James Graham at this date had not attained full age and the contemporary bp. of Brechin was not John (who appears here as a witness) but William Meldrum (1488–1514 × 1516) (Watt, *Fasti*, 41). This house was established by James Fotheringham, who granted two sisters, in name of the rest of the sisters, St. James chapel which he had founded, 8 March 1501/2 (Bryce, *Grey Friars*, i, 395–6; ii, 273–4). In Aug. 1560, the house was sold and its land leased by the magistrates (*ibid.*, i, 397; Maxwell, *Old Dundee*, 69, 183). Its last prioress, Isobel Wishart, 'of the place sumtyme situat besyde the burgh of Dunde', was granted a nun's portion within the priory of North Berwick, 16 May 1566 (*RSS*, v, no. 2830). The magistrates of Dundee were confirmed in possession of its properties, 14 April 1567 (*ibid.*, v, no. 3417).'

SUPPOSED FOUNDATIONS

Sciennes. Brockie (p. 1524) gives a charter (apparently from Tweedie) of Margaret Knox, daughter of Uchtred Knox of Ranfurly and widow of Cuthbert Purves, burgess of Edinburgh, granting her lands of Sciennes, for the erection of a hospital for twelve poor and ailing women, to six sisters from the convent of Aberdour (who, later in the charter, appear along with a prioress), 28 March 1496. This charter, as well as others purporting to deal with this house (Brockie, pp. 1525, 1526, 1527) is spurious (two of these refer to the *abbess* of Sciennes; and one (p. 1526) mentions a preposterous grant to the house of £1000 Scots). The Appendix to Spottiswoode, *Hist. of Ch. of Scotland* (1677 edn.), (p. 17), and Hay (Scotia Sacra, p. 218) also give this as a Franciscan foundation. The only house at Sciennes, however, was one of Dominican nuns (*q.v.*).

Southannan. Brockie (p. 1531, quoting from Tweedie, gives a charter of William, Lord Semple, founding at Southannan a house where the poor and sick will be cared for, for twelve sisters from Sciennes (above). ('This house or convent I have constructed and built after the venerable abbess of Sciennes had constituted and decreed twelve sisters of the same foundation (*instituti*) to occupy the same with the venerable Margaret Semple, my daughter, lawfully constituted their prioress . . . '.) The date is given as 'in festo Sancti *Mungo* Episcopi et Patroni Glasguensis diocesis', 1546; but a medieval charter would undoubtedly have 'Sancti *Kentigerni*'. This charter is not authentic. Again, the statement (Brockie, p. 1533) that this house was reduced to ashes at the Reformation is absurd. The only ecclesiastical buildings on record at Southannan are a chapel of St. Anandi [*sic*] with a chantry in its graveyard, mentioned, 5 June 1509 (*RMS*, ii, no. 3354).

SUPPOSED NUNNERIES

(ORDER UNSPECIFIED)

Aberdeen. A convent and ch., dedicated to St. Catherine, and built by 'the Constable of Aberdeen', are said to have stood on St. Catherine's Hill here (Hay, *Scotia Sacra*, 218; *Aberdeen-Banff Coll.*, 205). There is no record evidence of such a foundation.

Crail. Hist. Mon. Comm. Rep. (Fife, etc.) (p. 66) notes a site as 'nunnery (remains of)'. This nunnery is apocryphal. Its supposed existence is due to a misinterpretation of the fact that the nunnery of Haddington held the parish ch. and certain properties at Crail.

Edinburgh, St. Mary of Placentia. D. C. A. Malcolm shows that this alleged nunnery is 'completely spurious', an invention of Maitland (see *History of Edinburgh*, 176) to account for the name 'Pleasance' (*Hist. Mon. Comm. Rep. (Edinburgh)*, 216).

Inchcailleoch. The tradition that this island in Loch Lomond was the site of a nunnery 'seems to rest on no better foundation than the name, which is said to mean "the island of old women" ' (*OPS*, i, 32). Even the *Scotichronicon*, which has a certain partiality for supposititious ofundations on Scottish islands, has the entry: 'Inchecalzoch, where [there is] a parish church' (*ubi ecclesia parochialis*: lib. ii, cap. x; *Chron. Bower* i, 46). References to the parish ch. (a rectory) are found in records (e.g. *Glas. Reg.*, i, lxvii, lxxv; *RMS*, i, App. 2, no. 1144 (10)). The careful account in *The Lennox* (i, 49–63), which gives details of this parish and its ch., does not so much as mention a nunnery.

Molista. The suggestion that this was the site of a nunnery (*OPS*, ii¹, 286) is based on the fanciful explanation of a place-name which is said to mean 'the town (or house) of the black old women'.

Murkle. The supposed nunnery here, at a place locally known as Glosters (*OPS*, ii², 748), cannot be authenticated from Scottish records.

Nunnery. This place-name occurs in the parish of Crawford, Lanarkshire (see *OPS*, i, 166). No explanation of its origin can be given, but it is safe to say that it does not mark the site of a religious house (cf. the place-name Abbey (p. 235)).

Nuntoun. At this place in the island of Benbecula, *OPS* (ii¹, 370) reports the former existence of a building 'locally believed to have been a nunnery'. The sole testimony for this is the statement of the *New Statistical Account*. It need not be taken seriously.

Papple. Remains near Papple farm-house in the parish of Whittinghame, East Lothian› have been described as a 'convent' (*Hist. Mon. Comm. Rep (East Lothian)*, 132). Both the Cistercian nuns of Haddington (*RMS*, ii, no. 610) and the nuns of St. Bothan's of the same order (*East Lothian Deeds*, p. 9) held lands in 'Popil', but the existence of a 'convent' is an unwarranted inference from these facts.

It may be noted that, according to the Wardlaw MS., Hugh, E. of Ross, intended to build a nunnery at Dingwall, 'if the towne had not hindered it' (*Chron. Frasers*, 81). There is no other evidence of a projected foundation at Dingwall. Again, in the context of the narrative, 'Hugh', E. of Ross (who held the earldom 1322/3–33) is almost certainly an error.

THE KNIGHTS TEMPLARS

GENERAL NOTES

THE main object of this military and international order was to protect pilgrims after the recapture of Jerusalem, where the first house was established in 1118. In 1128 the professed knights, who were bound by the three perpetual vows, adopted a rule similar to that of the Cistercians. The lack of records makes the history of the Templars in Scotland difficult to trace. The order was introduced into Scotland by David I (1128I × 153), who granted certain liberties to the knights which subsequent kings confirmed and enlarged (*Regesta Regum Scottorum*, i, nos. 80–1, 287; cf. Edwards, 'Knights Templar in Scotland' in *Trans. Scot. Eccles. Soc.*, iv (1913), 37; *Torphichen Chrs.*, 6, in which date of introduction is given (without record authority) from *c.* 1128 to 1153). A vague reference which may point to the order holding land in St. Andrews, occurs 1126/7–1158/9 (*St. Andrews Liber*, 124). The number of Templar houses in Scotland has been exaggerated (e.g. by Spottiswoode, 435, whose account of them is inaccurate and misleading). It is clear by the record of the proceedings against them in Scotland (in 1309) that the order had only two major houses in Scotland, one of the Templars stating in examination that he had lived 'in various houses' of the order in England since his reception into it, also at 'Culther' (Maryculter) and at 'Blancrodoks' (Balantrodoch) in Scotland (*Spottiswoode Soc. Misc.*, ii, 11). Nevertheless, it should not be too readily assumed that these were the only Templar foundations. The knights held lands and property in many parts of Scotland and, if the English pattern was followed (see Knowles and Hadcock, *Medieval Religious Houses, England*, 290–7), lesser houses, usually under a preceptor and two or more professed brethren, may have been established at places such as Carnbee in order to supervise these. The Templars' revenues in Scotland are said to have amounted to 300 marks (Larking, *The Knights Hospitallers in England*, 201). Following general accusations against the Templars in 1307–8 and proceedings against them in various countries, similar action was initiated in Scotland, *c.* 1309. The whole order was suppressed in 1312, the greater part of their possessions passing to the Knights Hospitallers.

HOUSES OF THE KNIGHTS TEMPLARS

Name	County	Fd.	Supp.
¶ BALANTRODOCH (TEMPLE)	Midlothian	1128–53	*c.* 1309
CARNBEE	Fife	?	*c.* 1309
MARYCULTER	Kincardine	1221–36	*c.* 1309

(The *Date* column heads Fd. and Supp.)

BALANTRODOCH (TEMPLE). Early writers (e.g. Spottiswoode, 435) who were apparently unaware that the later medieval and modern Temple is identical with Balantrodoch, have sometimes treated 'the Temple' and Balantrodoch as two separate houses. This was the principal seat of the Templars in Scotland. There is no record of its fd'n., but the assumption (Spottiswoode, 435) that this was due to David I (1128 × 1153) is undoubtedly correct (*Regesta Regum Scottorum*, i, nos. 80–1, 287). The earliest reference is probably in 1175–99, when Brother Raan (?Ranulphus) Corbet, 'master in the land of the King of Scots of the House of Temple', grants a charter with the consent of 'our brethren of Plentidoc [*sic*]' (*Glas. Reg.*, i, no. 41). 'Plentidoc' is almost certainly a garbled form of the name 'Balantrodoch'. This charter—of a toft in Glasgow granted to the Templars by Bishop Jocelin—is witnessed by a brother-almoner, a brother-preceptor and two other brethren. An explicit reference to the master and brethren of the Temple of Balintrodoch occurs in 1237 (*Newb. Reg.*, 160). After the suppression of the Templars, 'Tempill of Balantrodoch' with the kirk became one of the baronies held by the Hospitallers (*Torphichen Chrs.*, 8) while, at an unascertained date, but possibly before 1426 (*CSSR*, ii, 129), the (former) Templar's church became parochial—a vicar of Temple is mentioned, 19 Sept. 1524 (*RMS*, iii, no. 275). That ch. was in use till the nineteenth c. and still exists in ruins.

CARNBEE. An instrument of sasine dated 15 March 1563/4 is said to have been effected 'at the templar-place of Carnbee, where the house thereof was wont to be' (*Laing Chrs.*, no. 769). No other reference to this fd'n. has been noted, and the veracity of the statement must remain in question.

MARYCULTER. This place in Kincardineshire is frequently confused with Culter in Lanarkshire. The house was founded by Walter Byset, 1221 × 1236 (*Kel. Lib.*, no. 233). A controversy with the abbey of Kelso (which held the parish ch. of Culter) regarding the newly built chapel of the knights, was settled, 4 Nov. 1287 (*ibid.*, no. 233; *Abdn. Reg.*, ii, 288 ff). Maryculter also became one of the baronies of the Knights of St. John, who also maintained a house here (see under Knights Hospitallers).

SUPPOSED FOUNDATIONS

There are numerous references to alleged houses of Templars in Scotland. These are exaggerated accounts of what were merely Temple lands such as are found in many parts of the country (see lists in *Torphichen Chrs.*, 7–55) or, in some cases, of appropriated chs. Those which are patently absurd have been ignored.

Aberdeen. Under the heading 'Templars or Red Fryers [*sic*]' appears the statement: 'Their convent and church stood in the northwest corner of the Castlegait' (*Aberdeen–Banff Coll.*, 203). The 'convent and church' are imaginary. The Templars merely had property here.

Aboyne. Described by Spottiswoode (435) as a 'considerable estate and house belonging to this order'. This is an exaggeration. The grant of the ch. of Aboyne to the Templars at Culter by Walter Byset was confirmed by Ralph, bp. of Aberdeen, 1239–42 (*Abdn. Reg.*, ii, 271) and by Alexander II, 15 April 1242 (*ibid.*, ii, 272). It is mentioned otherwise as a ch. held by the Templars (*Templaria*, 5, 7; *Torphichen Chrs.*, 9).

Culter. Morton (*Monastic Annals*, 144) and others have confused Maryculter (sometimes called simply Culter) in Kincardineshire, where there was one of the two Templar houses, with Culter in Lanarkshire, which had no such connection with the Templars.

Forvie. This ch. is described as 'formerly the Knights Templars now King's College' (*Aberdeen–Banff Coll.*, 217). There was certainly no Templar house here and the ch. is not otherwise mentioned as held by the Templars.

Inchinnan. This was a parish ch. held by the Templars and afterwards by the Hospitallers (*Templaria*, 5, 7; *Torphichen Chrs.*, p. 9; *CPL*, viii, 504).

Ladykirk (Ayrshire). The mention of the 'preceptory' of Our Lady Kirk of Kyle, 28 Sept. 1505 (*RSS*, i, no. 1128) has given rise to the idea that it was a Knights Templars' church. This was in fact a secular chapel, founded *c.* 1446 by John Blair (*CPL*, ix, 548). Offerings made at it and payments to its priests by James IV are recorded frequently from 1488 onwards in the *Treasurer Accts.*, i–iv. The term 'preceptory' was by no means applied merely to the houses of the Templars and Hospitallers. It is a common synonym for the mastership of a hospital and is also used in connection with a monastic cell (*v.* Gadvan under Cistercian Dependencies). Here it apparently refers to the office of the head of a quasi-collegiate group of priests serving this chapel. It may be noted that the description of Ladykirk as an 'old monastrie now ruinous' (Macfarlane, *Geog. Coll.*, i, 409) is entirely misleading.

Oggerstone. Given by Spottiswoode (435) as a 'fort and barony' belonging to the Knights. But this refers to Ogerston in England (*VCH.* Hunts, iii, 229).

St. Germains. Spottiswoode (435) speaks of it as belonging to this order. It was, however, a Bethlehemite hospital. See under Hospitals.

Tullich. Spottiswoode (435) calls it a residence of the Knights. It was in fact a parish ch. held by the Templars and latterly by the Hospitallers (*Templaria*, 5, 7; *Torphichen Chrs.*, p. 9).

THE KNIGHTS HOSPITALLERS

GENERAL NOTES

THE Hospital of St. John of Jerusalem was in being by the early twelfth century, and the brethren, who were originally infirmarians, were under the three perpetual religious vows and the order of St. Augustine. Its members cared for the poor and the sick and later provided escorts of knights to protect pilgrims to the Holy Land. The professed members were divided into three groups: the knights, the armed serving brothers and the brother chaplains. Members of the order, which like the Templars was international, were subject to the Grand Master. The order was introduced into Scotland by David I, c. 1144 × 1153. Endowments in various parts of the kingdom were granted to the order and to administer these, lesser houses known as commanderies, or as in England, preceptories, may have been established. Unfortunately in regard to the Hospitaller's records 'the archives of the Scottish commanderies seem absolutely lost and no trace of them exists' (*Cartulaire général des Hospiteliers de S. Jean de Jerusalem*, i (1890), clx). But there are more incidental references to the Hospitallers than to Templars and sixteenth-century rentals supply considerable particulars of their lands and possessions in Scotland, including those who came to them on the suppression of the Templars, c. 1309. In 1338 the normal revenues of the order in Scotland are given as 200 marks (Larkings, *The Knights Hospitallers in England*, 129).

HOUSES OF THE KNIGHTS HOSPITALLERS

Name	County	Fd.	Date T.	Sec.	
KIRKLISTON	West Lothian		1560		
MARYCULTER	Kincardine	+1309	c. 1513		Ex Templars
*‡TORPHICHEN	West Lothian	c. 1144 × 1153	1560	1563/4	

KIRKLISTON. The house of Kirkliston is recorded as being 'recently annexed' to the Commandery of Torphichen, 31 March 1513 (*James IV Letters*, no. 553). The barony of Kirkliston was held by the Hospitallers in the sixteenth c., but no other reference to a house therein has been noted (*Torphichen Chrs.*, 8–55).

MARYCULTER. Formerly a house belonging to the Knights Templars, which passed with the suppression of that order (*q.v.*) to the Hospitallers, c. 1309, the house is described as 'recently annexed' to the Commandery of Torphichen, 31 March 1513 (*James IV Letters*, no. 553). If accurate this description would seem to indicate that the original fd'n. became Hospitaller.

TORPHICHEN. A grant of the land of 'Torphigan' to the Knights Hospitallers by David I (1124–53) proves the truth of Spottiswoode's assertion (438) that David founded this house (Dugdale, *Monasticon Anglicanum*, ii, 551). The Hospitallers also received from Malcolm IV a full toft in every burgh of his realm (*Regesta Regum Scottorum*, i, no. 193); and their possessions were confirmed by Alexander II on 30 June 1231 and 12 June 1236, and by Alexander III, on 17 Jan. 1283/4 (*RMS*, ii, no. 1791). In 1338 their lands and possessions (like those of the Templars which passed to the Hospitallers on the suppression of that order, *c.* 1309) are described as destroyed and burned during the long continued war (Larkings, *Kts. Hosp. in England*, 129). The Pope on 10 Feb. 1356 issued letters conservatory of the Hospitallers in Scotland (Reg. Aven, 133, fo. 150v–1). The prior of the order in England claimed to be protector of the order in Scotland during a dispute over the preceptorship in course of which one of the rival litigants claimed in June 1513 that he would 'augment the membership of the order, revive the service of the order in Scotland, extinct for so many years, and repair the houses and half-buried chs. of the order' (*James IV Letters*, nos. 346, 385, 420–1, 423–4, 478, 535, 553–4). The preceptorship by this period is evidently the sole office connected with this order, and in all but name the office appears to have become secularized long before the Reformation. Included among the possessions of the house were the baronies of Torphichen, Thankerton, Denny, Kirkliston, Balantrodoch Temple and Maryculter with a large number of smaller lands and five parish chs. (Aboyne, Inchinnan, Kinbethock Towie, Maryculter and Tullich) (*Torphichen Chrs.*, 8–55). On 25 Jan. 1563/4, Q. Mary granted to the praeceptor James, Lord St. John, the lands and baronies belonging to Torphichen, these having been incorporated in one barony. (*RMS*, iv, no. 1499).

SUPPOSED FOUNDATIONS

Ancrum. The Knights of St. John are said to have had a preceptory or hospital here (Mackinlay, *Place Names*, p. 368). This is mere conjecture. Ancrum Spittal (*q.v.*) was a secular foundation.

Edinburgh. The 'Preceptory' mentioned *Hist. Mon. Comm. Rep. (Edinburgh)* (1951), 126, no. 75, is an exaggerated description of property held by the order.

Kinkell. The tradition that the knights of St. John had a commandery here is incorporated in a sixteenth c. account of the fd'n. of Kinkell in 1420 in which reference is made to the benefice as '*plebaniam seu militum Hierosolimitanorum*' (*Abdn. Reg.*, ii, 253).). There is no evidence to support this statement, and the benefice appears in the fourteenth c. as an independent parsonage (*CPL*, iii, 151; *CPP*, i, 113).

HOSPITALS

General Notes

THE compilation of a list of medieval Scottish hospitals involves considerable difficulties; and although the list which follows includes a few items not previously noted, nothing like finality can be claimed for it. 'Border-line' cases are inevitable and some items which have been listed are barely admissible, while certain others relegated to the 'uncertain' category are placed there with hesitation. In framing such a list, it is necessary to be wary of the suggestion that where the name 'Spittal' survives, a medieval hospital must have existed. Not infrequently it can be verified that 'Spittal' indicates a medieval site; but the name may also indicate a site which is post-Reformation. In certain cases, it has apparently become attached to hospital lands at a distance from the establishment to which they belonged. In a number of instances, its occurrence admits of no explanation. It may be noted that 'Maison Dieu' appears likewise as a name attached to land or property in places where no hospital of such a designation is recorded.

Dedications. The following abbreviations are used:

St. John B.	=	St. John the Baptist
St. John E.	=	St. John the Evangelist
St. Mary M.	=	St. Mary Magdalene
St. Mary V.	=	St. Mary the Virgin

Types. The following abbreviations are used:

L = Lepers.	A = Almshouse, in most cases
P = the Poor.	for resident poor people.
S = the Sick.	Am = As last, for bedesmen.
T = Travellers and Pilgrims.	Aw = As last, for bedeswomen.

A hospital was sometimes of dual or mixed type, e.g. for the Poor and the Sick (indicated thus: PS).

A hospital sometimes changed its type, e.g. from Lepers to the Poor (indicated thus: L–P).

Rules. Some hospitals were in charge of religious orders or of brethren (in one case, sisters) under a rule. Thus the Trinitarians originally held several hospitals, others were in some sense Augustinian, one was Bethlehemite (i.e. in the hands of the order of *Cruciferi cum Stella*, not the fifteenth-c. order of St. Mary of Bethlehem), and another of the order of St. Anthony of Vienne. These orders are shown thus: (Trinitarians) . . . (Vienne).

Some hospitals attached to monasteries were clearly secular, e.g. St. Leonard's, attached to Holyrood abbey.

The contraction 'Contd.' signifies that the hospital remained in existence after the Reformation.

HOSPITALS

Name	County	Dedication or designation	Fd.	Date Termd. or Sec.	Type	Dependent on or Rule
ABERDEEN	Aberdeen	Leper House	−1333	Contd.	L	
,,	,,	St. Anne	−1519	?	Aw	
,,	,,	St. Mary	1531/2	Contd.	Am	
,,	,,	St. Peter	−1179	1541+	S	
,,	,,	St. Thomas the Martyr	1459	Contd.	PS	
ADNISTON (AULDENESTUN) see LEGERWOOD						
ALDCAMBUS see OLDCAMBUS						
ANCRUM	Roxburgh		?	1545	?	
ANNAN	Dumfries		−1258	?	?	
ARBROATH	Angus	Almshouse	1178	1531+	A	Arbroath abbey
,,	,,	St. John B.	−1352	1519+	?	
ARDROSS	Fife		−1154	?	PT	North Berwick nunnery
ARRAT	Angus	St. Mary M.	−1412	?	P	
AYR	Ayr	Leper Houses	−1448	?	L	
,,	,,	St. Leonard	−1420	1506+	?	
BALGOWNIE	Angus	St. Mary(?)	−1418	Contd.	?	
BALLENCRIEFF	East Lothian	St. Cuthbert	−1291	−1481	?	
BANFF	Banff		−1544	−1589/90	L	
BARA	East Lothian		c. 1340	?	?	
BERWICK		Leper House	−1238×49	?	L	
,,		Maison Dieu	−1287	1484+	P	
,,		St. Edward	−1234	−1456	PS	Trinitarians
,,		St. Leonard	−1297	?	?	
,,		St. Mary M.	−1296	−1431−32	P	
BIGGAR	Lanark	Almshouse	1545/6	?	Am	Biggar collegiate church
,,	,,	St. Leonard	−1446	−1545	?	
BRECHIN	Angus		−1267	Contd.	P	

Name	County	Dedication or designation	Fd.	Date Termd. or Sec.	Type	Dependent on or Rule
CAMBUSLANG	Lanark	St. Leonard	−1455	?	?	
CARNWATH	Lanark		15 c.	?	Am	Carnwath collegiate church(?)
CAVERS see RULEMOUTH						
COCKBURNSPATH	Berwick		−1511	1581+	?	
CORSTORPHINE	Midlothian	St. John Baptist	−1538	1568+	Amw	
COVINGTON	Lanark	Almshouse	−1468	?	A	
CREE	Kirkcudbright		−1186	?	?	Held by Dundrennan abbey
CROOKSTON	Renfrew		−c. 1180	?	S(?)	
DALHOUSIE (=LASSWADE; POLTON)	Midlothian	St. Leonard	−1500	1564+	S(?)	
DALKEITH	,,	Maison Dieu	1396	?	P	Dalkeith collegiate church
DOONSLEE, see see AYR, ST. LEONARD						
DUMBARTON	Dunbarton		15 c.(?)	16 c.(?)	Am	Dumbarton collegiate church
,,	,,	Leper house	−1489	16 c.(?)	L	
DUNBAR	East Lothian	Maison Dieu	?	16 c.	P	Dunbar collegiate church or Trinitarians, v. notes.
DUNDEE	Angus	Leper house	−1498	−1552	L	
,,	,,	Maison Dieu	−c. 1390	1554+	PS	Trinitarians v. notes
,,	,,	St. Anthony Abbot	1443	?	?	
,,	,,	St. John B.	−1442/3	16 c.(?)		
DUNFERMLINE	Fife	Almshouse	−1488	?	A	
,,	,,	St. Catherine	−1327	1569+	A	Dunfermline abbey
,,	,,	St. Leonard	Uncertain	Cont.	Amw	
DUNGLASS	East Lothian	St. Mary and St. John B.	1443×67	?	P	Dunglass collegiate church.
DUNKELD	Perth	St. George	−1506	Contd.	P	
DUNS	Berwick		−1274	?	?	
EARLSTON	,,		−c. 1160	?	?	
EDINBURGH	Midlothian	Kirk o' Field	c. 1510	1544–7(?)	?	Probably attached to St. Mary in the Fields collegiate church.

Name	County	Dedication or designation	Fd.	Date Termd. or Sec.	Type	Dependent on or Rule
EDINBURGH	,,	Leper house	−1477	1544–7(?)	L	
,,	,,	St. Giles	−1541	1544–7(?)	?	
,,	,,	St. John B.	−1392	−1438(?)	?	
,,	,,	St. Leonard	−1239			Holyrood abbey
			1493 (reconstituted)	−1580/1	Am	
§ ,,	,,	St. Mary M.	−1537	Contd.	P	
,,	,,	St. Mary V.	−1438(?)	1583+	Aw	
,,	,,	St. Mary and St. Paul	1469	Contd.	Am	
,,	,,	St. Thomas M.	1541	Contd.	Am	
,,	,,	Trinity College	−1460	1567	Am	Trinity College
EDIRDOUER see KILLEARNAN						
EDNAM	Roxburgh	St. Leonard	−1178	−1627	Am	
ELGIN	Moray	Leper house	−1391	?	L	
,,	,,	Maison Dieu	−1237	1594/5	P	
FAIL	Ayrshire		−1560	?	P	Trinitarians
FAIRNINGTON	Roxburgh		−1511	1594+	?	
FORRES	Moray	Leper House	−1560	1565+	L	
FORTUNE	East		−1270	?	?	
GEILSTON	Dunbarton		−1560	1582+		
GLASGOW	Lanark	Blacader's (St. Nicholas, St. Serf, St. Machutus)	c. 1524–5	−1605	P	
,,	,,	St. Nicholas	c. 1464	Contd.	Am	
,,	,,	St. Ninian	c. 1359 or 15 c.	1636	L	
HADDEN	Roxburgh		−1432	?		
HADDINGTON	East Lothian	Almshouse	c. 1478	?	A	
,,	,,	Leper House	−1470	?	L	
,,	,,	St. Laurence	−1312 1470–2 (refounded)	see notes	A	
,,	,,	St. Mary	−1319	?	?	
HAMILTON	Lanark	St. Thomas M.	−1496	?	?	
HARELAW	Dumfries	St. Thomas M.	−1195	?	L	
HELMSDALE	Sutherland	St. John B.	−1362	?	?	Kinloss abbey
HOLYWOOD	Dumfries	St. John B.	−1362	1561+	Am	Lincluden collegiate church.
HORNDEAN	Berwick	St. Leonard	c. 1240	?	A	Kelso abbey
HOUSTON	East Lothian		−1296	?	?	Trinitarians
HUTTON	Berwick	St. John	−1296	1542	?	
INVERKEITHING	Fife		−1196	?	?	Dryburgh abbey.

Name	County	Dedication or designation	Fd.	Date Termd. or Sec.	Type	Dependent on or Rule
JEDBURGH	Roxburgh	Almshouse	−1553	1575+	A	Jedburgh abbey
,,	,,	Maison Dieu	−1296	Contd.	P	
KELSO	,,		−1260	?	P	Kelso abbey
KILLEARNAN	Ross		−1299 ×1310	?	?	
KILPATRICK	Dunbarton		c. 1173	1518+	P	
KINCARDINE O'NEIL	Aberdeen	St. Mary	1244+	c. 1330	P	
KINGCASE	Ayr	St. Ninian	14 c.(?)	Contd.	L–A	
KINGHORN	Fife	St. James	−1478	?	P	
KIRKWALL	Orkney		−1560	?		
LANARK	Lanark	St. Leonard	−1249	Contd.	A	
LASSWADE, ST. LEONARD see DALHOUSIE						
LASSWADE	Midlothian	St. Mary V.	1478	?	PST	
LAUDER	Berwick	St. Leonard	1175× 1189	c. 1432(?)	Amw	
LEGERWOOD	Berwick		−1177(?) or −1296(?)	?	L(?)	
LEITH	Midlothian	St. Anthony	1418	1591	PS	Vienne
,,	,,	Holy Trinity	1555	Contd.		
LINCLUDEN see HOLYWOOD						
LINLITHGOW	West Lothian	Almshouse	−1448	Contd.	A	
,,	,,	Almshouse, St. Mary V.	1496	1561+	A	
,,	,,	St. Mary M.	−1335	−1591	P	
LOCH LEVEN	Kinross	St. Mary V.	c. 1214		P	Trinitarians
METHVEN	Perth		1550	?	PS	
MONTROSE	Angus	St. Mary V.	c. 1245; refounded 1516 for Friars Preachers.	contd.	L–P	
MUSSELBURGH	Midlothian	St. Mary M.	−1386	?	LP	
NENTHORN	Roxburgh		−1542	1542(?)	?	
NEWBURGH	Aberdeen		c. 1261	?	A	
NORTH BERWICK	East Lothian	Almshouse	154	Contd.	A	
,,	,,		−1154	?	PT	North Berwick nunnery.
OLDCAMBUS	Berwick		−1214 × 16	?	L	
PEEBLES	Peebles	Almshouse (I)	1462	?	A	
,,	,,	Almshouse(II)	1464	1549(?)	A	
,,	,,	St. Leonard	−1305	Contd.	P	
PERTH	Perth	St. Anne	−1488	1586	P	
,,	,,	St. Katherine	1523	1567(?)	PT	
,,	,,	St. Leonard	−1184	1543+	?	Annexed to Charterhouse.

Name	County	Dedication or designation	Fd.	Date Termd. or Sec.	Type	Dependent on or Rule
PERTH	,,	St. Mary M.	−1327	1543+	P	Annexed to Charterhouse
,,	,,	St. Paul	1434	1580×83	PTS	
PILRIG	Midlothian		1448	?	P	
POLLOK	Renfrew	St. Mary M.	−1417	?	?	
POLMADIE		St. John	−1285	1427/8 or 1453/4	Amw	Perhaps transferred to Dumbarton and attached to the collegiate church.
POLTON see DALHOUSIE						
PORTINCRAIG	Angus		−1187–9	?	?	
PORTMOAK	Kinross	St. Thomas	Mentioned −1184	?	P	Probably superseded by Loch Leven, St. Mary.
QUEENSFERRY (NORTH)	Fife		−1165	?	?	Attached to Dunfermline abbey.
RATHVEN	Banff		1224–6	Contd.	L–Am	
ROXBURGH	Roxburgh	Maison Dieu	−1305	Contd.	?	
,,	,,	St. John	−1330	?	?	
,,	,,	St. Mary M.	−1319	?	?	
,,	,,	St. Peter	−1286(?)	?	?	
RULEMOUTH (SPITTAL-ON RULE)	Roxburgh	St. Mary(?)	−1425/6	1545	L	
RUTHERFORD	,,	St. Mary V. or St. Mary M.	−1276	?	?	Granted to Jedburgh abbey.
ST. ANDREWS	Fife	St. Leonard	1144	1512	PT–Amw	Erected into St. Leonard's College.
,,	,,	St. Nicholas	−1127	1583+	L–P	Granted to the Friars Preachers.
ST. GERMAINS	East Lothian	St. Germain	−1170×80	1577+	P	Bethlehemite. Granted to King's College, Aberdeen.
ST. MAGNUS	Caithness	St. Magnus	−1358	Contd.	?	
ST. NICHOLAS (BOHARM)	Banff	St. Nicholas	−1235	Contd.	PT	
SEGDEN	Berwick	St. Mary	13 c.	−1379	Am(?)	Augustinian.
SHOTTS	Lanark	St. Catherine	−1476	?	P	

Name	County	Dedication or designation	Fd.	Date Termd. or Sec.	Type	Dependent on or Rule
SMAILHOLM	Roxburgh		−1492	1542	?	Granted to Dryburgh abbey
§ SOUTRA	Midlothian	Holy Trinity	1164	1583/4	T–P	Augustinian
SPITTAL (CAITHNESS) see ST. MAGNUS						
STIRLING (OVER HOSPITAL)	Stirling	Almshouse	−1482	Contd. (to −1610)	A	
,,	,,	Leper House	−1464	*c.* 1513(?)	L	
,,	,,	Mary of Gueldres	1449 × 1462	*c.* 1463	P	
,, (NETHER HOSPITAL)	,,	Spittal's	−1546	Contd.	A	
,,	,,	St. James	−1221 × 1225	−1606	?	Granted to Cambus-kenneth abbey.
TEVIOTDALE, ST. MARY IN, See RULEMOUTH						
TORRANCE	Lanark	St. Leonard	−1296	1546+	?	
TRAILTROW	Dumfries	St. James	−1363(?)	1574+	P	
TURRIFF	Aberdeen	St. Mary and St. Congan	1272/3	1412	A	
UPSETTLINGTON see HORNDEAN						
UTHROGLE	Fife	St. John B.	−1293	1462(?)	?	Annexed to Trinity College, Edinburgh.
WHEEL	Roxburgh		mentioned 1348	?	?	
WIGTOWN	Wigtown		−1557	Contd.	?	

ABERDEEN, LEPER HOUSE. The *mons hospitalis* (Spitalhill) mentioned in 1333 (*Abdn Reg.*, i, 54; cf. i, 432) was undoubtedly the site of this hosp. which occurs as 'the houses of the lepers', 1 July 1363 (*ibid.*, ii, 283). The land called 'masyndow' on 1 Sept. 1459 (*St. Nich. Cart.*, ii, 329) may have belonged to this house. On 18 Aug. 1574, the magistrates and council were ordered by the Regent to collect a rent of land belonging to the lepers 'betwix New and Auld Aberdeen' and with the proceeds to have the leper house thatched and repaired; provision is also made for the maintenance of the house and the support of the male and female lepers (*RPC*, 1st ser., ii, 391–3). The house was in ruins in 1661 and in 1718 its lands were sold to King's College (McPherson, *The Kirk's Care of the Poor*, 169).

ABERDEEN, ST. ANNE. A hosp. for poor ladies situated at Footdee to which a chapel was added by Alexander Galloway, official of Aberdeen, in 1519 (*Aberdeen Council Register*, i, 96; cf. *Aberdeen Description*, 19). A reference to land pertaining to 'badeis wyffis' occurs in the mid-sixteenth c. (*Abdn. Reg.*, ii, 213).

ABERDEEN, ST. MARY. Fd. by Gavin Dunbar, bp. of Aberdeen, outside (to the west of) the cathedral burial ground, 23 Feb. 1531/2; for twelve old men (*Abdn. Reg.*, i, 401–6; *RMS*, iii, no. 1145). A master who was to 'performe the poyntis of the said fundatioun so far as is allowabill be the present lawis of this realme' was appointed 18 May 1573 (*RSS*, vi, no. 1965), and payments to this hospital are recorded during the sixteenth and seventeenth c. (*ER.* xvi, 158; *ibid.*, xviii, 58, 76; *ibid.*, xxiii, 352; *Aberdeen Council Register*, iii, 345). It continued to exist until the eigtheenth c. (*Aberdeen Description*, 22; *Aberdeen–Banff Coll.*, 156).

ABERDEEN, ST. PETER. Fd. by Mathew, bp. of Aberdeen (1172–99); for 'infirm brethren' (*Abdn. Reg.*, i, 11). In 1256 there is also a reference to 'the sisters living therein' (*ibid.*, ii, 39). In 1427 on the grounds that masters of the hospital had been applying the revenues to their own use without regard to the poor, Henry, bp. of Aberdeen diverted most of the endowments for the foundation of two chaplainries of the cathedral, one of whom was also to administer sacraments to the parishioners of what became the parish of Aberdeen–Spittal (*ibid.*, ii, 226–7; Cowan, *Parishes*, 2). The erection which was confirmed by the Pope on 18 Jan. 1436 in consideration 'that for forty years or more the hospital had been assigned to secular clerks' did not lead to the total suppression of the hosp. which retained certain endowments (*Abdn. Reg.*, ii, 226–9; Reg. Supp., 318, 95). The sick were still being maintained in 1541 (*Powis Papers*, 127–9) by which time the 'hospitale kirk of Sanct Petir' had been annexed to the sub-chantership of Aberdeen cathedral which had been established 1526 × 1534 (Watt, *Fasti*, 17; *RSS*, v, no. 2836, 2851).

ABERDEEN, ST. THOMAS MARTYR. Fd. in the Netherkirkgate by master John Clat for reception of the poor and infirm with a master, 28 May 1459 (*Abdn. St. Nich. Cart.*, i, no. lxxxiv; ii, 393). Payment to the bedesmen is recorded in 1596–7 (*Spalding Club Misc.*, v, 120); and disciplinary action by the kirk session against two of the inmates occurs in 1606 (*Aberdeen Ecclesiastical Records*, 56). It was apparently still in use after 1660 (*Aberdeen Discription*, 16).

ADNISTON (AULDENSTUN), see LEGERWOOD.

ALDCAMBUS, see OLDCAMBUS.

ANCRUM. Macfarlane (*Geog. Coll.*, ii, 158) refers to a hospital beside 'Ancrum'. The only evidence of a hosp. here comes from a list of places 'brent, rased and cast downe' during Hertford's invasion in 1545: one of the three 'spitelles and hosbitalles' destroyed is given as 'Angeram Spittel', burned on 14 Sept. (*LP Henry VIII*, xx2, nos. 456, 533). References to the mains (*terrae dominicales*) of Spittal, 'called Ancrum–Spittal', are found from 6 July 1566 to 31 May 1670 (e.g. *RMS*, iv, no. 1737; *HMC 12th Rep.*, App. Pt. viii, 151; *Roxburgh Retours*, nos. 126, 253). The statement that 'there appears to have existed [here] an establishment of the Knights Templars the remembrance of which is preserved in the name "Ancrum–Spittell" '(*OPS*, i, 304) is entirely unwarranted.

ANNAN. The hosp. appears in a charter of donation to St. Bees priory *c.* 1258 (*St. Bees Reg.*, 354). Held in lay patronage, 13 Oct. 1446 (Reg. Supp., 413, fo. 295v). There is also a mention 15 Feb. 1609 of hosp. lands in Annan parish 'which formerly belonged to pre-ceptory of Trailtrow and the hospital within the parish of Annan' (*RMS*, vii, no. 21). The history of this hospital is otherwise obscure.

ARBROATH, ALMSHOUSE. The almonry of the abbey of Arbroath was rather unusually situated outside the monastic precincts, lying close to the chapel of St. Michael (*Arb. Lib.*, ii, no. 60). Its fd'n. was presumably coeval with that of the abbey in 1178, but early references are lacking. It does, however, frequently appear on record during the fifteenth and sixteenth c., the last recorded occurrence being dated, 10 April 1531 (*ibid.*, ii, no. 174, 214, 753). An inspection of 1464 gives some indication of the scope and purpose of this fd'n. (*ibid.*, ii, no. 160).

ARBROATH, ST. JOHN BAPTIST. Appears in 1352 as the hosp. of St. John Baptist, '*iuxta Aberbrothoc*' (*Arb. Lib.*, i, no. 352). In 1464 and again in 1485, it is called the chapel of St. John (*ibid.*, ii, nos. 160, 267). An obligation for the payment of annates due from this hosp. was made 30 June 1519 (Vat. Arch., Introitus and Exitus, 559, fo. 42v).

ARDROSS. At Earlsferry, the north end of the ferry on the Firth of Forth (see NORTH BERWICK, below). Fd. by Duncan, fourth E. of Fife,–1154, for poor people and travellers;

and granted by Duncan, fifth E., to the nuns of North Berwick,—1177 (*N.B.Chrs.*, no. 3). The land of the hosp. was confirmed to the priory by Malcolm, E. of Fife,–1199, and by William I, *c.* 1213 (*ibid.*, no. 7; *SHS. Misc.*, iv, 308–9; *Regesta Regum Scottorum*, ii, no. 516).

ARRAT. This hospital in the diocese of Brechin first occurs 10 Dec. 1412 (Reg. Aven., 340, fos. 694–5v) and as a hospital dedicated to St. Mary Magdalene again appears on record, 29 Sept. 1440 (Reg. Supp., 368, fo. 59v). It occurs again on 8 July 1444 as the hospital of the poor of St. Mary Magdalene de Arroch (*ibid.*, 398, fo. 70). The text is corrupt but it appears that the location was Arrat. There was at Arrat a chapel, dedicated to St. Mary Magdalene, which was united to the altar of the Holy Cross in the ch. of Brechin on 12 Aug. 1435, although this intention was apparently not fulfilled until 11 June 1451 (*Brech. Reg.*, i, nos. 46, 81). These annexations make no mention of a hosp. The chapel '*cum domibus edificiis*' is referred to in 1591, but no further specific reference to a hospital (*ibid.*, ii, no. ccclxxvii).

AYR, LEPER HOUSES. These are first mentioned on 1 April 1448 when it was ruled by Ayr burgh council that there should only be 'four sekmen at ye spetale' because the town was oppressed by the expense of their upkeep (SRO, Ayr Burgh Court Book, i (1428–78), fo. 50v). Again, at Easter 1452, it repeated its decision to support only four lepers and 'al ye housis to be tane down', two alone to be maintained in the future (*ibid.*, fo. 59v). These may be the old spittals referred to 5 June 1503 (SRO, Court Book of Barony of Alloway (1492–1538), fo. 42) as near the Spittalbog to the north of Ayr Common (not to be confused with St. Leonard's hosp. to the south on the Corrochan, or modern Slaphouse, burn as shown by Pont in his map of Kyle in Blaeu's atlas). They are probably also identical with the cripple's lodge of 1547–8 and the God's house referred to about the same date (Pryde, *Ayr Burgh Accounts*, 104, 105, 109, 115).

AYR, ST. LEONARD. A charter of James II refers to an endowment of this hosp. with the lands of Collinhatrig in Dumfriesshire, as made by Robert, duke of Albany (d. 1420) and William, bp. of Glasgow (1408–25) (*Glasgow Reg.*, ii, no. 347). The hospital or chapel of St. Leonard near the burgh of Ayr is referred to as ruinous when associated with an indulgence, *c.* 11 July 1425 (*CSSR*, ii, 104–5). This is evidently the same as the hosp. of St. Leonard of Doonslee beside the burgh of Ayr which occurs 25 May 1506 (*RSS*, i, no. 1266).

BALGOWNIE (EASSIE). The hospital or chapel of Balgony, in St. Andrews diocese, is mentioned, 20 Aug. 1418 (*CSSR*, i, 16). This is almost certainly the hosp. of Balgownie, in the parish of Eassie, Angus, which appears frequently at a later date (Eassie was in the diocese of St. Andrews). There is a reference to a chapel of the Blessed Virgin Mary, Balgownie, in the parish of Eassie, 5 Aug. 1450 (*Panmure Reg.*, ii, 236), and to the 'chapel or poors hospital of St. Mary the Virgin' in the parish ch. of Eassie, 8 March 1476 (Reg. Supp. 735, fos. 248–248v). By this date the hosp. with all its fruits had been leased to members of the family of Lyon (*ibid.*). From 4 Oct. 1499 (*RSS*, i, no. 418), numerous presentations to the mastership of this hosp. reveal that the office was held by a succession of the members of that family. There are references to it (as the preceptorship) till 1695 (*Forfar Retours*, no. 418). This hosp. was clearly at Balgownie in Angus and not at Balgonie in Fife. It is specifically described as in the sheriffdom of Forfar, 17 May 1529 (*RSS*, ii, no. 97).

BALLENCRIEFF (RED SPITTAL). The master or warden of this hosp. swore fealty to Edward I in 1291 and 1296 (*CDS*, ii, nos. 308, 823). It was, however, of considerably earlier date; there is a somewhat indefinite reference in 1296 to its fd'n. by the ancestors of Robert de Pinkeny (*ibid.*, ii, no. 857). It is called the poor hospital (*rubeum nuncupatum*) in a bull of 12 March 1390 in which it is stated that the statutes of foundation laid down that it is a perpetual benefice, to be assigned to the secular clergy of the dioceses of Dunkeld and Glasgow (Reg. Aven., 262, fos. 420–420v). The patronage of this hosp., commonly called the Red Spittal, is mentioned 20 April 1421 (Fraser, *Douglas*, iii, no. 60) and 6 March 1422/3 (SRO, RH6/258). But it was apparently defunct and part of its lands granted to the collegiate ch. of Dunglass by 13 June 1481, since on that date 'Redspetall' was one of the prebends constituted in that ch. (*ibid.*, no. 496; cf. *Thirds of Benefices*, 28; *APS*, iv, 663 etc.). The lands of 'Easter and Wester Spittal alias Roid-Spittell' mentioned 15 March 1533/4 (*RSS*, iv, no. 2569) and later (e.g. Fraser, *Haddington*, i, 25; *Haddington Retours*, no. 12) were evidently former properties of the hosp.

BANFF, LEPER HOUSE. There was a medieval leper house, referred to as extinct 2 March 1589/90, near the vicar's glebe and the Carmelite monastery. A related reference to the lands of Spittalmyre, 14 July 1544 would point to the existence of the leper house at that date (SRO, GD 185/2/10, 21, Forglen Writs, Box 2, Bundles 10, 21).

BARA. A hosp. (*domus hospitalis*) is mentioned, *c.* 1340 (*Yester Writs*, no. 24).

BERWICK, LEPER HOUSE. Evidently fd. by the gild of Berwick before the mayorality of Robert de Bernham in whose term of office an ordinance was passed to the effect that no lepers were to enter the gates of the town as alms were collected for their sustenance in a proper place outside the burgh (*Ancient Burgh Laws*, i, 72; Scott, *Berwick-upon-Tweed*, 467). Robert de Bernham was mayor in 1238 and 1249, and possibly on other occasions (*ibid.*, 478). No other reference has been found.

BERWICK, MAISON DIEU. Fd. by Philip de Rydale in the time of Alexander III (*Rot. Scot.*, i, 266a). His generous benefactions to the master, chaplains and poor of this hosp. are confirmed by Edward I, 24 Nov. 1300 (*CDS*, ii, no. 1176). In 1287 and 1291, the master was engaged in a suit concerning the hospital's lands in Bowsden (Palgrave, *Docs. Hist. Scot.*, i, nos. xviii, cxii). It appears, in 1328, as having its Scottish possessions restored (*CDS*, iii, no. 962). At the end of 1333 a petition of the master, poor brethren and sisters of the Maison Dieu to the English king and his council shows that their ch. and house were destroyed during the siege of the town (*ibid.*, iii, no. 1105). A grant of it by James I to his chaplain, Thomas de Lawedre, is provisionally dated 8 June 1425 (*HMC, 12th Rep.*, App. pt. viii, 174). On 26 July 1408 the bp. of Durham admitted William Fox, priest, as master of the hosp. dedicated to Our Lord, St. Mary Virgin, St. John Apostle, St. John Evangelist, St. Andrew Apostle and All Saints, to which he had been presented by the mayor, community and twelve 'jurators' of Berwick (Langley, *Registrum*, i, no. 90). On 24 Aug. 1482, Alexander Lye was granted custody of 'Mesuneu' within the town of Berwick, and as master of the hosp. appears 28 Aug. 1484 (*Cal. Pat. Rolls (1476–85)*, 313; Hodgson, *History of Northumberland*, II, ii, 503–4). A further appointment to the 'Meason Dieu' of Berwick, 17 May 1543, probably concerns disused hosp. buildings or nearby quay to which name Maison Dieu long applied (*LP Henry VIII*, xviiii, 366, no. 72; Scott, *Berwick-upon-Tweed*, 348–50).

BERWICK, ST. EDWARD. 'The hospital of the bridge of Berwick'. Charters deal with the grant, –1234 of the ch. of Kettins to this hosp. for the maintenance of the sick (*Yester Writs*, nos. 9, 12), or the poor (*ibid.*, no. 11) dwelling there. Henry III granted protection without term for the master and brethren of the house of St. Edward on the bridge of Berwick, 1 Aug. 1246 (*Cal. Pat. Rolls, Henry III*, iii, 484). The designation '*Domus Dei*' was applied to this hosp. and a grant of rents to the master and brethren of the Domus Dei on the bridge of Berwick was confirmed by Edward I, 6 July 1281 (*Cal. Pat. Rolls, Edward I (1272–81)*, 448). Trinitarians had settled in Berwick by 1248 (*Yester Writs*, no. 14), and it is possible that they were established in this hosp. soon after their arrival, though it is only from 1306 there is evidence of their possessing Bridge House (*Hist. Papers and Letters from Northern Registers*, no. cxi). Certain identification of the house of Trinitarians with this hosp. comes only from 1386 (*CPL*, iv, 253). Attempts at this period to re-grant the ch. of Kettins 'annexed of old to the Domus Dei of Berwick' (*RMS*, i, no. 838) to the newly founded Trinitarian hosp. of Dundee proved unsuccessful (Cowan, *Parishes*, 93–94). In 1456 the buildings of the Trinitarian house are described as greatly ruined (*CPL*, xi, 47–8), and on 3 Feb. 1473/4 this house which is described as long wasted 'so that no brother of our order is able to dwell there', was annexed to the Trinitarian house of Holy Cross Peebles (*q.v.*) by the Head Minister of the order in Paris (Renwick, *Peebles Aisle and Monastery*, 71–4; *CPL*, xiii, 491). A letter under the privy seal, 1 July 1529 mentions 'the hous of God that wes possedit [possessed] thare [i.e. at Berwick] of the said religioun be the ministeris and brether thairof that is distroyit and put down' and goes on to refer to the 'translatioun and applicatioun of the rentis . . . of the . . . place [i.e. of the Trinitarians] and hous of God of Berwik and Kytternin [Kettins] to the place of Peblis [Peebles]' (*RSS*, ii, no. 203). No evidence for any revival of Trinitarian activities in Berwick, and identification of the chapel of Ravensdale, dissolved in 1539, as a Trinitarian hosp. is unwarranted (see Berwick, Dominican Friars). It is clear that this hosp. was always a separate fd'n. from the Maison Dieu.

BERWICK, ST. LEONARD. In 1297(?), the master and brethren petition Edward I and his council for the restitution of land in Liddesdale, of which they had been dispossessed (Palgrave, *Docs. Hist. Scot.*, ii, no. cccxx). This is the only reference to this hosp. which has been found.

BERWICK, ST. MARY MAGDALENE. The master of this hospital had restitution of lands from Edward I in 1296 (*Rot. Scot.*, i, 25). On 6 June 1356 it is mentioned as a poor's hosp. which had been destroyed by the Scots; Edward II, who has had it in his hands, restores it (*ibid.*, i, 794). Appointments to the mastership are recorded till 1448 (*ibid.*, ii, 128; *Fasti Dunelmensis*, 188). A reference to the ch. of the hosp. of St. Mary the sanctuary of which had been violated before 8 Aug. 1411 probably relates to this fd'n. (Langley, *Registrum*, i, no. 210). It may have ceased to function as a hosp. by 1431/2 when it was called a free chapel (*Cal. Pat. Rolls, Henry VI* (1429–36), 131). By 1437 the hermitage of Segden was annexed to the free chapel of St. Mary Magdalene (*ibid.*, (1435–1441), 97). The free chapel with the hermitage annexed is last noted in 1453 (*CDS*, iv, no. 1251). See SEGDEN below.

BIGGAR, ALMSHOUSE. According to the fd'n. charter of the collegiate ch., 16 Jan. 1545/6, six bedesmen with a house assigned to them, are to be attached to it, while the fourth prebendary is to act as their preceptor (*Spalding Club Misc.*, v, 300, 302). This provision was made *de novo* and had no relation to the older hosp. (below). The almshouse was still not erected in 1547 (*ibid.*, v, 314).

BIGGAR, ST. LEONARD. A precept of sasine for infefting Robert, Lord Fleming in the patronage of the ch. and hospital of Biggar was granted, 31 May 1446 (*Wigtown Charter Chest*, no. 409). The hosp. is again mentioned, after a struggle over the patronage between the Hays of Yester and the Flemings of Biggar, 28–9 May, 12 July 1470 and 22 Feb. 1472 (*ibid.*, no. 420; *Yester Writs*, nos. 117, 155, 157, 160; *RMS*, ii, no. 995). The latter was extinct or extinguished, 16 Jan. 1545/6, when, by a somewhat curious arrangement, the founder of the collegiate ch. grants the land of Spittal, which had apparently formed the hosp's endowment, to the first prebendary of the college, who though designated prebendary of the hospital of St. Leonard, is to be master of the college's song school (*Spalding Club Misc.*, v, 299). The new almshouse, of which the college's fourth prebendary was to act as preceptor, probably replaced this institution (see above).

BRECHIN, MAISON DIEU. Fd. –1267 (probably 1261–7) by William de Brechin whose charter refers to St. Mary's chapel of his foundation, and to the master, chaplains and the poor people serving God continually there (*Brech. Reg.*, i, no. 3; *Panmure Reg.*, ii, 205). According to a petition of 15 May 1463, the hosp. of St. Mary was accustomed to be ruled by laymen (Reg. Supp., 530, fo. 14v). There are frequent references to this fd'n., which may have been a dual establishment with a Little and Great Maison Dieu (*Brech. Reg.*, ii, no. cclxxxii), during the fifteenth and sixteenth c. (*ibid.*, i, no. 89; ii, nos. xxxvi, liii, lxxvii, cclxii). The ch. of the BVM or Masondew was refounded in 1517 with the consent of the preceptor. It is related in the crown charter of confirmation that previous masters had failed to reside and had applied revenues to themselves; it is to be refounded with a priest-master to take the grammar school, two chaplains holding no other benefices as collector and steward, four poor men over sixty not having wives (SRO, Dalhousie Muniments, GD 45/16/958). On 20 June 1572, ecclesiastical endowments in Brechin were vested in the burgh authorities (*RMS*, iv, no. 2079), but bedesmen were evidently still being maintained in 1582 (*ibid.*, v, no. 597) and there are references to the preceptory (mastership) till at least 1636, when the office was conjoined with a mastership in the grammar school (*Panmure Reg.*, ii, 321–2).

CAMBUSLANG. Fd. before 9 Feb. 1454/5 when the patronage of the hosp. of St. Leonard was granted by James, ninth E. of Douglas to James, Lord Hamilton (*HMC 11th Rep.*,

App. pt. vi, 17). The only further indication of a hosp. is from the occurrence of the place-name Spittal in post-Reformation records (EU MS. Dc. 4.32, fo. 15, *OPS*, i, 61; *Lanark Retours*, no. 308).

CARNWATH. A hosp. for eight bedesmen is said to have been founded here by Sir Thomas Somerville at the beginning of the fifteenth c. (*OPS*, i, 126, which does not give the source of this statement). If the place still called Spittal, at some distance from Carnwath, marks its site, it is difficult to regard it as having a connection with the collegiate ch. there. From 1524 onwards Spittal appears as in lay possession (*Carnwath Court Bk.*, *passim*); this would suggest that the hosp. was extinct before that date.

CAVERS, see RULEMOUTH.

COCKBURNSPATH. A hosp. is mentioned here from 27 Aug. 1511 (*RMS*, ii, no. 3635) to 16 June 1581 (*ibid.*, v, no. 218).

CORSTORPHINE, ST. JOHN BAPTIST. A small hosp. was attached to the collegiate ch. for bedesmen and bedeswomen at least by 1538. In 1568 two 'beidmen' and two 'wemen of ye college of corstorphine', hospitallers of the hosp. there, litigated regarding an annual rent due from tenants at the Overbow, Edinburgh (SRO, Edinburgh Commissariat Decreets, iii, fo. 17). In the same year they claimed this rent was of the patrimony of Corstorphine hospital for 'xxx at the leist xx at the leist x zeris nixt and immediately preceding 1558' since which date they had lacked payment (*ibid.*, fo. 68v).

COVINGTON. Fd. and endowed for a certain number of poor by James Lindsay, provost of Lincluden collegiate ch. between 1448 and 19 Nov. 1468, on which date an indulgence was sought for its expansion (Watt, *Fasti*, 364; Reg. Supp. 633, fo. 222).

CREE. The hosp. of 'Crithe' appears among the possessions of Dundrennan abbey, 18 Oct. 1305 (*CDS*, ii, no. 1702). 'Macraith de ospitali' occurs as a witness at Dundrennan during the episcopate of Christian, bp. of Galloway (*Holy. Lib.*, 20) and fd'n. can thus be assigned to a date before his death in 1186. Nothing is known of its history, but this site is probably indicated by the name Spittal in the parish of Kirkmabreck (see *RMS*, vi, no. 1122 (25 Dec. 1600); *Kirkcudbright Retours*, no. 256 (30 Sept. 1652).

CROOKSTON. A charter of the prior and convent of Paisley, *c.* 1180, concedes to the infirm brethren of the hosp. which Robert Croc has built in his land that they may have a chaplain and a chapel (*Pais. Reg.*, 77). This hosp. is said to have stood on the west side of the Levern Water, between Old Crookston and Neilston (*OPS*, i, 68).

DALHOUSIE, ST. LEONARD. References to the patronage of the chapel and hosp. of St. Leonard, within the barony of Dalhousie, are found from 20 May 1528 (*RMS*, iii, no. 590) to 27 July 1666 (*ibid.*, xi, no. 939). This is evidently the same as the hosp. of St. Leonard 'besid the brig of Laswaid' mentioned 20 July and 31 Aug. 1500 (*RSS*, i, no. 551, *Prot. Bk. Young*, no. 1080), and also identical with the hosp. of St. Leonard of Polton, situated near the bridge of Lasswade, the chapel of which appears, 7 May 1505 (*ibid.*, no. 1530). It is called the chaplaincy of St. Leonard *alias* the preceptory of Polton, 20 Oct. 1564 (SRO, Dalhousie Muniments, GD 45/16/321).

DALKEITH. Fd. by Sir James de Douglas, beside the chapel of St. Nicholas (later the collegiate ch.) as a '*domus dei sive hospitale*' for six poor people, 27 June 1396 (*Mort. Reg.*, ii, no. 208).

DOONSLEE, see AYR, ST. LEONARD.

DUMBARTON. A hosp. for men and women, which may have been transferred here from Polmadie, was probably attached to the collegiate ch. of Dumbarton from its fd'n., *c.* 1454 (see under Secular Colleges). A 'bedswomanis place' is mentioned 10 July 1526 (SRO, Prot. Bk. Forsyth, fo. 161–161v) and on 26 May 1539 a vacant bedemanship in the collegiate ch. is gifted by George Stirling of Glorat (Dumbarton Charters and Documents, no. 88). Further references to the hosp. occur 12 March 1551/2 and 1 Feb. 1552/3 (*RMS*, iv, nos. 683, 747). Deeds of gift of bedemanships continue until 11 Feb. 1627 (Dumbarton Charters and Documents, no. 92). By this date the hosp. itself may have ceased to exist and the building of a new hosp. was the subject of a letter dated 27 Sept. 1633 (*ibid.*, no. 44).

DUMBARTON, LEPER HOUSE. Not specifically mentioned as such; 'The spittale land liand besid ye toun of dunbartane' which had been leased by a leper was the subject of a legal action on 23 Feb. 1489/90 (*ADC*, 124) and there are frequent references from 27 Nov. 1494 (*ADA*, 185) to both male and female lepers leasing the 'spitelland liand abowne ye akynbare (SRO, B16/1/1, Prot. Bk. Mathew Forsyth, fos. 19, 63, 106, 164, 176). They probably also had a chapel as the lands of 'chappeltoun' are later associated with the lands of 'akinbar' (*ibid.*, fo. 267).

DUNBAR. A 'massindiew [Maison Dieu] or hospitall', said to be associated with the collegiate ch., is mentioned in an undated (probably sixteenth c.) record (BM. Harl. MS. 4637 C, fo. 189). As, however, 'Lie Masondew' appears among lands leased by the minister and convent of the Trinitarian house of Peebles, 1 June 1558 (*RMS*, iv, no. 3037), it may have originally been connected with the house of that order at Dunbar.

DUNDEE, LEPER HOUSE. Mentioned 20 June 1498 (*RMS*, ii, no. 2446). It stood on the river bank at the east end of the town (Maxwell, *Old Dundee*, 68). There is a reference to the hosp. or houses of the lepers, 30 Aug. 1540 (*Dundee Chrs.*, 30); but in 1552, the building had become ruinous and uninhabitable (Maxwell, *Old Dundee*, 68); and although, in 1556, the Town Council ordained its repair, this does not seem to have taken place. In 1564 its land was being leased for agricultural purposes (*ibid.*).

DUNDEE, MAISON DIEU. About 1390 Sir James Lindsay granted a tenement in Dundee to the Trinitarians for a hosp. and a Maison Dieu. This grant is incorporated in and confirmed by an undated charter (1390 × 1398) of Robert III, who also bestows on the hosp. (which is described as for the infirm, aged and ailing) the ch. of Kettins 'annexed of old to the Domus Dei of Berwick' to be held by it while Berwick remains in the hands of the English (*RMS*, i, no. 838). This part of the grant at least appears to have been inoperative, and the ch. of Kettins eventually passed with other revenues of the Trinitarian house at Berwick to the ch. of the Holy Cross at Peebles (*q.v.*) by a grant of 1473/4. It is impossible to say how long the Trinitarians held this hosp. but their tenure may have been short-lived. For some time before the Reformation the Town Council appointed the master and chaplain (Maxwell, *Old Dundee*, 65). It was burned by the English in 1548 (*ibid.*, 113) and various property of the Almshouse and its chapel, hidden during the English invasion, was restored in 1551 (*ibid.*, 66). There is a reference in 1553 to the Almshouse and 'the puir sick men thereof' (*ibid.*, 67), and the master of the almshouse occurs, 26 Oct. 1554 (Dundee Burgh Archives, Record of Burgh Head Courts).

DUNDEE, ST. ANTONY ABBOT. On 30 May 1443 Andrew Gray, lord of Foulis, and John Skrymgeour, constable of Dundee, knight, in honour of God, BVM and Blessed Anthony, ab., confirmed to the canons of Vienne certain lands near Dundee for a hosp. with six beds (SRO, GD 137/3809, Scrimgeour-Wedderburn Writs).

DUNDEE, ST. JOHN THE BAPTIST. The chapel or hosp. of St. John Baptist occurs 10 March 1442/3 (*Brech. Reg.*, i, no. 53). St. John's chapel, otherwise called the Rood chapel, is not associated with a hosp. thereafter. It stood considerably to the east of the leper house outside the burgh boundary. The chapel seems to have become derelict by 6 March 1561/2 (Maxwell, *Old Dundee*, 16n, 54, 177).

DUNFERMLINE, ALMSHOUSE. On 5 Aug. 1488 mention is made of a loft house outside the east gate above the 'almus hous' (*Dunfermline Burgh Recs.*, no. 2). No other reference has been found.

DUNFERMLINE, ST. CATHERINE. The almonry of the abbey was situated as at Arbroath, outside the monastic precincts, lying beyond the west part of the burgh and close to the chapel of St. Catherine. 'Our almshouse outside the port adjacent to the chapel of St. Catherine' occurs 10 March 1327 in a charter of the ab. of Dunfermline granting victuals from the mon. which are to be given to the poor (*Dunf. Reg.*, no. 370). The chapel, which was granted to the almshouse on that date, was destroyed and demolished before 23 Dec. 1420 when the buildings were in course of reconstruction at the instance of the almoner of Dunfermline abbey (*ibid.*, *CSSR*, i, 238). The land of the almshouse of Dunfermline is mentioned in a precept, 8 Nov. 1512 (*Laing Chrs.*, no. 289). Eleemosynary lands were leased by the commendator and almoner on 20 March 1565/6, part of the return from which was to be used for the repair of the '*Sacellum dive Katherine*' (*RMS*, iv, no. 2514). The hosp. with its buildings, garden etc. were granted in feu by the almoner to Alan Coutts, chamberlain of the monastery, 14 March 1568/9 (*ibid.*, iv, no. 2969).

DUNFERMLINE, ST. LEONARD. At the south end of the town. Early references to a hosp. of St. Leonard found in the records of Dunfermline abbey refer to the hosp. of St. Leonard, Perth (*q.v.*). There is little doubt that this was a medieval fd'n., but specific references to it seem only to be found after the Reformation. Thus several appointments to widowships are recorded from 1590 (*Dunfermline Court Bk.*, 187), while St. Leonard's hosp.and its almoner, widows and bedesmen appear, 9 Nov. 1615 (*Laing Chrs.*, no. 1736). The almoner appears as a party to various land transactions until 1636 (*ibid.*, nos. 1853, 1856, 1863-4, 2198). The chapel is said to have been wrecked by Cromwell's soldiers after the battle of Pitreavie, July 1651 (*Dunfermline Burgh Recs.*, xxix). The hosp. is mentioned until 1 April 1651 when it was evidently in a state of disrepair, and its lands till 1723 (*Dunfermline Court Bk.*, 191).

DUNGLASS. Erected shortly after the fd'n. of the collegiate ch. (*q.v.*) c. 1443/4, an indulgence for this hosp. for the poor and infirm, which names Sir Alexander Home as founder, was granted on 28 April 1467 (Reg. Supp., 609, fo. 65v). A bull of Pope Sixtus IV, dated 5 Aug. 1480, also refers to the poor's hosp., which, with a chapel of St. Mary and St. John Baptist, Sir Alexander Home had built near the collegiate ch. (Theiner, *Vet Mon.*, no. dcccclxxi; *CPL*, xiii, 271).

DUNKELD, ST. GEORGE. George Browne, bp. of Dunkeld (1484-1514/5), revived and augmented an earlier fd'n. (Myln, *Vitae*, 41-2). The hosp., which was for a master (a canon of Dunkeld) and seven poor folk (*ibid.*, 42) is first mentioned in diocesan accounts in 1506 (*Dunkeld Rentale*, 80). There are references to the hosp. in 1536 (Reg. Supp., 2204, fo. 77; 2205, fo. 66v) and to the master of the hosp. of St. George in 1606 (*HMC 7th Rep.*, Pt. II, App., 716) and 1608 (*RMS*, vii, no. 416).

DUNS. Occurs in 'Bagimond's Roll' in 1274/5 (*SHS, Misc.*, vi, 33) and in a taxation roll of the same century (*Cold. Corr.*, cx). It is called the poorhouse of Dons in a petition of 22 Nov. 1378 (Reg. Supp., 56, fo. 129). The hosp. with its appropriated ch. of Ellem occurs 13 Oct. 1394 (*CPPP*, i, 617). The master of the hosp. of Marie Magdalene of Douns occurs 12 Oct. 1492 (*HMC Rep.—Duns castle etc.*, no. 182); but it appears as the chapel of St. Magdalene, 2 July 1552 (*ibid.*, no. 186). On April 26 1699 Alexander Home of Linthill includes in a disposition 'the ald house called the Magdalene chapel' and four acres of land around it, acquired by the deceased William Home of Linthill, the disponer's father, from Margaret Douglas, daughter and heir of the deceased Archibald Douglas, servant to the earl of Morton (*ibid.*, no. 194).

EARLSTON. Mentioned only in a charter of Walter de Lyndesay to Kelso, c. 1160 (Raine, *North Durham*, App. no. clxiv).

EDINBURGH, KIRK O' FIELD. A hosp. attached to this collegiate ch. which was fd. c. 1510 (see EDINBURGH, St. Mary in the Fields under Secular Colleges) is mentioned 1544×1547 (*Midlothian Chrs.*, xxxvii). It is said to have been burned and destroyed by the English in the same period (*ibid.*, cccvii).

EDINBURGH, LEPER HOUSE. At the north port adjacent to Trinity college (*Prot. Bk. Young*, no. 1396). Payment to lepers is mentioned in 1477 and later (*St. Giles Reg.*, 134, 163, 177, 188) and these are identified as 'the lippir folkis of Sanct Ninian's chapell' in

1522 (*ibid.*, 215; cf. 222) and finally in 1529 (*ibid.*, 253). A '*domus Sancti Nicholai*' occurs in 1369 (*ibid.*, 278), but this could have been in Leith. The greater part of the chapel was burnt and the ornaments destroyed by the English, 1544 × 1547 (Edinburgh City Archives, Chrs. by the Commendators of Holyrood, no. 53). A commission was appointed to enquire into the 'estait and ordour of the awld fundation of the lipper hous', 30 Sept. 1584 (*Edinburgh Recs., 1573–89*, 352), but it had obviously ceased to function long before that date.

EDINBURGH, MAISON DIEU, see EDINBURGH, ST. THOMAS.

EDINBURGH, ST. ANDREW, see EDINBURGH, ST. THOMAS.

EDINBURGH, ST. GILES. The suggestion that this fd'n. was only a residence for the provost and curate of St. Giles is inaccurate. The hosp. is first mentioned in 1541. The curates of St. Giles were almoners and the ab. of Kilwinning was patron of one of the beds (SRO, Prot. Bk., Brounhill, ii, fos. 9–10). According to a charter of 2 July 1566, headed the hospital of St. Giles Kirk sett in feu ferm', the hosp., which lay within the cemetery of the ch. of St. Giles, had been burned by the English (1544 × 1547) and was ruinous and in need of repair (*St. Giles Reg.*, no. 152).

EDINBURGH, ST. JOHN BAPTIST. There are references to the tenement of the hosp. of St. John Baptist in charters, one of 1392 and another undated (*St. Giles Reg.*, nos. 19, 157). In 1438 and 1453 the hosp. was probably extinct when the ch. or chapel of St. John Baptist is mentioned (*Laing Chrs.*, nos. 118, 137). It was granted by the vicar of St. Giles on 18 Nov. 1464 to the Greyfriars (*q.v.*) who later replaced it with a bigger ch. in the same area (*St. Giles Reg.*, no. 81).

EDINBURGH, ST. LEONARD. 'The brethren of the hospital of St. Leonard Edinburgh' are parties to a controversy, 1219 × 1239 (NLS. MS. 34, l, 3a, fo. xcviv; cf. *Dunf. Reg.*, no. 220). David II (1328–1370/1) granted this hosp. to Holyrood Abbey (*RMS*, i, App. 2, Index A, no. 1668; *CPL*, xii, 734). This grant was confirmed by Robert III, 18 Jan. 1390/1 and Pope Clement VII, 28 May 1391 (*CPL*, xii, 730–5). On 19 June 1420 it was claimed that the union had been achieved by simony and a petition for its dissolution was made to the Pope (*CSSR*, i, 149–50). This was not effected, and the union was confirmed by papal bull on 3 Feb. 1470 (*CPL*, xii, 730–5). However, the proposal for dissolving the union was revived on petition of James III and papal bulls to effect this were issued 10 March and 2 May 1472 (*CPL*, xiii, 12–13; Cameron, *Apostolic Camera*, 172); but, on 18 July 1493, the hosp. was reconstituted by Robert Ballantyne, ab. of Holyrood, for six poor or aged men in the almshouse on the south side of St. Leonard's chapel in the village of that name (*Holy. Lib.*, 234–44) and on 3 Sept. 1494, the ab. duly gave six inmates of this almshouse sasine of two crofts and an annual rent (*Prot. Bk. Young*, no. 730). The hosp. beds were situated in the chapel vestibule and a brother hospitaller who was received into the hosp., 1 Jan. 1554/5, was shown where he might place his bed there, and was assigned his own garden (SRO, Prot. Bk. Robeson 1551–57, NP 1/14, fo. 94v). A similar procedure was followed 19 Feb. 1557/8 (*ibid.*, fo. 223v). A gift of a bedemanship, 8 Jan. 1580/1, refers to 'the place of the said hospital where the chapel formerly stood' (Edinburgh City Archives, Chrs. by the Commendators of Holyrood, no. 189). A preceptor of this hosp. occurs in 1591/2 and 1592 (*Yester Writs*, nos. 896, 903).

EDINBURGH, ST. MARY MAGDELENE. In the Cowgate, opposite the Greyfriars a chapel and hosp. for a chaplain and seven poor men were founded by Michael McQueen, burgess of Edinburgh (d. after 3 Jan., 1537/8: Prot. Bk. Brounhill, i, 48) and his wife Janet Rynd, whose confirmation charter by which she conveyed the chapel and hosp. in trust to the Edinburgh Hammermen is dated 12 Feb. 1547/8 (*Hist. Mon. Comm. Rep. (Edinburgh)*, 41–4, *q.v.* for a good account of this fd'n.; cf. also *RMS*, iii, nos. 2262, 2513; *RSS*, ii, no. 4325). Michael McQueen left £700 on his deathbed and his widow at length provided £2000 to purchase annual rents, including £40 from the whole lands of Carnwath and its mill (but not the Spittal lands in *The Carnwath Court Book*—recorded much earlier). This rent was sold to Bp. William Stewart of Aberdeen, one of McQueen's executors, as recorded in the Acts of the Lords of the Council, by Hugh, Lord Somerville, in Jan. 1540/1. The hosp. is then said to be 'newlie biggit and to be biggit to be institute eftir ye forme of ye fundacioun and erectione be ye said Reverend fader as executour forsaid or his executours to be maid' (Lockhart of Carnwath documents, SRO, GD247/16/Bundle K, now in NLS). An additional fd'n. by Isobel Mauchane provided four extra places in the Cross-house, apparently adjacent in Candlemakers' Row (*RMS*, iv, 950). Frequent payments to the hosp. and its bedesmen appear on record between 1544 and 1560 in which year a collector to the bedesmen was appointed by the Hammermen (*Edinburgh Hammermen*, 119, 134, 147–8, 150, 172–3). This hosp. survived the Reformation.

EDINBURGH, ST. MARY, ST. MARY'S WYND. This was not a nunnery, as has sometimes been assumed (e.g. Spottiswoode, 464), but an almshouse for poor women. Cf. references to 'the hospital of the Blessed Virgin Mary in the Wynd commonly called St. Mary's Wynd and the poor dwelling therein' (in 1484) (*RMS*, ii, no. 1600); 'the poor sisters of the hospital of St. Mary's Wynd outside the gates' (in 1535) (*St. Giles Reg.*, no. 135). Spottiswoode (464) states that 'in the chartulary of St. Giles', the nuns of St. Mary's Wynd are recorded'. But the sisters mentioned these are clearly not nuns but bedeswomen. (The use of the term 'sister' for a bedeswoman is illustrated by a reference to the granting of sasine to 'Marion Cockburn, sister of the Virgin Mary in St. Mary Wynd, in name of the other sisters, bedeswomen of the said hospital' (*Prot. Bk. Foular*, iii, no. 346.) On 30 May 1438 James [II] K. of Scots petitions for an indulgence for a hosp., which has been founded (with accommdation for forty-eight inmates) by the provost and community of Edinburgh (Reg. Supp., 348, fo. 28v) But identification of this hosp. with that of St. Mary for which James II sought the indulgence is questionable. The location of this hosp., possibly in order to avoid such confusion, is invariably stated, and the failure in 1438 to describe the inmates as female would also seem to weigh against such an identification. Appointments of bedeswomen are recorded till at least 1583 (*Edinburgh Recs., 1573–89*, 314). In 1585 the magistrates provided for using its chapel as a poor children's shelter (*ibid.*, 479). The latest reference to it—the payment of a deceased bedeswoman's due—occurs 19 Dec. 1589 (*Edinburgh Recs., 1589–1603*, 11).

EDINBURGH, ST. MARY AND ST. PAUL. There are divergent accounts of this hosp. It is described, 3 Feb. 1469/70 as a poor's hosp. which Archibald Crawford, ab. of Holyrood, had newly erected with a chapel dedicated to St. Paul (*CPL*, xiii, 761). The corresponding petition of the same date implies that this was a refoundation and states that Archibald had 'erected anew a certain poor's hospital with contiguous chapel which he wished dedicated to St. Paul' (Reg. Supp., 652, fos. 288 ff.). The phraseology is ambiguous, but in the event the hosp. appears to have been dedicated to St. Paul while the chapel was dedicated to St. Mary (*ADC*, 505, cf. 235). It was apparently in association with this chapel that Thomas Spens, bp. of Aberdeen (c. 1459–90) founded his hosp., reputedly for twelve poor men, in 1479, not many months before his death (*Edinburgh Recs., 1573–1589*, 136–8; Arnot, *History of Edinburgh*, 247). Another account states that this fd'n. was for decayed burgesses (Boece, Vitae, 54). The hosp. of our Lady founded by the late Bp. Spens occurs Feb. 1484/5 (*ADC*, *107). The two hospitals would appear to have become united, and may indeed have shared the same building from the outset, a fact which would explain the variety of designations applied to this hospital, e.g. 'the hospital of St. Mary of St. Paul', 7 Oct. 1488, 20 March 1490/1, 6 July 1514 (*Prot. Bk. Young*, nos. 127, 414, 2042); 'the hospital of the Blessed Virgin called St. Pauls, situated near Trinity College, at the end of Leith Wynd', 6 September 1501 (*ibid.*, 1159); 'the hospital of St. Mary the Virgin and St. Paul', in 1508 (*Prot. Bk. Foular*, i, no. 469). Again it is described as St. Paul's 'Werk' [building], which is specifically identified with Our Lady Hospital, e.g. in 1518, when it appears as 'the place or hospital of the Virgin Mary and St. Paul called St. Paul's werk' (*ibid.*, ii, no. 111); in 1579 when it is designated 'the hospitall of Oure Lady, callit Sanct Paullis Wark' (*Edinburgh Recs., 1573–89*, 137–8), with other similar mentions till 1608 (e.g. *ibid.*, 1573–89, 564; *ibid.*, 1604–26, 43). New statutes for the master and bedesmen were made by the Town Council in 1582 (*ibid.*, 1573–89, 564). The hospital was apparently rebuilt in 1619 and developed in the seventeenth c. as a workhouse or house of correction; it is said to have continued thus till 1750. See *Edinburgh Recs., passim; Hist. Mon. Comm. Rep.* (*Edinburgh*), 184. The building of 1619, however, survived; in it, in 1805, James Ballantyne established his press and there the Waverley novels were printed.

EDINBURGH, ST. THOMAS MARTYR. In the Watergate (Canongate burgh), as shown in *Edinburgh Commissariot Records*, i, 288 when several bedesmen are recorded. The hosp. is said to have been fd. in 1541 by George Crichton, bp. of Dunkeld (1526–1543/4), a former ab. of Holyrood for two chaplains and seven bedesmen: the chaplains were to serve the altars of St. Andrew and St. Catherine and the hosp. is sometimes referred to as the hosp. of SS. Andrew and Catherine. Seven almsmen received annual rents from property in Bell's Wynd in April 1541 and at Robinson's Inns in Jan., 1543/4 (Prot. Bk. Strathauchin, ii, fos 134v135v iii, fo. 167v). All the manses and chambers founded near the monastery as well as the Bell's Wynd tenement were destroyed by the English in 1544, as a charter testifies in 1558 when repairs were contemplated (*RMS*, v, 1242). The collector and master of the hosp. of St. Thomas 'beside Halirudhous' leased two upper rooms in the tenement at the head of Bell's Wynd (SRO, Abbrev. Feu Chrs., ii, 280). There are references to the lands of St. Thomas in the Canongate in 1489 (*Prot. Bk. Young*, no. 289) and Gavin Chrichton's land was founded for the chapel of St. Thomas (no. 1635) by April 1506 (cf. nos. 1616, 1618; *Laing Chrs.*, no. 1911). On 4 Feb. 1560/1, the Town Council ordered their treasurer to make a payment to the bedesmen of 'St. Andros hospitale' (*Edinburgh Burgh Recs., 1557–71*, 98). This hosp. survived the Reformation; there is a record of a presentation by the then bp. of Dunkeld, to a bedesmanship in 1564 (*Prot. Bk. Grote*, no. 265) and a master was appointed in 1580 (*RSS*, vii, no. 2430). The 'bedrellis' or hospitallers of the hosp. of SS. Thomas and Andrew in the almshouse founded by George, bp. of Dunkeld, appear in a charter of 2 Nov. 1622 (*Laing Chrs.*, no. 1911), and in 1666 there is a reference to the patronage of the hosp. of St. Andrew and St. Katherine near Holyroodhouse (*Edinburgh Retours*, no. 1152). The siting of the house in Bell's Wynd makes it clear that the Maison Dieu (Spottiswoode, 475) is to be identified with this fd'n.

EDINBURGH, TRINITY COLLEGE. Fd. by Mary of Gueldres, widow of James II, for thirteen poor people. This hosp. was part of the establishment of the collegiate ch. of the Holy Trinity, the fd'n. of which preceded a bull of 23 Oct. 1460 (*Midlothian Chrs.*, 58). The queen's foundation charter is dated 25 March 1462 (*ibid.*, 46 ff.).The inmates were endowed in part from the hosp. of Uthrogle (*q.v.*). On 10 June 1504 thirteen 'oratours and beidmen' of 'the king's hospitaile of the trinite colleg besyd the burgh of Edinburgh' subscribe a document (*ibid.*, cix). On 12 Nov. 1567, Sir Simon Preston, provost of Edinburgh, had a grant (evidently on behalf of the burgh) of the college ch. and hosp., with the proviso that this should not prejudice the bedesmen (*RMS.*, iv, no. 1802). At the same time the Town Council made provision for the erection of a new hosp. (*Edinburgh Recs., 1557–71*, 243–4). In 1578 the Council made preparations for housing in it twelve aged and sick people (*ibid., 1573–89*, 77). The new hosp. was apparently completed before 1587, when the older building, which was in a ruinous condition, was to be devoted to some 'profitable use' (*Edinburgh Trinity Chrs.*, no. xx).

EDIRDOUER. See KILLEARNAN.

EDNAM. There is a reference to a donation to the master and congregation by Ada, countess of Northumberland and Huntingdon (d. 1178) (*Dryb. Lib.*, no. 161). Payments are recorded to the master, in 1327 (*ER*, i, 67) and later. It is called the hosp. of St. Laurence of Ednam 25 Sept. 1426 and 31 Jan. 1437, when the Edmonstons of Ednam are referred to as patrons (*RMS*, ii, no. 62; Reg. Supp., 331, fo. 228). This gives some substance to the suggestion of Spottiswoode (475) that the hosp. was founded by that family. The English burned this hosp., 26 Oct. 1542 (*LP Henry VIII*, xvii, nos. 998(2), 1136). Brockie (p. 1105) is wide of the mark in describing it as 'reduced to ashes by the fury of fanatics' [i.e. Reformers]. The patronage of it is mentioned 16 Jan. 1573/4 (*RMS*, iii, no. 2987) and as late as 22 Nov. 1649, when there is also a mention of the lands of Spittle 'called from of old the lands of the place of the hospital of St. Leonard of Ednam' (*Roxburgh Retours*, no. 197). In 1627, however, there were no bedesmen at the hosp. (*Rep. on State of Certain Parishes*, 196). The hosps. of St. Leonard and St. Laurence are clearly the same institution.

ELGIN, LEPER HOUSE. About 1391 'land called Spetalflat, beside the houses of the lepers of Elgin' is mentioned (*Moray Reg.*, no. 117).

ELGIN, MAISON DIEU. Fd. by Andrew, bp. of Moray (1222–42), –1237 (*Moray Reg.*, nos. 39, 116, 117; NLS, MS. 34.7.2). In 1390 this was one of the buildings burned by the 'Wolf of Badenoch (*Moray Reg.*, no. 303). It is described as the '*domus dei*' near the walls of Elgin, 13 Oct. 1394 (Reg. Aven., 278, fos. 286–7). The office of hospitaller of the Domus Dei called St. Mary appears on record, 1 Dec. 1436 (Reg. Supp., 329, fo. 202), and it is described, 23 Sept. 1440 as the hospital of Elgin commonly called Maysendieu (*ibid.*, 367, fo. 290v). In 1445 it is said to have been long void and wont to be assigned to secular clerks as a perpetual benefice, though originally founded for the maintenance of poor brothers and sisters (*CPL*, ix, 480). On 17 Nov. 1520, James, bp. of Moray, granted it to the Blackfriars of Elgin (NLS, MS. 34.7.2) and this union was confirmed by the Pope, 21 June 1521 (Reg. Supp., 1744, fos. 192–192v). But although, 1561–72 its revenues appear as pertaining to the Blackfriars, there is about this time a record of payment to three bedesmen (*Thirds of Benefices*, 32, 109, 133), and, in 1567, a gift of the preceptory to Robert Douglas (*RSS*, v, no. 2416). Finally James VI, because the lands and rents of the hosp. since the Reformation, have been applied to the particular use of certain persons without respect to the poor for whom it was founded, grants the hosp. to the provost and council for the provision of a preceptor who will teach music and other liberal arts and for placing in it as many poor as are provided for by the first fd'n., 22 March 1594/5 (*RMS*, vi, no. 249).

FAIL. This Trinitarian fd'n. had four bedesmen attached to the monastery. There is a reference to expenses of meal in the Assumption of the Benefices. 'Extraordinar that ye minister ([i.e. the Trinitarian minister] gives out to four ald men of the convent ever ane of the four xi bollis meil' and 'four auld beidman of ye convent' (EU MS. Dc. 4. 32, fos. 48, 52v).

FAIRNINGTON. Early references are apparently to a chapel here. Not till 27 Aug. 1511 is there a reference to the lands of 'Fermyngtoun' with the hosp. of the same (*RMS*, ii, no. 3635). A crown presentation to the 'beidmanship of the hospital of St. Leonard in Farnyntoun' appears, 4 Dec. 1566 (*RSS*, v, no. 3116). There are later mentions of the hosp. to 1 Oct. 1594 (*RMS*, v, no. 215; *APS*, iii, 257, 259, 409; Fraser, *Buccleuch*, ii, 251).

FORRES, LEPER HOUSE. The '*domus leprosorum*' is mentioned in a resignation of lands 25 March 1564 and again in a similar transaction by a merchant of Forres, 28 April 1565 (SRO, NP 1/18, Protocol Book of William Douglas, 1555–79, fos. 48v, 66v). This was presumably a pre-Reformation fd'n.

FORTUNE. In the parish of Athelstaneford, East Lothian. 'The whole land that was of the hospital of Fortun' was among the lands bestowed, *c.* 1270 by Cristiana de Mubray upon the Trinitarian monastery of Houston (*q.v.*) which she had founded. Her donation was confirmed by Alexander III, 26 January 1271/2 (*PSAS*, 1887–8, 28). This grant may imply that the hosp. was extinct. It cannot be taken to indicate a connection of the hosp. with the monastery. 'The lands of the hospital of Fortoun' appear in a much later confirmation of Cristiana's donation, by James V, 8 Jan. 1541/2 (*RMS*, iii, no. 2569); but the reference is of course retrospective.

GEILSTON. On 3 Aug. 1563 and again in 1582, a spittal at Geilston in the parish of Cardross, Dunbartonshire is called the 'Ostellarie de Brigend'. It was undoubtedly of pre-Reformation origin (SRO, GD 242/15; *Retours–Dunbarton*, no. 100).

GLASGOW, BLACADER'S HOSPITAL (I). Roland Blacader, sub-dean of Glasgow cathedral founded a chaplaincy in the nave of the ch. of Glasgow (the cathedral), at the altar of St. John Baptist and St. Nicholas, the chaplain to be master of the hosp. for casual poor and indigent people founded by Blacader in the city of Glasgow, near the Stablegreen, *c.* 1524–5. The hosp., dedicated to St. Nicholas, St. Serf and St. Machutus, was to have six beds and was to be looked after by a keeper and his wife chosen by the chaplain (*Glasgow Protocols*, no. 618; *RSS*, iii, no. 1401; *Glas. Reg.*, ii, no. 495; *Glasgow Chrs.*, i, pt. 1, 13). It survived the Reformation and by an act of 8 Nov. 1589, the provost, bailies and council ordered an inspection of the hosp. and appointed a master, who became bound to uphold the fd'n. (*Glasgow Recs.*, 1573–1642, 147–8). 'In 1605 the crafts of Glasgow acquired all rights in the 'rwynit and decayit hospitall' which they proposed to rebuild for the use of poor craftsmen (*Glasgow Chrs.*, i, Pt. I, 54, *Glasgow Protocols*, nos. 619–620). The new hosp. was, however, built on another site, and the land on which the ruinous hosp. was situated was feued by the crafts in 1610 (*ibid.* no. 621).

GLASGOW BLACADER'S HOSPITAL (II), see below, p. 197.

GLASGOW, ST. NICHOLAS. Fd. by Andrew de Durisdere, bp. of Glasgow (c. 1456–71), for a priest and twelve old men, the hosp. erected in honour of God, the Virgin and St. Nicholas, is described as newly founded 31 March 1464 (*CPL*, xi, 662). References to a later fd'n. refer to Blacader's hosp., which was dedicated to St. Nicholas. The hosp. was later extended into an adjoining building which is usually referred to as the back alms-house to distinguish it from the original St. Nicholas hosp., which is sometimes called the fore almshouse. Patronage of the former belonged to the bp., of the latter to the town (*Glasgow Recs., 1573–1642*, 155). A donation on 1 June 1501, for the maintenance of a bed, of which the patronage was to lie with the council, may be one step in this extension of the hosp. (*Glasgow Chrs.*, i, Pt. II, 92–6). The 'bak place of the Almus howse' was certainly in use before 26 March 1531 (*Glasgow Protocols*, nos. 1064, 1135). On 26 March 1567 by a charter, which was confirmed 28 Feb. 1581/2, donations of three pounds and twenty shillings respectively were made to the 'twelf puir men in the foir almoushous' and the 'foure puir men in the backhous of the said almoushous' (*Glasgow Chrs.*, ii, 534–9, 561–3). The 'back almshouse' was deserted before 1600 (*ibid.*, ii, 56n); the hospital continued till the eighteenth c. but on 10 Dec. 1778 the preceptor reported that 'all the old houses which originally belonged to the said hospital (except the chapel) have for many years been totally ruinous and uninhabitable' (*Glasgow Protocols*, xi, 103n). See *Glasgow Chrs.*, i, Pt. I, xlvi ff.

GLASGOW, ST. NINIAN. At the south end of Glasgow bridge. Said to have been founded c. 1350 (*OPS*, i, 19); but probably the fd'n. took place in the following century. The earliest records found mention men and women lepers in the hospital and poor lepers dwelling there, 30 June and 1 July 1485 (*Glasgow Chrs.*, ii, 465–8). On 31 May 1494, William Stewart, canon and prebendary of Killearn founded a chaplaincy in St. Ninian's chapel, 'constructed by him and built anew' at the lepers' hospital beside the bridge of Glasgow (*Glas. Reg.*, no. 469). This chapel is also mentioned as newly built, 16 Aug. 1491 (*Glasgow Chrs.*, ii, 472). On 26 March 1567 by a charter, which was confirmed 28 Feb. 1581/2, a donation of twenty shillings was granted to the 'lipper men . . . dwelland at the south part of the brig' (*ibid.*, ii, 534–9, 561–3). The hosp. was granted to the city by Charles I, 16 Oct. 1636 (*ibid.*, i, Pat. II, 387). It continued to be used until the latter half of the seventeenth c. (*Glasgow Protocols*, vi, 97n).

HADDEN. This hosp. had been granted by its patron, James de Hadden, to Dryburgh abbey before 7 Aug. 1432 (Reg. Supp., 279, fo. 51v). No further reference has been found.

HADDINGTON, ALMSHOUSE. On 11 June 1478 an indenture is made between the Grey-friars of Haddington and John Haliburton, vicar of Greenlaw, concerning an almshouse erected by him in the Poldrait of Haddington (Bryce, *Grey Friars*, ii, 13).

HADDINGTON, LEPER HOUSE. In terms of the refoundation of St. Laurence's hosp., 1470–2, a chalder of victual is to be given by its master, at the two yearly terms, to the lepers of Haddington, dwelling in the leper house (Haddington Burgh Writs). This prerequisite of the lepers passed to the burgh; an act of parliament of 1592 empowered the provost and magistrates to uplift it (*APS*, iii, 580).

HADDINGTON, ST. LAURENCE. Mentioned in 1312 (*CDS*, iii, 405). It seems originally to have been dependent on St. Andrews priory (*St. Andrews Copiale*, 93). A payment to the master of the hosp. of Haddington is recorded, 26 Feb., 1327/8 (*ER*, i, 73); and 'St. Laurence's hospital beside Haddington' is described as in receipt of alms 'from of old,' 29 Sept. 1337 (*CDS*, iii, no. 1427). On 20 Nov. 1469, master Richard Guthrie, the King's almoner general, was appointed (*APS*, ii, 97) to put into operation an act of 9 Oct. 1466 for the reformation of hospitals (*ibid.*, ii, 86); and his visitation and reconstitution of this hosp. are recorded in an undated charter among the burgh writs. (Its date can be deter-mined by the fact that Guthrie appears in it as abbot of Arbroath, an office to which he was appointed, 3 Nov. 1470 and in which he died before 31 Jan. 1471/2 (*Arb. Lib.*, ii, nos. 186–7; Reg. Supp., 675, fo. 264v.) A letter of James IV to Pope Julius II, *c.* 1511, asked that this hosp., said, in what may be a rhetorical statement, to have been founded and endowed by his ancestors for the use of the poor, should be converted into a house of Augustinian Friars Observantines (*James IV Letters*, no. 471; the date suggested for this letter, July 1512, is too late); and the Pope on 13 Oct. 1511, suppressed the hosp. and erected a house of this order (*LP Henry VIII*, i², 1522). But, because these friars did not take up residence, James V bestowed the hosp. on a secular clerk, who appears as master 1513–14, and requested of the Pope Leo X the severance of the hosp. from incorporation in the order of friars (*Ep. Regum Scotorum*, i, 193–4; *James V Letters*, 8; *ER*, xiv, 62). It is certain that Friar James Wyndiyettis, who appears as master 1 July 1511–20 July 1512 (*ER*, xiii, 396, 496) was an Augustinian; but the friars who appear between 1515–16 and 1544–45 as receiving payments on behalf of the hosp. were wardens of the Franciscan house at Haddington (*ibid.*, xiv, 206; xviii, 74). On 29 Aug. 1532, the hosp. was annexed to the Dominican nunnery of Sciennes, Edinburgh (*Edinburgh Sciennes Lib.*, no. iv). A master of the hosp. whose office was presumably nominal continued to receive a payment from the burgh till 1558–9 (*ER*, xix, 86). The lands of the hosp. were leased, 15 Feb. 1556/7 (*HMC 14th Rep.*, App., Pt. III, 42–3) and 15 Feb. 1562/3 (*Edinburgh Sciennes Lib.*, no. ix) and thereafter became permanently secularized. See *East Lothian Trans.*, vi (1955), 9–18).

HADDINGTON, ST. MARY. A warden of this hosp. was nominated 30 July 1319 (*CDS*, iii, no. 657). No other reference has been found.

HAMILTON, ST. THOMAS MARTYR. This hosp. was, in the late fifteenth c., attached to the collegiate ch. of Hamilton. On 7 March 1496/7 the six prebendaries of the college granted a charter of assedation of the lands of Spittalgill with the mill of Spittal in the barony of Lesmahagow (Stonehouse parish). The reddendo is four merks Scots with attendance and suit paid to the courts of the hosp. of St. Thomas Martyr (SRO, Bargany Writs, GD 109/1265).

HARLAW, LEPER HOUSE. An agreement between the monks of Kelso abbey and the lepers of Harlaw, who were evidently attached to the chapel of St. Thomas the Martyr at Harlaw, had been reached before 4 July 1195 when William I confirms the ch. of Maxwell with the chapel to Kelso (*Kel. Lib.*, no. 409; *Regesta Regum Scottorum*, ii, no. 379). Refer-ences continue until 1232, but no indication of its continuance beyond this date. (*Kelso Liber*, no. 279).

HELMSDALE. William, E. of Sutherland, is said to have bestowed on Kinloss abbey the hosp. of St. John Baptist at Hebnisden, 21 May 1362 (Ferrerius, *Historia*, 27–8; *Kinloss Recs.*, xxxix–xl). This has been identified with the hosp. of St. John at Helmsdale, the master of which is mentioned in 1471 (Forres Chs., cited *OPS*, ii², 731), which is sub-sequently described in 1509 and 1514 as the chaplaincy of St. John of Helmsdale (*ibid.*). It was united to Dornoch cathedral by 1509 (Fraser, *Sutherland*, iii, 42) and had become a prebend before 1558; in 1578 there is a reference to a chaplaincy, the chapel of St. John the Baptist of Helmsdale (*OPS*, ii², 731).

HOLYWOOD OR DERCONGAL. The fd'n. of a poor's hosp. within the enclosure or limits of the Premonstratensian monastery of Holywood, previously contemplated by Edward de Bruce, was made by Archibald de Douglas (Archibald 'the Grim'), lord of Galloway, be-fore 1362 when Sir Walter de Byger, chamberlain, occurs as master of the '*domus dei de Dalqwowill*' [Dercongal] (*ER*, ii, 115). The foundation was confirmed by Robert II, 2 June 1372 (*RMS*, i, no. 483). On the petition of the founder, it received papal confirmation on 26 Oct. 1379 (Reg. Supp., 54, fos. 156–7; cf. *CPP*, i, 538; Reg. Aven., 215, fos. 242–3). This hosp. governed by a secular priest and with eighteen poor bedesmen, and situated near the nunnery of Lincluden 'at a distance of a mile or thereabout' was annexed to the collegiate ch. erected on the suppression of the nunnery, the number of bedesmen increased to twenty-four and the provost of the college made master of the hosp. on the petition of

Archibald de Douglas, 7 May 1389 (*ibid.*, 259, fos. 471–2v). A papal letter of 19 Nov. 1434 refers to the hosp. of St. John Baptist in Lincluden, annexed to the provostship (*CPL*, viii, 493). A bedesman of the 'masyn dew of Linclowdane' appears in an action 11 July 1494 (*ADC*, 374). A rental of 1561 mentions twenty-four bedesmen who were evidently still being maintained at that date (McDowall, *Chronicle of Lincluden*, 114).

HORNDEAN. About 1240 Robert Byseth, lord of Upsetlington, granted to Kelso abbey the hospital of St. Leonard, founded in his territory beside Tweed, opposite Horwerden (*Kel. Lib.*, no. 240). The hosp. of Horndean is mentioned, *c.* 1300, as held by Kelso, with provision for a chaplain and two poor people (*ibid.*, 467).

HOUSTON. In 1296, the master of the hosp. of the Holy Trinity of Houston, in the county of Haddington, swore fealty to Edward I (*CDS*, ii, no. 823) and had restitution of its lands from him (*Rot. Scot.*, i, 25). This hosp. was an adjunct or identical with the Trinitarian house of Houston (*q.v.*).

HUTTON. The warden of this house came to Edward I's peace in 1296 and had its lands restored (*Rot. Scot.*, i, 25). The fact that it is described, on that occasion, as the hosp. of St. John of 'Hoton' has given rise to the fanciful idea that it belonged to the Hospitallers (cf. *Berwickshire Hist.*, xvi (1896–8), 12). The hosp. was granted with the ch. of Hutton to Dunglass collegiate ch., 26 April 1451 (*HMC, 12th Rep.*, App. pt. viii, 127). Hutton Spittal appears in a list of places burned by the English in 1542 (*Hamilton Papers*, i, xci).

INVERKEITHING. A bull of 15 March 1196 confirms, among other possessions of Dryburgh abbey, 'the hospital of Innerkethyn' (*Dryb. Lib.*, no. 250). The hospital land near Inverkeithing mentioned *c.* 1400 (*Dunf. Reg.*, no. 397), belonged to the hosp. of North Queensferry (*q.v.*); but this hosp. was still in existence, 9 April 1453 when it is referred to in an altar charter of that date (NLS, Hutton Coll., vi, 105). The sickman's yard still appears on record in 1550, but no definite indication of a hosp. (Stephen, *Hist. of Inverkeithing*, 516).

JEDBURGH, ALMSHOUSE. This fd'n., which may have been one of the hospitals mentioned in 1296 (*Rot. Scot.*, ii, 172) was dependent on the abbey of Jedburgh and was quite distinct from the Maison Dieu (*q.v.*), the patrons of which were the Kers of Cessford. By virtue of a charter by John, ab. of Jedburgh, 1 July 1553, 3s. 4d. was to be paid '*ad domum elemosinarum*' (SRO, GD 40/13/3). On 24 April 1567 it is described as '*domus elemosynarie vocata almeryhous*' (SRO, GD 40/13/9) and on 17 Dec. 1575 it is called 'ye almoushous of ye abbay of Jedburght' (SRO, Charters of Jedburgh Abbey, CH 6/6/3, fo. 26).

JEDBURGH, MAISON DIEU. In 1296, the master of this hosp. had restitution of lands from Edward I (*Rot. Scot.*, i, 25). Provision to the mastership occur 19 March 1536 and 16 Dec. 1538 (Reg. Supp., 2206, fos. 7v–8; 2254, fo. 111). The patronage of the hosp. is mentioned in 1684 and 1696 (*Roxburgh Retours*, nos. 282, 318).

KELSO. The house of poor in Kelso is mentioned in 1260 (*Kel. Lib.*, i, no. 173); and there are several references to 'almarie lands' in the 'towne of Kelso', *c.* 1567 (*ibid.*, ii, 523–4, 526–9).

KILLEARNAN. The patronage of the '*domus hospitalis de edirdouer*' belonging to Elizabeth Bisset, widow of Andrew de Bosco, was, *c.* 1299–1310, transferred to William, E. of Ross (*Munro Writs*, no. 1). Edirdouer was the old name of the parish of Killearnan (Cowan, *Parishes*, 101), and the site of this hosp. was presumably near the modern place-name Spittal in this parish (*OPS*, ii², 525, *Ross and Cromarty Retours*, no. 156).

KILPATRICK. Bede Ferdan, *c.* 1173, held a great timber house near the graveyard of Kilpatrick, in return for receiving and feeding guests; three other holders of the ch. lands had a similar arrangement (*Pais. Reg.*, 166). About 1418 this site is styled the 'hostillar house at ye west end of ye kirk (Lees, *Abbey of Paisley*, clxii and cf. cxxxvi 'the ostlar hous wyth the zard at the west end of ye kyrk [1521]'). The land of the chapel of Wester Cochno, the 'belwarthill' was let to two tenants, *c.* 1515/6. Both had to keep a bed at all times *pro pauperibus* and maintain the chapel (*ibid.*, cxxvi). In 1518 'the chapelland of

Boquhanran was likewise 'wyth ane bed to trawellouris for goddis sak and fundouris wyth all fredomys usit of before (*ibid.*, cxxix).

KINCARDINE O'NEIL. Fd. by Thomas Durward (d. 1231), the erection, which was dedicated to St. Mary, was confirmed by his son Alan Durward, 3 March 1433/4 (*Abdn. Reg.*, ii, 268–9). In 1330 the hosp. with its appropriated churches was erected into a prebend of Aberdeen cathedral by Bp. Alexander de Kyninmund (*ibid.*, i, 51, 64–5; ii, 252). The hosp. was apparently extinguished by this date; a papal bull to the master and poor brothers, assigned to 2 June 1359 (*ibid.*, i, 83) should be dated 1251. The lands of Spittal in the sheriffdom of Kincardine are mentioned in March 1554/5 (*Brech. Reg.*, ii, 386).

KINGCASE. Despite the traditional connection of this hospital with Robert I, the terms and date of fd'n. are unknown. A copy of the fd'n. charter is said (*ADCP*, 201) to be in the register of Paisley, but does not appear there. The earliest reference to it seems to be in a charter of James II granting to Hugh Wallace and his heirs, 'hospitallers' of the house of 'Kilcase', the lands of Spitalshiels, 'even as the hospitallers of the said house were endowed and infeudated therein from of old by the king's predecessors', 14 Feb. 1451/2 (*RMS*, ii, no. 328). The term 'hospitaller' has nothing to do with the Knights Hospitallers. It is used (see SOUTRA) of an inmate of a hospital. In the case of the Wallaces, it implies that they had come to hold the hosp. as a heritable possession (see *Prestwick Recs.*, 128). That the hosp. 'is of auld foundit of King Robert the Bruce' (*ADCP*, 207) and that it has been 'usit by thame sen the deces of king Robert the Bruce' (*ibid.*, 201) are assertions quoted in 1524 by way of resisting claims to bedesmanships in the hosp. But the proceeding in this case show that bedesmen had been customarily admitted to it, a practice which, on 30 July 1535, the Lords of Council sought to check by instructing commissioners of the abp. of Glasgow to visit the hosp. with powers to remove the non-leprous and to put lepers in their place (*ibid.*, 443). But although 'seik lipper folkis in Kingcais' are mentioned in 1603 (*Prestwick Recs.*, 129), this fd'n. became, with the disappearance of leprosy, a hosp. for the sick and poor, and, as such, was in existence till the eighteenth c. (*ibid.*, 127, 129). The head of this hosp. is frequently called prior; e.g. on 26 Jan. 1538/9, there is a reference to the prior of the hosp. of St. Ninian of Kinkais (*RSS*, ii, no. 2871).

KINGHORN. A charter of Robert Peirson, burgess of Kinghorn, 20 July 1478, makes, in supplement of the maintenance of the poor in the new hosp. and a chaplain in the chapel of St. James, a grant of the land on which the chapel and hosp. are built (*RMS*, ii, no. 1407). Sir David Persone, chaplain of the chaplainry of St. James at Kinghorn constituted procurators to resign it into the hands of the patrons, the bailies on 23 Aug. 1485 (*Prot. Bk. Young*, no. 12).

KIRKWALL. A hosp., which may have been pre-Reformation in origin, is mentioned 18 Dec. 1581 (*RMS*, v, no. 309).

LANARK. The land of the brothers of the hosp. appears in a charter which is evidently of the reign of Alexander II (1214–49) (not of the time of William the Lion; as in *OPS*, i, 48) (*Dryb. Lib.*, no. 216), while payments to the 'master of the hospital of Lanark, described from 1365 as St. Leonard's are recorded from 1327 (*ER*, i, 71) till 1559 (*ibid.*, xix, 87). There is a reference, in 1482, to a hosp. of St. Laurence at the burgh of Lanark (*RMS*, ii, no. 1531), but this would appear to be an error for St. Leonard's. On 9 Nov. 1392, Robert III granted the hosp. and its lands to Sir John Dalziel (*ibid.*, i, no. 864); but a precept of sasine by James IV, for infefting Archibald, E. of Angus in the barony of Braidwood, 8 May 1497, includes the patronage of this hosp. (Fraser, *Douglas*, iii, no. 149). A precept of sasine by Archibald Douglas of Glenbervie for infefting his son William Douglas of Kemnay in the barony of Braidwood likewise includes the patronage of the hosp. (*Laing Chrs.*, no. 690). On 20 Feb. 1632, Charles I gave the patronage of the preceptorship to the burgh authorities (*Lanark Recs.*, 325–6); and, on 15 Nov. 1636, its lands were acquired by the magistrates and Town Council for the poor of the burgh and parish (*ibid.*, 370).

LASSWADE, ST. LEONARD, see DALHOUSIE.

LASSWADE, ST. MARY. On 11 March 1477/8, the Pope, on petition of master Robert Blackadir, rector of the parish ch. of Lasswade, who proposed to institute a hosp. at his ch., under the invocation of St. Mary of Consolation, for the poor, pilgrims and the infirm, gave faculty for building it (Theiner, *Vet. Mon.*, no. dccclxv; Cameron, *Apostolic Camera*, 193). An indulgence was granted 4 April 1478 to those who visit the ch. and assist the construction of the hosp. (Theiner, *Vet. Mon.*, no. dccclxiv).

LAUDER. This hosp. was fd. by Richard de Moreville, constable of Scotland 1175 × 1189 (*Dryb. Lib.*, 267–9; *HMC 5th Rep.*, App. 613). The idea that it was a hospital for leprous monks is fanciful. The fd'n. was for infirm brothers and sisters, 'brother' and 'sister' being a usual designation of beneficiaries of hospitals. The master of this hosp. had restitution of lands from Edward I in 1296 (*Rot. Scot.*, i, 25). The hosp., described as for the poor, was granted by its patron James de Lauder to the abbey of Dryburgh and this grant was subsequently confirmed to the abbey, on the petition of Archibald, fourth E. of Douglas and 'of the vale of Lawedre,' by the Pope on 30 Dec. 1429 and 7 Aug. 1432 (*CSSR*, iii, 67–8, 243). The hosp. does not appear to have survived this union. But there appears to have been another and much later hosp. in this parish. See Thirlestane below.

LEGERWOOD. The warden of this hosp. swore fealty to Edward I in 1296 (*CDS*, ii, no. 823). This appears to be the only clear reference to it. An undated charter of Walter, son of Alan, steward of the k. of Scots (d. 1177), grants an endowment of land 'to God and St. Mary and the hospital of Auldenestun and the infirm brethren dwelling there' (*Melr. Lib.*, i, no. 80). The charter does not name the abbey of Melrose as participating in this grant but the donor gives warrandice 'to the aforementioned [*prenominatis*] [*sic*] monks'. By another undated charter, which makes no mention of the hospital the steward conveys 'to God and the church of St. Mary of Melrose' the identical lands and privileges specified in the foregoing charter (*ibid.*, no. 81). No satisfactory explanation of these transactions can be given. It has been assumed that Melrose abbey held this hosp.; but this remains uncertain and no further mention of it is made in the Melrose charters. Again, Walter's first charter (no. 80) is endorsed 'charters of the lepers of Moricestun [Morriston]'; and part of the endowment is 'the casement of the wood of Birkenside [now Birkhillside] and the wood of Liggardewude [Legerwood].' These place-names, as well as Auldenestun (Adniston, in a map of 1831), are found in the parish of Legerwood, and it is tempting to identify the hosp. mentioned in 1177 with that which appears in 1296. This identification, while probable, is unverified.

LEITH, ST. ANTHONY. A hosp. for the poor and infirm, dedicated to St. Anthony, and with a hermit of St. Anthony as its rector is said to be newly founded, but inadequately endowed, in a papal grant of indulgence, 30 July 1418 (*CSSR*, i, 12–13). The founder may have been Sir Robert Logan of Restalrig who is frequently credited with founding in 1430 the conventual house of the order of St. Anthony of Vienne, of which the initial fd'n. appears to have been a precursor (Rogers, 'St. Anthony's Monastery at Leith', *Trans. RHS*, v, 384, citing NLS. MS. 34. 3. 12, fo. 11). Logan's part in the fd'n. of the conventual house appears to have been restricted to granting the land on which the house was built, and the actual fd'n. involving the constitution of the house and the erection of its buildings were carried through by James, I, K. of Scots (Reg. Supp. 349, fo. 298v). A papal letter of 8 Feb. 1443/4 (*CPL*, ix, 405), confirms that James I began to build it about fourteen years previously. It was erected for canons of the Augustinian Order of St. Anthony of Vienne—a preceptor and four canons are mentioned in 1443/4 (*CPL*, ix, 406) —and designed for the poor and those suffering from St. Anthony's desease (erysipelas). In 1505 a letter of the preceptor to the General of the order declares that pestilence had carried off all the brethren except himself and another and refers to the destitution of this house (*James V Letters*, no. 19). Sometime before 1526 a new organization, or confraternity of St. Anthony's, which included brethren and sisters, was formed with a right to elect a fit confessor of any order (Roger, *St. Anthony's Monastery*, 392 ff.). The death of one of the brothers is recorded and the master ordered to admit another in his place, 6 Aug. 1565 (*RSS*, v, no. 2246). On 28 March 1591 the preceptory was suppressed and granted with the place, lands and other possessions of St. Anthony's to Mr. John Hay (*RMS*, v, no. 1850). Some of the rents of the hospital continued, however, to be applied to charitable aims. See John Smith, 'Notes on the Augustinian House of St. Anthony, Leith', *PSAS*, lxix (1929-30), 275-90.

LEITH, HOLY TRINITY. Fd. in 1555 as a hosp. for seamen by the corporation of the ship-masters and mariners of Leith (Irons, *Leith and Its Antiquities*, i, 303, 306). The hosp.'s fd'n. was confirmed after the Reformation by a royal grant of 10 May 1566 (*RSS*, v, no. 2814). Its funds appear to have been misappropriated thereafter, but this was rectified in 1636 (Irons, *Leith and Its Antiquities*, i, 303-4). For the subsequent history of the hosp., see John Mason, *History of Trinity House of Leith* (Glasgow, 1957).

LINCLUDEN, see HOLYWOOD.

LINLITHGOW, ALMSHOUSE (I). An almshouse was in existence before 1448 (Ferguson, *Ecclesia Antiqua*, 347). This is apparently to be identified with the almshouse in the Kirk-gate which appears in 1578, and which evidently continued in being until its destruction during the Cromwellian period (*ibid.*, 330; *Prot. Bk. Johnsoun*, no. 953).

LINLITHGOW, ALMSHOUSE (II). On 14 May 1496 Henry de Levingtoun of Middle Binning granted a tenement 'to the chapel to be built anew in the place of his seven perches at the east end of the burgh of Linlithgow, in the Middleraw . . . with an alms-house (*cum una domo hospitali elemosine*)' (*RMS*, ii, no. 2333). This donation was confirmed under the great seal, 18 Nov. 1496 (*ibid.*). The hosp. and the chapel of the BVM with which it was associated, lay outside the east part of the burgh, reference being made to the chapel in 1553, and to the chapel and hosp., which was also dedicated to St. Mary, on 23 Aug. 1561 (*Prot. Bk. Foulis*, no. 213; *Prot. Bk. Thounis*, no. 45).

LINLITHGOW, ST. MARY MAGDALENE. Spottiswoode (467) declares that this hosp. was 'formerly governed by the Lazarites'. Of this there is no evidence. It seems originally to have been dependent on St. Andrew's priory (*St. Andrews Copiale*, 129). There are thirteenth-c. references to a toft held by the order St. Lazarus in the burgh (*Newbottle Registrum*, nos. 184-5); but no connection between this toft or this order and St. Mary Magdalene's hosp. is indicated. The hosp. is first mentioned 26 Dec. 1335, when Edward III claimed to appoint a warden (*Rot. Scot.*, i, 392). The suggestion that it provided for pilgrims is apparently mere guesswork, based on the fact that there was a 'Pilgrims' Hill' in the vicinity. In fact in origin this hosp. may have been for lepers as payments to the Lazar House as distinct from the almshouse, of Linlithgow are recorded in the mid-fifteenth c. (Ferguson, *Ecclesia Antiqua*, 347). According to a charter of 12 June 1528, this was a poor's hosp., with a chapel and cemetery (*RMS*, iii, no. 721). A master of this hosp. is mentioned 28 Feb. 1563/4 (*Prot. Bk. Thounis*, no. 181), but its revenues were utilized by the crown, 31 May 1568 and 2 April 1571 (*RSS*, vi, nos. 285 1142); and its lands alienated before 1 June 1591 (*RMS*, v, no. 1875).

LOCH LEVEN, ST. MARY. Fd. by William de Malvoisin, b. of St. Andrews (1202-38), for the reception of the poor and needy (SRO, RH6/48). The hosp. was in existence, *c.* 1214, when the founder granted it the ch. of Moonzie (*ibid.*, RH6/23). This donation was confirmed 1225-36, by the pr. of St. Andrews (*St. A. Lib.*, 175), who also exempted it from the payment of teind (except certain teinds due to the ch. of Portmoak); it is here described as the hosp. 'beside the bridge of Lochleven' (*ibid.*, 176). This fd'n. became known as Scotlandwell. On 2 Oct. 1244, its chapel was dedicated by David de Bernham, b. of St. Andrews (Anderson, *Early Sources*, ii, 535), who, 2 Jan. 1250/1, granted the hosp. with its appropriated chs. of Moonzie and Carnock, to the Trinitarians (SRO, RH6/48). See Scotlandwell.

METHVEN. A charter by David Haliburton, provost of Methven collegiate ch. since 1549, for the erection from the fruits of the provostry, of a hosp. for five sick and aged poor, was confirmed by the crown, 2 Sept. 1550. (*RSS*, iv., no. 869).

MONTROSE. A hosp. here is mentioned 1246 × 1265 (*Arbroath Liber*, i, 337). It is said to have been a royal fd'n. and for lepers (*Ep. Regum Scotorum*, i, 290), but both these state-ments may be queried. In a letter of James IV to Pope Julius II, asking for an indulgence for those who visit it, it is described as for the poor (*James IV Letters*, no. 334; cf. *ibid.*, no. 417). On 18 Aug. 1512, the same king empowered his counsellor and secretary, master Patrick Panter, mentioned in 1507 as preceptor of this hosp. (*RMS*, ii, no. 3121), to alter the fd'n. because Panter had redeemed the hosp. out of the hands of 'secular potentates', recovered its alienated lands and rebuilt the ch. and buildings (*ibid.*, ii, no. 3765). On 14 Nov. 1516 James V granted Panter authority to institute a new foundation of the hosp. in favour of the Friars Preachers (*ibid.*, iii, no. 113); and new petitions of the duke of Albany (on behalf of James V) to Pope Leo X for the grant of the hosp. and its lands to the Dominicans are granted, 18 May 1517 and 5 June 1513 (*James V Letters*, 45; Reg. Supp. 1610, fos. 189-190v) (see MONTROSE, under Dominican Friars). But, on 10 May 1524, because the situation of the hosp. in the public street proved disturbing to the friars, the king ordained their return to their old location. The Dominicans, nevertheless, retained the hosp. building until the period of the Reformation, but on 22 Feb. 1559/60 a letter of Francis and Mary approved of their ejection and appointed the Blackfriar's place to be distributed to the poor once more, a hosp. to be erected thereupon 'according as tyme and expenssis of the superexcressens giff any beis will suffer' (*HMC, 5th Rep.*, App. 640). But the hosp. had continued to exist under the Dominicans and donations to the institution are recorded in 1523, 1538 and 1543 (Low, *Memorials of the Parish Church of Montrose*, 34-6, citing Index of Deeds, 63, 71-7, 85). The hosp., which was granted the revenues of the friary of Inverbervie 23 July 1571 (*RSS*, vi, no. 1217), continued after the Reformation.

MUSSELBURGH, ST. MARY MAGDALENE. This hosp., which is described as caring for the poor and for lepers, appears 24 and 25 March 1386 when it is said to be in a ruinous condition on account of war (Reg. Aven., 243, fos. 125v-126; 244, fos. 72v-73). It is described as a poor's hosp. 28 Feb. and 21 March 1428 (*CPL*, viii, 19, 26). It was still in existence in 1561 when a payment to 'the lipper men at ye madgelenes beyond Mussilbrugh' is recorded (*Dunf. Reg.*, 454).

NENTHORN. Nenthorn Spittal appears in the list of places burned by the English in 1542 (*Hamilton Papers*, i, xci; *LP Henry VIII*, nos. 998(2), 1136(2)).

NEWBURGH (ABERDEENSHIRE). Fd. by Alexander Cumyn, E. of Buchan, for six poor men, with a chaplain, *c.* 1261 (*Abdn. Reg.*, ii, 276; *Aberdeen-Banff Coll.*, 371-2).

NORTH BERWICK, ALMSHOUSE. Not to be confused with the hosp. pertaining to the priory, this hosp., which in 1560 lay within the patronage of Lauder of the Bass, is first mentioned, 11 March 1541/2, when its founder is named as Robert Lauder of Bass (SRO, Prot. Bk. Symson, ii, fo. 135v, in Haddington Burgh Recs.). It is described in 1542 as newly fd. for almsmen (Prot. Bk. Brounhill, ii, fos. 70v-71; cf. James Young, *Notes on Historical references to the Scottish Family of Lauder* (Glasgow, 1884). In a charter of 15 Feb. 1543/4 there is reference to the master of the chaplaincy of the 'poore brether or hospitalares' of the hosp. of North Berwick founded by Robert Lauder of Bass of temple lands in Elbottle and Morham, both in East Lothian (Rental of Templelands (SRO), fo. 39). The hosp. was dedicated to St. Mary V. (SRO, Biel Writs., GD. 6/1221). In 1560 an appointment is recorded to the chaplaincy of the hosp. of the 'poor brethren' (*N.B. Chrs.*, 76-7), and on 12 June 1573 an annual pension to the hosp., said to have been founded by Robert Lauder of the Bass, received confirmation (*RSS*, vi., no. 1992).

NORTH BERWICK. At the south end of the ferry on the Firth of Forth (see Ardross above). Founded -1154 by Duncan fourth E. of Fife for poor people and pilgrims, and granted by Duncan fifth E. of Fife to the nuns of North Berwick, -1177 (*N.B. Chrs.*, no. 3). The land of the hosp. was confirmed to the priory by Malcolm, earl of Fife, -1199, and by William I, *c.* 1213 (*ibid.*, nos. 7; *SHS, Misc.* iv, 308-9; *Regesta Regum Scottorum*, ii, no. 516). It is not mentioned thereafter.

OLDCAMBUS. A donation to this hosp. and the lepers dwelling there made by David of Quixwood, who may have been its founder, was subsequently confirmed by William I, 1216 × 1214 (Raine, *North Durham*, App. nos. lix, clxxxvi). It is also mentioned in a thirteenth c. inventory. (*Cold. Corr.*, lxxxix).

PEEBLES, ALMSHOUSE (I). On 25 Oct. 1462 land was granted for an almshouse of which the chaplain of Our Lady Chapel was to be 'tutour and sursear' (*Peebles Chrs.*, 146–7). The 'land callit the almoushous' near 'our Lady Chapel' occurs, 30 Oct. 1549 (Renwick, *Peebles during the Reign of Queen Mary*, 158). It appears to have been supervised from St. Leonard's (cf., *ibid.*, 36).

PEEBLES, ALMSHOUSE (II). On 1 Oct. 1464, land was granted by the magistrates, at the request of the master of the Cross Kirk (the Trinitarian priory) for the building of an almshouse (*Peebles Chrs.*, 151). The 'halmushus' in Briggait is mentioned on 31 March 1545 and was probably burnt in 1549 (Renwick, *Peebles during the Reign of Queen Mary*, 11, 33).

PEEBLES, ST. LEONARD. Situated at Chapel yards, near Horsburgh about two miles east of the burgh (Renwick, *Peebles during the Reign of Queen Mary*, 66, citing Peebles Burgh Records, 1549–65, fo. 77). Lands pertaining to the hosp., but not hosp. itself, were situated in west end of burgh (*Peebles Chrs.*, 170–1). This was a poor's hosp. founded before 1305 (*ibid.*, 170–1; *CDS*, ii, no. 1695). It appears, 1396–8, as St. Lawrences' hosp. (*ER*, iii, 392, 419, 450), but it is mentioned as St. Leonard's hosp. till 1395 (*ibid.*, ii, 365) and from 1406 (*ibid.*, iv, 24; *CSSR*, iii, 222). An appointment to the preceptorship on 5 Feb. 1557/8 (*RSS*, v, no. 331; *Peebles Chrs.*, 248) calls the preceptorship perpetual, but this refers to the nature of the benefice, and in no sense implies that the benefice had become secularized. On 5 Oct. 1592 the synod of Lothian ordered a visitation of the hosp. of Peebles (SRO, Synod of Lothian Recs., fo. 50v).

PERTH, ST. ANNE. Fd. before 1488 when a dispute arose over a presentation to the hosp. and its chapel. From the circumstances it would appear that the hosp. had been founded by one of the Rollos of Duncrub (*ADC*, 96; *Scots Peerage*, vii, 180–6). The chapel of St. Anne with which it was associated was destroyed in 1559, but the hosp. appears to have survived and the revenues of the chaplaincy as it was donated 'of auld' was given to the poor of the hosp., 4 June 1580 (*RPC*, 1st ser., iii, 288–9). In 1586 the inmates were removed to a new hosp. (Fittis, *Eccles. Annals of Perth*, 283).

PERTH, ST. KATHERINE. Fd. 19 June 1523, by John Tyrie, provost of the collegiate church of Methven, for poor travellers (SRO, King James Hospital Inventory, 52; cf. Fittis, *Eccles. Annals of Perth*, 291). It was associated with St. Katherine's chapel and was probably included with the lands, houses etc., of that chapel disposed to Patrick Murray of Tibbermuir, in 1567 (*ibid.*, 292).

PERTH, ST. LEONARD. The chapel of the hosp. of St. Leonard is mentioned in a bull of 1184 (*Dunf. Reg.*, no. 239), and the hosp. in 1227 (*ibid.*, no. 214). The abbey of Dunfermline evidently had a controlling interest in the chapel from the revenues of which the hosp. was apparently endowed. There was also an attachment between the hosp. and St. Leonard's nunnery (*q.v.*). The master of the hospital is mentioned in *c.* 1360–1, 1403 and 1411 (*RMS*, i, App. ii, no. 1368; Fittis, *Eccles. Annals of Perth*, 278). About 1434 the hosp. with the nunnery was annexed to the charterhouse of Perth, and on 24 April 1438 the prioress of St. Leonard's resigned all claims to it (*ibid.*, 278–9). The transference of the hosp. to the Carthusians raised the problem of its endowment and this may explain a composition over the revenues of St. Leonard's chapel between the Charterhouse and Dunfermline Abbey in 1466 (*ibid.*, 278–9; *Dunf. Reg.*, no. 472). In the event the hosp. was not suppressed and the Charterhouse evidently assumed responsibility for the continuance of payments to it from the chapel, these being recorded until 1542/3 (*ER.*, xvii, 51, 471–2; xviii, 53–4).

PERTH, ST. MARY MAGDALENE. Persistently described as a nunnery, but clearly designated in records as a hosp. of which the master had payments made to him from 1327 (*ER*, i, 66). On 24 Nov. 1425, it is described as a poor's hosp., wont to be governed 'by secular laymen' (*per laicos seculares*) (*CSSR*, ii, 121). As in the case of Perth, St. Leonard (*q.v.*), the abbey of Dunfermline evidently had a controlling interest in the chapel from the revenues of which the hosp. was apparently endowed. About 1434 the hosp. was annexed to the Charterhouse at Perth and this union necessitated a composition over the revenues of the chapel of St. Mary Magdalene between the Charterhouse and Dunfermline abbey in 1466 (Fittis, *Eccles. Annals of Perth*, 275; *Dun. Reg.*, no. 472). In the event the hosp. was not suppressed and the Charterhouse evidently assumed responsibility for the continuance of payments to it from the chapel, these being recorded until 1542/3 (*ER*, xvii, 51, 471–2; xviii, 53–4).

PERTH, ST. PAUL. Fd., 25 Dec. 1434, by John Spens of Glendouglas, burgess of Perth, for strangers, the poor and the infirm (Reg. Supp., 308, fo. 16; Fittis, *Eccles. Annals of Perth*, 288). On 6 July 1435 the founder supplicates for an indulgence (Reg. Supp., 308, fo. 16), which was granted on the following 17 Sept., to all who visit and give alms for the chapel of the hosp. (*CPL*, viii, 552). The chapel may have been destroyed at the same time as the Perth religious houses in 1559 (Fittis, *Eccles. Annals of Perth*, 289). But the hosp. appears to have survived and the revenues of the chaplaincy as was donated 'of auld' was granted by James Moncreif its patron to 'the puir within the hospitale of Sanct Paule' on 4 June 1580 (*RPC.*, 1st ser., iii, 288). An attempt to refound the hosp. on this site in 1583 did not succeed (Fittis, *Eccles. Annals of Perth*, 289).

PILRIG. In 1448 Sir William Crichton, in association with the preceptor of St. Anthony's Leith, proposed the fd'n. of a hosp. for six poor at Pilrig, Midlothian (*St. Giles Reg.*, 82). No further reference has been noted, and the fd'n. may not have taken place.

POLLOK, ST. MARY MAGDALENE. Finlay of Albany is said to have petitioned for the fruits of the hosp. of St. Mary Magdalene of Polmadie in 1417 (*St. Andrews Copiale*, 389), but this seems to be a blunder for Pollok, also in the lordship of Darnley. The master of Polmadie hosp., dedicated to St. John, was William de Cunningham from 1404–*c.* 1428, when he was succeeded by Robert, canon of Glasgow (*Glas. Reg.*, nos. 322, 338). The lands, 'lie Magdalenis', are mentioned in 1545 (*RMS*, iv, no. 111). In later documents they are associated with Magdalenemuir and Spitlemeadow (Fraser, *Pollok-Maxwell*, 38, 68, 152).

POLMADIE. On 28 May 1316 Robert I conceded to the master, brethren and sisters that they might freely enjoy the privileges they were wont to use in the reign of Alexander III (1249–1285/6) (*Glas. Reg.*, no. 265). This hosp. was dedicated to St. John (*Foedera*, iii, 786). On 9 Dec. 1390 a petition to be admitted a brother of the hosp. states that it is administered by the parish ch. of Strathblane (Reg. Supp. 78, fo. 9v). In 1394, the Pope was petitioned to appropriate the hosp. 'in which for a long time nothing has been done for the poor', to the choir of Glasgow cathedral for the maintenance of a music master and choristers (*CPP*, i, 614). This was apparently ineffective and on 12 Jan. 1427/8 John, b. of Glasgow, erected the hosp. and its appropriated ch. of Strathblane into a prebend of Glasgow cathedral; this had papal consent, 5 Dec. 1429 (*Glas. Reg.*, no. 338). During the fourteenth c. the earls of Lennox had asserted their right to present to the hosp. but formally renounced this 16 Feb. 1440/1, probably to facilitate the erection of the prebend (*ibid.*, no. 344). But, on 3 Jan. 1453/4, the Pope appointed mandatories on the petition of Isabel, countess of Lennox, to erect a collegiate ch. at Dumbarton and to transfer to it this hosp., founded by her predecessors and described as 'neglected and forgotten and turned from its original purpose' (*CPL*, x, 623–4). This transference appears to have taken place. See DUMBARTON, above.

POLTON, see DALHOUSIE.

PORTINCRAIG (BROUGHTY FERRY). Gillebride, E. of Angus (+1187–9), gave land to Arbroath abbey to build a hosp. (or inn) here (*Arb. Lib.*, i, nos. 52, 53). The grant of land was confirmed by his son earl Gilchrist and by William I, 1201 × 1205 (*ibid.*, i, nos. 50–51; *Regesta Regum Scottorum*, ii, no. 456). A further royal confirmation, 25 Feb. 1213 and another by Malcolm, Earl of Angus, 1214 × 1226 appear to be the last contemporary notices of this grant, and the fd'n. may have remained unfulfilled (*ibid.*, ii, no. 513; *Arb. Lib.*, i, nos. 1, 53). The original donation is re-confirmed by the crown 1 Jan. 1436/7 (*ibid.*, ii, 544–5) but the reference is retrospective.

PORTMOAK, ST. THOMAS. Described as 'at the bridge of Portmoak' and 'for the reception of poor people', –1184 (*St. A. Lib.*, 146). This seems to be the only reference. This hosp. may have been superseded by Loch Leven, St. Mary (above).

QUEENSFERRY (NORTH). It is impossible to say whether this was one of the 'dwellings' for pilgrims and the poor said by Turgot to have been built by Queen Margaret 'upon either shore of the sea that separates Lothian and Scotland' (i.e. the Firth of Forth) (Anderson, *Early Sources*, ii, 77). An endowment of lands to this hosp. could either be a grant of Malcolm III (c. 1085 × 1093) or of Malcolm IV (1153 × 1165) (*Dunf. Reg.*, no. 250; *Regesta Regum Scottorum*, i, 282). It does not seem to be mentioned later than 14 July 1233 (*Dunf. Reg.*, no. 268), but its land near Inverkeithing (*ibid.*, no. 250), is the subject of a charter, c. 1400 (*ibid.*, no. 397).

RATHVEN. Fd. by John Byseth for a chaplain, seven lepers and a servant, 1224–6 (*Moray Reg.*, no. 71). In a charter of 19 June 1226 the head of the house is called 'prior' (*ibid.*, no. 72). The hosp. should not be confused with the ch. of Rathen which was granted to the chapter of Aberdeen by Edward I in 1327/8 (*Abdn. Reg.*, ii, 150). This hosp., which was dedicated to St. Peter, was erected, with the greater part of its revenues, into a prebend of Aberdeen cathedral in 1445, but nevertheless continued to support three bedesmen (*ibid.*, ii, 253; Reg. Supp., 416, fo. 213). This was supplemented by the restoration of three prebends for bedesmen in 1536, an action which evidently restored the hosp. to its original state, and this remained unchanged even with the appropriation of the vicarage of Rathven to the collegiate ch. of Cullen in 1543 (Cramond, *Church and Churchyard of Rathven*, 83–6; Cramond, *Church and Churchyard of Cullen*, 35–55; *RSS*, iii, no. 1420). The hosp. continued at the Reformation as an institution for the poor (SRO, Book of Assumption, fo. 393v). Its bedesmen's pensions are mentioned, c. 1563 (*Aberdeen–Banff Illustrations*, ii, 145) and its existence is noted till the nineteenth c. (*ibid.*, ii, 143–4). It is, in fact, stated that the last bedesman died in 1859 and the house was demolished in 1886. See Cramond, *History of the Bede House of Rathven* (Buckie, 1890), 13; this work traces its post-Reformation history.

ROXBURGH, MAISON DIEU. About 1145, David I granted land to the hosp. of Roxburgh (*Kel. Lib.*, no. 372). It is impossible to say whether this was identical with the Maison Dieu. In Edward I's parliament of Sept. 1305 a petition of the master of the Maison Dieu (that he and his brethren might enjoy its rents and possessions) was presented (*Mem de Parl.*, no. 368; see introduction to *Rotuli Parliamentorum Anglie Hactenus Inediti*; ed. Richardson and Douglas, Camden Society, for revised date). A payment to the master of part of the Scottish king's grant for the fabric of the hospital's ch. is recorded in 1327 (*ER*, i, 67–68). This hosp. was situated some distance north-east of Roxburgh. The description of it as for pilgrims and for the diseased and the poor (*OPS*, i, 462) is exaggerated. 'Massendew' is mentioned as one of the places burned by Hertford's forces, 17 Sept. 1545 (*LP Henry VIII*, xx², nos. 456, 533). This place is given as on the Kale water; but the location may be erroneous, as no hosp. is known to have existed there and the Maison Dieu is probably that of Roxburgh. Mentions of the patronage of this hosp. continue till at least 1696 (*Roxburgh Retours*, no. 318).

ROXBURGH, ST. JOHN. There is a reference to this hosp. in 1330 (*Kel. Lib.*, no. 491) and again 28 June 1426; the original fd'n. appears to have occurred in the reign of Alexander III (1249–86) (*CDS*, iv, no. 991). It may have been associated with St. John the Evangelist's church in Roxburgh castle.

ROXBURGH, ST. MARY MAGDALENE. Mentioned in 1319 when a master was appointed (*Cal. Pat. Rolls*, ii (1317–21), 381).

ROXBURGH, ST. PETER. Mentioned 28 June 1426, the hosp. appears to have been fd. in the reign of Alexander III (1249–86) (*CDS*, iv, no. 991).

RULEMOUTH, SPITTAL-ON-RULE. 'There is another hospital for lepers at the mouth of the water of Rule called Rule Hospital' (Macfarlane, *Geographical Coll.*, iii, 156). On 5 March 1425/6, an inquest on an alleged case of leprosy was held in the chapel of the hosp. of 'Roulmouth' (Minto Chrs., cited *Hawick Trans.*, (1903), 43). This was the hosp. of St.

Mary in Teviotdale, mentioned, 28 Dec. 1510 (*RSS*, i, no. 2171) 'Rowle Spittell' was one of the places burned by Hertford's forces, 16 Sept. 1545 (*LP Henry VIII*, xx², nos. 456, 533). Confirmatory evidence for its dedication to our Lady is forthcoming in 1586 when it is described as on the West of the Teviot water (SRO, GD 157/163).

RUTHERFORD. Mentioned in 1276 (*Newb. Reg.*, no. 187). Its dedication is given as St. Mary the Virgin in 1296 (*Rot. Scot.*, i, 25), and as St. Mary Magdalene, in 1395 and 1444 (*RMS*, i, no. 933); *Melr. Lib.*, ii, no. 566). It was granted by Robert III to Jedburgh abbey, 6 May 1395, the right of presentation being said to have belonged to the crown since its foundation (*RMS*, i, no. 933). In this grant, which was confirmed by the Pope, 9 Sept. 1395, it was stipulated that the hosp. should be served in future by one of the canons of Jedburgh, but if by chance the hosp. is destroyed on account of war, prayer for the king was to be in the monastery until the place of Rutherford was restored (Reg. Aven., 280, fos. 367v–368). There is an appointment to the mastership 18 May 1426 and a legal transaction within the hosp. is recorded 16 Nov. 1444 (*Melr. Lib.*, ii, no. 566).

ST. ANDREWS, ST. LEONARD. In 1144 Robert, bp. of St. Andrews, assigned the hosp. of the Culdees to the canons of the newly founded priory and endowed it for the reception of visitors and pilgrims (*St. A. Lib.*, 123). In 1183 it is described as for the reception of visitors, the poor and pilgrims (*ibid.*, 58). Then, and later, it is called the hosp. of St. Andrew (or probably of St. Andrews), and, 1158–62, the new hosp. (*ibid.*, 127). It is first mentioned as St. Leonard's in 1248 (*ibid.*, 103). These designations apply to one and the selfsame hospital (Herkless and Hannay, *College of St. Leonard*, 10, 12). It is said to have been occupied eventually by old women and also by poor men (*ibid.*, 16–17). On 20 Aug. 1512, Alexander Stewart, abp. of St. Andrews, erected the hosp. and ch. of St. Leonard into the college of that name (*ibid.*, 16–17, 128 ff.) See ST. LEONARD'S COLLEGE.

ST. ANDREWS, ST. NICHOLAS. A donation was made to this hosp. by Roger, b. of St. Andrews, −1127 (*RMS*, iii, no. 2032). It was a leper hosp. (*ibid.*, iii, no. 2032; see no. 883). It is described as a house of lepers 14 March 1438 (Reg. Supp. 343, fo. 121v), but it is called a poor's hosp. 12 May 1438 (*ibid.*, 348, fo. 157). In 1529 St. Nicholas's was united to the Dominican house at St. Andrews (Macfarlane, *Geneaal Coll.*, ii, 186). and there is a reference, 1568–72 to an annual rent paid to the Blackfriars for the 'crypellis, lamyt, blynd and pouir' of this hosp. (*Thirds of Benefices*, 241). It was apparently still in use in 1583, when an endowment of victual was made to the 'poor folk, present and to come' (St. And. Univ. Chs., cited *St. Andrews Copiale*, 409).

ST. GERMAINS (ST. GERMAN'S). This was the only Scottish fd'n. of the Bethlemite order. A charter of Robert de Quinci relating to land in Tranent is witnessed (*c.* 1170 × 1180) by two canons of Bethlehem and another canon witnesses a charter of Walter de Chartres belonging to the same period (SRO, GD, 241/254; *Kel. Lib.*, ii, no. 344). The fd'n. of the house can be confidently assigned to this period, possibly *c.* 1170, and it is possible that the founder may have been Robert de Quinci himself. Ralph prior of this house is mentioned, −1219 (*Dunf. Reg.*, no. 155). In the fifteenth c. the hosp. and its revenues were a constant source of litigation (Reg. Supp., 287, fo. 103; 306, fo. 71v). On 7 Dec. 1470 the master is accused of permitting laymen with their wives and families to live there as in a private house (*ibid.*, 662, fo. 53v). At length on 9 Feb. 1495/6, a bull of Pope Alexander VI, which describes the hosp. except the chapel as ruinous, while its fruits are secularized, grants, at the instigation of James IV its revenues to the newly erected university of Old Aberdeen (later King's College), with provision for the maintenance of one religious and three poor people at the hosp. and likewise of three poor students in the university (*Aberdeen Fasti*, no. 4). A charter of 12 Aug. 1507 is granted by William, bp. of Aberdeen, chancellor of the university and 'master of the house of the hospital of St. German's . . . annexed to the new college of the Blessed Virgin Mary in the said university' (*RMS*, v, no. 868). There is a reference to the chaplain or preceptor of the chapel of St. German's, 12 Aug. 1577 (*ibid.*, iv, no. 2744). It should be noted that a papal letter of 11 Dec. 1474 (*CPL*, xiii, 462) refers to the hosp. of St. German in the diocese of Abedeen, 'which has been from of old in the presentation of the priory of St. Germanus at St. German's . . . in the diocese of St. Andrews'. This statement which seems to indicate a second foundation under the same invocation in the diocese of Aberdeen undoubtedly involves a blunder.

Cf. Cameron, *Apostolic Camera*, 181. The only hosp. of St. German's was in the diocese of St. Andrews.

ST. MAGNUS (CAITHNESS). Doubtfully identified with a site 'hospitale' which occurs in 1290 and evidently lay between Helmsdale and Wick (Stevenson, *Documents*, i, 184; Durkan, 'Care of the Poor: pre-Reformation hospitals'; in *Essays of Scottish Reformation*, 116; see Obsdale). Its first certain appearance as the hosp. of Caithness is 11 Feb. 1358 (*CPP*, i, 326) and as the poors hosp. of Skyburgh, 5 Sept. 1376 (Reg. Vat., fo. 439). It reoccurs, 23 Sept. 1440, when it is called St. Magnus de Skymer, and 1 June 1448 when it appears as St. Magnus Martyr (Reg. Supp., 367, fo. 290v; *ibid.*, 427, fo. 17v). It is almost certainly this hosp. which is referred to as the poor's hosp. of St. Mary, Caithness diocese, 3 Feb. 1474/5 (*CPL*, ix, 465). There was attached to it a ch. mentioned as 'the rectory of the church of [Spittal] called the hospital of St. Magnus in Caithness', 27 March 1547 (*RSS*, iii, no. 2228). It was leased with its revenues, by the master, 5 and 24 March 1580/1 (*Munro Writs*, no. 97). The patronage of the hosp. which pertained to the earldom of Caithness is mentioned till 1644 (*OPS*, ii2, 757–8; *RSS*, v, nos. 3034, 3296; *APS*, v, 154). See *Hist. Mon. Comms. Rep. (Caithness)*, no. 89.

ST. NICHOLAS (BOHARM). 'Beside the bridge of Spey', fd. by Muriel de Polloc for the reception of poor travellers (*Moray Reg.*, no. 106). In 1232 Alexander II made provision for a chaplain and clerks serving in the chapel of St. Nicholas (*ibid.*, no. 110). The hosp. does not appear in a dated record until 1235 (*St. A. Lib.* 326), but must have been in existence previously. The master is mentioned in a charter, 10 June 1471 (*Cawdor Bk.*, 53). The buildings are said to have survived the Reformation and 'in considerable extent' until removed for the rebuilding of the bridge (*Aberdeen–Banff Illustrations*, ii, 277–8).

SCONE, ST. JOHN THE APOSTLE. Lands which Robert Blund of Perth gave to the hosp. of St. John the Apostle of Scone were the subject of a composition which the abbot and convent of Scone made with the donor's sister and nephew, 1206 × 1227 (*Scone Lib.*, no. 169).

SEGDEN. This house has been erroneously located at Seggieden, near Perth. Thus, Spottiswoode (479) speaks of it as 'situated upon the River Tay in the shire of Perth'. (The only connection of that place with a religious house was that the lands of Seggieden were granted to the friars preachers of Edinburgh, 11 Feb. 1546/7 (*RSS*, iii, no. 2143).) This was an Augustinian hosp. at or near Berwick. Segden was the former name of Follydean, a small valley down which a stream runs into the North Sea about two miles north of Berwick (Scott, *Berwick-upon-Tweed* . . . (1888), 348; Br. M. Maps 186.h.1 (24)). The hospital must have stood in or near this valley at the beginning but there is some evidence that its site was changed later. An inquisition into the hospital's possessions in 1367 contains a reference to land next to it 'in its enclosure within the cemetery of Berwick', which seems to indicate that the hosp. was actually in the town by that time (*CDS*, iv, no. 135; *Cal. Inquis. Miscell.*, iii (1348–77) no. 647). A confirmation of a grant of 1335 shows that the advowson of the chapel of Segdene had belonged to the Lindsay family (*CDS*, iii, no. 1159), and, up to 1349, two chaplains 'of the order of the house of Segden in Scotland' had a chantry on an island on Windermere (*Cal. Inquis. Miscell.*, iii, no. 167), which was also part of the possessions of the Lindsays of Lamberton in the thirteenth c. It is possible that a member of this family was founder of the hosp., particularly as Segden is near Lamberton. 'Hermit brethren' were already established on the isle of St. Mary, Windermere, by 1272 (*Cal. Inquis.*, i, Henry III, no. 820), but it is not clear that they were then in any way connected with Segden. The earliest reference to the hosp. occurs in a thirteenth-c. taxation roll where it appears simply as 'Seggeden' (*Cold. Corr.*, cxvi). In 1296 the master of the house of St. Austin of Seggedene swore fealty to Edward I and a writ was issued for the return of the house's lands (*CDS*, ii, no. 823; *Rot. Scot.*, i, 25). In 1311 Edward III gave the hermit of Seggedene 100s. in alms to glaze the windows of his chapel (*CDS*, iii, no. 218). On 20 Dec. 1333 reference is made to a tenement of Berwick acquired from the brethren of Seggedene (*Cal. Inquis, Miscell.*, ii (1307–49), no. 1402), and in 1338 Edward III granted protection for two years to the master and brethren of the house, 'who depend for their subsistence on charity, collecting alms in churches' (*Cal. Pat. Rolls, Edw. III (1334–1338)*, 572). A warden of the hosp. was appointed by the English king in 1362 (*ibid.*, *Edw. III (1361–1364)*, 215), but, on the Scottish side, John de Peblis was said to hold the administration of the hermitage in 1363 and 1365 (*CPP*, i, 417, 506). In 1379 Segden was described as the king's free chapel (*Rot. Scot.*, ii, 15), and, though it was again termed hospital in 1431 (*Cal. Pat. Rolls, Henry VI (1429–1436)*, 131), it seems probable that it had already ceased to function as such before the earlier date. The hermitage of Segden was annexed to the free chapel of St. Mary Magdalene at Berwick (formerly the hosp. of St. Mary Magdalene, *q.v.*) by 1437 (*ibid.*, *Henry VI (1436–1441)*, 97), and it is last noted in 1453 (*CDS*, iv, no. 1251). Segden seems to have been a hosp. and hermitage of Augustinian friars, but there is no evidence that it was in any way connected with the friary of that order in Berwick.

SHOTTS (BERTRAMSHOTTS). On 30 April 1476 a bull of Sixtus IV confirms the erection and measures for the endowment of the chapel of St. Catherine (created by the ordinary a parish ch.) and the poor's hosp. fd. by James de Hamilton at Bertramshotts (*HMC 11th Rep.*, App., Pt. vi, 48; *CPL*, xiii, 489–90). The hosp. was erected *c.* 1471 and payment to the master is recorded from that date to 1476 (*ER*, viii, 15, 175, 244, 278, 358). Later grants of the patronage of the ch. of Bertramshotts make no mention of the hosp. (*RMS*, ii, nos. 1794, 3635).

SMAILHOLM. Fd. before 30 Dec. 1429 when the grant of the hosp. to the abbey of Dryburgh by Archibald, fourth E. of Douglas and lord of Smailholm, its patron, was confirmed by the Pope (*CSSR*, iii, 67–8, 243). It evidently continued as a hosp. and 'Smalham Spettell' appears in a list of places burned by the English in 1542 (*Hamilton Papers*, i, xci; *LP Henry VIII*, xvii, nos. 998 (2), 1136 (2)). There are also entries of Smailholm Spittal in rentals of Dryburgh abbey, *c.* 1540 onwards (*Dryb. Lib.*, 340 etc.) and elsewhere as late as 17 March 1637 (*Roxburgh Retours*, no. 165), but the reference in those cases is to land so designated.

SOUTRA. Said to have been founded by Malcolm IV in 1164, for lodging travellers (*Scotichronicon*, lib. viii, cap. vii (*Chron. Bower*, i, 453)). But the foundation was probably somewhat earlier; there is a charter of King Malcolm to Soutra, 1162 × 1164 (*Regesta Regum Scottorum*, i, 244–5), which is not the fd'n. charter. In a bull of Pope Gregory IX, 20 Sept. 1236, specific mention is made that the rule of St. Augustine, instituted in the hosp., shall be observed in perpetuity (*Midlothian Chrs.*, 36), and the fact that it is designated the house or hospital of the Holy Trinity from –1164 (*Regesta Regum Scottorum*, i, 244–5) merely indicates its dedication and gives no support to the suggestion that it should be regarded as Trinitarian. Cf. the supplications of the master and brethren for confirmation of the privileges granted by Pope Gregory IX (above) 27 May 1420 (*CSSR*, 199) and for the right to wear rochets 'after the manner of other canons of the same order', 10 June 1420 (*ibid.*, 207). But, on 7 Oct. 1444 its deterioration was such that doubts were expressed whether it should follow the rule of St. Augustine and the opinion was given that it was more likely to have been founded as a hosp. for the reception of the poor rather than as a religious place (Reg. Supp., 400, fo. 34.) No mention is made of the Trinitarian order in this petition (cf. Dunlop, *James Kennedy*, 408). On 28 Nov. 1450 the Pope appointed a mandatory to deal with the petition of Melrose abbey for the appropriation to it of Soutra hosp. (Reg. Supp., 446, fo. 264v; *CPL*, x, 501). This did not take place as the hosp. had already been annexed *c.* 1449 to the newly erected secular dignity of chancellorship in St. Andrews cathedral (*q.v.*) which occurred ten years or more before 3 Nov. 1459 (Reg. Supp., 525, fo. 192). The hosp. appears as the chancellor's prebend in 1454 (*CPL*, X, 164) and the 'chancellorship of St. Andrews, called Soltre' is said to be vacant, 14 Feb. 1459/60 (Reg. Supp., 527, fo. 161). But, on the petition of Mary of Gueldres, the widowed queen of James II, Pope Pius II united the hosp. by his bull of 23 Oct. 1460 (*Midlothian Chrs.*, 58–61) to her new foundation of Trinity College and hosp., Edinburgh. The queen's charter of 25 March 1462 provides that the provost of Trinity College, who is to hold the ch. of Soutra, will maintain three poor people living there (*ibid.*, 65); references to the 'hospitallers' (i.e. residents in the hospital) of Soutra are found in 1531 and as late as Feb. 1583/4 (*ibid.*, 102, ciii). In the seventeenth c. the hosp. of Soutra is described as 'alluterlie [completely] ruynd' (Bisset, *Rolment of Courtis*, ii, 123). Although Soutra is said to have been founded as a hosp. for travellers (above) there are many indications from the thirteenth c. onwards (e.g. the appropriation of chs. to it for the maintenance of the poor

(*Midlothian Chrs.*, 13, 15, 17)), that it was a poor's hosp. and it is so described in the fifteenth c. (Reg. Supp., 291, fo. 138; 293, fo. 237v). Although its career as a well-endowed regular hosp. was terminated in the fifteenth c., the maintenance of 'hospitallers' was a continuance of its traditional association with the poor. The description of it as a 'hospice' on the tablet affixed to the remaining fragment of its buildings is hardly accurate.

SPITTAL (CAITHNESS), see ST. MAGNUS.

STIRLING, ALMSHOUSE (THE OVER HOSPITAL). Dedicated to St. Peter, the hosp. was in existence before 7 March 1482. (*Stirling Trans.*, (1898–9), 156; *Scot. Antiq.*, x, 170). It was situated on the east side of the parish ch. beside the burial ground and is mentioned as a poor's hosp. (with a chaplain) on 17 Feb. 1540/1 (*Stirling Chrs.*, *1124–1705*, no. xlii), and again 28 Feb. and 1 May 1610, when it was ruinous and proposed to be rehabilitated (*ibid.*, no. lii). A hosp. mentioned in 1296 and 1327 is more likely to be that of Stirling, St. James (*q.v.*) (*Stirling Trans.*, (1898–9), 159–60).

STIRLING, LEPER HOUSE. There are frequent references to this house from 1464 until 1513, but nothing is heard of it after this date, and it certainly does not appear to have survived the Reformation (*ER.*, vii, 246, 393; *ibid.*, xiii, 274, 568; *Stirling Trans.* (1910–11), 120). It lay at the east end of Stirling, and in 1497 is called the grantgore 'at the toune end of Strivelin' (*ER*, xiii, 568; *TA*, i, 378).

STIRLING, MARY OF GUELDRES. Situated on the castle hill, this hosp. was fd. by Mary of Gueldres, queen of James II before 1462. The account of the queen's chamberlain in Stirlingshire for 1461/2 shows payments to six minor canons in the queen's hospital '*in monti castri de Strivelyn*,' and also six poor persons near the castle gate (*ER*, vii, 60). The hospital is again noted in 1462/3 (*ibid.*, vii, 85, 188) but royal gifts appear to have ceased with the queen's death in 1463 (*Stirling Trans.* (1910–11), 121).

STIRLING, THE NETHER HOSPITAL. Commonly called Spittal's Hospital from its foundation by Robert Spittal, tailor to James IV. Its reputed date of erection is 1530 and it was definitely founded by Spittal before 1546 (*Stirling Trans.*, (1897–8), 79; *ibid.* (1905–6), 42; cf. *ibid.* (1891–2), 9 ff. which attempts to disprove Spittal's part in the foundation). It continued in being after the Reformation. On 18 March 1738 the council as patrons of the hospital ordered the repair of this almshouse 'which lately fell down' (*Stirling Recs.* (*1667–1752*), 242).

STIRLING, ST. JAMES. In all probability this is the hosp. sited at Causewayhead mentioned in a composition of 1221 × 1225 (*Dunf. Reg.*, no. 216). It would appear from an entry in an inventory of records of 1282 that the hosp. was in royal patronage and had been held by Master Abel de Golyn (1249 × 1254) before he became bp. of St. Andrews (*APS*, i, 110). This again would appear to be the hosp. of 1296 (*Stirling Trans.* (1891–2), 5) and 1327 (*ER*, i, 67), but it is not until 10 March 1402/3, when Robert III granted the hosp. of St. James 'at the end of the causeway of the bridge of Stirling', to Cambuskenneth abbey, that it is first mentioned by dedication (*Camb. Reg.*, no. 108). The patronage of this hosp. was bestowed upon the magistrates and community by James II, 24 June 1456 (*Stirling Chrs.*, 1124–1705, no. xxiii). But it apparently continued to be held by Cambuskenneth, for, with its lands, it is included among the properties of that abbey incorporated, by act of parliament, 1606, in a temporal lordship (*APS*, iv 345). It is said to have been destroyed at the Reformation and never rebuilt (*Stirling Trans.* (1891–2), 5); and the Town Council made regulations regarding the removal of the stonework of St. James's chapel, 2 Nov. 1567 (*Stirling Chrs.*, 210).

TEVIOTDALE, ST. MARY IN, see RULEMOUTH.

TORRANCE. The warden of this hosp. swore fealty to Edward I in 1296 and had its lands restored (*CDS*, ii, no. 823; *Rot. Scot.*, i, 26). It is associated in some way with the ch. of Torrance. Thus, it is designated the hosp. of the chaplaincy of Torrens and alternatively the hosp. or chapel without cure of Torrens, 30 June 1439 (Reg. Supp., 359, fos. 107v, 108v); and the hosp. of the ch. of Torrance, 29 Sept. 1512 (*RSS*, i, no. 2435). By this period the ch. appears to have achieved parochial status and a presentation to the parsonage, chaplaincy and hosp. of Torrance is recorded, 5 Aug. 1531 (*ibid.*, ii, no. 977). The parsonage, which evidently included the hosp., was united to the collegiate ch. of Restalrig before 1532, and apparently supported a prebend within that college (*RMS*, iii, no. 3210). A presentation to the parsonage and preceptory of Torrance, 5 May 1546 is apparently the last specific reference to the preceptory (*RSS*, iii, no. 1648). In post-Reformation record the benefice is accounted part of the parish of Kilbride (*RMS*, viii, no. 1840). Brockie (p. 1096) mistakenly locates this hosp. near Peebles.

TRAILTROW. There is a reference to a poor's hosp. here, 20 April 1455 (*CPL*, xi, 261), but a reference in a petition of 1363 to 'a certain hospital, having a parish church annexed' almost certainly refers to this hosp. (*CPP*, i, 446). Preceptors of it are mentioned till 27 Sept. 1574 (*RMS*, iv, no. 2311); one of these is designated (in 1501) preceptor of St. James of Trailtrow (*HMC 15th Rep.*, App., Pt. viii, 59). It was evidently extinct before 15 Feb. 1609 when there is a mention of lands formerly held by this hosp. (*RMS*, vii, no. 21); and although this hosp. and its lands are mentioned till 1696 (*Dumfries Retours*, no. 346), obviously these had long been secularized.

TURRIFF. Dedicated to St. Mary and St. Congan, this hosp. was fd. by Alexander Cumyn, E. of Buchan for a master, six chaplains and thirteen poor people, 6 Feb. 1272/3 (*Abdn. Reg.*, i, 30–4). With the end of the Cumyn line of the earls of Buchan in 1342 (*Scots Peerage*, ii, 259–60) the patronage passed to the crown. On 17 Oct. 1379 Robert III granted the ch. of Turriff and the almshouse with the right of the presentation of its master to Coupar-Angus abbey (Reg. Aven., 229, 377v–8), but despite papal confirmation of the hosp. and ch. in 1382 and of the ch. in 1389 (*ibid; ibid.*, 259, fo. 457; *Coupar Angus Chrs.*, no. 119), the grant was ineffective. Instead the patronage evidently passed to the Stewart line of the earls of Buchan (*Scots Peerage*, ii, 262–3), and in 1412 Gilbert, bp. of Aberdeen, with the consent of John Stewart, E. of Buchan, erected the hosp. with its revenues into a prebend of Aberdeen cathedral (*Abdn., Reg.*, i, 213–4). No provision was made for the continuation of the hosp., notice of which does not appear in the charter of erection, and the hosp. may have already decayed. A reference in 1521 to the leasing of the ch. lands '*pro policia et hospitalitate*' may be no more than common form, and cannot be taken to indicate the hosp.'s continuance (*ibid.*, i, 386).

UPSETLINGTON, see HORNDEAN.

UTHROGLE. Gifts of alms to this hosp. are recorded 20 Nov. 1293 and 16 February 1293/4 (Stevenson, *Documents*, i, 410, 414). It is called the poor's hosp. of St. John the Evangelist of Hothtyrrogale, 5 May 1380 (Reg. Aven., 222, fo. 505v; *CPL*, iv, 238). It is again mentioned in 1394 (*CPP*, i, 615) and 1420, when it is described as 'the hospital of St. John, Ouctherogale' (*CSSR*, i, 223). It was united, with its associated chapel and some of its teinds, to Trinity College, Edinburgh, for the maintenance of the bedesmen there, 10 July 1462 (*Midlothian Chrs.*, 64, 67; Cameron, *Apostolic Camera*, 142, 240, 278). The chapel of St. John the Baptist of Utherogall appears 16 Oct. 1543 (*Midlothian Chrs.*, 109), but no further reference to a hosp.; the 'chaplancie of Ouchtarogall' again appearing by itself on 31 May 1581 (*ibid.*, 236).

WHEEL. This site is in south-west Roxburghshire and is described as 'between the Wheel causeway and Peel burn, one mile south of the hill known as Wheelrig Head' (Watson, 'Wheel Kirk, Liddesdale,' *Hawick Trans.*, 1914, 20). The chapel 'del Quele' in Scotland is mentioned, 5 Aug. 1347 (*CDS*, iii, no. 1500) and it is designated the hosp. or free chapel 'del Whele,' 26 May 1348 (*ibid.*, iii, no. 1552). The brothers and sisters of the hosp. house and Domus Dei of 'Welle' occur 31 Aug. 1386 (*Durham Wills and Inventories* (Surtees Soc.), i, 40). On 3 Dec. 1600, Quheil ch., formerly in possession of Jedburgh abbey is described as 'waist' (*Hawick Trans.*, 1914, 20).

WIGTOWN. CRIPPLE HOUSE. In the community's hands in 1557, when references to a lease of the croft pertaining to the 'crepill hous' occurs in a contemporary rental (SRO, Wigtown Rental Book, fos. 28v, 30). It occurs again in 1559 and 1577 and is still mentioned in 1599 (*ibid.*, fos. 32, 88, 121).

INCOMPLETE FOUNDATION

Aberdour, St. Martha. Called St. Mary's (Cameron, *Apostolic Camera*, 221). Fd. 9 July 1474, by James E. of Morton, for the maintenance of the poor and the entertainment of pilgrims and wayfarers; and on 22 July following, the ab. and convent of Inchcolm intimated that they had given permission to John Scot, vicar of Aberdour and canon of that abbey, to take over the care and administration of the proposed hospital (*Mort. Reg.*, i, no. 231). As the project had not been realized, the earl granted the lands for the building of a hosp. to four sisters of the Third Order of St. Francis, 16 Oct. 1486 (*ibid.*, i, no. 233); but a bull of 23 June 1487 extinguished the name and rights of the hospital (Theiner, *Vet. Mon.*, no. dccclxxxiv).

Edinburgh. A seven-year project for hosp. with priest, surgeon, medicinar, and forty beds is mentioned in 1552 (*Edinburgh Recs.*, ii, 170–1).

UNCERTAIN AND UNAUTHENTICATED FOUNDATION

Aberdeen, Maison Dieu. On 1 Sept. 1459, there is a reference to *land* called 'Masyndow' (*Abda. S. Nich. Cart.*, ii, 329). This was in the vicinity of the house of the Trinitarians, who may have had a hosp. on this site. Evidence, however, is wholly lacking. A later hosp. for decayed burgesses was founded (in 1632) on the site of the Trinitarian monastery (McPherson, *The Kirk's Care of the Poor*, 164).

Aberdeen, St. Anthony. A papal letter, dated in *CPL* (ix, 412) 8 Jan. 1443/4, which is said to record a petition of the ab. and convent of St. Anthony, Vienne, and the preceptor of St. Anthony's, Leith, containing that 'the brethren of the houses of Dundee and Aberdeen (and others) . . . on account of certain churches, chapels, oratories, etc., of theirs, dedicated to St. Anthony, ask and receive alms', and which nominates mandatories to check this practice, has been taken to indicate that there were houses of the order of St. Anthony at the places named. This was not the case. A supplication of the above abbot and convent and preceptor, 6 Jan. 1444, shows that the alleged offenders were the Friars Minor of Dundee and the Friars Preachers of Aberdeen (Reg. Supp., 394, 77).

Alyth. The lands of the town of Alyth and the hospice ('*Ostlaria*') of the said town occur in a grant, 11 Aug. 1468 (SRO, Airlie Inventory, GD/6/12/5). The status of this hospice is questionable.

Arnbeg. Land called the Spittal of Arnbeg, in the parish of Kippen, is mentioned, 26 Jan. 1686 (*Perth Retours*, no. 943). There is, however, no evidence of a hospital here.

Arngibbon. There is a reference to land called the Spittal of Arngibbon, 7 Sept. 1550 (*RMS*, iv, no. 517) Cf. *OPS*, i, 38. This land may have belonged to a hosp. There is nothing to show that it was the site of one.

Auchintorlie. Although the lands of Spittal are mentioned along with those of Auchintorlie, e.g. 14 Oct. 1550 (*RMS*, iv, no. 530), no evidence of a hosp. in this locality is forthcoming.

Auchterderran. From 30 April 1511 (*RMS*, ii, no. 3567) there are references to the lands of Spittal in this parish. Cf. also *Fife Retours*, no. 129 (20 April 1603); *RMS*, vii, no. 1058 (13 March 1627). No evidence of a hosp. here can be found. In the late sixteenth c. the lands of Dundonald (Fife) and Spittal were held *in capite* of the 'prebendary' or chaplain of the St. Katherine aisle in the ch. of Wemyss, which ch. itself was annexed to Trinity college hosp. in Edinburgh (SRO, Boswell of Balmuto Writs, GD 66/1/102 and 110).

Balfron. The occurrence of the name Spittal in this parish permits of no specific explanation.

Banff. The hosp. or bedehouse for eight poor women (*Aberdeen–Banff Illus.*, ii, 114) was, in all likelihood, a post-Reformation fd'n.

Blairspittal. The lands so named along with the Spittal in the barony of Buchanan(?). 18 Feb. 1685 (*Perth Retours*, no. 936) can hardly be regarded as the site of a hosp.

Cairnwell. There is said to have been a hosp. called Sheen Spidell or Old Hospital, on the road over the Grampians (*Aberdeen–Banff Coll.*, p. 642; *Aberdeen–Banff Illus.*, ii, 84). No record attesting its existence has been found.

Cameron. On 30 Dec. 1387, Thomas, lord Erskine, farmer and warden of the lands and possessions of St. John of Jerusalem confirmed a letter of wadset (undated) by Donald de Porta to Gilchrist de Bannori (? initial uncertain) of the hosps. of Cameron and Stokrog [near Cameron, Dunbartonshire, given as Stockrothart in Blaeu's atlas] for 4 merks sterling to be paid at Dumbarton for 1*d.* blench (Seal of Torphichen appended; *SRO*, Mar and Kellie, GD 124/1/420: abstract in *HMC Mar and Kellie*, i, 8). The kirklands commonly called 'Spittell of Campbroun' were granted to Arthur Darleyth in 1571 (Fraser, *Colquhoun Chartulary*, 316–7).

Crailing. 'An hospital and church or chapel existed at an early though unknown date at a place called Spital in Nisbet, now occupied by the modern mansion of Monteviot' (*OPS*, i, 387). But the sources cited for this statement (viz. *APS*, iv, 500, 538 and *Retours*) do not bear it out. *APS* refers to the joining of the churches of Crailing, Nisbet and Spittell in one parish, 9 July 1606. There is no indication of the location or nature of 'Spittell'. Again, the references to Spittal in the Roxburgh retours (nos. 126, 253) do not apply to this site, but to Ancrum Spittal, which was, in fact, the only hospital in the locality.

Cullen. 'There was a hospital at Cullen which may have been associated with the collegiate church' (*Aberdeen–Banff Illus.*, ii, 136–7). This connection is highly probable, although proof of this is confined to references in the foundation charter of the college (*q.v.*) to the 'Bede's Myir' (Crammond, *Church and Churchyard of Cullen*, 43, 47). Bedesmen of an unidentified bedehouse, which may have been pre-Reformation, occur 8 Jan. 1611 (Cramond, *Annals of Cullen* (1894), 23, 49). Other bedehouses at Cullen were undoubtedly of later fd'n. Thus, William Lawtie (d. 1657) endowed a bedehouse for poor men and women (decayed farmers and farmers' widows) (McPherson, *The Kirk's Care of the Poor*, 165). Again, a hosp. is said to have been fd. for men by the family of Findlater, while another was founded for women 'by the present earl of Findlater his deceast Countess' (*Aberdeen–Banff* Illus. ii, 135–6). In the Old Statistical Account is a reference to a bedehouse for eight old men, which is said to be ruinous and removed (*ibid.*, ii, 137 *n.*). The fact that the earldom of Findlater was not fd. till 1638 suggests that fd'ns. by this family were not earlier than the seventeenth c.

Dalnaspidal. The existence of a hosp. here is merely a surmise from the place-name ('the field of the hospital'). Nothing is known of any such foundation.

Drymen. The lands of Spittal of Drymen called Craginschedrach are mentioned, 12 July 1548 (*RMS*, iv, no. 227) and 18 Nov. 1646 (*Stirling Retours*, no. 186), while other references to Spittal lands in this parish occur till 13 Feb. 1685 (*ibid.*, no. 295; cf. *OPS*, i, 38). No explanation of these place-names can be given, as evidence of a hosp. here is wholly lacking.

Dunblane. A reference in 1516 to the 'hous and croft with the pertinens, callit the Spittell Croft, and Merzonis akir at the brigend of Dunblane' may point to the existence of an extinct hosp. on that site (Fraser, *Stirlings of Keir*, 307).

Dundee, Hospice. 'For cases of severe or protracted sickness the abbey [of Coupar Angus] owned a hospital at Dundee where medical aid could always be obtained' (*Coupar Angus Rental* (ed. Rogers), i, xlvii). In this statement, imagination runs riot. It is true that the entry in the Rental Book of Coupar Angus, on which it purports to be based, is translated: 'At Pentecost, 1469, the hospital of Dundee is let to William Tullach . . .' (*ibid.*, i, 145); but reference to the original (SRO, Registrum Assedationum, etc., B. Marie de Cupro, 1443–1458, 12v) reveals that the phrase is 'Hospitium Dunde'. Likewise, the alleged mention of the garden of the hospital of Dundee in 1464 (*Cupar Angus Rental*, i, 147) is in fact a mention of the garden of the *hospitium* there (Registrum, 13v). There is no doubt that the so-called hosp. was simply the abbot's lodging in Dundee. It is correctly mentioned as 'hospitium nostrum' (*Cupar Angus Rental*, ii, 205). Oddly enough, in a reference to the abbot's lodging at Perth (*ibid.*, ii, 64), the word *hospitium* is given and correctly translated.

Dundee, St. Anthony, see *Aberdeen, St. Anthony* (above).

Eckford. There is a local tradition of the existence of a leper hosp. in this parish, and a rivulet flowing into the Kale water is known as the Spittal or Spittalend burn. *OPS* (i, 397) also refers to a place called Spittalbank or Hospital Lands. No evidence of such a hospital has been found. 'Massendew' is mentioned as one of the forty-four places on the 'river of Kale' burned by the English, 17 Sept. 1545 (*LP Henry VIII*, xx², nos. 458, 533). But it is difficult to accept this as a reference to a hosp. at Eckford. It is more likely to be an erroneous reference to the Maison Dieu of Roxburgh.

Edinburgh, Maison Dieu. 'There was likewise some women appointed to sollicit the sick in the Hospitall of Bell's Wynd in Edinburgh, which was called l'Hotel Dieu', says Fr. Richard Augustine Hay (cited in *Edinburgh Siennes Liber*, 67). St. Thomas's hosp. owned land here (Prot. Bk. Strathauchin, ii, fos. 134v–135v; *RMS*, v, 1242). All contemporary references, however, locate it in the Cowgate, near or on the site of the later hosp. of St. Mary Magdalene. Land of 'Massondew' near Galowgate (*sic*, for Cowgate) is mentioned 6 April 1444 (SRO, Newbattle Inventory, i, no. 68; cf. *RMS*, ii, 1923, 2014); These confirm that it was in the Cowgate adjacent to the Greyfriars. It may have been property of the hosp. of St. John Baptist (*q.v.*).

Elgin. In 1360 John, bp. of Moray, gave to four chaplains in the cathedral a 'piece of land . . . held of the brethren of St. Lazarus outside the walls of Jerusalem' (*Moray Reg.*, no. 236). There is likewise a reference to 'Lazarus Wynd' as a boundary of land, 25 June 1590 (*RMS*, v, nos. 1742, 1743). The Lazarites apparently held land at Elgin; but there is no evidence that they had a house there.

Fala. A charter of 13 May 1513 refers to 'the lands of Edmonstoun and Ednam, with the gift of churches and chaplainries and the right of patronage of the hospital of Fawlo' (*RMS*, ii, no. 3844). There is said, in 1627, to have been a fd'n. of four bedesmen in Fala, which was apparently defunct and of which no information was available (*Rep. on State of Certain Parishes*, p. 65). This statement may point to the existence of a hosp. here, though it may also be due to confusion with the neighbouring hosp. of Soutra (*q.v.*). On the other hand, the ch. of Fala was held by the hosp. of Ednam (*ibid.*, p. 65), and it is possible that 'hospital', in the 1513 charter, is an error for 'church'.

Forda (Fordam). In the narrative of the endowments of Holyrood abbey in David I's 'Great Charter', 1128–53 (*Holy. Lib.*, no. 1), the phrase appears: 'Hamere and Forda (or Fordam) with their proper marches and the hospital with a carrucate of land' (*Hamere et Fordam cum suis rectis divisis et hospitale cum una carrucata terre*). Lawrie annotates this as follows: '*Fordam*: Forda, a land in Whitekirk, where, it seems, there was a hospital for travellers.' (Lawrie, *Charters*, 385). But there are two points of dubiety here. The hosp. is an item separate from Hamere and Forda; and when these are mentioned elsewhere (e.g. *Holy. Lib.*, nos. 2, 27 and p. 169), there is no reference to a hosp. Further, there is nothing to bear out the statement that this was a hospital for travellers. This hosp. can only be regarded as unidentified.

Fyvie. The idea that there was a hosp. here is due to a wrong entry in the index of *Abdn. Reg.* (ii, 374). 'Hospitale S. Petri' clearly does not refer to Fyvie, but to the hosp. of that dedication at Aberdeen (*ibid.*, ii, 226–7). A charter of 20 June 1427 refers to the appropriation of the vicarage to the 'monks in the religious house built on the land of Ardlogy, beside the *church* of the Blessed Peter of Fyvie' (*ibid.*, ii, 225); but there is no mention in this or any other record of a hosp. under this invocation at Fyvie.

Glasgow. Roland Blacader, subdean of Glasgow cathedral, bequeathed £100 for the erection of a hospital beside the collegiate church of St. Mary and St. Anne (Our Lady College), but the bequest apparently was not carried into effect (Glasgow *St. Mary Liber*, lxxii).

Glendye. The occurrence of the place-name Spittal in this locality admits of no explanation. Evidence of a hosp. is entirely lacking.

Glenmuick. There is said to have been a hosp. at the east end of Loch Muick, where there is a pass, called the Caiple Month, to the hills of Clova (Angus) (*Aberdeen–Banff Coll.*, p 640). Its existence cannot be verified.

Glenshee. The earliest reference found is to the lands of 'Spittale of Glensche' in a charter of sale by David Wemyss, lord of Strathardill [Strathardie], etc., 10 October 1542 (Fraser, *Wemyss*, ii, no. 197). The possibility that there was a chapel in Glenshee is suggested by the mention of the Chapel-crofts in 1615 (*RMS*, vii, no. 1156) and 1641 (*Perth Retours*, no. 498). No evidence of a hosp. here has been discovered.

Gosford. The supposition that there was a hosp. here is due to the mention of the lands of Gosford along with those of Ballencrieff (where there was a hosp.), e.g. 20 April 1421 (Fraser, *Douglas*, iii, no. 60). Cf. references to the lands of Ballencrieff, Gosford and Spittall (i.e. land formerly belonging to the hospital) in 1551/2 and 1607 (*RMS*, iv, no. 151; vi, no. 1961). There was no hosp. at Gosford.

Hamilton. Land of St. Mary of Bethlehem is mentioned in 1369 (*Glas. Reg.*, no. 311).

Harehope. The fact that, in 1296, the master of the house of St. Lazarus of Harop had letters from Edward I, directed to the sheriff of Edinburgh, for restitution of his houses' lands (*Rot. Scot.*, i, 25) has given rise to the supposition that this house was situated in Scotland. It has thus been located at Harehope, in the parish of Eddleston in Peeblesshire (*OPS*, i, 217). This is erroneous; the house in question was undoubtedly the hospital of Harehope in Northumberland. On 15 June 1376, Robert II granted to his son John, E. of Carrick, the lands of Prestisfelde, St. Giles' Grange and Spetelton, in the sheriffdom of Edinburgh, which were in the king's hands by reason of the forfeiture of the brethren of Harehope, these brethren being at the faith and peace of the king of England and against the faith and peace of the king of Scots (*RMS*, i, no. 582). From this charter it appears not only that the brethren belonged to an English house but also that the lands held by them in Scotland were not those of Harehope in Eddleston parish. The assertion that this was a foundation of David I (*OPS*, i, 211) is likewise unwarranted; it is recorded that Waldeve, son of Edward, gave Harehope (in Northumberland) to the brethren of St. Lazarus (1178+) (*CDS*, i, no. 1712; Hodgson, 'The Hospital of St. Lazarus and the Manor of Harehope', *Archaeol. Aeliana*, 3rd ser., xix (1922), 77). There is again, no ground for the statement: 'It is sufficiently certain [*sic*] that the "Harehope" of this charter (i.e. *RMS*, i, no. 582) is the . . . monastery of Holmcultram . . . which was commonly called also by the name of "Harihop" ' (*OPS*, i, 212). *OPS* relies unduly on a confused account in the *Scotichronicon* (*Chron. Bower*, ii, 161): 'The monks of Harehope, otherwise Holme, founded by a grant of . . . King David . . . to which had been annexed certain lands in Lothian, near the royal town of Edinburgh, namely, Spitalton and "Sant Gilysis" Grange' (*Medieval Religious Houses: England and Wales*, p. 362).

Hassendean. Morton, referring to the settlement of a controversy between Jocelin, bp. of Glasgow, and William the Lion regarding the patronage of Hassendean ch., declares: 'They agreed that the revenues and property of the said church shall be devoted to some work of charity. The bishop therefore, with the consent of the king, conferred the patronage thereof, with its lands, tithes and dues, upon the convent of Melrose, to be used in founding and maintaining a house of hospitality at Hastenden [Hassendean] for the reception and entertaining of the wayfaring poor and pilgrims journeying to Melrose abbey. The hospital was afterwards called Monks' Tower' (Morton, *Monastic Annals*, 272). But Bp. Jocelin's charter (*Melr. Lib.*, no. 121) says nothing about a 'house of hospitality' at Hassendean. The bp. grants this ch. to Melrose 'for the reception of the poor and of pilgrims coming to the house of Melrose'; and, again, 'for the perpetual uses of the poor and of pilgrims'. In other words, the bp.'s donation was not intended to supply a hospice *at Hassendean*; its motive was to augment *at Melrose* the provision for the poor and pilgrims coming *there*. Further, the building known as 'Hassendean Tower otherwise Monks' Tower' was a secular building, viz., a tower or fortalice (*OPS*, i, 318).

Kilmadock. The teinds of 'the spitale within the parichoune of Kilmadock' were set by David prior of Inchmahome in 1488 according to a case heard, 5 May 1491 (*ADA*, 147). Spittalton and Upper Spittalton are near Coldach; the lands of 'Coldouche Eister *alias* Spiltetoun' are mentioned (*Perth Retours*, no. 442).

Kintore. There is a reference, in 1551, to four roods of land called the Hospital of Kintore (*Abdn. Reg.*, i, 454). This land was so called because, as appears from a charter of 1499, it was held by the hosp. of St. Thomas the Martyr at Aberdeen (*Aberdeen–Banff Illus.*, iii, 239).

Kirkcowan. The place-name Spittal occurs in this parish, but no explanation of it can be given.

Lanark. Spottiswoode (477) says of the Lazarites that 'Lanark belonged likewise to this sect [*sic*]'. There is, however, no evidence of property held by this order at Lanark.

Leith. In 1327 Newbattle abbey was to maintain 'the house which bears the black cross of the hospital' (*domum que nigram crucem hospitalis portat*); an obligation which stemmed from a grant of land to the monks by Gilbert son of Henry in Leith in the early thirteenth c. (*Newb. Reg.*, nos. 50, 270).

Leith, St. Nicholas. 'The fort of Leith had a chapel dedicated to St. Nicholas. . . . The precise date of its erection is not known, but it is believed to have been founded after A.D. 1493. Adjoining it was the hosp. of St. Nicholas. The chapel and the hosp. were much damaged in 1544 when the English attacked Leith' (Mackinlay, *Dedications* (*NS*), p. 434). This chapel, described as on the north side of the water of Leith (*Prot. Bk. Young*, no. 844), is frequently mentioned from 23 Sept. 1488 (*ibid.*, no. 123). But no mention of a hosp. associated with it has been found and such a foundation must be regarded as very probably conjectural. The earliest indication of a hosp. (apart from St. Anthony's) at Leith would appear to be on 11 Nov. 1657 (*Edinburgh Recs.*, *1655-65*, p. 70; cf. *ibid.*, p. 181) and this was evidently post-Reformation.

Mauchline. There are references to a *hospitium* here, 2 March 1533/4 and 1 Sept. 1535 (*RMS*, iii, nos, 1369, 2569). On both occasions it occurs in the phrase 'the place, houses and hospice of Mauchline'; and there are apparently no other references to it. What this *hospitium* was is entirely uncertain. It may have been a lodging for visiting representatives of Melrose abbey or for the 'master' who probably supervised that abbey's property in this neighbourhood (see Mauchline, under Cistercian Houses). It may have been an inn for travellers.

Maybole. A reference to *lands* called the 'Masonedew', 9 October 1574 (*RMS*, iv, no. 2746), may point to the existence of a hosp., perhaps connected with the collegiate ch. But of this there is no definite evidence.

Monymusk. This is given in the heading of a charter (perhaps taken from the endorsement) *Abdn. Reg.*, ii, 264) which reads: 'Ad reformandum hospitale siue Kildey de Monymusk' ('Kildey' is a mutilated form of 'Keledei', i.e. Culdees, with whom the charter is concerned); and also in the index to *Abdn. Reg.* There is, however, no reference to a hospital in the text of the charter and no mention elsewhere of a hosp. at Monymusk. 'Hospitale' is a blunder.

Obsdale. A site 'hospitale' which evidently lay between Helmsdale and Wick is mentioned in 1290 (Stevenson, *Documents*, i, 184). The context makes it clear that this was not the hosp. at Helmsdale, and it is equally unlikely to refer to the hosp. of St. Magnus which lies well off the route between Helmsdale and Wick. The site is much more likely to be located on the coastal plain between these places. In this respect Obsdale which has been identified with the lands of Hospitill which appear in 1384, 1490 and in several post-Reformation sources, appears to most nearly fit the requirements (*OPS*, ii², 469). There is no positive evidence of a medieval hosp. here. The only fd'n. connected with Obsdale which is on record is a chaplainry in Fortrose cathedral, mentioned 6 Nov. 1547 (*RSS*, iii, no. 2529), 21 July 1570 (*Munro Writs*, no. 84), 10 May 1583 (*RMS*, v, no. 588).

Papa Stour. The structures of which the foundations remain on Brei Holm, an islet fifty feet distant from Papa Stour, and which are known locally as the 'leper houses' (see *Hist. Mon. Comm. Rep.* (*Orkney and Shetland*), iii, 156) have been supposed to be of medieval origin. Professor Gordon Donaldson informs me that while an eighteenth-c. leper settlement (rather than a hosp.) here is well documented, he has found no reference to a medieval hosp.

Perth, Hospice. See *Dundee, Hospice* (above).

Rutherglen. The lands of Spittal and Spittalquarter, in the vicinity of Rutherglen, mentioned, 21 Nov. 1607 (*RMS*, vi, no. 1991) and 20 Dec. 1617 (*Lanark Retours*, no. 118) were probably associated with the hosp. of Polmadie (*q.v.*). No evidence of a hosp. at Rutherglen is forthcoming.

Sanquhar. The supposition that there was a hosp. here (which may have originated with Spottiswoode (478-9)) is based on a reference to the warden of the 'New Place of

Senerwar', who, in 1296, swore fealty to Edward I (*CDS*, ii, no. 823). But it is not at all certain that this is an indication of a hosp. (though the warden is described as a chaplain); the chaplainry of St. Nicholas called the New Wark situated in the barony of Sanquhar in Dumfriesshire is mentioned in 1554 (SRO, Deeds, 6; cf. *Thirds of Benefices*, 23-4, 296). A local historian (Brown, *Hist. of Sanquhar*, pp. 53-4) purports to give the situation of this hosp., but this needs verification. Brockie's statement (p. 1097) that there was a hosp. of Sanquhar erected 'as is supposed', by the ancient lords (*reguli*) of Galloway, is mere romancing.

Selkirk. According to Brockie (p. 1092), David, prince of Cumbria and E. of Northumberland (i.e. the future David I) wished to convert the former site of the monastery at Selkirk (see under the Order of Tiron) into a hosp. for the poor and sick and this hosp., governed by the monks of Kelso, remained till the Reformation. These statements would seem to be unfounded. No mention of a hosp. here has been traced.

Snawdon. See *Thirlestane* (below).

Spittal (in the parish of Penicuik). This place-name survives, but evidence of a hosp. is entirely lacking. H. F. Brown ('Newhall on the North Esk', *SHR*, xvi (1919), 178) mentions an alleged *hospitium* for travellers here, but does not attempt to authenticate it.

Stewarton. There are references to the lands of 'le Spetale' (also called le Spittalis and Spittale) in the lordship of Stewarton (with some variants), 30 June 1452 and later (*RMS*, ii, nos. 583, 751, 1876, 3371). The significance of this place-name does not transpire. No evidence of a hosp. in this vicinity has been found.

Stockrodger. See *Cameron.*

Stonehouse. 'On the eastern side of the parish . . . at a place still called Spittal, stood formerly an hospital which is said to have been endowed with the lands of Spittal' (*OPS*, i, 109). These lands are mentioned as in the barony of Stonehouse, 10 March 1657 (*Lanark Retours*, nos. 266, 267; cf. *ibid.*, no. 328). There was no hosp. here; the lands in question pertained to the hosp. of Hamilton, St. Thomas Martyr (*q.v.*).

Stoneykirk. The place-name Port of Spittal occurs in this parish, but no explanation of this can be given (*Ayrshire-Galloway Coll.*, 2nd ser., x, 28).

Strathblane. There are several references, in 1429, to a poor's hospital here (*CPL*, viii, 101-2; Cameron, *Apostolic Camera*, 97). These are errors for Polmadie (see above).

Tarves. The hosp. here for four poor men (*Aberdeen-Banff Coll.*, 330) was very probably post-Reformation. The fd'n. is attributed to William Forbes of Tolquhon (*floruit, c.* 1584(?)) (*ibid.*, 330). But it should be noted that the fifth laird of Tolquhon, 1509-27, was also William Forbes (*House of Forbes*, 394).

Thirlestane. A ruined building to the east of the farmhouse of Thirlestane has been identified with a hosp., evidently for poor men and women, to which references are found, 1674-1701, in the Lauderdale estate account books (*HBNC*, xvi (1896-8), 23-4). It has been stated that 'there is a strong probability that it dates from pre-Reformation times' (*ibid.*, 23). In support of this is adduced a reference to 'Spittle Snawdoun' near Thirlestane, 12 April 1557 (*ibid.*, 24), though an earlier mention might have been cited, viz., in a charter, 15 April 1541[1], which refers to the incorporation by the ab. of Dryburgh of this and other lands in the tenandry or lordship of Spittale (*RMS*, iii, no. 2332). The lands of Spittale Snawdoun are also mentioned as lying near the burgh of Lauder, 23 February 1562/3 (*Dryb. Lib.*, 298, 299). But it is impossible to say what this place-name signifies. It may indicate the existence of a pre-Reformation hospital at or near Thirlestane. On the other hand, there is nothing to suggest an association of the lands of Snawdon with the older hospital at Lauder (*q.v.*).

Trefontains. There is a mention here of a ch. or hosp. (see under Cistercian Nuns). But the existence of a hosp. must be regarded as unconfirmed.

---

[1] This charter as printed (*RMS*, iii, no. 2332) gives 'Spittle, Snawdoun', i.e. as two separate items. But it has been confirmed that the comma has been inserted in error and is not in the original.

CATHEDRALS

GENERAL NOTES

INFORMATION regarding the history, constitution and personnel of the Scottish cathedrals is very unequal and, in some instances, e.g. Lismore, altogether meagre. For only four of the medieval bishoprics—Aberdeen, Brechin, Glasgow and Moray—is a chartulary available; for others we have to be content with random references. Again, the foundation or restoration of a see is often difficult to date with precision and may precede by a considerable interval the establishment of a cathedral and the setting up of a chapter. In certain cases below, the foundation (or restoration) of the see is indicated by 'S'; the foundation of the cathedral by 'C'. Where bishops and archdeacons held canonries, these are included in the figures given for 'canons'. It is virtually impossible to distinguish between chaplains and vicars and the numbers of these are mainly given as identical. Deacons and sub-deacons (except when given as vicars) as well as acolytes, etc., are included with choristers under 'other clergy'. Where there are isolated references to cathedral personnel, especially in the case of chaplains and vicars, the date is given in brackets. Only at Dunkeld and Kirkwall can an accurate number of chaplains be mentioned at a specific date.

The following contractions are used: v.=vicars; ch.=chaplains; d.=deacons; sd.=subdeacons; ac.=acolytes; chr.=choristers; sac.=sacrist.

(I) SECULAR CATHEDRALS

Name	County	Minimum income 1561	Date of foundation	Canons 1560	Vicars Chaplains	Other clergy, choristers etc.
*‡ABERDEEN	Aberdeen	£5170	–1157	30	20 (1506) 24 (1540)	2d 2sd 2 ac. (1506) 6 chr. 1 sac. 8 chr. (1540)
*‡BRECHIN	Angus	£1250	–1150	14	17 (1453)	6 chr. (1429)

201

Name	County	Minimum income 1561	Date of foundation	Canons 1560	Vicars Chaplains	Other clergy, choristers etc.
‡DORNOCH	Sutherland	£1166	c. 1147 × 51(S)	13	10 (c. 1225 ?)	
			1222–3 × 45(C)		4 (1497) 3 (1561)	
‡DUNBANE	Perth	£640	c. 1155(S) 1237 + C	16	9 (1522) 12 (1532/3)	
*‡DUNKELD	Perth	£3400	c. 1114– c. 1120(S)	22	13	6 chr.
*ELGIN	Moray	£5000	c. 1114– c.1120(S) 1207–08 (Spynie) (C) 1224 (Elgin)	25	17 ch. (1350) 25 ch. (1350+) 18–19 v (1489) 14 ch. (1566–72)	some
*FORTROSE (ROSEMARKIE)	Ross and Cromarty	£2100	1127–31	21	5 + v (1255) 3 ch. (1543–6)	some
‡GLASGOW	Lanark	£4400	c. 1114–18 (S) 1136(C)	32	11– numerous	4 + chr.
ISLES	Inverness	?	× 1079	See notes		
‡KIRKWALL	Orkney	£1100	× 1035	14	6 (–1544) 13 (1544)	6 chr. (1544)
‡LISMORE	Argyll	?	1183 × 1189		9–12(?)	

ABERDEEN. The traditions that a see was fd. at Mortlach (*q.v.*) by Malcolm II in 1011 (as given e.g. *Chron. Bower*, lib. iv, cap. xlvi (i, 227) or by Malcolm III in 1063 (as given *Abdn. Reg.*, i, 3) and that the see was transferred by David I to Aberdeen in 1125 (*ibid.*, ii, 227) are discussed *ibid.*, i, xi ff; Skene, *Celtic Scotland*, ii, 378; Lawrie, *Charters*, 230, 354, cf. G. Donaldson, 'Scottish bishops sees before the reign of David I', *PSAS*, lxxxvii (1952–3), 115. While early charters which support these traditions are spurious or suspect, the 'monasterium de Murthillach' is listed as a possession of the ch. of Aberdeen in a papal bull granted 10 Aug. 1157 and may well have been the monastery or minster which tradition associates with the earliest bps. (named Bean, Denortius and Cormac) until their successor Nechtan moved the site of the see to Aberdeen before 1131 × 1132 (Watt, *Fasti*, 1, 5; I. B. Cowan, 'The medieval church in the diocese of Aberdeen', *Northern Scotland*, i, 19–23; Jackson, *Gaelic Notes*, 20, 60–1). On 10 Aug. 1157 his successor, Edward, received authority from Pope Adrian VI to institute monks or canons in his cathedral (*Abdn. Reg.*, i, 6). This may have been an attempt to found a regular chapter either to serve a cathedral which was destitute of clergy or as a means of utilizing an existing body of clergy. In fact no chapter seems to have been formally constituted, although the evidence produces a few stray canons in the early thirteenth c., and two monks of Aberdeen' who may have been connected with tentative plans for a regular chapter occur, 1238–42 (*ibid.*, i, 272). In the event the clergy of the 'city' with the archdeacon, who first appears 1172 × 1179, at their head, appear to have had equal rights with the bp.'s clerks; and the latter only gradually called themselves a chapter and adopted a common seal. At first the two groups intermingled and when the chapter and the clergy of the city were convoked for an episcopal election in 1239 they appointed seven delegates, of whom four were from the chapter and three from the clergy. Thereafter the clergy were excluded and in the following election in 1247 only the dean and chapter were involved.

By this time the Aberdeen chapter had 'a sophisticated corporate character'. This development can be traced from the first appearance of a dean who, initially inferior to the archdeacon in the last quarter of the twelfth c., rose to a position of pre-eminence in the chapter about 1240; it can also be seen in the appearance of a treasurer in 1228 × 1239 and of a chanter and a chancellor in 1240 (Watt, *Fasti*, 5–6; Cowan, *op. cit.*, 23–5). In that year the chapter consisted of the four dignitaries and seven ordinary canons (*Abdn. Reg.*, i, 15). By 1243 the bp. and archdeacon (now clearly inferior to the dean) also appear as members of a chapter which then numbered thirteen (*St. A. Lib.*, 304–5). It is at this figure that the first formal recorded constitution of the chapter was promulgated by Bp. Ramsay, with an allocation of prebends to each of the canons (*Abdn. Reg.*, ii, 38–49). This process had reputedly been started by Bp. Edward (1147 × 1151–71) and continued by his successors. Thereafter, the development of the chapter can be traced through an outline sketch written in 1527 which depicts fairly accurately the successive increase in prebends (*ibid.*, i, 236–55). A fourteenth prebend, Crimond, was added in 1262; four further prebends were erected by Bp. Henry de Cheyne: Lonmay in 1314, Aberdour in 1318, Forbes in 1325 and Ellon in 1328. The hospital of Kincardine o' Neil (*q.v.*) became a prebend in 1330 and five further prebends were added by Bp. Alexander de Kinimund II: Invernochtie in 1356, Philorth in 1361, Methlick in 1362, Tullynestle in 1366 and Drumoak in 1368. The early fifteenth c. saw further additions with the hospital of Turriff (*q.v.*) in 1412 and the ch. of Kinkell and Colstone in 1420 and 1424 respectively. The last two additions to the chapter, according to the 1527 account, took place in 1445 when prebends were created from the revenues of the hospital of Rathven (*q.v.*) and the ch. of Monymusk. By 1445, therefore, Aberdeen had a cathedral chapter consisting of four dignitaries, an archdeacon and twenty-four simple canonries, one of which was held by the bp. (*RSCHS*, xiv, 41–42; Cowan, *op. cit.*, 27–33). Only one further prebend was to be added, although prebends *ad vitam* appear from time to time (*RSCHS*, xiv, 38–39). This was the prebend of the sub-chanter which first appears in the sixteen c. founded upon the revenues of Aberdeen—Spittal (see under Hospitals, ABERDEEN–ST. PETER). A sub-chanter is first found in 1533/4 and as the prebend is unmentioned in the 1527 account, it may have been founded between 1527 and 1534 (Cowan, *op. cit.*, 33). With this addition the cathedral constitution had been completed; an establishment of thirty canons consisting of four dignitaries, sub-chanter, archdeacon and twenty-four prebendaries.

BRECHIN. The first recorded bp. appears *c.* 1160 (Lawrie, *Charters*, 180); but the origins of the see, though uncertain, are probably earlier (see p. 46 above; Donaldson, 'Scottish bishops' sees', 113–14). This was the site of a community of Culdees who with a prior at their head formed a chapter together with certain other unspecified clerks during the twelfth and early thirteenth c. (*Arb. Lib.*, i, no. 188; Theiner, *Vet. Mon.*, no. xix). By 1246 a college of canons had emerged, apparently by an act of Bp. Gregory (1218–42) referred to in a papal bull of 18 Feb. 1250 which refers to the fact that 'the brethren who have wont to be in the ch. of Brechin were called Keledei and now by change of name are styled canons' (*Lind. Cart.*, no. xcix). Probably the four major dignities in addition to the older office of archdeacon, which first appears 1189 × 1198, were founded at this time, the dean appearing in 1248, the chanter in 1246, the chancellor in 1274 and the treasurer between 1219 and 1246 (Watt, *Fasti*, 42–49). There were at least six or seven prebends by 1274–5 when one (Kilmoir) and possibly two simple prebends are noted in addition to the dignitaries and archdeacon previously recorded (*SHS, Misc.*, vi, 52–3, 69–70). In the first formal definition of the state of the chapter, eleven prebends including now a sub-deanery, are recorded, two of the five simple prebends being founded on the vicarage revenues of Brechin and the remainder on revenues derived from the chs. of Buttergill, Guthrie and Kilmoir (*Brech. Reg.*, i, no. 15). To these were added Lethnot in 1384/5; Glenbervie in 1422, the parsonage of Brechin as the prebend of the bp. before 1435 and Finhaven in 1474. The extinction of the prebend of Guthrie in 1479 on the erection of the collegiate ch. of Guthrie (*q.v.*) reduced the total and the number of prebends stood thereafter at fourteen (*RSCHS*, xiv, 29–30, 42).

DORNOCH. The see was probably founded by David I, *c.* 1147 × 1151, as part of a deliberate move by that king to detach the area north of the river Oykell, which had been under the political influence of the E. of Orkney and may have been ecclesiastically under the bps. of Orkney, from its Norse loyalties (Watt, *Fasti*, 62). Its first recorded bp., Andrew, had been a monk of Dunfermline and appears to have taken fellow monks north with him with the possible intention of founding a monastic cathedral (*Dunf. Reg.*, no. 23; Lawrie, *Charters*, no. cxxxii; Watt, *Fasti*, 58, 62). Nothing came of this intention and the whereabouts of the cathedral under the early bps., who appear to have resided at the episcopal manor of Halkirk, is unknown (*ibid.*, 62). Only with the establishment of Scottish line of earls of Caithness after 1231, and during the episcopate of Gilbert de Moravia (1222-3-1245), was the ch. of Dornoch rebuilt and developed as the cathedral of the diocese. In place of the single priest who had previously served the church, an establishment of ten canons headed by the bp. and including four dignitaries and the archdeacon was proposed. The surviving draft of this constitution is undated, but the proposals contained in it were confirmed in essence by a papal bull issued 21 March 1238 × 20 March 1239 (*ibid.*, 62; *Bannatyne Misc.*, iii, 17–21; *Reg. Gregoire IX*, no. 4423). This constitution utilized as prebends all the existing parish chs. of the diocese which were not mensal or common chs. and it may have taken some time to fully implement. However, it seems to have been fully operative by 1274-5 by which date an additional prebend of Assynt, which had possibly been disjoined from the parish of Criech, had been added to the four simple prebends of Cannisby, Dunnet, Olrig and Kildonan, the latter being held in terms of the original constitution by the ab. of Scone to whose abbey the ch. was appropriated (*SHS, Misc.*, vi, 51–2, 68–9; *Bannatyne Misc.*, iii, 17–21; Cowan, *Parishes*, 9). At some unknown date before the Reformation, the revenues, either in whole or in part, of the hospital of Helmsdale (× 1558) and the chaplaincy of Kinnald (× 1560) were utilized to endow two further prebends, making a final establishment of thirteen prebends in all (*RSCHS*, xiv, 35–6, 42–3). The bp. and the dignitaries were bound to provide priests as their vicars (i.e. in the cathedral) and the simple canons vicars in deacon's orders (*Bannatyne Misc.*, iii, 11–14, 17–21) see, also *OPS*, ii², 601 ff.; Skene, *Celtic Scotland*, ii, 382–4.

DUNBLANE. There was an early fd'n. here (*q.v.*), but the presence of Culdees cannot be authenticated. A Culdee community was, however, situated at Muthill (*q.v.*), and the early history of the see may have been associated with that site rather than with Dunblane itself. The first recorded bp. occurs in 1155, but the see might have been reconstituted rather than founded at about this date (Watt, *Fasti*, 75; Donaldson, 'Scottish bishops' sees', 116). The first archdeacon on record 1165 × 1171 used the title 'Muthill' and while his successors used Dunblane and Strathearn as their title, Dunblane did not become the standard title until the mid-thirteenth c. (Watt, *Fasti*, 88). Early bps. exhibited the same duality and Bp. Osbert (1226 × 1227–31) not only used the title 'of Strathearn' in place of Dunblane but concentrated on the Strathearn section of his diocese in which Muthill lay rather than on the Menteith section in which Dunblane itself lay (*ibid.*, 78–9). Deans of Dunblane found from *c.* 1170 onwards are apparently of the early type who were of lesser status than the archdeacons, and the separation of the diocese into two sections of Menteith/Dunblane and Muthill/Strathearn is reflected in the appearance of deans for both sections in the thirteenth c. (*ibid.*, 79–80, 91). Malgirhe, designated as canon, witnesses a charter of Bp. Simon *c.* 1190 in company with one of the Culdees of Muthill and would seem himself to be identifiable with Malgirk de Mothel who in turn may be identical with Malkirg, prior of the Culdees of Muthill in the early thirteenth c. (*Inchaff. Chrs.*, nos. i, iii, xiii; *N.B. Chrs.*, 12). Even without this identification, it would appear that a comparable situation to that at Brechin existed in this diocese whereby a community of Culdees with a prior at their head formed a chapter together with the archdeacon, deans and other clergy of the diocese for whom the right of election is claimed in 1234 (*Inchaff. Chrs.*, lx).

However, the conversion of the Culdees into canons which occurred at Brechin did not occur here, possibly because of a reversion in favour of Dunblane during the episcopate of Bp. Clement (1233–58). This bp. found the ch. at Dunblane roofless, its property alienated to laymen and served not by a college of clergy, but just by 'a certain rural chaplain'; he obtained a papal mandate 11 June 1237 to bp. of Glasgow and Dunkeld to make provision for the bp. from the fourth part of the teinds of the parishes of his diocese, out of which he was to assign portions for the dean and canons whom the mandatories were to institute. Alternatively, they were to assign to the bp. the fourth part of the teinds of the parishes of his diocese held by laymen and to transfer the see to the mon. of St. John [Inchaffray], the canons of which are to have power to elect the bp. when the ch. of Dunblane is vacant (*Inchaff. Liber.*, xxx; *Arb. Lib.*, i, 176; Theiner, *Vet. Mon.*, no. xci). The latter course was not followed; for soon after (1 July 1238), the ch. of Kippen was assigned as a simple prebend (*Inchaff. Liber.*, xxxi) and, on 29 Jan. 1239/40 the dean and chanter along with the older-established archdeacon are found acting as the chapter of Dunblane and using a capitular seal (*Inchaff. Chrs.*, no. lxvii). On the latter date also, the ab. of Cambuskenneth was granted a canonry of Dunblane (*Cam. Reg.*, no. 125) and about the same time (1238–1240) similar agreements were concluded with other interested monasteries who held appropriated chs. in the diocese. The ab. of Arbroath became a canon, the ab. of Inchaffray, chanter and the ab. of Lindores may likewise have become a canon (*Inchaff. Chrs.* no. xxxvii, *Arb. Lib.*, i, no. 241; Theiner, *Vet. Mon.*, no. ccclxxxvi). In consequence the fourth part of the teinds due from chs. annexed to these houses were remitted by the bp., and eventually only five chs.—Balquhidder, Comrie, Fossoway and Tulliallan whose quarters went to the bp. and Tullibole whose quarter went to the dean—paid the dues stipulated in the 1237 mandate (*RSCHS*, xiv, 34).

It is not certain whether the newly established chapter managed immediately to exclude the other diocesan clergy from participating in episcopal elections (Watt, *Fasti*, 79) but an election of 1296 was made by the abs. of Cambuskenneth Inchaffray and Arbroath (as canons), the dean, archdeacon, chancellor, treasurer (first found in 1274) and two other unidentified canons (*CPL*, i, 567). A gradual build-up of the chapter occurred thereafter and prebends of Aberfoyle, Abernethy, Balquhidder, Comrie, Glendevon, Kippen Logie-Atheron and Monzie appear in the course of the fifteenth and sixteenth c. Only the erection of Kippen can be assigned with certainty to the period before 1296 and with the exception of Abernethy founded 1427×1465, the others may have been founded before or after that date (*RSCHS*, xiv, 43). A sub-deanery with an annexed vicarage of Muthill appears in 1468 (Reg. Supp., 626, fo. 144), and, omitting the ab. of Lindores, the final state of the chapter was four dignitaries, the archdeacon and eleven prebends. With the omission of the abbots, a reconstitution of the chapter in 1663 which found it 'most convenient to continue the ministers [of] these kirks who were formerly of the chapter in the same statioun degree and place as they were of old' (NLS, MS. 34.4.8) confirms this as the final constitution. Nine chaplains are recorded 14 May 1522 (*HMC, Rep. Var. Collins*, v, 70) and twelve chaplains (of the choir), 18 Jan. 1532/3 (*RMS*, iii, no. 1257).

DUNKELD. This was the site of an early bishopric (see below). The bishopric is said to have been revived by Alexander I (1106/7–24) (Dowden, *Bishops*, 47). The succession of bps. begins *c.* 1114 or *c.* 1120 (Watt, *Fasti*, 94), but the first casual, isolated mention of the name of a bp. (Donaldson, 'Scottish bishops' sees', 112) is insufficient evidence to confirm this speculation. Originally the diocese included the territory of the diocese of Argyll which was separated from it 1183×1189 (see Lismore; Myln, *Vitae*, 8). A community of the early church apparently continued to function here in the twelfth c., but whether it was a community of Culdees, as late tradition averred, is not proven (see under Early Foundations). There is no certain evidence that they ever formed a chapter for the see, although they may have constituted the bishop's *familia*. The Dunkeld tradition of sixteenth c. was that a new college of secular canons was established in the reign of David I (1124–53), but no such college existed until the following century (Watt, *Fasti*, 101). Nevertheless, a papal confirmation, apparently at the request of the bp., 7 June 1163 gave the right to elect the bp. to the 'canons of Dunkeld' who may be identifiable with the personnel of the original community (Fraser, *Wemyss*, ii, 1–3). No clerk with this designation appears in surviving twelfth c. witness lists (Watt, *Fasti*, 101), but at an episcopal election of 1211, the archdeacon who first appears on record in 1177 presided over a synodal assembly including both the 'chapter' and 'all the clergy' of the diocese (*ibid.*, 101). The nature of the 'chapter' is uncertain but does not appear to have been restricted to any particular group of clergy as an act of the chapter 1214×1223 (still under the archdeacon and including a dean who is inferior to him in status) indicates a wide membership with a synodal character (*ibid.*, 101). Shortly afterwards clergy came to be designated as canons, and one is occasionally referred to as chanter, but the archdeacon appears to have retained his precedency until *c.* 1230. At about that time Bp. Gilbert and not Bp. Geoffrey his successor (cf. Myln, *Vitae*, 10) converted the synodal diocesan chapter into a collegiate body at the cathedral. A dean (who had previously been one of the canons) is found presiding over the 'chapter of Dunkeld' in place of the archdeacon 1231×1236, and it is the dean and chapter who elected Bp. Geoffrey 1236; the dean had certainly become superior in status to the archdeacon by 21 Dec. 1238 (Watt, *Fasti*, 102). On that date the dean, chanter, treasurer, sub-dean, sub-chanter and one canon appear on record and while the office of chancellor does not appear until 1274, it is difficult to believe that it was not in existence at this earlier date. (*Inchaff. Chrs.*, 56–57; SHS, Misc., vi, 48).

Further developments followed in the episcopate of Geoffrey (1236–49), who added the ch. of Crieff as a prebend, and sixteenth c. tradition may be correct in attributing to him the introduction of chapter statutes on the model of Salisbury and encouraging the develop- of a large resident community of clergy (Myln, *Vitae.*, 9–10). By 1274 in addition to prebends pertaining to the six dignitaries, archdeacon and canon of Crieff, seven other simple prebends—Caputh, Craigie, Fongarth, Inchmagrannoch, Menmuir, Moneydie, and Ruffel—had been erected either by or subsequent to the original fd'n. (*SHS, Misc.*, vi, 47–49). Myln declares that the building of the cathedral was begun by Bp. William Sinclair (1309/10–1337) (*Vitae*, 13); this ch., which must have replaced an earlier cathe- dral, was dedicated by Bp. Thomas de Lawder in 1464 (*ibid.*, 22–3). Seven more simple prebends were added between 1274 and 1506 when the state of the chapter is recorded as, a dean, chanter, chancellor, treasurer, archdeacon, sub-dean, sub-chanter and fifteen canons (Myln, *Vitae*, 2, 55–68). Of the seven, three—Aberlady, Alyth and Muckersie— were erected 1452 × 1469 (*ibid.*, 24), and another, Ferdischaw, which had apparently previously been a prebend, was reconstituted as such 1484 × 1506 (*ibid.*, 41–42). The remaining three prebends—Fearn, Forgandenny and Lundeiff appear for the first time during the fifteenth c. and may have been constituted during that period. This is con- firmed as the final state of the chapter in 1564 (*Dunkeld Rentale*, 346–51).

ELGIN. Early bps. of Moray may have existed before *c.* 1114 or *c.* 1120 when the first bp. appears on record, but this is far from certain (Watt, *Fasti*, 214; Donaldson, 'Scottish bishops' sees', 115). Little is known about the early history of the see, but the appearance of an archdeacon between 1179 and 1188 and the occurrence of a dean who is inferior in status would suggest that any chapter was of synodal nature with the archdeacon as its head (Watt, *Fasti*, 218, 237). Before the appointment of Bp. Brice de Douglas in 1203 the earlier bps. of Moray had no fixed place for their see, but alternated between Birnie, Spynie and Kineddar, all of which are near Elgin (*Moray Reg.*, no. 46). Following a papal mandate of 7 April 1206 Bp. Douglas fixed his see at Spynie (March 1207 × June 1208) (*ibid.*, nos. 45–46). But, following upon another papal mandate of 10 April 1224 trans- ferred the see to Elgin where the cathedral was founded 19 July 1224 (*ibid.*, nos. 26, 57, 58; *Vet. Mon.*, no. lii). On 17 June 1390 it was burned, along with the canons' and chap- lains' houses, by the 'Wolf of Badenoch' (*Moray Reg.*, no. 303). Bp. Douglas's foundation at Spynie in 1208 was for a community of eight canons, including the dean, chanter, treasurer, chancellor and archdeacon with three ordinary canons maintained by the prebends of Dipple and Ruthven, Inveravon and Urquhart and Spynie and Kintray (*ibid.*, no. 46). The constitution of the cathedral was modelled on Lincoln (*ibid.*). 'It is an interesting fact that the earliest account of the constitution of Lincoln that now appears anywhere is to be found in the document supplied [i.e. *ibid.*, no. 48] . . . at request by the dean and chapter of Lincoln to the dean and chapter of Moray' (Dowden, *Medieval Church*, 65).

The erection of new prebends was undertaken following the transference of the cathedral. A sub-dean and a sub-chanter appear in 1225 (Watt, *Fasti*, 231, 233), and papal authorization for four simple prebends was granted on 20 April 1224 (*Moray Reg.*, nos. 55, 67). These arrangements were formalized 5 May 1226 when the arrangements of 1208 were slightly altered as one of the simple prebends, Inveravon and Urquhart, was allocated to the chancellor whose existing prebend, derived from the lands of Fothervais (Ferness), was granted to the bp. (as a canon). The sub-deanship and sub-chantership were now added to the four dignitaries and archdeaconry and with the further addition of eight new simple prebends—Aberlour and Botriphnie, Advie and Cromdale, Botarie and Elchies, Brachlie and Petty, Dunbennan and Kinnoir, Inverkeithy, May and Rhynie —the establishment reached a total of eighteen (*ibid.*, no. 69). Two further prebends— Croy and Lunan and Insh and Kingussie— were added later in 1226 (*ibid.*, no. 68) and Duffus became a prebend before 1237 (*ibid.*, no. 81). A further constitution before the end of Bp. Andrew's episcopate in 1242 reveals the addition of two further prebends, Duthil and another derived from one hundred shillings of the vicarage revenues of Elgin (*ibid.*, no. 81). Twenty-three canons therefore existed before 1242 and little change took place thereafter. Prebends *ad vitam* appear from time to time, and another additional prebend of Kincardine, which continued as such, appears in 1537 (*RSCHS*, xiv, 39; *RSS*, ii, no. 2412). The final addition of Unthank as a prebend in 1542 raised the number of canonries to twenty-five (*Moray Reg.*, no. 474; *RSCHS*, xiv, 44). Bp. Andrew also made provision for seventeen vicars of whom seven (priests) were to be provided by the chancellor, treasurer, archdeacon, sub-dean and sub-chanter and two canons; five (deacons) by five of the canons, and five (sub-deacons) by the five remaining canons. The eighth canon (of Croy) was to act as bp.'s vicar and the sub-dean and sub-chanter are apparently regarded as vicars of the dean and chanter (*Moray Reg.*, no. 81). This number seems to have varied little; in 1489, arrangements are made for the payment of eighteen vicars (stallers) and a sacrist (*ibid.*, no. 210). How far these correspond with the seventeen resident chaplains mentioned, 1331–50 (*ibid.*, no. 277) it is impossible to say. The chaplainries numbered twenty-five shortly after this date (*ibid.*, no. 278). The number of boy-choristers is not given but provision is made, in 1489, for their instruction (*ibid.*, no. 210).

FORTROSE (ROSEMARKIE). There was apparently an early fd'n. here (*q.v.*) but the presence of Culdees is not authenticated. The see of Ross, usually designated as Rosemarkie in the twelfth c., first appears on record 1127 × 1131 but may antedate this period and St. Duthac (d. 1065) may have served as a bp. in this area though connected with Tain rather than with Rosemarkie (Watt, *Fasti*, 226). Little information is forthcoming on the development of the chapter which probably came into existence in the early thirteenth c. The dean and chancellor are found between 1212 and 1233 and the archdeacon appears in the latter year (Watt, *Fasti*, 271, 277, 285). A charter of 1 Feb. 1226/7 is signed by the bp. of Ross (as canon), the dean, treasurer, archdeacon (who is also a canon), two canons of Ross, a canon who is also parson of Ardersier and another canon of Ross who is also a canon of Moray (*Moray Reg.*, no. 75). The chapter was evidently well established by this date and a papal mandate 29 May 1235 stating that there were only four prebends in the ch. of Ross evidently refers to the similarly named Irish diocese (Theiner, *Vet. Mon.*, no. lxxx; Gwynn and Hadcock, *Medieval Religious Houses Ireland*, 96; cf. Watt, *Fasti*, 271). By 9 Feb. 1255/6 a deanery, chantership, chancellorship, treasurership, archdeaconry, sub-deanery and sub-chantership with their associated prebends and several undesignated simple prebends were in existence in ch. of Rosemarkie (situated in modern Fortrose) when papal confirmation of these and of statutes governing the conduct of the cathedral community was granted by Pope Alexander VI (Theiner, *Vet. Mon.*, no. clxxxii). According to this document, the dean is to be elected 'as in the church of Sarum', but there is no further suggestion that Salisbury is the model of the cathedral constitution. It is not until the fourteenth and in most cases the fifteenth c. that it is possible to identify most of the simple prebends although some clearly existed at an earlier date. The ab. of Kinloss was a canon of Ross in respect of the appropriated ch. of Avoch before 5 Jan. 1324/5 and in the same century four other prebends—Contin, Cullicudden, Logie Easter and Newnakle with Roskeen—have been noted. Seven more prebends—Alness, Dingwall, Kilmuir-Easter, Kiltearn, Kincardine, Kirkmichael and Lemlair—appear in the following century and yet another, Kilchrist, does not appear as such until 1560 (*RSCHS*, xiv, 44–45). All in all, twenty-one prebends involving the revenues of thirty-one chs. have been accounted for and as these, with six chs. pertaining to the chapter in common, account for every ch. in the diocese, this total may be accepted with some finality (*RSCHS*, xiv, 25–6, 36, 44–5; Cowan, *Parishes*, 218).

GLASGOW. Three bps. bearing this title occur in the eleventh and early twelfth c. but they may in practice have been suffragan bps. of the abp. of York within his diocese and may have had nothing to do with Glasgow itself (Watt, *Fasti*, 143). The see was apparently revived by Earl David (afterwards David I) *c.* 1114 × 1118 (*ibid.*, 143; Donaldson, 'Scottish bishops' sees,' 114, 116). There seems to be no suggestion of Culdees at Glasgow; and apart from its legendary association with St. Kentigern, its connection with the early ch. is difficult to define (see GLASGOW and GOVAN under Early Foundations). Early bps. were involved in resisting the metropolitan authority of York and this was not resolved until the status of direct subjection to Rome as a *filia specialis* was obtained for the see of Glasgow in 1175 and confirmed in 1176 and 1192. The see was placed under the metropolitan authority of St. Andrews 14 Aug. 1472 and itself achieved archiepiscopal and metropolitan status 9 Jan. 1492 (Watt, *Fasti*, 143–4). The ch. of Glasgow was dedicated 7 July 1136 (*Chron. Holyrood*, 119). It was possibly thereafter that Bp. John (1118–47) established a group of secular canons at Glasgow supported, both by a common fund, and the allocation of individual prebends, the former means of endowment possibly preceding the creation of prebends. However, at least four and possibly as many as six prebends were founded by Bp. John from a miscellaneous range of revenues including the chs. of Glasgow, Hamilton (later allocated to the dean), Renfrew and possibly Govan, a prebend which John's successor Herbert may have augmented rather than fd. 1147–64 (*Glas. Reg.*, nos. 7, 28, 66). As the common fund, in which a seventh canon whose prebend was fd. by Bp. Herbert was allowed to participate, had been originally divided among six canons it seems likely that John's original fd'n. had been for six canons (*ibid.*, no. 66). The single archdeacon of this period who first appears 1126 × 1127 may have been head of this community which nevertheless appears to be collegiate rather than synodal in character (Watt, *Fasti*, 152, 170). A dean, who first appears 1159 × 1164 was thereafter regarded as head of the community of canons, and the dean and canons confirmed their right to elect the bps. of Glasgow 1174 (*ibid.*, 152).

No formal act of constitution of the chapter survives but the other dignitaries appear comparatively late in the twelfth and early thirteenth c.—the chantership 1179 × 1221, the chancellorship 1249 × 1258 and the treasureship 1195 × 1196 (Watt, *Fasti*, 156, 160, 164). Simple prebends were added during the same period. Carnwath, which later became the treasurer's prebend, was erected 1180 × 1186, Morebattle by 1228 and between 1233 and 1258 the ch. of Peebles was assigned to the archdeacon of Glasgow (*Glas. Reg.*, i, nos. 52–53, 89, 147). The ch. of Old Roxburgh had become a prebend by 1304 and Campsie may have been the chancellor's prebend by 1267 (*CDS*, ii, no. 1502; *Kel. Lib.*, no. 229). Eddleston may have been a prebend before 1233 although confirmation is not certain until 1394 (Keith, *Scottish Bishops*, 238; *CPP*, i, 590), while the division of the diocese into two archdeaconries Jan. × March 1237/8 was followed by the allocation of the prebend of Morebattle to the newly created archdeacon of Teviotdale and the chs. of Peebles and Manor to the archdeacons of Glasgow 1233 × 1257 (Cowan, *Parishes*, 151–2; Watt, *Fasti*, 170, 174). In the absence of a constitution, the state of the chapter at the end of the thirteenth c. is hard to determine as most of the early prebends based on miscellaneous revenues appear, with the exception of Barlanark, to have been suppressed as endowments based on parish chs. became more readily available. By 1189, during the episcopate of Bishop Jocelin, there were at least seven canons as well as the dean and archdeacon (*Glas. Reg.*, i, no. 29), and that bp. dedicated the cathedral which he had built anew 6 July 1197 (*Melrose Chron.*, 103). In 1248 there were at least four dignitaries, an archdeacon and nine simple prebends (*CPL*, i, 257).

The constitution of the cathedral of Salisbury was, with certain modifications, adopted as a model for Glasgow in 1258, earlier attempts to adopt this constitution having met with little success (*Glas. Reg.*, i, nos. 28, 207, 208, 211, 213–14). In 1259 four dignitaries, two archdeacons, a sacristan and seven canons are listed (*ibid.*, i, no. 208). The sub-deanery which does not appear to have been in existence at this date appears in 1266 and holds the prebend of Cadder and Monkland before 1350 (*ibid.*, no. 212; *CPP*, i, 201). By 1325 four dignitaries, two archdeacons and ten canons are listed (*Glas. Reg.*, i, no. 273); in 1401 twenty-three prebends are listed. Of these Ashkirk (× 1390), Ayr (× 1327), Cardross (× 1371), Erskine (× 1358), Glasgow Secundo (× 1379), Moffat (× 1375) and Stobo (× 1349) had earlier been recorded as prebends but Ancrum, and Carstairs both appear for the first time on this list (*RSCHS*, xiv, 45–46; *Glas. Reg.*, i, no. 320; Reg. Aven., 198, fo. 367). On the other hand Durisdeer, which appears as a prebend × 1375, does not appear on this list (Cowan, *Parishes*, 56). Polmadie was erected as a prebend in 1427/8, only to be extinguished in 1453/4 (*RSCHS*, xiv, 28, 46). Six new prebends—Cambuslang, Eaglesham, Killearn, Kirkmahoe, Luss and Tarbolton—were added by Bp. John Cameron, 1429–*c.* 1430 (*ibid.*, xiv, 45–46), and these were joined by a further three—Sanquhar (× 1460), Cumnock (× 1453) and Douglas (× 1460)— in mid-century (*ibid.*, 45–6). In the same period a sub-chantership was erected by Bp. Andrew de Durisdeer 1455 × 1471, and the prebend of Durisdeer annexed to it (Watt, *Fasti*, 169). Thirty-two prebends existed at this period. An attempt by the bp. in 1487 to obtain the prebend of Barlanark as an episcopal prebend and create an additional prebend of Dryfesdale in lieu was unsuccessful (*RSCHS*, xiv, 23). An additional prebend of Mearns is listed in 1501/2, but does not reappear, and although thirty-three prebends are again listed in 1571, the additional prebend in this instance, Baldernock, neither appears as a prebend before or after this date. Both erections appear to be prebends *ad vitam* (prebends created only for the lifetime of the incumbent), and the final state of the chapter would appear to be four dignitaries, sub-dean, sub-chanter, two archdeacons and twenty-six canons, giving thirty-two prebends in all (*RSCHS*, xiv, 26–29, 45–46).

Isles. Alternative titles used by the bps. of the Isles who appear × 1079 include Skye, Man, Sudreys and Sodor. These bishops appear to have recognized metropolitan authority of York until 1153, when they were placed under Nidaros/Trondheim; some bps. continued to seek confirmation from York or (exceptionally) Dublin until early thirteenth c. The rights of Trondheim were reduced to a nominal level after 1349 when a papal grace excused the bp. from a personal visit to Trondheim to profess obedience. Two separate lines of bps. based on Man and the Isles respectively emerge as a result of the Great Schism from 1387 onwards (Watt, *Fasti*, 197–202). The see was thereafter treated as other Scottish bishoprics as falling under papal authority (*ibid.*, 203) until placed under the metropolitan authority of St. Andrews, 14 Aug. 1472 (*ibid.*, 197). The right to elect the bp. was held by monks of Furness abbey from grant of Olaf, K. of Man in 1134 and finally confirmed by Pope Innocent IV, 1244. This right was challenged from time to time and rejected by Alexander III, K. of Scots, in 1275. Simon, bp. of the Isles (1226–48) began to build the cathedral of St. German at Peel, Isle of Man, which existed by 1231, but the chapter of secular clergy who are found acting in episcopal elections thereafter appear to be of a synodal nature representing the clergy of the island rather than a cathedral chapter; an archdeacon, who first appears 1188 × 1190, possibly acting as their head rather than a cathedral dignitary, of which no others are known to exist (*ibid.*, 201–2, 207). Even before the split occasioned by the Great Schism, a separatist trend is observable in the Scottish part of the diocese. A group of canons of Snizort along with the clergy of Skye elected a bp., 1326 × 1331. This community may have had a continuous existence from the eleventh c. when an earlier bp. of Skye is recorded. The clergy there certainly provided a cathedral chapter of some sort for the bp. of Sodor in Scotland after the split of 1387, though by 1433 Bp. Angus de Insulis was petitioning the Pope to authorize him to transfer his cathedral ch. from Snizort (Suusperdy) to some honest place within the diocese and of creating a community of twelve canons with as many prebends (Watt, *Fasti*, 207; *RSCHS*, xiv, 23–24). Two ordinary prebends have been found thereafter in Strath on Skye in 1450 and Kingarth in Bute in 1463 (Cowan, *Parishes*, 112, 190), but both revert to their original status and archdeacon is still the only dignitary found (*ibid.*, Watt, *Fasti*, 207). Iona abbey (see under Monastic Cathedrals) was to become the cathedral of the Scottish diocese in 1498, but this was not successful, and successive bps. held the abbey *in commendam*. There is no evidence to prove that the Benedictine monks ever formed the chapter; indeed a Sodor chancellor appears as a secular dignity by 1541, in addition to the archdeaconry, and a dean may also have existed before 1560 (Watt, *Fasti*, 207–9).

Kirkwall. Early bps. of Orkney, the first of whom was appointed before 1035, recognized metropolitan authority of York in early eleventh c. Hamburg-Bremen supplied three bps. in the period 1043 × 1072; then York appointed three 1073–*c.* 1112, but the last nominee failed to gain possession and an alternative bp. appointed *c.* 1112 probably accepted metropolitan authority of Lund. A plan in 1151 to place this diocese under St. Andrews as metropolitan was rejected in favour of putting Orkney under Nidaros/Trondheim in 1153 (Watt, *Fasti*, 247; R. G. Cant, 'The Church in Orkney and Shetland and its relations with Norway and Scotland in the Middle Ages', *Northern Scotland*, i, 1–18). It remained under Trondheim until after political transfer of Orkney and Shetland to Scotland 1468–9, and was then put under new metropolitan see of St. Andrews, 17 Aug. 1472 (Watt, *Fasti*, 247). The first known cathedral was situated at Christ's Kirk, Birsay 1048 × 1065, from which it was moved to Kirkwall following the erection of the cathedral of St. Magnus founded by Earl Rognvald in 1137 (Anderson, *Orkneyinga Saga*, lxxxiv–lxxxviii). The move was not immediate and for some years after 1135 the bp. was resident on Egilsay where there was a ch. dedicated to St. Magnus (Cant, 'Church in Orkney and Shetland', 4–5). Part of the new cathedral at Kirkwall existed by 1155 and archaeological evidence would appear to suggest that a monastic ch. with a Benedictine community may originally have been intended, but this plan was altered when it was decided to institute a chapter of secular canons in the early thirteenth c. (Watt, *Fasti*, 254).

First indication of a chapter is at election of Bp. Henry in 1247, and although there is no evidence whether this chapter was of a synodal or collegiate character, the fact that Henry was a canon of Orkney when elected would seem to point to the latter type. A group of such canons is identifiable from then on, and possessed a sufficiently corporate character by 1266 to be appointed to receive annual payments for the K. of Norway from the K. of Scots (Watt, *Fasti*, 255). Prebends came to be attached to these canonries; four of these

Stronsay, Sandwick, Holy Cross, Sanday and one identified only by the name of its holder appearing on record in 1327–8 (Ian B. Cowan, 'Two early Scottish taxation rolls', *Innes Review*, xxii, 8–9, 11). A further ten named prebends have been identified in the fifteenth and early sixteenth c., two of these Birsay and Harray and Tingwall, Whiteness and Weisdale being held by the archdeacons of Orkney and Shetland respectively (*RSCHS*, xiv, 46). These are the only known dignitaries in this period, archdeacons of Shetland appearing from 1215 and of Orkney from 1309, and it has been suggested (Watt, *Fasti*, 255) that of the two, that of Shetland was established first, and as the holder of the senior office, when the community of canons of Kirkwall was being developed, became the customary president of the chapter. A total establishment of thirteen canons is a possibility but it is unlikely that the number remained constant. Sandwick never reappears as a prebend and others such as Kirkwall–St. Olaf and Stronsay–Lady only appear in the fifteenth c. Nevertheless, ten prebends can be identified in the sixteenth c., two of these pertaining to the respective archdeacons and eight to canons who appear in groupings of six in 1539 and 1544. In that year Bp. Reid gave his cathedral a new constitution 28 Oct. 1544 asserting (with no mention of either archdeacon as such) 'that only six canons and as many chaplains . . . were known hitherto to be erected within the same'. A comparison of the prebends recorded in 1539 and 1544 reveals, however, that in only four cases do the prebends correspond, and the inference must be that either the bp.'s statement is not entirely reliable, or if it is accurate that the number of canons was maintained at six by interchanging, as the occasion arose, the chs. which could be used, as prebends. If this was the case, it might also explain the assertion that what pertained by the foundation to each of the canons was unknown (*RSCHS*, xiv, 39–40, 47). The new constitution established a chapter comprising of four dignitaries, with a provost as head, archdeacon, sub-dean, sub-chanter, seven other canons, thirteen chaplains and six boys (*RMS*, iii, no. 3102). The bp. obtained the revenues of Kirkwall–St. Olaf, as an episcopal prebend, but no provision was made for the archdeacon of Shetland, some of whose former revenues went to the provost (Watt, *Fasti*, 255). Members of the old chapter continued to retain their prebends and this constitution, which allowed for fifteen canons in all, did not become immediately operative and was apparently not fully implemented until *c.* 1588/9 (*RSCHS*, xiv, 24–25).

LISMORE. The diocese of Argyll of Lismore was formed by subdivision from Dunkeld 1183 × 1189 (*Chron. Bower*, i, 356–7; *Le Liber censuum de l'eglise romaine* ed. Paul Fabre and L. Duchesne, Paris, 1889–1910, i, text, 230–2, ii, 101, 106). The see was located on the island of Lismore in Loch Linnhe apparently from 1225 and probably from time of erection of the diocese (cf. *PSAS*, xc, 209; *TSES*, xv, pt. i, 41–50). The view that the see was first located at Muckairn on the south side of Loch Etive (Skene, *Celtic Scotland*, ii, 408) seems to be based on the interpretation of the place-name Killespeckerrill as 'the church of Bishop Harold' and is entirely conjectural. A reference to the dean and chapter of Lismore in 1203 (*CPL*, i, 15) can be no more than 'common form'. A dean found in 1240 is apparently of the early type who were of lesser status than the archdeacons who first appear 1230 × 1236 (*PSAS*, xc, 219; *Pais. Reg.*, 135–6). On 7 July 1236, the bishopric which had been in charge of the bp. of the Isles, is said to be in great poverty (Theiner *Vet. Mon.*, no. lxxxiv). The see was vacant for at least seven years before 23 Dec. 1248 when the Pope empowered the bps. of Dunblane and Glasgow to arrange an election (*ibid.*, no. cxxxix). On 2 Jan. 1249 authority was given to transfer the see from the island of Lismore to a safer and more convenient place (*ibid.*, no. cxl). The king was said to be willing to endow a new cathedral ch., and Alexander II's gift of the ch. of Kilbride (near modern Oban) on his deathbed, 3 July 1249, may have been a move to this end (*PSAS*, xc, 218, cf. 210); but the king's death in fact prevented any move from Lismore. A canon of the ch. appears by 27 Sept. 1250 (*Pais. Reg.*, 134) and notice of the dean and 'all the chapter' occurs in 1251 (*RMS*, ii, no. 3136). But the electoral chapter, under the presidency of a dean from at least 1262 × 1264 (*Reg. Urbain IV*, iii, no. 1496), appears to have remained of a synodal character until the mid-fourteenth c., when as late as 26 Sept. 1357 the bp. could not produce a common chapter seal *quia totus clerus eligit* (*APS*, i, 294; *CDS* iii, no. 1650); yet some kind of lesser chapter of a collegiate character was emerging within the synodal framework before then—the seal of some kind of chapter was attached to an episcopal act 18 Nov. 1327 (*Pais Reg.*, 137). Clarification of this situation was undoubtedly required after a double episcopal election in 1342 when the 'chapter' (presumably those clergy associated with the cathedral) acted separately from the 'clergy of the city and diocese' (Dowden, *Medieval Church*, 37). It was probably thereafter during the episcopate of Bp. Martin de Argyll (1342–62), and presumably after 1357 (see above) that a fully constituted secular chapter emerged with three dignities in addition to the deanery and the old office of archdeacon appearing by the late fourteenth c. (Watt, *Fasti*, 29–34). Simple prebends were erected at the same time; there were originally four in number, making a total of nine canonries, to which Bp. Martin added Kilcolmkill as a tenth prebend (Reg. Aven., 230, fo. 232v). The four original prebends were apparently Glassary, Kilberry, Kilmartin and Kilmodan (Cowan, *Parishes*, 74, 94, 104–5). The precentorship, initially held by the prior of Ardchattan, became a secular benefice *c.* 1371, and this may have marked the finalization of the early constitution (*CPP*, i, 584; *CSSR*, ii, 112). Further prebends of Kilmore (1380) and Kilchousland (*c.* 1426–8) were subsequently erected (Cowan, *Parishes*, 97, 106). If the priors of Ardchattan relinquished their rights even to a simple canonry a total establishment of twelve prebends is possible. However, this was subject to fluctuation. Kilchousland had ceased to be a prebend before 1508 and the continuance as such of Kilmore and Kilcolmkill remains doubtful. On the other hand, prebends for life were not unknown, as for example in 1506 when the ch. of Knoydart was erected by the Pope '*in canonicatum et prebendam ad vitam*' (*RSCHS*, xiv, 37–38, 47). This uncertainty may reflect a situation parallel to that in the Irish diocese of Cloyne, in which there was 'no fixed number of canons' (*CPL*, xiv, 67).

In an attempt to revive the fortunes of the see, the cathedral of which was said to be ruinous and deserted, having neither bp. nor chapter, James IV proposed to the Pope on 22 April 1512 that the cathedral be moved from Lismore to Saddell, the property of the old Cistercian abbey of which (*q.v.*) had been united to the bishopric in 1507–8 (*James IV Letters*, no. 446; *James V Letters*, 364). Nothing came of this proposal. Although no resident chapter may have been present in Lismore, the corporate character of the chapter was retained. An uninterrupted succession of dignatories was maintained, the archdeacon and two canons attest a charter, in 1557, and the four original prebends—Glassary, Kilberry, Kilmartin and Kilmodan—which may have been the only permanent prebends remained in existence at the Reformation (Watt, *Fasti*, 29–36; SRO, RH6/1691; Cowan, *Parishes*, 74, 94, 104–5).

(II) MONASTIC CATHEDRALS

Name	County	Minimum income 1561	Date of foundation
St. Andrews	Fife	£12,500	1144
Whithorn	Wigtown	£2540	1175 × 1177

St. Andrews. For the history of the bishopric of St. Andrews during the 'Celtic' period, see Skene, *Celtic Scotland*, ii, 323 ff; for names of early bps. in the tenth and early eleventh c. at least some of whom were probably associated with the ch. of St. Andrews, see Hadden and Stubbs, *Councils*, II, i, 173–4. The last of the authenticated Celtic bps., Fóthad, d. 1093. In 1109 Turgot began the line of medieval bps. (Watt, *Fasti*, 289–90). Two groups of clergy neither of whom served the high altar of the then cathedral ch. (i.e. the modern St. Rule's ch.) were then in existence. One group consisted of *personae*, who were married clergy of some kind who did not lead a communal life, while the other was a community of thirteen Culdees who celebrated their offices at a side altar of the ch. of St. Andrew and may have shared in the duty of electing the bp. along with the other clergy of the city and the diocese (*ibid.*, 299–300). Plans for the re-allocation of the endowments of these clergy and the foundation of a cathedral community of Augustinian canons seem to have been underway in 1124 but the new community was not finally established until 1144, the church thereafter passed to the regular canons but plans, *c.* 1150, that they should also absorb the property of the Culdees were never implemented and by the mid-thirteenth c. the Culdee community had been transferred into the chapter of the collegiate ch. of St. Mary on the Rock at St. Andrews (*q.v.*) (G. W. S. Barrow, 'The Cathedral chapter of St. Andrews and the Culdees in the twelfth and thirteenth centuries', *Journ. Eccles. Hist.*, iii, 23–39; Watt, *Fasti*, 299–301).

A separate issue in dispute was occasioned by the claim of the priory to exclusive rights in episcopal elections which had been granted to them by a papal bull of Eugenius III on 30 Aug. 1147 (*St. A. Lib.*, 48–50). Two elements challenged this privilege—the two archdeacons and the Culdees or chapter of St. Mary. At least one archdeacon, and probably both, were coeval with the Augustinian community and successive archdeacons of St. Andrews and Lothian were probably members of the chapter along with the canons from the first. Thirteenth c. disputes were resolved in the archdeacon's favour and by mid-century their place in the chapter was unchallenged (Watt, *Fasti*, 301). The Culdee claims, on the other hand, were not raised until the thirteenth c. and appear to be a matter of ecclesiastical politics to which the canons were from time to time forced to bow. These had been effectively resolved in favour of the chapter by 1271 although claims on behalf of the Culdees continued to be made until 1332 (*ibid.*, 301). A place was eventually found for the provost of St. Mary's on the Rock by papal privilege of 24 Jan. 1386 that the holder of this benefice should henceforth have a place in the choir and chapter as a third secular dignitary along with the two archdeacons (Reg. Aven. 245, fo. 397v). A fourth secular dignitary was the chancellorship erected 1447 × 1449 (Reg. Supp., 525, fo. 192) but this was shortlived and the benefice was dissolved 1461 × 1462 (Watt, *Fasti*, 302–4). For the relationship between the bps. of St. Andrews and their diocesan chapter see Mark Dilworth, 'The Augustinian Chapter of St. Andrews', *Innes Review*, xxv (1974), 15–22.

WHITHORN. A succession of eighth-c. bps. is recorded until 790(see p.51 above).Thereafter the bishopric appears to have lapsed until its revival, probably by Fergus of Galloway *c.* 1128 (Watt, *Fasti*, 129). Bishops recognized the metropolitan authority of York from this date to 1355, after which no bp. offered obedience to York and the see was treated as other Scottish bishoprics as falling under papal authority until placed under the metropolitan authority of St. Andrews 14 Aug. 1472, and then transferred to province of Glasgow 9 Jan. 1492 (*ibid.*). The status of the ch. from which Bp. Gilla-Aldan took his title in 1128 is obscure. A community associated with a 'minster' already situated on this site may have been in existence at this date and the *canonicos iam regulares* who were replaced by Premonstratensian canons introduced by Bp. Christian in 1175 × 1177 may have been canons of this early institution (*TDGAS*, 3rd series, xxvii, 104–5). On the other hand, arguments have been advanced for a shortlived Augustinian community preceding that of the Premonstratensians, but there is no firm evidence to support this contention (Watt, *Fasti*, 133–4). The regular community at the cathedral probably from the first shared the duty of electing the bp. with the archdeacon and some or all of the secular clergy of the diocese. Disputes arose in thirteenth c. but after these were resolved it was stated in 1293–4 to be the custom in Galloway for election to be in the hands of the prior and chapter of Whithorn together with all the clergy of the diocese. This right was exercised in 1326, and although subsequent elections were held by a body simply described as 'the chapter', it is far from certain that the prior and convent of Whithorn alone were meant by this terminology (*ibid.*, 134–5).

INCOMPLETE FOUNDATIONS

Iona. A request made by the crown to the Pope that Iona abbey should be erected as the see of the bp. of the Isles until 'his principall kirk in the Ile of Man be recoverit fra Inglismen' was made 1 April 1498, but this was not successful. Successive bps. from 1499 held the abbey *in commendam*, but there is no evidence that the Benedictine monks of Iona ever formed a cathedral chapter (Watt, *Fasti* 207; see under IONA and Bishopric of the Isles).

As appears above (pp. 202, 204, 209), Aberdeen, Inchaffray and Kirkwall might have, but did not, become the site of monastic cathedrals.

SECULAR COLLEGES

GENERAL NOTES

WITH such exceptions as Restalrig and St. Mary on the Rock, St. Andrews (destroyed by the Reformers), St. Mary in the Fields, Edinburgh and Peebles (destroyed by the English) and the Chapel Royal at Stirling (rebuilt in 1594), the Scottish collegiate churches (i.e. their buildings) survived the Reformation and more than half their number, in whole or in part, are still extant. No column appears in the following list to show the date at which these churches ceased to function in their collegiate capacity because it may be assumed that, in general, their career as secular colleges was closed with the abolition and outlawry of the mass by the acts of Parliament of 1560 and 1567 (*APS*, ii. 535; iii. 22). Many continued as parish churches; some which had not previously been parochial became so. It should be noted that for some time after the Reformation presentations to prebends and chaplainries in collegiate churches continued to be made. This was due to the act of parliament of 1567 (*ibid.*, iii, 25) which ordained that such benefices might be granted, as bursaries, to students at the universities.

SECULAR COLLEGES

Name	County	Minimum income (1561)	Date F	D	Pre-bends etc.	Chaplains	Clerks choristers etc.
‡ ABERDEEN							
ST. NICHOLAS	Aberdeen		1540			22–16–?	
ABERNETHY	Perth	£240	1328–31		6–11–7		3
‡ BIGGAR	Lanark		1545/6		9		4
§ BOTHANS	E. Lothian	£162	1421		5–7		
‡ BOTHWELL	Lanark	£423	1397/8		7–10		2
§ CARNWATH	Lanark		1424		7(?)		
¶‡COLDINGHAM	Berwick		1473	1488	dean		
‡ CORSTORPHINE	Midlothian	£434	1429		5–9		4
‡ CRAIL	Fife		1517		12		probably some
‡ CRICHTON	Midlothian	£233	1449		9–14		4
‡ CULLEN	Banff		1543		7–8		2
‡ DALKEITH	Midlothian		1406		6–13		3
DIRLETON	E. Lothian		1444		Some		
DUMBARTON	Dunbarton	£340	c. 1454		7		

213

Name	County	Minimum income (1561)	Date	F	Pre-bends etc.	Chaplains	Approximate no. of Clerks, choristers etc.
DUNBAR	E. Lothian	£690	1342		10		some(?)
* DUNGLASS	E. Lothian	£160	1443/4(?)		3–13(?)		4
DUNROSSNESS	Shetland		?		several		
‡ EDINBURGH ST. GILES	Midlothian		1466–9		16–18	numerous	4
EDINBURGH ST. MARY IN THE FIELDS	Midlothian		c. 1510		11		
EDINBURGH TRINITY COLLEGE	,,	£532	–1460		9–11		2
‡ FOWLIS (EASTER)	Angus		1453		8		
GLASGOW OUR LADY COLLEGE	Lanark		1525		9–12		3
GUTHRIE	Angus		c. 1479		5		
‡ HADDINGTON	E. Lothian		c. 1540			numerous	
HAMILTON	Lanark		1450/1		7–9		
§ INNERPEFFRAY	Perth		1506–42		some		
§ KILMAURS	Ayr		1413–		9(?)		2
§ KILMUN	Argyll		1441		6–8		
* LINCLUDEN	Kirkcudbright	£540	1389		9–13		
MARKLE	E. Lothian		c. 1450		some		
* MAYBOLE	Ayr		1381/2		3–5		1
§ METHVEN	Perth	£790	1433		6–10	5	4
§ PEEBLES	Peebles		1541		13		2
§ RESTALRIG	Midlothian	£530+	1487		7–12(?)		2
‡ ROSLIN	,,		c. 1450		6		
ST. ANDREWS, ST. MARY ON THE ROCK	Fife	£500	c. 1250		7–14		
SEMPLE, or LOCHWINNOCH	Renfrew		1504		7		
* SETON	E. Lothian		1492		7–9		3
STIRLING, CHAPEL ROYAL	Stirling	£1270	1501		19–28		6
‡ STIRLING, HOLY RUDE	Stirling		–1546			numerous	
STRATHMIGLO	Fife		c. 1527		?		3
§ TAIN	Ross	£100	1487		6–7		5

ABERDEEN, St. NICHOLAS. This large parish ch., the rectory of which was assigned to the sixth prebend of the cathedral in 1256 (*Abdn. Reg.*, ii, 40), had, in the fifteenth c., a considerable body of chaplains. For these, regulations were made by Ingeram de Lindesay, bp. of Aberdeen (1441–59) (*Abdn. St. Nich. Cart.*, i, no. cxxii), a step which has been regarded as 'nothing less than the constituting of St. Nicholas' a collegiate church' (*ibid.*, ii, xxvi); but this is an exaggeration. In 1491, when there were twenty-two chaplains (*ibid.*, i, no. cxxiv), the ch. was prematurely described as collegiate (*RMS*, ii, no. 2033). About this time, the number of chaplains was apparently reduced to sixteen (*Abdn. St. Nich. Cart.*, i, no. cxxv). New statutes made on 14 July 1519 (*ibid.*, i, no. cxxvi) contemplate a quasi-collegiate organization; while thirty-four stalls were ordered for the new choir (*ibid.*, ii, 346) which was evidently completed early in the sixteenth c. But it was not till 28 March 1540 that William Gordon, bp. of Aberdeen, with the consent of the dean and chapter gave the vicarage of St. Nicholas to 'the College of the Chaplenis of the said

Sanct Nicolas Kirk . . . for sustentatioun of ane provest' (*ibid.*, ii, 381), thus completing the collegiate constitution of the ch. This provostry was demitted by John Collinson in 1578 (Reg. Pres., i, fo. 151).

ABERNETHY, ST. BRIDE. The community of Culdees (see under Early Religious Foundations) here was succeeded by Augustinian canons, who are said to have formed a priory in 1272 or 1273 (*Scotichronicon*, lib. x, cap. xxxiii; *Chron. Bower*, ii, 120) (see under Augustinian canons). This priory appears in turn to have been transformed, in the earlier fourteenth c., into a college of secular canons. A canon of Abernethy, who is not designated as a regular is mentioned in 1325 (Reg. Vat., 78, fo. 351; *CPL*, ii, 243), and a secular canon appears in 1345 and 1349 (*CPP*, i, 89, 145). The head of this house is entitled provost on 17 March 1351 (*Lind. Lib.*, App. v, 45), but occurs as prior *c.*1380 and this is the normal designation until mid-fifteenth c. (*RMS*, i, App. i, no. 141; Fraser, *Douglas*, iii, 397; *CPP*, i, 579; *CSSR*, iii, 190; Fraser, *Weemys*, ii, 69). Margaret, countess of Angus (eldest daughter and co-heiress of Sir Alexander Abernethy, who married John Stewart, E. of Angus, *c.*1328) is described in 1364 as patron of the ch., lineal descendant of the original founders, lords of Abernethy (*CPL*, iv, 213). This statement probably relates to the fd'n. of the priory as in 1467 it is claimed that the collegiate ch. was founded, built and endowed by the earls of Angus (Reg. Supp., 616, fo. 132 v). As this would have been after the marriage of John Stewart, first E. of Angus, to the Abernethy heiress in 1328, the possible date of erection is between this event and the earl's death in 1331, as in the period between that date and 1345, his successor was a minor (*Scots Peerage*, i, 169–170). The statement that the college was founded by George, E. of Angus, *c.*1450 (*Midlothian Chrs.* iv) is erroneous, although further endowments may have come from the Douglas line of the earls of Angus. The collegiate foundation was initially for a prior and five canons; and the number of the latter was raised to ten on the prospective increase of the churches' income. But as this augmentation did not take place, the bp. of Dunblane, 8 Feb. 1364/5, reduced the number to the original five (*CPL*, iv, 214–5). As a result of a petition of the pr. and chapter the Pope commissioned the bp. of St. Andrews to inquire into the circumstances of the college, 8 April 1373 (SRO Vat. Trans., i, 102) and, on 31 Oct. 1375, confirmed the reduction (*CPL*, iv, 214–5). Three choristers occur, 8 September 1547 (*Prot. BK. Gaw*, no. 5). After the Reformation the provost and five canons, whose prebends are detailed as Balmanno, Colsy and Balmanno, Colsy, Pettinbrog and Pitmedden, granted a charter in Nov. 1577, but at least one further prebend, Foirevinschip, also appears in post-Reformation records (*RMS*, iv, nos. 149, 1545, 2737; *Thirds of Benefices*, 15–16).

BIGGAR, ST. MARY AND ST. NICHOLAS. Mooted in 1539 (*James V Letters*, 368; *Wigtown Charter Chest*, no. 522), the college was founded in the parish ch. by Malcolm, Lord Fleming, 16 Jan. 1545/6 for a provost, eight prebendaries, and four choristers (*Spalding Club Misc.*, v, 196 ff). The first of the prebendaries was to be called canon of the hospital of St. Leonard; the second was to be instructor of the grammar school and have the lands of Auchynreoch as his prebend; the third prebendary, founded on the lands of Garnegabir and Auchyndavy, was to be sacristan; the fourth prebendary mainly based on rents from Drummelzier, was to have charge of the poor men. The remaining four prebendaries, one of whom held the prebend of the Lady altarage of Kirkintilloch (*RSS*, vii, no. 1685) were to be maintained from revenues from the parish ch. of Biggar. No further prebends appear to have been created before the Reformation and little evidence for the existing prebends is found thereafter (*Wigtown Charter Chest*, no. 602). A hospital was attached to this college. See under Hospitals.

BOTHANS, ST. CUTHBERT. Spottiswoode (466), whose account of the fd'n. is inaccurate and confused (see *Yester* below), gives this erroneously as 'Botham'. It is also mistakenly called 'St. Bothans' (e.g. *Midlothian Chrs.*, iii)—this is the name of a Cistercian nunnery in Berwickshire; but Bothans in East Lothian had no connection with this saint; its patron was St. Cuthbert. The erection by Henry, bp. of St. Andrews, of the college in this parish ch. is dated 22 April 1421, following a petition of Sir William Hay, sheriff of Peebles, Thomas Boyd, Eustace de Maxwell, and Dougald McDowall, co-lords of the lordship of Yester and patrons in turn of this ch., made 1 Aug. 1420, and with provision for a provost and four chaplains (*Yester Writs*, nos. 53, 55). On 6 Aug. 1440 this erection, which a papal petition claims had been, and at that date remains, for a provost and two chaplains, is said to have been opposed by Robert (*sic*) Boyd, 'one of the patrons, older than the others and to whom presentation legitimately pertained for the first time to come'. As a result an unsuccessful attempt was made to restore the ch. to its former state (Reg. Supp., 366, fo. 77; 368, fo. 214 v). Two additional chaplaincies, one at St. Mary's altar also referred to as the prebend of Blans, and the other at the altar of the Holy Cross, were added 30 July 1447 and 23 Jan. 1535/6 (*Yester Writs*, nos. 85–7, 92, 522). Both these remained as prebends at the Reformation (*ibid.*, nos. 855A, 1606). Other prebends found at this time are Morham and Kirkbank, both of which were included as such in the original fd'n., the prebend of St. Edmund which may also have been part of the initial establishment and the prebend of St. Cosmo and St. Damian, to which only a post-Reformation reference has been found (*ibid.*, nos. 55, 116A, 152, 763A, 1058; *Thirds of Benefices*, 28). Of the chaplaincy of St. Nicholas on 24 March 1470 (Reg. Supp., 654, 233 v) and the prebend of the altar of St. Ninian to which a presentation was made, 27 March 1470, no further references have been noted (*Yester Writs*, nos. 152–3). Presentations to the titular provostship continue until 1630 (Watt, *Fasti*, 343–4).

BOTHWELL. The petition of Archibald, E. of Douglas, for the erection of this parish ch. to collegiate status, with a provost and six prebendaries, was granted by the Pope, 21 Feb. 1397/8 (Reg. Aven., 304, fo. 541 v). This was confirmed 18 May 1410 (*ibid.*, 335, fos. 223–223 v). Spottiswoode (466) and *OPS* (i, 54) give the date of foundation as 10 Oct. 1398 and the number of prebendaries as eight and this appears to have been the actual number endowed (see below). On 4 October 1447 the parish ch. of Hawick was erected into an additional prebend (*Glasgow Reg.* ii, nos. 349–50); a papal mandatory was appointed to confirm this erection and provision for two boy clerks, 30 Jan. 1477 (*CPL*, x, 340–1). At the Reformation, in addition to this prebend, eight others entitled Crookburn, Hassilden, Kittymuir, Netherfield, Newton, Overtoun, Stonehouse and Strathaven are recorded with the provostry to which titulars continue to be appointed until the early seventeenth c. (Book of Assumption, 259 v, *Thirds of Benefices*, 18–19; Watt, *Fasti*, 344–6).

CARNWATH. The list appended to the *Scotichronicon* (*Chron. Bower*, ii, 541) MS. lists and Spottiswoode (466) ascribe this fd'n. to Thomas de Somerville. Spottiswoode also states that the fd'n. was for a provost and six prebendaries and gives the date as 1424 (this is followed by *OPS* (i, 126).) The date is also given as 1425–30 (*Memorie of the Somervilles*, i, 166). An aisle is extant, but apart from reference to a prebendary in 1516 and to a 'prebendary of the isle of Carnwath' at the Reformation (*OPS*. i, 126; *RMS*, iii, no. 106), this college does not seem to be mentioned in records. Indeed the total absence of any holder of the provostry (Watt, *Fasti*) would suggest that a single canon was the sole member of this 'college'. See Carnwath under Hospitals.

COLDINGHAM. Erected 3 April 1473 when, as part of revised plan for the suppression of Coldingham priory (*q.v.*), the Pope consented that only a portion of the priory's revenues should be applied to the chapel royal of St. Mary on the Rock, St. Andrews, the other part being applied to the erection of an additional chapel royal at Coldingham as a collegiate ch. with a dean and prebendaries (Theiner, *Vet. Mon.*, no. dccclvii; *CPL*, xiii, 19). Nothing was done to erect prebends, other than the deanery, and although the dean, John Hume, went to Pope Innocent VIII, after his coronation on 16 Sept. 1484, on the understanding that he would arrange for the erection of additional prebends, he misused royal letters of recommendation. Instead he obtained a revocation of the proceedings subsequent to the mandate of 3 April 1473, the partially erected collegiate ch. being formally suppressed (*CPL*, xiv, 46–47). Parliament on 26 May 1485 decided that the Pope should be asked to overturn his act of revocation and adhere to the scheme of 3 April 1473 (*APS*, ii, 171). But although the Pope eventually agreed to this 28 April 1487, and parliament declared it was treason to try to upset the erection of a collegiate ch. at Coldingham, the restoration of the political fortunes of the Humes on the death of James III on 11 June 1488 saw the end of this scheme to restore and complete the collegiate ch. (*CPL*, xiv, 47–48; *APS*, ii, 179). See Watt, *Fasti*, 346–8.

CORSTORPHINE, ST. JOHN BAPTIST. This collegiate ch. originated in a chapel in the cemetery beside the parish ch.; the foundation of three chaplaincies there was confirmed under the great seal, 25 Feb. 1425/6 (*Midlothian Chrs.*, 293–5). Two more chaplains and two clerks were added, 20 May 1429 (*ibid.*, 295–8); and an inscription in the ch. attributes the fd'n. to that year. The foundation charter is not extant, but a college of a provost, four other priests and two choristers had been founded by Sir John Forrester before 26 June 1436, when in order to augment this establishment by another four or five priests, a petition for the appropriation of the parish ch. of Ratho was presented to the Pope (Reg. Supp., 323, fo. 238 ᵛ). A petition in a similar vein was again presented 7 Jan. 1436/7 (*ibid.*, 331, fo. 148 v; cf. *CPL*, viii, 595). The proposed union of Ratho was not immediately effective, and it was not until 1443 that the scheme was revived in order that five additional chaplains might be sustained, one of whom was to serve in the parish ch. of Ratho (Cowan, *Parishes*, 168). Even this scheme was not fully implemented, and following upon a petition by Sir John Forrester on 10 June 1444 (Reg. Supp., 397, fo. 173) that the establishment might be nine priests and two boys, the bp. of St. Andrews, in terms of a bull of Eugenius IV, sanctioned, on 30 Oct. 1444, the addition of four chaplains (instead of five as originally proposed) and laid down the endowment for each of the prebendaries (Cowan, *Parishes*, 168; *Midlothian Chrs.*, 298–304; cf. *CPL*, viii, 595; x, 476). No further additions appear to have taken place and the eight chaplaincies thus instituted were maintained in pairs by prebends known as Half Dalmahoy and Half Haltoune and Half Bonnyton and Half Platt (the four original prebends) and Half Gogar and Alderstone and Ratho-byres and Half Nortoune (based on the teinds of Ratho) (*Thirds of Benefices*, 27, 31, 39, 278).

CRAIL, ST. MARY. The first indication of the proposed erection of a college in the parish ch. is apparently a charter recording the vicar's consent to the erection of the vicarage into a provostry, 3 March 1516/17 (*Crail Register*, no. 102). The erection was initiated by a petition, dated 7 and 8 June 1517, and directed to Andrew [Forman], abp. of St. Andrews, by Jonet, prioress of the Cistercian nunnery of Haddington (which held the church of Crail) and William Myrton, vicar of Lathrisk, for the confirmation of their proposals for a provostry, ten prebends (seven of which—two at the altar of St. Mary the Virgin, two at the altar of St. Michael and the remaining three at the altars of St. James the Apostle, St. Nicholas and St. Bartholomew (later designated as St. John Baptist) had been founded by Myrton) and a clerkship, of which the endowments are set forth (*ibid.*, no. 101; cf. no. 53). The other prebends were those of the vicar-pensioner and the chaplains at the altars of the Holy Cross and Our Lady (*ibid.*, no. 101). On 20 June following, the abp. ratified the collegiate foundation (*ibid.*, no. 103). Another version of the abp's. charter (*St. Andrews Formulare* i, no. 288) names the bailies, councillors and community of Crail and the parishioners of the ch. as among the petitioners. These are mentioned (*Crail Register*, no. 101) in respect of their consenting to the erection of the two existing chaplaincies of Holy Cross and Our Lady into prebends as the prioress of Haddington appears consenting to the annexation of the vicarage to the provostry (*ibid.*, nos. 47, 101). But in an undated charter of the above abp. of St. Andrews confirming additional statutes for the college, Myrton is designated its 'first and principal founder' (*St. Andrews Formulare*, i, no. 290; cf. *Crail Register*, no. 121). The creation of an additional prebend was authorized by the abp., 20 June 1517 (*ibid.*, no. 103). This appears to have been effected before 6 Aug. 1518 when a prebendary of St. John the Apostle appears (*ibid.*, no. 54) while a charter of James V credits Myrton with founding eight prebendaries in the college (*ibid.*, no. 104). Eleven prebendaries enter into a obligation on 16 Dec. 1536 (*Laing Chrs.*, no. 412). The abp's. charter of 20 June 1517 provides for instituting four choristers (*Crail Register*, no. 103), and although there is no further mention of these, one of Myrton's charters of endowment, 22 Oct. 1520, assigns the charge of the song school to the second prebendary (*ibid.*, no. 47) and another, 9 Nov. 1525, makes provision for a grammar school (*ibid.*, 12). Chaplaincies of St. Stephen and St. Katherine, which occur on 23 September 1553 and 7 May 1566 respectively, may have been further additional prebends (SRO, Liber Officialis Sanctiandree Principalis, fo. 285; SRO, Court BK of Crail (B 10/8/4), fo. 3). On 10 May 1587 James VI grants to the bailies and councillors of Crail, for the maintenance of the ch., school and hospital of the burgh, the collegiate ch., with its benefices and properties (*RMS*, v, no. 1197).

CRICHTON, ST. KENTIGERN. Fd. in the parish ch. by William, Lord Crichton, chancellor of Scotland, 29 Dec. 1449, for a provost, eight prebendaries and two boy choristers. Provision was made for the prebendaries, one of whom was the parish clerk of Crichton who was to be sacristan, while six others were to be maintained by prebends entitled Crichton, the first and second prebendaries of Middleton, Lochorwart (later known as Vogrie: *RMS*, vi, no. 425), Ford and Ogston. The name of an eighth prebend is blank in the fd'n. charter (*Midlothian Chrs.*, 305–12). In 1450 the founder is said to have notably augmented the original fd'n. (*ibid.*, cxiii–cxv; *CPL*, x, 64; xi, 290), but details of this are lacking. A prebend of Halkerston fd. by the provost of that name for the praeceptor or master of the grammar school, is recorded 13 Oct. 1488 (*RMS.*, ii, no. 1784; *St. Andrews Formulare*, i, 203–4). A further prebend of 'Quhithous' occurs 28 February 1551/2 (SRO, Prot. Bk. Strathauchin, iv, fo. 24 v) At least four other prebends—of the master of the song school, of the old ch. of St. Kentigern, of the tenement of Edinburgh and of Arniston—appear in post-Reformation sources (*RMS*, iv, no. 2169; *RSS*, v, no. 2531). At least two further choristers were also added to the original fd'n. (*RMS*, iv, no. 2169). If one of these additional prebends is to be equated with the unidentified prebend of the original foundation, the final constitution appears to have consisted at least of a provost, thirteen canons and four choristers.

CULLEN, ST. MARY. Founded in the parish ch. by Alexander Ogilvy of Findlater, Alexander Dick, archdeacon of Glasgow, John Duff of Muldavit, the bailies, councillors and community of Cullen, and the parishioners of the ch., 23 April 1543, for a provost, six prebendaries entitled St. Anne, Holy Cross, St. Mary, St. John the Baptist, St. Andrew and St. Mary Magdalene and two boy choristers (Cramond, *Church and Churchyard of Cullen*, 34–55). On 1543 the crown ratified the incorporation and erection of the 'auld chaplainrie of five pundis' (*HMC 3rd Rep.*, App. 404). Feus of their lands and revenues granted by four of these prebendaries to the cleik register, Alexander Hay in 1582/3 were confirmed by the town, 5 July 1583 (*RMS*, vi, no. 582).

DALKEITH, ST. NICHOLAS. On 21 June 1406 six chaplains, one of whom was to be provost, were endowed in the chapel of St. Nicholas by Sir James de Douglas, lord of Dalkeith (*Midlothian Chrs.*, 313; *Mort. Reg.*, ii, 324). The prebends of the six canons were to be maintained from prebends of Dechmont and Holden, Quilt and Fethane, Hornbruke, Lochurd and Kirkurd, Spittalhauch and sixthly Ingalstoun (*Midlothian Chrs.*, 313–9). A petition by James, E. of Morton to erect further prebends from the revenues of three parish chs. in the collegiate ch., which is said to have been founded for a provostship and five canonries, resulted in a papal mandate to effect this, 9 Nov. 1475 (*CPL*, xiii, 467–8). This was effected, 17 May 1477 when in addition to three clerks or choristers, five further prebends for a sacrist and prebendaries of Newlands, Romanhouse, Bordland and Mordington were erected (*Mort. Reg.*, ii, no. 230). Two further chaplains or prebendaries, entitled Holy Rood and St. John the Baptist were added, 20 July 1503 (*RMS* ii, no. 2789; v, no. 612). This collegiate ch. became the parish ch. of Dalkeith, 1 Oct. 1467 (*ibid.*, cxvi). As early as 1396 a hospital was attached to St. Nicholas' chapel (see under Hospitals).

DIRLETON. This ch. is said to have been established by Sir Walter Haliburton in 1444 (Spottiswoode, 467). A similar statement is made in the list appended to *Scotichronicon* (*Chron. Bower*, ii, 541), where it is added: 'Here he established a provost, but nothing was done for the project' (*hic constituit praepositum sed nihil factum ad propositum*). The name of a provost (John Burgon) is given in that year (SRO, Wallace-James Notes [GD 1/413] x, pt. 1, p. 201) and a somewhat irregular succession of provosts can thereafter be established (Watt, *Fasti*, 352). There are also references to the provostry from 1539 (*St. Andrews Rentale*, 55); in 1561, it is described as 'the provostry of the chapel of the castle of Dryltoun, situated near the castle of the same' (*N.B. Chrs.*, 82). This was obviously a small fd'n. although a grant of the patronage of the provostry and chaplaincies of Dirltoun, 17 Oct. 1570, would seem to indicate that the college had been served by clergy other than the provost (*RSS*, vi, no. 961). The provostry was secularized at the Reformation and titular provosts continue to appear on record until at least 1632 (Watt, *Fasti*, 352).

DUMBARTON, ST. MARY. The chapel of the Blessed Virgin Mary was granted, 11 May 1453, by the bailies, council and burgesses of Dumbarton to Isabel, duchess of Albany and countess of Lennox, for the erection and creation of a collegiate ch. (Dumbarton Charters, no. 85). On the following day the duchess entered into a bond to restore the chapel to the bailies, if she should fail to found her proposed college (*ibid.*, no. 86). Following a petition by the duchess, a papal mandate was issued for the erection of the chapel of St. Mary (not of St. Patrick, as given by Spottiswoode (468) into a collegiate ch. with a provost, and a sufficient number of chaplains, 3 Jan. 1453/4 (*CPL*, x, 623-4). At the Reformation it was endowed for a provost and six prebendaries (EU, ms. Dc. 4. 32, fo. 36). The provost and four prebendaries appear by name in 1567, the prebend of one of these having been described in 1563 as that of Bonhill (*Thirds of Benefices*, 268; *RSS*, v, no. 1368).

DUNBAR. Patrick, fifth E. of Dunbar, is said to have founded a collegiate ch. here in 1218 (*Scots Peerage*, iii, 252), while Spottiswoode (467) attributes the foundation to George, E. of March, in 1392. Both statements are erroneous. The fd'n. charter shows that the college was founded in the parish ch. by Patrick, ninth E. of Dunbar, and second or fourth E. of March, 21 Sept. 1342, for a dean, an archpriest and eight canons, who were to hold the prebends of Belton, Chirnside, Dunbar, Duns, Linton, Pinkerton, Pitcox and Spott (*SHS. Misc.*, vi, 89-97). In 1501 the archpriestship and the five prebends of Belton, Dunbar, Duns, Pinkerton and Spott were appropriated to the chapel royal at Stirling (*Hist. Chapel Royal*, 4, 14), but this was not successful and presentations to these prebends continue to refer to them as lying within the college of Dunbar (*RSS*, ii, no. 3755; iii, no. 1649). At the Reformation the college remained as originally constituted and titular provosts continue on record until 1580 (*RMS*, vi, no. 1773, Watt, *Fasti*, 355). See *SHS Misc.* vi, 81-109.

DUNGLASS, ST. MARY. On 30 Nov. 1423, Alexander Home made certain donations to the chapel of St. Mary of Dunglass and 'the presbyters there serving God' (*HMC 12th Rep.*, App., pt. viii, 123); and this chapel was the nucleus of the collegiate ch. The date of the collegiate fd'n. is given as 1403 (*Midlothian Chrs.*, iii) and also as 1450 (Spottiswoode, 468). The former date appears in the fd'n. charter but is clearly an error. It occurs as a college, 2 February 1448/9 (Fraser, *Buccleuch*, ii, 39). On 22 Aug. 1450, James II confirming the charter granted in 1423 by Alexander Home, father of Sir Alexander Home, refers to the chapel as lately founded as a collegiate ch. (*HMC. 12th Rep.*, App. Pt. viii, 123-4). Sir Alexander Home is named as founder in a papal confirmation of the fd'n., 2 Jan. 1451 (*ibid.*, 127-8; Reg. Supp., 450, fo. 36); and the date of the founder's charter, 12 March 1403, may thus be intended for 12 March 1443 (1443/4). According to this writ, the college was fd. by Sir Alexander Home in the chapel of St. Mary of Dunglass for a provost, three chaplains and four boy-choristers (*HMC 12th Rep.*, App. viii, 124-6). One of the chaplains was to be maintained from the revenues of Kello and the other two from returns from 'Balwlsy and Gordounshall' in Fife (*ibid.*). The former continued to constitute a prebend in the collegiate church, but other revenues may have subsequently been found for the other chaplains as further endowments were received by the college. Between 5 Aug. 1450 and 11 Jan. 1451/2, lands in Chirnside, Oldhamstocks, the hospital of Hutton or Red Spittal (*q.v.*) and Trefontains were granted to the college (*ibid.*, 126-7), and were subsequently used to endow prebends. In a similar fashion the grant on 8 June 1460 of the lands of Wester Upsetlington resulted in the foundation of two further prebends, which are later described in a variety of ways such as the prebend of the 'half fischeing and half landis' of Upsetlington, 'the fishings of the West ford of Norham' or simply Upsetlington (*RSS*, vii, no. 1228; *HMC, Milne Home MSS.*, 55, 75). Nine prebends —two each of Trefontains and Upsetlington with Kello, Chirnside, Red Spittal, Oldhamstocks and Oldcambus, in which lands had also been acquired—are mentioned in 1481 (SRO, *RH* 6/496). Another prebend of Vigorushauch was endowed in 1503 (*HMC, 12th Rep.*, App. viii, 177-8). At least two other prebends, Barnside and Dewingham, also existed, and the total complement at the Reformation may have been a provost and twelve prebendaries (*ibid.*, 55, 181, 239; *RSS*, vii, nos. 590, 1042; *RMS*, vi, no. 1559; *Laing Chrs.*, no. 1866, SRO, Book of Assumptions, fo. 169 v). It appears to have been burnt by the English, 16 August 1544 (Raine, *North Durham*. xix). A hospital was attached to this ch., which also held the hospital of Hutton (see under Hospitals). See *East Lothian Trans.*, iv (1948), 15-17.

DUNROSSNESS. The gift of a prebend called the Cross Stouk in the 'college kirk' of Dunrossness occurs 21 June 1590 (RSS, lx, 141) and the 'prebendarie callit the Croce Kirk foundit within the college kirk of Dunrossness in Yeitland' appears 24 Aug. 1604

(*Shetland Court Bk.*, 155). The 'Croce stowk' is mentioned as a benefice separate from the vicarage of Dunrossness in 1561 (*Thirds of Benefices*, 2, 48). Though there are no pre-Reformation references, the foregoing seems to show that this was a collegiate ch. Other 'stowks' mentioned in Shetland—the 'small stowk in Northmavin callit St. Michaelis Stowk' (Goudie, *Shetland Antiquities*, 157) and on 24 Aug. 1604, 'Sanct Laurens stowk within the parochin of Northmaving'; the 'stouk and stouk landis of Asta within the parochin of Tingwall' and 'Sanct Piteris stouk in the Fair Yle'—may have been prebends of this ch. (*Shetland Court Bk.*, 155).

EDINBURGH, ST. GILES. On 19 June 1419 Pope Martin V appointed a mandatory to deal with the petition of the provost, bailies and community of Edinburgh for the erection of this parish ch. to collegiate status. The thirteen perpetual chaplaincies already in the ch. were to be converted into prebends, and other prebends, including a provostship, were to be erected (*CSSR*, i, 77–8; *CPL*, vii, 136). This had no result, although a further petition to this end was made on 16 Dec. 1423 (*CSSR*, ii, 41–2). A further chaplaincy, dedicated to St. Michael was founded by Patrick Lesouris in 1454 (*St. Giles Reg.*, 103). On 21 Oct. 1466, James III assented to a proposal similar to those previously made (*RMS*, ii, 887) but several years elapsed before fd'n. was completed. A petition to the Pope for the erection of the college was granted 22 Feb. 1467/8 and on 26 Feb. 1468/9, Pope Paul II granted the petition of the magistrates and community for its erection for a provost, sacrist and minister of the choir, one or both of whom may have been accounted as canons, fourteen prebendaries and four choristers (Reg. Supp., 620, fo. 229; Theiner, *Vet. Mon.*, no. dcccxxxviii). One of these prebendaries was to be maintained by the provost and was to act as his vicar while the others were maintained by prebends known as Ravelston, Craigcrook, Merchiston [St. Catherine], Grotall, St. Andrew, St. Michael [Lesouris], St. Michael de Monte Tomba, the Holy Rood, St. Salvator, St. John the Baptist [St. John Evangelist], St. Nicholas, Holy Rood of Lucca [Black Rood or Holy Blood] and St. Sebastian (*St. Giles Reg.*, xxxi–xxxii). The ch. of Kirknewton was erected as an additional prebend in 1472 (Cameron, *Apostolic Camera*, 172). No further prebends were erected and prebends of St. John the Evangelist, St. Catherine and St. Gregory which appear in 1508, 1552 and 1579, with the exception of the last, which may be an error, are to be identified as above. (*St. Giles Reg.*, c, ci, cxiii). The provost, vicar and fourteen other prebendaries witness a charter in 1526/7 (*ibid.*, 221). Forty-nine altars in this ch. are listed (*ibid.*, xciv–xcv), but this figure is probably not entirely accurate. Titular provosts occur until 1566 (Watt, *Fasti*, 357).

EDINBURGH, ST. MARY IN THE FIELDS. Called a chapel in 1428 (*Arb. Lib.*, ii, 57), but described as a church in 1498/9 (*St. Giles Reg.*, no. 112). The date of its fd'n. as a collegiate ch., dedicated to BVM of Consolation (SRO, Liber Officialis Sanctiandree Principalis, fo. 247), is indicated by the facts that, on 21 March 1510/11, there is reference to the prebendaries (*Midlothian Chrs.*, 261), that, on 19 Sept. 1511, lands passed to its possession for the building of houses for the 'master' of the ch. *pro tempore* and chaplains (*ibid.*, 261–2) and that, on 20 Oct. 1512, there is further mention of the provost and prebendaries (*ibid.*, 262–3). In litigation between the abbey of Holyrood and the provost of this ch. in 1523, it was claimed that the abbey, which held the patronage of St. Mary's in the Fields, had had it erected into a collegiate ch. (*ADCP*, 178). Assertions that it was founded by master David Vocat, who was a chaplain in this ch. in 1509 (EU. Ms. Db. 6, 19; NLS., MS. 22, 1, 14; *Midlothian Chrs.*, cxi, appear to be based upon the fact that Vocat, who is rather improbably described as provost of the college in 1527 (*ibid.*, cf. Watt, *Fasti*, 257), supported an altar in the ch. in 1518 and is credited in 1528 with founding four prebends within the college (SRO Prot. Bk. Otterburn, fo. 3; SRO Prot. Bk. Meldrum, fos. 706–7). The foundation at the Reformation is said to have consisted of a provost and ten prebendaries (NLS, MS., 31, 3, 13). Prebends which have been identified include those of St. Andrew, St. Ann, St. Mary Magdalene, St. Mathew, St. Roche, Name of Jesus, *Domina nostra prima*, and by implication *Domina nostra secunda* (*Midlothian Chrs.*, cx–cxi, *RSS*, vi, no. 2595, 2824; vii, no. 1897). The prebendaries' houses and the hospital attached to them (*q.v.*) are stated to have been destroyed by the English 1544–7 (*Midlothian Chrs.*, xxxvii). On 21 June 1563 a contract is recorded between the provost of Kirk o' Field and the Town Council for the sale to the latter of the buildings (*Edinburgh Recs.*, 1557–71, 163); and on 9 Aug. 1564, the council arranged for the purchase of the stonework, which was being taken down, 'owther [either] for the hospitall or for ane vniuersite to be maid in the said Kirk of Feild' [*sic*] (*ibid.*, 182). The provostry was granted to the provost, bailies etc. of Edinburgh 18 March 1581 (Reg. Pres., ii, 73) and the college which developed into Edinburgh University was built upon the site. See *Midlothian Chrs.*, xxxiii–xlii, 261–72.

EDINBURGH, TRINITY COLLEGE. A bull of Pope Pius II, 23 Oct. 1460, annexes the hospital of Soutra (*q.v.*) to the college and hosp. of the Holy Trinity fd. by Mary, Q. of Scotland [Mary of Gueldres, widow of James II] (*Midlothian Chrs.*, 57; *Edinburgh Trinity Chrs.*, no. 1). The fd'n. had taken place somewhat before this date; and the queen's charter 25 March 1462 (which is no doubt the fd'n. charter), ordained the constitution of the college and assigned the endowments (*ibid.*, 64 ff; *ibid.*, no. 11). Provision was made for a provost, eight chaplains and two choristers as well as for thirteen bedesmen (see Trinity College Hospital). The first prebendary had the title of master of the hospital of the Holy Trinity, the second was called the sacristan, the others were the prebendaries respectively of Browderstanis, Strathmartin, Gilstoun, Ormiston, Hill and Newlands. Two additional prebends, one of which was to be allocated to a dean, while the other, as noted in a papal confirmation of 1504, was assigned to a sub-dean, were provided, 14 Nov. 1502 by the appropriation of the parish ch. of Dunnottar (*ibid.*, no. vi; *Midlothian Chrs.*, 143). A letter of James V to Pope Clement VII, 23 March 1531/2 desired an indulgence for penitents visiting Trinity College, where the provost had planned to bring the rest of the ch. into keeping with the nobly constructed choir (*James V Letters*, 217). The prebendaries houses are said to have been destroyed by Reformers in 1559 (Lesley, *History*, 275). The establishment remained as a provost and ten prebendaries at the Reformation, titular provosts holding office until 1585 (*Midlothian Chrs.*, nos. 82, 85, 86, 106, 203, 205, 213; Watt, *Fasti*, 359). On 12 Nov. 1567, James VI granted the ch. and hospital to Sir Simon Preston, provost of the city and the provost, bailies, councillors and community, as his successors (*Edinburgh Trinity Chrs.*, no. x) but this was not accomplished until 25 June 1585, this being confirmed by another royal grant, 26 May 1587 (Reg. Pres., ii, 134, 172; *Edinburgh Trinity Chrs.*, no. xiv). This ch., 'the last and finest Gothic fragment in Edinburgh', was made parochial *c.*1580 and continued in use till 1848, when it was removed to make a site for the Waverley Station (see *Midlothian Chrs.*, xxix–xxxi; Cockburn, *Memorials* (1909 edn.), 414*n*). See *Midlothian Chrs.*, xii–xxxii; *Edinburgh Trinity Chrs.*, 57–258.

FOWLIS (EASTER), ST. MARNOCK. A petition of 27 Jan. 1450 reveals that the parish ch. of Abernyte had recently been demitted in order that its fruits might be united to a college which Andrew, lord Gray, intended to found '*in sua villa de Folles*' (Reg. Supp., 439, fo. 272). This part of the plan was not effected (Cowan, *Parishes*, 4, 70–1), but an inscription in this ch., which indicates that it was built in 1453, supports a fd'n., possibly under a presiding prebendary (cf. Roslin) at about this date (*Chron. Bower*, ii, 541, NLS, MS. 33, 2, 12, fo. 9, Spottiswoode 468). According to an inventory of 1775, the parish ch. of Ballumby was annexed to the collegiate ch. of Fowlis by the bp. of St. Andrews, 30 April 1460 (SRO, Murray of Ochtertyre Writs (GD 54/2/170), item no. 95). A reconstitution of the college was approved by the Pope, 12 April 1511 (Reg. Supp., 1361, fos. 231 v–232). This may not have been immediately effected and a note (NLS, MS. 34, 3, 11) which attributes the collegiate fd'n. to Patrick, lord Gray, who succeeded to the title in 1514, as well as the confirmation of this foundation and consecration of the ch. to James Beaton, abp. of St. Andrews (1522–39) may be substantially correct, in so far as it refers to the erection of a provostry and reconstitution of the college. The first mention of provostry, along with seven prebendaries is found in 1538 (Prot. Bk. Ireland, fo. 42). Prebends which have been identified are Ballumby, Cuthilbank and Bowhouse, Easter and Wester Keith, Ladyet, Over Smithton and the parish clerkship, the holder of which appears to have been a prebendary (*ibid.*, fos. 43, 57 v; SRO, Prot. Bk. Harlaw, fo. 20 v; SRO, Murray of Ochtertyre Writs, items 97, 100, 115).

GLASGOW, OUR LADY COLLEGE. Fd. by James Houston, subdean of Glasgow. There are indications from 20 Feb. 1522/3 that the fd'n. was contemplated (*Glasgow, St. Mary Lib.*, xii, 79, 80, 83 *n*). On 29 April 1525, the abp. of Glasgow approved the fd'n. of this ch., the building of which had begun (*Glasgow Chrs.*, ii, 494–7). The original fd'n. was for a provost, nine prebendaries and three choristers who were supported by the prebend of that name (*Glasgow, St. Mary Lib.*, xv–xxi, 6–7). The nine individual prebends were known as Holy Trinity (which pertained to archpriest), sacristan, St. Anne (which pertained to the master of the Song school), St. Mary, St. James the Apostle, St. Roche, St. Kentigern, St. Nicholas (founded by Nicholas Witherspoon) and St. Andrew the Apostle (*ibid.*, xv–xxi, 23–37). Two further prebends, the Name of Jesus and St. Martin, were added by Martin Reid, 20 March 1548/9 (*ibid.*, xix–xx, 38–42). On 2 Aug. 1570, the ch., which is described as ruinous, was feued to one of the burgesses by the provost and bailies of Glasgow (*Glasgow Chrs.*, ii, no. lxi). It was subsequently reacquired and the building was used as a parish ch. from 1592 to 1793 when it was destroyed by fire. See *Glasgow, St. Mary Lib.*, *passim; Glasgow Chrs.*, i, pt. I, lix–lxi).

GUTHRIE, ST. MARY. The date of fd'n. has been given as *c*1456 (*Midlothian Chrs.*, iv), but this is too early. Spottiswoode (468) describes Sir David Guthrie of that ilk as founder and the latter is thus designated in a charter which also shows that his death took place before the proposed foundation was complete (*RMS*, ii, no. 2910). On 19 May 1479 the Pope, in response to a petition of Sir Alexander Guthrie, Sir David's son and successor, containing that his late father enlarged and adorned the parish ch. of Guthrie, then a prebendal ch. of Brechin cathedral, with a view to its erection into a collegiate ch., consented to the extinction of the prebend and the erection of the ch. for a provost and four canons, who were to be maintained by prebends based upon one third of the parsonage revenues of Guthrie for one canon, the vicarage revenues of Guthrie for another, the fruits of the parish ch. of Kirkbuddo for a third canon and from immovable goods belonging to Alexander for a fourth (*CPL*, xiii, 137–9; Reg. Supp., 782, fo. 70–71). Annates were to be paid in the name of the provost and chapter of Guthrie, 'newly erected into a collegiate church', 24 July 1483 (Cameron, *Apostolic Camera*, 207). Only three of these prebends, besides the provostry, were at first erected, but provision was made for a fourth canonry, 30 September 1505 (*RMS*, ii, no. 2910). A prebend of Hiltoun and Langlandis and another of Little Loure occur in 1573 (NLS, 31.3.12, fo. 97) but which is to be equated with the prebend originally based upon part of the parsonage revenues of Guthrie, and which is the sixteenth century foundation is uncertain.

HADDINGTON, ST. MARY. About 1540, the priests of this large parish ch., already mentioned, 20 May 1537, as 'the college Kirk of Haddington' (Wallace-James's MS. Notebooks, SRO, Miscell., i, 77), were, on the initiative of the bailies, councillors and community, formally constituted as a college, under a president (*St. Andrews Formulare*, ii, no. 435). There is a reference to the 'prebendars of the College Kirk', 5 Dec. 1540, and another to the 'president of the College Kirk', 22 May 1541 (Wallace-James's MS. Notebooks, SRO, Miscell., i, 83, 85 (from burgh records).

HAMILTON, ST. MARY. The fd'n. in the parish ch. by James, Lord Hamilton, confirmed by Pope Nicholas V, 4 Jan. 1450/1 (*CPL*, x, 75–76; *HMC, 11th Rep.*, pt. 6, 47–8; Theiner, *Vet. Mon.*, no. dcclvii), was for a provost and six chaplains. Two existing chaplainries in the ch. also appear to have been converted into prebends (*OPS*, i, 106; Hamilton of Wishaw, *Lanarkshire*, 17). One of the eight prebends is described in 1506 as the 'prebendal sacristary or treasurership' (*Glasgow Dioc. Reg.*, i, no. 196) and there is also reference to the prebend of the parish clerkship (*St. Andrews Formulare*, i, 263). Three chaplains were to be hired for seven years to sing continually for the soul of John, E. of Lennox, 13 Feb. 1530 (*HMC, 3rd Rep.*, 393). The title and office of the prebends were suppressed 8 Jan. 1668, and this was followed by the suppression of the provostry on 23 Feb. 1672 (*APS*, vii, 519; viii, III).

INNERPEFFRAY. This ch. is not noted by Spottiswoode nor in MS. and other lists. A chapel of St. Mary is mentioned, 28 Nov. 1365 (*Inchaffray Chrs.*, 128) and 10 May 1483 (Anderson, *Oliphants*, no. 37); and, on 3 Feb. 1506/7 (or 4 Feb., according to *ibid.*, no 77), four chaplainries were endowed there by John, lord Drummond (*RMS*, ii, no. 3048). It thus appears to have been a chantry which acquired collegiate form. On 25 Oct. 1542, this is called a collegiate ch. (*ibid.*, iii, no. 2825); and there is litigation over the provostry, 11 Feb. 1548/9 (*ADCP*, 581). There are references to provosts in 1562 and 1567 (NLS. MS. 16.1.1; *RMS*, iv, no. 2378), and to a 'provost or principal chaplain of the church of the

Blessed Mary of Innerpeffray' (Macfarlane's Notes (NLS, MS.), 34). Titular provosts continue on record until 1592 (Watt, *Fasti*, 361–2).

KILMAURS. The date of fd'n. is given as 13 May 1403 (Spottiswoode, 469; NLS. MS., 35.4.16, fo. 9), but this is the date on which three chaplainries were endowed in the parish ch. by William Cunningham, lord of Kilmaurs (SRO Glencairn Chrs., no. 17). The endowment of three further chaplainries on 14 May 1413 may have been the origin of the college, which, according to one source, was for a provost, six prebendaries and two singing boys (NLS, Hutton Collections, vii, 101; McNaught, *Kilmaurs Parish and Burgh*, 325–8). Spottiswoode (469) on the other hand claims that there were eight prebendaries. The fd'n. charter is not apparently extant, and the occurence of a provost on 8 Jan. 1462 is the first intimation of the erection of the college (Watt, *Fasti*, 362). Four prebends, Bellahill, Chirretreheuch, Fluiris and Bankheid, and Kilmaurs, have been identified from post-Reformation sources (*RMS*, iv, no. 221, *Laing Charters*, no. 1320). As its patron, the E. of Glencairn, was a prominent protestant, this college may have ceased to function as such, even before the Reformation.

KILMUN, ST. MUND. The document entitled '*fundatio Collegii de Kilmun*' (NLS, MSS, 22.1.14, 217; 34.3.11, 156 printed in *RMS*, ii, no. 346) and dated 4 Aug. 1442, is a charter of endowment rather than of foundation. On 5 Aug. 1441, the Pope granted the petition of Sir Duncan Campbell of Lochawe for the confirmation of the erection of the parish ch. of St. Mund into a collegiate ch. for five chaplains, one of whom was to be provost, and a parochial chaplain who was to take part in divine services with the other chaplains (Reg. Supp., 375, fo. 124). Annates paid in the name of the provost and these five chaplains 'to be constituted in the parish church of St. Mund . . . on its erection into a collegiate church' are recorded, 5 Oct. 1441 (Cameron, *Apostolic Camera*, 129). The provost and seven chaplains of the college appear 6 July 1452 (*RMS*, iv, no. 791, cf. *OPS*, ii² 71). These additional chaplainries may have been endowed from the revenues of the parish ch. of Kilmalieu of which possession was confirmed to the college by the Pope, 26 March 1466 (*CPL*, xii, 242–4). At least one prebend seems to have been supported by this ch. at a later date, while yet another was upheld by the revenues of the parish ch. of Kilmelfort (*RSS*, vi, no. 1915; SRO, RH6/ 1691).

LINCLUDEN. Originally a Benedictine nunnery. See under Benedictine Nuns. On 7 May 1389 the Pope, on the petition of Archibald de Douglas, lord of Galloway, commissioned the bp. of Glasgow to suppress the nunnery and to erect a collegiate ch. for a provost, eight priests and twenty-four bedesmen (Reg. Aven., 259, fos. 471-2 v). A bull of privileges to the provost was issued 25 January 1395/6 (*ibid.*, 300, fo. 80 v; *Scot, Antiq.*, viii, 67–8). The date of the fd'n. is given erroneously as 1413 (*Midlothian Chrs.*, iv). An additional chaplainry of the Blessed Virgin Mary was founded, 22 Sept. 1429 (*RMS*, ii., no. 133). At least four other prebends—Kirkandrews (× 1447/8), Kirkbride (× 1487), Lochmaben (1447 × 1449) and Tinwald (× 1498)—were erected in the course of the fifteenth c. (Cowan, *Parishes*, 117, 118, 135–6, 198). Kirkandrews was disjoined on its annexation to the Chapel Royal at Stirling (*q.v.*) in 1501, and while another prebend, Parton, was apparently added 1525/6 × 1541, this appears to have been ineffective (*ibid.*, 117, 162). The final composition of the college would thus appear to be a provost and twelve prebendaries. On 3 June 1508 the Pope consented to the annexation of the provostry of Lincluden to the Chapel Royal at Stirling (Reg. Lat., 1208, fo. 289; *Hist. Chapel Royal*, cxlv); but the union was dissolved before 14 July 1529 (Watt, *Fasti*, 365). A hospital was attached to this ch. See HOLYWOOD HOSPITAL. On Lincluden, see *Dumfriesshire Trans.*, xxiii, 190–5.

MARKLE, ST. MARIOTA. It is stated of this fd'n. in Prestonkirk parish that 'Dr. J. G. Wallace-James . . . has notes of charters c.1450 in which St. Mary . . . is named as the titular of the provostry' (MacKinlay, *Dedications (non-scriptural)*, 499–500). No such references have, however, been found in Wallace-James' notes (now in SRO). In title deeds of the barony of Hailes it is customarily described just as a chapel, not as a collegiate ch. (*RMS*, ii, no. 3635; v, no. 218, vi, no. 166). As such it is on record from 27 Aug. 1511 (*ibid.*, ii, no. 3635) to 12 May 1653 (*Haddington Retours*, no. 233). Clergy with the title of provost are, however, found from 28 July 1515 (*Lag. Chrs.*, no. 76; Watt, *Fasti*, 366). The provostship and prebendaries are mentioned, 8 Nov. 1569 (*Haddington Retours*, no. 388) but no information is forthcoming as to the number of prebends.

MAYBOLE, ST. MARY. On 29 Nov. 1371, a chapel of St. Mary was founded by John Kennedy of Dunure beside the churchyard of the parish ch., for three chaplains and a clerk (*RMS*, i. nos. 378, 428). A college was founded in this chapel by Kennedy with the consent of the bp. of Glasgow shortly before 2 Feb. 1382 when a mandate to confirm the erection was granted by Pope Clement VII (Reg. Aven., 229, fo. 188 v). On the same date it is stated that the greater part of the building has been completed (*ibid.*, 229, fo. 188). The ratification of the erection in virtue of the papal bull was effected and the constitution established as a provost, two chaplains and a clerk (*Cross. Chrs.*, i, no. 21). A fourth chaplainry was endowed, 18 May 1451 (*RMS*, ii, no. 446) and on 24 April 1516, a fifth prebend was founded by Egidia Blair, widow of James Kennedy of Row (SRO, Airlie Writs, i, no. 246; *Glas. Reg.*, ii, nos. 492–3). At least five prebendal stalls existed in the college at the Reformation, one of which evidently pertained to the provost (*RMS*, iv, no. 2377). The college continued to function for a time after the Reformation, mass being publicly celebrated there at Easter 1563 (Pitcairn, *Trials*, 1a, *427–8).

METHVEN. Fd. in the parish ch. by Walter Stewart, E. of Atholl, Caithness and Strathearn for a provost, five chaplains and four boy choristers, 1 May 1433 (*CPL*, vii, 460–1). An endowment for the erection of a prebend from the lands of Easter and Wester Busbies was granted to the then provost John Tiry by James IV, 15 Oct. 1510 (Morris, *Provostry of Methven*, 34–40). Thereafter, and before 18 July 1516, Tiry erected no fewer than eight further prebends from the fruits of his provostry. One of these prebends was assigned twenty bolls of meal, three were allotted twenty pounds and the other four received sixteen pounds annually (*ibid.*, 112–3; cf. *RSS*, i, nos. 2782, 2798). The duties of vicar pensioner, who is sometimes designated as *vicarius prebendarius de Methven* (Morris, *Provostry of Methven*, 99) was probably held by one of the eight prebendaries. In addition to these, the prebendary of Busbies, and the original five chaplains, were being maintained at the Reformation at which the establishment appears to have consisted of the provost, nine prebendaries and five chaplains (*ibid.*, 99, 112–3). See T. Morris, *The Provostry of Methven* (Edinburgh, 1875).

PEEBLES, ST. ANDREW. A college consisting of a provost, who was to be parson of Lyne (Cowan, *Parishes*, 141–2), twelve prebendaries and two choristers was founded in the parish ch. by the bailies, councillors and John Hay of Yester on 28 May 1541 (Vat. Arch., Resignationes A, 87, fos. 160v–1; *Peebles Chrs.*, 61–4). The fd'n. was ratified by Mary, Queen of Scots, 8 June 1543, the twelve prebendaries being named as those at the altars of St. Mary in Childbirth, Holy Rood, St. Michael, St. Mary Major, St. Peter and St. Paul, St. John Baptist, St. Mary of Geddes Aisle, St. Andrew, St. James, St. Laurence, St. Martin and St. Christopher (*ibid.*). No post-Reformation references to the altars of St. Martin and St. Peter and Paul have been noted, but St. Peter's chaplain occurs in 1555 and St. Martin's still existed, 15 Jan. 1557/8 (Renwick, *Peebles in Reign of Queen Mary*, 8, 37), and the constitution at the Reformation may still have consisted of the provost and twelve prebendaries (cf. *Peebles Chrs.*, 91; *OPS* i, 299). On 17 Dec. 1560, this ch. is said to have been 'brint and distroyit be Yngland xii yeris syne or thairby' (i.e. *c*.1548) (*Peebles Chrs.*, 264).

RESTALRIG. A petition by John Frissell, 6 May 1487, for the erection as a collegiate ch. of the ch. of the Holy and Indivisible Trinity and St. Mary the Virgin within the bounds of the parish ch. of Restalrig which James III had built and endowed, was granted and this was confirmed by papal bull on 13 Nov. 1487 (Reg. Supp., 870, fos. 264–5; *CPL*, xiv, 211–3; *Midlothian Chrs.*, 273, ff). This fd'n. is sometimes styled a chapel royal. In 1487, the ch. is called 'the king's chapel beside the parish church of Restalrig (*ER*, ix, 540), and 1497, the dean is designated as of 'the chapel royal of Restalrig (*ibid.*, xi, 2). The initial fd'n. was for a dean and an unspecified number of prebendaries (*CPL*, xiv, 211–13). Prebends were not however, established until 1512 when following upon a request for the renewal and confirmation by Pope Julius II of the privileges granted to this ch., founded by his father, James IV presented the dean of Restalrig to the ch. of Rothesay in Bute which was subsequently divided into six prebends known as Bute *primo* to Bute *sexto*

(*James IV Letters*, no. 440, *RSS*, i, no. 2394; *Midlothian Chrs.*, lv; Cowan, *Parishes*, 174). On 18 Oct. 1512, two further prebends, one known as the Kingis Werk (*Opus Regale*) and the other as St. Triduans aisle, were fd. by the king (*Midlothian Chrs.*, 278–80). These erections were confirmed, 10 Oct. 1515, by James V, who also made provision for another prebend to be entitled Ross in memory of the first provost of the college, who had subsequently become bp. of that diocese (*ibid.*, 280–90). Other prebends included that of St. Jerome and another undesignated prebend founded in memory of provost Thomas Dickson who died in 1513 (*ibid.*, lv–lvi). The latter remains unidentified, but the others remained at the Reformation (Book of Assumptions, fo. 155 v; *RSS*, v, no. 3068; *Midlothian Chrs.*, lviii). According to a charter of 1552 the prebendaries houses had been 'burned and almost destroyed' by the English (*HMC. Rep.*, *MSS. in Various Collns.*, v, 68). In 1560 the ch. was ordered by the Reformed General Assembly to be demolished (*BUK*, i, 5).

ROSLIN, ST. MATHEW. The suggestion that this celebrated ch., founded by William, E. of Caithness and Orkney, in 1446, was from the outset collegiate, is frequently made (e.g. Spottiswoode, 471; Hay, *Sainteclaires*, 26). It was certainly under construction at this date, but it was probably not until the early 1450s that it possessed a collegiate constitution (*Hist. Mon. Comm.* (*Midlothian and West Lothian*), 100, 106). It is described in 1456 as a 'college kirk' (*Bannatyne Misc.*, iii, 96). Its erection under a presiding prebendary with six other prebendary priests and three humble clerks, choristers of whom one should be sacrist, was confirmed by the Pope, 12 Feb. 1477 (Reg. Supp., 747, fos. 75–6; cf. Spottiswoode, 471). Again, charters of 10 Dec. 1476 and 5 Jan. 1491/2 refer to the 'preses' or 'presidens' and prebendaries (*RMS*, ii, nos. 1270, 2076; Hay, *Sainteclaires*, 83). The formal erection of this ch. to collegiate status is attributed to Andrew Forman, abp. of St. Andrews (d. 11 March 1520/1) in an undated charter which purports to erect it, on the petition of Sir William Sinclair, into a 'perpetual college' for a provost and four prebendaries (*St. Andrews Formulare*, i, no. 389). As this document cannot have been issued before 18 May 1521, it must have been given by Abp. James Beaton, Forman's successor (*ibid.*, i, 348 n). This charter, which must be regarded as providing for a reconstitution of the college under a provost, was probably granted about the same time as a charter by Sir William Sinclair providing manses for the provost, sacrist and the third and fourth prebendaries 5 Feb. 1523/4 (*Midlothian Chrs.*, 328–31). The two prebendaries are described as serving the altars of St. Andrews the Apostle and St. Peter the Apostle, while the provost and Sacrist served those of St. Mathew and the blessed Virgin Mary (*ibid.*). The dedications of the remaining two prebendal altars is unascertained, but as the college contained six altars, the existence of a first and second prebendary, other than provost and sacrist, may be assumed (*Hist. Mon.Comm.* (*Midlothian and West Lothian*) 106).

ST. ANDREWS, ST. MARY ON THE ROCK (KIRKHEUGH). This college was a development of the community of Keledei (*q.v.*), whose head and members are thus described, 7 Nov. 1250: 'Master Adam de Malkarviston conducting himself as provost of the church of St. Mary of the city of St. Andrews and the Keledei conducting themselves as canons' (NLS, MS., 15.1.18, fo. 30); while a bull of 7 April 1251 refers to the provost and secular chapter of St. Mary's (*Inchaff. Chrs.*, 154). Its creation as a collegiate ch. can probably be attributed to 1248–9 (G.W.S. Barrow, 'The clergy at St. Andrews', in *The Kingdom of Scots*, London, 1973, 229). The culdean prebends were apparently converted into the prebends of the new fd'n., whose membership comprised a provost and more than six canons (*ibid.*, 216–23). In 1344 it is still designated 'St. Mary of the Culdees' (*CPL*, iii, 150, 152). This ch. had the dignity of a chapel royal. It is difficult to say when it acquired this status, but it may have been so regarded from the time of its inception as a secular college. A seal dated 1286 × 1296 suggests it was so regarded at that time, and there is reference in a mandate of Edward I, 10 Sept. 1298, to the 'provostry of the king's free chapel of St. Andrews' (*CDS*, ii, no. 1017). On 24 Jan. 1385/6, Pope Clement VII granted a petition of Robert II, who desired that the provost of the chapel royal should, like the two archdeacons of St. Andrews, be given a stall, a place in the cathedral chapter, and a voice in elections (Reg. Aven., 245, fo. 397). Attempts were made in the fifteenth c. to have the revenues of the priory of Coldingham annexed to this ch. (see COLDINGHAM). Its status as a chapel royal may have ceased with the erection of the Chapel Royal at Stirling (*q.v.*) to the deanship of which, the provostship of this ch. was personally conjoined between 1501 and 1504 (Watt, *Fasti*, 335). This ch. is said to have had a provost and ten prebendaries (Spottiswoode, 469; NLS., MS., 35.4.16). Martine says at least nin (*Reliqiuae*, 217). The exact number of prebends is difficult to determine. At least three of the thirteenth c. culdean prebends—Cairns and Cameron, Kinglassie and Kingask, ar Lambieletham—continued as such (*St. A. Lib.*, 318; *Thirds of Benefices*, 13) and the prebends of Durie and Rumgally, Kinkell, and Kinaldy all based on the revenues of lands situated in the near vicinity of St. Andrews may have likewise been original prebends, in providing a total complement with the provost of seven (*ibid.*, 13; *RSS*, ii, no. 229). On 5 April 1425, Henry, bp. of St. Andrews 'having regard to the fewness of persons in the Chapel Royal of St. Mary . . . who are seven in number and not more' endowed a new prebend of Fetteresso (*St. A. Lib.*, 407). The erection of another prebend in the college in which there are stated to be only eight prebends, and which is attributed to Archbishop Forman (d. 1520/1) (*St. Andrews Formulare*, i, no. 131) is in fact a charter of erection of the parish ch. of Strathbrock as a prebend, *c.* 1435 × 1436, by Henry, bp. of St. Andrews (Cowan, *Parishes*, 191).The erection of at least five further prebends—Arbuthnot (× 1447), Ballingry (× 1461), Benholm (× 1477), Dysart (1477) and Idvies (× 1547)—can be substantiated (Cowan, *Parishes*, 8, 12–13, 16, 57, 84). The charter of erection of an additional prebend, apparently granted by Abp. Forman is given in *St. Andrews Formulare* (i, nos. 121–2), but it is uncertain whether this took place, but at least thirteen simple prebends existed at the Reformation. This ch. is said to have been pulled down by Reformers in June 1559 (Lesley, *History*, 273). See Barrow, 'The clergy at St. Andrews', in *The Kingdom of the Scots*, 212–32.

SEMPLE, or LOCHWINNOCH. Fd. by John, Lord Semple, 21 April 1504, for a provost, six chaplains of Nether Pennal, Upper Pennal, Auchinlodmond, Nether Schelis, Lochwinnoch and Chapeltown, a sacrist and two choristers (*Glas. Reg.*, ii, no. 483). The original fd'n. appears to have remained unaugmented, although further information about these chaplainries is sparse (*Laing Chrs.*, no. 1971).

SETON. On the petition of George, Lord Seton, Pope Paul II gave a mandate for the erection of this parish ch., on its voidance by the then rector, into a collegiate ch. for a provost, six canons, a clerk and two choristers (*CPL*, xii, 346). However, the rector of the ch. is still described as such, and not as provost, in 1482 (*ER*, ix, 176). Moreover, although the ch. is styled 'collegiate' in 1488 (*Prot. Bk. Young*, no. 119), the bull of fd'n. was not granted till 22 Dec. 1492 when following the petition of George [II], Lord Seton, on 29 Nov. 1492, Pope Alexander VI appointed mandatories to carry out the erection as the ch. was now vacant (Reg. Supp., 965, fos. 203–3 v; 966, fo. 9 v; NLS. MS. 15.1.19, no. 15). This mandate was executed in 1493. Details of the erection, including the allocation of the endowments between the provost and six prebendaries, are included in a contemporary vernacular copy of the fd'n. chapter (J. Durkan, 'Foundation of the collegiate church of Seton', *Innes Rev.*, xiii (1962), 71–76. Two additional prebends, known as Harperdean *primus* and *secundus* were endowed *c.* 1540 by Lady Janet Hepburn, their erection being confirmed by John Hamilton, abp. of St. Andrews, in 1556 (*ibid.*, 72–3).

STIRLING, CHAPEL ROYAL. A constitution for a collegiate ch. was being formulated at the turn of the fifteenth–sixteenth c., when a body of clergy was assembled under the temporary headship of David Trail, who is described (10 July 1499 x 14 July 1501) as 'provost of the new college in the castle of Stirling' (*ER*, xi, 314, f. 318). On 2 May 1501 Pope Alexander VI, on the petition of James IV, sanctioned the erection of the Chapel Royal of St. Mary and St. Michael, Stirling, into a collegiate ch. for a dean, sub-dean, sacrist, sixteen canons and six choristers. The provostry of St. Mary on the Rock, St. Andrews, was to be erected into the deanery of the Chapel Royal, Stirling to form a joint dignity, the holder having pre-eminence in both chs. This constitution was put into effect 6 Sept. 1501. Provision was also made for the partial appropriation of the revenues of Restennet priory (*q.v.*) of certain prebends of Dunbar (*q.v.*) and of some fifteen parish chs. and their associated chapels (*Hist. Chapel Royal*, no. 1). Not all these unions were effective (*ibid.*, cxxxiv; Cowan, *Parishes*, 22, 37–8, 50, 55, 56, 61, 110–11, 164). In 1502 one of the canonries was erected into a chantership (Hist. Chapel Royal, no. 2), and in 1504 a treasurership and ten lesser canonries were added (*ibid.*, no. 8). A sub-chantership is mentioned in 1506 and although not mentioned thereafter may be equated with the later office of master of the bairns (*RSS*, i, no. 1341; Watt, *Fasti*, 340–1, *Hist Chapel Royal*, cxxi); between 1507 and 1512 an archdeaconry was erected (*ibid.*, 341), and in 1512 a chancellor appears (*James IV Letters*, 476).

On 3 July 1504, on the petition of James IV, Pope Julius II revoked the union of St. Mary on the Rock and the Chapel Royal and united the deanery to the bishopric of Galloway [Whithorn], so that the bp. of that diocese would be dean of the Chapel Royal (Reg. Vat., 984, fos. 70–1; *Hist. Chapel Royal*, nos. 15, 17). On 3 Oct. 1506 and 6 April, 1507, James IV is found asking the Pope and the Cardinal of St. Mark that the dean should have his title altered to bishop and that the priory of Inchmahome (*q.v.*) should be annexed to the episcopal *mensa* (*James IV Letters*, nos. 52, 53, 101). These requests are assumed to have been granted on 1 March, 1507/8 when the king intimates his desire that besides Inchmahome priory, the priory of Restennet (which evidently had not yet been appropriated) and the provostry of Lincluden should be annexed to it (*ibid.*, no. 156). The Pope, 3 June 1508, consented to these appropriations (Reg. Lat., 1208, fo. 289), but, on 8 Nov. following K. James is found mentioning, in a letter to the Cardinal of St. Marks, that the annexation of Restennet had not taken effect (*James IV Letters*, no. 195; cf. no. 201. On 1 March 1507/8, the king had asked that the bp. of Galloway and the Chapel Royal should be inferior to no other (*ibid.*, no. 156) and, on 1 Aug. 1511, requested the Pope to confirm the privileges of the bp. of the Chapel Royal, conferring upon him jurisdiction over the king and his household, as well as over annexed chs. of royal patronage, and their parishioners and to declare that the Chapel Royal, in this respect, covered all the palaces of his kingdom (*ibid.*, no. 209). A further letter to the Pope, 9 April 1512, mentions that the suit of the abp. of Glasgow against the Chapel Royal and its privileges had been quashed by the Pope and asks that a suit involving the provostry of Lincluden should be dealt with similarly (*ibid.*, no. 241).

Before 14 July 1529, despite efforts of James V to the contrary (*ADC*, xxxvii, 151), Inchmahome and Lincluden had been disjoined from the Chapel Royal (*James V Letters*, 161; cf. *RSS*, ii, no, 210; Watt, *Fasti*, 345). There is a reference to the union of the abbey of Tongland to the bishopric of Galloway and of the Chapel Royal, by bulls of Pope Clement VII, 14 Jan. 1529/30 (Brady, *Episcopal Succession*, i, 208); and from 1529 to 1541 James V appears as attempting to secure this (*James V Letters*, 162, 425; *Ep. Reg. um. Scotorum*, ii, 115–19). The constitution at the Reformation is uncertain, but the college at that date would appear to consist of dean, sub-dean, sacrist, chanter, chancellor, treasurer, sub-chanter or master of the bairns, archdeacon and prebendaries of Balmaclellan, Crieff *primo* and *secundo*, Glenholm and Kells (Watt, *Fasti*, 335 –41; Cowan, *Parishes*, 13, 39, 75–6, 92, 112, 120–1, 186, 211). Six further prebendaries, making a complement of at least nineteen canons, were maintained from the fruits of the parish ch. of Ayr and its chapels of Alloway, Coylton and Dalrymple, these usually being designated Ayr *primo* to Ayr *sexto*, although on occasions Coylton *primo* and *secundo* replaces Ayr *primo* and *sexto* as the designation of these prebends. In addition nine of the ten lesser canonries, which were projected in 1504, were erected, five being maintained from revenues in Strathbran and four from revenues in Castellaw (*Hist. Chapel Royal*, cxxxiii). After the Reformation the Chapel Royal because it was 'ruinous and too little' was to be 'utterly rased' in 1594 and a new chapel erected. (*ibid.*, lxxxi).

STIRLING, HOLY RUDE. This parish ch. which possessed at least fourteen altars and as many chaplains had a new choir built by the magistrates, town council and community in the early sixteenth c. (*Stirling Chrs.*, no. xxxvii, p. 247; *Stirling Recs.* (*1519–1666*), 18, 323–4; *HMC Rept.*, (*Stirlingshire*), i, 129–40); and before 1546, a college of priests choristers which had been previously founded was constituted with the vicar perpetual as president and a sub-president as his deputy (*St. Andrews Formulare*, ii, 172).

STRATHMIGLO. On 31 March 1527 mention is made of a proposal by Sir William Scott of Balweary to set up a college in this parish ch. (*ADCP*, 257). The patronage of the provostry and prebends is confirmed to him, 5 March 1528/9 (*RMS*, iii, no. 760), and to his son, 30 April 1548 (*ibid.*, iv, no. 200). The number of prebends is not known, but there is a reference to three choristers (*ADCP*, 257).

TAIN, ST. DUTHAC. This college originated in the chapel of St. Duthac which was adjacent to the parish ch. It is described as a collegiate chapel after its destruction by fire in 1427 (Macdonald, *The Clan Donald*, i, 542; cf. NLS MS. 35.4.12a, Macfarlane's Collns.). By a charter of 10 Oct. 1457, James II endowed a chaplainry in what is designated 'the collegiate church of St. Duthac of Tain' (*Fraser Papers*, 220). It is usually referred to as a collegiate chapel and certainly there was no provost, but it is quite clear that the clerics of Tain lived a collegiate existence long before the fd'n. of their collegiate ch. as such. On 12 Sept. 1487, with the assent of his chapter and at the instigation of James III, Thomas, bp. of Ross, erected it—'for the increase of the divine worship of the chapel or collegiate church of the blessed confessor bishop Duthac of Tain' into a collegiate ch. for a provost, five prebendaries or canons of Newmore, Dunskeath, Tarlogie, Morangie and Cambuscurry, two deacons or sub-deacons, a sacrist and assistant clerk and three boy choristers (Durkan, 'The sanctuary and college of Tain', *Innes Rev.*, xiii (1962), 152–6). A transaction took place in the choir of the collegiate ch. 8 Oct. 1487 and the bp's. charter was confirmed under the great seal, 3 Dec. 1487 (Fraser, *Cromartie*, ii, 324 (Cromarty Chrs., no. 526); *RMS*, ii, no. 1694). An additional chaplainry was founded and maintained by an endowment of ten pounds granted by James IV (*RSS*, iii, nos. 182, 195), but this apparently remained the constitution until the Reformation (*Thirds of Benefices*, 3, 210–211; *RMS*, vi, no. 771).

INCOMPLETE FOUNDATIONS

Darnley. On 24 Feb. 1421/2, the Pope granted a petition of John Stewart, Lord Darnley, for the annexation of the parish ch. of Tarbolton to a college of six priests which he proposed to found in the territory of 'Derneley' (*CSSR*, i, 283). The fd'n. did not take place, and it remained a chapel (EU. DC. 4, 32, fo. 10).

Douglas. On 27 March 1423 the Pope was petitioned by Archibald, E. of Douglas, to sanction the erection of the parish ch. of Douglas into a collegiate ch. under a dean (*CSSR*, ii, 15); and, again on 7 Aug. 1448, the Pope granted a petition of William, E. of Douglas, for the fd'n. of a collegiate ch. with a provost and thirteen prebendaries (*CPL*, x. 429). Although an indulgence is granted to penitents who give alms for the completion and maintenance of this ch., described as 'erected by papal authority into the collegiate church of St. Bride, Douglas, which William, E. of Douglas, has at great cost caused to be new built', 1 Feb. 1450/1 (*ibid.*, x. 84), and although there are mentions of a provostry, 31 Jan. 1488/9 (Fraser, *Douglas*, iii, no. 119; *RMS*, ii, no. 1827) and 5 July 1499 (Fraser, *Douglas*, iii, no. 152), it does not seem to have acquired collegiate status and is mentioned simply as a parish church, 7 March 1483/4 and 16 June 1506 (*RMS*, ii, nos. 1586, 2974).

Falkirk. On 24 Feb. 1449/50, the Pope consented on the petition of Alexander Livingstone, to the erection of a collegiate ch. for a provost and six canons; but, because objection was made by the king and the abbey of Holyrood, which held this (parish) ch., the consent was withdrawn, 1 June 1450 (Reg. Supp., 434, 279; 442, 228 v).

Linlithgow. In 1430 a proposal was made at the instigation of James I that the parish ch. should be erected into a collegiate ch. with a provost and twelve prebendaries. Endowments were to include the fruits of the vicarage of Linlithgow and the revenues of the chs. of Calder-Comitis and Strathbrock (Reg. Supp., 262, fo. 234; *ibid.*, 268, fo. 127 v). These plans never materialized, the death of the king in 1437 probably seeing the end of the project.

St. Andrews, Holy Trinity. Sir John Lindsay, son of Sir William Lindsay, lord of the Byres, who had been responsible for the removal of the ch. to a more commodious site, petitioned the Pope, 27 May 1433, that he might found and endow a college of secular canons in the ch. This was conditional on the patronage of the ch. being transferred from the priory to himself (Reg. Supp., 286, fo. 221). Opposition from the priory would almost certainly be forthcoming, and no doubt because of this, the scheme came to nothing.

St. Ninian's. A charter of James V, 28 June 1528, made provision for the erection by the abbot of Cambuskenneth, the sheriff of Stirling and the *generosi*, nobles, knights and parishioners of St. Ninian's for the erection of a college in this parish ch. (*RMS*, iii, no. 601). The project does not seem to have matured.

UNCERTAIN AND SUPPOSED FOUNDATIONS

Arbroath. References are found between 1561 and 1572 to the provostry of Our Lady in Arbroath (*Thirds of Benefices*, pp. 10, 167, 235). There is no other mention of a secular college in Arbroath, but the reference may be to a chantry 'beside the bridge' of that town of which a principal chaplain of the Blessed Virgin Mary is mentioned, 4 Jan. 1519/20 (*Arb. Lib.*, ii, no. 583).

Arbuthnott. This ch., mentioned as collegiate (e.g. McGibbon and Ross, *Eccles. Archit.*, iii, 235), was simply a parish ch.

Auchterless. Given by Dempster (*Apparatus* i, 77) as a collegiate ch., fd'n. by David Dempster of Auchterless, in 1403. There is no evidence of this and Dempster's statements are notoriously unreliable.

Brechin. References to a college (e.g. 4 Sept. 1503 (*RSS*, i, no. 977) and to a collegiate ch. (e.g. 7 Nov. 1512 (*ibid.*, i, no. 2440)) are explained by the fd'n. made by Walter, E. of Strathearn, Athole and Caithness, Lord of Brechin and of Cortachy, 22–31 Oct. 1429, of an association of four priests and six choristers serving in the cathedral, for whom a residence is provided (*Brech. Reg.*, i, nos. 33, 34).

Dysart. Prebends of the collegiate ch. of Dysart are mentioned in 1568 (*More Gleanings from the Records of Dysart* (Edinburgh, 1862) 24).

Houston. Keith declares that this is referred to in the Register of the Privy Seal as a provostry (*Hist. of Affairs of Church and State in Scotland*, iii, 511). But the reference is to the ministry of Houston (*RSS*, ii, no. 1069), i.e. Houston in East Lothian. There is, however, a puzzling reference, in a charter of 1525, to a pensionary provost in the parish church of Houston (*Glas. Reg.*, ii, no. 497), i.e. Houston in Renfrewshire. No other indication of a provostry here has been noticed.

Kennethmont. Given by Dempster (*Apparatus*, i, 77) and Hay (Scotia Sacra, 384) as a collegiate ch. founded by Andrew Dempster. The parish ch. was appropriated to Lindores abbey (*Lind. Cart.*, no. ii, etc.). No evidence of a college in it or elsewhere is forthcoming.

Kirkcudbright, St. Andrew. A chapel, dedicated to St. Andrew, was fd. before 12 Aug. 1517 by William Wardlaw, rector of Dalry who received a precept of confirmation on that date (*RSS*, i, no. 2928). A chaplain, or chaplains, were to be sustained from returns within the burgh, and evidently four such chaplains were maintained. Although chaplains referred to as 'prebendaries and stallaris' occur in 1580, no provostry or college is mentioned, and the fd'n. evidently remained a chapel (SRO, Abbrev. Feu Charters, ii, fo. 121, *RMS*, v. no. 86).

Perth. There is a reference, 11 Jan. 1547/8, to the chaplainry of the altar of St. Fillan founded within the collegiate ch. of Perth (*RSS*, ii, no. 2601). This is an exaggeration of the status of the parish ch. of Perth.

Tullibardine. Frequently given as a collegiate ch. Thus, Spottiswoode (473) declares that it was founded by Sir David Murray of Tullibardine, in 1446, for a provost and several prebendaries; while Hay refers to its foundation as a collegiate ch. in 1447 (NLS. MS. 35.4.16, 10). But it is described as a chapel, 30 Oct. 1455 (*HMC 7th Rep.* App., 708) and 21 March 1618 (*Perth Retours*, no. 255). There is no record of its being made collegiate.

Yester. Given by Spottiswoode (473) as a collegiate ch. This is a blunder due to that writer's failure to recognize that the medieval parish of Bothans is identical with the post-Reformation parish of Yester. The statements made by him concerning the suppositious college of Yester are more nearly correct, as applied to the authentic college of Bothans, than those made in the paragraph dealing with the latter (which he calls 'Bothan' (466).

In his *Commentary on the Rule of St. Augustine* (SHS, ed., p. 73), Richardinus [Richardson] has a reference to 'that most holy and most religious college of the Lord of Borthwick', with an indication that it was dedicated to St. Kentigern. This college defies identification. The most obvious interpretation of the reference would be that it applies to the ch. of Lochorwart (now Borthwick), which had St. Kentigern as its patron. But this was not a collegiate ch. Again, it might be taken to apply to the neighbouring collegiate ch. of

Crichton (to which Lochorwart was appropriated), which was also under the invocation of St. Kentigern. But, in that case, it is not clear why the college should be described as 'of the Lord of Borthwick'.

ACADEMIC SECULAR COLLEGES

GENERAL NOTES

THE five medieval academic colleges of Scotland in existence at the Reformation with the exception of St. Leonard's College, St. Andrews, have continued to the present day.

Name	County	Date Fd.	Termd.	Personnel
‡ABERDEEN KING'S COLLEGE	Aberdeen	−1500		See notes
GLASGOW THE COLLEGE OF ARTS	Lanark	1450/1		See notes
ST. ANDREWS THE PEDAGOGY	Fife	1430	1537/8	See notes
ST. ANDREWS ST. JOHN'S COLLEGE	Fife	−1416	1537/8	See notes
¶‡ST. ANDREWS ST. LEONARD'S COLLEGE	Fife	1512	1747	See notes
ST. ANDREWS ST. MARY'S COLLEGE	Fife	1537/8		See notes
‡ST. ANDREWS ST. SALVATOR'S COLLEGE	Fife	1450		See notes

ACADEMIC SECULAR COLLEGES

ABERDEEN, KING'S COLLEGE. The petition of James IV for the erection of a *studium generale* at Old Aberdeen was sanctioned by Pope Alexander VI on 6 Feb. 1494/5 and a bull to this effect was issued 9 Feb. 1494/5 (Reg. Supp., 1000, fos. 8 vi–82 v; *Aberdeen Fasti*, 1). The fd'n. of a college was probably envisaged from the start and first mooted in an instrument of 22 May 1497 when certain sums are 'to be applied to the support of the collegiate church, to be founded by the bishop in the said university' (Rait, Universities of Aberdeen, 29). The founder, William Elphinstone, bp. of Aberdeen, in 1497 suggested originally one lecturer in each of five faculties (theology, decrees, imperial and civil law, medicine, arts), six students and six priest chaplains (*Aberdeen Fasti*, 14). There is a reference in 1499 to 'our new college . . . of the B.V.M. in Aberdeen university' (*ibid.*, 28) and more precisely 'B.V.M. in her Nativity' (*ibid.*, 31). In that year, 1500, an inscription over the west door of the King's College chapel indicates that building was begun then in the spring (Rait, *Universities of Aberdeen*, 30). In the projected foundation there was no mention of a principal and there were almost as many founded teachers as students. The second foundation of 17 Sept. 1505, proposed a college of thirty-six persons: a master or licentiate in theology to be principal; a canonist; a civilist; a mediciner; a subprincipal, regent in arts; a grammarian; five theologian students (one a regent in arts); thirteen arts students; eight student priest prebendaries (students in any faculty, one to be cantor another sacrist); and four choristers (*Aberdeen Fasti*, 54, 60). On 18 Dec. 1529, Gavin Dunbar, Bp. of Aberdeen, cites a further fd'n. by Elphinstone drawn up before his death and incomplete, extending the foundation to forty-two persons: the first six as before; six theology students (some of them regents); arts students and priest prebendaries as before; and six choristers. (*Aberdeen Fasti*, 82–106). St. Germains hospital (*q.v.*), with certain reservations, was appropriated to the college, which survived the Reformation as an educational establishment: the college's dedication of B.V.M. in her Nativity reflected its debt to the Bethlehemite revenues, acquired for it by the king's goodwill. See further *Fasti Aberdonensis* (Spalding Club, 1854); Rait, *Universities of Aberdeen* (1895).

GLASGOW, THE COLLEGE OF ARTS. On the petition of James II, and on the initiative of Bishop Turnbull, a *studium generale* was authorized by a bull of Pope Nicholas V, 7 Jan. 1450/1 (*Glas. Mun.*, i, 3–5). There came into being on the High Street site almost immediately a school for the faculty of arts and in Oct. 1453, this building was repaired and furnished with benches (*ibid.*, ii, 182). On 6 Jan. 1459–60, this rented pedagogy, whose ultimate superior was James, lord Hamilton, was gifted outright by him to found a college of arts, but as yet it had no chapel or oratory of its own (*ibid.*, i, 9–12). Archbishop Blackadder's will of 1508, however, left money to build a ch. in Glasgow college in honour of the Names of Jesus and Mary (*Innes Review*, xxiii, 147).) This college is sometimes referred to as the Pedagogy, and in time, with the early disuse of the Old Pedagogy in the Rottenrow, the terms became interchangeable (cf. Mackie, *University of Glasgow*, 43 ff). Likewise its head is at different times styled principal regent in the faculty of arts; principal regent of the college of arts; principal regent of the pedagogy; and principal regent of the university and pedagogy (Watt, *Fasti*, 378–9). Its educational functions were uninterrupted by the Reformation.

ST. ANDREWS, THE PEDAGOGY. On 26 March 1430 Henry Wardlaw, bp. of St. Andrews proposed, as chancellor of the university, to grant a tenement for building a college for the Faculty of Arts (*St. Andrews Acta*, 26–27). The donation was effected on 9 April 1430 (*Univ. Evidence*, iii, 351), and the intention was clearly to link up the new fd'n. with that of St. John's college (see below) in whose chapel the members of Wardlaw's fd'n. were to celebrate masses for the soul of their founder (Cant, *University of St. Andrews*, 16). The word 'pedagogy' is not mentioned in Wardlaw's charter. What he intended evidently was 'a college of arts' to separate the arts students from the theologians. The effort to replace private pedagogies by one united pedagogy was not a complete success, for in Nov. 1432 the faculty had to recognise a second pedagogy (presumably a private concern) and thereafter fell back on the plan of maintaining its own official house and of supervising houses of individual masters (*St. Andrews Acta*, 33). The new premises were not ready for use till about 1435 (*ibid.*, xix), but thereafter the Pedagogy and St. John's college became so closely associated as to become almost one. The Pedagogy slowly declined during the fifteenth c. Towards the end of the century there were renewed building operations, but the Pedagogy suffered by comparison with the endowed colleges. It incorporated the old theological schools of St. John's and the law schools were adjacent in the same complex, yet the main burden of its maintenance fell on the arts faculty. From 1525 it received no more students, although in 1554 two St. Mary's men are described anachronistically as Pedagogy students (*St. Andrews Univ. Recs.*, 122, 152). An attempt to reorganize it by the appropriation of the ch. of Tarvit to the Pedagogy on 25 April 1512 'for the purpose of erecting it into a college' were thwarted by the erection of St. Leonard's College (Cant, *University of St. Andrews*, 28–9; *Univ. Evidence*, iii, 365–7). This scheme was revived on 4 Oct. 1523, but not brought to fruition until 12 Feb. 1537/8 when a papal bull founded St. Mary's College (see below) in the Pedagogy, an action which was completed on 7 Feb. 1538/9 when the principal of the Pedagogy was inducted as first principal of St. Mary's (*St. Andrews Acta*, cclxiii).

ST. ANDREWS, ST. JOHN'S COLLEGE. On 22 Jan. 1418/19, Robert of Montrose, rector of Cults, granted a tenement and certain annual rents to found a 'college of theologians and artists' dedicated to St. John the Evangelist (*Univ. Evidence*, iii, 350). The college buildings are, however, mentioned as early as 19 June 1416 and they might even be identical with 'the schools of theology' mentioned on 8 Dec. 1414 (*St. Andrews Acta*, 2, 7). The schools of theology were obviously common property unlike the early arts pedagogies which were rented or owned by different masters. The canon lawyers had their own schools. The only officer mentioned in the 'foundation' charter is the master who was to appoint a chaplain or chaplains to celebrate masses for the soul of the founder in the college chapel, of which there is no specific mention in the Montrose grant. The first master, Laurence of Lindores, is the only one to appear on record (Watt, *Fasti*, 381). The college may be regarded as a type of chantry of which the revenues were to be employed for the maintenance of masters in the university faculties of Theology and Arts (Cant, *University of St. Andrews*, 14–15). But a full collegiate organization never developed and with the fd'n. in 1430 of the Pedagogy (see above) whose members were to celebrate masses for their founder in the chapel of St. John's, the two colleges became so closely associated as to become almost one (*ibid.*, 16). The building was probably still in use in 1456 and 1461 (*St. Andrews Acta*, 115, 117, 147), but became derelict thereafter. In 1497 practical measures were taken to rebuild the chapel (*ibid.*, 261). When the Pedagogy was replaced by St. Mary's College in 1538, the chapel continued to be used for some time as the common 'south school' of the university (St. Andrews University Muniments [1569], SMB 15/9). The site of St. John's college was utilized in 1612 for the building of a common hall and library for the university (Cant, *University of St. Andrews*, 17, 60).

St. Andrews, St. Leonard's College. Fd. by Alexander Stewart, abp. of St. Andrews and John Hepburn, prior of St. Andrews, who erected the hospital (*q.v.*) and ch. of St. Leonard into 'the college of poor clerks of the church of St. Andrews' on 20 Aug. 1512 (Herkless and Hannay, *Coll. of St. Leonard*, 128 ff). The prior and convent added certain endowments, 1 Feb. 1512/13 (*ibid.*, 130 ff) and the foundation was confirmed by James IV, 23 Feb. 1512/13 (*ibid.*, 134—5). Papal confirmation of this fd'n. is wanting, but it was confirmed by Cardinal David Beaton as legate, 28 Nov. 1545 (*ibid.*, 177 ff). The original fd'n. provided for a 'master and principal director' (who was to be a canon of the cathedral), four chaplains (two to act as regents), twenty scholars in arts and six in theology (*ibid.*, 129); this was subsequently altered in 1544 to a principal, two priests, four regents and a variable number of scholars (*ibid.*, 145 ff). At the Reformation the college continued to fulfil its educational functions. It was united with St. Salvators in 1747. See Herkless and Hannay, *College of St. Leonard*, Cant, *University of St. Andrews*, 28 ff.

St. Andrews, St. Mary's College. Permission to found a college under the patronage of St. Mary of the Assumption was granted by the Pope to James Beaton, abp. of St. Andrews, on 4 Oct. 1525, but no further action was taken at that time. It was suggested that subjects taught would be theology, canon and civil law, physics, medicine and the other liberal disciplines (Reg. Supp., 1870, fos. 124ᵛ–125). This more than absorbed all the Pedagogy area schools; and the ancient ch. of St. John was to be absorbed, re-dedicated and given collegiate standing. If Abp. Beaton hoped for royal confirmation for his foundations or even for further papal authority, his personal difficulty with James V and not merely episcopal procrastination held it up. The scheme was later revived by Beaton, the bull of foundation by Pope Paul III being dated 12 Feb. 1537/8 (*Univ. Evidence*, iii, 357). The 'New College' was placed in the old Pedagogy and the assimilation of that institution was completed on 7 Feb. 1538/9 when the principal of the Pedagogy became first principal of St. Mary's (*St. Andrews Acta*, cclxiii). There is evidence of some continuing uncertainty on Beaton's part in documents issued within a few days of each other in Feb. 1538/9. One list includes a principal (theologian), sub-principal, mediciner, four regent students in theology, six choir chaplains and four singers; another excludes the mediciner, but includes a canonist and civilist (St. Andrews University Muniments, St. Mary's Writs, MB 1. P. 1. 17; MB 15. no. 1). Following a further petition of John Hamilton, abp. of St. Andrews, 26 Aug. 1552 (Reg. Supp., 2766, fos. 118ᵛ–121ᵛ), a further revision of the constitution was approved and this was completed by the issue of a new charter in 1554. This provided for a provost (a doctor of theology), a licentiate and a bachelor in theology, a canonist, eight theological students, three professors of philosophy, an orator, a grammarian, sixteen poor students and three household staff; thirty-six in all. No provision was made for boy singers and no overt provision for medicine and civil law (*Univ. Evidence*, iii, 360–6; Cant, *Univ. of St. Andrews*, 36–7). The college survived the Reformation, but was restricted to the study of theology in 1579 (*ibid.*, 41).

St. Andrews, St. Salvator's College. The fd'n. charter was granted by James Kennedy, bp. of St. Andrews, 27 Aug. 1450, providing for a provost, who was to be a master of theology, a licentiate and a bachelor of theology, four masters of arts, all priests, to study for the bachelorship in theology and teach philosophy, and six poor clerks (*Univ. Evidence*, iii, 270 ff; Cant, *Coll. of St. Salvator*, 54–60; Dunlop, *James Kennedy*, 274–5). The fd'n. was confirmed by Pope Nicholas V, 5 Feb. 1450/1 (Theiner, *Vet Mon.*, no. dcclix). Three prebends—Cults, Kemback and Dunino—were included in this original foundation, which was slightly amended by a revised charter in April 1458 (Cant, *Coll. of St. Salvator*, 66–80; cf. *Midlothian Chrs.*, iv). The ch. was consecrated in Oct. 1460, but other buildings were still incomplete (*St. Andrews Acta*, 139; Theiner, *Vet. Mon.*, no. dccciv). At least seven further prebends were added before the Reformation. Two of these—Lasswade, unsuccessfully erected in 1465 and 1468, maintained a canon only 1478–80, and Tyninghame, newly erected in 1485—proved to be transitory (Cowan, *Parishes*, 128, 203). Prebends which apparently maintained their status were Cranston (x 1464), Keith-Marischal (1469), Forteviot (1495), Kinnell (1510) and Kinnettles (1514). Kinnell had been previously associated with the prebend of Cranston in 1464, but ceased to be connected before 1473 (*ibid.*, 38, 69, 92, 114–5). Thirty chaplaincies appear to have existed by 1475 and numerous others were added before the Reformation. On 7 June 1533 some statutes were drawn up by the university Rector to subject the choir chaplains more strictly to the college provost. Shortly after a song school was initiated to teach the founded choirboys, two of whom the provost was to maintain. Even so there continued to be problems concerning the status of non-regent chaplains. (Cant, *Coll. of St. Salvator*, 21–31). At the Reformation the ecclesiastical functions of the college came to an end, but it continued to fulfil its educational purpose. The college was united with St. Leonards in 1747 (*ibid.*, 167–200).

DOUBTFUL AND REJECTED FOUNDATIONS
(*not previously included*)

Abbey. Two places in the south of Scotland bear this name: (1) Abbey, to the west of the village of Forth, in the parish of Carstairs, Lanarkshire. The source of this name has not been discovered; but it may definitely be said that there was no religious house on this site. (2) Abbey, on the Cliffhope burn, north of Saughtree, in Liddesdale. Mr. George Watson has shown that this was probably not used as a place-name till 1726, and that there is insufficient evidence 'to warrant one's assuming that "the Abbey" was a structure built for ecclesiastical or sacred purposes'. See his article, 'The Abbey, Upper Liddesdale', *Hawick Trans.*, (1916), pp. 32–3. The name, it has been suggested, is due to the possession by Jedburgh abbey of lands in this area (*Berwickshire Hist.*, (1887–9), pp. 461–3).

Buchan. On 18 Oct. 1221, the Pope grants protection to the prior and canons of St. James's, Buchan, with confirmation of their possessions, especially the churches of St. James, All Saints, St. Andrew, Buchan and Chenigale, with their chapels and appurtenances (*CPL*, i, 83). There is no known house of regular canons in the district of Buchan, Aberdeenshire, nor are any of the appropriated churches recognizable. 'Buchan' here may be an orthographical error for a place-name elsewhere than in Scotland.

Charterhouse. See MAKERSTOUN, under the Carthusian Monks.

Holy Island. Opposite Lamlash, on the east coast of Arran. The Book of Clanranald states that Ranald, K. of the Isles and Argyll (d. *c.* 1207) founded the monastic order of Molaise (*Reliquiae Celticae*, ii, 157). Monro, in 1549, speaks of this as 'ane . . . little ile callit the yle of Molass, quherin there was foundit by Johne, Lorde of the iles, ane monastery of friars which is decayit' (*Western Isles*, 48). The alleged founder was probably 'the good John of Islay', who died in 1380 (*Arran Bk.*, ii, 74). But the existence of a house of friars here must be regarded as very doubtful; and there is no evidence of any other form of (medieval) monastic establishment. The island was associated with the Celtic saint, Molaise.

Inchcolm. It is said that there was a hermit in this island before the foundation of the Augustinian monastery in 1123 (*Scotichronicon*, lib. v, cap. xxxvii (*Chron. Bower*, i, 287)).

Inchkenneth. This island is said to have had a monastery (*OPS*, ii¹, 316), but of this there is no evidence. Even *Scotichronicon*, which is prone to locate supposititious religious houses in the Isles, does not mention a monastery here; his statement is: 'The island of St. Kenneth of which and in which there is a parish church' (lib. ii, cap. x (*Chron. Bower* i, 45–6)). Monro (*Western Isles*, 52) does not mention a monastery. The whole lands belonged to the nunnery of Iona (*ibid.*, *OPS*, ii¹, 316, 317) and the idea of a monastery may have originated in its connection with Iona (*OPS*, ii¹, 316).

Inchmarnock. Of this island, lying between Bute and Kintyre, *Scotichronicon* says: 'Inchemernoc or the island of St. Mernoch; and there [is] a cell of monks' (lib. ii, cap. x (*Chron. Bower* i, 45)). *Origines Parochiales* (ii¹, 223) calls Inchmarnock 'the site of a chapel or monastery'. Monro (*Western Isles*, 48) does not mention a monastery here; and there is no evidence of such a fd'n. The island, however, had a parish ch., which, on 17 Jan. 1390/1, Saddell abbey obtained by exchange from Crossraguel abbey, by which it had been previously held (*Highland Papers*, iv, 142–4).

Kar. On 15 Feb. 1220/1, Henry III ordered the justiciar of Ireland to allow the monks of the order of Vaudey, dwelling at Kar in Galloway, to buy corn, etc., in Ireland for their sustenance (*CDS*, i, no. 795). Charters in *Melrose Liber* (i, nos. 192–5) deal with the grant by Thomas de Colville, in the early thirteenth c. and certainly –1223, of the land of 'Keresban' to the abbey of Vaudey. This land is described as in Galloway (*ibid.*, i, no. 195), but was probably in south Ayrshire, since it extended to the river Doon. In none of these records is there any suggestion that the monks of Vaudey were resident on this land. In 1223, Vaudey abbey, finding the possession of this land useless and a source of danger, gave it to Melrose Abbey in perpetual lease (*ibid.*, i, *loc. cit.*).

Kennethmont. There is said to have been a cell (the order is not specified) here which was burned down at the Reformation (*Aberdeen–Banff Coll.*, 200). (cf. the statement that there was a collegiate ch. here. See under Secular Colleges. But no evidence of any ecclesiastical fd'n. other than the parish ch. is to be found. Kennethmont was one of the chs. granted by the founder to Lindores abbey, 1188–9 (*Lind. Cart.*, no. ii) and is frequently mentioned in the Lindores charters.

May. Lawrie makes the statement, 'It is possible that on the Isle of May, in the beginning of the twelfth century, there was a small fraternity of culdees or monks of the old Scottish church' (Lawrie, *Charters*, 387). This is purely conjectural.

Rothesay. MacGibbon and Ross (*Eccles. Archit.*, iii, 418) refer to the ruined ch. here as 'St. Mary's abbey'. This was not a monastic building but evidently the medieval parish ch.

Scone. The editor of the *Scone Liber* states that the 'monastery of Scone, a foundation of unknown antiquity of the Culdees or followers of St. Columba . . . was reformed by King Alexander I' (*Scone Lib.*, ix). Likewise A. O. Anderson, in a note on the entry in the Chronicle of Melrose (s.a. 1115): 'the church of Scone was given over to canons' (*Melrose Chron.*, 65), declares that the abbey of Scone had formerly been occupied by Céli-Dé (*ES*, ii, 160 *n*). There is no explicit evidence for these statements.

Texa. 'Helentexa' (the island of Texa), according to *Scotichronicon* (lib. ii, cap. x; *Chron. Bower*, i, 45)), had a cell of monks. Monro (*Western Isles*, 26) says of 'Tigsay' that it has 'a kirk in it', but the 'cell' is no doubt apocryphal.

Thirlestane. A ruinous building east of the farm of Thirlestane has been described as a 'convent' (Thomson, *Lauder and Lauderdale*, 69; *HBNC*, xviii (1901–2), pp. 267, 292); and it is alleged that 'to this' Sir Richard Maitland gave all the lands which Walter de Gilling held in his fee of Thirlestane, as well as pasturage there (*HBNC*, xviii (1901–2), 267). But Maitland's charter, *c.* 1260, makes no mention of a religious house at Thirlestane. It indicates plainly that his benefaction was made to Dryburgh abbey (*Dryburgh Liber*, no. 124). The 'convent' is an antiquary's invention; and the building in question was probably a hospital (*v.* p. 165). *Hist. Mon. Comm. Rep.* (*Berwick*), 106, refers to it as a chapel.

Upsettlington. The site of a 'convent chapel' at Chapel Park is listed (*Hist. Mon. Comm. Rep.* (*Berwick*), 102). There was, however, no religious house in this vicinity.

The pseudo-medieval names of certain mansion-houses may be noted here:

Crawford Priory. South-west of Cupar, Fife. This name is attached to a mansion-house built in 1813. There was never a priory on this site and the name appears to be fanciful.

Inchrye Abbey. In north Fife, near Newburgh. The mansion-house thus designated was built in the nineteenth c. The name is fanciful.

Ross Priory. On the east side of Loch Lomond. It is called 'Ross' in 1793 (Ross Estate Muniments, no. 1163). Scott, writing to the proprietor (his friend and colleague, Hector Macdonald Buchanan), addresses his letters which are unreliably dated, both to 'Ross', and 'Ross Priory' (*Letters of Sir Walter Scott*, iv, 469; vi, 173; ix, 213). The latter name was probably invented in the early nineteenth c. and perhaps after an addition had been made to the building in 1810 (see Smith, *Strathendrick*, p. 277).

Rossie Priory. In the Carse of Gowrie, west of Dundee. This name is attached to a mansion-house begun in 1807. There is a reference in a charter of Malcolm IV (1153–65) to the 'abbacy' (*abbatia*) of Rossie (*St. A. Lib.*, 200), which points to the existence of a (defunct) Celtic religious house; while 'Rossinclerach' and its ch. were granted to the priory of St. Andrews by Bishop Ernald, 1160–2 (*ibid.*, p. 126). But no medieval priory existed at Rossie and the name applied to the mansion-house is without historical justification.

These names, products of the age of Scott, were probably adopted in imitation of English mansion-houses (e.g. Nostell Priory) which had a better claim to such designations.

APPENDIX I

RELIGIOUS HOUSES IN THE ISLE OF MAN

THE following notes on the Manx houses owe much to the kind and assiduous assistance of Mr. B. R. S. Megaw, former Director and Librarian of the Manx Museum, Douglas.

The edition of the *Chronicle of Man* cited below is that of P. A. Munch (1860).

THE CISTERCIAN MONKS

Name	Rank	Valuation (1540)	Date Fd.	D.	Dependent on
MIRESCOG			1176	*c.* 1200 (?)	Rievaulx (?)
RUSHEN	Abbey	£215	1134/5	1540	Furness

MIRESCOG. In Kirk Christ Lezayre parish. Later called Sulby Grange. Mr. Megaw informs me that the supposed siting of this house at Ballamona (see Tanner and others) is incorrect. It is stated that, in 1176, 'Godred, king of Man, gave as an offering to . . . abbot Silvanus (i.e. of Rievaulx) part of the land of Mirescog. He immediately built a monastery there, but in process of time all the land with the monks was granted to the abbey of St. Mary of Rushen' (*Chron. Man*, 13–14). It has been suggested that there was still a mon. here in 1249. But the passage on which this supposition is based speaks of an island in the wood of Mirescog; a mon. at Mirescog is not mentioned in this connection (*ibid.*, 24).

RUSHEN. It is said that, in 1134, Olaf K. of Man, gave to Ivo, ab. of Furness, part of his land in Man for the constitution of an abbey in the place called Russin (*Chron. Man.* p. 7–8). This date is also found in a list of Cistercian foundations (*JBAA*, xxvi (1870), 358), where it is called '[the abbey] of Mann'. Janauschek (p. 101) assigns the foundation to 10 Jan. 1134(/5). In *Furness Coucher Book* (i, 11), the date is given erroneously as 1238. It may be noted that 'the abbey of Man' is included with Furness among the abbeys subject to the ab. of Savigny which are confirmed to him by Pope Anastasius IV, 20 April 1154 (*Patr. Lat.*, 188, col. 1054). The abbey is stated to have been transferred in 1192 to Douglas, but the monks returned to Rushen four years later (*Chron. Man*, p. 15). The ch. was dedicated by Richard, bp. of Sodor, in 1257 (*ibid.*, p. 27). In 1275, when a Scottish force subdued the island, the abbey suffered considerable spoliation (*Annals of Furness* in *Chrons. of Stephen*, etc., 570); and it was again despoiled in 1316 during an invasion of Man by Richard de Mandeville and his associates from Ireland (*Chron. Man*, 28). This house was dissolved by arbitrary act of Henry VIII (since the act of 1539 did not apply to Man), 24 June 1540, when the ab. and six brethren were removed from the abbey (*PRO* Roll of Accounts (Isle of Man—Dissolutions (1540)); *v.* T. Talbot in *Manx Sun*, 24 Nov. 1894, p. 8; A. W. Moore, *Hist. of Isle of Man*, i, 351). It was granted by the Crown to Thomas Hungate of the Household, 18 March 1543/4 (*L. P. Henry VIII*, xviii[1], 557). The statement that it was the last mon. to be dissolved (as in Tanner and *Manx Society*, xii, 57) should be extended to cover the other Manx houses (below). (The last house to be dissolved in England was Waltham, on 10 April 1540.)

THE FRANCISCAN FRIARS

Name	Valuation (1540)	Date Fd.	D.
BEMAKEN	not given	1367	1540

BEMAKEN. In Kirk Arbory parish. On 7 Dec. 1367, following on the petition of the provincial and brethren of the Friars Minor of the province of Ireland, and William Montague, E. of Salisbury, which contained that, since there was no place of that order in the diocese of Sodor, the earl proposed to assign one to the friars in the *villa* of St. Columba in Man. Pope Urban V appointed the bp. of Sodor mandatory to license the provincial and friars to accept this place and to build there a ch. and the necessary offices, with provision for twelve friars (*CPL*, iv, 75; *Chron. Man*, (Appendix) 179–180, where the papal letter is printed *in extenso*). Tanner gives the date of fd'n., as 1373 (cf. *Manx Society*, xii, 54). The property was apparently seized by Henry VIII in 1540, along with the other religious houses in Man. The friary was granted by the Crown to Thomas Hungate of the Household, 18 March 1543/4 (*L.P. Henry VIII*, xviii[1], 557).

THE CISTERCIAN NUNS

Name	Rank	Valuation (1540)	Date Fd.	D.
DOUGLAS	Priory	£58	−1226	1540

DOUGLAS (ST. MARY). The supposed dedication of this house to St. Bridget is doubtful, unless it was additional to the dedication to St. Mary. Reginald, K. of Man (1187–1226) is named as founder and the house is described as Cistercian in an inquisition of 1414 (recorded in an abstract of 1511) (*Journal of Manx Museum*, ii, no. 27, p. 21). Robert [Bruce], K. of Scots, is said to have stayed at the nunnery, 20 May 1313, on an expedition to Man (*Chron. Man*, p. 27). In 1422, the prioress of Douglas appears as one of the barons of Man called to do fealty (*Lex Scripta of the Isle of Man*, 5). The dissolution took place, 24 June 1540, when the prioress and her three sisters 'departed' from the priory (PRO Roll of Accounts (Isle of Man—Dissolutions (1540)); *v.* T. Talbot, *Manx Sun*, 24 Nov. 1894, 8; A. W. Moore, *Hist. of Isle of Man*, i, 351). Douglas priory was granted to Thomas Hungate of the Household, 18 March 1543/4 (*LP, Henry VIII*, xviii[1], 557).

HOSPITAL

Name	Dedication	Date Fd.	D.
BALLACGNIBA	uncertain	−1153(?)	?

BALLACGNIBA. In Kirk Marown parish. Perhaps fd'n by Olaf I, K. of Man, between 1134 and 1153; his wife was a daughter of Fergus of Galloway, and *Chron. Man*, p. 9 (*s.a.* 1142) implies his introduction of Galloway settlers in Man. This hospital is mentioned along with the ch. of St. Ninian of Ballacgniba (St. Trinian's) and the ch. of St. Runar (Kirk Marown) as granted by Olaf II to Whithorn priory in Galloway, 1193–1215 (B. R. S. Megaw, 'The Barony of St. Trinian's in the Isle of Man', *Dumfries. Trans.* 3rd ser.

xxvii (1950), 176 ff). and it may have been associated with the former ch. Its further history is unknown.

ADDITIONAL NOTE

Mr. Megaw informs me that a place-name found at Peel (at least as early as 1703), viz. Boaly Spittal, is evidently *Boayly Spittal*, i.e. 'place of the hospital', but there is no record of a hospital, medieval or otherwise, at this site.

CATHEDRAL

Name	Date of foundation	Personnel
ST. GERMAN	−1231	no information available

ST. GERMAN (PEEL). The inception of the building of the cathedral of St. German, in the island of St. Patrick, is attributed to Simon, bp. of Sodor (1229/30–1247/8) (*Chron. Man*, p. 23, 29). It is mentioned in a bull of Pope Gregory IX to that bp., 30 July 1231 (*SHR*, viii (1911), 259). In the entry *s.a.* 1247/8, it is stated that, after Simon's death, Laurence, archdeacon in Man, was elected bp. 'with the common consent and assent of the whole Manx chapter' (*Chron. Man*, p. 23). Munch declares: 'As it is certain that no chapter existed before, it is evident that this important institution was founded by Simon, and closely connected with the erection of the new cathedral' (*ibid.*, App., 142). The chapter is also mentioned in papal letters, e.g. in 1253 (*CPL*, i, 284) and 1393 (*CPP*, i, 577); but this may be no more than 'common form'; in any case, no particulars of the constitution of this chapter can be found. It is to be noted that, in 1134, Olaf I granted the election of the bp. to the ch. of Furness (*Manx Society*, vii, 1–2) and that, in a papal mandate of 15 Feb. 1244/5, this right is said to belong to the ab. and convent of Furness (*CPL*, i, 206). But it is impossible to believe that the 'chapter' of the chronicler's statement was a monastic one. The term is probably used here not of a cathedral but of the totality of the clergy of the diocese. It is thus possible that Munch has read too much into the chronicler's statement. On 3 Jan. 1363/4, Pope Urban V granted the petition of William, bp. of Sodor, who had represented that his cathedral ch. and precincts had been occupied as a fortress by the lord of the Isle of Man, during the wars between England and Scotland, so that the bps. had suffered greatly and divine service had ceased and who supplicated that the Pope would require the said lord to restore the cathedral to the bp. (*CPP*, i, 394). Again, the Pope granted licence, on 24 Oct. 1392, to Sir William de Scrope, lord of the kingdom of Man and the Isles, to build a castle in the place called 'Patrikysholm' near and belonging to the ch. of Sodor, whose buildings had been destroyed by invasion and could not, through the slenderness of its means, be repaired, whereby divine worship had been almost entirely diminished and divine offices for long had not been celebrated. Scrope, it is said, intended to repair the ch., to which the castle would serve as a defence (*CPL*, iv, 432). On the same date, the Pope issued an exhortation for alms for the repair of the ch. of Sodor (*ibid.*, iv, 433). From the third decade of the fifteenth c. the diocese was resolved into two parts. See ISLES under Cathedrals.

CELTIC FOUNDATION

St. Leoc. In 1153 a bull of Pope Eugenius III confirms, among other possessions, to Furness Abbey: 'In Man, by gift of . . . Olaf, king of the Isles, the lands of Carneclet as far as the monastery of St. Leoc . . .' (*Manx Soc.*, vii, 10–11). This monastery, of which nothing seems to be known, was probably a Celtic foundation. The reference here is presumably to its site and does not necessarily imply that it was still in being.

APPENDIX II

THE SCHOTTENKLÖSTER
(Contributed by the Rev. Mark Dilworth, OSB)

GENERAL NOTES

No account of medieval Scottish monasticism is complete without mention of the occupation of various monasteries in south Germany, the so-called *Schottenklöster*, by Scottish monks in the early sixteenth century. Some attempt should therefore be made to outline the history of these houses and explain how they came to be occupied by Scots. It is a story probably unique in the annals of monastic life. To understand their origin one must go back to the early centuries of Irish Christianity when it was the custom for monks to go into voluntary exile, preaching the gospel as they went. Irish missionaries evangelized not only Britain but wide regions of western and central Europe, and monasteries for Irish monks exclusively were founded on the Continent from the seventh century on. Whatever rule was followed in them to begin with, it was the Rule of St. Benedict which eventually prevailed, as it was to do even in the Celtic homelands. Gradually too the activity of these monks in exile became focused on what is now south Germany.

Ratisbon (Regensburg) on the Danube had long been a centre of Irish activity, and here in 1075–6 an Irish monk called Marianus Scotus founded the monastery of Weih-Sankt-Peter. His community flourished and after his death the larger abbey of St. James's was founded in the town. A most remarkable period of expansion then followed, during which no fewer than seven monasteries for Irish monks were founded in German lands in a few decades from about 1135. Henceforth almost all Irish monks going into exile were channelled into this group of monasteries centred on St. James's in Ratisbon and observing the Benedictine rule. In 1215, when the Lateran Council ordered Benedictines of each kingdom or province to unite into congregations and hold general chapters at regular intervals, a special arrangement was made grouping these Irish monasteries together under the authority of the Ratisbon abbot, on a basis of nationality and not of region.

The Irish were known as *Scoti* up to the eleventh century; so too naturally were the Irish monks on the Continent and the Irish settlers in

240

the west of Scotland. After the Norman Conquest, however, a change in meaning took place: Ireland and the Irish became known as *Hibernia* and *Hiberni*, while *Scotia* came to denote the country of the *Scoti* north of Forth and Clyde and eventually the whole of present day Scotland. The Irish monks in the Ratisbon group of houses, however, did not abandon their old name. Although in documents they frequently used *Hiberni* as an alternative to *Scoti*, their monasteries continued to be known universally as the *monasteria Scotorum*. In spite of being on German soil they did not accept German recruits, and in spite of the continued use of the name *Scoti* all their links were with Ireland.

This unusual congregation of Gaels in exile flourished until the fourteenth century, but began to break up after 1400. Recruitment from Ireland proved unsatisfactory, some houses passed into German hands and others sank into decay. By 1500 only the Ratisbon abbey had a community, and a small one at that, while the three other surviving monasteries had each a solitary Irish monk elected to act as superior by the Ratisbon chapter. Meanwhile in Scotland the belief had grown that these Scotic monasteries were foundations made by and for Scots from Scotland; it was part of the version of history which ascribed the origin of the Franco-Scottish alliance to Charlemagne and was of a piece with the mythical line of Scottish kings stretching back to the fourth century B.C. The *Schottenklöster* 'myth', first found in Walter Bower's chronicle in the mid-fifteenth century, remained in manuscript but the story was evidently well known and was to feature in all the productions of sixteenth-century Scottish historians.

Meanwhile too there had been a steady growth of colonies or groups of expatriate Scots in Germany. Around Ratisbon in particular Scots traders were numerous and had been receiving citizenship of the town since 1493. In 1500 they entered into an agreement with the Irish abbot for the erection of a confraternity of Scots with an altar dedicated to St. Andrew. Thus the *Schottenklöster* myth was brought to Ratisbon by Scots who held it firmly and had positions of influence. The retention of the title of *Scoti* now had fateful consequences. There was a serious dispute over the Ratisbon abbey in 1514–15, the upshot of which was a decision from Rome that this *monasterium Scotorum* belonged by right to Scottish monks and should be restored to them. John Thomson, the Scot provided as abbot by Rome, had to overcome the opposition of interested parties in Ratisbon who had hoped to gain possession of the abbey themselves, but eventually he was successful. One must surely credit the Scots resident in Ratisbon with some influence in the affair, as regards both the Roman decision and the favourable outcome in Ratisbon itself.

In acquiring the Ratisbon abbacy the Scots gained control of the entire congregation, because as abbot-general Thomson had jurisdiction over the other houses and there was no Irish community to offer resistance in any of them. He appointed Scots as superiors to each in the same way as the Irish chapter used to do. By 1520 the takeover was complete and in 1523 four superiors and seven other monks took part in a chapter to confirm the election of Thomson's successor. It was a promising beginning and augured well, but neither civil nor ecclesiastical conditions were conducive to a vigorous monastic life. War, the Reformation and internal disputes combined to thwart any growth; in fact by the middle of the century two houses were completely destroyed and the Ratisbon abbey itself was damaged by fire. Monastic life of any kind was all but extinct in the *Schottenklöster* when in August 1560 the Reformation Parliament sat in the monks' Scottish homeland.

This was not the end. The Scots citizens of Ratisbon again exerted their influence, while Bishop John Lesley, ambassador of the Queen of Scots in Rome, worked to retain the monasteries for his nation. Ninian Winzet, appointed abbot of Ratisbon in 1577, gathered a community of expatriate Scots around him, and he and Lesley made vigorous efforts to regain former houses of the congregation or, failing that, to obtain compensation for their loss. Winzet's monks included both pre-Reformation Scottish religious and young products of the Counter-Reformation. By the end of the century the Scots had three abbeys, which remained in their hands and played a not undistinguished part in the ecclesiastical and cultural life of Germany until the nineteenth century.

A general outline of the period before 1515 and the growth of the 'myth' is found in M. Dilworth, *The Scots in Franconia* (1974) 11–19, 212–15. For the status of the Irish houses at the time of the takeover see the same author's 'The Schottenklöster at the Reformation', *Essays on the Scottish Reformation 1513–1625*, ed. D. Roberts (1962) 241—4. Events within the monasteries from 1515 to 1577 are covered in some detail in Dilworth, 'The first Scottish monks in Ratisbon,' *Innes Review*, xvi, (1965) 180—98. The recovery or attempted recovery of the monasteries in the years 1577–83 is outlined in *The Scots in Franconia*, 24–30. Of value for the background in the towns of Ratisbon and Erfurt is Dr Ludwig Hammermayer's long article, 'Deutsche Schottenklöster, schottische Reformation, Katholische Reform und Gegenreformation in West- und Mitteleuropa (1560–1580)', *Zeitschrift für bayerische Landesgeschichte* 26 (1963) 131–255. All these works give references to primary sources.

In the following list the houses are divided into two groups according to whether they ever had Scottish monks in residence or not. Other houses claimed for the congregation by various writers, but for which no documentary evidence exists, have been omitted. Any source references are intended to be in addition to those listed above. It only remains to say that, at the present stage of research, there are still great uncertainties as regards the history of many of these *Schottenklöster* but the vicissitudes of the Reformation in the various German territories go far to explain the history of each house in the sixteenth century.

THE SCHOTTENKLÖSTER

CONSTANCE, ST. JAMES. Fd. 1142. It remained in Irish hands until the abbacy fell vacant in 1518; a Scottish abbot was then appointed from Ratisbon. The buildings suffered damage at the hands of the Zwinglians in 1526 and were at least partially demolished in 1530. In 1533 the Scots abbot ceded all rights to the abbey and it was then completely demolished. The Ratisbon Scots in 1607 reopened the matter and succeeded in obtaining compensation from the Constance town authorities in 1609 (*Scots in Franconia*, 43–44).

ERFURT, ST. JAMES. Fd. *c.* 1137(?). It remained in Irish hands until the last Irish abbot died in 1517. David Cumming, a Scot, was appointed ab. in early 1518 by John Thomson and in 1521 was *Judex et Conservator* of Erfurt university, an office traditionally held by the Scotic ab. In 1524 Cumming leased the buildings of the *Schottenkloster* school to the Protestant senate. Scots abbots remained in possession, though under increasing difficulties, until 1561 and the Catholic diocesan officials then administered the revenues. A Scot, William Chalmers, was appointed ab. in 1577 by Roman authority but was obliged to leave the town the following year. In 1581 the Ratisbon chapter elected as ab. of Erfurt one of its own members, John Hamilton, formerly a monk of Paisley. Thereafter the house remained in Scottish hands and dependent on the Ratisbon abbey until its secularization in 1819.

KELHEIM, ST. JOHN. Fd. 1232. It was perhaps never fully a monastery and certainly never attained the rank of abbey. It remained in Irish hands until 1515 though probably for a considerable time before then no monk had resided. It passed into possession of the Scots and in the early seventeenth c. had a monk in residence (*Scots in Franconia* 42, 46). The Ratisbon Scots retained possession of the property until 1862.

RATISBON, ST. JAMES. Fd. *c.* 1110. A community of Irish monks was in possession until 1515. On 31 July 1515 the holy see provided John Thomson, of the diocese of St. Andrews and resident in Rome, to the abbacy. Thomson then assumed authority over the remaining houses of the congregation. A dozen mks. (including the superiors of the three dependent houses) are found in 1523 and 1525. Ab. David Cumming visited Scotland in 1528–9 and enlisted James V's support for his plans. The community declined in numbers in the 1530s. In 1538 ab. and chapter entrusted the financial administration of the house to the town authorities and in 1542 the Scottish abp. of Armagh, Robert Wauchope, attempted to gain possession of the house. Only two mks. are found in 1546, the year in which a fire destroyed much of the buildings. In the early 1550s the ab. was involved in a bitter dispute with the only other Scots mk. in the town, the prior of St. Peter's, and from 1555 the ab. was the sole Scots mk. in Ratisbon. A Scots ab. remained in possession, however, until 1576. On 13 June 1577 Ninian Winzet was provided to the abbacy by Rome; by March 1580 there were six other mks. and a college for youth had been established. Thereafter the abbey had a Scottish community until it was suppressed in 1862 by agreement between the Bavarian government and the holy see.

RATISBON, ST. PETER (Weih-Sankt-Peter). This ancient ch., belonging to the abbess of Obermunster, was given in 1075–6 to Marianus Scotus, who gathered a community round him. It never became an abbey but its prior took the place of the claustral prior of St. James's and the abbess of Obermunster retained rights of patronage and presentation, an arrangement that survived into the Scottish period. John Denys, monk of Newbattle, was prior by 7 Dec. 1515 and was installed in office at the end of 1516 though not yet in peaceful possession. A series of Scottish priors is found from then until May 1552, when the priory was razed to the ground to make way for fortifications. Ninian Winzet later entered into negotiations with the Obermunster abbess over compensation for its loss (Winzet's *Certane Tractates*, ed. J. K. Hewison, Scottish Text Society 1888–90, vol. 1, p. lxv).

WURZBURG, ST. JAMES. Fd. by 1142. It passed into the hands of German monks when the last Irish ab. died in 1497 but monastic life ceased in 1547 (*Scots in Franconia*, 20–1). Lesley and Winzet made unsuccessful attempts to regain the abbey in 1578–83. In 1595 the bp. of Würzburg invited the Ratisbon Scots to inaugurate monastic life in it once more; the monastery was solemnly handed over on 30 April and a new fd'n. charter signed on 2 May (*ibid.*, 32–9). The abbey remained united with the Ratisbon community until 1615 (*ibid.*, 41–8) but thereafter links were fraternal rather than juridical. The mon. had a Scottish community until it was suppressed in the secularization of 1803.

FOUNDATIONS WHICH WERE NEVER SCOTTISH MONASTERIE

Eichstatt, Holy Cross. Fd. by 1166. It never attained abbatial status and though it remained in Irish hands it probably had no monk resident in the decades before 1515. The Scots ab. of Ratisbon asserted his claim to it in 1545. In 1566 most of its income was allotted to the new diocesan seminary, and the Ratisbon ab. two years later agreed to accept an annual sum in compensation. When Lesley and Winzet made efforts to recover the property, all they could obtain was a small annual payment. In the early seventeenth c. the house became a Capuchin friary, which it still is today.

Memmingen, St. Nicholas. Fd. 1167. It may never have attained abbatial status and for most of the fifteenth c. was no longer a monastery. The buildings were completely demolished *c.* 1500. It was the only house the Scots never tried to recover or obtain compensation for.

Nuremberg, St. Giles. Fd. 1140. It was handed over to German monks in 1418 and passed into the possession of the Lutheran town senate in 1525. Lesley and Winzet tried to recover the property in 1578–83 and a further unsuccessful effort was made in 1629 (*Scots in Franconia*, 65, 147).

Vienna, Our Lady. Fd. 1155. Handed over to Austrian monks in 1418. Lesley and Winzet claimed the abbey in 1578–83 and the Würzburg or Ratisbon Scots made efforts to recover it in 1624–30, 1641 and the 1670s (*Scots in Franconia*, 62–64, 85, 108). It has remained in the possession of Benedictine monks and is the only *Schottenkloster* still a monastery today.

APPENDIX III

THE INCOME OF THE SCOTTISH RELIGIOUS HOUSES: THE SOURCES
(Contributed by Professor Gordon Donaldson)

The records which preserve the figures for the values of the Scottish religious houses arose from the Crown's interest in and management of the ecclesiastical revenues at the Reformation. By arrangements made in 1561 all persons holding benefices retained their fruits with the exception of one-third, which was collected to augment the revenues of the Crown and make payments to the clergy of the reformed church. This 'assumption of thirds' involved the gathering in of rentals of all benefices in Scotland, except those in the diocese of Argyll and the Isles and a number which were fraudulently or negligently omitted. The 'Books of Assumption', in which these records were recorded, have not survived in a complete form. What may be regarded as the principal volume, in H.M. General Register House, Edinburgh, covers the east coast counties as far north as Moray, with the Borders and Perthshire. It was written in or about 1605, but the rentals in it mostly belong to 1561. Two volumes written at an earlier date, one in the Register House and one in the National Library of Scotland (MS. 31.3.12), together deal with the same parts of the country as that 'principal' volume. For a complete set of figures (lacking, however, the details of the rentals), we must turn to the Accounts of the Collectors of Thirds of Benefices, which begin in 1561.

The values given in the present volume are based on the figures printed in the *Accounts of the Collectors of Thirds of Benefices, 1561–1572* (Scottish History Society), with some supplementary information from 'The New Enterit Benefices', 1573–1586', *Scottish Historical Review*, xxxii, 93–8. The figures given there for the various revenues in money and kind have been compared with the figures, derived from both the Books of Assumption and the Collectors' Accounts, which were printed by Bishop Keith (*History of Church and State in Scotland* (Spottiswoode Society), iii, 374 ff.), and in a few instances verification has been sought in the MS. Books of Assumption themselves. A money equivalent of the revenues received in kind has been calculated from the figures for the sale of victual and other fruits for the year 1561, as printed in the *Accounts of the Collectors of Thirds*.

The valuation on which the third was assessed represented certain deductions from the gross value—the portions which continued to be paid to the monks, the salaries of officers on the estates and in the precincts of the house, contributions to the College of Justice, and some other items. In the case of the abbey of Dunfermline, such deductions amounted to £714 (see, in general, *Accounts of the Collectors of Thirds*, xiv–xv). Rentals specially prepared for the 'assumption' were no more likely to exaggerate the revenues than is an income tax return today. With these qualifications, and bearing in mind that Scots money was, by 1561, worth only one-fifth of the corresponding sterling, the figures now printed do afford some indication of the value of the Scottish houses and a basis for comparison among them.

INDEX OF RELIGIOUS HOUSES

ABBREVIATIONS FOR ORDERS, ETC.

A	Augustinian Canons		H	Hospital
B	Benedictine Monks		KH	Knights Hospitallers
BC	Cluniac Monks		KT	Knights Templars
BT	Monks of the Order of Tiron		MC	Monastic Cathedral
C	Cistercian Monks		NA	Augustinian Nuns
CA	Carthusian Monks		NB	Benedictine Nuns
EF	Early Foundations		NC	Cistercian Nuns
FA	Friars, Augustinian		ND	Dominican Nuns
FC	Carmelite		NF	Franciscan Nuns
FCr	Crutched		P	Premonstratensian Canons
FD	Dominican		SA	Secular College (Academic)
FF	Franciscan		SC(i)	Secular Canons (Cathedral)
FFO	Franciscan Observant		SC(ii)	(Collegiate Church)
FS	of the Sack		T	Trinitarian
G	Gilbertine Canons		U	Uncertain Order
			V	Valluscaulian Monks

Numerals, in *italics*, after the abbreviation of Order denote the number of such establishments, if more than one.

Abbreviations shown in *italics* denote incomplete, uncertain, supposed or rejected foundations.

Alternative names are shown in brackets.

Index of Religious Houses